The
Chicago Symphony Orchestra

THEODORE THOMAS

The
Chicago Symphony Orchestra

Its Organization
Growth and Development

1891-1924

By
PHILO ADAMS OTIS

BOOKS FOR LIBRARIES PRESS
FREEPORT, NEW YORK

First Published 1924
Reprinted 1972

INTERNATIONAL STANDARD BOOK NUMBER:
0-8369-6742-9

LIBRARY OF CONGRESS CATALOG CARD NUMBER:
79-37904

PRINTED IN THE UNITED STATES OF AMERICA
BY
NEW WORLD BOOK MANUFACTURING CO., INC.
HALLANDALE, FLORIDA 33009

*To the Memory of
Theodore Thomas*

IN making this dedication to Mr. Thomas, where can a loftier sentiment be found than that expressed by Ignace J. Paderewski:

"Scarcely any man in any land has done so much for the musical education of the people as did Theodore Thomas in this country. The nobility of his ideals, with the magnitude of his achievement, will assure him everlasting glory."

LIST OF ILLUSTRATIONS

	PAGE
THEODORE THOMAS	Frontispiece
HANS BALATKA	10
CROSBY OPERA HOUSE	13
GEORGE BENEDICT CARPENTER	15
ROSE FAY THOMAS	24
CHARLES NORMAN FAY	28
THEODORE THOMAS	38
MUSIC HALL (WORLD'S COLUMBIAN EXPOSITION)	45
CHORAL (FESTIVAL) HALL (WORLD'S COLUMBIAN EXPOSITION)	47
PHILO ADAMS OTIS	57
THEODORE THOMAS	58
ANNA MILLAR	60
GEORGE H. WILSON	73
FREDERICK J. WESSELS	83
THEODORE THOMAS	99
ARTHUR MEES	103
JOSEPH ADAMS	109
FREDERICK STOCK	118
HENRY E. VOEGELI	120
ADOLPH W. DOHN	123
NATHANIEL KELLOGG FAIRBANK	139
ORCHESTRA HALL	147
ORCHESTRA HALL, INTERIOR	150
THEODORE THOMAS	158
CHARLES DAVIDSON HAMILL	163
CHARLES H. HAMILL	167
FLORENCE LATHROP PAGE	184
FESTIVAL TOUR—WESSELS, STOCK AND OTIS	186
FREDERICK STOCK	209
DANIEL HUDSON BURNHAM	241
ALBERT ARNOLD SPRAGUE	266
ELIZABETH SPRAGUE COOLIDGE	272
NANCY SPRAGUE	279
BRYAN LATHROP	281
GEORGE EVERETT ADAMS	296
HORACE S. OAKLEY	300
ERIC DELAMARTER	311
GEORGE PUTNAM UPTON	319
MILWARD ADAMS	364
CLYDE MITCHELL CARR	366
THEODORE THOMAS MEMORIAL	372

PRELUDE

My musical memories, covering a period of sixty years, start with the first symphony concerts in Chicago (1860-1868) given by the Philharmonic Society, under the direction of Hans Balatka, a good musician and an able Conductor. I attended the concerts in the season of 1862-1863, enjoying the music very much, although it was quite beyond my comprehension, it being the first Orchestra I had ever heard.

This work includes the details of the organization (1890) of The Orchestral Association, its membership, Boards of Trustees, *personnel* of the Orchestra, and the names of the men and women of Chicago whose loyal and generous support has made the Orchestra possible.

The chapter on the Bureau of Music at the World's Columbian Exposition (1893) is introduced in answer to the malicious charges brought against Theodore Thomas by the Exposition authorities and Chicago newspapers. It never seemed to me that he had an adequate defense, only one voice at the time being raised in his behalf— that of George P. Upton, of the *Chicago Tribune*. Though the work of the Bureau and its unjust treatment at the hands of the National Commission have long since passed into history, I have thought it best to review this unhappy period in Mr. Thomas' life, to show that this man, whose whole life was passed in proclaiming the gospel of good music to the community, lived above dishonest methods in his art.

As I recall the closing years of our leader's life, it all seems like the finale of an "Unfinished Symphony." The people of Chicago, out of the fullness of their hearts and in grateful appreciation for the work Mr. Thomas had done for the cause of music in America, had given him an Orchestra and a permanent hall for his concerts. The end to which his life had been given was now at hand, when he could develop his Orchestra along larger and broader lines, but death intervened and his work stopped. This is a sad but not uncommon experience, when men give their lives to great and noble causes and then pass away without seeing their fulfillment.

Theodore Thomas had another ideal which he did not live to see fulfilled—the establishment of the Pension and Invalid Fund. Years passed, and this dream came true through the thoughtful generosity of Mrs. Elizabeth Sprague Coolidge, Bryan Lathrop and other devoted friends of the Orchestra.

The workmen change, but the work must go on. The mantle of Mr. Thomas fell (1905) upon a worthy successor, Frederick Stock, who for nineteen years has carried on the high standards and maintained the traditions of his great predecessor.

Much of the data for this work has been gathered from my journals, which note many musical events in Chicago during the past fifty years, including all the regular concerts of the Orchestra in each season, the important concerts of the Apollo Musical Club, and other Chicago concerts in which the Orchestra has appeared. A few concerts have been noticed; space would not permit me to mention all.

Three works have been of great service: "Theodore Thomas. A Musical Autobiography," by George P. Upton (1905); "Musical Memories," by George P. Upton (1908); "Memoirs of Theodore Thomas," by Rose Fay Thomas (1911).

P. A. O.

1857-1872

Musical conditions in Chicago (1857)—The Philharmonic Society—Our first Orchestra, and its Conductor—Hans Balatka, the forerunner of Theodore Thomas—First Appearance of the Thomas Orchestra in Chicago.

When my father, James Otis, brought his family to Chicago in 1857, the city was just emerging from the chrysalis state of a village, and was fast assuming the appearance of a thriving western town. Some attempts had been made to develop the musical resources of the city, though of a limited character; a few churches had two-manual organs and good choirs; a singing society, the Musical Union, had given its first concert in April (1857); and a season of orchestral concerts by the Philharmonic Society, under the leadership of Henry Ahner, was then in progress.

Another singing society, the Mendelssohn, should now be mentioned, to do honor to three of its founders (1857), enthusiastic workers in the cause of good music in our city: George P. Upton, critic, author and the first President (1872) of the Apollo Musical Club; Adolph W. Dohn, who came to Chicago in 1854, first Conductor of the Mendelssohn Society (1858) and of the Apollo Musical Club (1872-1874), and first editor (1891-1894) of the program book of the Chicago Orchestra; Charles D. Hamill, President of the Apollo Musical Club (1886-1887) and a member of the first Board of Trustees (1891) of the Chicago Orchestra.

The Philharmonic Society, established by Julius Dyhrenfurth in 1850, gave its first concert on September 4 of that year. Mr. Dyhrenfurth was followed by various conductors until 1856, when Henry Ahner, a trumpet player in the old Germania Society of New York City, came to Chicago, organized practically a new orchestra from the best players of the Great Western and Light Guard Band and from ex-members of the old Philharmonic Society. He gave concerts until 1858, and then, discouraged by lack of appreciation and financial support, gave up the work. "Never," says Mr. Upton, "was there a musician of more honest purpose, a gentleman of finer quality than Henry Ahner."

In 1860 a new Philharmonic Society was organized through the efforts of John G. Shortall, E. I. Tinkham, Samuel Johnson and other music lovers, with Hans Balatka, then living in Milwaukee, as Conductor—the result of a visit Mr. Balatka made (1857) to Chicago to conduct the Northwestern Sängerfest.

The first concert was given November 11, 1860, in Bryan Hall, to a crowded house. Before the close of the first season Hans Balatka was the musical hero of the day; his concerts were "all the rage"; people turned away at every performance! Chicago then began to take on airs, and to believe that it would soon "rival Boston and New York as a musical center." For six years the society, under Balatka's leadership, flourished, doing excellent work until the Seventh Season, when the public grew indifferent and the attendance declined to such an extent that the board of trustees was without funds and disbanded the society; but not through any fault of the Conductor. Mr. Balatka, a sincere, earnest musician, the forerunner of Theodore Thomas, introduced much of the higher class of music to his audience.

In 1868 Mr. Balatka reorganized the Philharmonic Society, giving its First Season of concerts in Farwell Hall, but with discouraging financial returns. He was not at all disheartened, but at once prepared for a Second Season.

The *Chicago Tribune* of November 24, 25 and 26, 1869, contained this advertisement:

"Farwell Hall, First Grand Symphony Concert of H. Balatka, Friday Evening, November 26."

In the same column, but a little below, appeared another advertisement:

THEODORE THOMAS' GRAND CONCERT ORGANIZATION
of
FORTY CELEBRATED MUSICIANS COMPOSING ALL THE EMINENT SOLOISTS OF HIS GREAT ORCHESTRA, WILL GIVE
THREE GRAND CONCERTS
in
FARWELL HALL
Saturday, November 27
Monday, November 29
Tuesday, November 30

HANS BALATKA

Mr. Thomas made his first visit to Chicago, says Mr. Upton in his "Musical Memories" (1908)—

"in 1854 as violinist in a small orchestra accompanying a concert troupe, composed of Ole Bull, Amalia Patti (contralto), Max Strakosch (pianist) and Bertucca Maretzek (harpist). In October, 1858, he made a second visit in the same capacity, in a concert troupe directed by Carl Anschutz, under the management of Ullman. It included Madame Schumann (soprano), Carl Formes (basso) and Ernest Perring (tenor)."

The orchestra with this "troupe" on the second visit, numbering twenty-one of the best players in the east, included among the first violins Theodore Thomas and Julius Mosenthal. Two concerts were given, and in the second Mr. Thomas played Vieuxtemps' "Rêverie."

His third visit (1869), when he came as Conductor, was destined to have a marked influence on the musical future of Chicago.

The appearance of the two orchestras on consecutive evenings afforded the local critics material for several weeks, in commenting on the respective merits of the two organizations, somewhat to the disadvantage of Mr. Balatka and his supporters, who openly declared that "Peregrine Pickle" (George P. Upton), the critic for the *Tribune*, was trying to break up their orchestra. I attended both concerts, and can heartily sustain "Peregrine Pickle" in his views, particularly as regards the different interpretations of Schumann's "Träumerei" by the two orchestras. Balatka's men played the number almost *forte*, with all the strings; the Thomas Orchestra gave it with a few strings, muted and *pianissimo*. Another matter I recall: Thomas' men remained seated during the performance. Balatka* adhered to the old usage in Germany, requiring the men to stand while playing.

Mr. Upton, many years later (1908), wrote of the playing by the Thomas Orchestra of the "Träumerei" in the concert on November 27, 1869:

"The difference in setting and reading, the precision, shading and tonal beauty, and particularly the '*pianis-is-simo*,' as Mr. Thomas calls it, at the close, all proclaimed a new musical departure for Chicago. The 'Träumerei' was the dawn of a new musical day for the west."

Mr. Upton said of this concert in the *Tribune* of the next day (Sunday), November 28:

---
*Hans Balatka died April 17, 1899, in Chicago.

"On the evening of the 7th of October, just twelve years ago, Carl Formes* gave a concert in Metropolitan Hall. It rained that night. It always rained in those times on the nights of the best concerts. . . . At that concert there was an orchestra which came from the east, and in that orchestra (conducted by Carl Anschutz) there were such names as Mosenthal, Besig, Bernstein, Mollenhauer, Bergman, Letsch and Thomas. That last name is Theodore Thomas in full, who played that evening Vieuxtemps' 'Rêverie' for violin. He has come up since those days, and before this meets your eye he will have introduced his splendidly trained orchestra to the Chicago public, a pleasure which will be repeated on Monday and Tuesday evenings of next week. If we can't support a home orchestra the next best thing is to support a foreign orchestra."

The last concert of the series was given on Tuesday evening, November 30, with a repetition of the "Träumerei." Again I quote from Mr. Upton in the *Tribune* of December 1:

"And now at the last moment come the people to hear Theodore Thomas' Orchestra; now when the last strains are dying away, come the Chicago public to hear such a performance as they never heard before, as they may never hear again. . . . This sudden spasm of musical enthusiasm should have commenced on Saturday night, when a comparative handful of people sat in that great hall and listened breathlessly to such playing as they had hardly dreamed of before. It was a revelation. . . . Dance music when played by such an orchestra is enticing enough to wake up a graveyard. We carry away with us alluring memories of that delicate dream work of Schumann's and the sound of the muted violins . . . and, best of all, the 'Allegretto' to the eighth symphony which Thomas selected for the encore to the 'Träumerei.' "

Mr. Thomas came again the following year (1870), giving seven concerts, November 7-14. The most notable of the series was that of November 14, a Beethoven program, which included the "Choral Fantasie," with Miss Anna Mehlig, pianist, assisted by a select chorus of 200 voices, This was the beginning of my friendship with Adolph W. Dohn, afterward Conductor of the Apollo Musical Club, who trained the Chorus, of which I was a member.

---

*In 1897 Mme. Kaselowska, a married daughter of Carl Formes, lived in an apartment building at No. 1207 West Twelfth Street. On learning who she was, I made several calls to gather some facts about her history. At that time she was a member of a German theatrical company, playing at McVicker's Theatre. She told me of her father and his wonderful voice, and that at the time of his death (1889) he was living in San Francisco. I was in San Francisco (1875), and heard him sing at the Occidental Hotel.

CROSBY OPERA HOUSE (1866)
From the Chicago Historical Society Collection.

Another series of concerts by the Thomas Orchestra was announced in Chicago, commencing Monday, October 9, 1871, at the Crosby Opera House. On Saturday, the 7th, the long line of ticket buyers at the box office on Washington Street (the Opera House was on the north side of Washington, between State and Dearborn Streets) indicated the interest of the public; but no one dreamed of the disaster which came in the great fire of Sunday and Monday, leaving Opera House, hotels, homes, banks and business houses in ashes. On Monday morning I left my home, which was then at No. 369 (now 1216) Michigan Avenue, to go over to State Street to note the progress of the conflagration, and there I observed a line of men walking north, carrying violins, 'cellos, trombones and other instruments. I learned, on inquiry, that they were members of the Thomas Orchestra, who had just arrived at the Twenty-second Street Station of the Lake Shore road. "We are going to the Opera House for rehearsal," replied one of the men. Mr. Thomas said, years later: "We got away from the burning city as best we could, and spent the time intervening before our next engagement, which was at St. Louis, October 21, in rehearsals." He became so involved financially by this disaster that some years passed before he recovered from the loss. During the twenty years which elapsed before Chicago gave him a permanent home for himself and Orchestra, he came again and again to our city, always receiving a cordial welcome and a generous support. Mr. Thomas once said of a musician who was reported to have died broken-hearted, "He had no Chicago to go to."

1872-1891

Organization of the Apollo Musical Club—Early concerts of the Club with the Thomas Orchestra—The Summer Garden Concerts, the creation of George Benedict Carpenter—His death and funeral services—Festivals of 1882 and 1884, conducted by Theodore Thomas—Testimonial tour of the Thomas Orchestra—Dedication of the Auditorium—Marriage of Theodore Thomas and Miss Rose Fay.

Early in 1872 Silas Gamaliel Pratt, a Boston pianist, came to Chicago to make this city his home. During the summer he suggested to George P. Upton and others the formation of a men's singing society after the order of the Apollo Club in Boston, founded by Benjamin J. Lang. A preliminary meeting and rehearsal were held one evening in the old frame church building, then at the southeast corner of Wabash Avenue and Sixteenth Street, occupied by Lyon & Healy's music store. A permanent organization was soon effected: George P. Upton, President; William Sprague, Vice-President; Charles C. Curtiss, Secretary; Frank A. Bowen, Treasurer; Warren C. Coffin, Librarian; Fritz Foltz, S. E. Cleveland and Philo A. Otis, Music Committee. Mr. Pratt conducted the early rehearsals, and then withdrew in favor of Adolph W. Dohn, who directed the first concert or reception (as it was then called) January 21, 1873, in Standard Hall. Mr. Dohn was the Conductor until 1875, when he was succeeded by William L. Tomlins.

Such were the simple beginnings of the Apollo Musical Club, now (1924) in its Fifty-third Season, known at home and abroad for its earnest work in the cause of music.

Some attractive concerts were given in the early days of the Club, with the assistance of Mr. Thomas and his Orchestra.

"February 16, 17 and 18, 1874: A series of concerts with the Apollo Club* and Germania Männerchor in McCormick Hall; Theodore Thomas and A. W. Dohn, Conductors. The first performance in America of Schumann's 'Paradise and the Peri' was given on Wednesday evening, the 18th. Soloists, Miss Clara

---

*The Apollo Musical Club was organized as a männerchor, but for the performance of large choral works an auxiliary chorus of women's voices was easily obtained. When William L. Tomlins became Conductor in 1875, the Club was changed to a mixed chorus.

GEORGE BENEDICT CARPENTER

Doria,* Mrs. O. L. Fox,† Mrs. O. K. Johnson, Mrs. T. E. Stacey, Miss Ella White, now Mrs. Jacob R. Custer, Miss Anna Lewis, Fritz Foltz,‡ L. A. Phelps and E. W. Reuling."

"June 5, 6 and 7, 1877: Festival of the Apollo Musical Club in the Tabernacle on Monroe Street. Conductors, Theodore Thomas and William L. Tomlins. Soloists, Mrs. H. M. Smith, Miss Annie Louise Cary, W. J. Winch and Myron W. Whitney. The important works given were 'Saint Paul,' Part First (Mendelssohn), and 'Israel in Egypt' (Handel)."

The Summer Garden Concerts (1877-1891) in the old Exposition Building on the Lake Front, conducted by Mr. Thomas, were a delightful feature of Chicago life in those days. The concerts inaugurated by Carpenter & Sheldon, who had organized and developed the Chicago "Star Lecture Course," were continued after the death (1881) of George Benedict Carpenter by Mrs. Carpenter and Milward Adams; later by Milward Adams alone.

One or two generations of concert-goers have come and gone since the days of the Summer Garden Concerts. Music lovers of the present day would smile at the simple life of their fathers and mothers, in the "seventies." We passed the months of July and August in the city, attending the Thomas Concerts in the evening, where it was always cool and where we heard good music. It was quite a prehistoric age in the way of transportation. There were no taxis, motor or trolley cars; we had horse cars. The young and frivolous paid twenty-five cents for admission to the concerts, and then gathered about the tables among the evergreen trees, partaking of lemonade and ice cream, while enjoying the strains of "The Beautiful Blue Danube." Spectacled young women and grave young men sat in the fifty-cent section and listened reverently to Bach, Beethoven and Brahms. The central location of the building, the informal and Bohemian character of the interior, the low prices of admission, with the charm of Mr. Thomas' programs—all combined to make the concerts very popular.

George Benedict Carpenter, to whom the credit for organizing the Summer Garden Concerts belongs, was one

---

*Miss Kathleen Barnett (stage name Clara Doria), daughter of John Barnett, the English composer, is now Mrs. Henry M. Rogers, and resides in Boston. Mrs. Rogers is an author of note, her principal works being "My Voice and I; or the Relation of the Singer to the Song" (1918), and "Memories of a Musical Career" (1919).

†Mrs. O. L. Fox died October 18, 1920, in Chicago. She had been for forty years a member of the Chicago Musical College.

‡Fritz Foltz, an early member of the Apollo Musical Club and member of the firm of Treat & Foltz, architects, died February 1, 1916.

of the foremost managers of his time in the lecture and concert field. He came to Chicago in 1866 from a farm, and began life as a clerk in the freight department of the Chicago & North-Western Railroad Company. My friendship with him dates from 1868 after he had given up his clerkship and had started on a literary career as a reporter on the Chicago *Republican;* later he became managing editor of the *Interior*, a weekly paper in the interest of Presbyterianism, now known as the *Continent*. Mr. Carpenter and I, having similar tastes, were much together in those days, and in our talks he advanced views on life and work which were remarkable for so young a man. In November, 1868 (he was then twenty-three years old), I heard him in an address on "Ideals" to a Literary Association composed of the young men of Chicago:

"Never dwarf your ideal down to your present life; but raise your life to the standard of your ideal. Do not doubt success. Never fence yourself in, in the fear of the future. You will have enough obstacles to climb without obstructing your pathway with doubts. O! I have such large faith in the young men and women of today. It is so grand to be living now and to be young."

On Thursday evening, January 6, 1881, the men of the Apollo Musical Club were rehearsing in Apollo Hall (Central Music Hall Building) for a performance of Berlioz's "Faust" with Mr. Thomas in February, when word came that Mr. Carpenter, Manager of Central Music Hall and the Club, was dying. He had been seriously ill for several days. Mr. Tomlins closed the rehearsal at once, and we went sadly home. Early the next morning, January 7, Mr. Carpenter passed away.

It was Mr. Carpenter who conceived (1877) the idea of Central Music Hall as a home for the Central Church, and who brought the idea to completion, with the Rev. David Swing (Professor Swing) as the first minister. Professor Swing, in his address at Mr. Carpenter's funeral, Sunday afternoon, January 9, 1881, related an instance of Mr. Carpenter's difficulties in securing the capital to erect the hall. "He urged me," said Professor Swing, "to write a letter to a leading citizen of great wealth, and secure his co-operation, with nine other men, in building the hall. The answer came back in exactly these words:

"Dear Sir: I cannot give your project one moment's attention.
"Yours truly.
"XXXX."

"And yet this hero in such work," continued Professor Swing, "induced me, a month later, to visit that same gentleman; and before the interview was over the success of the Music Hall was assured. The will of George B. Carpenter often has made life grow out of ashes."

It is sad that Mr. Carpenter did not live to see some of the "Ideals" we talked of fifty years ago realized; but he was a dreamer and, like all dreamers, lived ahead of his time. In the language of stage-folk, "The advance agent was making dates too far ahead of the show." Thus by a process of evolution the way was being prepared for the coming of the new Orchestra.

Berlioz's "Damnation of Faust," for which we were rehearsing on that sad Thursday evening when we heard George Carpenter was dying, had its first performance in Chicago by the Apollo Musical Club February 28, 1881, in Central Music Hall; Theodore Thomas, Conductor. Soloists: Miss Fanny Kellogg (soprano), W. C. Tower (tenor), Franz Remmertz (baritone) and W. H. Clark (bass).

The Chicago Biennial Musical Festival Association was organized in 1881 to give a Festival in 1882, with Nathaniel K. Fairbank, President; George L. Dunlap, Vice-President; Philo A. Otis, Secretary; Charles D. Hamill, Chairman of Music Committee; George Sturges, Treasurer, and Milward Adams, Business Manager.

The First Festival was held in the Exposition Building, May 23, 24, 25 and 26, 1882, under the direction of Theodore Thomas; William L. Tomlins, Chorus Director. Soloists: Mme. Amalie Materna and Mrs. E. Aline Osgood (sopranos); Miss Annie Louise Cary* and Miss Emily Winant (contraltos); Italo Campanini, William Candidus and Theodore J. Toedt (tenors); George Henschel, Franz Remmertz and Myron W. Whitney (basses); Clarence Eddy (organist); F. Dietz (trumpet); festival chorus of 900; festival orchestra of 174.

May 23, Tuesday evening, miscellaneous program for soloists, chorus, organ and orchestra, including "The Jubilate" (Handel).

---

*Annie Louise Cary, a famous singer of other days, died April 4, 1921, at Norwalk, Connecticut, at the age of seventy-nine. She was the widow of Charles M. Raymond, a former New York banker.

May 24, Wednesday matinée, for soloists and orchestra.
May 24, Wednesday evening, "The Messiah" (Handel).
May 25, Thursday matinée, for soloists and orchestra.
May 25, Thursday evening, after intermission, the ninth symphony (Beethoven).
May 26, Friday matinée, for soloists and orchestra— Wagner program.
May 26, Friday evening, "Mass in C Minor" (Schumann) and "The Fall of Troy," from "Les Troyens" (Berlioz).

The proportion of loss on the Festival to each of the fifty subscribers to the Guarantee Fund was $184.20.

The echoes of the final chorus in Berlioz's "Troyens" had scarcely died away when we began to plan for another festival.

The officers of the Festival Association held several conferences with Mr. Thomas when he returned in July for the Summer Garden Concerts, and practically decided on the works the chorus would study during the coming winter; but no action was taken about dates and soloists for the Second Festival until the Conductor came for the Summer Garden Concerts in 1883. A joint meeting was then held July 13, at the Chicago Club, with Mr. Thomas, the officers of the Chicago and Cincinnati Festival Associations and Charles E. Locke, Manager of the Festival Tours of the Thomas Orchestra, to arrange details for the Festival of 1884, to be held May 27, 28, 29, 30 and 31, 1884, in the Exposition Building; Theodore Thomas, Conductor; William L. Tomlins, Chorus Director; Milward Adams, Business Manager. Soloists: Mme. Amalie Materna, Mme. Christine Nilsson and Miss Emma Juch (sopranos); Miss Emily Winant (contralto); Hermann Winkelmann and Theodore J. Toedt (tenors); Emil Scaria and Franz Remmertz (basses); Clarence Eddy (organist); festival chorus of 900; festival orchestra of 170.

The Festival was held, as in 1882, in the south end of the Exposition Building. Many alterations were again required, in order to convert the building into a concert hall. A stage for chorus and orchestra with necessary dressing rooms had to be constructed, and the rest of the space arranged for seating an audience of 6,500 people. It being the year for the presidential election (1884),

Chicago had been chosen as the convention city. The Festival Association arranged with the two National Committees that the Republican Convention should use the hall in June, and the Democratic Convention in July, the two committees sharing with the Festival Association in the cost of alterations. One factor we had not taken into account—the weather. The month of May, 1884, was unusually cold, and there being no heating plant in the building, performers and audience suffered in consequence.

I went to Cincinnati Thursday (the 22nd) to hear the last concert of their Festival, the sixth, and to report to Mr. Thomas on conditions in Chicago, returning with soloists, Conductor and Orchestra by special train after the concert Saturday night. It was quite warm in Cincinnati, but on arriving at Kankakee Sunday morning a cold wind from Lake Michigan met us, and at once I thought of the Exposition Building: How could we give the concerts in that cold place? We arrived in Chicago at noon, and in the evening, though it was cold, Mr. Thomas held a rehearsal on the stage for the Orchestra. The next morning there were snowflakes in the air. My journal will indicate some of the difficulties we experienced with the Exposition Building:

"May 26, Monday A. M.: To the building, so cold and damp; then to Dalton's on State Street to get stoves put up in chorus dressing room and two in main hall; chorus and Orchestra rehearsal at 12:00; men wore hats and overcoats.

"May 27, Tuesday A. M.: Weather still cold; to the building. Hamill and I spent the whole morning working about the hall. First concert in evening; about 6,000 in attendance; very cold. The G minor symphony (Mozart) magnificently played. Mr. Thomas stopped Remmertz and Orchestra in 'The Creation'; called out to a man in the gallery, 'Close that door; draft on soloists!' Chorus fine; Mr. Thomas took 'The Heavens are Telling' at a furious *tempo;* never heard it given so fast before; we could hardly follow him.

"May 28, Wednesday: Rehearsal at 12:00 noon for 'The Redemption' (Gounod) and 'Tannhäuser'; large enthusiastic audience in the evening; 'Tannhäuser' went well, especially 'March and Chorus.' The 'Pilgrims' Chorus' (men) ended on the pitch—unusual even in Vienna (so Frau Materna told me). The 'Septet' in first act was delightful.

"May 29, Thursday: Wagner matinée—attendance of at least 6,000, in spite of the newspaper complaints: 'Too much Wagner.' The most unpopular program draws the largest house.

"A small house in the evening to hear the 'Requiem' (Berlioz); good work by the chorus. 'Lachrymosa' very effective. Winkelmann sang the tenor solo in the 'Sanctus' with great breadth; recalled three times. 'Tuba Mirum' and 'Rex Tremendæ' brought applause from Mr. Thomas.

"Such a small audience! Bitter cold!

"May 30, Friday: The Music Committee decided to change the program for tonight; cut out the 'Te Deum' (Handel), all but two numbers, substituting the 'Tannhäuser' selections sung on Wednesday night.

"May 31, Saturday matinée: The Children's Choir (1,000) was the attraction; their singing a revelation, especially in the Cherubini number, 'Like as a Father.' Mr. Tomlins called out again and again. Winkelmann sang the aria from 'Iphigénie en Tauride' (Gluck)—a glorious melody. In the evening 'The Redemption' (Gounod); large house."

The reader can now understand why the Association did not undertake another Festival. The Exposition Building could not be used again on account of the cost of the alterations and the lack of proper lighting, seating and heating facilities, and it was too large for the best choral and orchestral results. There was but one opinion, however, as to the Orchestra: that it was the largest and most efficient that Mr. Thomas had ever brought to Chicago, and in the matter of auxiliaries of wind and percussion instruments required for the performance of the "Requiem" (Berlioz) probably had not been surpassed in this country.

The Secretary's report showed receipts, $65,747.77; expenses, $71,565.17, with a loss of $5,817.40, representing $98.60 to be paid by each of the subscribers to the Guarantee Fund. In a permanent hall, and with our own Orchestra, the Festival would have shown a profit. The people were eager to hear the music; the temperature of the building kept them away; not the newspaper clamor of "Too much Wagner." The signatures to the Guarantee Fund were easily obtained; no one refused.

The Board of Management of the Apollo Musical Club ordinarily employed a local orchestra for its concerts, but for important works secured the Thomas Orchestra when it was on a western tour and dates could be arranged. We had planned to give "Elijah" for the last concert of the thirteenth season (1884-1885), but on learning that Mr. Thomas would close the season of the

New York Choral Society, April 21, 1885, with a new work, "The Rose of Sharon" (Mackenzie), and would then start on a festival tour in May to San Francisco, we determined to secure him and his Orchestra, and to substitute "The Rose of Sharon" for "Elijah."

Two concerts were arranged:

"May 21, Thursday evening, in Central Music Hall, Mackenzie's 'Rose of Sharon,' Theodore Thomas, Conductor. Soloists: Miss Emma Juch (soprano) in place of Madame Fursch-Madi; Miss Hattie J. Clapper (contralto); William J. Winch (tenor), and Max Heinrich (bass)."

MAY 22, FRIDAY EVENING, EXTRA CONCERT
PART I.
"Stabat Mater,". . . . . *Rossini*
SOLOISTS: MISS EMMA JUCH, MISS HATTIE J. CLAPPER, WILLIAM J. WINCH* and MAX HEINRICH; WILLIAM L. TOMLINS, Conductor.

Miscellaneous selections for soloist (Miss Emma Juch) and Orchestra, under the direction of Mr. Thomas, occupied the second part of the concert.

Mr. Winch, in a letter dated August 12, 1918, from his home in Windsor, Vermont, writes of his artistic career:

"My residence in London (1880-1886) was full of interest. I was the first to sing Dvořák's songs to an English audience. Liszt told me I was the first man he ever heard sing his 'Lorelei.' I enjoyed an intimate acquaintanceship with Theodore Thomas, having made a three months' tour with him in the spring of 1885, from Portland, Maine, to San Francisco."

My own remembrance of Mr. Winch dates from the "Peace Jubilee" (1872) in Boston, when he was one of the "Bouquet of Artists."

The report of the Music Committee at the Annual Meeting of the Apollo Club a few weeks later contained some caustic comments on the indifference of our music lovers to Mackenzie's work:

"The dear people of Chicago who love to go to a Thomas concert did not come out at all on Thursday and Friday nights. The audience on Friday night was the smallest Mr. Thomas ever had in Chicago. The great composers, great soloists, great organists and great pianists of this city showed no desire whatever to hear Mackenzie's work on Thursday evening, written for the Norwich Festival (1884), the most important oratorio ever heard in England since Mendelssohn brought out 'Elijah' at Birmingham forty years ago."

*William J. Winch died February 19, 1919, in Boston, Massachusetts.

In 1889 the people of Chicago gave Mr. Thomas a great reception in connection with the testimonial tour tendered him by the principal cities of our country. The *Chicago Tribune* of May 19, in commending the tour, expressed the hope that: "Mr. Thomas might be our orchestra leader in the near future—a consummation devoutly to be wished."

In harmony with this movement a letter was addressed to Mr. Thomas, signed by many of his friends in Chicago, expressing the "cordial hope that you will include this city in the list to be honored by one or more of these concerts; and in case of an affirmative response, we will pledge you a cordial, hearty and thoroughly appreciative welcome."

Early in October I was in New York, and on the morning of October 9 met Mr. Thomas with the two men who were promoting the testimonial tour, David Blakely and John D. Elwell.* In answer to their inquiry as to what we were doing in Chicago about the concerts, I replied: "We will welcome Mr. Thomas with sold-out houses."

In the evening I went over to Brooklyn to attend the first of the testimonial concerts (Rafael Joseffy, soloist) at the Academy of Music, in a program of a popular character: overture ("Tannhäuser"), selections from "The Damnation of Faust" (Berlioz), "Träumerei" (Schumann) and other numbers. Mr. Joseffy played delightfully, his principal number being Liszt's "Fantasie on Hungarian Airs," for piano and orchestra.

The audience was so small that I can now, after an interval of many years, easily understand why Mr. Thomas chose to accept the call which Chicago made him two years later.

---

*While busy with the details of the testimonial concerts, I received this letter:

"THE THOMAS TESTIMONIAL TOUR
"John D. Elwell, *Chairman*
"David Blakely, *Secretary*
"*Committee on Arrangements.*
"New York, October 18, 1889.

"My Dear Mr. Otis:

"I enclose you a leaf from a letter which takes your name in vain.

"I don't suppose you want thanks any more than I do, but all the same, you must know that 'the Old Man' has a very warm place in his heart for you. He is going to do splendidly in many places, thanks to hard work, and I am sure Chicago won't be behind.

"Always with kind regards,
"Very truly yours,
"Jno. D. Elwell."

On my return home I set to work in earnest to redeem my promise that we would "welcome Mr. Thomas with sold-out houses." A note was accordingly sent to all the signers of our letter, asking them to show their appreciation of Mr. Thomas by "practically taking the entire house for both nights."

With the co-operation of Charles D. Hamill and Milward Adams, then Manager of the Auditorium, I organized an active campaign to promote the testimonial concerts, and so successfully that on the day the box office opened (October 21) Central Music Hall had been sold out for both evenings.

Mr. Thomas accepted the invitation from Chicago, and as he regarded this as a popular movement and desired to give the people an opportunity to express their preferences for the music to be performed, he prepared three programs. The ticket holders were requested to send their choice, in writing, to Theodore Thomas, care of Milward Adams, at the Auditorium; the two programs receiving the largest popular vote to be performed. The people made a good choice:

OCTOBER 25, 1889, FRIDAY EVENING

Overture, "Coriolanus," . . . . *Beethoven*
Adagio, "Prometheus," . . . . *Beethoven*
        Violoncello Solo by Victor Herbert
"Invitation to the Dance," . . . . . *Weber—Berlioz*
Symphonic Poem, "Les Préludes," . . . . . *Liszt*
        INTERMISSION
Concerto, E Minor, ... *Chopin—Tausig*
        Rafael Joseffy
"Heart Wounds," }
"Spring," . . . } . . . . *Grieg*
        String Orchestra
"Waldweben" ("Siegfried"), }
"Ride of the Valkyries," . } . . . . . . *Wagner*

OCTOBER 26, SATURDAY EVENING

Overture, "Flying Dutchman," . . . . . . *Wagner*
Symphony No. 8, F Major, ... *Beethoven*
        INTERMISSION
Concerto, A Minor, ... *Schumann*
        Rafael Joseffy
Funeral March, ... *Chopin—Thomas*
Serenade No. 3, D Minor, ... *Volkmann*
        Violoncello Solo by Victor Herbert
        String Orchestra
Hungarian Rhapsody No. 3, ... *Liszt*
"In the Garden," }
"Dance," . . } . . . . *Goldmark*

With the dedication of the Auditorium, December 9, 1889, Chicago possessed a hall suitable for all important occasions, national conventions, opera, concerts of the Apollo Musical Club and a home for a permanent Orchestra, did we but have as a leader, in the words of Martin Luther:

> "The right man on our side,
> The man of God's own choosing."

Such a leader was found, and eventually, through the influence and generosity of our strong friends of music, Theodore Thomas came to Chicago—in the autumn of 1891. In the meantime a happy event occurred, which I find noted in my journal:

"May 7, 1890: 7:30 Wednesday evening to the Church of the Ascension, wedding of Miss Rose Fay and Mr. Thomas—service conducted by the Rev. E. A. Larrabee; delightful program of organ music by Clarence Eddy, including the march from the Concertstück (Weber) and portion of the fifth symphony (Beethoven). After the ceremony, to the reception at the home of C. N. Fay, 43 Bellevue Place. All of the musical and social world were there.

"In the words of Sir Walter Scott, 'The Hour's come, and the Man.'"

ROSE FAY THOMAS

FIRST SEASON
(1891-1892)

Charles Norman Fay tells the story of the organization, incorporation and first Board of Trustees of the Orchestra—First concerts—Mr. Thomas conducts Berlioz's "Faust" for the Apollo Musical Club—The Orchestra assists the Apollo Musical Club in its Twentieth Anniversary.

To Theodore Thomas we must ascribe all honor as the founder of our Orchestra, but to Charles Norman Fay, a man endowed with a genius for organization and executive work, is due equal honor for the first thought of the Orchestra. From 1879 to 1887 Mr. Fay was Vice-President and General Manager of the Chicago Telephone Company; 1887 to 1889, President of the Chicago Gas Company; later President of the Chicago Arc Light and Power Company until it was absorbed by the Commonwealth Edison Company (1893). It was Mr. Fay who suggested to Mr. Thomas the formation of a permanent Orchestra in Chicago, and who provided the ways and means for his coming as its Conductor.

The story of the organization of the Orchestra was told by Mr. Fay in the February (1910) number of the *Outlook:*

"In August, 1877, I was unexpectedly called to Chicago to protect business interests involved in a failure precipitated by the railway strike and riots of that year. I did not know when I started that I could even enter the town, and gentlemen from the country were supposed to take their lives in their hands in the mob-ridden streets of what had once been called 'the Garden City.'

"I got there safely, however, and found as quiet a burg as ever seemed to drowse, and very hot. That evening, wandering out for a breath of air, I came upon the old Exposition Building, down on the Lake Front, and from its open doors and windows floated, instead of shots and battle cries, the divinest music. Theodore Thomas was giving there his first Chicago season of Summer Garden Concerts, and for the first time I heard a great orchestra.

"I moved to Chicago that autumn, and he came again for Summer Garden Concerts in 1880, and every year thereafter, except 1884, until 1891, when he brought his Orchestra to Chicago for good— for exceeding great good—and played there until he died in 1905.

---

*By permission of the Outlook Company.

"I became personally acquainted with Mr. Thomas in 1881, and the acquaintance ripened into intimacy. One day in 1889 I met him on Fifth Avenue, and we turned in to the old Delmonico's. He looked worn and worried, and I asked him why. There were reasons enough. There was mortal illness in his home; the American Opera Company, that short and melancholy chapter of good music and bad management, had swept away his savings; and, almost worst of all, he had been obliged to give up his own permanent Orchestra. To use his own words, 'I have had to stop engaging my men by the year, and now I play with scratch orchestras. In order to keep my old Orchestra together I have always had to travel constantly, winter and summer, the year around, and year after year. Now I am fifty-three, too old to stand the traveling. New York alone cannot support my Orchestra, so it has had perforce to be disbanded.'

"For a moment, so bitter was his tone, I had nothing to reply, but finally I said: 'Is there no one, no rich and generous man, to do here in New York as Major Higginson has done in Boston—keep your Orchestra going, and pay the deficit?'

" 'No one,' he answered. 'I have told them often, those who say they are my friends, that for good work there must be a permanent Orchestra; and for a permanent Orchestra, which will not pay, there must be a subsidy. My work is known. I am old now, and have no ax to grind. But they do not care. They think I have always kept the body and soul together somehow, and that I always will—that I have nowhere else to go. They treat me as a music merchant, a commercial proposition, subject to the laws of supply and demand.'

"My thoughts went back to those ten years of Summer Garden Concerts, and to some powerful and devoted friends of Mr. Thomas and his music at home, and I asked, 'Would you come to Chicago if we could give you a permanent Orchestra?' The answer, grim and sincere, and entirely destitute of intentional humor, came back like a flash: 'I would go to hell if they gave me a permanent Orchestra.'

"Well, Chicago has always resembled the west end of the next world in this, among other things, that it is wide open to good company.

"And then and there were roughed-out in talk the general principles of an agreement under which the Theodore Thomas Orchestra has lived, moved and had its being in that city for eighteen years":

That he would bring an Orchestra to Chicago, of which he should have absolute control, and that he would make his own programs without reference to box office receipts;

That an Association should be organized to provide ways and means, including a guarantee against loss, of $50,000 per annum for three years; that there should be no entangling alliances of any kind with piano houses,

First Season—1891-1892

musical colleges or newspapers; that the members of the Orchestra should be given contracts for twenty-eight weeks in each year, and that there should be a series of symphonic concerts Friday afternoon and Saturday evening every week, for twenty weeks in each season.

"When I returned to Chicago after this talk [continued Mr. Fay] it did not take long to find support for the plan outlined above. The Orchestral Association, a 'corporation not for pecuniary benefit,' was formed under Illinois law, consisting of five members: N. K. Fairbank, E. B. McCagg, A. C. Bartlett, Charles D. Hamill and myself, of which N. K. Fairbank, a leader in all the liberalities, was President, and I was Vice-President and factotum. Fifty gentlemen, headed by the late Marshall Field, gave me their signatures to a guarantee of $1,000 per annum each for three years against any deficit resulting from our operations.

"Artistically the success of our undertaking was great and cumulative. Relieved from the necessity of constant travel, exhausting both to himself and his men, and for the first time in his life free from the business cares of so large a concern; able to search the world for master-musicians—young men—vigorous and enthusiastic; rehearsing four times a week and playing twice; inspiring them with artistic purpose and a proud *esprit de corps*, Mr. Thomas developed his Orchestra from year to year as a gardener develops a splendid rose. Always, but especially in his later years, the astonishing virtuosity of his Orchestra, its dramatic power and effect, the dazzling beauty and blending of its tone color, its perfection of quality and shading, well deserved César Thomson's epigram, 'I have seen many a man direct an orchestra, but never heard a man *play on* one before,' and Paderewski's exclamation, 'I have played that concerto a hundred times, but never *heard* it before in my life!'

"Such comments were not novel. Years before, Anton Rubinstein had said to William Steinway, after his tour across the United States with the old Thomas Orchestra: 'I little thought to find in this new country the finest Orchestra in the world! Man for man, the orchestra of the Conservatoire in Paris is perhaps equal to them, but unfortunately they have not Theodore Thomas to direct.'

"Fortunate it was that we had artistic success to buoy us up, for financially our record was melancholy enough."

The first meeting for the incorporation of The Orchestral Association was held at the Chicago Club, December 17, 1890, and a Board of five Trustees elected to serve for one year, or until their successors were elected: A. C. Bartlett, C. Norman Fay, N. K. Fairbank, Charles D. Hamill and Ezra B. McCagg.

Officers: N. K. Fairbank, President, and C. Norman Fay, Vice-President. Milward Adams was appointed Manager, and P. A. McEwan, Secretary and Treasurer.

Mr. Fay presented the Guarantee Fund of $50,000 he had secured, and the contract with Mr. Thomas. The contract covered two important items:

"ARTICLE II—Thomas agrees to furnish all the orchestral music, but not the instrumental solos and vocal numbers, except when the same are in the Thomas library.

"ARTICLE III—The Trustees reserve the right to furnish the Orchestra for the opera performances (Auditorium) with or without Thomas as Conductor."

Mr. Thomas' library was indeed a valuable addition to the working forces of the Association. The scores and orchestral parts of the works needed to give the concerts could have been acquired by loan or purchase, but with some delay and cost in money.

For the first six seasons the Association furnished the Orchestra to the opera companies in the Auditorium at a compensation covering the weekly salary list; a welcome addition to the revenues of the Association, but always "without Thomas to conduct." The opera companies brought their own conductors, thus relieving Mr. Thomas of much exacting and arduous work.

In response to a request for data regarding the early meetings of the Trustees and how he secured the signatures to the Guarantee Fund, Mr. Fay wrote:

"BOSTON, MASSACHUSETTS, October 20, 1916.
"DEAR OTIS:

"As to the early meetings of the Trustees, I do not remember very much about them. My impression is that the first was held in E. B. McCagg's office, as I made him one of the five original incorporators because he was a lawyer. Hamill was the only active man of the five besides myself. Fairbank, Bartlett and McCagg did what we asked them, and I suppose the minutes of the Association will reveal what that was. Hamill and I used to meet casually at the Chicago Club, where he was always to be found, and I used to lunch. I would tell him what I was about, and he generally said 'All right.'

"I started originally to get a guarantee of $50,000 a year for three years from ten men at $5,000 apiece. I, of course, was to be one of them, and the first consent I got was from Marshall Field at his summer home at Pride's Crossing. Then Fairbank consented, and George Pullman, which made four of us. I went to Ferd. Peck, and he urged me to make the subscription $1,000 apiece from fifty men, instead of $5,000 apiece from ten men. It happened just then that the Commercial Club gave an excursion to see the new buildings at Fort Sheridan, and I put a subscription paper in my pocket, and talked the matter up on the train going and coming, having first secured Marshall Field's signature as a starter. Field

CHARLES NORMAN FAY

First Season—1891-1892

himself was there, and told the others to come along, and I got nineteen signatures that day. After that it was merely a matter of running around until I completed the fifty-one who actually signed; but two of them never paid up at all, though they took the credit as guarantors just the same.

"Always cordially,
"C. N. Fay."

GUARANTORS

J. McGregor Adams.	S. A. Kent.
Allison V. Armour.	Edson Keith.
George A. Armour.	Henry W. King.
Philip D. Armour.	Walter C. Larned.
S. E. Barrett.	Victor F. Lawson.
A. C. Bartlett.	L. Z. Leiter.
Henry W. Bishop.	J. Mason Loomis.
T. B. Blackstone.	Franklin MacVeagh.
E. W. Blatchford.	Ezra B. McCagg.
John M. Clark.	Cyrus H. McCormick.
Charles Counselman.	O. W. Meysenburg.
R. T. Crane.	Thomas Murdoch.
Columbus R. Cummings.	Eugene S. Pike.
N. K. Fairbank.	Henry H. Porter.
C. Norman Fay.	O. W. Potter.
Henry Field.	George M. Pullman.
Marshall Field.	Norman B. Ream.
Charles W. Fullerton	Martin A. Ryerson.
Lyman J. Gage.	Byron L. Smith.
John J. Glessner.	Albert A. Sprague.
T. W. Harvey.	Otho S. A. Sprague.
William G. Hibbard.	Charles H. Wacker.
H. N. Higginbotham.	John R. Walsh.
Charles L. Hutchinson.	Norman Williams.
Dr. Ralph N. Isham.	Carl Wolfsohn.
Albert Keep.	

In the spring of 1891 Mr. Thomas gave a series of "Farewell Concerts" in the east before entering on his new work in Chicago. He extended the tour to Chicago, and appeared at the Auditorium with his "Unrivaled New York Orchestra," in a series of "Six Popular Concerts at Popular Prices" for the week commencing March 23, bringing an orchestra of fifty-six players, with Italo Campanini, Max Bendix and Victor Herbert as soloists. He came again with his Orchestra for another series of concerts, commencing April 27, bringing Miss Marie Jahn, of the Metropolitan Opera Company, and Max Bendix as soloists.

The *Chicago Tribune* had a few comments on the latter concerts:

"The Orchestra is some six or eight less in number than in March, and inferior to the other; the playing lacking that superior finish which made the former concerts the finest Mr. Thomas has given in several years."

To my mind he was simply "trying out" his players, in order to select the men needed for the new Orchestra he finally assembled for his First Season in Chicago.

Mr. Thomas was much annoyed at this time over the action taken by the Musicians' Union at its convention held in Milwaukee on March 21, regarding the contract he had made with The Orchestral Association of Chicago. The union maintained that this Orchestra being a Chicago enterprise, all of its players should come from Chicago, and not from New York or abroad.

A resolution was accordingly presented by a delegate from the Chicago Local, calling on Local No. 1 of New York, to annul this contract, as being detrimental to the character and standing of the musicians of Local No. 4 in Chicago, in that it violated the Alien Labor Contract Law by bringing foreign players to Chicago, to the exclusion of Chicago men. In case Mr. Thomas refused to cancel the contract, then Local No. 1 of New York should hold Mr. Thomas amenable to the laws of the local, and discipline him accordingly. On the assurance of the New York delegates that they would call on Mr. Thomas and undertake necessary action in the matter, the resolution was withdrawn.

While this last series of concerts was in progress I called with Mr. Tomlins (Conductor of the Apollo Musical Club) on Mr. Thomas at the Auditorium, just as he had finished his rehearsal, to discuss with him some concerts for next season; but we did not find him in an amiable mood. The newspapers were not at all friendly over the playing of the Orchestra, and the rehearsal that morning had been unsatisfactory.

"This is not a rehearsal at all," he declared; "I only wish to be sure that nothing happens." He then went on to speak of the Orchestra he was to bring for the Chicago concerts in the autumn, and of the action by the Musicians' Union at its recent meeting in Milwaukee:

"I shall select my players where I find them; and will bring them from New York or go to Europe for them if necessary. If there are good men in Chicago I will use them. I do not work for money or business. I work only for art."

First Season—1891-1892

Mr. Thomas opened a Summer Night Series at the Madison Square Garden in New York, July 6, 1891, playing forty-two concerts in all, ending on August 16. His work in the east being finished, the Conductor turned his face to the west—to Chicago, a city which for twenty years had always given him a cordial welcome, and which now furnished him a permanent Orchestra, and ultimately with an endowment unequaled in the annals of music.

The first public recognition of the Conductor of the new Orchestra came from the Apollo Musical Club, in a reception tendered by the members to Mr. and Mrs. Theodore Thomas, Wednesday evening, October 14, 1891, in the Apollo Club rooms, Central Music Hall. Mr. Thomas said in his note accepting this invitation:

"October 8, 1891.
"DEAR MR. OTIS:
"Your very kind and friendly letter has been received. Mrs. Thomas and myself will be glad to avail ourselves of the opportunity of meeting the members of the Apollo Club, and appreciate the honor they do us.
"Sincerely yours,
"THEODORE THOMAS."

A society editor said of the reception:

"Musical Director William L. Tomlins and President Philo A. Otis, with a number of the members and one hundred guests, extended to Mr. Thomas and his bride of a year (*née* Miss Rose Fay, of our city) a hearty and cordial greeting."

The prospectus issued by Manager Adams announced that:

"The First Season (1891-1892) of the Chicago Orchestra will consist of twenty concerts, each concert preceded by a public rehearsal, to be given in the Auditorium under the direction of Theodore Thomas. The talent engaged to make up the Chicago Orchestra is of the very finest order."

The Orchestra assembled by Mr. Thomas for his First Season numbered eighty-six men, of whom twenty-four were from Chicago, showing that the Conductor had kept faith with the union: "If there are good men in Chicago I will use them."

The prices of the season tickets were as follows:

For the twenty concerts, $30, $20 and $10, according to location; boxes seating five, $200.

For the twenty public rehearsals, $20, $15 and $10, according to location; boxes seating five, $150.

The first concerts were given on Friday afternoon, October 16, and Saturday evening, October 17, with Rafael Joseffy, soloist:

A Faust Overture, ...	*Wagner*
Symphony No. 5, Opus 67, ...	*Beethoven*

INTERMISSION

Concerto No. 1 for Pianoforte and Orchestra, . .	*Tschaikowsky*
Dramatic Overture, "Husitska,"	*Dvořák*

Program notes by Adolph W. Dohn.

A Sunday editor said of the First Program:

"The Orchestra will enable Chicago to take rank in the music world commensurate with her standing as one of the great cities of the country. The playing is beyond adverse criticism. . . . Such precision, such unity of attack, such accuracy is marvelous, when it is remembered that one fortnight ago the first rehearsal had not yet been held. Theodore Thomas worked wonders, and the end is by no means yet."

There was some interruption in the Chicago series of concerts that autumn, in consequence of out-of-town dates for the Orchestra, and a five weeks' engagement with the Italian Opera.

The Orchestra, however, assisted the Apollo Musical Club in the "Annual Christmas Performance" of Handel's "Messiah," in the Auditorium, Thursday evening, December 25, under the direction of William L. Tomlins. Soloists: Mrs. Jennie Patrick Walker (soprano), Mrs. Pauline Rommeiss Bremner (contralto), William J. Lavin (tenor) and Emil Fischer (bass); Ch. Rodenkirchen (trumpet), and Clarence Eddy (organist).

The concert was repeated on the following (Friday) evening for the "Wage Workers," with Mrs. Genevra Johnston Bishop in place of Mrs. Walker, who could not appear in consequence of illness.

At the concerts of January 1 and 2, 1892, Fifth Program, Mr. Paderewski appeared in a great performance of Rubinstein's concerto for pianoforte No. 4 in D minor.

SEVENTH PROGRAM, JANUARY 22 AND 23
POPULAR CONCERTS
SOLOISTS:

MRS. JULIE WYMAN	JOSEPH SCHREURS (Clarinet)
VIGO ANDERSEN (Flute)	BRUNO STEINDEL (Violoncello)

EDMUND SCHUECKER (Harp)

The program included:

"Tarantelle" for Flute and Clarinet,	*Saint-Saëns*
Fantasia, "Le Désir" (Violoncello),	*Servais*
Aria, "Samson et Dalila,"	*Saint-Saëns*
"Fantasia di Bravura" (Harp),	*Schuecker*

Mr. Thomas and the Orchestra assisted the Apollo Musical Club in a performance of Berlioz's "Faust" at the Auditorium on Monday evening, February 15. Soloists: Miss Ida Klein, Italo Campanini, William Ludwig and W. N. Porteous.

The concert was repeated on the following evening to the "Wage Workers."

The "Faust" performances were good as to band and soloists, but the chorus was sadly lacking. The "Easter Hymn" and "Slumber Song" were well sung, but we did not have men enough for "The Soldiers' Chorus," and there were too few rehearsals for the new members to learn the music. Mr. Thomas placed the tenors and basses directly in front of him and in the center of the chorus. Before the concert began he stepped in front of the men, telling us, "We have some hard work to do; look right at me! Never mind your music; all will go right."

It was "hard work," and we found it so in "The Soldiers' Chorus." But what a band! Eighty-seven in all. Never before had we heard the "Hungarian March," "The Dance of the Sylphs" and "The Will-o'-the-Wisps" as they were played at the "Faust" concerts.

Mr. Ludwig was not a German, as his name might indicate, but a genial Irishman, born in Dublin. His father's name was "Ledwich," but "as the people could not always get the name right," said the baritone, "I changed it to Ludwig." He came to New York in 1886 as a member of the American Opera Company, at the instance of the Musical Director, Mr. Thomas, to sing Mephisto in Gounod's "Faust" and some Wagner *rôles*, notably "The Dutchman," in which he had been very successful with the Carl Rosa Opera Company in London. Mr. Thomas said of Ludwig as Mephisto, that "in dress, action and voice he was the personification of Satan himself." Those who heard Berlioz's "Faust" may recall Ludwig's energetic singing of the passage, "Mark well the time, ye fiddlers of hell," in the recitative to the

"Serenade," and "The Ride to Hell," in which Mephisto invokes his "slaves in hell's dominions." He was no less successful as "The Dutchman." Ludwig told me, "I caught the idea of the part as I heard Santley sing it in London. When Santley retired he gave me his wardrobe, and thus I learned to dress the part."

Italo Campanini was the soloist February 19 and 20, Eleventh Program:

Aria, "Iphigénie en Tauride," . . . . *Gluck*
Song, "Adelaide," . . . . *Beethoven*

Winkelmann sang the Gluck aria at the Chicago Musical Festival (1884), but Campanini interested me much more. Lifting up his mighty voice, he sang the glorious melody as Orpheus sang when he went into the forest, followed by the birds, the trees, the lions and the deer; reminding me of William De Morgan's words in his story "Somehow Good," that "it is impossible to make Gluck's music anything but a foretaste of heaven."

FIFTEENTH PROGRAM, MARCH 18 AND 19
THIRD POPULAR CONCERT
SOLOIST: EMIL LIEBLING*

Concertstück, Opus 79, ... *Weber*

Mr. Thomas arranged a program of works by American composers for April 8 and 9, Eighteenth Program, George E. Holmes, soloist:

Symphony No. 2, "Im Frühling," Opus 34,
Aria from "St. Peter," "O God, My God, Forsake Me Not," . . . . . . } . *John K. Paine*

INTERMISSION

Dramatic Overture, "Melpomene," . . *George W. Chadwick*
Romance, "Deep in My Heart,"
 from "Otho Visconti," . . . . *Frederick Grant Gleason*
Symphonic Poem, "Francesca da Rimini," . *Harry Rowe Shelley*

The First Season of the Chicago Orchestra closed with the Twentieth Program ("Request"), April 22 and 23:

Introduction, Second Part ("Christmas Oratorio"), . . . *Bach*
Symphony No. 3, in F, ... *Beethoven*
Marche Funèbre, ... *Chopin—Thomas*

INTERMISSION

Overture, "Tannhäuser," . . . . *Wagner*
Theme and Variations from D Minor Quartette,. . . *Schubert*
"Les Préludes," . . . . *Liszt*

---

*Emil Liebling, artist and musician and a sincere friend of other days, was born April 12, 1851, in Pless, Germany. He came to Chicago in 1872, and was well known as player, teacher and writer. Mr. Liebling died January 20, 1914, in Chicago.

First Season—1891-1892

The Apollo Musical Club finished its season with the Twentieth Anniversary Concerts in recognition of the twenty years of work by the Club, and as a tribute to its Conductor, William L. Tomlins. The subject had been under consideration by the Board of Management for a year or more, and became a certainty when the Chicago Orchestra was established. We had decided to call the occasion a "Festival," until Mr. Thomas told us that under the rules of the Musicians' Union the word "Festival" would entitle the members of the Orchestra to increased compensation; hence the use of the word "Anniversary." The series consisted of three concerts in the Auditorium, for which our chorus of 500 voices was enlarged to 800 for the performance of the "Creation," "Hymn of Praise," and the "Passion Music." We had the assistance of Mr. Thomas and the entire Chicago Orchestra:

"May 17, Tuesday evening: 'The Creation' (Haydn). Soloists: Mrs. Clementine de Vere (soprano), Charles A. Knorr (tenor) and William Ludwig (bass); Clarence Eddy (organist); William L. Tomlins (Conductor).

INTERMISSION

"The Requiem (Berlioz): Soloist: Charles A. Knorr; Theodore Thomas (Conductor).

"May 18, Wednesday evening: 'Acis and Galatea' (Handel). Soloists: Mrs. Clementine de Vere (soprano), Edward Lloyd (tenor), and Gardner S. Lamson (bass). 'Hymn of Praise' (Mendelssohn). Soloists: Mrs. Clementine de Vere and Miss Helen Buckley (sopranos) and Edward Lloyd (tenor); William L. Tomlins (Conductor).

"May 19, Thursday evening: St. Matthew Passion Music (Bach), under the direction of Theodore Thomas. Soloists: Mrs. Genevra J. Bishop (soprano), Mme. Amalia Joachim (contralto), Edward Lloyd (tenor), Gardner S. Lamson and A. F. Maish (basses); Clarence Eddy (organist)."

The Anniversary Concerts come back to me so clearly, as I look over the pages of an old journal (1892) with notes of rehearsals and performances. Edward Lloyd, the best English oratorio tenor of his day, came to America in April to fill engagements with the Handel and Haydn Society of Boston, the Cincinnati Festival Association, and the Apollo Musical Club of Chicago. His singing of "Love Sounds the Alarm" in "Acis and Galatea," "The Sorrows of Death" in the "Hymn of Praise," and the part of the "Narrator" in the "Passion Music" was a revelation to American audiences. My journal notes:

"May 17, Tuesday: The large chorus did well in 'The Creation.' When we came to the 'Requiem' the extra chorus was sent off the stage. The Apollo Club sang it alone; audience appreciated it. The 'Tuba Mirum' produced a profound sensation, the bands and drums coming in at the exact moment.

"May 18, Wednesday evening: 'Acis and Galatea' did not go well; the extra chorus uncertain in attack, not knowing their parts; Lloyd in great form. The aria, 'Love in Her Eyes Sits Playing,' had to be repeated. The large chorus sang better in 'The Hymn of Praise'; more familiar with the music.

"May 19, Thursday evening: The 'Passion Music' went well. The singing of the boys in the first chorus much helped by four trumpets. Mr. Thomas conducted so quietly—a masterpiece of work. Audience did not understand Bach's work, though they appreciated the 'Chorales.' Mr. Lloyd's singing was a delight. Went to Mr. Thomas' room at intermission with check for his services. At first he declined to accept it: 'I am glad to help the Apollo Club'; but on my reminding him of the work he had done for the Club, accepted the money. He was so gracious about it."

The work of the Orchestra in the First Season was of a high order, as might be expected from such a body of players when taken in hand by Theodore Thomas. Everything was satisfactory but the attitude of the public.

"The dear people of Chicago who love to go to a Thomas Concert"—who flocked to the Exposition Building to hear his Orchestra in the "Summer Garden" period; who were always asking, "When are we to have our permanent Orchestra and hall?"—manifested but little interest in the Orchestra when it was established. Manager Adams made special efforts to sell season tickets, by a thorough canvass of the business and residence districts of Chicago, paying a commission of fifty cents to one dollar on every ticket sold. The canvassers met with the usual objections of that period: "Too much Wagner! Too many symphonies! Will not Mr. Thomas give us some 'Ball Room' and 'Request Programs'?"

There was a strong argument against season tickets, and it was often presented: "The Auditorium is so large, one can always get a seat; there is no need to buy tickets six months in advance."

With all his efforts the Manager could report only $17,500 in sales of season tickets, including boxes. The first sign of financial difficulties was suggested at a meeting of the Trustees, December 20, 1891, when it was voted:

"That the Treasurer be authorized to borrow from the First National Bank of Chicago such sums as may be necessary, not exceeding $20,000, to pay salaries and current expenses, and to execute the Association's notes therefor to the order of said bank, provided that Messrs. Fairbank and Fay endorse said notes, as they volunteer to do."

The largest attendance was at the first concerts, October 23 and 24, with Joseffy, soloist, $4,847; the Paderewski concerts, Fifth Program, January 1 and 2, 1892, yielded $4,373.75. The smallest attendance was on April 8 and 9, Eighteenth Program (American composers), with George E. Holmes, soloist, $598. The Twentieth, and last, Program (Request), April 22 and 23, drew $1,608.

The report of the Treasurer for the First Season (1891-1892), ending June 30, 1892, was, to use Mr. Fay's words, a "melancholy exhibit," covering twenty weeks of Chicago concerts, five weeks of Italian Opera and three weeks "on the road." The total expense for salaries of Conductor and Orchestra, Auditorium rent, soloists, advertising and business management was $129,328.69. The receipts from Chicago and out-of-town concerts, Italian Opera, Apollo Club and other engagements were $85,715.28, leaving a loss of $53,613.41 for the fifty-one guarantors to meet.

FIRST SEASON
(1891-1892)
SOLOISTS

CLARINET: Joseph Schreurs.
FLUTE: Vigo Andersen.
HARP: Edmund Schuecker.
HORN: Hermann Dutschke.
PIANOFORTE: Miss Adele aus der Ohe, Mme. Julia Rivé King, Mrs. Fannie Bloomfield Zeisler; Adolph Carpé, Rafael Joseffy, Emil Liebling, Ignace J. Paderewski.
VIOLA: August Junker.
VIOLIN: Max Bendix.
VIOLONCELLO: Bruno Steindel.
VOCAL: Misses Marguerite Hall, Medora Head, Ida Klein, Mrs. Clementine de Vere, Mrs. Julie Wyman; Antonio Galassi, Italo Campanini, Emil Fischer, George Ellsworth Holmes. William Ludwig.

SECOND SEASON
(1892-1893)

Opening of the Columbian Exposition—The Seventh and Eighth Programs (Beethoven) enjoyed by "the plain people"—Working Men's Concerts—Mr. Thomas' experiences as Musical Director of the Bureau of Music at the Exposition—His resignation.

The First Season was not a happy one for Mr. Thomas. Chicago had given him a magnificent Orchestra with a generous provision for its support during the first three seasons, but his programs did not interest the people; the attendance at the concerts depended mainly on the soloists; there was a large deficit. The comments of a writer to the *Times* on the "Request Program" of the concerts of April 22 and 23, the last of the First Season, indicate how little appreciation press and public had for the work of Mr. Thomas:

"The requests, it is fair to presume, came from habitual attendants at the concerts, and the general character of the selections asked indicates plainly enough the taste of the attendants. . . . If it be desirable to educate 'the masses' to a liking for any certain style of music, sound policy dictates that some effective means be adopted for bringing 'the masses' aforesaid within the reach of educative influences, and that the uniform and exclusive offering of what they will not tolerate is hardly to be reckoned among effective means. Mr. Thomas and his advisers seem to think otherwise, and if the Orchestral Association members are willing, for their own gratification, to pay the cost of what has been given them, nobody else has any right to object."

All this of a man whom "the masses" a few years later came to love and esteem for his sturdy, honest belief in his art. It was "the masses" who assisted in building a permanent home for the Orchestra, and on the death of our leader (1905) it was "the masses" that joined with the whole world in paying a loving tribute to his memory.

The Trustees were not disheartened by the large deficit and the adverse opinion of the newspapers. With faith still unshaken and with the earnest conviction that their cause was worthy of support by the Chicago people, they began preparations for the Second Season.

THEODORE THOMAS

Second Season—1892-1893

Early in June the prospectus for the Second Season (1892-1893) was issued by Milward Adams, Manager, announcing nineteen Friday afternoon and twenty Saturday evening concerts in the Auditorium, under the direction of Theodore Thomas.

The "Associate Members" and "option tickets" referred to in the prospectus were methods adopted by George B. Carpenter for promoting the season ticket sales of his lecture courses:

"The Orchestra will be guaranteed for two years more by the men whose names appear on the first page of this prospectus. In order that their efforts and liberality may result in permanently establishing the Orchestra in this city, the Trustees desire to create a permanent body of Associate Members, not less than five hundred in number, whose annual subscription shall take the place of this guarantee after its expiration. They, therefore, offer Associate Memberships upon the following plan:

"Associate Members to pay an annual membership fee of $100, and to receive therefor two reserved seats for each matinée and evening concert of the entire series, and twenty option tickets which can be exchanged at the box office without charge for any unsold seat for any concert during the season. These tickets will all be transferable.

"The Orchestra for the Second Season will comprise eighty-six musicians. Its *personnel*, while in the main the same as last year, will be much improved in the strings."

The World's Columbian Exposition was opened Friday, October 21, 1892, in the Liberal Arts Building, with stately ceremonies, including an important program of music. The musical exercises were under the direction of Theodore Thomas, Director of the Bureau of Music at the Exposition, who assembled some unusual choral and instrumental forces for the occasion: The Apollo Musical Club and Auxiliary, Children's Chorus, German, Swedish and Welsh Societies, church choirs, etc., in all about 3,500 voices, with Orchestra including six harps, and bands numbering 300 players, in addition to 100 drummers for the Chadwick "Ode." The important numbers in the order of exercises were:

"Columbus March and Hymn," . . . . *Paine*
"Dedicatory Ode" (Harriet Monroe), ... *Chadwick*
"The Heavens are Telling," . . . . *Haydn*
Cantata, "To the Sons of Art," . . . . *Mendelssohn*
                      Men's Voices
   Sung while the Director General was presenting medals to the master artists of the Exposition.

"Hallelujah Chorus," . . . . *Handel*
Dedicatory Oration . . . . *Henry Watterson*
"The Star Spangled Banner."
Chorus, "In Praise of God," . . . . *Beethoven*
National Salute.

I was a member of the Apollo Musical Club, and made a few notes on the Inaugural Exercises:

"October 21, Friday: A glorious autumnal day; to the Van Buren Street pier at 8 A. M. for boat on the lake to the Exposition, special for Mr. and Mrs. Thomas and guests; among them Mr. and Mrs. George W. Chadwick, Mr. and Mrs. A. W. Dohn, George H. Wilson, Secretary of the Bureau of Music of the Exposition, and Mrs. Wilson, and Mr. and Mrs. Sigmund Zeisler; arrived at the Fair Grounds 9 A. M. Mr. Thomas started the rehearsal at once on the immense stage. Strange echo in building when the bands began to rehearse Paine's 'March'—disappeared when the crowd got in for the performance; rehearsed until 11:30; then intermission. Exercises were to begin at 12:30; noted guests and speakers did not arrive until 2:20; Paine's 'March' and Chadwick's 'Ode' very impressive; followed by the 'Hallelujah Chorus'; best sung of all the selections; everybody knew the music; each chorus number preceded by roll of 100 drummers; Mendelssohn's 'Sons of Art' for men's voices well sung; had to omit 'The Heavens are Telling'; from the chorus seats we could not hear a word the speakers said; an immense crowd; home by boat."

In consequence of the Inaugural Exercises occurring on Friday, October 21, the first concert (Popular) of the Second Season was deferred until Saturday evening, October 22:

Overture, "Der Freischütz," . . . . *Weber*

> Marche Funèbre, ... *Chopin*
> IN MEMORY OF
> THE LATE GEORGE WILLIAM CURTIS,
> THE GENEROUS PATRON AND ELOQUENT ADVOCATE OF MUSIC

Suite from the Ballet, "Casse-Noisette" (New), . . *Tschaikowsky*
Fantasie for Violoncello, "O Cara Memoria," . . . *Servais*
      BRUNO STEINDEL
Intermezzo, "L'Amico Fritz" (New), ... *Mascagni*
Waltz, "Seid umschlungen Millionen" (New), . *Johann Strauss*
     INTERMISSION
Overture, "William Tell," . . . . *Rossini*
Angelus, ... *Liszt*
    (First Time)
Boabdil (New), ... *Moszkowski*
    STRING ORCHESTRA

Mr. Thomas prepared a Beethoven celebration for the concerts of December 16 and 17, Eighth Program, in memory of the one hundred and twenty-second anniversary of the composer's birth; with the assistance of Miss Minnie Fish (soprano), Mrs. Minna Brentano (contralto), Charles A. Knorr (tenor), George E. Holmes (bass) and 200 members of the Apollo Musical Club. The program consisted of the music to Goethe's "Egmont" and the ninth symphony (Beethoven). The singers were at a disadvantage at the Friday concert in being placed on the stage in such a way that we could not see the Conductor; some of the men could not attend the concert on account of business duties. On Saturday night, however, conditions were better; there was a larger attendance on the part of the men; the Conductor's stand had been moved out into the house, so everyone could see Mr. Thomas. When we rose to sing, all doubts and fears seemed to vanish as we looked at him. His presence on the stand inspired confidence; it was an inspiration. "Never mind the music! Look right at me! It will all go right," were his words at the last rehearsal. Everything did go right.

What an audience it was, as seen from the stage! The vast Auditorium filled with "the plain people," "the masses," eager to enjoy the feast of glorious music prepared by Mr. Thomas.

A few months before, the newspapers were giving the Trustees some advice as to "the effective means" they should employ for bringing "the masses within the reach of educative influences," mildly suggesting that "the uniform and exclusive offering of what they will not tolerate" (works, for example, of Bach, Beethoven, Berlioz and Brahms) "cannot be reckoned among effective means." Mr. Thomas and "his advisers" went steadily on their way, however, regardless of the newspapers. After the performance of the ninth symphony one of the critics, having "seen a great light," was in a more amiable mood:

"It is most encouraging, both to the Trustees and all lovers of musical art, to see the steadily increasing patronage which is being bestowed upon these truly superb concerts."

The Popular Concerts, December 23 and 24, Ninth Program, introduced a new soloist (soprano) from Milwaukee—Mrs. Martha Werbke-Burchard—in a Wagner program.

ELEVENTH PROGRAM, JANUARY 27 AND 28
Soloist: William H. Sherwood

Concerto in C Minor, Opus 185, ... Raff

The first of a series of three "Workingmen's" or "People's" Concerts was given by the Orchestra in the Auditorium on Monday evening, January 30, 1893, bringing out a crowd of "Wage Workers." The *Tribune* had some kind words about the concert:

> "The audience last night left not a vacant place in boxes, parquet and balcony. A more appreciative company of listeners the great Conductor and his men may have had, but certainly none that ever followed their work more closely or evinced a keener desire to understand and appreciate their work."

The means adopted by "Mr. Thomas and his advisers" for bringing "the masses" under "educative influences" will be best illustrated by the program of the "Third People's Concert" at the Auditorium, Monday evening, March 20. The nominal prices of admission, twenty-five, fifteen and ten cents, had much to do, undoubtedly, with bringing out the large audience; but the quiet, rapt attention of the 4,000 "Wage Workers" showed that they came to hear the music, and that it was a class of music they would "tolerate" and were trying to appreciate:

Symphony No. 3, "Eroica," Opus 55, ... Beethoven
Vorspiel, "The Meistersingers,"
"Waldweben," . . . . Wagner
"Siegfried's Rhine Journey," .

INTERMISSION

Symphonic Poem No. 1, "Rouet d'Omphale," Opus 31, *Saint-Saëns*
Concerto for Piano, No. 1, in E Flat, ... Liszt
A. Hyllested

Suite from the Ballet "Casse Noisette," . . . *Tschaikowsky*

At the concerts of March 3 and 4, 1893, Sixteenth Program, Mr. Paderewski was the soloist, playing his own concerto in A minor to enthusiastic audiences and filling the house on both occasions.

Mendelssohn's "Elijah" was given by the Apollo Musical Club Monday evening, March 13, to the "Wage Workers," and to the regular subscribers on Tuesday evening, March 14. William L. Tomlins, the Musical Director, had the assistance of Mme. Lillian Nordica

Second Season—1892-1893

(soprano), Mrs. Christine Nielson-Dreier (contralto), Italo Campanini* (tenor) and Plunkett Greene (bass); the entire Chicago Orchestra; Clarence Eddy (organist). Owing to illness, Mr. Campanini was unable to appear on Monday evening, his place being taken by Charles A. Knorr, but he recovered so that he was able to sing on Tuesday evening.

For the Twentieth and last Program (Wagner), April 14 and 15, Mr. Thomas was assisted by Mme. Lillian Nordica (soprano), Charles A. Knorr (tenor) and George E. Holmes (bass).

The report of the Treasurer, P. A. McEwan, for the Second Season was another disappointment, showing how little interest the people had in the concerts:

"The total expenditures were $121,937.82, including $93,250.61 for salaries of Conductor and Orchestra. The Chicago concerts yielded $56,469.25 (an increase of $10,000 over the First Season), to which may be added the earnings of out-of-town, Apollo Club and other concerts, $14,087.39, a total of $70,556.64 in receipts, with nothing from the Italian Opera Company in consequence of the burning of the Metropolitan Opera House in New York, leaving the loss, $51,381.18, for the guarantors to pay."

The Paderewski concerts, as usual, brought the largest single sales: Friday afternoon, March 3, 1893, $936; Saturday evening, March 4, $2,337.50; total for the week, $3,273.50.

The Beethoven Celebration, single sales, Friday afternoon, December 16, 1892, $736.50; Saturday evening, December 17, $1,772.25; total for the week, $2,508.75. The last concerts, single sales, on Friday afternoon, April 14, 1893, $955.50; Saturday evening, April 15, $1,676.25; total for the week, $2,631.75. The sale of season tickets brought $27,000, of which $17,500 came from Associate Members.

---

*Under date of December 6, 1916, Cleofonte Campanini wrote me:
"Dear Mr. Otis:

"Replying to your letter of the 29th ultimo, the death of my brother occurred on November 13, 1897, at Parma, Italy, where he was born. His body was interred in Parma, in a plot given by the municipality, where Paganini, the world's greatest violinist, and Bottesini, the famous contra-bass player, are also buried."

Cleofonte Campanini, Musical Director of the Chicago Grand Opera Company, died December 19, 1919, in Chicago.

SECOND SEASON
(1892-1893)
SOLOISTS

CLARINET: Joseph Schreurs.
FLUTE: Vigo Andersen.
HARP: Edmund Schuecker.
PIANOFORTE: Mrs. Fannie Bloomfield Zeisler; Ferruccio Busoni, Ignace J. Paderewski, Xaver Scharwenka, William H. Sherwood.
VIOLIN: Max Bendix, Franz Esser, J. Marquardt, Theodore B. Spiering.
VIOLONCELLO: Louis Amato, Bruno Steindel.
VOCAL: Miss Minnie Fish, Mrs. Minna Brentano, Mrs. Martha Werbke-Burchard, Mmes. Ragna Linné, Lillian Nordica; George Ellsworth Holmes, Charles A. Knorr, Whitney Mockridge.

THE WORLD'S COLUMBIAN EXPOSITION

This chapter on the musical events at the Exposition is introduced to answer the charges of bribery and dishonesty brought by the Exposition authorities and Chicago newspapers against Theodore Thomas, the Director of the Bureau of Music. Theodore Thomas was the first Conductor of his day; a man of iron will, "steadfast, immovable" as to the character of his programs, whom I at first feared, then respected and at last loved for his honesty in everything which pertained to his art. For thirty-five years I was associated with him in concert work in Chicago, as a member of the Board of Management of the Apollo Musical Club, as Secretary of the Festival Association (1882-1884) and in later years as Secretary of the Board of Trustees of the Chicago Orchestra, thus being afforded the opportunity to become familiar with every detail of the work, pay-rolls of the Orchestra, engagement of soloists, etc. In all these years I never heard of Mr. Thomas accepting bribes from members of the Orchestra, soloists, piano houses or manufacturers of musical instruments. Theodore Thomas, as I knew him, was a man of stern integrity, having rigid ideas as to business honor, and could not be bought with any sum of money. The statements made by the newspapers during the Exposition as to these charges against Mr. Thomas were absolutely false, and a reflection on the character of a man who was strictly honest in business and art.

MUSIC HALL—INTERIOR
At the World's Columbian Exposition, 1893. Built for Theodore Thomas

Second Season—1892-1893

Old Chicagoans will recall the days when the present Jackson Park was simply a wilderness. They will recall the transformation scene which took place when the Park was given over to Daniel H. Burnham, John W. Root and Frederick Law Olmstead, to prepare grounds and buildings for the World's Columbian Exposition. In the hands of these master workmen the wilderness was made to "blossom as the rose." At their command there sprang up in these waste places stately buildings for the arts and crafts, amid waterways, wooded islands and beds of flowers. Music had its place in this fairy scene, with architecture, sculpture and painting, thus making the Chicago Fair of 1893 the greatest exhibition of modern times.

Early in 1892 the Directors of the Exposition created the Bureau of Music, consisting of Theodore Thomas, Musical Director, William L. Tomlins, Choral Director, and George H. Wilson, Secretary.

In order to assist the Musical Director in his plan of showing to the world the progress of music in this country, the Directors of the Exposition made generous provision for a Recital Hall, Music Hall and Festival Hall (with organ) for the larger choral performances; with proper appropriations for salaries of the members of the Bureau, Orchestra, soloists and all other expenses of the musical work connected with the Fair. The Musical Director further announced a scheme of fourteen varieties of concerts, including daily free concerts by the Exposition Orchestra and by visiting orchestras; choral and children's concerts; Amateur Musical Club concerts; chamber concerts, symphony concerts, etc.

On September 24 an invitation was issued by the Bureau of Music to all the important choral societies in the United States and Canada, inviting them to visit Chicago and give performances as guests of the Exposition. A bulletin was also issued, with a list of the noted composers and soloists who had been invited to appear.

This was truly a broad and comprehensive plan, but "Mr. Thomas' experiences with expositions," says Mr. Upton,* "was unfortunate"; and through no fault of his. The Conductor said in his "Autobiography" that his plan of music for the Philadelphia Exposition (1876)

---

*"Theodore Thomas. A Musical Autobiography," by George P. Upton (1908).

"was a dismal failure." At the Chicago Fair he was hampered by the National Commission, composed of Congressmen whose views were not altogether in accord with his own.

As a member of the Apollo Musical Club I took part in all its performances at the Exposition, but not in an official capacity, though I remained in the Club as an active member until 1897. The reader may be interested in some notes I made on the music during the Exposition:

"May 1, 1893, Monday: Opening of the Exposition; crowds of people going to the Lexington Hotel early in A. M. to see President Cleveland start with the procession; with other Apollo members, took Illinois Central train to Sixtieth Street; then to the Administration Building to hear the exercises in front of the building; Paine's 'March' played by the band, Mr. Thomas conducting. Then to the Woman's Building to sing Mrs. H. H. A. Beach's 'Jubilate.' Only 150 Apollos turned out, not enough to do the work properly; Orchestra of 100, Mr. Thomas, Conductor. Mrs. Potter Palmer then read her address; the Duke and Duchess of Veragua and other notables on the platform."

"May 16, Tuesday P. M. Heard the Boston Symphony Orchestra in Music Hall. The Exposition is now under way. Sunday opening and the outrageous attacks on Mr. Thomas still continue to be topics for the newspapers. The *Evening Post* and *Herald* are especially bitter, calling on the Conductor to resign on account of the wretched harp and piano business."

"May 24, Wednesday P. M.: To Festival Hall to sing 'Elijah' with the Apollo Club. When the concert was about to begin it was found that the chorus had no music; the copies had been sent to the wrong hall. Mr. Tomlins explained the situation; said the Club would sing without the music. We sang the first three numbers from memory; then the copies came."

"June 10, Saturday P. M.: Festival Hall; concert given by Exposition authorities in honor of the Spanish Princess, Eulalie; Exposition Orchestra conducted by Mr. Thomas, with Edward Lloyd, Apollo Club and Children's Chorus; the audience by invitation. The Princess and her party came late, stayed in their box five minutes and then left, much to the disappointment of the people."

"June 16, Friday P. M.: To Festival Hall to sing with the Apollo Club in the 'Passion Music' (Bach). Where was the Apollo Club? Only half the membership turned up; the other half probably out on the lagoons or on the Midway. The half who did come might as well have stayed away; Bach's work was not well sung; had not been properly rehearsed; delightful singing by Edward Lloyd, as the 'Narrator.' Other soloists: Mrs. Agnes Thomson, Miss Bella Tomlins, George E. Holmes and M. Bushnell; Exposition Orchestra of one hundred; Mr. Thomas conducted."

"July 13, Thursday: Festival Hall; Bach's 'Stronghold Sure' and Wagner selections made up the program. Miss Medora

CHORAL (FESTIVAL) HALL
At the World's Columbian Exposition (1893), as Seen from the Wooded Island; from the Chicago Historical Society Collection.

Second Season—1892-1893

Henson, Miss Mary Louise Clary and George E. Holmes, soloists. Exposition Orchestra, Mr. Thomas conducting; chorus made up of members of Western Choral Societies; I sang with the tenors from Omaha."

"July 14, Friday P. M.: To Festival Hall to take part in the last concert by the Western Societies; 'Judas Maccabæus' (Handel) conducted by Mr. Tomlins; two numbers from the 'Requiem' (Berlioz) conducted by Mr. Thomas. What a great Conductor he is! to take these inexperienced singers through Berlioz's work with hardly a rehearsal! The 'Tuba Mirum' with four bands created a deep impression."

"July 25, Tuesday: A scandalous article in the *Herald* about Mr. Thomas and his library, and the salary he is receiving from the Exposition. The newspapers do not think full scores and band parts cost anything, and that Mr. Thomas should furnish this music without charge."

I wrote an answer showing it was not fair that Mr. Thomas should furnish all this music without compensation, and took it to the *Journal*. The editor said he was not in sympathy with Mr. Thomas, but would publish my article as "news."

Another article appeared in the *Herald*, August 3, regarding Mr. Thomas and his salary:

"It is too bad that Theodore Thomas should experience any difficulty in getting his $20,000 a year from the Exposition treasury. If his friends speak the truth this salary was not asked for by the Musical Director of the World's Fair. It was forced upon him by his admirers in the Directory. He himself did not specify any salary, nor did he, indeed, express any desire for the position itself. He yielded only to the importunities of members of the Directory who insisted that he should accept the place. These members afterward felt that Mr. Thomas' services were worth more than the $12,000 a year which it was originally intended to pay him, and they added $8,000 a year more, Mr. Thomas presumably protesting vigorously all the time."

I find some more notes:

"August 8, Tuesday: The Bureau of Music at the Fair is in difficulties. Mr. Thomas has resigned, and has gone to his summer home at Fair Haven, Massachusetts. No more choral concerts; the Orchestra will continue for a time."

"August 12, Saturday: Bohemian Day at the Exposition; to Festival Hall to see Dr. Dvořák and hear the United Bohemian singers. It is sad not to see Mr. Thomas in his customary place; the Russian conductor, Hlavac, on the stand. Address from the Bohemian governor of Wisconsin. In the soloists' room I met Dr. Dvořák, and introduced him to Mayor Harrison. Dvořák then went on the stand amid the cheers of his countrymen, and conducted his symphony in G major."

What was the cause of this "hue and cry"? Where did this persecution of Mr. Thomas start? In accepting the directorship of the Bureau of Music at the Exposition, he made the positive condition that the music should be under his control entirely, and should be kept apart from the commercial and political influences which dominated the National Commission. The roll of drums and the sound of cannon in the national salute at the inaugural exercises in October, 1892, had no sooner died away than the storm broke out in the piano section of the Liberal Arts Building, which was to involve the great Conductor in a mass of controversies, accusations and falsehoods, and finally bring down in ruins the whole fabric of music which he had planned as the crowning event of his life.

In the winter following the inaugural ceremonies, dissatisfaction was brewing in the section of the Liberal Arts Building devoted to the musical trade exhibit, due in part to the discontent among the exhibitors with the space allotted them, and in part to the intense rivalry existing between dealers in the same line of trade, notably the piano houses. A number of New York piano manufacturers, including Steinway & Sons, declined to make exhibits for another reason—they did not wish to submit their pianos in a contest for awards, with a politically appointed jury. The other piano firms demanded of the Exposition authorities that the Steinway piano, if not exhibited, should not be used in the concerts in Music Hall. They charged the Director with writing a letter to the harp players of the Exposition Orchestra, threatening them with discharge if they played certain instruments.

At a meeting of the National Commission, April 28, 1893, whose members were well advised in politics and trade competition, but knew nothing of art, the complaints of the music trade exhibitors were promptly sustained in this resolution:

"That no piano should be used on the Exposition grounds, except those represented by firms that made exhibits at the Fair."

Several riders were attached to this resolution; one may be noted:

"If any Steinway pianos are announced for concerts in the Exposition grounds, the Director-General (Davis) is authorized to send teams and dump the pianos outside the gates."

Second Season—1892-1893

Another one pertained to Mr. Paderewski:

"The bills announcing Mr. Paderewski's appearance at a concert with the Exposition Orchestra, and using the Steinway piano, to be taken down and Mr. Paderewski's name erased."

The Commission appointed a committee to investigate the charges against Mr. Thomas, and summoned him to appear and show cause why he should not be removed from the control of the Bureau of Music. The committee met on May 8, with Mr. Thomas in attendance, whose "statement," as Mrs. Thomas has written in her "Memoirs of Theodore Thomas," "was concise, manly and straightforward, as might have been anticipated from anyone who knows his character."

Mr. Thomas told the committee very plainly that he should use the best instruments possible in his Orchestra, whether made by Smith or Jones. That the Steinway firm made an instrument which was the best, and that he would use it. Furthermore, that he had never written any letter to his harp players forbidding them to use the Lyon & Healy harp, and that he had never heard of such a letter until he read it in the papers. That the men in his Orchestra might play any instrument they desired. "That is the right of all artists."

By this time the Bureau of Music had been separated from the Department of Liberal Arts and placed in charge of a Music Committee, consisting of "art lovers in Chicago, personal friends of Mr. Thomas, who were ready to endorse his actions to the letter." "The National Commission," continued Mrs. Thomas, "was therefore powerless to remove him, so long as the Music Committee refused to co-operate in the matter."

This unhappy experience might have been avoided, had the musical trade people been willing to make one simple concession. Long before the Exposition opened, the Musical Director had invited a number of foreign artists in the name of the Exposition to honor it with their presence, and give concerts. It was too late now to recall the invitations, and he could not honorably notify these artists that they must use such instruments as the National Commission ordered. The concession asked by Mr. Thomas was one that the National Commission and the musical trade exhibitors could not, in honor and fairness, ignore: That for the half dozen concerts only in which the foreign artists were to appear, they be allowed to make their own selection as to the pianos they would use, and that for the remaining concerts, during the progress of the Fair, the rule of the National Commission would be observed. Mr. Paderewski had something to say on this subject, in a letter from New York dated April 28:

> "I must emphatically deny that I am bound by contract or agreement, either in writing or verbally, to the use of any particular make of piano. In this respect I am at perfect liberty to follow my convictions and inclinations, and this privilege I must be free to exercise in the prosecution of my artistic career. Throughout the wide world any artist is permitted to use the instrument of his choice, and I do not understand why I should be forced to play an instrument of a manufacture strange to me, which may jeopardize my artistic success. I simply prefer to play the instrument which is my own and on which I have already played sixty concerts."

Mr. Paderewski did appear as announced, at the inaugural concert in Music Hall, May 2, playing his own concerto and on his own piano (Steinway—brought into the Exposition grounds during the night) with the Exposition Orchestra under the direction of Theodore Thomas, regardless of the threats of the World's Fair Director that any Steinway pianos found on the Exposition grounds would be dumped outside the gates of the Exposition. The exhibiting firms, however, declined to make the concession asked for by Mr. Thomas regarding the other concerts to be given at the Fair in the autumn, at which Saint-Saëns, Hans Richter, Arthur Nikisch, Massenet and other artists had been engaged to appear. The mind of the average member of Congress cannot understand (and it is useless to explain) why Mr. Saint-Saëns should prefer to play a piano of his own selection rather than one imposed on him by the National Commission. As Mr. Thomas said, it is a question of art, pure and simple, with which politics and trade competition have nothing to do. Nevertheless, the exhibiting firms continued to besiege the National Commission for Mr. Thomas' removal, and on May 17 Director-General Davis formally asked for his resignation:

> "DEAR SIR: In compliance with a resolution adopted this day by the World's Columbian Exposition, I have to request your resignation as Musical Director in the Department of Liberal Arts.

Second Season—1892-1893

"You will please turn over all property, records and documents belonging to and appertaining to your office to the Chief of the Department of Liberal Arts.

"Respectfully yours,
"GEORGE R. DAVIS,
"Director-General."

Mr. Thomas did not think it necessary to respond at once to this demand from the National Commission, for the reason that the Bureau of Music was now under the control of the Music Committee. He continued his work accordingly, giving every concert announced excepting the last, on August 12, Bohemian Day, which was conducted by Mr. Hlavac. The Musical Director would gladly have laid down his baton in May when he was asked to resign, but for the 114 members of the Exposition Orchestra whom he had engaged for the period of the Fair, many having families to support, it being necessary that they should earn something during the summer months. He could not, therefore, desert them at this moment and leave them to the tender mercies of the Exposition authorities, to be summarily discharged at their pleasure.

From the *Herald* of July 26:

"Thomas is tiresome. His music fails to draw crowds. Fair managers talk of cutting his big Orchestra up into little bands in the different buildings. Must reduce expenses."

After four months of this daily irritating struggle to meet the unjust and cruel charges of dishonesty, incompetence and bribery made by the National Commission, the Director of Music at the Fair laid down his baton and tendered his resignation in a letter dated August 12, 1893, to James W. Ellsworth, Chairman of the Committee on Music. Under the circumstances this letter was a model, setting forth clearly the condition of the Bureau of Music at the Fair, and with no reference whatever to the scurrilous charges made against him. He thought it best that his elaborate scheme of music should be given up, "in consequence of the discouraging business situation," and "the reduction of expenses of the Fair," which obliged "the Bureau of Music to cancel all future engagements with foreign artists and organizations, and to abandon all future festivals." He further suggested that "for the remainder of the Fair, music should not be given as an art, but be treated merely on the basis of an amusement." A Sunday paper of August 13 had this comment on Mr. Thomas' resignation:

"With the long delayed but at last effectual termination of the Theodore Thomas *régime* at the World's Fair ends a chapter blotted with evidences of greed, arrogance and incapacity. If Mr. Thomas did not enter on his campaign at the Fair in the calm determination to subordinate the great trust imposed on him to his own artistic whims and prejudices, to reward his friends and punish his enemies, and above all to fill his purse in some way or in any way, the strange and forbidding facts pointing to these conclusions should be explained away immediately."

When the financial clouds had passed by and the people began to come to the Fair in thousands, the National Commission realized that they had made a mistake in discharging the Musical Director and ending the work of the Bureau of Music. Early in the autumn a request was sent to Mr. Thomas to return and resume the work of the Bureau, though in a somewhat different form, putting the Orchestra in one of the music halls, and on a percentage basis. But the Conductor was worn out bodily and mentally with the experiences of the summer, and declined to leave his home in Fair Haven, Massachusetts.

Thirty years have passed since the Chicago Exposition of 1893, that wondrous fairy scene in white, on the borders of Lake Michigan. The stately buildings have disappeared; many of the master workmen are gone, but the work of their hands will not be forgotten, nor will the glorious music be forgotten, though much injustice was shown Theodore Thomas by the National Commission and many bitter words were uttered by the Chicago press.

THIRD SEASON
(1893-1894)

Mr. Thomas declines an offer from Mr. Higginson to conduct the Boston Symphony Orchestra—Nathaniel K. Fairbank resigns as President of The Orchestral Association, and is succeeded by George E. Adams—Resignation of E. B. McCagg as Trustee— Succeeded by Allison V. Armour—Eleventh Cincinnati Festival —Mr. Thomas declines an offer from New York City—Resignation of A. C. Bartlett as Trustee—Succeeded by Philo A. Otis— George H. Wilson appointed Secretary.

The World's Fair of 1893, in bringing fame and prestige to our city, brought in its train a horde of speculators, adventurers and workmen, who promoted all manner of enterprises, from shows on the Midway to World's Fair hotels and steam heated flat buildings. The close of the Fair in October found the city filled with an army of human derelicts, homeless and penniless, who slept through the cold nights of the winter in the corridors of the City Hall and in the police stations. It was not an auspicious time to suggest symphony concerts, when the needs of these freezing, starving people were the first demand on the public, nor did the heavy deficit of The Orchestral Association for the Second Season, the collapse of the Bureau of Music at the Fair, the enforced resignation of Mr. Thomas and the bitter newspaper comments thereon, constitute a cheerful outlook for a Third Season of the Orchestra. It was the last year of the three years' guarantee, and the thoughts of all friends of the Orchestra were centered on the future of the Orchestra, so that it was not at all strange that Mr. Thomas had grave doubts on the subject, and was disposed to remain at his home in Fair Haven for the winter and give up his work in Chicago. The newspapers continued to be unkind, as the following excerpt will show:

"During two seasons, with every possible influence united in his behalf, a deficiency of about $80,000 was created for the liberal guarantors of the Chicago Orchestral Association to pay out of their own pockets. The prospects for a Third Season under the gloomy auspices now existing are such that unless Mr. Thomas is lost to all sense of gratitude he will relieve the friends who have stood by him from any further unreasonable and hopeless expense."

On his return to Fair Haven after the collapse of the Bureau of Music at the Exposition, with all his hopes and ideals shattered, Mr. Thomas feared that his artistic career was ended. It was then with real pride that—

*"He received a letter from Mr. Henry L. Higginson, of Boston [says Mrs. Thomas], offering him the conductorship of the Boston Symphony Orchestra. This was the one position he had longed for for years, and which exactly suited his needs. Boston was a cultivated city, and its orchestra one of the best. There no missionary work was needed, but on the contrary the first law of its being was 'a symphony on every program.'

"But when he thought of his Chicago friends, of the large sums they had already given, the hard work they had done, the earnest desire to create a truly great musical institution, he knew that now he could not honorably leave them until the Chicago Orchestra was either permanently established, or abandoned. His reply to Mr. Higginson was therefore in the negative."

The Exposition not closing until October 31, and the Auditorium being occupied every afternoon and evening with the spectacular play "America," the autumn had well advanced before the Association could resume its work. Mr. Thomas' experiences at the Exposition, though bitter and trying, had one compensation at least in the Exposition Orchestra, which somehow kept together after he had resigned, though under different conductors. He did not, therefore, have to assemble new players for his winter work.

The program of the first concerts, November 24 and 25, contained a new work, Charpentier's charming suite, "Impressions d'Italie," which brought, in a few weeks, a letter to Mr. Thomas* from the composer:

"My friend Amato† has written me of your performance of my work, 'Impressions d'Italie,' in Chicago. Permit me to thank you, and to add also the compliments of my publisher, M. Tellier. I am very happy that the work has made a success, and I know all that I owe to you in the matter."

The resignation of P. A. McEwan, Secretary and Treasurer of the Association, was accepted at a meeting of the Trustees, Friday afternoon, November 24, at the Chicago Club, with sincere regrets and with the thanks of the Trustees for the faithful and satisfactory performance by Mr. McEwan of his duties. Charles E. Anderson was elected to fill the vacancy.

---

*"Memoirs of Theodore Thomas," by Rose Fay Thomas (1911).
†Louis Amato, member of the violoncello section of the Orchestra.

Third Season—1893-1894

Madame Amalie Materna, who came to Chicago during the Exposition (1893) was the soloist December 22 and 23, Fifth Program (Wagner), singing the recitative and prayer of Elizabeth ("Tannhäuser") with great fervor and dramatic intensity.

Saint-Saëns' "Samson et Dalila," was given by the Apollo Musical Club, Thursday evening, February 1, 1894, in the Auditorium, under the direction of William L. Tomlins. Soloists: Mary Louise Clary (contralto), J. H. McKinley (tenor), George E. Holmes (bass) and Karleton Hackett (baritone); Clarence Eddy (organist) and the Chicago Orchestra.

E. A. MacDowell was the soloist February 9 and 10, Eleventh Program, playing his concerto No. 1 in A minor.

THIRTEENTH PROGRAM, FEBRUARY 23 AND 24
Soloist: Mlle. Adele Aus der Ohe

Concerto for Pianoforte and Orchestra, No. 1, ... *Liszt*
Piano Solos:
    (a) Nocturne, E Flat, ... *Napravnik*
    (b) Waltz, E Minor, ... *Chopin*

At a meeting of the Trustees held on February 26, the resignation of Nathaniel K. Fairbank as President of the Association was accepted. On motion of Mr. Fay this resolution was adopted:

"That the resignation of Mr. Fairbank as Trustee and President of The Orchestral Association be accepted with regret and with the hearty thanks of the Association for his personal labor and financial aid in the cause of good music, not only to this Association, but to every organization of kindred purposes which has dignified the history of Chicago."

On motion of Mr. Hamill, George E. Adams was elected Trustee and President to fill the vacancy caused by the resignation of Mr. Fairbank.

Mr. Fay then presented the resignation of Ezra B. McCagg as Trustee, and, on motion, Allison V. Armour was elected to fill the vacancy.

Mr. Thomas introduced two artists April 13 and 14, Sixteenth Program—Plunkett Greene, the English baritone, who delighted the audience by his singing of a set of old country songs, notably the Welsh melody "All through the Night"; and Henry Schoenfeld, a young composer and former resident of Chicago, who conducted his "Pastoral" symphony in G major. This work received the prize of $500 offered the previous year by the National Conservatory of Music of New York City.

The Apollo Club closed its season Thursday evening, April 26, with a performance of Max Bruch's "Frithjof" and Horatio W. Parker's "Hora Novissima," in the Auditorium, under the direction of William L. Tomlins. Soloists: Miss Antoinette Trebelli (soprano), Mrs. Katharine Fisk (contralto), Ben Davies (tenor) and George E. Holmes (bass); Clarence Eddy (organist) and the Chicago Orchestra.

While rehearsing "Frithjof" my thoughts went back to the early days when the Club was a männerchor and we gave the work under the direction of A. W. Dohn, What a delight it was when we began the study of this thrilling song of the North!

Wilhelm Middelschulte, the organist of the Orchestra, and soloist at the concerts of April 27 and 28, Eighteenth Program, received an ovation after his performance of the Guilmant concerto. He played quietly and easily, with a clear, crisp touch and a broad, dignified style.

NINETEENTH PROGRAM, MAY 4 AND 5

"The ninth symphony (Beethoven), with the assistance of the Apollo Musical Club. Soloists: Mrs. Minnie Fish-Griffin (soprano), Miss Fanchon H. Thompson (contralto), Charles A. Knorr (tenor) and George E. Holmes (bass); Max Bendix (violin)."

I made a few notes on the Saturday night performance:

"Magnificent work by the Orchestra! Rain came down in torrents, and we had a small house. About 150 Apollo members turned out. Singers not well placed on the stage; we could not all see the Conductor. Mr. Thomas had the choral part of the symphony transposed from D major to C major, one whole tone lower. This made it easier for the singers; less strain on the voices; but much of the life and brightness of the music was gone."

The Third Season closed May 11 and 12, Twentieth Program, with the two largest houses of the year. Mme. Emma Eames, soloist.

The future of the Orchestra would seem to have been assured, judging from a slip inserted in the program book:

"ANNOUNCEMENT

"The Trustees of The Orchestral Association take pleasure in announcing that its Fourth Season of concerts, twenty weeks, will begin with Friday afternoon, October 12, and Saturday, October 13, 1894."

An editor on the following Sunday was in a more hopeful mood over the work of the Orchestra:

PHILO ADAMS OTIS

Third Season—1893-1894

"The three seasons of the present Orchestra have been the most remarkable in the musical history of Chicago, from an artistic point of view. Mr. Thomas gathered the greatest artists of the world from the first orchestras of Europe; he trained them as only he can; and from the beginning there has been a steady progress throughout toward artistic perfection, until the close of the third year shows an organization which is unrivaled."

A meeting of the Trustees was held on Monday, May 16, at 2:00 P. M. at the Chicago Club. Mr. Fay presented the resignation of A. C. Bartlett as Trustee, which, on motion of Mr. Hamill, was accepted,

"With the thanks of the Association for Mr. Bartlett's most valuable services from the commencement of the Association's work."

On motion of Mr. Hamill, Philo Adams Otis was elected to fill the vacancy caused by Mr. Bartlett's resignation. On motion of Mr. Hamill, it was voted that George H. Wilson be engaged as Secretary of the Association for the ensuing year. It was further resolved that:

"Advertisements be permitted upon the programs for the season of 1894-1895, and that Mr. Wilson be instructed to make arrangements therefor."

The report of the Treasurer for the Third Season was another "melancholy exhibit"; the earnings of the Orchestra ($66,000), including $10,200 received from the Italian Opera Company, were far from paying $88,000, the salaries of the men. The loss on the season was $49,000.

THIRD SEASON
(1893-1894)
SOLOISTS

HARP: Edmund Schuecker.
ORGAN: Wilhelm Middelschulte.
PIANOFORTE: Mlle. Aus der Ohe; Edward A. MacDowell.
VIOLIN: Max Bendix (twice), Henri Marteau (twice).
VIOLONCELLO: Bruno Steindel.
VOCAL: Mrs. Minnie Fish-Griffin, Miss Fanchon H. Thompson, Mmes. Katharine van Arnheim, Emma Eames, Amalie Materna; Charles A. Knorr, George E. Holmes, Plunkett Greene.

Mr. Hamill and I left Chicago on Thursday evening, May 24, 1894, to attend the closing concerts of the Eleventh Cincinnati Festival. We arrived early the next morning, Friday, going to the Burnet House, where we had breakfast with some of the soloists, Miss Antoinette Trebelli, Ben Davies and Watkin Mills; later to rehearsal in Music Hall for Orchestra and soloists.

At the matinée Ben Davies was in glorious voice, and sang well in the aria from "Der Freischütz" (Weber). After the intermission Miss Trebelli carried the house by storm with her singing of the "Polonaise" from "Mignon" (Thomas). My seat was in the front row, close to the first violins. After the Orchestra had played the "Hungarian Dances" (Brahms) Max Bendix leaned over and whispered, "Mr. Thomas wishes to see you after the concert." When Plunkett Greene came out to sing his songs with the piano I followed Mr. Thomas to the artists' room. He began at once:

"I have something to say to you; let me think; I am so busy; every moment is occupied. The New York committee is here about their orchestra for next season, and they want me to go on to New York and conduct. Well, I see you do not quite understand the situation. Please find Hamill and tell him I wish him to walk with me to the Queen City Club after the concert this evening."

At this point the Conductor went on to conduct "Les Préludes" (Liszt), the last number on the program.

"Does Mr. Thomas really intend to leave us to go to New York and conduct the new Orchestra, and is that to be the end of our work in Chicago?" With thoughts of this character in mind, I started for the hotel to find Mr. Hamill. As he was not in his room, I left a note telling him of Mr. Thomas' request. After the concert that evening we met at the Queen City Club at the supper given by the Directors of the Festival to Mr. Thomas and the soloists, and discussed the situation. On the train home the next day (Sunday) we talked of little else. Fortunately for us, Mr. Thomas decided the matter himself, and in a most thoughtful, generous way. There were many reasons why it was for his own welfare and that of his family that he should accept the call from New York. "He declined," says Mrs. Thomas, "for the same reason that led him to decline the Boston invitation": He could not leave his Chicago friends, in view of the generous support they had given him, and in view of their earnest "desire to create a truly great institution."

A Snapshot of Theodore Thomas Leaving the Hall after a Festival Rehearsal in Cincinnati.

FOURTH SEASON
(1894-1895)

Resignation of Milward Adams, Manager of the Orchestra—George H. Wilson succeeds Adolph W. Dohn as editor of the program book—Miss Anna Millar appointed Manager of the season ticket sale—Philo A. Otis elected Treasurer—Cyrus Hall McCormick, Chairman of the Committee appointed on enlarging the work of the Orchestra, makes a report—Bryan Lathrop elected Trustee and Vice-President—The tours of the Orchestra over the "Highway"—Fatiguing work for Mr. Thomas —Complimentary dinner in his honor by friends of the Orchestra.

The summer of 1894 will be long remembered by those who had the work in hand of preparing for another season of the Orchestra. The times were hard, though the city was gradually recovering from the wild, disastrous speculations of the World's Fair period. Then came the July railroad strikes and riots, which brought the United States troops to Chicago for the protection of life and property. It was certainly an inauspicious time to suggest symphony concerts. But in season and out of season, the friends of the Orchestra have never failed in their loyalty to its interests.

Milward Adams, the Manager of the Orchestra through its first three seasons, tendered his resignation in April, and was succeeded by George H. Wilson, Secretary of the Bureau of Music at the World's Fair. Though Mr. Wilson's position with the Orchestra was that of Secretary of the Association, his duties now covered the general work of management, advertising, press notices and out-of-town concerts. The resignation of Mr. Adams was accepted by the Trustees with genuine regret. He was a warm friend of Mr. Thomas, and through the Summer Garden Concerts and other engagements for the Thomas Orchestra had been a strong factor in shaping the events which brought the Conductor to Chicago (1891) and led to the formation of the new Orchestra.

Another change on the official staff was caused by the resignation of Adolph W. Dohn, editor of the program book for the first three seasons. The duties of preparing the program notes and securing the advertisements now devolved upon Mr. Wilson.

Before the close of the Third Season a "Fund for the Support of the Orchestra" had been started to replace the original three-year guarantee, which expired with the last concerts of that season, May 11 and 12, 1894. The new guarantee aggregated $30,850, in sums from $50 to $1,000 each, one-half payable on January 1, 1895, and the other half April 1, 1895. The Trustees realized that the new fund would not cover the loss on the coming season, but hoped for a wider interest in the concerts on the part of the general public.

With this in mind, Miss Anna Millar was engaged by the Trustees to take in hand the sale of Associate Memberships and season tickets. She entered upon this work at once, seriously and earnestly, making a thorough canvass of residence districts, stores and offices, with the result that the advance sale of tickets for the Fourth Season indicated a great increase over that of any previous season.

The dates heretofore announced for the opening of the Fourth Season of twenty weeks of the Chicago Orchestra, October 12 and 13, were changed to October 19 and 20 at a meeting of the Trustees held Friday afternoon, June 22, at the office of President Adams in the Woman's Temple. Present: Messrs. Adams, Fay, Hamill and Otis; Secretary Wilson by invitation.

The prospectus for the Fourth Season, prepared by Secretary Wilson, appeared in July:

"The Trustees are happy to announce that the Orchestra will be continued during the season of 1894-1895; that Mr. Thomas will remain as Conductor, and that there will be no change of importance among the eighty-six musicians composing the Orchestra—a body of players of unsurpassed excellence."

Miss Millar opened her office as Manager of the season ticket sale at Lyon & Healy's music store soon after the close of the Third Season, and before the summer had set in, had secured upwards of $30,000 in signatures for tickets for the Fourth Season. But it was another matter to persuade people who had signed for tickets to come to her office and redeem their promises. Many

ANNA MILLAR

people declined to take the tickets, chiefly on account of financial difficulties, as my journal shows:

"July 5, Thursday: Season tickets for the Orchestra concerts in such a large hall as the Auditorium do not interest the public now. Concerts are too far off. I visit the box office two and three times a day to help in the work. Miss Millar declares it is impossible to sell tickets; people much agitated over the labor troubles and the riots. Will it end in revolution and bloodshed? United States troops and the State Militia are in camp on the Lake Front."

A meeting of the Trustees was held on Tuesday afternoon, September 4, at the office of President Adams, in the Woman's Temple. Present: Messrs. Adams, Hamill and Otis; Secretary Wilson by invitation. Philo A. Otis was elected Treasurer, Charles E. Anderson having resigned.

"October 1, Monday: In response to the advertisements in the papers yesterday, the returns were better at the box office; $1,385 collected today. Some people who signed for season tickets now want to give them up. I spent most of the day at Lyon & Healy's; have delivered many of the tickets personally and collected the money. We have $20,000 in season tickets laid aside for people who do not seem to value their signed agreements."

"October 19, Friday: First afternoon concert; we had $514.75 in single sales; last year, $199.75; playing of the Orchestra today was delightful."

Overture "Sappho" (New), Opus 44, ... *Goldmark*
Symphony No. 7, A Major, Opus 92, ... *Beethoven*

INTERMISSION

Serenade No. 1, D Major, Opus 9, ... *Fuchs*
(For String Orchestra)
(First Time at These Concerts)
Vorspiel, "Die Meistersinger von Nürnberg," . . . *Wagner*

The large audience on Friday was encouraging, and indicated an increasing interest in the Orchestra on the part of the people; but the vacant seats on Saturday night were a source of anxiety to the Trustees.

"October 26, Friday: Second afternoon concert: Mrs. Lillian Blauvelt, soloist. A good house; $529 in single sales; last year $185. The delightful weather brought out a crowd of ladies."

"November 2, Friday: Third afternoon concert; rained all day; at 3:00 P. M. it came down in torrents. Still we had $340 in single sales, as compared with $223 last year."

At the concerts of November 30 and December 1, Seventh Program, Arthur Foote's concerto for violoncello and orchestra was played by Mr. Steindel.

On Saturday evening, at the intermission, a meeting of the subscribers to the "Fund for the Support of the

Orchestra" was held in the smoking room of the Auditorium; present, George E. Adams, C. Norman Fay, Charles D. Hamill, Bryan Lathrop, Albert A. Sprague, Philo A. Otis, O. W. Norton, Edward Norton, T. B. Blackstone and A. C. Bartlett. A short address was made by Mr. Adams on the work of the Orchestra, with suggestions as to increasing the interest of the public in the Association by securing more subscribers to the fund and enlarging the membership of the Board of Trustees. At an adjourned meeting held on the following Saturday evening, December 8, President Adams appointed a committee to formulate a plan of action to be presented at a future meeting of the Association: Cyrus H. McCormick, John J. Glessner, Charles L. Hutchinson, H. H. Kohlsaat, Daniel H. Burnham, O. W. Norton and Henry B. Stone.

"December 12, Wednesday: Meeting of Trustees, 3:00 P. M., at the office of President Adams. Present, Messrs. Adams, Hamill, Fay and Otis. Treasurer Otis made a report on the finances, showing the funds would hold out until January 1st next, when the first half of the subscription money would become due."

The Ninth Program, December 14 and 15, though one of the best Mr. Thomas ever made, and interesting to musicians, was not so to the casual concert-goer:

Overture ("Fidelio"), ... *Beethoven*
Symphony No. 3, "Eroica," Opus 55, ... *Beethoven*
INTERMISSION
Prelude and Closing Scene ("Tristan and Isolde"), . . *Wagner*
Bacchanale ("Tannhäuser"), ... *Wagner*
"Kaisermarsch," . . . . *Wagner*

It was my duty as Treasurer of the Association to draw the money every Monday morning from our bank (the Northern Trust Company) and pay the men of the Orchestra. On Monday after the above concerts I drew $2,925 for the pay-roll of the previous week—$2,515 for the regular men and $410 for the extra men—carrying the money in a newspaper to the Auditorium, and giving it to Henry Sachleben* (one of the violoncello players and "factotum" for Mr. Thomas), who distributed it to the men. Mr. Thomas, seeing me at the wings of the stage, at once came down from his stand and, walking through

---

*Henry Sachleben was associated many years with Mr. Thomas and his Orchestra, having charge of all the engagements of the men. He had been a member of the Chicago Orchestra since the First Season (1891-1892). He returned to New York in 1898, and there his death occurred in February, 1899.

the Orchestra, called out: "Well, how did you like our program last week?"

The men were looking right at me, and I hardly knew what to say in reply. At first I thought he was a little sarcastic, fearing Sachleben might have shown him the sketch of a program I had prepared, with a view of filling the vacant seats on Saturday nights. I managed to say: "It was one of the best you have ever given us, Mr. Thomas, and showed how a program can be made from the works of two masters only."

Then he came across the stage to the wings where I was standing, and began to speak sadly of the indifference of the public and the lack of interest manifested by the people in his work. To which I replied: "I think you are mistaken, Mr. Thomas. The people are becoming more and more interested in the concerts. What an education last week's concerts afforded, in showing the contrast between the severely classical style of Beethoven and the gorgeous coloring of Richard Wagner."

We then discussed the soloists for the rest of the season. He said of soloists generally: "I am always willing to help deserving people. When an artist of reputation appears at one of my concerts and does not succeed, the artist suffers. But when I take some one unknown and he or she makes a failure, then I am the one to suffer. We are about to look through Dvořák's overture, 'Nature.' You had better stay and hear it." With this the Conductor went back to his work.

César Thomson was the soloist at the concerts of December 21 and 22, Tenth Program, playing the Bruch concerto for violin, No. 1, in G minor, Opus 26, and after the intermission, Paganini's Grand Fantasie.

The committee appointed on December 8 made its report to the subscribers to the Guarantee Fund on December 26, at a meeting held in the Corn Exchange National Bank. Cyrus H. McCormick, as chairman of the committee, stated:

"Your committee begs leave to recommend the following plan of reorganization of The Orchestral Association:

"1. By-laws to be amended so that all subscribers to the 'Fund for the Support of the Orchestra' shall be known as 'Governing Members'; each member contributing $50 shall be entitled to one vote at the Annual Meeting for the election of Trustees.

"2. That a complete canvass be made for a subscription of $40,000 annually in sums of $50 to $1,000 each.

"3. That the subscription be for three years, payable on January 1 and March 1 in each year."

At subsequent meetings of the Association during the months of January and February, 1895, the above amendments to the by-laws were adopted, with a further amendment increasing the number of Trustees from five to nine, and creating an Executive Committee consisting of three members of the Board of Trustees "clothed with such powers as the Board may from time to time confer." On Saturday, January 19, Trustees, according to the new by-laws, were elected for the ensuing year as follows:

George E. Adams, Bryan Lathrop, Philo A. Otis, Allison V. Armour, Daniel H. Burnham, C. Norman Fay, William A. Fuller, Charles D. Hamill and Charles H. Wacker.

Executive Committee: Charles D. Hamill, C. Norman Fay and Philo A. Otis.

The Trustees met Wednesday afternoon, January 23, and elected George E. Adams, President; George H. Wilson, Secretary, and Philo A. Otis, Treasurer. In consequence of illness Mr. Lathrop could not be present, but came to the adjourned meeting Saturday afternoon, January 26, and was then elected Vice-President. Charles H. Wacker declining to serve, the Trustees met on Saturday afternoon, February 2, and elected Henry B. Stone, Trustee.

FOURTEENTH PROGRAM, JANUARY 25 AND 26
  SOLOISTS: MLLE. CARLOTTA DESVIGNES
      W. C. E. SEEBOECK

Concerto for Pianoforte No. 2, D Minor, ... *Seeboeck*
Recitative and Aria, "Pleurez, Mes Yeux," from
    "The Cid," . . . . *Massenet*
Aria, "Amour, Viens Aider," from "Samson et Dalila," *Saint-Saëns*

Eugène Ysaye was the soloist February 1 and 2, 1895, Fifteenth Program, playing the violin concerto No. 3 in B minor, Opus 61 (Saint-Saëns), and after the intermission the "Scotch Fantasia" (Bruch).

Early in January a letter came from the Rev. W. G. Clark, Secretary of the People's Institute, at the corner of Van Buren and Leavitt Streets, in regard to opening

Fourth Season—1894-1895

their new auditorium with a concert by Mr. Thomas and the Orchestra. I set out to try my hand in managing this affair, Mr. Thomas having visited the Institute and reported favorably on the hall. Arrangements were thereupon made for the concert. I suggested that we would play for them on this basis: The first $100 of the receipts to be allowed Mr. Clark for expenses; the next $500 to go to us, and we would divide the balance equally. Mr. Clark said he would not make any promises, but would do his best to create an interest in the concert among their people; anyway, we could be sure of his "blessing." The concert was announced for St. Valentine's Day, February 14, and had it been properly worked up among the friends of the Institute the audience would have been larger. Mr. Thomas gave them one of his best "Popular Programs," which included the "Tannhäuser" march (Wagner), Handel's "Largo" (solo by Max Bendix), fantasia for harp (Saint-Saëns), played by Edmund Schuecker, and "The Beautiful Blue Danube" (Strauss). It was a bitter cold night, and the audience, as I had feared would be the case, was small. At the intermission I went into the box office to "count up," and there realized the meaning of the nursery rhyme phrase, "The cupboard was bare." I took all there was ($96.30), a meagre return indeed for our work, but we pleased the people.

The Rheinberger concerto (organ), No. 2, in G minor was the solo number February 22 and 23, Eighteenth Program. This work by the famous master of counterpoint in Munich was played for the first time in America by one of our foremost organists, Clarence Eddy, whose interpretation of the concerto was of the highest order, showing great breadth and repose.

Rafael Joseffy was the soloist March 1 and 2, Nineteenth Program:

Introduction and Fugue, ...	*Lachner*
Hornpipe, . . . ⎫	
Larghetto, . . ⎬	*Handel*
Allegro Molto, . ⎭	
Concerto No. 2, B Flat, ...	*Brahms*
INTERMISSION	
Symphony No. 2 in C Major, Opus 61, ...	*Schumann*

At the intermission on Saturday night I found Mr. Thomas in a delightful mood over the enthusiasm of the audience: "What a charming contrast the Handel numbers," said the Conductor, "make with the Brahms concerto. Handel's music, written a hundred and fifty years ago, is still grateful, and so characteristic of the composer and his time."

Two works were given by the Apollo Musical Club in the Auditorium, Thursday evening, March 7, under the direction of William L. Tomlins: Handel's "Israel in Egypt" (selections) and Arthur Sullivan's "Golden Legend." Soloists: Mrs. Corinne Moore-Lawson (soprano), Miss Fanchon H. Thompson (contralto), H. Evan Williams (tenor), George W. Fergusson and John H. Cameron (basses); the Students' Musical Club, Clarence Eddy (organist) and the Chicago Orchestra.

The Twentieth Program, last concerts, March 8 and 9, was one that Mr. Thomas loved to prepare, containing the "Pastoral Symphony" (Beethoven) and selections from Wagner. I have never seen him conduct with so much fire and enthusiasm, nor had the Orchestra ever played with greater spirit than in the concerts of the last two weeks. This Fourth Season, in which Mr. Thomas produced more novelties than have appeared in symphony concerts in Berlin or Vienna, finished half a century of work which he had given to the cause of good music in America. At the conclusion of the Saturday night concert he was called again and again to the Conductor's stand, in response to the demands of the delighted audience.

The sale of boxes, Associate Memberships and season tickets for this year approached $35,000, through the efforts of Miss Millar, bringing a corresponding increase in the single ticket sales; the largest attendance being at the César Thomson, Ysaye and Joseffy concerts. The last concerts, without soloists, brought $1,154 on Friday afternoon, March 8, and $1,170 on Saturday evening, March 9, together with a flood of "option tickets" which were sure to appear when the attractions proved strong enough.

The program book did not yield the profit we had anticipated. Mr. Wilson's duties as Manager of the Orchestra caused frequent absences from the city in arranging the out-of-town dates, thus making it impossible for him to give any time toward securing adver-

Fourth Season—1894-1895

tisements. This part of the work was turned over to solicitors, who proved to be irresponsible and failed to make proper returns in their collections; some of the advertisers were worthless. A well known firm of tailors contracted for their card in the book, for which the solicitors accepted in payment three trade certificates, worth $25 each, and redeemable in clothes. When the card had run several weeks with no cash forthcoming, I inquired into the matter and discovered the facts. The Trustees not being in the habit of buying their clothes by trade certificates, these documents were returned and the space canceled.

It is now time that some reference should be made to the origin, growth and development of the out-of-town concerts, which have always constituted an important feature of each season's business, in exploiting the Orchestra and giving the men a few weeks' additional salaries. The Thomas Orchestra of other days was among the first of its kind to "take the road," and our present system of management is the result of a process of evolution, growing out of Mr. Thomas' own experiences. No one understood the details of transportation, hotels, baggage and other features of the business so well as Theodore Thomas. He knew the best points on the "Highway" * east and west, the size of the stage and seating capacity of every important hall in this country. To leave Chicago in the morning for St. Louis (for example), arriving in the afternoon in time for the music-stands and instruments to be taken to the hall and placed on the stage; in time for the men to reach their hotels, get dinner, dress and go to the hall; play a Bach and Wagner program, and after the concert take a "special" for Kansas City, arriving there in time for a matinée the next day; and finally to collect enough money from local managers to pay salaries and expenses—all this to the layman would seem impossible. But to Mr. Thomas, who had learned this work in the school of bitter experience, "All things were possible."

Concert managers along the "Highway" do not often give guarantees to visiting "attractions." They prefer to divide the receipts—eighty per cent to the "attraction"

---

*An appropriate expression used by Mrs. Thomas in her "Memoirs of Theodore Thomas."

and twenty per cent to the manager, out of which he furnishes hall, ticket sellers, and the advertising. The "attraction" to provide all programs, circulars and posters. It was on this basis that the out-of-town business of the Orchestra had been conducted during the first three seasons. In accordance with the instructions of the Trustees, Miss Millar and Mr. Wilson secured guarantees from local societies and ladies' clubs for many of the concerts on the eight weeks' tour at the close of the Fourth Season. The circulars needed for working up interest in the tour were prepared by Mr. Wilson, with suggestions by Mr. Hamill and myself. Mr. Thomas had an intense dislike of any praise of himself. One afternoon I sent a draft of a circular we had prepared to Mrs. Thomas (Mr. Thomas being "somewhere" on the "Highway"), for her approval. It was returned with this note on the envelope, which, with due apologies to Mrs. Thomas, I will here insert: "If you ever intend to get this printed, you had better not show it to Mr. Thomas for suggestions, for he will not object if he does not see it."

With proper modifications the document was finally printed and sent on its way.

My diary has this note:

"March 11, Monday: To the Lake Shore Station at 10:30 A. M. to see Mr. Thomas and the men off for Kalamazoo. Miss Millar in charge."

The tour covered many of the principal places on the "Highway" (Kalamazoo, Detroit, Cleveland, Toronto, Columbus, St. Louis, Burlington, St. Paul and other towns, ending at Milwaukee), and all went well, excepting that, owing to our inexperience in such matters, and the carelessness of the printer in shipping, the house programs and circulars in some places, on several occasions went astray. There was some confusion at Pittsburgh as to the concerto Miss Aus der Ohe was to play. I find this note in my journal:

"April 1, Monday: Fay called at my office; said Mr. Thomas and Miss Millar had an exciting time at Pittsburgh. The people there were determined to have the Tschaikowsky concerto. Mr. Thomas would not play it, for the reason I had supposed—he did not have time to rehearse it; men did not know the work. Schumann concerto played instead."

Fourth Season—1894-1895

The tour yielded, after paying transportation and hotel bills, $16,469.53, to be applied towards salaries for the eight weeks; but the fatigue and annoyance Mr. Thomas experienced were so trying that he had serious thoughts of resigning. In a letter to Mrs. Thomas, from Burlington, Iowa, he wrote: "This traveling must stop for me, and I have asked Norman [Fay] to notify the Trustees that next year will be my last." And again from Minneapolis: "Can anyone blame me if I say that I cannot do this work any more? I feel that I must leave after next winter, and if we have no offer from Boston or New York, then we will go to Fair Haven or to Europe and wait until something comes along." On another occasion he wrote from Indianapolis: "I have been trying to write for two days, but we are in the cars pretty much all day—nasty old cars—and this is as hard a trip as I ever made. I don't see how I can do this any more. Nearly all our large instruments have been broken by rough handling on the trains, and for two days we have had no dinner—only a bit of sausage and bread. This sort of traveling is not natural or right, and I cannot continue to live this way after this year."

One of Mr. Thomas' maxims, and one we often quoted in the office, was: "To accomplish one great thing, a hundred details must be attended to; not one of them can be neglected."

Had this rule been enforced on the tour, Conductor and Manager would have avoided much trouble and anxiety.

Mr. Thomas did not present his resignation, although, as Mrs. Thomas says, "he was in earnest about it, not only on account of the traveling, but on account of his health, which was beginning to be seriously affected by the Chicago climate."

After his return to Chicago and prior to his departure for a summer in Europe, the Trustees and friends of the Orchestra gave him a dinner at the Chicago Club. The occasion was one of good-will and good cheer, and such thorough affection was manifested for himself and such enthusiasm for the cause for which they were all working, that he did not have the heart to push his resignation then:

"May 14, Tuesday evening: Dinner at the Chicago Club. Mr. Hamill presided in the absence of President Adams; round table decorated with flowers and ferns; a silver punch bowl* in the center, the gift to Mr. Thomas from thirty-six ladies in Chicago, headed by Mrs. John J. Glessner.

"Present: Marshall Field, George M. Pullman, C. Norman Fay, George A. Armour, Martin A. Ryerson, Daniel H. Burnham, H. H. Kohlsaat, John J. Glessner, Robert A. Waller, E. P. Ripley, William A. Fuller, Philo A. Otis, Charles L. Hutchinson, A. C. Bartlett, T. B. Blackstone, N. K. Fairbank, Charles D. Hamill, H. N. Higginbotham and Albert A. Sprague."

The report of the Treasurer, Philo A. Otis, for the Fourth Season (1894-1895) now ending, presented at a meeting of the Trustees Friday evening, June 14, 1895, again showed a large deficit:

Receipts		Expenses	
Chicago concerts	$ 64,695.50	Salaries of Conductor and Orchestra	$ 93,664.04
Out-of-town concerts (net)	16,489.53	Auditorium rent	12,000.00
Apollo Club, other local engagements, program book, etc	5,736.79	Soloists	2,725.00
		Business management	7,388.28
	$ 86,921.82	Advertising, etc.	5,618.43
Loss on season	34,473.93		
	$121,395.75		$121,395.75

The subscriptions to the "Fund for the Support of the Orchestra" covered $30,800 of the loss.

---

*The bowl, ladle and pitcher were presented to Mr. Thomas at his home a short time before the dinner, by a group of ladies:

Mrs. George A. Armour.
Mrs. S. E. Barrett.
Mrs. A. C. Bartlett.
Mrs. Hugh T. Birch.
Mrs. T. B. Blackstone.
Mrs. L. A. Coonley.
Mrs. A. N. Eddy.
Mrs. Clarence Eddy.
Miss Frances Glessner.
Mrs. John J. Glessner.
Mrs. Charles D. Hamill.
Mrs. J. A. Hunt.
Mrs. C. L. Hutchinson.
Miss Elizabeth Isham.
Mrs. R. N. Isham.
Mrs. Edson Keith.
Mrs. Henry W. King.
Mrs. Bryan Lathrop.
Mrs. Edward F. Lawrence.
Mrs. Ezra B. McCagg.
Mrs. Cyrus H. McCormick.
Mrs. Philo A. Otis.
Mrs. A. A. Parker.
Mrs. Henry H. Porter.
Mrs. Orrin W. Potter.
Mrs. George M. Pullman.
Mrs. Martin A. Ryerson.
Miss Skinner.
Mrs. Albert A. Sprague.
Mrs. Henry B. Stone.
Mrs. H. O. Stone.
Mrs. William B. Walker.
Mrs. Meridyth Whitehouse.
Mrs. Norman Williams.
Mrs. Henry J. Willing.
Mrs. H. M. Wilmarth.

FOURTH SEASON
(1894-1895)
SOLOISTS

HARP: Edmund Schuecker.
ORGAN: Clarence Eddy.
PIANOFORTE: Rafael Joseffy, Hans von Schiller, W. C. E. Seeboeck.
VIOLA: August Junker.
VIOLIN: Max Bendix, Eugene Boegner, César Thomson, Eugène Ysaye.
VIOLONCELLO: Bruno Steindel.
VOCAL: Mrs. Lillian Blauvelt, Misses Carlotta Desvignes, Electa Gifford; Max Heinrich.

FIFTH SEASON
(1895-1896)

The "Committee on Reorganization" issues an appeal to the public for Governing Members—Resignation of Secretary George H. Wilson, who was succeeded by Philo A. Otis—P. A. McEwan elected Treasurer—Miss Anna Millar appointed Business Manager of the Orchestra—Frederick Stock a member of the Orchestra—Mr. Thomas and the Orchestra assist the Apollo Musical Club in a performance of Berlioz's "Faust"—The eastern tour of the Orchestra, and comments of the critics—Dinner to Mr. Thomas in honor of his half century of work for music in America.

After four years of work the period of formation had passed, and Mr. Thomas found that he had an Orchestra equaled by few in Europe, and by only one, possibly, in America, the Boston Symphony Orchestra. With increased attendance at the concerts and the strong support of Governing Members, the future of the Orchestra seemed assured. On March 1, 1895, a letter was issued to the people of Chicago, inviting them to become Governing Members, in accordance with the suggestions of Mr. McCormick's committee:

"The Orchestra, now in its Fifth Season, has been supported by approximately sixty men and women, whose contributions will aggregate nearly $184,000 at the close of the present season.

"In our judgment it is not well for the Orchestra, nor is it fair to those whose support has carried it thus far, that it should continue indefinitely to be sustained by so few for the benefit of all. At the suggestion, therefore, of a committee, of which C. H. McCormick was chairman, The Orchestral Association (the corporation controlling the Orchestra) has recently been reorganized as follows:

"All contributors to the fund for its support are made Governing Members, with voting power at all meetings of the Association, proportionate to the sums contributed.

"Mr. McCormick's committee also recommended that a canvass be made to secure Governing Members, whose subscriptions should aggregate $40,000 per annum for at least three years.

"As we have said before, the Chicago Orchestra has become an institution the equal of anything of the kind in the world, of which Chicago is justly proud. The very moderate prices of admission now charged might perhaps be raised, but this, in our judgment, is inexpedient and undesirable. The galleries, crowded with people of modest means at fifty cents and twenty-five cents

GEORGE H. WILSON

admission, are a source of great satisfaction to the supporters of the Association, and afford the purest pleasure and most unquestionable benefit to the thousands who occupy them during the season.

"It seems to us best to provide for any deficit by donation, rather than by a raise of prices. We therefore cordially invite and earnestly urge you to join us and become a Governing Member, contributing a moderate amount, say $250 per annum, and we beg you to use your influence among your friends, that they may do likewise.

"The favor of a reply is requested, addressed to George E. Adams, President, The Temple, Chicago.

"Respectfully yours,

BRYAN LATHROP.	E. B. MCCAGG.
MARSHALL FIELD.	HENRY W. KING.
CHARLES L. HUTCHINSON.	T. B. BLACKSTONE.
MARTIN A. RYERSON.	GEORGE E. ADAMS.
CHARLES NORMAN FAY.	WILLIAM A. FULLER.
HENRY B. STONE.	JOHN J. GLESSNER.
CYRUS H. MCCORMICK.	DANIEL H. BURNHAM."

While we did not secure the $40,000 asked for in this letter, the responses were sufficient to justify the Trustees in signing contracts for the Fifth Season.

Plans for the new season were adopted at a meeting of the Trustees in the office of Daniel H. Burnham, Monday afternoon, May 13, after the close of the Fourth Season. Present, Messrs. Fay, Burnham, Hamill and Otis. It was voted that:

"The Chicago season of concerts be lengthened to twenty-two weeks, thus shortening the time of the Orchestra on the road; prices of Associate Memberships to remain at $100, as before, with ten option tickets in place of twenty."

The resignation of George H. Wilson,* Secretary of the Association, was accepted, and Philo A. Otis was elected in his stead.

Other changes in the staff of the Association may now be noted: P. A. McEwan to succeed Philo A. Otis as

---

*In a letter dated April 5, 1917, Mrs. K. D. N. Wilson writes of her husband's life:

"George H. Wilson, born in Lawrence, Massachusetts, February 18, 1854, came to Boston when quite a lad to study the piano and organ. He sang in the chorus at the Gilmore Peace Jubilee (1872); later he was a member of the Apollo Club, Handel and Haydn Society and other musical organizations in Boston.

"Mr. Wilson came to Pittsburgh in 1895, when the new Carnegie Institute, including the Music Hall, was dedicated, and was connected with the Institute until his death. For twelve years he was Manager of the Pittsburgh Orchestra and also the Art Society, the oldest organization for promoting music and art in Pittsburgh.

"He managed two Cincinnati Festivals, and was at work on the third when death came upon him, in Pittsburgh, March 18, 1908."

Treasurer, and Miss Anna Millar as Manager of the Orchestra, her duties to begin July 1.

Miss Millar spoke of her plans for the next year, which would include a two weeks' trip of the Orchestra to New York City. She started at once for the east, and on May 31 I had a telegram asking if she might "close with the Metropolitan Opera House people for a series of concerts in the spring of 1896." After consultation with the Executive Committee I sent an answer advising her "not to make any contract without consulting Mr. Thomas." However, she returned from New York City on June 10, and reported that arrangements had been made for an eastern trip in March, 1896, including concerts in New York, Philadelphia and Brooklyn, and that Mr. Thomas had approved.

The summer of 1895 was no more auspicious for the sale of season tickets than was the previous summer. The people had not altogether recovered from the reckless speculation of the World's Fair, and the times continued to be hard. I spent an hour or more each day at the box office at Lyon & Healy's, assisting in the delivery of tickets and collecting money. An entry in my journal will explain the character of the work:

"July 15, Monday: Last day in which ticket holders can renew their subscriptions. Miss Millar reports $15,000 in orders thus far, not including boxes. Worked in the evening with Miss Millar and Mr. McEwan, Treasurer, in adjusting changes asked by ticket holders. It was like a game of chess; moving people about in order to give everybody an aisle seat."

A meeting of the Trustees was held on Monday, October 21, at 9:30 A. M.; present, Messrs. Adams, Lathrop, Fay, Stone and Otis. On motion of Mr. Stone it was voted that this announcement be made to the public:

"Box office prices of tickets will be increased on occasions when important soloists appear; not to apply to season ticket holders."

The first afternoon concert on Friday, October 25, brought a large audience to hear the lovely music. The program book, edited by W. S. B. Mathews, appeared in a new cover, with an attractive article entitled "Intermezzo," containing gossipy notes on the composers and their works. Many familiar names, with a few new ones, appeared in the list of the Orchestra in the program book. One new member must be noted, Frederick Stock, sitting quietly among the viola players, who was destined to succeed Mr. Thomas as the honored and beloved Conductor of the Orchestra.

The people turned out in force this week, filling the house both afternoon and evening. There were no attractions other than the Orchestra, our leader and the glorious music:

POPULAR PROGRAM

Prelude, Chorale and Fugue, ... *Bach*
(Arranged for Orchestra by J. J. Abert)
Introduction to Third Act, ⎫
Bacchanale, ... ⎬ "Tannhäuser," . . . . *Wagner*
Minuet, ⎫
Finale, ⎬ From String Quartet in C, No. 9, . . . *Beethoven*
Symphonic Poem, "Sarka," . . . . *Smetana*
(First Time)

INTERMISSION

Suite, "Mozartiana,". . . . . *Tschaikowsky*
Three Dances, Written for "Henry VIII," . . *Edward German*
(First Time)
Intermezzo, "Cavalleria Rusticana," . . . . . *Mascagni*
ORCHESTRA AND ORGAN
Overture, "Jubilee," . . . . *Weber*
ORCHESTRA AND ORGAN

One morning I came to the Auditorium after the rehearsal to see Mr. Thomas, and in speaking of Massenet's opera "Thaïs" and the incidental solo (violin), "The Meditation," I asked his opinion of this French music. He said:

"You know what I think of most French operas. Massenet's work is probably the highest form of modern French music, but the soul cannot live on such sweet things, any more than the body can live on tarts and puddings. I cannot ignore 'Thaïs'; if I did, then I would be ignored. If I had my way nothing of the kind should ever be played; but it is my duty to give the people the highest forms of art in each school."

Much more he said, but I cannot now recall his words.

"November 7, Thursday, 2:30 P. M.: Meeting of the Trustees in President Adams' office. All rejoiced over the outlook for the season in the report made by Miss Millar—season sale, $40,500, and the sale of single tickets thus far about double that of last season."

In the evening a reception was given in Steinway Hall by Mr. and Mrs. Thomas to the Trustees and friends of the Orchestra, to meet the ladies who presented Mr.

Thomas with the silver punch bowl, ladle and pitcher just before his departure for Europe. The program by the Orchestra contained several novelties; one may be noted—

Serenade in D Major, Opus 11, ... *Brahms*
    (First Time)

    DEDICATION OF THE BOWL
  (Mr. Thomas made the punch, and Allison V. Armour carried the bowl on the stage).

Selection from "Hänsel and Gretel," . . . *Humperdinck*
    (First Time)
    a. SONG OF THE LITTLE SANDMAN.
        MRS. PROCTOR SMITH
    b. THE CHILDREN'S PRAYER.
        MISS ELECTA GIFFORD AND MRS. SMITH
    c. DREAM MUSIC.
        THE ORCHESTRA

Meditation, "Thaïs" (New), ... *Massenet*
    VIOLIN OBBLIGATO BY MAX BENDIX

Turkish March, ... *Mozart*
    THEODORE THOMAS, CONDUCTOR

The Fourth Program, November 15 and 16, contained a work which was of an unusual character at that time, though familiar to concert-goers of the present day—"Till Eulenspiegel" (Strauss).

Lyman B. Glover, of the *Times-Herald*, called Strauss' rondo—

"The most fantastical piece of musical horse play that ever found a place in one of Mr. Thomas' concerts. Professor Mathews, who explains the jokes and cracks the hard nuts on the program for the benefit of those who wear false teeth in their intellect, declares that 'Till Eulenspiegel' was an old German jester, whose name became a synonym for all sorts of comical pranks. . . . Members of the Orchestra who have never been known to smile since the band was organized, seemed quite convulsed by the fantastic and exceedingly difficult composition."

"Friday P. M.: After the concert met Miss Millar and Mr. Fay; went to Mr. Thomas' room—told him he could not rehearse in the Auditorium week after next—German Opera coming. I had already secured Central Music Hall for Tuesday, Wednesday and Thursday. He was much annoyed—'I must have a rehearsal Monday.'"

This was one of the trials we had then to meet, in not having our own hall. Later we secured Turner Hall, on North Clark Street; and there Conductor, Orchestra, with music and instruments, had to go for rehearsal—a great inconvenience and some expense.

Franz Ondricek (violin) was the soloist November 29 and 30, Fifth Program, playing the Dvořák concerto for violin and orchestra, Opus 53. A little man, as I now think of him, a typical Bohemian, and though not as brilliant a player as Ysaye, he displayed talents of a very high order. On Saturday night his fellow-countrymen in Chicago came out *en masse*, and after the concert presented him with a silver wreath.

Some of the Trustees were in Mr. Thomas' room at the intermission, and attention was called to the opera season now in progress at the Auditorium, and the small attendance on the Wagner nights. The Conductor remarked, "Wagner did not write his operas for traveling companies."

The Annual Meeting of the Association was held Wednesday at 4:00 P. M., December 11, in the south parlor of the Auditorium Hotel. The resignation of William A. Fuller as Trustee was accepted with regrets and with the thanks of the Association for the interest he had taken in its affairs. Charles R. Corwith was elected to fill the vacancy. Officers and Trustees for the ensuing year were then elected.

During the autumn the Apollo Musical Club had been preparing for another performance of Berlioz's "Faust" at its third concert, Monday evening, February 3, 1896, to be conducted by Mr. Thomas. At the last rehearsal, Monday evening, January 27, which he had in hand, we experienced trouble with the "Soldiers' Chorus"—it had never been done right. One of the tenors called out, "You are taking it faster, Mr. Thomas, than we are accustomed to sing it in our rehearsals." Mr. Thomas answered, "It must be sung like a march, as the French sing it." With that he left the stand, marched up and down the stage, shouting out the music, and thus gave us the right idea of the rhythm. After the rehearsal he talked to us about Berlioz:

"I met Berlioz in Paris years ago, and he showed me much attention, presenting me with a copy of the 'Requiem,' with his autograph. Poor Berlioz! He was not appreciated by the Parisians. His music was liked better in Petrograd and Vienna than in Paris. The Franco-Prussian war did much to open the eyes of the French people in musical matters. The Germans were at that time making Wagner their idol. The French then looked about for one of their composers whom they could exploit, and took up Berlioz. 'Faust' is thoroughly French music, but it lacks unity. Berlioz is like Liszt in many ways, brilliant but sometimes noisy. Of the two men Berlioz has the most invention and will live the longest."

The Apollo Club had given "Faust" a number of times in other years, but the performance on February 3 was the best we had ever undertaken, the choral numbers being sung with vigor and finish. The soloists, Mrs. Eleanor Meredith (Marguerite), W. H. Rieger (Faust), Max Heinrich* (Mephisto) and Charles W. Clark (Brander), sang delightfully, but to my mind Mr. Thomas was the greatest artist of them all. It was a pleasure to sing with him. We were never once in doubt as to our risings and sittings and the entrance of an important theme; he always gave us the signal. The "Easter Hymn" was gloriously sung, and when it was finished we knew he was pleased! His face fairly beamed with pleasure.

FOURTEENTH PROGRAM, FEBRUARY 7 AND 8
SOLOIST: EMILE SAURET
Concerto for Violin and Orchestra, Opus 64, . . *Mendelssohn*

EIGHTEENTH PROGRAM, MARCH 13 AND 14
SOLOIST: IGNACE JAN PADEREWSKI
Concerto No. 1, E Flat, ... *Liszt*

"March 15, Sunday, 9:30 A. M. To the Lake Shore Station to see Mr. Thomas and the Orchestra off for New York by special train; Miss Millar in charge."

The eastern tour covered eleven concerts:
Tuesday evening, March 17, Metropolitan Opera House, New York.
Wednesday evening, March 18, Academy of Music, Brooklyn.
Thursday evening, March 19, Academy of Music, Philadelphia.
Friday evening, March 20, Academy of Music, Brooklyn.
Saturday afternoon, March 21, Metropolitan Opera House, New York.
Saturday evening, March 21, Metropolitan Opera House, New York.
Monday evening, March 23, Metropolitan Opera House, New York.
Wednesday evening, March 25, Metropolitan Opera House, New York.
Thursday evening, March 26, Metropolitan Opera House, New York.
Friday afternoon, March 27, Academy of Music, Brooklyn.
Saturday evening, March 28, Metropolitan Opera House, New York.

The eastern tour had been, throughout the winter, a matter of some anxiety to Mr. Thomas in regard to the

---
*Max Heinrich died August 9, 1916, in New York City.

"regular" and "extra" men, who made up his Orchestra. He had taken the "regular" men only on the ordinary tours along the western "Highway," but for this New York visit it was necessary that the whole band should go. In order to get the men in proper condition he placed on the Chicago programs of the winter all the numbers to be played in the east. When the time came for the Orchestra to start, everything had been so carefully rehearsed that "there was not a musician in the Orchestra," Mrs. Thomas says in her "Memoirs," "to whom every lightest shade of expression was not as familiar as household words."

"The visit of the Chicago Orchestra to New York City," continues Mrs. Thomas, "was a success, and the warmth of his welcome, the large and appreciative audiences and the beautiful tributes which came to him touched Mr. Thomas deeply." After the second concert in New York a large silver loving cup was presented to him, dedicated to "The Great Conductor, the True Man and the Cherished Friend," from Ignace J. Paderewski. All the musicians and music lovers in New York joined in giving Mr. Thomas at the final concert a silver centerpiece, designed by Paulding Farnham, of Tiffany & Co., and presented in a graceful speech by Gerritt Smith.

Mrs. Thomas gives the comments of some of the newspaper men on this visit of the Orchestra to New York, but let us look on the other side of the picture and note the views of other critics who were not so friendly to Mr. Thomas:

"The Chicago Orchestra is a well trained organization of mediocrities."

"If Mr. Thomas had a better Orchestra he would naturally make better music."

Speaking of his interpretation of Dvořák's "New World" symphony:

"It would require half a column to enumerate the things Mr. Thomas does not know about this work."

These cruel words coming from a city he had always looked upon as his home were unjust and untrue and must have hurt the Conductor keenly, if he had read them. A western editor replied:

"The New York critics usually convey the impression that their own Orchestra is composed entirely of Ysayes, Saurets, César Thomsons, Paderewskis and Joseffys."

However, Mr. Thomas had one friend, Henry T. Finck, of the *Evening Post*, who said kind words of the Chicago Orchestra:

"Brilliant when brilliancy was called for, at other times dignified and classic, delicate and tender, dreamy and romantic, or dramatic and thrilling, as in Mr. Thomas' own arrangement of Chopin's 'Funeral March.' In consequence of this versatility, which revealed the genius of the Conductor, there was a surprise in store for the audience at every concert, and it was not until the last had been given that anyone could feel sure that he really knew the full capacity of the Chicago Orchestra and its Conductor."

From New York City the Orchestra returned to Chicago, and after a few days' rest started on another tour: Ann Arbor on Tuesday evening, April 7; Columbus, Wednesday evening, April 8; Akron, Thursday evening, April 9; Cleveland, Friday evening, April 10, and Toledo, Saturday evening, April 11.

While the Orchestra was playing in some Ohio town, I had word from the Auditorium management that, the hall having been engaged the early part of the week of April 13 by Loie Fuller, the "skirt and wing dancer," Mr. Thomas could not hold his rehearsals on the Auditorium stage on the following Monday and Tuesday. I at once secured Central Music Hall, and advised Miss Millar at Columbus. Monday morning, the 13th, Henry Sachleben came to my office with a message that "the old man" wished to see me at once. On arriving at Central Music Hall, I found him discussing with Frederick Grant Gleason the *tempi* of his symphonic poem, "Edris," to be given April 17 and 18, Nineteenth Program. The Conductor soon turned to me: "Let us go over to one of the boxes and talk." He began at once about the necessity of a permanent hall for his rehearsals and concerts: "I cannot stand the strain of work and responsibility unless I can have regular rehearsals. It is out of the question to have rehearsals in one place and give concerts in another."

I told him that for the present we must put up with conditions as they were, and that there was nothing to do but to make the best of the situation.

"I have now my permanent Orchestra," he replied, "and I hope we will soon have a permanent hall; if not, I must give up the work." With that he returned to the stand to rehearse Mr. Gleason's "Edris."

The Conductor's words sank deep into my heart; he was perfectly right. At the meeting of the Executive Committee on Friday afternoon of that week the matter was brought up and informally discussed. We could take no action; must simply wait.

At the concerts of May 8 and 9, Twenty-second, and last, Program, Beethoven's ninth symphony was played in the second part of the program. Soloists: Miss Electa Gifford (soprano), Miss Fanchon H. Thompson (contralto), George Hamlin (tenor) and Charles W. Clark (bass); Max Bendix (violin), and the Apollo Musical Club.

FIFTH SEASON
(1895-1896)
SOLOISTS

PIANOFORTE: Mrs. Fannie Bloomfield Zeisler; Ignace J. Paderewski.

VIOLIN: Max Bendix, Martin Marsick, Franz Ondricek, Emile Sauret.

VIOLONCELLO: Bruno Steindel.

VOCAL: Misses Electa Gifford, Marguerite Hall, Fanchon H. Thompson, Mrs. May Phœnix-Cameron, Mme. Amalie Materna; Charles W. Clark, George W. Fergusson, George Hamlin.

A complimentary dinner was given to Mr. Thomas on Friday evening, May 8, at the Chicago Club, in honor of the completion of his fifty years of musical work in America. Among those present were:

GEORGE E. ADAMS.	WILLIAM R. HARPER.
CHARLES D. HAMILL.	H. H. KOHLSAAT.
ALBERT A. SPRAGUE.	C. NORMAN FAY.
ADOLPHUS C. BARTLETT.	HENRY B. STONE.
JOHN J. GLESSNER.	ROBERT A. WALLER.
WILLIAM A. FULLER.	ALLISON V. ARMOUR.
PHILO A. OTIS.	FRANKLIN MACVEAGH.
JAMES W. ELLSWORTH.	CYRUS H. MCCORMICK.
DANIEL H. BURNHAM.	WILLIAM B. WALKER.
A. C. MCCLURG.	EDSON KEITH.
BRYAN LATHROP.	

After the dinner came words of love and congratulations from Trustees George E. Adams, Charles D. Hamill and Bryan Lathrop to our Conductor for the great work he had done in the cause of good music in our country, to which Mr. Thomas responded, showing his appreciation of the cordial and generous support he had received from the people of Chicago in establishing our Orchestra.

SIXTH SEASON
(1896-1897)

Mr. Thomas urges the need of a new hall—The Trustees decide not to leave the Auditorium at present—Organization of a chorus with Arthur Mees as Assistant Conductor—Frederick J. Wessels elected Treasurer—Arthur Mees succeeds W. S. B. Mathews as editor of the program |book—Promenade concert for the benefit of the Orchestra.

Mr. Hamill and I had many conferences with Mr. Thomas during the winter to consider some plan for interesting the general public in our concerts. The Conductor insisted that a smaller and permanent hall for rehearsals and concerts would solve the problem. Mr. Hamill suggested that a chorus of two hundred voices for the performance of short works with Orchestra might interest the people, and that an Assistant Conductor be engaged to prepare the chorus.

Mr. Thomas was right regarding the urgent need for a permanent hall, as former experiences with the Auditorium management had shown, and some action was, therefore, taken during the summer months. The Trustees were called to Mr. Burnham's office on June 24 to consider plans he had prepared for a Music Hall to be erected on Michigan Avenue by Charles C. Curtiss. Though the proposition had some attractive features as to rental and other details, it was not thought advisable to proceed with the plan, for reasons set forth at a meeting of the Trustees on December 3. President Adams at this meeting read a letter from Ferdinand W. Peck, President of the Auditorium Association, stating that the rental now paid the Auditorium by The Orchestral Association was the salvation of the Auditorium. It was further stated by Mr. Adams that many friends of the Orchestra were largely interested in the Auditorium. In deference to their wishes the proposition for the new Music Hall was abandoned.

In the meantime it had been decided (July 3) by the Trustees to proceed with the organization of the chorus, and that Arthur Mees be engaged as Assistant Con-

FREDERICK J. WESSELS

Sixth Season—1896-1897

ductor. At this meeting the resignation of P. A. McEwan, Treasurer, was accepted, and Frederick J. Wessels,* Secretary of the Apollo Musical Club, was elected in his place. The work of assembling the chorus was entrusted to Mr. Hamill and myself. We did not undertake this task with much enthusiasm; having had an experience of twenty-five years in chorus work in Chicago, we knew some of the difficulties to be encountered. Mr. Hamill and I were at Cincinnati, in May, for the Festival, and the question of forming a chorus and securing an Assistant Conductor came up for discussion at a luncheon with Mr. Thomas at the St. Nicholas Hotel. It had been the talk in Chicago that the Apollo Club was in difficulties, and that we could have two hundred of their members for our chorus. We learned subsequently that this was not true; hence the two hundred discontented members of the Club did not flock to our colors. I told Mr. Thomas and Mr. Hamill plainly that the salary of the Assistant Conductor and the expenses of the chorus would be a very material addition to the cargo of our already heavily laden craft. "We had better keep to orchestral work," I continued, "and when we need a chorus the Apollo Club will gladly help us out, as they have done before."

In July I wrote to Mr. Thomas regarding the prospects of forming the chorus, asking his views as to the works to be performed and the soloists needed. He replied:

"FAIRHAVEN, MASSACHUSETTS, July 30, 1896.

"DEAR MR. OTIS:

"I was glad to receive your letter of the 21st, and have your opinion on the various chorus questions. We fully agree though on all points, probably because we both have experience in the matter and no side interests. You will excuse me if I do not enter into any discussion about chorus matters in this letter, for I fully discussed the subject with Miss Millar. I want to acknowledge your letter and do want your advice on one point. The Grieg work ('Olaf Trygvason') will answer all your demands and 'fill the bill' wholly. The chorus parts, which are very good, cost twenty-five cents a copy, while the piano score costs ninety cents. The American chorus singer is used to having a piano score to sing from—an unknown thing in Europe—and our chorus will sometimes have to sing from parts instead of scores. But the question

---

*Mr. Wessels was admitted to membership in the Apollo Musical Club in 1881; appointed Assistant Secretary of the Club (1891) and elected Secretary (1892).

is whether it would be advisable to have parts instead of scores for the first concert. Will you please inform me by telegraph, that I may have the music imported? What date do you expect to have the first rehearsal take place?

"It would be very desirable to select and announce the three choral works, and I have given Miss Millar a list of works for you and Mr. Hamill to choose from. If you think 'The Creation' would be an attraction, all right as far as I am concerned, but do remember, please, that we must have three good soloists; besides the two you mention, we need also as good a soprano. Do you mean to give the whole work ('Creation') or only the two first parts, with a symphony?
"Yours sincerely,
(Signed) "THEODORE THOMAS.

"P. S.—Do you think the chorus can assist in a Beethoven and Wagner night, in addition to the three choral concerts? Say the 'Ballade' or 'Spinning Song' from 'The Flying Dutchman' and fantasia for piano, chorus and orchestra by Beethoven, and the 'Prisoners' Chorus' from 'Fidelio' for the other composers' night."

I replied that we would leave the program entirely to his discretion, and would not undertake "The Creation" this season.

The prospectus for the Sixth Season, issued by the Manager, Miss Anna Millar, dated September 8, 1896, announced that the season would consist of twenty-two matinées on Fridays at 2:15 o'clock and twenty-two evening concerts on Saturdays at 8:15 o'clock.

"In order to open to the public a most interesting field of musical literature seldon heard in this country, consisting of short works for chorus and orchestra, the Association has undertaken the formation of 'A Special Chorus,' and has been fortunate enough to secure that well known and excellent musician, Arthur Mees, as Assistant Director. The chorus will take part at intervals in the season's programs, and will give principally novelties."

The important matter now was the organization of the chorus. A letter was sent September 1 to the press and to amateur and professional singers, signed by Mr. Thomas, announcing the arrival in Chicago of Arthur Mees, Assistant Conductor, and that Mr. Mees would be in attendance at Apollo Hall, Central Music Hall Building, on Tuesday and Friday afternoons and evenings, commencing September 8, to receive applicants for admission to the chorus. It was the eve of a presidential election, and the city was aflame with excitement over the rival parties—Bryan and "Free Silver!" McKinley and "Protection!"—but it was not a favorable time to talk of symphony concerts and chorus rehearsals. I made a few notes at the time regarding our progress in selecting a chorus:

"September 8, Tuesday: In P. M. to Apollo Hall; examination of voices for the chorus; Mees, Wessels and myself in attendance. Only a few came.

"September 9, Wednesday P. M.: We are not having any returns from Mr. Thomas' letter asking for members for the chorus. Mees was greatly disappointed yesterday, and expressed himself so in plain words. We heard in the P. M. eighteen people; many of them no good. Last evening only seven applied; what is to be done? Plenty of men with good voices singing in campaign meetings."

The first rehearsal of the chorus was held Monday evening, October 5, in Apollo Hall, under the direction of Mr. Mees, with ninety-five singers present. This was disappointing, but we believed the attendance would increase when the elections were over and people had returned to rational occupations of leisure. The attendance did increase at subsequent rehearsals, through the influence of the Chorus Committee, Charles D. Hamill, D. A. Noyes, Louis Spahn, F. J. Wessels and myself; but with all our efforts we could not interest musical people. In numbers and tone production the chorus was never what we had expected.

The season ticket sale that year, under Miss Millar's management, yielded $47,500, the largest since the organization of the Orchestra, and right in the face of the hard times caused by Bryan and his doctrine of "Free Silver."

There were some changes in the *personnel* of the Orchestra: Max Bendix,* concertmeister, had retired and was succeeded by Ernest Wendel, who came to Mr. Thomas with a note from Dr. Joachim: "Here is the right man for you, the only thing against him being his youth."

---

*One of my happy remembrances is associated with the Chicago Summer Garden Concerts given by Theodore Thomas in other days, and hearing Max Bendix in some delightful solo work—notably in the "Meditation" (Bach—Gounod), which I heard then for the first time.

Max Bendix, born March 28, 1866, in Detroit, Michigan, acquired his education in New York, Cincinnati and Berlin. On his return (1886) to America he was engaged as concertmeister of the orchestra in the Manhattan Opera House, New York; later with the Theodore Thomas Orchestra, and was retained in this position when Mr. Thomas organized (1891) the Chicago Orchestra. After leaving Chicago (1896) Mr. Bendix returned to New York, where he has since resided, engaged in concert and other professional work. Mr. Bendix was Conductor of the Orchestra at the St. Louis Exposition, 1904, at the San Francisco Exposition, 1915, and conducted the St. Louis Municipal Orchestra, 1920.

Leopold de Maré, who had played third horn heretofore, was promoted to the position of first horn. One of the new members, Alfred Quensel (flute), came from the Philharmonic Orchestra in Berlin, and is still with us (1924) in this, the Thirty-third Season.

The Sixth Season opened with a flourish of trumpets and a burst of melody on Friday afternoon, October 23, a lovely autumnal day. Mr. Thomas had prepared a great feast for his audience, which included two new modern works: Fanfare Inaugural (new), by Gilson, and Symphonic Poem (Thamar), by Balakirew (first performance).

The program book, with a new editor, Arthur Mees, the Assistant Conductor (W. S. B. Mathews* having resigned), furnished the audience with some attractive reading. Mr. Mees is a scholar as well as a conductor, and his analyses of the works heard at the concerts of the week showed research and study.

The concert on Saturday evening, October 31, Second Program, had a patriotic ending which was not put down in the bill. During the week Mr. Thomas had received a request signed by the Trustees and friends of the Orchestra to play "The Star Spangled Banner" at the close of this concert, in recognition of the presidential election, then near at hand. He arranged accordingly that the chorus should occupy the first rows of seats in the parquet. At the conclusion of the last number, Massenet's suite, "Les Erinnyes," when the audience was about to leave, a roll of the drums was heard, softly and quietly, increasing "louder and louder, until everyone wondered," says Mrs. Thomas, "what was coming next." At last Mr. Thomas turned toward the audience, motioned for them to rise and sing, and with the full power of the Orchestra, organ, chorus and four thousand people in the audience, all joined in one stupendous maelstrom of sound, "The

---

*My friendship with Mr. Mathews dates from 1869, when he was organist (1867-1893) of the Centenary M. E. Church. He had just established a series of organ recitals on Saturday afternoons, with the assistance of local organists and singers. The recitals were very popular, and continued until the great fire of 1871. Mr. Mathews was musical critic of the *Chicago Times*, the *Daily News* and the *Chicago Tribune* (1878-1886), and was the author of a number of instructive works on musical subjects. One may be noted: "How to Understand Music" (two volumes, 1880-1888). William Smythe Babcock Mathews was born May 8, 1837, at Loudon, New Hampshire; died April 1, 1912, at Denver, Colorado.

Sixth Season—1896-1897

Star Spangled Banner" was given such a presentation as is not often heard.

Clarence Eddy was the soloist November 6 and 7, Third Program, playing the fantasia (organ and orchestra) by Saint-Saëns and the toccata by Capocci.

Jan van Oordt, the Dutch violinist, the soloist November 13 and 14, Fourth Program, brought us large houses; we had $972 at the door on Friday afternoon.

Moriz Rosenthal (piano), who was announced for November 27 and 28, Sixth Program, was taken seriously ill at the Auditorium, and was unable to appear. Massenet's suite, "Les Erinnyes," was substituted, Bruno Steindel playing the incidental solo.

The offices of The Orchestral Association were moved in the previous season from Room 1304 in the Auditorium Tower to Room 804 Isabella Building (now No. 21 East Van Buren Street), a place indelibly stamped on my memory with sad thoughts of our finances.

The Annual Meeting for the election of Trustees and Officers was held in the Isabella Building Wednesday afternoon, December 9. The report of the Treasurer, Frederick J. Wessels, for the Fifth Season, ending June 30, 1896, was read and ordered printed; copies to be sent to the Governing Members:

"Expenditures $133,286.12, including $95,719.04 for salaries of Conductor and Orchestra, and $13,200 for rental of the Auditorium. The Orchestra earned $80,877.25 from the Chicago concerts, and $25,249.14 from all other sources, leaving a loss of $27,159.73 for the Governing Members to pay.

"To meet this deficit the Trustees had subscriptions from Governing Members for $23,700, leaving a balance of $3,459.93 to be carried forward, making a total deficit to date, including previous seasons, of $8,520.55.

"The out-of-town concerts yielded $30,165.25, under Miss Millar's effective management. After deducting expenses for transportation, hotels and baggage, $10,729.32, there was a balance of $19,435.93, towards paying salaries of the Orchestra.

". . . A notable success was the taking of the entire Orchestra of 100 men to New York, Brooklyn and Philadelphia, playing there during a season of two weeks, with profit to the treasury and gain to the reputation of the organization. Notwithstanding the crucial test of seven concerts in ten days in the city of New York, the box office receipts tell the story of the popular verdict, while the Director was overwhelmed with attentions at the hands of old friends, and was publicly presented with beautiful and valuable testimonials."

The deficit of $8,520.55 at the close of the Fifth Season was carried for a time with a note of the Trustees for $7,000 at the bank, which we had to pay in October out of the ticket sales. The season sale for the current year ($47,500) was encouraging, but the single sales had steadily declined:

December 4, 1896, Friday, symphony program	$ 347.00
December 11, 1896, Friday, Nordica, soloist	2,000.00
December 12, 1896, Saturday, Nordica, soloist	2,300.00
January 15, 1897, Saturday, Godowsky, soloist	381.00
January 22, 1897, Friday, Brueckner Symphony	326.00
January 23, 1897, Saturday, "A blizzard from Dakota"	281.00

At the concerts of December 18 and 19, Ninth Program, the chorus made its first appearance in a Beethoven program which included the fantasia for piano (Hans Bruening, soloist), chorus and orchestra, and the march and chorus from "The Ruins of Athens"; Arthur Mees, Conductor. The chorus, though small (125 voices), sang with vigor and clear attack, showing the care taken in the selection of the singers and the thorough training given them by Mr. Mees.

"February 2, 1897, Tuesday: Meeting of the Trustees at 2:30 P. M.; Treasurer Wessels made a report showing a probable deficit of $15,000 for the year. Mr. Thomas told Miss Millar that 'if the deficit must be carried until next season, I shall resign.' Various opinions expressed by Trustees as to the declining receipts: 'heavy programs,' 'too much new music,' and 'hard times.'"

On the subject of financial conditions in Chicago and throughout the country, the *Chicago Tribune* said there were 40,000 people in Chicago that winter (1896-1897) in actual destitution and want. It was the middle class that was suffering; the clerk, salesman and bookkeeper who were out of work. When times are good these people always fill the gallery at our concerts.

We felt encouraged after the concerts of February 5 and 6, Sixteenth Program, when Mme. Carreño gave a great performance of the Beethoven concerto No. 5 in E flat, Opus 73, the Friday concert yielding $1,100, and the Saturday night concert $1,348.

Mme. Georgine von Januschowsky, Miss Sue Aline Harrington, George Hamlin and D. Ffrangcon Davies took part with the chorus, February 12 and 13, Seventeenth Program, the women's voices being especially effective in the "Spinning Chorus and Ballad" from

Sixth Season—1896-1897

"The Flying Dutchman" (Wagner), conducted by Mr. Mees. The selections from "Parsifal" (Wagner) for solo voices, chorus and orchestra, conducted by Mr. Thomas, made a profound impression on the audience.

The boy violinist, Bronislaw Huberman, soloist February 19 and 20, Eighteenth Program (Request), created a sensation by his extraordinary work. It seemed almost beyond belief that this child could play Mendelssohn's concerto with the art and technique of an older performer. He was no mere infant prodigy, no *Wunderkind*, but an artist with divine talent.

The Italian Opera Company, after some uncertainty caused by poor business in New York City, began a season of six weeks at the Auditorium on March 1, employing the Chicago Orchestra. The Trustees now had ample time to consider the affairs of the Orchestra and make provision for a deficit of at least $15,000 at the close of this season. A meeting of the Trustees was held:

"March 9, Tuesday, 2:30 P. M.: Present, Messrs. Fay, Hamill, Stone and Otis—Mr. Thomas and Miss Millar* by invitation. Mr. Thomas suggested that if there is no opera next year, Miss Millar should go to San Francisco to work up a guarantee for six weeks of concerts next spring (1898).

"March 10, Wednesday: Trustees met in P. M.; decided on a Promenade Concert for April 27, and to make an appeal to the public for its support. Mr. Hamill reported an interview with Mr. Grau, who stated there would be no opera next year in America; 'give the people a rest.' The Directors of the Metropolitan Opera Company of New York would decide this later."

The regular concerts of the Orchestra were resumed at the close of the opera season on April 9 and 10, Nineteenth Program, the chorus taking part with Orchestra and organ (Wilhelm Middelschulte, organist) in the overture "A Mighty Fortress" (Nicolai) and in selections from "Tannhäuser" (Wagner).

"April 21, Wednesday evening: To the Auditorium; Apollo Club concert under the direction of William L. Tomlins:
'Stabat Mater,' . . . . *Dvořák*
'Swan and Skylark,' . . . . *A. Goring Thomas*

---

*Miss Millar left Chicago on March 14 for California, hoping she could arrange a series of concerts on the Coast for the spring of 1898. "It was a disappointing trip," she said in a letter (1917). "There was no hall at that time in San Francisco suitable for our concerts. The largest theatre was being used for a stock opera company; the people did not care for orchestral concerts. One or two men appeared to be interested, but unfortunately they were not able to swing it alone or to greatly influence others."

"Soloists: Miss Ella Russell (soprano), Mrs. Katharine Fisk (contralto), Ben Davies (tenor) and George E. Holmes (bass); Wilhelm Middelschulte (organist) and the Chicago Orchestra."

The chorus again assisted the Orchestra, April 23 and 24, Twenty-first Program, in Grieg's dramatic work, "Olaf Trygvason," Mr. Mees conducting. Soloists: Miss N. Estelle Harrington (soprano), Miss Sue Aline Harrington (contralto) and Edward H. Dermitt (bass).

With all our efforts we found it difficult to interest musical people in the chorus of the Orchestra, partly on account of business and professional engagements which interfered with the attendance of the singers at the Friday concerts, but mainly through sheer indifference. It would seem that from the large population of our city we might surely assemble 250 young men and women who would love to sing under such leaders as Theodore Thomas and Arthur Mees. We could only secure 127 voices to sing Grieg's work: forty-three sopranos, thirty altos, twenty-four tenors and thirty basses; one-half the number we had expected. However, the chorus had been carefully drilled by Mr. Mees, and held their own against the Orchestra of ninety players. There was a small audience on Friday afternoon, and a still smaller one on Saturday night. Grieg's music did not interest the people.

Early in March invitations were issued to the 4,000 names on the Charity Ball list:

THE TRUSTEES OF
THE ORCHESTRAL ASSOCIATION
Request the Honor of Your Subscription to and Presence at a Promenade Concert to be Given by

MR. THEODORE THOMAS
With the Assistance of the Orchestra and Chorus of the Association, for the Benefit of Its Treasury at the Auditorium on Tuesday Evening, April 27, 1897, at Quarter Past Eight o'Clock.

PATRONESSES

MRS. GEORGE E. ADAMS.	MRS. HENRY W. KING.
MRS. GEORGE A. ARMOUR.	MRS. H. H. KOHLSAAT.
MRS. HUGH T. BIRCH.	MRS. EZRA B. MCCAGG.
MRS. CHAUNCEY J. BLAIR.	MRS. CYRUS H. MCCORMICK.
MRS. W. J. CHALMERS.	MRS. POTTER PALMER.
MRS. ARTHUR J. CATON.	MRS. ROBERT W. PATTERSON.
MRS. HENRY DIBBLEE.	MRS. GEORGE M. PULLMAN.
MRS. AUGUSTUS N. EDDY.	MRS. ROBERT A. WALLER.
MRS. JOHN J. GLESSNER.	MRS. NORMAN WILLIAMS.

Sixth Season—1896-1897

The Promenade Concert grew out of a suggestion made by Mr. Thomas at a Trustees' meeting in February, when ways and means were being devised for meeting the deficit. The Auditorium, richly decorated with flowers and flags, with the vast parquet floored over, was an attractive sight on the eventful evening. Mr. Thomas planned a program which represented three features: (1) concert music with the Orchestra; (2) a pageant, introducing the chorus and leading up to the minuet; and (3) dance music by Strauss, in which all could take part:

Jubilee Overture,	*Weber*
Dances from the Suite "Henry VIII,"	*German*
Polonaise, A Flat Major,	*Chopin—Thomas*

INTERMISSION

March and Chorus ("Tannhäuser"),	*Wagner*
Introduction and Bridal Chorus ("Lohengrin"),	*Wagner*
March ("Lohengrin"),	*Wagner*

CHORUS AND ORCHESTRA

INTERMISSION

March, "Triumphal Entrance of the Boyards,"	*Halvorsen*
Minuet ("Don Giovanni"),	*Mozart*
(Danced by Thirty Couples in Court Costume)	
Waltz, "On the Beautiful Blue Danube,"	*Strauss*
Waltz, "Artists' Life,"	*Strauss*
Polka Schnell,	*Strauss*

General Dancing

It was a beautiful picture as the thirty couples of society belles and beaux, dressed after the period of the ancient French court, a shimmer of powdered hair, lace, velvet and satin, came forward to take their places in the stately minuet. Among the dancers may be noted:

MRS. C. H. WILMERDING.	MR. C. H. WILMERDING.
MRS. WILLIAM P. HUNT.	MR. C. NORMAN FAY.
MRS. GEORGE S. WILLITS.	MR. WILLIAM P. HUNT.
MRS. E. S. ADAMS.	MR. ERNEST WALKER.
MRS. S. LEROY.	MRS. F. REMINGTON.
MISS HOSMER.	MRS. EAMES MACVEAGH.
MISS LAURA WILLIAMS.	MR. H. J. WHIGHAM.
MISS MINNA THOMAS.	LIEUT. DUNCAN.
MISS MARGARET ABBOTT.	LIEUT. STEVENSON.
MISS CHARLOTTE SILSBEE.	MR. CHARLES H. HAMILL.
MISS MARIE OWENS.	MR. ARTHUR BOLTON.
MISS LOUISE BURKE.	MR. ROBERT MCKAY.
MISS EDITH DEXTER.	

One important feature was lacking in this Promenade Concert—the enthusiasm of a large audience; the financial result was indeed disappointing. Four thousand tickets at $5 each were issued with the invitations; less than five hundred were sold.

"April 30 and May 1: Twenty-second Program; last concerts. A fairly good house, but many option tickets were used. Steindel played delightfully in Massenet's 'Les Erinnyes.'"

The Apollo Musical Club celebrated its Twenty-fifth Anniversary by a performance of Mendelssohn's "Elijah" as an extra concert, Monday evening, May 10, in the Auditorium, William L. Tomlins, Conductor. Soloists: Miss Jenny Osborn (soprano), Miss Sue Aline Harrington (contralto), George Hamlin (tenor), Plunkett Greene (bass); Wilhelm Middelschulte (organist); the Chicago Orchestra.

SIXTH SEASON
(1896-1897)
SOLOISTS

ORGAN: Clarence Eddy, Wilhelm Middelschulte.
PIANOFORTE: H. Bruening, Leopold Godowsky; Mme. Teresa Carreño.
VIOLIN: Jan van Oordt, Carl Halir, Bronislaw Huberman.
VIOLONCELLO: Bruno Steindel, Leo Stern.
VOCAL: Mmes. Lillian Nordica, Georgine von Januschowsky, Misses N. Estelle Harrington, Sue Aline Harrington; D. Ffrangcon Davies, Edward H. Dermitt, George Hamlin.

SEVENTH SEASON
(1897-1898)

Miss Millar makes a trip to Europe and engages Josef Hofmann for a series of concerts—Death of Henry B. Stone and George M. Pullman, sincere friends of the Orchestra—The chorus of the Association takes part in the ninth symphony—Mr. Thomas expresses his views on modern music at a dinner given to Alexandre Guilmant—The Orchestra again makes an eastern tour—Bryan Lathrop meets a financial emergency.

The offices of the Association were removed to our former quarters in the Auditorium Tower on May 1, 1897, and through the courtesy of the Auditorium Association we had the rental free. Once settled in these comfortable rooms, which we occupied until the completion (1904) of Orchestra Hall, we had time to consider the condition of our finances. A few Governing Members met on the afternoon of May 7, at the Chicago Club, to make provision for meeting the deficit of $13,500 on the Sixth Season. It was agreed that the Orchestra should continue, and that a new guarantee of $25,000 be obtained. There was some discussion about lengthening the Chicago season to twenty-four weeks and thus reduce the time on the road from six to four weeks. This question was settled by the Executive Committee at the next meeting:

"May 25, Tuesday, 2:30 P. M. Meeting of Executive Committee: Messrs. Hamill, Fay and Otis. It was decided that Miss Millar should go to Europe at once to secure artists for out-of-town tour next spring. Chicago season to be twenty-two weeks. If Miss Millar can fill in six weeks of outside business, no need to lengthen Chicago season."

The prospectus for the Seventh Season appeared in June, announcing twenty-two weeks of concerts, beginning October 22 and 23, and that the season ticket sale would open, as usual, at Lyon & Healy's. By July 1 orders for renewals to the amount of $28,000 had been received; on October 15 this amount had increased to $50,000, the largest advance sale since the Orchestra was established.

It is a sad experience of every season, that we lose from our Governing Members, by death, removal from the city and other causes, strong friends, without whose aid we could not carry on the Orchestra. It was only by the personal endorsement of the Trustees that we succeeded in doing a business in the previous season of $135,000 on our slender resources. Before the concerts had started in the autumn, the Trustees were called together October 21 to record the death of two of our best friends—Henry B. Stone, July 5, and George M. Pullman, October 19. At this meeting the following minute was adopted:

"The Trustees of The Orchestral Association, during last summer's intermission of their sessions, learned with unfeigned sorrow of the tragic death of one of their own number, the lamented Henry B. Stone. Before commencing another season's work they desire to record in simple language, as befits the nature of the man, their respect for a strong character, a loyal associate and a lover of the true, the beautiful and the good in every form, especially in music.

"To this record the Trustees are compelled, in grief, to add that of the passing away of George M. Pullman, a great man, a lover of art and music and of the concerts of the Orchestra; from its very inception one of the Guarantors and Governing Members of this Association, and of late, because of his leadership in its moral and financial support and his unhesitating endorsement of its work and purposes in their integrity, its most potent and valued friend."

Miss Millar returned from Europe in October, having secured Josef Hofmann for the eastern tour of the Orchestra in the spring of 1898.

The chorus resumed its work on Monday evening, September 20, Mr. Mees devoting a portion of the evening to instructing the new voices in sight reading, using in this work chalk and blackboard, after the manner of the old-time singing school teacher.

New voices were added to the chorus in the next two weeks, so that on October 16 we could take up the study of the ninth symphony (Beethoven) and the One Hundred and Fourteenth Psalm (Mendelssohn).

The first concerts of the season, October 22 and 23, opened with "The Festival March" for chorus and Orchestra, written by Hugo Kaun, in which he introduced, with great effect, "The Star Spangled Banner."

The program book, with Arthur Mees again as editor, gave the *personnel* of the Orchestra for the Seventh

Seventh Season—1897-1898

Season, showing, as new men in the ranks Leopold Kramer, from Vienna (taking the place of Ernest Wendell, resigned), and Emil Baré, from Essen, concertmeisters. August Junker (first viola) having gone to Tokio, Japan, as a member of the faculty of the Imperial School of Music in that city, he was succeeded by J. Keller.

Giuseppe Campanari, soloist October 29 and 30, Second Program, sang the aria, "Vision Fugitive" (Massenet) and the prologue to "Pagliacci" (Leoncavallo), Mr. Mees conducting. Mr. Campanari was a member (1885-1893) ('cello) of the Boston Symphony Orchestra, and a good singer also. He has often been seen leaving his seat in the Orchestra to stand before the audience and delight the people with his glorious voice and style.

The women's voices of the chorus, assisted by Miss Helen Buckley and Miss N. Estelle Harrington, took part in the Fifth Program, November 26 and 27, in "A Midsummer Night's Dream" (Mendelssohn).

Eugène Ysaye was the soloist December 3 and 4, Sixth Program, playing the Beethoven concerto in D major.

At the Annual Meeting, held on December 8 in the Auditorium Tower, the Trustees heard from the Treasurer another sad tale of our finances for the Sixth Season (1896-1897), but no action was taken further than to have the report printed and sent to Associate and Governing Members:

RECEIPTS		EXPENSES	
Chicago concerts	$ 81,449.25	Business management, advertising, etc.	$ 17,867.02
Out-of-town, Apollo Club, etc.	5,871.66	Auditorium rent	12,000.00
Program book	1,424.06	Salaries of Conductor and Orchestra	94,454.44
Italian opera	15,000.00	Soloists	4,417.00
Promenade concert	2,328.85	Chorus	4,371.59
Loss on season for Governing Members to pay	27,036.23		
	$133,110.05		$133,110.05

To meet the loss the Trustees had subscriptions from Governing Members of $22,100, leaving a balance of $5,070.13 to be provided. This, added to the deficit of

$8,520.55 for the previous season, made the total deficit $13,590.68 to date. The $15,000 from the Opera Company was a welcome addition to our receipts.

SEVENTH PROGRAM, DECEMBER 10 AND 11
Soloists: Bruno Steindel and Edmund Schuecker

Concerto for Violoncello, Opus 104, ... *Dvořák*
Fantasie for Harp, Opus 35, ... *Schuecker*

Beethoven's ninth symphony was given December 17 and 18, Eighth Program, with the chorus of the Association, assisted by Mrs. Genevieve C. Wilson (soprano), Mrs. Christine N. Dreier (contralto), George Hamlin (tenor) and George E. Holmes* (bass). Beethoven's music did not interest the people at all, and there were small houses at both concerts.

Raoul Pugno, the French pianist, made his first appearance in Chicago with the Orchestra January 14 and 15, 1898, Twelfth Program, playing the Grieg concerto, and showing himself to be an artist of the highest order. Pianists of the present day, who play without notes and suffer from nervousness in doing so, from fear of defective memory, may take courage and profit by the example of Mr. Pugno. He had a copy of the concerto before him, and referred to it when necessary, quietly and without embarrassment.

All students of organ and theory of music came to the concerts of January 21 and 22, Thirteenth Program, filling the Auditorium on both occasions to hear Alexandre Guilmant, the eminent French organist. His numbers were the concerto No. 1 (Handel) and his own symphony for organ and orchestra No. 1, Opus 42. This quiet, silver-haired Frenchman had the rare power of making the instrument sing and speak in tones of poetic beauty, so that the listener never thought of the organ, but only of Guilmant, the player.

One of our enthusiastic lovers of music, and an accomplished organist, Charles D. Irwin, gave a dinner on Friday evening, January 28, to Mr. Guilmant, at the Union League Club. At Mr. Irwin's request I called on Mr. Thomas to ask him to be one of the guests and thus show honor to the illustrious French artist. At first he declined, being under the doctor's orders; but at the con-

---
*George Ellsworth Holmes, one of our best local baritones, died March 24, 1898, in Chicago.

cert that afternoon he said he would be happy to accept. The other guests were Frederick Grant Gleason, Samuel Kayser, Napoleon Ledochowski, Clarence Eddy and myself. It was a delightful occasion, with plenty of good cheer, accompanied by a continuous conversation on literature and art. Never have I heard Mr. Thomas talk so long and so well. It was Gleason who started a discussion: "Do you not think, Mr. Thomas, that Mozart and Beethoven will become antiquated, and that Wagner will be the composer of the future?"

Gleason's question, like the red flag flaunted in the face of a bull, roused the Conductor to action, and at once he was ready for battle. For one half hour we listened to a vigorous discourse on the art the Conductor loved so well. Leaving his seat at the table, he walked about the room, constantly talking of the ancient and modern schools. Few of the men that evening ever heard such a comparison of the art of the old writers with that of Richard Wagner: "Bach, Handel, Mozart and Beethoven were sons of God! Wagner was an egotist! All sensuousness! Beethoven worked for humanity. There are three epochs in the history of art; (1) the Greek; (2) the period which produced Shakespeare; (3) the period which gave the world Beethoven."

All this was set forth by Mr. Thomas, partly in vigorous German and partly in English. Mr. Guilmant was an eager listener through this discussion. As he could not speak German at all, and very little English, Mr. Ledochowski interpreted for him. The French artist did not entirely agree with Mr. Thomas, though he spoke delightfully and tenderly of Bach and Handel; he could well do this, for we had never heard the Handel concerto played as Guilmant played it at the concert that afternoon. "Surely, Mr. Thomas, you cannot ignore the author of 'Lohengrin' and 'Siegfried,' works the French people are now learning to appreciate. I am told you were the first to play Wagner's music in America."

The Conductor would not yield, but held sturdily to his views that Mozart and Beethoven would live, and that Wagner might not.

After reaching home I could not rest until I had set down some of the things said that evening. . Many changes have occurred in the years that have passed since Mr. Irwin gave this delightful dinner. Guilmant,* Ledochowski† and Gleason‡ are gone; our leader also, but his work abides. The Orchestra lives, an enduring monument to his genius.

The chorus of the Association, Mr. Mees conducting, appeared February 18 and 19, Fifteenth Program, in the chorale and chorus from the "Reformation Cantata" (Bach) and in the One Hundred and Fourteenth Psalm (Mendelssohn), Wilhelm Middelschulte, organist. This was the best work the chorus had done since it came under the direction of Mr. Mees two years before; the two hundred voices showing a rich, sonorous tone and singing with good attack and finish. Henri Marteau was the soloist, playing the Dubois concerto for violin in D minor.

The eastern tour of the Orchestra had now been arranged by Miss Millar, covering a series of concerts in New York, Brooklyn, Boston, Philadelphia, Washington and Baltimore.

"February 21, Monday evening, Auditorium: A furious storm all day, but I managed to hear the Apollo Club, their Second Concert, Twenty-sixth Season; miscellaneous selections for the first part; Stanford's 'Requiem Mass' occupying the second part. Soloists: Miss Mina Schelling (soprano), Miss Mary Louise Clary (contralto), George Hamlin (tenor) and Pol Plançon (bass). William L. Tomlins conducted, assisted by Wilhelm Middelschulte (organist) and the Chicago Orchestra."

"February 24, Thursday evening, dinner at the Chicago Club to Mr. Thomas, preliminary to the eastern trip of the Orchestra. Present: Messrs. Adams, Corwith, Hamill, Lathrop, Otis and Walker. Talk was on the guarantee for the next three years; $6,000 now subscribed. Mr. Thomas expressed disappointment in the size and work of the chorus; decided not to continue the chorus next year on account of the cost."

---

*Alexandre Guilmant died March 30, 1911, in Paris.

†Count Napoleon Ledochowski, one of our best local pianists and teachers, came to Chicago in 1868. He belonged to an illustrious French family, his grandfather, Baron de Ménéval, having been Secretary (1802) to the First Consul. Las Cases in his "Memoirs" says:

"Ménéval's title, when attached to the First Consul, was Secretary of the Portfolio; . . . a man of gentle and reserved manners, very discreet, working at all times and at all hours. . . . Ménéval being in a very indifferent state of health, worn down by fatigue from application and requiring some interval of repose, the Emperor gave him a situation in the household of the Empress Maria Louisa."

In the second codicil to Napoleon's will (St. Helena, April 24, 1821), "Item No. 12, 50,000 francs were bequeathed to 'Baron Ménéval.'"

Count Ledochowski's father came to Paris after the partition of Poland, and married the daughter of Baron Ménéval. The Count was born in Paris in 1845, and died in Chicago, October 20, 1917.

‡See footnote on page 121 for the life and work of Frederick Grant Gleason.

THEODORE THOMAS

Seventh Season—1897-1898

"February 27, Sunday, 8:00 A. M.: Orchestra started for New York in special train. Much depends on the drawing power of Josef Hofmann in making the tour a success. If he does not interest the public, there will be a loss."

Mr. Thomas was in the best of spirits and in a happy mood. I have never seen him more so in starting on a tour of the "Highway." He had an Orchestra of one hundred men, larger than on the trip last season; all the programs had been carefully prepared and rehearsed, and for soloists he would have Mme. Nordica, Eugène Ysaye and Josef Hofmann. He was looking forward with keen delight and a little anxiety to the eastern tour, especially the "Musical Stronghold of America" (Boston), where he had not played with his Orchestra in sixteen years. "In the ordeal of playing there," says Mrs. Thomas, "the ordeal of playing in New York was forgotten." The critics were, as on the former visit, divided in their opinions on the work of the Orchestra; a few were friendly, some distinctly hostile, while others were indifferent. A writer on the *Harper's Weekly* said of the first concert in New York:

"The concert was what one expected—an object lesson as to what rich ensemble perfectness a permanent, well balanced orchestra (even if not one of all-round exceptional material) can attain by learning and minding only its own business, and by doing so under a great director's continued care. . . . The evening was a triumph for the Chicago Orchestra and a welcome to its Director, which must have moved even Mr. Thomas, at least a trifle."

Mr. Thomas had good friends among the newspaper men in Boston. After the first concert the critic of the *Boston Journal* said:

"I have never heard, in this country or in Europe, so admirably balanced, so thoroughly musical a performance of Mozart's immortal symphony as that led by Mr. Thomas last night."

Mr. Thomas had other friends in the east who gave him a cordial welcome, but the "dear people" (known as "the general public") did not care to hear this collection of "western mediocrities." The paid admissions to the concert on March 11 at the Academy of Music in Brooklyn were a little more than sufficient to pay Nordica's fee of $1,275.

The receipts of the concert on March 22 in Providence, R. I., did not pay Ysaye's fee of $850. The public was not at all interested in Josef Hofmann at $750 for each concert, with traveling and hotel expenses extra.

The Orchestra returned from the tour and resumed the Chicago concerts:

"Seventeenth Program, April 1 and 2: Josef Hofmann, soloist, played with wonderful spirit and fire the concerto No. 4 in D minor, by Rubinstein. A large audience at each concert; receipts $1,497 for the week."

The particulars of the eastern tour were given to the Trustees:

"April 6, Wednesday P. M.: Present, Messrs. George E. Adams, Armour, Hamill, Burnham and Otis. Loss on eastern tour $15,000. The excessive fees paid soloists and unusual expenses caused the loss on the tour. Question is now, how to finance the five remaining weeks of concerts. Decided to borrow $10,000 more at the bank, making the total indebtedness at the bank $20,000. Nordica and Ysaye received $10,000 between them for the concerts on the eastern trip; Hofmann $3,000."

I made a few notes regarding the closing concerts of the season:

"Nineteenth Program, April 15 and 16: 'German Requiem' (Brahms) given in the second part of the program; Mrs. Minnie Fish-Griffin (soprano) and Charles W. Clark (bass), soloists; Wilhelm Middelschulte (organist) and the chorus of the Association."

"Twenty-first program, April 29 and 30. The war with Spain is the all-absorbing topic; the eyes of the world are turned toward America; Havana blockaded; very little interest in the concerts.

"Selections from 'Parsifal' occupied the second part of the program; George Hamlin and Joseph S. Baernstein, soloists, and the chorus of the Association. At intermission (Friday) I went to Mr. Thomas' room and informed him that there were not men enough of the chorus present to give 'Parsifal.' 'If that is so, go on the stage, call all the men off and I'll play it without the chorus.' I went out, met 'Mac' (McNicol), the librarian, who said: 'There are a number of the men already on the stage, and the women are coming in fast,' which I reported to the Conductor. We managed to get through 'Parsifal,' but it was, to say the least, a scratch performance.

"Saturday evening the men turned out in force, and we had a good performance; but such a small house; only $242 at the door."

"Twenty-second, and last, Program, May 6 and 7: Josef Hofmann played Beethoven's concerto No. 4 in G major; Charles W. Clark sang Wotan's Farewell from 'The Valkyrie' (Wagner); good houses; $1,400 at the door Saturday night."

Mendelssohn's "Elijah" was given by the Apollo Musical Club in the Auditorium, Tuesday evening, May 17, as a farewell concert to their Conductor, William L. Tomlins, assisted by Miss Jenny Osborn (soprano), Miss

Seventh Season—1897-1898

Bessie Campbell (contralto), George Hamlin (tenor) and Ffrangcon Davies (bass); Wilhelm Middelschulte (organist) and the Chicago Orchestra.

Mr. Tomlins began his duties as Conductor of the Club, May 1, 1875, and after many years of earnest, vigorous work raised the Club from a men's singing society to a place among the first choral societies in America. He was succeeded May 1, 1898, by Harrison M. Wild, Conductor of the Mendelssohn Club and organist of Grace Episcopal Church, Chicago.

The report of the Treasurer for the Seventh Season (1897-1898), ending June 30, 1898, showed a large deficit. The entire earnings of the Orchestra, $102,500, did not pay the Auditorium rent ($11,000) and the salaries ($96,000) of Conductor and Orchestra, without mention of business management, soloists, chorus ($4,500) and other items, making total expenditures $141,674.66. The loss on the season, $39,150, was partly covered by subscriptions from Governing Members ($24,425). The balance, $14,725.67, added to the losses on former seasons made a total (less accounts receivable and cash) of $28,364.35 for the Trustees to provide.

The Trustees now had to consider how to carry this load of indebtedness and undertake another season; how to provide the cash with which to pay some pressing claims: $20,000 due the Commercial National Bank; $6,250 due Mr. Thomas, and $2,000 to the Auditorium. It was Bryan Lathrop who finally met the situation quietly and calmly. Mr. Lathrop was sincerely attached to the Orchestra and its Conductor, and had a strong faith in the importance of the work Mr. Thomas was doing. In the meantime a resolution had been passed by the Trustees on April 25, authorizing "the Treasurer to sign contracts with the members of the Orchestra for another season." At this meeting Messrs. Burnham, Lathrop and Hamill were appointed a committee to formulate some suggestions as to the finances for the coming season and "to call a meeting of the friends of the Orchestra at once." The present emergency was met by Mr. Lathrop at a meeting of the Trustees on June 15, by offering to advance his own subscription of $1,000 and that of Mrs. Thomas Nelson Page of $1,000 on the guarantee for the Eighth Season, and to loan the Association $5,000 on its note, to be paid from the ticket sales in the autumn, thus enabling the Treasurer to pay all immediate claims. This generous action was gratefully accepted by the Trustees, and the President or Vice-President was authorized to execute the necessary note to Mr. Lathrop.

SEVENTH SEASON
(1897-1898)
SOLOISTS

HARP: Edmund Schuecker.

ORGAN: Alexandre Guilmant.

PIANOFORTE: Raoul Pugno, Alexandre Siloti, Josef Hofmann (twice); Miss Laura Sanford.

VIOLIN: Eugène Ysaye, Leopold Kramer, Emil Baré, Henri Marteau.

VIOLONCELLO: Bruno Steindel, Jean Gerardy.

VOCAL: Mme. Lillian Nordica, Miss Helen Buckley, Miss N. Estelle Harrington, Mrs. Genevieve C. Wilson, Mrs. Christine N. Dreier, Miss J. S. Jacoby, Mrs. S. Swabacker, Mrs. Minnie Fish-Griffin; Giuseppe Campanari, George Hamlin (twice), George E. Holmes, Pol Plançon, Charles W. Clark (twice), J. S. Baernstein.

ARTHUR MEES

EIGHTH SEASON
(1898-1899)

Chorus of the Association disbanded—Arthur Mees returns to New York City—Dinner at the Chicago Club by Trustees to friends of the Orchestra—$55,000 subscribed for the Orchestra—Trustees issue a statement of the finances of the Orchestral Association since its organization (1891), with list of subscribers to the Guarantee Fund.

The program of the first concerts, October 14 and 15, contained four numbers that were especially interesting:

Overture, "Don Juan,"	Mozart
(With Concert Ending by Theodore Thomas)	
"Eine Faust Overture,".	Wagner
Symphonic Variations, ...	Parry
Suite from the Ballet "Casse Noisette," . . .	Tschaikowsky

The graceful "Nut Cracker" suite by Tschaikowsky had not been heard since Mr. Thomas played it in the concerts of the First Season. The witchery and exquisite coloring of the dainty melodies, with the incessant movement of the dances, will always appeal to the listener. The new instrument in the Orchestra, the celesta, introduced by Mr. Thomas in the work of the Russian master, was well played by Miss Jeannette Durno, and added interest.

The men of the Orchestra, whose names are almost household words at our concerts, were in the best form, and played magnificently.

With the disbanding of the chorus and the departure to the east of Mr. Mees,* the Assistant Conductor, the

---

*Dr. Arthur Mees, a well known name among American musicians, was born February 13, 1850, in Columbus, Ohio, and died April 26, 1923, in New York City. His studies were pursued in Berlin with Kullak (piano) and Weitzmann in musical theory. On his return to America he assisted (1880) Theodore Thomas in training the Cincinnati Festival Chorus, and later was Assistant Conductor of the American Opera Company under Mr. Thomas. From 1887 to 1896 he wrote the analytical program notes of the New York Philharmonic Society. On his return from Chicago to New York he conducted the Mendelssohn Glee Club (1898-1904) and, in 1913, the Bridgeport Oratorio Society. In 1897 Dr. Mees married Sarah Marguerite Howell, who survives him. He received the degree of Doctor of Music from Alfred University, New York.

The *New York Times*, in noting the passing of Dr. Mees, said: "He was a thorough musician and a constant friend to students. As a writer he had a gift of clear analysis and expression. His loss is a grievous one, not only to his friends, but to American music."

editorial chair of the program book became vacant, and was filled by the Trustees appointing Hubbard William Harris. The new editor, a pupil of Frederick Grant Gleason in musical theory, and a member of the faculty of the American Conservatory of Music, came well equipped for the work.

The Trustees held several meetings early in October to discuss ways and means for paying the $30,000 of indebtedness. We were much encouraged by the season sale, which under Miss Millar's management approached $57,000 (larger than that of any former season), clearly indicating an increased interest on the part of the general public in the work of the Association. The Trustees dined on Friday evening, October 21, at Mr. Lathrop's residence, and there decided to give a dinner on November 4 at the Chicago Club to the friends of the Orchestra, and then make an appeal for funds to pay the debt. Daniel H. Burnham was appointed Chairman of a "Committee on Organization," and began at once a thorough campaign, assigning a list of men for each Trustee to call upon and urge their presence at the dinner. We met at his office every day to report on the men we had seen, and to receive new assignments of names. Mr. Burnham's plan was to secure forty men to attend the dinner, but some were out of town, and others pleaded previous engagements. I made a few notes on this memorable dinner:

"November 4, Friday: The Trustees met in private room of Club at 6:00 P. M. and arranged that at close of dinner, George E. Adams should state object of meeting; Bryan Lathrop to follow; Dr. Harper to close. Before going to the dining room Mr. Burnham asked the Trustees what they would give—various answers. Allison Armour quietly remarked, 'You have not asked me what I shall do.' *Lunga pausa.* 'Put me down for $5,000.' We were quite overcome with this unexpected gift. Then followed the dinner, at which were present:

GEORGE E. ADAMS.	MARSHALL FIELD.
JOSEPH ADAMS.	WILLIAM A. FULLER.
ALLISON V. ARMOUR.	JOHN J. GLESSNER.
OWEN F. ALDIS.	CHARLES D. HAMILL.
C. T. BOYNTON.	PRESIDENT W. R. HARPER.
WILLIAM L. BROWN.	CHARLES L. HUTCHINSON.
CLARENCE A. BURLEY.	DR. RALPH N. ISHAM.
DANIEL H. BURNHAM.	H. H. KOHLSAAT.
WILLIAM T. CARRINGTON.	BRYAN LATHROP.
CHARLES NORMAN FAY.	FRANK O. LOWDEN.

Eighth Season—1898-1899

Henry C. Lytton.
Cyrus H. McCormick.
Arthur Orr.
Charles T. Otis.
Philo A. Otis.

Martin A. Ryerson.
Albert A. Sprague.
William B. Walker.
Theodore Thomas.

"After the speeches came the subscriptions; in less than one-half hour the whole $30,000 was subscribed. Mr. Lathrop then suggested that an additional $30,000 be secured for a reserve fund for future losses, if any. In another half hour $17,500 was pledged for the fund. I have never seen such enthusiasm; such generosity; the money came so easily."

Mr. Armour had previously advised Mr. Lathrop and other Trustees what he intended to do at the dinner, so that his gift of $5,000 was not entirely unexpected. But when he announced his intention of leaving Chicago for an indefinite time, and must resign from the Board of Trustees, we were surprised, and realized that the Orchestra was about to lose one of its best friends. At the next meeting of the Trustees, Wednesday afternoon, November 9, in Mr. Burnham's office, there being present Messrs. Lathrop, Burnham, Fay, Hamill, Otis and Walker, the resignation of Allison V. Armour was presented, and accepted with the sincere regrets of the Trustees. Frank O. Lowden was thereupon elected to fill the vacancy.

Subscriptions soon came from other generous friends, making a total of $55,000, which paid the $30,000 debt in full and added $25,000 towards a working capital or reserve fund for the Orchestra, in the event of loss.

The time had now come when the general public, the people who go to concerts and who were the real beneficiaries in this great work, should do their part. The prices of admission from the beginning of the Orchestra had been so low that it was impossible to continue the concerts on the sales from admission tickets alone. A committee, consisting of Messrs. Lathrop, Fay, Hamill and Otis, was appointed by the Trustees at a meeting on November 9 to prepare a statement of the receipts and expenditures during the eight seasons of the Orchestra, and to revise the prices of admission. The report of the committee appeared in the program book of the concerts of December 9 and 10, Fifth Program, during which the audience, while looking through the report, heard some delightful work by the soloist for the week, Moriz Rosenthal, in his interpretation of Liszt's concerto No. 1 in E flat.

	SINGLE	SEASON
Associate Membership, two seats for afternoon and evening..............................	....	$120.00
Season seats for afternoon or evening concerts:		
Main Floor, first four rows.................	$1.00	20.00
Main Floor, fifth row to tunnels...........	1.50	30.00
Main Floor, back of tunnels...............	1.00	20.00
Main Balcony, first two rows..............	1.00	20.00
Main Balcony, next seven rows............	1.00	15.00
Main Balcony, balance....................	.75	10.00

TO THE PATRONS OF THE CHICAGO ORCHESTRA:

The Orchestral Association begs to lay before you the following information:

The gross expenditures during the first seven years were...........................	$884,962.85
The gross receipts were...................	597,258.09
Gross deficit, June, 1898..............	$287,704.76

Then followed a list of:

"the generous friends of music and lovers of Chicago who have contributed to the support of the Orchestra since its organization (1891), including the forty-nine subscribers to the original three-year guaranty and all who have subscribed (1894-1898) as Governing Members:

George E. Adams..$	4,000.00	William L. Brown..$	300.00
J. McGregor Adams	2,974.98	T. B. Blackstone...	5,772.43
Joseph Adams.....	300.00	Daniel H. Burnham	1,250.00
Milward Adams....	297.45	W. H. Burnet.....	200.00
Owen F. Aldis.....	750.00	E. B. Butler.......	850.00
Mrs. Samuel W. Al-		John S. Carpenter..	50.00
lerton...........	750.00	W. J. Chalmers....	100.00
Mrs. Barbara Armour	500.00	John M. Clark.....	2,974.98
Allison V. Armour..	7,272.43	Mrs. Henry Cor-	
George A. Armour..	2,974.98	with............	2,500.00
Philip D. Armour..	2,974.98	Charles Counselman	2,974.98
Auditorium Ass'n..	594.90	R. T. Crane.......	2,974.98
A. C. Bartlett.....	5,772.43	Michael Cudahy...	300.00
S. E. Barrett......	3,974.98	Columbus R. Cum-	
Frank T. Baird....	150.00	mings...........	2,974.98
E. W. Blatchford...	2,974.98	Clarence Eddy.....	1,100.00
Mrs. Hugh T. Birch	5,000.00	J. W. Ellsworth....	300.00
Henry W. Bishop..	2,974.98	John M. Ewen.....	300.00
C. K. G. Billings...	100.00	C. Norman Fay....	7,867.33
Chauncey J. Blair..	500.00	N. K. Fairbank....	2,974.98
J. Harley Bradley..	100.00	John A. Farwell....	400.00

Eighth Season—1898-1899

Marshall Field.....$	6,272.43	Mrs. Mahlon D. Ogden............$	400.00
A Friend.........	2,522.43	Charles T. Otis....	400.00
William A. Fuller..	2,797.45	Philo A. Otis......	1,000.00
C. W. Fullerton....	4,974.98	Mrs. Thomas Nelson Page.......	7,000.00
Lyman J. Gage....	3,000.00	R. F. Pettibone....	50.00
John J. Glessner...	7,272.43	Eugene S. Pike....	3,750.00
S. E. Gross........	1,000.00	O. W. Potter......	3,224.98
W. E. Hale........	750.00	Henry H. Porter...	4,500.00
William G. Hibbard	3,000.00	George M. Pullman.	7,000.00
H.N. Higginbotham	3,974.98	Norman B. Ream..	2,974.98
Charles L. Hutchinson............	6,272.43	Martin A. Ryerson.	6,500.00
Dr. R. N. Isham...	2,974.98	W. H. Schimpferman...........	100.00
J. M. W. Jones....	750.00	Leo Schlesinger....	400.00
Albert Keep.......	3,000.00	Henry G. Selfridge.	100.00
Sidney A. Kent....	2,974.98	Byron L. Smith....	3,000.00
Edson Keith......	3,772.43	Albert A. Sprague..	5,872.43
Henry W. King....	4,272.43	O. S. A. Sprague...	3,000.00
H. H. Kohlsaat....	2,000.00	Henry B. Stone....	1,500.00
Walter C. Larned..	2,974.98	Mrs. H. O. Stone..	600.00
Bryan Lathrop....	4,000.00	Mrs. Mary D. Sturges............	750.00
E. F. Lawrence....	375.00	Theodore Thomas..	297.45
Victor F. Lawson..	3,750.00	Charles H. Wacker.	3,224.98
T. J. Lefens.......	250.00	William B. Walker.	750.00
Levi Z. Leiter......	7,000.00	Robert A. Waller..	750.00
John R. Lindgren..	150.00	John R. Walsh.....	2,913.49
J. Mason Loomis...	2,974.98	Ezra J. Warner....	1,000.00
Franklin MacVeagh	4,250.00	Mrs. Henry J. Willing............	1,250.00
Ezra B. McCagg...	4,272.43	Norman Williams..	3,000.00
A. C. McClurg.....	250.00	George H. Webster.	250.00
Cyrus H. McCormick..........	7,272.43	W. H. Winslow....	500.00
Thomas Murdoch..	2,974.98	Caryl Young......	200.00
O. W. Meysenberg.	2,974.98		
Edward Norton....	200.00		
O. W. Norton.....	1,700.00		

Total..................................$254,311.79

"To this may be added unpaid pledges which are considered good to the amount of................. 1,250.00

Grand total............................$255,561.79

Deficit.. 32,142.97
Assets thought to be good, say..................... 2,142.97

Net deficit for seven years.......................$ 30,000.00

"Commencing the eighth year with this heavy burden, the Association was forced to appeal again to its friends, who have in response recently contributed toward a fund of $60,000 to pay the above deficit and provide a working capital, as follows:

Allison V. Armour	$5,000.00	William B. Walker	$2,000.00
George E. Adams	2,000.00	Philo A. Otis	1,000.00
Bryan Lathrop	2,000.00	Martin A. Ryerson	5,000.00
Daniel H. Burnham	2,000.00	Cyrus H. McCormick	2,500.00
Charles R. Corwith	2,000.00	Harold F. McCormick	2,000.00
C. Norman Fay	2,000.00	William L. Brown	2,000.00
Frank O. Lowden	2,000.00	Mrs. A. N. Eddy	500.00
Arthur Orr	2,000.00	S. E. Barrett	500.00
Charles L. Hutchinson	1,000.00	Ezra J. Warner	500.00
Owen F. Aldis	1,000.00	Mrs. S. W. Allerton	500.00
W. T. Carrington	1,000.00	Byron L. Smith	250.00
Marshall Field	1,000.00	E. P. Ripley	250.00
A. C. McClurg	1,000.00	J. S. Hannah	500.00
John J. Glessner	1,000.00	Norman B. Ream	500.00
Albert A. Sprague	1,000.00	John A. Spoor	250.00
Theodore A. Kochs	1,000.00	Mrs. Geo. M. Pullman	1,000.00
M. W. Kirk	1,000.00	Henry H. Walker	100.00
Henry C. Lytton	1,000.00	Huntington W. Jackson	100.00
Joseph Adams	250.00	Chauncey Keep	100.00
Clarence A. Burley	250.00	W. J. Pope	100.00
George B. Harris	250.00	E. A. Driver	100.00
C. T. Boynton	1,000.00	John H. Wrenn & Co.	250.00
Charles R. Crane	1,000.00	Mrs. Conrad Seipp	250.00
A. C. Bartlett	500.00	T. J. Lefens	250.00
Charles T. Otis	500.00	Henry A. Blair	100.00
William A. Fuller	500.00	Mrs. Thomas Nelson Page	1,000.00
David Rutter	500.00		
Mrs. A. J. Caton	500.00		
Total			$55,850.00

"The Association hopes soon to receive the balance of the $60,000. The Association, however, cannot forget that its basis of operations is still unsound. Unless a change is made, a few short years will certainly put The Orchestral Association in the extreme peril it has just, *for the third time*, escaped. It cannot count upon the endless generosity of a few."

The Committee recommended:

"That the Trustees adopt a schedule of prices of admission which would fully meet the expenses of the Orchestra, if every seat in the house were sold for the season. This cannot, of course, be counted on, but as the interest in the concerts grows and widens we may reasonably hope in time to approach this condition."

The Annual Meeting was held on Wednesday, December 14, at 4:00 P. M., in the offices of the Association in the Auditorium Tower. On motion of George E. Adams, Article II of the by-laws was amended to read as follows:

"The management of the Association shall be exercised by a Board of fifteen (15) Trustees, elected at the Annual Meeting of

JOSEPH ADAMS

Eighth Season—1898-1899

the Governing Members, to hold office for one year, and until their successors are elected and qualified."

The Trustees reviewed the report of the Treasurer, Frederick J. Wessels, for the Seventh Season, as shown on page 101, and recalled Mr. Lathrop's prompt and generous action in providing means to meet the obligations of the Association, then maturing.

At the adjourned meeting held Wednesday, December 21, at 2:30 P. M., in the office of Daniel H. Burnham in the Rookery Building, a Board of fifteen Trustees was elected:

GEORGE E. ADAMS.	CHARLES D. HAMILL.
JOSEPH ADAMS.	THEODORE A. KOCHS.
DANIEL H. BURNHAM.	BRYAN LATHROP.
WILLIAM L. BROWN.	FRANK O. LOWDEN.
WILLIAM T. CARRINGTON.	ARTHUR ORR.
CHARLES R. CORWITH.	PHILO A. OTIS.
C. NORMAN FAY.	WILLIAM B. WALKER.
JOHN J. GLESSNER.	

Here we must note the performance of a work quite new to a Chicago audience at the concerts of December 23 and 24, Seventh Program: symphony in B minor, Opus 58, after Byron's "Manfred," by Tschaikowsky.

The "Manfred" symphony was given by Mr. Thomas for the first time in America, December 4, 1886, at the Metropolitan Opera House, New York City. The program book of our concerts contained this note:

"This program includes a work both important and new to these concerts—Tschaikowsky's 'Manfred' symphony. The magnitude of this remarkable composition entitling it to extensive notice, the entire space allotted to the program notes has been exhausted in the consideration."

The new Board met Mr. Adams at luncheon on Wednesday, December 28, at the Chicago Club, there being present: Daniel H. Burnham, William L. Brown, Charles R. Corwith, C. Norman Fay, Charles D. Hamill, Frank O. Lowden, Philo A. Otis, William B. Walker; Theodore Thomas by invitation.

The returns from the ticket sales in the past few weeks were indeed meagre:

December 16, Friday afternoon, single sales, $198.
December 17, Saturday evening, single sales, $178.
December 23, Friday afternoon, single sales, $163.
December 24, Saturday evening, single sales, $155.

"January 19, 1899, Thursday: Letter from Mr. Thomas: 'If you are not too old to be out early in the morning, will you attend a banquet and "show" to be given by the members of the Orchestra on Saturday evening at Fisher's Garden?' Reply: 'I am not too old to be out early in the morning, if I am in company with Mr. Thomas.'"

"January 21, Saturday evening: With Fay, Hamill, Orr and Thomas to the banquet and 'show.' After the banquet, the 'show' by the men. Amato* came on the stage, bringing a double-bass; from an opening in the back he drew out his dress coat, put it on and played a solo. Then followed the 'Peasant's' symphony (Mozart), played by six of the men, dressed in the costumes of Mozart's time—wigs, powder, lace ruffles, etc. At 3 A. M. Mr. Thomas played (violin) a jig for Frank Ernest Wagner to dance. It was 'very early in the morning' when the guests started for home."

"Eighteenth Program, March 10 and 11: The feature of this week's concerts was the 'Faust' symphony (Liszt), for men's voices and Orchestra, with the Mendelssohn Club and George Hamlin (tenor), soloist; delightful work on the part of Mr. Hamlin and the Club. William H. Sherwood,† soloist, played Saint-Saëns' concerto for pianoforte No. 2, in G minor."

"March 13, Monday P. M.: Meeting of Executive Committee to consider leasing the Studebaker Theatre for some of the concerts next season, the Auditorium being too large. Hamill and Lathrop were appointed a committee to consult with Mr. Thomas on the matter."

Twentieth Program, March 24 and 25; Lady Hallé (widow of Sir Charles Hallé) soloist, playing the Mendelssohn concerto for violin, Opus 64.

The Orchestra assisted the Apollo Musical Club in the performance of Haydn's "Creation" in the Auditorium, Thursday evening, April 6, under the direction of Harrison M. Wild. Soloists: Miss Helen Buckley (soprano), Ben Davies (tenor) and Joseph Baernstein (bass); Wilhelm Middelschulte (organist).

"April 7, Friday evening: Dinner to Mr. Thomas at the Chicago Club by the Trustees, prior to his departure with the Orchestra on the southern tour. Present: George E. Adams,

---

*Louis Amato, a member of the Orchestra, violoncello section (1891-1900), and soloist in the Second and Eighth Seasons, came to America (1890) and was engaged by Mr. Thomas (1891) for his new Orchestra in Chicago. While in Chicago Mr. Amato organized the French Choral Society, giving several concerts with orchestra. He returned (1901) to Paris as first 'cellist at the Grand Opéra; died in Paris, December 19, 1913.

†William Hall Sherwood, founder of the Sherwood School, died January 13, 1911, in Chicago.

Eighth Season—1898-1899

Joseph Adams, D. H. Burnham, W. T. Carrington, C. Norman Fay, John J. Glessner, Charles D. Hamill, Philo A. Otis and William B. Walker."

"Twenty-second and last Program, April 7 and 8: A flood of option tickets on Saturday evening, but we had $862 in cash at the door."

The out-of-town concerts of the Orchestra in the Eighth Season, under Miss Millar's management, covered: Winona, Wisconsin, November 30, St. Paul and Minneapolis, December 1 and 3 (four concerts); Milwaukee, January 24, 1899.

In the spring tour: Lafayette, Indiana, April 10; Terre Haute, April 11; Muncie, April 12; Bloomington, April 14; Louisville, April 15; Atlanta, Georgia, April 17-19 (four concerts); Nashville, April 20-21 (three concerts); yielding a net return of $7,086.79 after paying hotel bills and transportation.

The receipts from the Chicago concerts not meeting our expectations, the Executive Committee decided to give a Children's Concert, hoping this would find special favor with the people who have been asking for "Popular Music" at "Popular Prices":

"The Trustees of The Orchestral Association beg to announce that they have arranged with Mr. Thomas to give an extra concert at the Auditorium on Saturday, April 22, at 2:30 P. M., presenting a program especially intended for *children*.

"Mr. Thomas was formerly in the habit of giving performances of this character in the city of New York, as a means of influencing the rising generation and bringing its members up to be not only lovers of music, but of good music. 'As the twig is bent, the tree inclines.' It has several times been suggested that a similar course of performances be inaugurated here.

"For the Trustees,

"Philo A. Otis, *Secretary*."

The program, one of Mr. Thomas' happiest efforts, included the "Air" (Bach), Little Suite, "Children's Games" (Bizet), "Träumerei" (Schumann), and the "Tannhäuser" March (Wagner), but was played to a small house. The total receipts were $1,305. Twenty-five per cent of this went to the Auditorium management for rent, leaving as our share some $970, out of which, after paying extra men and advertising, we had less than $600.

EIGHTH SEASON
(1898-1899)
SOLOISTS

BASSOON: M. Bachman.
CLARINET: Joseph Schreurs.
HORN: Leopold de Maré.
OBOE: F. Starke.
ORGAN: Clarence Eddy, Wilhelm Middelschulte.
PIANOFORTE: Mme. Teresa Carreño; Moriz Rosenthal, Emil Sauer, William H. Sherwood.
VIOLIN: Lady Hallé; Emil Baré, Willy Burmester, Leopold Kramer.
VIOLONCELLO: Louis Amato.
VOCAL: Mme. Marcella Sembrich; George Hamlin.

NINTH SEASON
(1899-1900)

Mr. Thomas' views on the works of young composers—Meeting of the Trustees to consider the Conductor's resignation, which he withdraws after suggestions by one of the Trustees—Bryan Lathrop succeeds George E. Adams as President of The Orchestral Association—Resignation of Miss Anna Millar—Frederick J. Wessels appointed Business Manager—A "young viola player" conducts the Orchestra on a southern tour, who is destined to be one of the great Conductors in the future—Death of Timothy B. Blackstone, a sincere friend of the Orchestra—Proposition to affiliate the Orchestra with the University of Chicago not approved by the Trustees.

The Eighth Season had not been satisfactory in the way of finances, though the programs were most attractive and the work of the Orchestra was of the highest order; but there was a singular indifference on the part of the people towards some of the concerts. Tschaikowsky's sumptuous "Manfred" symphony brought the smallest houses of the season. Rosenthal and Carreño proved attractive, but the people did not care for Emil Sauer and Lady Hallé, two distinguished artists who deserved better recognition.

The season ticket sale—twenty-two weeks—showed a loss of $4,000 as compared with the previous season, though there was a good attendance at the first concerts, October 20 and 21. The program contained one novelty, the symphonic poem by Dvořák, "The Wild Dove," and two numbers suggesting reminiscences of the Summer Garden Concerts and delighting the audiences—Bizet's suite, "L'Arlésienne" and the "Blue Danube Waltz," in memory of Johann Strauss, whose death occurred June 9, 1899, in Vienna.

"Second Program, October 27 and 28: I brought a new work to Mr. Thomas at the Friday concert, by a young English composer whom I met this summer, hoping Mr. Thomas would look it over. 'I have a pile so high,' he answered (indicating with his hands), 'waiting to be looked over; there should be a school for orchestra in Chicago where young composers can get their works performed. I cannot undertake at our concerts to play anything but the works of recognized authors.' "

"November 16, Thursday evening: At the opera to hear Calvé, Campanari, Susanne Adams and De Lucia in 'Carmen'; met Wessels after first act, who handed me a letter from Mr. Thomas, tendering his resignation, to take effect May 1, 1901. Bizet's lovely music had little interest for me after reading this letter."

On the following Wednesday I met some of the Trustees at Mr. Burnham's office, and read Mr. Thomas' letter. We were surprised and much disturbed over his decision, but decided to take no action at present:

"MR. PRESIDENT AND GENTLEMEN:

"I consider it my duty to acquaint you with a decision I have arrived at, and to give you all the time possible in which to make your arrangements.

"I wish to return to the east after the season of 1900-1901. I regret more than I can tell you that I cannot end my life of usefulness here in Chicago, where I have met more friendships and public spirit than anywhere else, but the climate does not allow me to end my life here happily.

"I wish to return to the east before my professional usefulness weakens, although I do not feel sure whether any work will offer itself there that I shall be willing to accept.

"I thank you for the kind feeling I have always met with from you, and above all I desire to express my appreciation of the generous support that you have given to music in this country, in your effort to establish an art institution of the highest standard in Chicago.

"In all sincerity, and with respect,

"THEODORE THOMAS.

"CHICAGO, November 14, 1899."

Not receiving any word from the Trustees in answer to his letter of resignation, Mr. Thomas sent me this note:

"DEAR MR. OTIS:

"I have to see you and have a talk with you. If you have certain hours at your office I will call on you.

"Yours sincerely,

"THEODORE THOMAS.

"Monday morning, November 27, 1899."

The next morning he came to my office in a very despondent mood, and sinking wearily into a chair asked, "have the Trustees acted on my letter of resignation?"

Going to the safe, I took the letter from a drawer and handed it back to Mr. Thomas, but he declined to take it: "No, Mr. Otis, I am in earnest. I am through. I

Ninth Season—1899-1900

cannot stand these continual attacks by the newspapers on my programs; the Chicago climate affects my hearing and makes my life a burden; the Auditorium is too large for symphony concerts; if I am to remain here we must have a smaller hall."

I could see that the real cause for his action was the attitude of the press.

"Why do you read the newspapers, Mr. Thomas? They do not pay the salaries of the Orchestra. The Trustees have never once commented on your programs. We have paid the losses cheerfully and without a word of complaint. Go on with your work; make the programs as you have always done, without regard to the newspapers."

Mr. Thomas was present at a meeting of the Trustees a few days later, and, speaking of the bitter attacks by the newspapers, said he must resign. Thereupon one of the Trustees, President of a steel corporation, and one of the "misguided lot of wealthy citizens" of Chicago, said quietly: "We do not wish to think of your resignation, Mr. Thomas. You are engaged to play only the great works of ancient and modern times, and nothing else. If there are any deficits in giving the concerts, we will take care of them."

Mr. Thomas never again suggested his resignation, but went on with his work, going "from strength to strength," with programs ever increasing in the favor of the people.

FOURTH PROGRAM, DECEMBER 8 AND 9

SOLOISTS: ALEXANDER PETSCHNIKOFF
ARTHUR DUNHAM

Concerto for Violin, Opus 35, ... *Tschaikowsky*
Fantasie Triomphale for Organ and Orchestra, . . . *Dubois*

The Annual Meeting for the election of Trustees and officers was held Wednesday, December 13, at 4 P. M., in the office of Daniel H. Burnham, there being present George E. Adams, Joseph Adams, Daniel H. Burnham, C. N. Fay, Charles D. Hamill, Bryan Lathrop, Frank O. Lowden, Arthur Orr, Philo A. Otis and William B. Walker.

Frederick J. Wessels, Treasurer, presented his report for the Eighth Season (1898-1899) ending June 30, 1899:

RECEIPTS		EXPENSES	
Chicago concerts	$ 84,424.25	Business management, advertising, etc.	$ 12,765.10
Out-of-town, Apollo Club and other engagements	10,186.79	Auditorium rent	11,000.00
Italian Opera Company	7,300.00	Salaries of Conductor and Orchestra	91,644.54
Program book, etc.	2,229.88	Soloists	5,400.00
Loss on season	16,668.72		
	$120,809.64		$120,809.64

"To this deficit on the season should be added that of former seasons, $28,364.35, with accounts charged off, making $46,067.57 to be provided. The Governing Members contributed $15,950, and the balance of the deficit, $30,117.57, was taken from the 'Special Fund,' which had grown to $59,650, leaving $29,532.43 on hand."

The Trustees met again on Tuesday, December 19, at 2:30 P. M., in the office of Daniel H. Burnham, when Trustees and officers were elected for the ensuing year. Present: George E. Adams, Joseph Adams, Daniel H. Burnham, C. N. Fay, Charles D. Hamill, Bryan Lathrop, Frank O. Lowden, Arthur Orr, Philo A. Otis and William B. Walker.

George E. Adams declining re-election, Bryan Lathrop was elected President. The Trustees accepted the resignation with sincere regret and with a resolution thanking Mr. Adams for his devotion to the interests of the Orchestra.

Charles R. Crane was elected to fill the vacancy caused by the resignation of Charles R. Corwith.[*]

"December 25, Monday, Christmas Day: In the evening to the Auditorium to hear the annual performance of 'The Messiah' by the Apollo Musical Club; Harrison M. Wild conducted. Soloists: Miss Lillian French (soprano), Mrs. Marie White-Longman (contralto), Glenn Hall (tenor) and Arthur Van Eweyk (bass); Wilhelm Middelschulte (organist), and the Chicago Orchestra."

The Trustees held another meeting on Saturday, December 30, to receive the resignation of Miss Anna Millar,[†] Manager of the Orchestra, on the ground of ill health.

On motion of Mr. Lowden, seconded by Mr. Fay, the following resolution was unanimously adopted:

---

[*]Charles R. Corwith died December 8, 1915, in Chicago.

[†]Miss Anna Millar is now (1924) Manager of the Kansas City Symphony Orchestra.

Ninth Season—1899-1900

"That the Board receives the resignation of Miss Anna Millar as Manager of the Orchestra with profound regret. It desires to express its appreciation of the very great services she has rendered to the Association, and its members unanimously hope for a speedy return of her health."

Frederick J. Wessels was appointed Business Manager, to succeed Miss Millar.

A work by a former member of the Orchestra had its first performance January 5 and 6, 1900, Eighth Program: Capriccio, by Adolf Weidig.*

The composer constructed the capriccio somewhat in the form of a scherzo, using charming themes of a contrasting character, all leading to a brilliant close. Mr. Weidig's work was given a delightful interpretation by Mr. Thomas and the Orchestra.

Edmund Schuecker (harp), a member of the Orchestra from the First Season (1891), tendered his resignation January 18, on account of illness. He came of a good musical heritage, his brother, Heinrich Schuecker, having been a member of the Boston Symphony Orchestra from 1886 until his retirement in 1913. Mr. Thomas cabled at once to Bremen for R. Suppantschitsch, who arrived for the concerts of February 23 and 24, Miss Helen Stone filling the position in the meantime.

TENTH PROGRAM, JANUARY 19 AND 20
Soloist: Miss Leonora Jackson

Concerto for Violin and Orchestra, Opus 77, . . . *Brahms*

The concerto is a *tour de force* for young artists, but Miss Jackson gave the work a vigorous interpretation.

ELEVENTH PROGRAM, JANUARY 26 AND 27
Soloist: Whitney Mockridge

Aria, "Lend Me Your Aid," from "La Reine de Saba," *Gounod*
Aria, "Onaway! Awake, Beloved!" from
   "Hiawatha's Wedding Feast," . . . *Coleridge-Taylor*

The Orchestra started Sunday morning, March 11, for a two weeks' tour in the south, filling engagements in Knoxville, Tennessee, Atlanta, Georgia, Birmingham,

---

*Mr. Weidig came to Chicago from Hamburg in 1892, and entered the first violin section of the Chicago Orchestra in the autumn of that year (Second Season). His father was a member of the City Theatre Orchestra in Hamburg, and in that city his son acquired his early musical training; later he studied in Munich with Rheinberger. He left the Orchestra at the close of the Fifth Season (1896) to become a member of the faculty of the American Conservatory of Music in this city.

Alabama, Montgomery, Alabama, Macon, Georgia, Charleston, South Carolina, Savannah, Georgia, Spartanburg, South Carolina, Asheville, North Carolina, Louisville, Kentucky, and Indianapolis, Indiana.

"Eighteenth Program, March 30 and 31: Orchestra returned from southern tour. Mrs. Katharine Fisk, soloist this week; one of her numbers from 'Sapho'—a forgotten opera by Gounod. The other selection from 'Samson et Dalila' (Saint-Saëns)."

Frederick Stock, a member of the Orchestra, conducted for all the soloists on the above-mentioned tour, and for Mrs. Fisk at the concerts of this week. At the intermission on Friday many people asked why Mr. Thomas allowed " a young viola player" to appear on the stand. The day was not far off, however, when this "young viola player" would take Mr. Thomas' place and become one of the great conductors of his day.

"Nineteenth Program, April 6 and 7: Ben Davies,* soloist, with the Mendelssohn Club in Liszt's 'Faust' symphony—a small house."

TWENTY-SECOND, AND LAST, PROGRAM, APRIL 27 AND 28

Soloist: Bruno Steindel

Concerto for Violoncello, Opus 33, ... Volkmann

Fair houses; $1,100 for the week.

The Orchestral Association sustained at this time a great loss in the death of Timothy B. Blackstone, one of its loyal friends and supporters. It was characteristic of his generosity to send us during the winter his check for $1,000, as his subscription to the "Fund for the Support of the Orchestra," when he had signed for only $500. The Executive Committee met on Monday, May 28, and passed this resolution, which the Secretary sent to Mrs. Blackstone:

"The Trustees of The Orchestral Association desire to place upon their records an expression of their gratitude for the constant and generous support of the late T. B. Blackstone, from the very inception of the Association up to the day of his death, May 26, 1900, together with their sense of the great loss sustained by the Orchestra, in common with every other Chicago institution of like liberal purpose."

---

*Mr. Davies is still an active member of his profession, and is constantly singing at concerts. The *Musical Times* (March, 1923) speaks of a recital given by Mr. Davies in London, February 10: "He made an admirable choice of artistic songs and sang them mighty well. Mr. Davies has the fervor and more than the art of a young man. His singing of 'Total Eclipse' was an object lesson."

FREDERICK STOCK

An important matter which might have solved the future of the Orchestra came before the Trustees on July 23, when Mr. Hamill made a statement regarding the proposition of Dr. Harper for an affiliation of the Orchestra with the University of Chicago in founding a School of Music, and read the correspondence between Mr. Thomas and Dr. Harper on the subject. The question had been already considered at an informal dinner at the Chicago Club a few evenings before, Dr. Harper being present. At the meeting on the 23rd, after a full discussion by the Trustees, George E. Adams offered a resolution, which was adopted:

"That the Secretary notify Dr. Harper that a meeting of the Trustees had been held this day, and that they did not feel justified in taking any action at present."

NINTH SEASON
(1899-1900)
SOLOISTS

ORGAN: Arthur Dunham.
PIANOFORTE: Leopold Godowsky, Mark Hambourg, Ignace J. Paderewski, George Proctor.
VIOLIN: Miss Leonora Jackson; Emil Baré, Leopold Kramer, Alexandre Petschnikoff.
VIOLONCELLO: Miss Elsa Ruegger; Bruno Steindel, Walter Unger.
VOCAL: Mrs. Katharine Fisk; David Bispham, Ben Davies, Arthur van Eweyk, Whitney Mockridge.

TENTH SEASON
(1900-1901)

Three matters considered by the Trustees—Henry E. Voegeli begins his work as assistant to Manager Wessels—The "Beethoven Cycle"—Death of Adolph W. Dohn—Funeral services—A bequest of ten thousand dollars from the estate of Franklin Rudolph—The Orchestra assists the Apollo Musical Club in the performance of Berlioz's "Te Deum."

In view of the large deficit on the Ninth Season, the Trustees realized that some new methods of finance must be adopted to insure the future of the Orchestra. We had already considered:

1. The necessity of increasing the list of Governing Members to fill the places of those who could not renew their subscriptions and of those removed by death.

2. The question of lengthening the Chicago season from twenty-two to twenty-four weeks, thereby shortening the time of the Orchestra on "The Highways" and conserving the health of the Conductor.

3. The question of a new and smaller hall, Mr. Thomas' suggestion as a solution of the future of the Orchestra. "I cannot do good work," he said, "in the Auditorium. The hall for symphony concerts should not seat over 2,500 people. With such a hall there will be a demand for season tickets."

The Trustees did not think the time had come for taking up the subject of a new hall, and as the plan of renting Studebaker Theatre for some of the concerts did not seem advisable, we continued to use the Auditorium.

Henry E. Voegeli* began his work as Assistant to Manager Wessels September 17, 1900.

The Tenth Season opened October 19 and 20, with a program of deligtful music. Two works were of special interest:

Symphonic Variations, Opus 24, ... *Georg Schumann*
Suite from the Ballet, "The Sleeping Beauty
   in the Wood," Opus 66A, ... *Tschaikowsky*

---

*Henry E. Voegeli, born in St. Louis, Missouri, came to Chicago in 1892. He served in the Spanish-American War (1898) as a member of the First Illinois Infantry, and at the close of the war returned to Chicago, taking the position of Secretary for a financial magazine, the *Chicago Banker*. In 1905 he was appointed Assistant Manager and Assistant Treasurer of The Orchestral Association.

HENRY E. VOEGELI

Tenth Season—1900-1901

A feature of this season was the "Beethoven Cycle,"* introduced by Mr. Thomas in commemoration of his ten years of work with the Orchestra:

FIFTH PROGRAM, NOVEMBER 23 AND 24
  First Concert of the "Cycle"
    SOLOIST: ERNST VON DOHNÁNYI
Concerto for Pianoforte No. 4, in G Major.

The symphonic poem, "The Song of Life," given at the concerts of November 30 and December 1, Sixth Program, had a real interest for me, through my long friendship with the composer, Frederick Grant Gleason, with whom I had worked in various musical associations ever since he came to Chicago. Mr. Gleason was a futurist, an impressionist, having given up long ago his faith in the primitives, and holding ideals as to the future of music which were somewhat revolutionary. I loved to hear him talk. He fully believed that his works would at some time be received and win recognition. Having seen the score of the poem and heard many of the themes and their development, I was fairly familiar with "The Song of Life" and ready for the performance. The poem is based on Swinburne's lines:

> "They have the night, who had, like us, the day;
> We, whom the day binds, shall have the night as they."

Does any mortal know what this means? Swinburne has some mystic meaning concealed by this barrage of words, and the music is in the same vein. The hearer, in his endeavor to find any connection between the poetry and music, cannot but be interested in the composer's treatment of his themes and the ease with which he makes use of the resources of the modern orchestra. Mr. Gleason† labored long and earnestly over the score,

---

*In a letter from Bethlehem, New Hampshire, June 2, 1900, Mr. Thomas writes to Mr. Wessels: " 'The Beethoven Cycle' gives me heartache, for the want of soloists. However, I hope to conquer the difficulties. I have not heard anything from you yet about the chorus which is needed for the series."

†Frederick Grant Gleason came to Chicago in 1877 as a member of the faculty of the Hershey School of Music, of which Clarence Eddy was the general director. Born December 17, 1848, in Middletown, Connecticut, Mr. Gleason spent much of his early life in the neighboring city of Hartford, as a pupil of Dudley Buck, going in 1869 to Leipzig to study with Moscheles and Richter. Mr. Gleason's principal works are the operas "Otho Visconti" and "Montezuma," the "Festival Ode" for orchestra and chorus, written for the opening (1889) of the Auditorium, and the symphonic poems "Edris" and "Song of Life." He was an idealist, a dreamer, though too much of a follower to be a leader. I have known many composers and musicians, but few so devoted to their art as was Frederick Grant Gleason. His death occurred December 6, 1903, in Chicago.

to which Mr. Thomas gave every care and attention in the performance.

The report of the Treasurer, Frederick J. Wessels, for the Ninth Season (1899-1900), ending June 30, 1900, was presented to the Trustees at the Annual Meeting on December 12:

RECEIPTS		EXPENSES	
Chicago concerts...$	85,094.50	Salaries of Conductor and Orchestra.$	95,099.73
Out-of-town, Apollo Club and other concerts.........	9,079.79	Soloists..........	5,850.00
Grand Opera Company...........	9,393.00	Business management and advertising..........	10,937.85
Program book.....	1,920.18	Auditorium rent...	11,000.00
Interest at bank...	999.07	Musical instruments	20.50
Loss on season.....	16,421.54		
	$122,908.08		$122,908.08

EIGHTH PROGRAM, DECEMBER 14 AND 15
Second Concert of the "Cycle"
SOLOIST: FRITZ KREISLER (Violin)
Concerto in D Major.

"December 20, Thursday evening: 'The Messiah' by the Apollo Musical Club, in the Auditorium, under the direction of Harrison M. Wild. Soloists: Mrs. Minnie Fish-Griffin (soprano), Mrs. Annie R. Thacker (contralto), Charles Humphrey (tenor) and William Ludwig* (bass); Wilhelm Middelschulte (organist), and the Chicago Orchestra."

"February 26, 1901, Tuesday: An old friend, Adolph W. Dohn, who taught music in our family in early days (1859), and an early organist and conductor in our city, passed away today."

My journal, February 28, Thursday, has this note about the funeral service of Mr. Dohn, which was held at his home, 165 Locust Street:

"William Sprague and I went together at 2:30 P. M. Among those present were Mr. and Mrs. Charles D. Hamill and Theodore Thomas. George P. Upton made an address with special reference to Mr. Dohn's 'stern honesty and sincerity in all that pertained to his art.'"

Adolph W. Dohn, "one of the best equipped musicians Chicago ever had," said Mr. Upton in his "Musical Memoirs," was born May 10, 1835, in Breslau, Silesia.

---
*William Ludwig died December 28, 1923, in London.

ADOLPH W. DOHN

He came to America in 1857, arriving in Chicago April 7, and in October was appointed organist in the new edifice of the First Presbyterian Church on Wabash Avenue at Congress Street, where he continued until 1859.

It was Mr. Dohn's ambition, however, to conduct, and the opportunity came through C. M. Cady, who secured him to lead the Musical Union, a new singing society, through the winter of 1857-1858. In 1858, through his own initiative, this young leader organized a larger chorus of fifty voices for the performance of Haydn's "Creation," with orchestra, Carl Formes, a famous bass singer of that day, being one of the soloists. Carl Anschutz was the Conductor, though Mr. Dohn led some of the numbers. This was an interesting occasion for Mr. Dohn, it being his first meeting with Theodore Thomas, who was one of the first violins in the orchestra. This concert led to the organization of the Mendelssohn Society, of which Mr. Dohn was Conductor until 1865. The Apollo Musical Club, dating from 1872, of which he was the first Conductor (1872-1874), owes much of its success to Mr. Dohn's "stern sincerity" and rigid discipline in his work as its Conductor in those early days.

In later years Mr. Dohn was much occupied in commercial life, but in heart and soul he was devoted to the art he loved so well.

Mr. Dohn's daughter, Pauline, married Franklin Rudolph, and on his death (1923) a generous bequest of $10,000 came from his estate to the Endowment Fund of The Orchestral Association.

"March 8 and 9, Seventeenth Program, last concerts of the 'Beethoven Cycle,' the ninth symphony, assisted by Mrs. Genevieve Clark Wilson (soprano), Mrs. Sue Harrington Furbeck (contralto), George Hamlin (tenor), Charles W. Clark (bass); Leopold Kramer (violin) and the Apollo Musical Club. 'The Benedictus' very impressive; the violin solo seemed almost celestial, soaring above soloists, chorus and Orchestra; great audience on Saturday night; $3,000 for the week."

April 9, Tuesday afternoon, meeting of the Trustees. It was voted to lengthen the Eleventh Season of Chicago concerts (1901-1902) to twenty-four weeks, thus reducing the time on the road for Conductor and Orchestra.

Two works were heard at the Apollo Club concert Monday evening, April 15, in the Auditorium, under the direction of Harrison M. Wild:

"Hiawatha's Wedding Feast," . . . . . S. Coleridge-Taylor
"Te Deum," . . . . Hector Berlioz

For the performance of the "Te Deum" the choral and instrumental forces were enlarged: Chorus (400), choir of boys (300), the Chicago Orchestra, Charles Gautier (tenor), soloist; Wilhelm Middelschulte (organist).

"Twenty-second, and last, Program, April 19 and 20. Soloist: Miss Maud Powell; Tschaikowsky's concerto for violin, Opus 35.

"Friday evening, April 19: Dinner by the Trustees to Mr. Thomas at the Chicago Club. Present: Joseph Adams, Burnham, Fay, Glessner, Hamill, Lowden and Otis; talk around the table was about gardening, farming, politics and a new hall."

The attendance this season was again disappointing, though some of the concerts with important soloists brought good houses.

	AFTERNOON	EVENING
November 23 and 24, 1900, Dohnányi, soloist	$ 771.50	$ 919.75
December 21 and 22, Burmeister, soloist	317.50	294.50
(Smallest houses of the season)		
February 1 and 2, 1901, Mrs. Zeisler, soloist	$ 982.50	$ 997.50
February 22 and 23, Request Program	547.50	1,000.00
March 1 and 2, Godowsky, soloist	550.00	600.00
March 8 and 9, ninth symphony	1,153.25	1,838.50
April 19 and 20, last concerts, Maud Powell, soloist	645.00	772.25

November 7-13, 1900, western tour, including Cedar Rapids, Iowa, and St. Paul, Minnesota.

December 31-January 5, 1901, Evansville, Indiana, St. Louis.

February 4-9, Anderson, Indiana, Louisville, Kentucky, etc.

March 11-15, Indianapolis, Fort Wayne, etc.

April 22-May 4, southern tour, Bloomington, Illinois, Nashville, Tennessee.

Three concerts were given in Milwaukee during the season: November 27, 1900, January 22, 1901, and April 9, 1901.

TENTH SEASON
(1900-1901)

SOLOISTS

CLARINET: Joseph Schreurs.

ORGAN: Wilhelm Middelschulte.

PIANO: Richard Burmeister, Ernst von Dohnányi, Ossip Gabrilowitsch, Leopold Godowsky; Mrs. Fannie Bloomfield Zeisler.

VIOLIN: Emil Baré (twice), Leopold Kramer (three times), Fritz Kreisler, Leon Marx; Miss Maud Powell.

VIOLONCELLO: Hugo Becker, Bruno Steindel, Carl Brueckner.

VOCAL: Mrs. Sue Harrington Furbeck, Mrs. Genevieve C. Wilson; Charles W. Clark (twice), George Hamlin.

ELEVENTH SEASON
(1901-1902)

The Executive Committee and its meetings—Theodore Thomas does not need any "Committee on Soloists"—President Lathrop "a tower of strength" in financial troubles—Six Historical Concerts planned by Mr. Thomas—The members of the Orchestra give a vaudeville for Mr. Thomas and the Trustees—The Northwestern University presents plans for a new hall—Dr. Harper again proposes a School of Music at the University of Chicago, but it is not favored by the strong supporters of the Orchestra.

The daily routine business of the Orchestra (advertising, printing, pay-rolls, hall rentals, etc.) has always been in charge of the Manager, Frederick J. Wessels, subject to the approval of the Executive Committee, composed (1901) of Charles D. Hamill (Chairman), C. Norman Fay, and the Secretary, with the President of the Board as member *ex-officio;* but the programs, engagement of soloists and members of the Orchestra have always been under the control of the Conductor. The Executive Committee has never interfered in these matters; the judgment of the Conductor was final, and the rule has held good since Mr. Stock became (1905) Conductor. This is in marked contrast with the usage in other cities having orchestras managed by ladies, with "committees" on soloists, programs, etc. Theodore Thomas, Conductor of the Chicago Orchestra, did not require the assistance of any "committees." The Secretary has often been interviewed by soloists and their friends requesting his influence with the "committee" for an appearance at the concerts.

"We have no 'committee on soloists' " was always my answer.

"No 'committee on soloists'! Who does engage the soloists?"

"Mr. Thomas makes all these engagements. That is his business."

The meetings of the Executive Committee held after the Friday concerts have always been interesting, especially in Mr. Lathrop's time, he never failing to be present when in the city. After the business of the meeting was finished there would follow half an hour of entertaining

Eleventh Season—1901-1902

talk on the work of the Orchestra, the soloists and the programs, in which he invariably took part and with keen interest. When the business in hand was important, President Lathrop was "a tower of strength" in our midst, and inspired confidence in the hearts of his associates. He met many financial situations, of a serious character, quietly and calmly. The loss on the eastern tour (1898) which seemed a mountain to some of us, had no terrors for him. In giving generously of his own means to the Orchestra, he had the rare power of inspiring others to give.

The Eleventh Season (twenty-four weeks) opened with serious business in hand for the consideration of the Trustees, in the depleted state of the Special Fund, caused by the deficit of previous seasons, leaving a balance in hand which, with the subscriptions from Governing Members, would barely meet the probable loss on the current season. The season ticket sale by the middle of October was under $50,000, and $4,500 less than at this time in the previous year, though the total sales were increased with the return of the people to the city for the winter months. Mr. Thomas was right; the Auditorium was too large for symphony concerts. A smaller hall would create a demand for season tickets.

The first concerts on October 25 and 26 brought the people out to hear a delightful program, which included:

Overture, "Oberon," . . . . *Weber*
Second Symphony in D Major, Opus 36, ... *Beethoven*
Tone Poem, "Macbeth," . . . . . . *Richard Strauss*

Charles Gregorowitsch was the soloist at the concerts of November 29 and 30, Fifth Program, playing Mendelssohn's concerto for violin, Opus 64.

The Annual Meeting for the election of Trustees and officers was held Wednesday afternoon, December 11, in Room 55 Auditorium Tower.

The resignation of Charles R. Crane, Trustee, was accepted, and Harold F. McCormick was elected in his place.

The Treasurer's report for the Tenth Season (1900-1901), ending June 30, 1901, was not encouraging, showing a loss of $27,000. To meet this we had subscriptions of $12,250 from Governing Members, leaving a balance to be supplied from our Special Fund, of which there was barely $14,000 left when all bills had been paid. The earnings of the Orchestra from Chicago, out-of-town and other concerts did not exceed $94,000; not enough to pay salaries. The item of $11,000 for rent of the Auditorium emphasized the need of a new hall.

Mr. Thomas prepared a series of six Historical Concerts for the Eleventh Season; the first, occurring on December 13 and 14 (Seventh Program), included works new to a Chicago audience; Charles W. Clark (bass), soloist:

"King Arthur," . . . . *Purcell (1658-1695)*
"Castor et Pollux," . . . . . . *Rameau (1683-1764)*
"Water Music," . . . . *Handel (1685-1759)*

The "Water Music" was composed for George I, to be played when the king went down the Thames on the royal barge to Whitehall. This was the first work in which Handel employed French horns, writing brilliant parts for these instruments. The music has no terrors for modern players who use the valve horn, but in Handel's time, with the hand horn then in use, the horn parts must have been very difficult.

After the concert on Saturday evening, December 21, an entertainment was given by the members of the Orchestra to Mr. Thomas and the Trustees at Kinsley's restaurant. Supper was served at eleven o'clock, followed by a vaudeville in which the men showed they had gifts in other lines as well as in music:

Director Streise has the Honor to Present

JACK SAM'S WORLD-FAMOUS
MAMMOTH EVELESS EDEN VAUDEVILLE
AGGREGATION

EXECUTIVE STAFF

DIRECTOR, ... Mr. B. Sharp
MANAGER, ... Mr. C. Flat
FINANCIAL SECRETARY, ... Mr. A. Natural
ADVANCE AGENT, ... Mr. A. Minor
STAGE MANAGER, ... Mr. Albert Major

PROLOG, ... *Mr. St. Louis Shorty*

No. 1. A Restaurant in Arkansas—Musical Pantomime in One Act.

THE TRAVELER, ... *Red River Bill*
WAITER, ... *Mr. Henry Clay Johnsing*
COOK, ... *Mrs. Lucy Snowball Johnsing*
PORTER, ... *Mr. George Washington Whitewash*

An attractive feature of the evening was the second movement in Beethoven's eighth symphony, played by the kitchen artists on their tin pans and dishes. Many

Eleventh Season—1901-1902

years later the symphony was given at a Popular Concert Thursday evening, November 30, 1922. Eric DeLamarter said in the program notes:

"This movement has a bit of intriguing local history, as well. During the early days of the Orchestra, Messrs. Zettelmann, Wintrich (today active members of the Orchestra) and Wagner, then of the percussion section, played this second movement on a collection of dishes and kitchen utensils at an Orchestra banquet. Report of Theodore Thomas' laughter of appreciation is an epic by itself. Mr. Zettelmann and Mr. Wintrich still have that 'kitchen symphony,' and they once told of their researches among the pawnshops to complete its chromatic scale."

No. 2. The Funny Trio. Introducing an Old Celebrated German Song.

No. 3. The Original and Only Symphony Band from the Philippine Islands (especially captured for this occasion).

Ein Märchen (A Fairy Tale),* . . . . *Fesoj Kus*
    1. LOVE AND SORROWS OF A KING'S CHILDREN.
    2. FARMERS HAVE A GOOD TIME.
    3. SAD MUSIC AND A JOLLY SOLO.
        Bombardino Obbligato by Mr. ALPHONSO TUBASMALL
    4. QUEEN'S CURSE (she doesn't feel very well)—VICTORY OF THE MOTHER-IN-LAW.

No. 4. Mme. Malibran, Jr. Aria from the Opera "Der Freischütz," . . . . *C. M. v. Weber*
    MANIPULATOR OF THE IVORIES: MR. EACH

No. 5. The Hungry Six.

No. 6. Exhibition Bout between Mr. Jim Jeffries and Mr. Terry McGovern.
    REFEREE, ... *Mr. Sleepy Eye*
    SECOND FOR JIM JEFFRIES, ... *Mr. O'Buss*
    SECOND FOR TERRY MCGOVERN, . . . *Mr. Tough Nick*
    NOTICE—On account of the short supply of wind, we are compelled to limit the fight to two rounds, and also prohibit *rag chewing*.

No. 7. Short Trio.
    OBOE: MR. FRITZ STRONG.
    HARP: MR. PERZEL LEBERKNOEDEL.
    TIN FLUTE: MR. PRETZEL LAGERBEER.

No. 8. Signor Garibaldi Kulicke (Paganini's ghost), the great violin virtuoso. Concerto for open strings, ... *McNicol—Hansen*

No. 9. Serenade by a Country Band—With Song and Trouble.

No. 10. Four of a Kind.

No. 11. The Four Run-away Monks. Introducing *their* little *prodigée*, ELSIE TROMBONINI
        (Hot Punch)

The wonderful sliding artist. Her first appearance in the Wild West.
        FINE

---

*A "skit" on Joseph Suk's "Fairy Tale."

But there was a shadow over the merry scene; sad news had come to Mr. Thomas during the concert preceding the vaudeville, of the death of his son, Franz C. Thomas, at Pensacola, Florida. The message came in a dispatch to the *Inter-Ocean*, and was brought by a reporter to Mr. Wessels early in the evening. When Mr. Thomas heard, at intermission, of his son's death, he simply asked that the men should not be told, as it would mar their pleasure at the banquet, and then went out to conduct the "Funeral March" from "Parsifal" with his customary care and vigor. Such was his iron will and stern sense of duty.

The subject of a new hall came up at a meeting of the Trustees, Saturday, December 29, at Mr. Burnham's office. The Northwestern University of Evanston, having purchased the Tremont House property at the southeast corner of Lake and Dearborn Streets, proposed to construct a Music Hall on the premises, seating 2,500 people, hoping it might be a home for the Chicago Orchestra and the Central Church. The Trustees were much pleased with the plans prepared by D. H. Burnham & Company, and authorized Mr. Fay to enter into negotiations for a lease.

It had been the hope of Dr. Robert D. Shepherd, President of the University, that such a hall should be built, as he stated at the dedication of the remodeled building, January 28, 1903:

"A noble dream that did not come true, and from which I shrank when I found it could not be unanimously supported by the Trustees of the University."

A Chicago pianist, Mrs. Ella Dahl Rich, a new name to our patrons, created quite a sensation at the concerts of January 3 and 4, 1902, Tenth Program, by her artistic interpretation of the concerto No. 1, in B flat minor, Opus 23 (Tschaikowsky).

January 31 and February 1, 1902, Third Historical Concert (Fourteenth Program): Miss Electa Gifford (soprano), soloist; the entire program from the works of Beethoven. The first part included the aria, "Ah! Perfido," Opus 46, and the symphony No. 3 in E flat, Opus 55. The second half of the program was devoted to the "Egmont" music, Opus 84; George Riddle (reader).

Fourth Historical Concert, February 21 and 22, Seventeenth Program: Mrs. Fannie Bloomfield Zeisler,

Eleventh Season—1901-1902

soloist, played Chopin's concerto for pianoforte No. 2, F minor, Opus 21 (1810-1849).

Fifth Historical Concert, March 14 and 15, Nineteenth Program: Owing to severe illness, Ludwig Breitner, announced to appear at this concert, was unable to leave New York City. In place of the concerto in E flat for pianoforte by Liszt, Mr. Thomas substituted "Tasso, Lamento e Trionfo" by the same composer:

"Symphonie Fantastique," Opus 14 A, . *Berlioz (1803-1869)*
Symphonic Poem No. 2,
"Tasso, Lamento e Trionfo," } . . . . *Liszt (1811-1886)*
"Lohengrin" Vorspiel,
"Die Meistersinger" Vorspiel, } . . . *Wagner (1813-1883)*

Sixth Historical Concert, March 28 and 29, Twenty-first Program. Harold Bauer, soloist:

Symphony No. 4, E Minor, Opus 98, . . *Brahms (1833-1897)*
Concerto in G Minor No. 2, Opus 22, . *Saint-Saëns (1835-1921)*
Symphony No. 6, "Pathetic," B Minor,
 Opus 74, ... *Tschaikowsky (1840-1893)*

Twenty-fourth, and last, Program, May 2 and 3. Mrs. Gertrude May Stein, soloist:

Recitative, "O My Consort,"
Aria, "Can I Bear This Anguish," } From "Orpheus," . *Gluck*
Aria, "Gerechter Gott!" from "Rienzi," . . . . . *Wagner*

There was but one question before the Trustees now, to use Mr. Burnham's words: "The condition and future of the Orchestra"; how to meet the deficit of $30,000 on the current season; how to finance the Orchestra through another season. Financially the Eleventh Season was disastrous, but musically it was a great success, with better programs than in any previous season, and with work of the highest order on the part of the Orchestra. The Trustees voted on April 23 to continue the concerts another year and to secure a loan at the Commercial National Bank for $25,000 to cover any loss. It was also voted that the Executive Committee should consider the question of an endowment and confer with President Harper, of the University of Chicago. Mr. Lathrop, in a letter to President Harper, May 9, had doubts as to the future of the Orchestra:

"For your information we beg to say that we, the Trustees of the Association, have rendered ourselves personally liable for the deficit of the Orchestra for the season just closed and for that to come, in order to secure time for placing the institution upon a permanent foundation, but if we do not succeed in doing so, our minds are fully made up to disband the Orchestra and make no further attempt to maintain it. It cannot longer be supported by annual begging."

In response to this letter a proposition was made by the University at a luncheon given by Mr. Lathrop on Tuesday, May 13, at the Chicago Club, to President Harper and the Executive Committee of The Orchestral Association. Mr. Hamill being ill, Mr. Fay and I were the only members of the committee present. Dr. Harper had a long cherished dream of a School of Music, to be attached to the University, with Theodore Thomas as the head and the Orchestra as an important adjunct. The purport of the luncheon was to consider again the affiliation of the Orchestra with the University. President Harper proposed that $1,000,000 be raised for the endowment of the School, of which the University would furnish one-half and the friends of the Orchestra should contribute the other half.

At the conclusion of the luncheon, Mr. Fay and I discussed the proposition of Dr. Harper, though it did not interest me at all.

"It will be a great loss to the musical interests of Chicago and the whole country," I said, "if the Orchestra becomes a part of the University."

"Why did you not tell Dr. Harper so?" answered Mr. Fay.

"Because," I replied, "I did not wish to show hostility to the opinions of Mr. Lathrop and Dr. Harper at this time, though I fully believe the people of Chicago will not consent to this disposition of Mr. Thomas and the Orchestra."

The whole subject came before the Trustees on Thursday afternoon, May 22, at Mr. Burnham's office, when Mr. Lathrop reported the result of his negotiations with Dr. Harper, and presented "A Memorandum of a Plan for the Co-operation of The Orchestral Association and the University of Chicago in Establishing a School of Music." On motion, the Trustees voted that the "Memorandum" be forwarded to President Harper.

The "Memorandum" prepared by Mr. Lathrop, though broad and comprehensive, did not appeal to the strong supporters of the Orchestra, who were to be responsible for one-half of the "Million-dollar Endowment" of the School. They feared that the Orchestra in its new field of labor might fall under the influence of conditions which would lower the standard of its work. Mr. Thomas, while in favor of the general plan for the School, insisted that the piano and voice should not be taught; these courses of study would antagonize other schools of music. He knew by sad experience the baneful influence of piano manufacturers and music houses in school and concert work. The University authorities declining to yield their position as to the piano and vocal departments, the School of Music was abandoned.

ELEVENTH SEASON
(1901-1902)

SOLOISTS

PIANOFORTE: Miss Augusta Cottlow, Mrs. Ella Dahl Rich, Mrs. Fannie Bloomfield Zeisler; Josef von Slivinski, Harold Bauer.
VIOLIN: Miss Olive Mead; Charles Gregorowitsch, Fritz Kreisler, Leopold Kramer, Emil Baré.
VIOLONCELLO: Bruno Steindel.
VOCAL: Miss Electa Gifford, Mrs. Gertrude May Stein (twice); Charles W. Clark, Ben Davies.
READER: George Riddle.

TWELFTH SEASON
(1902-1903)

A permanent home suggested for the Orchestra—Bryan Lathrop buys the land and conveys it to three Trustees—Horatio W. Parker soloist in the Twelfth Program—Mr. Fay writes "An Appeal to the Chicago Friends of Music" for a new hall—Death of Nathaniel Kellogg Fairbank, the first President of the Orchestral Association.

The "Memorandum of the Plan for the Co-operation of The Orchestral Association and the University of Chicago in Establishing a School of Music" provided that the "Million-Dollar Fund" (of which the friends of the Orchestra were to contribute one-half) should be expended in acquiring ground centrally located for the construction thereon of a hall for the use of the School. Before the summer (1902) was over, and while negotiations with the University were still pending, this thought occurred to some of the Trustees: "Why not go among our friends and secure funds for the purchase of ground and the erection of our own hall as a permanent home for the Orchestra?"

Old residents will recall Leroy Payne's livery stable, built in the "Seventies," at 165-173 (old numbers) Michigan Avenue, between Jackson Boulevard and Adams Street, and directly opposite the entrance of the Exposition Building. The stable was a lounging-place for "old-timers" of the South Side, who drove down in the morning, left their buggies, surreys or stanhopes in Mr. Payne's care and, after business hours, returned for their "rigs" to go home. These premises, with another livery stable on the north, making a frontage of 105 feet on Michigan Avenue, occupied the space between the Pullman Building and the Railway Exchange.

Mr. Burnham, the promoter and builder of the Railway Exchange, had for a long time desired to secure the Payne premises in order to protect the north light of his building. This property had also been considered by Mr. Lathrop as a possible location for the University School of Music, but when it became evident that the

School could not be established, he determined to act for the Orchestra, and on November 26 purchased the property for a consideration of $450,000. Later the title was held by Daniel H. Burnham, John J. Glessner and Bryan Lathrop as Trustees for The Orchestral Association, who, with seven other Trustees—George E. Adams, William L. Brown, William T. Carrington, Harold F. McCormick, Frank O. Lowden, Arthur Orr and Albert A. Sprague—carried the entire purchase price, by cash and their personal notes, share and share alike, until 1905, when the Association secured a loan for the completion of the hall.

Thus, through the forethought of Bryan Lathrop, Daniel H. Burnham and their associates, we find the beginnings of Orchestra Hall, which has proved a blessing to Chicago in promoting the spiritual, educational and musical life of the people.

In the meantime the season ticket sale had been in progress, but with results not at all satisfactory. Many old subscribers declined to renew, for the usual reasons: "We do not need to take tickets for the season; we can always get seats in the Auditorium when we wish to go."

Before the middle of October we had $31,000 from Associate Memberships and other season ticket holders, and $9,000 from the boxes—a total of $40,000, which was later increased to $50,000. There were (1902-1903) 1,440 seats on the main floor of the Auditorium, 1,454 in the main balcony, 950 in the two galleries and forty boxes seating 240, a total of 4,084 seats. The entire season sale this year, covering seventy-three Associate Memberships representing 146 seats for each concert, the forty boxes and all other individual season ticket sales for afternoon and evening, with the single sales, did not make an average attendance of 2,200 at each concert, leaving room for 1,500 more people at every concert. These facts will afford thoughtful people some strong arguments as to why there was need of a smaller hall.

At the first concerts, October 17 and 18, there was no soloist, only our leader, the Orchestra and the glorious music. The program included the symphony No. 4 in B flat (Beethoven), and, after intermission, "Death and Transfiguration" (Strauss) and Wagner's "Tannhäuser" overture.

Mr. Thomas introduced a new symphonic poem, "Barbarossa" (Hausegger), October 31 and November 1, Third Program, founded on a legend attaching to Frederick I (1190), the Holy Roman Emperor, who was called "Barbarossa" by reason of his long red beard, and who did wondrous things for his people. The work was magnificently played and aroused enthusiasm on Friday, but none on Saturday night—all the world had gone to the Coliseum, it being the last day of the Horse Show!

Delightful soloists were heard in the next three weeks:

November 7 and 8, Fourth Program: Concerto (piano) No. 1, E minor, Opus 11, by Chopin, Ossip Gabrilowitsch, soloist.

November 14 and 15, Fifth Program: "Variations Symphoniques" (violoncello) by Boellman; Bruno Steindel, soloist.

November 21 and 22, Sixth Program: Concerto (piano) No. 9, E flat, by Mozart; Raoul Pugno, soloist.

The Annual Meeting of the Association was held Wednesday afternoon, December 10. I find this note in my journal:

"Hamill, Fay and myself only members present in person, but with proxies we re-elected the old Board of Trustees (excepting Carrington—resigned) to serve for the coming year; two vacancies to be filled.

Mr. Wessels' report for the Eleventh Season (1901-1902), ending June 30, 1902, showed a large deficit:

"The balance, $13,729.07, of our Special Fund was exhausted when salaries, Auditorium rent ($12,000) and other expenses for the season had been paid. The earnings of the Orchestra from all the concerts were only $91,763.72, nearly $3,000 less than in the Tenth Season. The loss on the Eleventh Season was $31,306.55, for which the Governing Members contributed $13,750, and after using the balance of the Special Fund there was still $3,827.48 for the Trustees to provide.

"Mr. Hamill reported that Mr. Lathrop has secured the Payne Livery Stable lot on Michigan Avenue, south of Adams Street; has organized a syndicate among Trustees to carry the property. Now if the friends of the Orchestra can raise another $500,000, we will have a new hall! What a chance!"

"January 1, 1903, Thursday, New Year's: In the P. M. to a reception and musicale at Mr. and Mrs. John J. Glessner's to meet Professor Horatio W. Parker, of Yale University. The program was given by Mr. Thomas and men of the Orchestra."

Professor Parker was the soloist January 2 and 3, Twelfth Program, playing his new concerto (Opus 55) for organ and orchestra. In order to make the contrast more effective between organ and orchestra the composer dispensed with the woodwinds, using brass and strings only. The "Andante," with enchanting solos for violin and horn, haunted me for days afterward. Professor Parker, one of the foremost of American musicians and composers, had never appeared at our concerts in the capacity of soloist, although two of his works had been given by Mr. Thomas—the concert overture, "Count Robert of Paris," in 1893, and "A Northern Ballad," in 1900.

Early in 1903 the Trustees made a frank statement to the people of Chicago regarding the needs of the Orchestra and the plans under consideration for its preservation. At a luncheon given by Mr. Lathrop on Tuesday, January 6, at the Chicago Club, to the Trustees and a few of the Guarantors, it was unanimously agreed that an endowment of $1,000,000 should be raised. Mr. Lathrop further stated that he had been advised by the large donors that they would not sign another Guarantee Fund, nor would they be responsible for any further deficits; but they would subscribe to any fund that would place the Orchestra on a self-sustaining basis.

In response to the request of the Trustees, an article by Mr. Fay, entitled "An Appeal to the Chicago Friends of Music," appeared in the morning papers of February 13, surprising the people with the statement that the Orchestra might be abandoned at the close of the season. Mr. Fay gave as an immediate reason for a new hall, "the excessive size of the Auditorium":

"We are practically certain that the concerts cannot go on in the Auditorium without entailing a continual annual deficit of between $25,000 and $30,000. We are equally certain that it is impossible to continue meeting this deficit, as heretofore, by the precarious expedient of subscriptions annually solicited.

"Of the fifty-one original Guarantors of the Association twenty-two have died, or left Chicago, or suffered financial reverses; and of the remainder only twelve continue to contribute regularly. Besides these original Guarantors, ninety other individuals have contributed once or more, of whom thirteen contribute regularly, making but twenty-five persons in all who have stood the strain of an annual appeal for aid. This number is not sufficient, and consequently grows smaller, under the belief that the Orchestra will somehow go on.

"Recognizing the emergency at the close of last season, we firmly resolved to disband the Orchestra at the close of this season unless an adequate endowment could be secured. It is almost needless to say that Theodore Thomas is in thorough accord with this decision. He has warned us for years that we were wasting effort and money unless our purpose was ultimately to found a permanent institution."

Then followed a description in detail of the new hall the Trustees contemplated building, the "Appeal" concluding with these earnest words:

"We shall, therefore, make the best fight we can during the next six weeks for the integrity of our Orchestra as it stands and its perpetuation hereafter. That is all the time we have.

"The exact situation today is, that the ten gentlemen who bought the ground have offered to head a subscription of not less than $750,000 with personal subscriptions of $10,000 each, aggregating $100,000. But it will require seventy-five such subscriptions to make up the total. We are, therefore, not over-sanguine of success. If, among those who have listened to the Orchestra all these years, there are voices to raise in its behalf, now is the time to raise them. If there is money to give, now is the time to pledge it.

(Signed)   DANIEL H. BURNHAM.
C. NORMAN FAY.
JOHN J. GLESSNER.
CHARLES D. HAMILL.
BRYAN LATHROP.
PHILO A. OTIS."

The audiences at the concerts in the afternoon of that Friday, February 13, and Saturday evening, February 14, Eighteenth Program, were in a serious mood when they read the "Appeal" in the program book and realized there might be only six more weeks of the Orchestra. It was a "Popular" concert, with two members of the Orchestra, Walter Unger and Enrico Tramonti, who made their first appearance as soloists. Mr. Unger played Popper's concerto for violoncello in E minor for the first time at these concerts.

Mr. Tramonti* chose for his number the "Marche Triomphale du Roi David" (Godefroid) and showed at once that he had earned the praise of the London critics when they spoke of him as the "Paganini of harp players."

---

*Enrico Tramonti was born October 6, 1876, in Palermo, Sicily. His father, a physician, had intended that the son should study civil engineering, but music was the desire of the young man's heart. At the age of thirteen he began the study of the piano, and two years later the harp with Bellotta, in Palermo, later with Labono, in Naples, finishing his studies with Godefroid, in Paris. He made his début (1896) before Queen Margherita of Italy, and in 1898, while on a tour in England, appeared before Queen Victoria, who was a musician of ability and a fine performer on the harp. Mr. Tramonti is still with the Orchestra (1924), having commenced his work February 1, 1902.

NATHANIEL KELLOGG FAIRBANK

Twelfth Season—1902-1903

Some notes taken on the closing concerts of the season will indicate the progress made in the campaign for funds to preserve the Orchestra:

"February 20 and 21, Nineteenth Program. Miss Maud MacCarthy, soloist, playing Mendelssohn's concerto for violin, Opus 64. . . . The continuation of the Orchestra the subject of talk on all sides. . . . Money coming in; $170,000 to date."

"February 27 and 28, Twentieth Program. Miss Mary Wood Chase, soloist; concerto for pianoforte in D flat (Sinding)."

"Mr. Fay addressed the audience on Saturday evening, March 7, telling the people plainly the Orchestra will be disbanded April 1 unless they respond to the call for a permanent fund. 'This is no "bluff," no vain threat on the part of the Trustees, but the sober truth. We cannot undertake another season without a permanent fund in hand to support the Orchestra.'"

"March 13 and 14, Twemty-second Program. 'Young People's Concerts'—with a program including the 'Peer Gynt' suite (Grieg), symphonic poem, 'Phaëton' (Saint-Saëns), and the 'Cockaigne' overture (Elgar); delightful work by the Orchestra."

Frank O. Lowden made an address at each concert:

"Chicago once built a city out of ashes and another out of dreams. You have shown what wonders you can perform in a crisis, and a crisis now confronts you. Shall Chicago, the city of great victories and few defeats, write 'defeat' for the first time, and that above its Orchestra, the greatest in the world?"

"March 20 and 21, Twenty-third Program. Rudolph Ganz, soloist, playing d'Indy's symphony for pianoforte and orchestra, Opus 25 (on a French mountain song)."

"Elgar's 'Dream of Gerontius' was given by the Apollo Musical Club in the Auditorium, on Monday evening, March 23, under the direction of Harrison M. Wild. Soloists: Mrs. Jenny Osborn-Hannah (soprano), H. Evan Williams (tenor) and Gwilym Miles (baritone); Wilhelm Middelschulte (organist), Arthur Dunham (pianist), and the Chicago Orchestra."

"March 27 and 28, Twenty-fourth and last Program. Hugo Heermann, soloist, playing the concerto for violin in D major, Opus 77 (Brahms).

"March 28: The morning papers announce the death yesterday (27th) of N. K. Fairbank, an early friend of the Orchestra."

Nathaniel Kellogg Fairbank, one of Chicago's foremost citizens and benefactors, born (1829) in Sodus, Wayne County, New York, came to Chicago in 1855 as the western representative of David Dow & Company, a New York grain and commission house. This was in the early days of the Board of Trade, which had just started in a plain wooden building on the south branch of the Chicago River at Madison Street.

Mr. Fairbank soon became an active member of the Exchange, and later organized the well known firm of

N. K. Fairbank & Company, with Joseph Sears and W. H. Burnet as partners, for the manufacture of lard.

Few men of his day did more than N. K. Fairbank in promoting the religious, educational and philanthropic life of our city, thus making the community a better place to live in. He gave $30,000 to assist George B. Carpenter in building (1877) Central Music Hall as a home for the Central Church, with the Rev. David Swing as the first minister. The small hall in this building, known as Fairbank Hall, was long associated with our local concert work. Mr. Fairbank gave freely of his time and money to the support of other institutions, notably St. Luke's Hospital and the Newsboys' Home.

He was active in the organization of The Orchestral Association, was its first President (1890-1894), and a generous contributor to its support.

"March 31: President William R. Harper, of the University of Chicago, was elected a Trustee, on motion of Harold F. Mc-Cormick, seconded by Arthur Orr, at a meeting of the Board held this Thursday P. M. in the office of Daniel H. Burnham."

The Trustees were now thoroughly agreed as to the need for the new hall, and that they might have the co-operation of the people of Chicago, blanks had been distributed for the past three weeks at the concerts, asking the patrons of the Orchestra for funds to be used by The Orchestral Association, "in purchasing ground and erecting thereon a Music Hall, provided that a total subscription of not less than $750,000 shall be secured," the subscriptions payable in one year.

TWELFTH SEASON
(1902-1903)
SOLOISTS

HARP: Mrs. Margaretha Wunderle; Enrico Tramonti.

ORGAN: Horatio W. Parker.

PIANOFORTE: Miss Mary Wood Chase, Mrs. Fannie Bloomfield Zeisler; Ossip Gabrilowitsch, Rudolph Ganz, Mark Hambourg, Frederic Lamond, Raoul Pugno.

VIOLIN: Miss Maud MacCarthy; Cornelius Franke, Hugo Heermann, Leopold Kramer.

VIOLONCELLO: Bruno Steindel, Walter Unger.

VOCAL: Misses Mabelle Crawford, Jenny Osborn, Mme. Kirkby Lunn; David L. Canmann, Glenn Hall, Anton van Rooy.

THIRTEENTH SEASON
(1903-1904)

The money coming in response to "The Appeal"—Trustees engage the Auditorium for another season and sign contracts with the men—Some "Misapprehensions" answered by the Trustees—Program book of first concerts calls for more subscriptions or the Orchestra must be disbanded—The Iroquois Theatre fire—The Association takes title to the Michigan Avenue property—Fourteenth Season of the Orchestra to open in new hall—The Sixteenth Cincinnati Festival.

From the day the Trustees made their "Appeal" money began to come from all classes, rich and poor, in sums from ten cents to $25,000, but so slowly that the Trustees made another appeal March 24:

"Already, up to March 23, over two thousand pledges have been given, aggregating $270,000. This great and spontaneous support is most encouraging, but we have yet a large sum to raise. We therefore urge the two thousand or more of our regular weekly audiences who have not sent in their pledges to do so at once. It looks as though we are going to win, but *every man and woman who loves the concerts must pull with us.*"

A strong factor in this work was the Auxiliary Committee of 100 members, appointed by the Trustees, Harry G. Selfridge, Chairman, and Max Baird, Secretary. The members of this Committee represented much of the important religious, educational, professional, social and commercial life of Chicago.

It may be of interest to note some details in the campaign for the fund:

"April 15, Wednesday, 1:00 P. M.: The Auxiliary Committee had luncheon at Kinsley's restaurant, with Messrs. Lathrop, Hamill and Otis, of the Trustees. Max Baird, Secretary of Committee, read reports from sub-committees, showing $375,000 now in sight."

"April 27, Monday: Trustees met at 12 o'clock (noon) in Mr. Lathrop's office, with Wessels, Treasurer, and Baird, Secretary of Auxiliary Committee; voted to engage Auditorium for another season and to sign contracts with the Orchestra. Mr. Lathrop announced that a guarantee of $20,000 had been signed."

"April 28, Tuesday: Busy all day with Orchestra matters. Met Fay at 9:30 A. M. in Milward Adams' office in the Auditorium to secure dates for next season; Adams in New York; had to wait until a telegram could be sent. Finally all arranged. First concerts

October 23 and 24; a break of two weeks in November and two weeks in March (1904) for opera."

There was a feeling of satisfaction on all sides that the concerts for another season were assured, and that we could now turn our attention to the campaign for the Building Fund. The canvass moved steadily on through the summer (1903), in which Trustees, committees, press and pulpit heartily joined, until the autumn came and the good work was practically accomplished. In the meantime views of the hall, from the plans of D. H. Burnham & Company, architects, showing an attractive exterior and interior, with seating capacity of 2,500, had appeared in the daily papers and acted as an incentive toward obtaining subscriptions.

Some friends of the Orchestra were not in sympathy with the thought of a new hall, believing it best to secure an endowment and remain in the Auditorium.

After twenty years of continuous use by the whole community, Orchestra Hall can now speak for itself. The building has been all that its founders promised, having given us an income from rentals of hall, stores and offices which has met the annual deficit on the concerts. Orchestra Hall has been a blessing to the whole community. It was the salvation of the Orchestra.

The season ticket sale opened early in June, resulting in receipts of $56,000 from Associate Members and box holders when the concerts began in October. The total sales, including single tickets, for the Thirteenth Season, aggregated $98,000, exceeding the previous season by $6,000, an increase due largely to the publicity given the concerts through the agitation for the new hall.

The program of the first concerts, October 23 and 24, included Beethoven's seventh symphony in A major and a new Russian work founded on a folk-melody, with variations by six of Russia's most distinguished living composers—Artcibouchefl, Wihtol, Liadow, Rimsky-Korsakow, Sokolow and Glazounow. Though the work of the Orchestra was of the highest order, and every number delightfully played, there was a feeling of unrest in the audience, due to the uncertainty of the future of the concerts. The program book contained a statement by Daniel H. Burnham, Vice-President of the Board of Trustees, that more subscriptions must yet be obtained before the new hall could be assured.

Thirteenth Season—1903-1904

"The pledges made now stand as follows:

33 of $5,000 to $10,000	$255,000.00
44 of 1,000 to 2,500	46,500.00
201 of 100 to 1,000	44,300.00
2,081 of 100 or less	20,254.50
5,708 club, society and list subscriptions turned in collectively	42,672.61
8,067 pledges in all for	$408,727.11

"It may not be amiss that the Trustees should express here the hope that the great Orchestra, built up by such lavish expenditure of time, hard work and money, may not disappear like a wreath of smoke, even though Chicago loses it, but may endure to delight some more fortunate community forever."

Mrs. Fannie Bloomfield Zeisler was the soloist November 13 and 14, Fourth Program, playing Grieg's concerto for pianoforte in A minor.

The following appeared in the program book regarding the Building Fund:

"The time set for announcing the success or failure of the effort to raise a fund to provide a permanent endowment for the Orchestra has expired. The last few weeks have, however, brought much encouragement.

"The pledges to the fund have reached nearly half a million dollars, and many further subscriptions are under consideration.

"The Trustees have therefore decided, with the approval of the members of the Orchestra, to extend the time to December 26."

The Trustees met for the Annual Meeting Wednesday afternoon, December 9, in Room 55 Auditorium Tower, and heard the report of the Treasurer for the Twelfth Season (1902-1903), ending June 30, 1903; it was again discouraging:

"The loss was $21,124.01, to which must be added the deficit carried from the Eleventh Season—$3,827.48—making a total of $24,941.49. To meet this we had subscriptions of $9,600 from the Governing Members, leaving $15,351.49 for the Trustees to carry; a better showing than that of the previous year, owing to an increase of $10,000 in receipts from Chicago concerts."

In the general discussion of the affairs of the Association which followed, Mr. Burnham spoke of the new hall: "We have $520,000 in sight, and are hopeful for the balance."

The people were so eager to hear "The Messiah" by the Apollo Club that two performances of the oratorio were given under Mr. Wild's direction in the Auditorium:

"December 25, Friday evening, Christmas Day. Mrs. Genevieve Clark Wilson (soprano), Mrs. Willard S. Bracken (contralto), Holmes Cowper (tenor) and Arthur Beresford (bass), soloists."

"December 27, Sunday evening, with Mme. Ragna Linné (soprano), Miss Mabelle Crawford (contralto), Theodore von Yorx (tenor) and Arthur Beresford (bass), soloists; Arthur Dunham (organist), and the Chicago Orchestra."

The destruction of the Iroquois Theatre by fire on Wednesday afternoon, December 30, the greatest disaster in the annals of the stage, whereby 570 people were crushed, trampled or burned to death, now comes into this record:

"The concert on Friday afternoon, January 1, 1904, Ninth Program, was given as usual, though it was a day of sorrow, and the whole city in mourning. George Proctor was the soloist, playing Liszt's concerto for pianoforte No. 1 in E flat. The audience was small, and there was little enthusiasm over the excellent performance by the soloist. By order of Mayor Harrison all theatres, including the Auditorium, were closed Saturday, January 2, for inspection."

In the midst of these sad conditions, with many of our patrons in mourning through the death of loved ones in the Iroquois fire, the Trustees must proceed with the new hall work:

"January 7, 1904, Thursday P. M.: Meeting of Trustees at Mr. Burnham's office. Present, Messrs. George E. Adams, Joseph Adams, Brown, Burnham, Fay, Glessner, Hamill, Harper, Lathrop, Otis and Walker."

The important business of this meeting was the consideration of the Building Fund, which had now reached the sum of $520,000—but not sufficient to provide for the cost of the land and the building. The Executive Committee was authorized to send requests to all subscribers to allow their subscriptions to stand, waiving the condition that a total of $750,000 be secured, and that the Trustees be allowed to borrow a sum not to exceed $200,000; on condition, however, that $650,000 be subscribed before sending out the requests.

TENTH PROGRAM, JANUARY 8 AND 9
SOLOIST: JACQUES THIBAUD
Concerto for Violin, No. 2, B Minor, ... Saint-Saëns

The Auditorium authorities finally convinced the Council Committee that the building was in accordance

Thirteenth Season—1903-1904

with the fire ordinances, and, with the approval of the Mayor, the concerts were resumed on Friday, January 15, Eleventh Program, with the Orchestra placed in front of the steel curtain, thus increasing the sonority and resonance, and showing clearly how much better the tone would be in a smaller hall. We looked for a large attendance, but the people did not come. Mr. Thomas received an ovation when he appeared on the Conductor's stand. The soloist, Carl Brueckner,* a member of the Orchestra from the Third Season (1893), and still with us (1924), played Svendsen's concerto for violoncello in D major. Other attractive numbers were the symphony in D minor (Dohnányi) and the suite "L'Arlésienne" (Bizet).

The concerts deferred by the closing of the Auditorium were given to the season ticket holders on Monday evening, January 18; Wednesday afternoon, January 20, and Thursday evening, January 21. At the latter concert Leopold Kramer played the Bruch concerto in G minor for violin. The attendance was not large, but those who came appreciated the better quality of tone from the Orchestra by its position in front of the steel curtain. Ferruccio Busoni was the soloist at the concerts of January 22 and 23, Twelfth Program, playing the concerto for pianoforte No. 5 in E flat (Beethoven). There was a good sale—$585 in single ticket sales on Friday afternoon, and $1,085 on Saturday evening.

The purchase of the Michigan Avenue lot by the Association was formally consummated at a meeting of the Trustees on Friday, February 26, the Association receiving title from the three Trustees, Messrs. Burnham, Glessner and Lathrop, subject to a mortgage of $350,000 held by the Northern Trust Company. D. H. Burnham & Company were appointed architects, and authorized "to construct a suitable building upon the said lot as soon as they shall have prepared plans for the same, approved by the Executive Committee, and are satisfied

---

*Mr. Brueckner was born in Ruedlingburg, Germany, in 1869; studied the 'cello under the tuition of Herlitz and later of Gruetzmacher in Dresden. Mr. Brueckner was principal 'cellist in the Hamburg Symphony Orchestra (Fritz Scheel, Conductor), which came to Chicago under the management of Dr. Florenz Ziegfeld, at the opening of the World's Fair (May, 1893), and for a few weeks gave a series of concerts in Battery D, a building on Michigan Avenue north of the old Exposition Building, but was soon disbanded for lack of support. In the autumn (1893) Mr. Brueckner became a member of the Chicago Orchestra.

that the finances of the Association justify them in letting contracts."

The program for the remaining concerts of the season contained attractive numbers for soloists and Orchestra:

"February 26 and 27, Seventeenth Program. Soloists: Miss Blanche Sherman, concerto No. 1, B flat minor, Opus 23-I, by Tschaikowsky, the Tschaikowsky symphony No. 5, and a new work, symphonic variations, by Frederick Stock, one of our viola players and Assistant Conductor of the Orchestra. The work was written in the summer of 1903 and dedicated to Mr. Thomas; delightfully played by the Orchestra."

"March 4 and 5, Eighteenth Program. Alfred Barthel* (oboe), soloist, playing Guilhaud's concerto. The concerts were "Popular," and brought good houses—$2,500 for the week. An insert in the program book announced the final decision of the Trustees "Relative to the Building Fund," stating that $625,000 had been subscribed, and asking all subscribers to allow their subscriptions to stand, waiving the condition that a total of $750,000 be secured. 'We shall commence needing money during April, and hope to collect the bulk of the present subscription on or before July 1 next. The Orchestra will be re-engaged at once, and the work of building pushed vigorously, in the expectation of opening the next season in the new hall.' "

"March 11 and 12, Nineteenth Program. Beethoven's ninth symphony occupied the second part of the program. Soloists: Miss Jenny Osborn (soprano), Mrs. Sue Harrington Furbeck (contralto), George Hamlin (tenor) and Albert Borroff (bass), and the Apollo Musical Club. The men of the Club could not all come out Friday afternoon, but were on hand in force Saturday night. The people enjoyed the music; $1,700 for the week.'

"April 1 and 2, Twentieth Program. Dr. Richard Strauss, Visiting Conductor, and his wife, Mme. Pauline Strauss de Ahna, soloist, in a program composed mainly of the composer's works. 'Death and Transfiguration' made a deep impression. The song, 'Morgen' was delightfully sung by Mme. Strauss. Great audiences; $4,600 for the week."

"April 15 and 16, Twenty-second Program. 'Young People's Concerts.' Leopold de Maré (horn), Alfred Quensel (flute) and Joseph Schreurs (clarinet), soloists. The program contained Saint-

---

*Alfred Barthel, a native of France, received his musical education at the Conservatories of Dijon and Paris, and graduated from the Paris Conservatory, winning the first prize. During his eighteen years' residence in Paris Mr. Barthel was a member of the leading orchestras (Colonne, Lamoureux and others). For six years he was first oboe at the Théâtre National de l'Opéra Comique and at the Société de Concert du Conservatoire. He was engaged as first oboe for the Chicago Orchestra in 1903, which position he still occupies. In 1907 Mr. Barthel was awarded a silver medal by the Académie des Sciences, Arts et Belles-lettres of France, an award seldom granted to an instrumentalist.

Mr. Barthel returned to Paris at the close of the Thirteenth Season, with the full expectation of remaining there the remainder of his life. His one year of work with the Chicago Orchestra had opened up attractions he could not withstand, however, and at the beginning of the Fourteenth Season we were delighted to see him in his old seat in the Orchestra.

ORCHESTRA HALL

Thirteenth Season—1903-1904 147

Saëns' 'Romanza' for horn and his 'Tarantelle' for flute and clarinet, Opus 6, all interesting to 'grown-ups,' but the 'young people' stayed away."

"April 29 and 30, Twenty-fourth, and last, Program. Miss Muriel Foster, soloist, who sang Elgar's 'Sea Pictures,' Opus 37, and Dr. Strauss' 'Hymnus,' Opus 33, No. 3, thrilling the audience with her glorious voice."

The Trustees announced in the program book:

"That the concerts of the Fourteenth Season, under the direction of Theodore Thomas, will be given in the new Music Hall on Michigan Avenue, between Adams Street and Jackson Boulevard, and will consist of twenty-four Friday afternoon and twenty-four Saturday evening concerts.

"The opening of the new hall—the permanent home of the Orchestra—will be an important event in the history of music in Chicago, and the first performance will be a dedicatory concert by Mr. Thomas and the Orchestra, designed to be worthy of the occasion. This concert, however, will not form a part of the regular series."

MAY 11, 12, 13 AND 14, SIXTEENTH CINCINNATI FESTIVAL
Theodore Thomas, Conductor

The formation of the Cincinnati Festivals was the work of Theodore Thomas, and their growth and development were due to his indomitable energy and the high ideals of his programs. The Festivals of 1873, 1875, 1878 and later (covering thirty-two years in all) were largely formatory, leading up to the Sixteenth (1904), the last he was to conduct—his final achievement. The program was of the highest order, including the Bach suite in B minor and Mass in B Minor, Elgar's "Dream of Gerontius," Berlioz's "Imperial Hymn," Beethoven's "Missa Solennis" and ninth symphony. Three of the soloists—Miss Agnes Nicholls, Miss Muriel Foster and William Green—seemed like old friends to me, I having heard them at the Birmingham (England) Festival in the previous October (1903) under the direction of Hans Richter: Mr. Green in the ninth symphony, Miss Nicholls and Miss Foster in the Bach Mass.

My notes on the Cincinnati Festival recall the effective work of the chorus at the evening concerts and that of the soloists at the matinées, Mme. Schumann-Heink in Liszt's song, "The Three Gypsies," with violin obbligato by Mr. Kramer, on Thursday, and Miss Foster's singing of Elgar's "Sea Pictures" on Saturday.

But with due regard to soloists and chorus, the strength of the Festival, to my mind, was Mr. Thomas and the Orchestra. Never have I heard the Beethoven eighth symphony played as at the first matinée! What a performance he gave us Friday evening of "Death and Transfiguration"! Did it suggest that his own "Transfiguration" might be soon at hand?

On Saturday morning I met Henry Wolfsohn, the New York manager, who had come to Cincinnati to see Mr. Thomas about bringing Felix Weingartner to America next season to conduct a series of concerts in New York, Boston and Chicago. Mr. Wolfsohn asked, "Will you not talk with Mr. Thomas and try to interest him in the scheme?" I met Mr. Wolfsohn again at the intermission in the afternoon, and after further discussion his scheme seemed to be a good business proposition if Mr. Thomas would consent. The question came before us a few months later after his death, but under such conditions, as will be seen, that we could not take Mr. Weingartner.

THIRTEENTH SEASON
(1903-1904)
SOLOISTS

CLARINET: Joseph Schreurs.
FLUTE: Alfred Quensel.
FRENCH HORN: Leopold de Maré.
HARP: Enrico Tramonti.
OBOE: Alfred Barthel.
PIANOFORTE: Miss Blanche Sherman, Mrs. Jeannette Durno Collins, Mrs. Fannie Bloomfield Zeisler; Ferruccio Busoni, George Proctor, Arthur Whiting.
VIOLIN: Miss Maud Powell; Leopold Kramer, Leon Marx, Jacques Thibaud.
VIOLONCELLO: Carl Brueckner, Bruno Steindel.
VOCAL: Misses Muriel Foster, Marguerite Hall, Jenny Osborn, Mme. Pauline Strauss de Ahna, Mrs. Sue Harrington Furbeck, Mme. Ernestine Schumann-Heink; Albert Borroff, George Hamlin.
VISITING CONDUCTOR: Dr. Richard Strauss.

FOURTEENTH SEASON
(1904-1905)

First six weeks of concerts given in the Auditorium—Dedication of Orchestra Hall a triumph for Theodore Thomas—His illness, "Death and Transfiguration"—Mrs. Thomas presents Mr. Thomas' library to The Orchestral Association—The life and work of Theodore Thomas—Death of Charles Davidson Hamill, a devoted friend of the Orchestra—Meeting of subscribers to the Building Fund—"Plan of Organization" approved—Election of fifteen Trustees, as provided by the new by-laws—Trustees elect Frederick Stock Conductor and change the name of the Orchestra to "The Theodore Thomas Orchestra"—Dedication of the Lyon & Healy organ in Orchestra Hall.

The ticket sale for the Fourteenth Season opened Monday morning, September 26, at Lyon & Healy's, with a line of eager buyers, indicating that things were at last coming our way. All doubts, misgivings and "misapprehensions" any of us had about leaving the Auditorium vanished as we watched the crowd of people at the box office.

All friends of the Orchestra were now in a hopeful frame of mind and in a mood to enjoy the program of the first concerts, November 4 and 5, in the Auditorium. In memory of Antonin Dvořák, whose death had occurred May 1, soon after the close of the Thirteenth Season, Mr. Thomas devoted the first part of the program to two works of the Bohemian composer—the "Carneval" overture and the symphony "From the New World."

"The dear people who loved to go to a Thomas Concert" in the Auditorium where "one could always get a seat," now saw "a great light," and soon realized that if they were to hear the Orchestra in the new hall they must become season subscribers. The programs, with noted soloists for the remaining concerts in the Auditorium, were very attractive:

    Second Program, November 11 and 12, Mme. Louise Homer.
    Third Program, November 18 and 19, Mrs. Fannie Bloomfield Zeisler.
    Fourth Program, November 25 and 26, Popular Concerts.
    Fifth Program, December 2 and 3, Leopold Kramer.

Sixth Program, December 9 and 10, last concerts in the Auditorium, Bruno Steindel.

When the first week in December came around the interior of the hall was still in disorder; floors covered with builders' material; tuners at work on the organ; atmosphere redolent with the odor of drying plaster. How could the dedicatory concert be given on the 14th? I said to Mr. Lathrop: "Let us secure the Auditorium for another week and defer the opening of the hall." It was finally decided to wait until after Tuesday, the 6th, of the following week, when Mr. Thomas would hold his first rehearsal in the hall and then consider the dedicatory concert. In the meantime architects and contractors had been busy—rubbish and material removed, stage in order, organ ready—and when Mr. Thomas and his men assembled Tuesday morning (6th) for rehearsal, they found a well equipped, attractive hall, perfect in the most essential detail—acoustics.

Mr. Thomas was an acknowledged authority on acoustics, and during the thirteen years the Orchestra had occupied the Auditorium he had continually experimented with sounding-boards and various methods of seating the men on the stage. Orchestra Hall, as we know it today, with its commodious arrangements for orchestra and chorus, is the joint creation of Theodore Thomas and Daniel H. Burnham. Mr. Thomas began his rehearsal on that Tuesday morning with some doubts and misgivings. The occasion was eventful, as the rehearsal was the supreme test of the acoustics, and it meant so much to him. The first number, the "Tannhäuser" overture, contained enough light and shade to bring out the defects in the hall, if there were any. At the conclusion of the rehearsal, "he turned," says Mrs. Thomas, "to the boxes at the other end of the hall, in one of which were seated Mr. Lathrop, Mr. Fay and one or two others, and shouted triumphantly, 'your hall is a success, gentlemen, a great success.' After which he sent the following cablegram to Mr. Burnham, who was at that time in Manila:

"CHICAGO, December 7, 1904.

"D. H. BURNHAM:
"Hall a complete success. Quality exceeds all expectations.
"THEODORE THOMAS."

ORCHESTRA HALL—INTERIOR

Fourteenth Season—1904-1905

The hall was still incomplete when Mr. Thomas began his regular rehearsals:

"December 13, Tuesday: Spent the morning in the hall with Mr. Lathrop and contractors; much to be done before the concert tomorrow night. Mr. Thomas began his regular rehearsals yesterday, 'but,' said the Conductor, 'it is like working on top of "The Ruins of Athens."' "

The afternoon papers announced that: "Charles D. Hamill, a prominent pioneer resident, and long identified with the Chicago Orchestra, was critically ill at his residence, 2127 Prairie Avenue."

The next morning (Wednesday) I called at Mr. Hamill's residence, and learned that my old friend and colleague was indeed very ill. The announcement of his illness at the Annual Meeting in the afternoon (14th) called forth from Mr. Lathrop and other Trustees testimonials of their affection and regard, and regrets that he could not be present at the dedication of the hall that evening.

At this meeting the former Board of Trustees was reelected, with the exception of William B. Walker, resigned; Max Baird taking his place.

The report of the Treasurer, Frederick J. Wessels, for the Thirteenth Season (1903-1904), ending June 30, 1904, was then received:

Receipts		Expenses	
Chicago concerts	$ 98,815.50	Business management	$ 5,729.77
Out-of-town concerts	4,741.02	Auditorium rent	12,000.00
Apollo Musical Club	2,352.00	Salaries of Conductor and Orchestra	101,090.00
Local engagements	3,858.05	Advertising	4,964.67
Program book	2,203.80	Soloists	6,100.00
Deficit	19,332.06	Miscellaneous concert expenses	664.99
		Accounts written off	753.00
	$131,302.43		$131,302.43

The loss on the Thirteenth Season, $19,332.06, the last the Governing Members were called upon to pay, was met by the men and women of Chicago who have so often cheerfully and unselfishly responded to the call of the Trustees:

GEORGE E. ADAMS.
JOSEPH ADAMS.
ALLISON V. ARMOUR.
MRS. HUGH T. BIRCH.
MRS. T. B. BLACKSTONE.
WILLIAM L. BROWN.
DANIEL H. BURNHAM.
WILLIAM T. CARRINGTON.
ESTATE OF HENRY CORWITH.
CHARLES R. CRANE.
HENRY DIBBLEE.
CHARLES NORMAN FAY.
MARSHALL FIELD.
WILLIAM A. FULLER.
JOHN J. GLESSNER.
GEORGE HAMLIN.
WILLIAM R. HARPER.
P. J. HEALY.
CHARLES L. HUTCHINSON.
CHAUNCEY KEEP.
EDSON KEITH.
BRYAN LATHROP.
VICTOR F. LAWSON.
LEVI Z. LEITER.
JOHN R. LINDGREN.
FRANK O. LOWDEN.
CYRUS H. MCCORMICK.
HAROLD F. MCCORMICK.
STANLEY MCCORMICK.
O. W. NORTON.
MRS. M. D. OGDEN.
ARTHUR ORR.
CHARLES F. OTIS.
PHILO A. OTIS.
MRS. THOMAS N. PAGE.
GEORGE M. PULLMAN.
MARTIN A. RYERSON.
JOHN A. SPOOR.
ALBERT A. SPRAGUE.
MRS. M. D. STURGES.
WILLIAM B. WALKER.
EZRA J. WARNER.
MRS. JULIA M. WATSON.
MISS M. S. WATSON.
ESTATE OF MRS. F. S. WILLING.

The Trustees thought the time had now come when the work of the Association should be enlarged, and with that in view it was resolved at this meeting:

"to adjourn the Annual Meeting to January 31, 1905, and that Bryan Lathrop, Philo A. Otis and C. Norman Fay be appointed a committee to report at this meeting on the business condition of the Association and a plan for its reorganization and future work."

At the dedicatory concert Wednesday evening, December 14, the Orchestra was assisted by the Apollo Musical Club and the Mendelssohn Club:

Dedicatory Address—HON. GEORGE E. ADAMS

"Hail! Bright Abode" ("Tannhäuser"), ... *Wagner*
CHORUS AND ORCHESTRA

Overture, "Tannhäuser," . . . . *Wagner*
Tone Poem, "Death and Transfiguration," . . . . *Strauss*
Symphony No. 5, C Minor, Opus 67, ... *Beethoven*
Hallelujah Chorus, "The Messiah," . . . . . . *Handel*
CHORUS AND ORCHESTRA

The speaker of the evening, George E. Adams, paid a worthy tribute to Mr. Thomas and the Orchestra:

"We have built here a noble hall of music. It is merely a material structure of brick and stone and steel. We have not, and we cannot, put into this building its living soul. That is a task for other hands than ours.

Fourteenth Season—1904-1905

"Mr. Thomas and gentlemen of the Orchestra, we hope and believe that it will stand for generations to come, but if it stands for centuries it will not outlast the beneficent influence which you have bestowed on the higher life of the American people."

It was a proud moment for Mr. Thomas when he appeared on the Conductor's stand at this concert. He had, indeed, worked for "the higher life of the American people." Orchestra Hall, the gift of the Chicago friends of the Orchestra, represented the fulfillment, the achievement of his life-long dreams and hopes that he might some day see his Orchestra established in its own home, and with an ample endowment. "Everything comes to him who waits!" And it came to Mr. Thomas—but it was too late.

The evening was a triumph for him such as has been given to few men. The spacious, commodious hall was a worthy monument to his genius, and the great audience showed their appreciation by calling him out again and again.

The "wearisome traveling" had now ended, but he was soon to start on another and longer journey "through the valley of the shadow of death." He had not been in the best of health in recent years. On his return to Chicago in October, from his summer home in New Hampshire, the members of the Executive Committee realized that he was slowly breaking down. It was a great disappointment to him that the hall was not ready, as had been announced, and that his preliminary rehearsals and the first six weeks of concerts must be given in the Auditorium. The changing of the Orchestra to the new hall, the experimental work of adapting the men to the new environment and seating arrangements on the stage, with an accompaniment of hammers and saws by the carpenters—all of this was trying to the nerves of the Conductor in his feeble condition.

The program of the Beethoven Anniversary, December 16 and 17, Seventh Program, was magnificently played by the Orchestra, but only the people on the stage realized the effort it cost Mr. Thomas.

The program included the fourth and seventh symphonies, the "Coriolanus" overture and the "Romanza" for violin (Leopold Kramer).

Mr. Thomas resumed his rehearsals on Monday morning, the 19th, with his customary vigor, apparently, although he had contracted a severe attack of *grippe* during the previous week. "When art or duty called he never considered himself," says Mrs. Thomas, "and so in spite of the fever and lassitude of the disease he arose from his sick bed every day, with his old indomitable will," and went forth to his work. I was at the hall on Monday, and again on Thursday, at the close of rehearsal, and met the Conductor as he was leaving the stage, hoping to find his cold wearing away, and his condition better; but he was far from well. I could see the fever in his system and feel it in the pressure of his hand, as he inquired earnestly about Mr. Hamill, and he was deeply moved when I told him of the serious illness of his old friend.

The "Popular" concerts on Friday and Saturday following, December 23 and 24, Eighth Program, were the last to be conducted by Theodore Thomas:

Overture, "In der Natur," Opus 91,	Dvořák
Larghetto, from Second Symphony,	Beethoven
Contrasts (the Gavotte, A. D. 1700 and 1900),	Elgar
Suite Pastorale,	Chabrier
Love Scene, from "Feuersnot,"	Richard Strauss

INTERMISSION

"Waldphantasie," Opus 83,	Zoellner
"Träume,"	Wagner
Symphonic Poem No. 1, "Le Rouet d'Omphale," Opus 31,	Saint-Saëns
Waltz, "Village Swallows,"	Joseph Strauss
Suite, "Sylvia,"	Delibes

With other Trustees I was in the Conductor's room at the intermission on Friday. He looked feeble and weary; but none of us realized that our beloved leader was about closing his earthly career and would soon be with the immortals.

Monday morning, the 26th, the man who had never missed a rehearsal or a concert through illness prepared to go to the hall; but the effort was too much. He returned to his bed, from which he was never again to rise, though there seemed to be some improvement in his condition on Tuesday and Wednesday. I made a few notes during these sad days:

"December 30, Friday A. M.: Called at the Orchestra office in the Auditorium. Wessels had just received message that pneumonia had developed; Mr. Thomas' condition serious. To the concert at 2:00 P. M. in the new hall. Mr. Stock conducted the

Ninth Program. A large house; everyone asking about Mr. Thomas. After the concert, to the Hamills'. Mrs. Hamill said her husband was very ill; no change in forty-eight hours.

"December 31, Saturday A. M. At Wessels' office; no further word about Mr. Thomas. As I left the Auditorium the sun was shining warm and bright. In all this gladness of nature it is hard to realize that Mr. Thomas is so ill! To his house, Bellevue Place. McNicol (the librarian) met me at the door: 'Just the same; no change; very uncertain.' At the concert in the evening, Orchestra Hall, met Dr. Ely (the physician in attendance): 'Mr. Thomas has slept during the day; his condition is better; I feel encouraged.'"

Sunday and Monday the city, the nation, the whole world waited anxiously but hopefully for news from the sick-room in Bellevue Place. Mr. Thomas seemed to be better on Tuesday, but at night a change came, and at five o'clock on Wednesday morning, January 4, 1905, the Master of Music, says Mrs. Thomas, "passed quietly and painlessly into the presence of the God he had served so faithfully and well."

The Trustees were called together at noon on Wednesday (the 4th) and voted to postpone the concerts of January 6 and 7, Tenth Program, and to give a Memorial Concert for Theodore Thomas, in Orchestra Hall on Friday afternoon, January 6, at three-thirty o'clock, to holders of season tickets only. It was decided also to accept the use of the Auditorium, by the courtesy of its Management, for a Memorial Concert to be given to the general public on Sunday afternoon, January 8, at three o'clock. At this meeting on January 4, "George E. Adams was appointed a committee of one to draft resolutions on the death of Theodore Thomas for the records of the Association and the daily papers."

The funeral services of Theodore Thomas were held in St. James Episcopal Church at eleven o'clock on Friday morning, January 6, conducted by the minister, the Rev. James S. Stone, assisted by the Rev. John Henry Hopkins, minister of the Church of the Epiphany. At the opening of the service Wilhelm Middelschulte, the organist of the Orchestra, played Bach's prelude in G minor. While the casket was being carried up the aisle, borne by members of the Orchestra, preceded by the honorary pall-bearers and officers of The Orchestral Association, and followed by the ministers and members of the family, the brass choir of the Orchestra, led by Frederick Stock, played the Luther chorale, "A Mighty

Fortress." After the service, organ and instruments played the chorale from the ninth symphony of Beethoven. Eight members of the Orchestra served as pallbearers: Robert Ambrosius, Leopold Kramer, Calvin Lampert, Louis Novak, Louis Mayer, Hans Parbs, Ernest Frank Wagner* and Otto Wolf. Honorary pallbearers: A. C. Bartlett, Marshall Field, John J. Glessner, Charles L. Hutchinson, Victor F. Lawson, Bernhard Listeman, Cyrus H. McCormick, A. A. Sprague, George P. Upton and Bernhard Ziehn.

The remains were placed temporarily in a vault at Graceland Cemetery; later were removed to Mt. Auburn Cemetery, Cambridge, Massachusetts.

The program of the Memorial Concert in the afternoon in Orchestra Hall, under the direction of Mr. Stock, consisted of selections Mr. Thomas had taught us how to enjoy:

Chorale, ... Bach—Abert
Symphony No. 3, "Eroica," Opus 55 (First Two Movements), ... Beethoven
Siegfried's Funeral March, from "Die Götterdämmerung," *Wagner*
Tone Poem, "Death and Transfiguration," . . *Richard Strauss*

The Memorial Concert was repeated Sunday afternoon, January 8, in the Auditorium to the men and women of Chicago who by their gifts had made Orchestra Hall possible.

It was no easy task to gather up the threads in the daily work of the Orchestra, with Mr. Thomas gone. The men resumed their regular rehearsals in the hall on Monday morning, January 9, with Mr. Stock, the Assistant Conductor, in charge. "Who will now take up the work of the Orchestra and be responsible to the people for the high standard Mr. Thomas had maintained? Who will be our leader?"

The Trustees met on the following day, the 10th, at 2:30 P. M., in Mr. Burnham's office, and voted:

"1. That annually hereafter, the Friday afternoon and Saturday evening concerts falling nearest the anniversary of his death shall be a memorial to the honored founder and leader of the Chicago Orchestra, Theodore Thomas.

"2. That Mr. Frederick Stock be appointed temporary Conductor of the Orchestra."

---

*Ernest Frank Wagner died February 20, 1922, at Alameda, California. He had been with the Orchestra from the First Season (1891); retired (1916) on a pension.

The Trustees were grieved to hear that Charles D. Hamill, Chairman of the Executive Committee, whose presence and counsel we needed so much, and who had been ill for some time, was now in a critical condition, beyond hope of recovery.

Mr. Lathrop presented a letter from Mrs. Thomas, indicating the generous intention of the family to donate the musical library of Mr. Thomas to The Orchestral Association:

"43 BELLEVUE PLACE, January 9, 1905.

"MY DEAR MR. LATHROP:

"No doubt the Trustees of The Orchestral Association are beginning to wonder what disposition Mr. Thomas made of his musical library in his will, and whether they are to have the use of his music in the future, as in the past, for the Orchestra.

"Mr. Thomas never gave me any definite instructions in regard to the library, except that part of it which he promised to the Newberry Library. But I think, nevertheless, that he intended that some time or other it should belong to The Orchestral Association. So I believe I am doing as he would wish, when I tell you that it is my intention to give the library—which he willed to me unreservedly—to the Association—especially as we were not able to make a large contribution in money towards the new Hall.

"The library is very large and valuable; its chief value, however, in my opinion, is that every score in it is marked by Mr. Thomas' own hand, and is a complete record of his own readings, embodying the result of his researches of a lifetime. As a reference library for students it ought to be of very great value.

"In making this gift to the Association I have the entire sanction of Mr. Thomas' sons, Hector and Hermann Thomas, who are as anxious to carry out their father's wishes as I am in the matter, and who gladly forego whatever money its sale might have brought in to them for the sake of furthering the great work of establishing his Orchestra permanently for all time, for which he labored all his life.

"Very sincerely yours,

"ROSE FAY THOMAS."

The bequest from the heirs of Theodore Thomas was most welcome. During his fourteen years as Conductor of our Orchestra he had furnished, from this library, the music needed for the concerts, and until the details of the bequest were perfected in December, 1905, the Association had the use of the library for all the intervening concerts—a truly welcome gift.

The resolutions prepared by George E. Adams for the records of the Association and the daily papers were approved by the Trustees:

"The Trustees wish it were possible to place upon their records a fitting tribute to the memory of their friend and leader, Theodore Thomas.

"They feel how inadequate any formal expression of regard and regret must be.

"The world knows what Theodore Thomas has done to inspire the American people with love of the highest form of the most spiritual of all the arts.

"Only those who were nearest to him knew the difficulties of his task, and the wisdom and patient courage with which he overcame them.

"We deplore his death as our own personal bereavement and an unspeakable loss to the higher life of our country; but we rejoice that such a man has lived and labored, and so far as in us lies we resolve that his labors shall not have been in vain."

THEODORE THOMAS

Theodore Thomas attained his position as the first Conductor of his time, not only by the high character of his programs, but by his practical knowledge of every detail in his work, whereby nothing was ever forgotten, nothing left to chance; a knowledge acquired in the stern school of experience. Guided by such standards men become great, be it in music, law or commerce; and in war, by following such standards, victories are won. His courage, iron will and determination to succeed are illustrated by a statement made in later life:

"I have gone without food longer than I should. I have walked when I could not afford to ride. I have even played when my hands were cold. But I shall succeed, for I shall never give up my belief that at last the people will come to me and my concerts will be crowded."*

Theodore Thomas was born October 11, 1835, the eldest of a large family of children, and the only one who showed any love of music. His father, Johann August Thomas, a musician of good standing, taught the boy to play the violin, and with such success that before he was seven years of age Theodore had appeared as a concert artist.

In 1845 the Thomas family emigrated to America, and "here Theodore was brought, a boy of ten, to educate himself and carve out his own career, as best he might." The struggle for a livelihood was then too intense for Theodore to entertain rosy thoughts of a future career. During the first year in New York he accepted any

---

*"Theodore Thomas. A Musical Autobiography," by George P. Upton (1905).

THEODORE THOMAS

engagements which would help him to earn a living, such as playing for dancing at balls and parties, often the whole night long. Other well known musicians beat the drum in street parades; fortunately Theodore never had to do that. It was a relief from this musical drudgery when he secured a position in the orchestra of an English theatre, thus affording him the opportunity to hear the works of Shakespeare and Beethoven, "two names which were ever afterward beacon lights in his career." Then followed an engagement for his father and himself to play first and second horns on board the warship "Pennsylvania" at Portsmouth, Virginia—an important factor in Theodore's education, for here he became familiar with the brass choir of the orchestra.

At the conclusion of this engagement (1849) Theodore started on horseback, "carrying his few belongings in a valise," for a concert tour in the south.* "He rode on a straight line," over fences and ditches, through streams and forests. Like young Lochinvar, he

"Stopped not for brake and stayed not for stone;
He swam the Esk River, where ford there was none."

On arriving at a town he would secure the dining room of the hotel for his concert, and then set out to put up posters announcing the appearance of "the wonderful boy violinist, T. T."

"When the time for the concert arrived," said Mr. Thomas, "I would stand at the door of the hall and take the money until I concluded that my audience was about gathered, after which I would go to the front of the hall, unpack my violin and begin the concert."†

In the summer of 1850 a German theatre was opened in New York with a good orchestra, in which Theodore was engaged as leading violinist—another important factor in his education. He thus became acquainted with the works of Goethe, Schiller and other German poets.

The next few years may be sketched together, years full of work for Theodore, but of a more congenial character, when he was first violin in the concert and operatic performances of Jenny Lind, Sontag, Grisi, Mario and other artists who came to America in the early

---

*"Memoirs of Theodore Thomas," by Rose Fay Thomas (1911).
†"Theodore Thomas. A Musical Autobiography," by George P. Upton (1905).

"fifties." Theodore played in the orchestra for Sontag, conducted by Karl Eckert, the most satisfactory Conductor of that period in New York. Mr. Thomas said afterwards, "The influence of Eckert laid the foundation of my future career."

Theodore made his first visit to Chicago* "in 1854 as violinist in a small orchestra accompanying a concert troupe, composed of Ole Bull," and other soloists. "In October, 1858, he made a second visit in the same capacity in a concert troupe directed by Carl Anschutz, under the management of Ullman," Carl Formes being the principal soloist.

In 1854 Mr. Thomas was elected a member (violin) of the New York Philharmonic Society, playing under Carl Bergmann and other Conductors until he began his own orchestral concerts in 1862.

In 1855 William Mason established his famous "Chamber Concerts" in New York, under the name of "Mason and Bergmann": William Mason (pianoforte), Carl Bergmann (violoncello), Theodore Thomas (first violin), Julius Mosenthal (second violin) and George Matzka (viola). In consequence of the withdrawal later of Bergmann, the concerts were continued under the name of "Mason and Thomas." Bergmann was succeeded by Frederick Bergner, the first 'cellist of that day. Bergner once said of Theodore Thomas, "One of the greatest violinists in the world was spoiled to become the greatest Conductor."†

With the organization of the "Chamber Concerts," the apprenticeship in Mr. Thomas' life ended. As first violinist in the "Mason-Thomas" concerts, "he was the master musician," says George P. Upton, "master in every sense, for he dominated that organization in its methods, its music, its programs and its progress." This may be called the formatory period, fitting him for his real life work, which began when he gave his first "Thomas Concert," May 13, 1862. He continued to give occasional orchestral concerts during the next two years "as opportunity offered," but he soon discovered that to maintain the standard he had in mind, he must have an orchestra

---

*"Musical Memories," by George P. Upton (1908).
†"Theodore Thomas. A Musical Autobiography," by George P. Upton (1905).

Fourteenth Season—1904-1905

of his own. This he set out to do, a penniless youth, without capital, without guarantors, by engaging his men and announcing his concerts, having perfect confidence that the public would support him. This new Orchestra gave its first concert December 3, 1864, in Irving Hall, and was called "The Theodore Thomas Orchestra," a name soon to become dear to music lovers in all sections of the country.

During the summer of 1866 Mr. Thomas inaugurated his first Summer Night Concerts at Terrace Garden in New York; a more attractive place was the new hall in Central Park Garden, which he dedicated May 25, 1868, inaugurating another series of concerts known as the Garden Concerts, attractive and educational, which continued until 1869. During the winter months he maintained his Symphonic Soirées and miscellaneous concerts to keep his men together and earn money for salaries.

In 1869 he started the famous tours of the Theodore Thomas Orchestra, along the great "Highway" through the eastern, southern and western states, "carrying with him," said the *New York Evening Post* (1873), "the power to make the finest music in the finest way." The tours continued through the winter months, in order that the Orchestra might be in New York for the Summer Concerts. The outcome of the yearly visits to Cincinnati was the organization of the Festivals, the first in 1873, the second in 1875, and the third in 1878, in the new Music Hall. The Festivals continued every two years until at the close of the sixteenth (1904) Mr. Thomas laid down his baton: the last he was to be permitted to conduct.

At the close of the Thirty-fifth Season (1877), when Leopold Damrosch was Conductor, the affairs of the Philharmonic Society were at a low ebb, musically and financially, while the symphonic concerts of Theodore Thomas were flourishing. In this emergency he was invited to take the conductorship of the Philharmonic, and accepted, thinking it best to give up his own flourishing concerts to make the Society again a power for music in New York.

After the Third Festival (1878) Mr. Thomas accepted the musical directorship of the Cincinnati College of Music. In 1880, owing to disagreement between the Board of Directors and himself regarding the conduct of the College, he tendered his resignation and returned to New York.

There was another city along the "Highway" where the visits of the Theodore Thomas Orchestra were always welcome, in the twenty-two years of travel from 1869 to 1891. That city was Chicago, which gave him the realization of his life wish, his heart's desire—a permanent Orchestra in its own home—and here he lived the last chapter in his art career.

On Sunday morning, January 8, 1905, following the death and burial of Theodore Thomas, the Rev. Frank Wakely Gunsaulus, D.D., from the stage of the Auditorium, where Mr. Thomas had long stood as Conductor of the Chicago Orchestra, addressed the people of Central Church on the life and work of our leader:

"We have said goodbye to a priest and prophet. It makes no difference that Theodore Thomas never acknowledged his divine call to a high and noble ministry. The art of interpreting great music comes as a duty, and Theodore Thomas, like a true minister, made it a privilege and joy. As Beethoven interpreted the involved and hidden values of the soul, so Theodore Thomas interpreted Beethoven."

Charles D. Hamill, Chairman of the Executive Committee, whose presence and counsel we now needed so much, died at his residence, 2127 Prairie Avenue, Wednesday afternoon, January 11, 1905. No one among the Trustees was more zealous in his support of Theodore Thomas and more enthusiastic in advocating the new hall, than was Mr. Hamill. The funeral services were held from the First Presbyterian Church, then at the corner of Indiana Avenue and Twenty-first Street, on Friday, January 13, at 12:30 P. M., conducted by the minister, the Rev. John Archibald Morison, D.D. The musical service, contributed by the brass choir of the Chicago Orchestra, under the direction of Mr. Stock, the choir of the church and the organist, Francis S. Moore, included:

Organ Prelude, Dead March ("Saul"), ... *Handel*
Two Chorales:
    "A Mighty Fortress," . . . . *Luther*
    From the Ninth Symphony, ... *Beethoven*
                BRASS CHOIR
Organ Postlude, Funeral March, ... *Beethoven*

Two favorite hymns of Mr. Hamill were sung by the choir of the church. The acting pall-bearers were five

CHARLES D. HAMILL

Fourteenth Season—1904-1905 163

sons and a nephew: Charles H. Hamill, Philip W. Hamill, Paul Hamill, Robert W. Hamill, Lawrence Hamill and Ralph C. Hamill.

Thirty years and more of my life have been associated with two men in the development of music in Chicago: Theodore Thomas and Charles D. Hamill; men who stood for high ideals in art. Mr. Hamill's first work in the musical life of our city was with the Mendelssohn Society (1858-1865), of which he was a founder, and Adolph W. Dohn the first Conductor. My recollections of Mr. Hamill date from a later period, in connection with a series of concerts given by Mr. Thomas and his Orchestra in November, 1870, in Farwell Hall. Mr. Hamill and I were members of a chorus assembled by Mr. Dohn to assist at the concert on November 14, in the performance of Beethoven's fantasia for piano (Miss Anna Mehlig, soloist), chorus and orchestra. Mr. Hamill became a member of the Apollo Musical Club in 1877, and in the season of 1886-1887 was its President. He was Chairman of the Music Committee in the May Festivals of 1882 and 1884, one of the founders of the Art Institute and a member of its Board of Trustees until his death. During his last illness his mind constantly dwelt on the completion of Orchestra Hall, to which he had given much time and thought during the closing year of his life.

At the request of the Executive Committee, Charles Norman Fay prepared this memorial to Mr. Hamill:

"One of the five charter members of this Association, and always active upon its Board of Trustees and Executive Committee, has this day, though he knew it not, followed his forty years' friend, Theodore Thomas, into the eternal rest. Among men prominent in Chicago's early life and growth almost the first lover and promoter of good music, our late associate supported with active influence and open purse every movement in aid of good art.

"It is therefore with high regard and deep personal feeling that we here write for the last time upon these records his honored name, and order that the concerts of the current week, as the final tribute he himself would have loved best, shall be given and announced 'In Memoriam' of him."

In accordance with this action of the Trustees, the program book for the concerts of January 13 and 14 contained this announcement:

CHARLES D. HAMILL

BORN
November 14, 1839
at Bloomington, Ind.

DIED
January 11, 1905
at Chicago, Ill.

"Mr. Hamill was one of the incorporators of The Orchestral Association, and served as a Trustee since its organization in 1890, and at the time of his death was Chairman of the Executive Committee.

"He was a friend of the late Theodore Thomas for more than forty years, and as a tribute to his memory the Orchestra will play before the regular program, January 13 and 14, the Beethoven Marcia Funebre from sonata, Opus 26, which was arranged for orchestra by Mr. Thomas."

In consequence of the death of Mr. Thomas the concerts of January 6 and 7, Tenth Program, were postponed to Monday afternoon, January 30, and Tuesday evening, January 31, Frederick Stock, Conductor. As it was impossible to secure Mr. de Pachmann (piano), the soloist announced, a revision of the program was necessary:

Huldigungsmarsch, ... *Wagner*
Symphony No. 4, Opus 36, ... *Tschaikowsky*
Scherzo, "L'Apprenti Sorcier," . . . . . . *Dukas*
Vorspiel, Act II, "Ingwelde," . . . . . . *Schillings*
Tone Poem, "Don Juan," Opus 20, ... *Strauss*

ELEVENTH PROGRAM, JANUARY 13 AND 14
SOLOISTS: LUDWIG BECKER
FRANZ ESSER

Marcia Funebre, from Sonata, Opus 26, . . . *Beethoven*
In Memoriam, CHARLES DAVIDSON HAMILL

Symphony, G Major, ... *Haydn*
Symphonie Concertante, E Flat, for Violin and Viola, . *Mozart*

INTERMISSION

Variations, Chorale "St. Anthony," . . . . . *Brahms*
Overture, "Leonore," No. 3, ... *Beethoven*

The Committee on Organization and By-laws, consisting of Mr. Lathrop, Mr. Fay and the Secretary, met in Mr. Lathrop's office Thursday afternoon, January 19, to prepare a report. We were at once confronted with the suggestion made by some of our best friends and sup-

Fourteenth Season—1904-1905

porters, that every contributor to the Building Fund should have a vote on the new plan of organization. We were not at all in sympathy with the idea of calling the 8,000 subscribers together in a "town meeting" to discuss important matters of the Orchestra, yet in deference to the wishes of the large givers, it was decided that such a meeting should be held.

The Committee on Organization and By-laws made its report at the adjourned Annual Meeting of the Association, Tuesday afternoon, January 31, 1905. In accordance with the recommendation of the committee, the members voted:

"That this adjourned meeting do further adjourn until Tuesday, February 28, 1905, at the office of the Association, in Orchestra Building, at 3:30 P. M.;

"That the Secretary be instructed to call a meeting of the subscribers of not less than $100 to the Orchestra Building Fund, to be held at the office of the Association, in Orchestra Building, on Monday, February 27, 1905, at 11:00 o'clock A. M.; that at that meeting the said subscribers be invited to express their approval or disapproval of the plan of organization."

"February 7, Tuesday: Spent most of the day trying to arrange dates for Felix Weingartner to conduct a pair of our concerts. It came about through Dr. Ziegfeld,* of the Chicago Musical College, who crossed the ocean last week from Hamburg with Weingartner. Dr. Ziegfeld told me Saturday we could get Weingartner, but for one date only—Saturday, February 18. I called Messrs. Lathrop and Fay together at the Chicago Club; decided not to take Weingartner: one concert would not allow all of our subscribers (Friday and Saturday) to hear him; if a foreign Conductor is chosen we would prefer Mottl, whom Mr. Thomas had spoken of as his possible successor."

The meeting of the subscribers to the Building Fund, held February 27 at 11:00 A. M. in the foyer of Orchestra Hall, with George E. Adams, Chairman, and Max Baird, Secretary, passed along as we had hoped, with no objections or comments. There were possibly twenty subscribers present (three of them women, the rest Trustees

---

*Dr. Florenz Ziegfeld, an international figure in the musical world, died May 20, 1923, at his home in Chicago. He was born June 10, 1841, in Jever, Duchy of Oldenburg. After completing his musical education he came to America, making his home in Chicago, and in 1867 founded the Chicago Musical College in Crosby's Opera House. My recollections of Dr. Ziegfeld date from the World's Peace Jubilee (June, 1872) in Boston, in which I took part as member of an auxiliary chorus from Chicago. The interest in the Jubilee centered largely about the foreign attractions—Johann Strauss, the band of the Garde Républicaine (Paris) and other European bands, all secured through the efforts of Dr. Ziegfeld, who was sent abroad on this important mission by Patrick S. Gilmore, Musical Director of the Jubilee.

and Governing Members), but as the Secretary held proxies representing subscriptions to the amount of $439,875, a majority of the total amount subscribed to the Building Fund, the "Plan of Organization," as recommended by the committee appointed at the Annual Meeting, was, on motion, adopted:

"That the Association shall hereafter consist of forty persons, whose names here follow, who shall be known as Members:

GEORGE E. ADAMS.
JOSEPH ADAMS.
EDWARD E. AYER.
MAX BAIRD.
A. C. BARTLETT.
A. G. BECKER.
CHAUNCEY B. BORLAND.
WILLIAM L. BROWN.
CLARENCE A. BURLEY.
DANIEL H. BURNHAM.
EDWARD B. BUTLER.
WILLIAM J. BRYSON.
FREDERIC A. DELANO.
C. NORMAN FAY.
JOHN J. GLESSNER.
CHARLES H. HAMILL.
PRESIDENT W. R. HARPER.
ARTHUR HEURTLEY.
C. L. HUTCHINSON.
DR. GEORGE S. ISHAM.
CHAUNCEY KEEP.
BRYAN LATHROP.
VICTOR F. LAWSON.
JOHN R. LINDGREN.
FRANK O. LOWDEN.
HORACE H. MARTIN.
CYRUS H. MCCORMICK.
HAROLD F. MCCORMICK.
STANLEY MCCORMICK.
O. W. NORTON.
ARTHUR ORR.
PHILO A. OTIS.
F. F. PEABODY.
H. H. PORTER, JR.
E. P. RIPLEY.
MARTIN A. RYERSON.
JOHN A. SPOOR.
ALBERT A. SPRAGUE.
WILLIAM B. WALKER.
CLARENCE M. WOOLLEY.

"The Members shall elect out of their number each year at the Annual Meeting, in the manner provided by the laws of Illinois, a Board of not exceeding fifteen Trustees, to which shall be committed the management of the Association and its affairs;

"That the said membership of forty persons when once elected shall be self-perpetuating; that is to say, vacancies occurring by death, resignation or disability shall be filled, from time to time, by the remaining Members at the Annual Meeting of the Association, or at special meetings called for that purpose, by a majority vote of those present at the meeting.

"Provided the foregoing plan shall have secured the approval of the majority of the subscribers represented in person or by proxy at the said subscribers' meeting of February 27, 1905, it shall be voted upon at the adjourned Annual Meeting of February 28, 1905."

The Orchestral Association held its adjourned meeting on the day following, Tuesday, the 28th, ratifying and adopting the "Plan of Organization" approved by the subscribers to the Building Fund at their meeting on the preceding day, the 27th; also, the by-laws presented and recommended by the Committee on Organization.

CHARLES H. HAMILL

The Association approved "The purchase by the Trustees of the land on which Orchestra Hall now stands, from Bryan Lathrop, John J. Glessner and Daniel H. Burnham, as Trustees, by deed dated February 27, 1904."

The Association then proceeded to the election of a Trustee to fill the vacancy on the Board caused by the death of Charles D. Hamill. The name of his son, Charles H. Hamill, was then placed in nomination, and on motion he was unanimously elected. At this point I must introduce a note from my journal:

"March 7, Tuesday: Cable from Felix Mottl, in answer to an offer from Fay, of February 16, to be Conductor. One word only—'No.'"

NINETEENTH PROGRAM, MARCH 10 AND 11
SOLOIST: VLADIMIR DE PACHMANN
Concerto for Pianoforte No. 2, F Minor, Opus 21, . . *Chopin*

Mr. de Pachmann had been announced as soloist for the week of January 6 and 7, but in consequence of the death of Mr. Thomas, the concerts were postponed.

A Board of fifteen Trustees, as provided in the new by-laws, was elected at a meeting of the Governing Members held Thursday afternoon, March 16, in the offices of the Association:

GEORGE E. ADAMS.
JOSEPH ADAMS.
MAX BAIRD.
WILLIAM L. BROWN.
DANIEL H. BURNHAM.
C. NORMAN FAY.
JOHN J. GLESSNER.
CHARLES H. HAMILL.

WILLIAM R. HARPER.
BRYAN LATHROP.
FRANK O. LOWDEN.
HAROLD F. McCORMICK.
ARTHUR ORR.
PHILO A. OTIS.
CLARENCE M. WOOLLEY.

The Members ratified and approved the agreement dated February 28, 1905, between The Orchestral Association and the Standard Office Company, adjoining Orchestra Building on the south, also the agreement with the Pullman Company, on the north, dated March 4, 1905, limiting the height, with other details of Orchestra Building, for which concessions the Standard Office Company and the Pullman Company each paid the Association $25,000.

The agreements with the Pullman Company and the Standard Office Company were arranged by Mr. Lathrop and Mr. Burnham early in the popular campaign for funds to construct Orchestra Hall, and the money received from these sources was a welcome addition to our Building Fund. It was expressly provided, however, that The Orchestral Association may increase the height of the hall with additional stories, on refunding the money paid by the Standard Office Company and the Pullman Company.

TWENTY-FIRST PROGRAM, MARCH 24 AND 25
SOLOIST: ERNEST SCHELLING

Concerto for Pianoforte, A Minor, Opus 54, . . . *Schumann*

After the Friday concert the Executive Committee held a conference with Mr. Stock in Mr. Burnham's office. Mr. Fay, as spokesman, asked Mr. Stock if he would give the Committee time to go abroad and secure either Mottl,* Weingartner or Richter as Conductor of the Orchestra. "If we cannot secure any one of these three men," continued Mr. Fay, "you, Mr. Stock, shall be Conductor." To this proposition Mr. Stock graciously assented. Thus the question of Conductor was satisfactorily arranged for the present.

TWENTY-THIRD PROGRAM, APRIL 7 AND 8
SOLOIST: IGNACE J. PADEREWSKI

Concerto for Pianoforte No. 2, F Minor, Opus 21, . . *Chopin*

Mr. Stock's symphonic poem, "Eines Menschenlebens Morgen, Mittag und Abend," dedicated to "Theodore Thomas and the Members of the Chicago Orchestra," was given its first performance at these concerts.

The Executive Committee met on Friday afternoon, April 7, for the first time in its new offices in Orchestra Hall. It was then voted that the concerts of the Fifteenth Season should begin October 21 and 22.

"April 11, Tuesday: Meeting of Trustees at 4 P. M. Frederick Stock unanimously elected Conductor. Trustees voted that the Orchestra should now be known as 'The Theodore Thomas Orchestra.'"

During the ten years Mr. Stock had been with the Orchestra, first as viola player, later as Assistant Conductor, he had shown himself to be a thorough musician, a composer of unusual attainments, and as a Conductor,

---

*Mottl had already declined Mr. Fay's offer, as we have seen, so there was little chance of securing him.

Fourteenth Season—1904-1905

the logical successor to Theodore Thomas. After careful consideration of the various foreign conductors, the Executive Committee was unanimous in recommending to the Trustees the election of Frederick Stock.

"April 12, Wednesday: All the daily papers heartily endorse the election of Frederick Stock as Conductor, and approve the change in name of the Orchestra."

TWENTY-FOURTH, AND LAST, PROGRAM, APRIL 14 AND 15

Mr. Stock received great applause as he came to the Conductor's stand.

Prelude, Chorale and Fugue, ... Bach
  (Transcribed for Orchestra, and the Chorale added, by J. J. ABERT)
Overture, "Leonore," No. 3, ... Beethoven
Symphony No. 4, E Minor, Opus 98, ... Brahms

INTERMISSION

Bacchanale from "Tannhäuser," . . . . Wagner
"Tristan and Isolde," Prelude and Isolde's Love-
  Death, ... Wagner
Kaisermarsch, ... Wagner

The Trustees made a ruling on the subject of encores, which appeared in the program book of the week:

"No orchestral number will be repeated except at a 'Popular' concert; soloists who appear but once will be given time for a single encore."

Two extra concerts were given in Holy Week, April 21 and 22, Friday and Saturday, under Mr. Stock's direction. The important numbers on Friday afternoon (Good Friday) were: The incidental music and funeral march from "Grania and Diarmid" (Elgar), Schubert's "Unfinished" symphony and Strauss' "Death and Transfiguration."

The program on Saturday evening contained popular selections which delighted the people: "Serenade," Opus 48 (Tschaikowsky), Hungarian Rhapsody No. 1 (Liszt), the "Scène Religieuse" (Massenet), ('cello obbligato by Bruno Steindel) and Mendelssohn's "Spring Song."

Two concerts with Wilhelm Middelschulte, soloist, dedicating the Lyon & Healy organ in Orchestra Hall, were given under Mr. Stock's direction, Thursday evening, April 27, and Friday afternoon, April 28. Mr. Middelschulte played on Thursday evening two numbers with Orchestra, Handel's concerto No. 1 and Saint-Saëns' fantasie, Opus 101, in D flat major; on Friday afternoon the Rheinberger concerto, Opus 137, and Thiele's "Theme, Variations and Finale" in A flat major.

FOURTEENTH SEASON
(1904-1905)
SOLOISTS

FLUTE: Alfred Quensel.
HARP: Enrico Tramonti.
HORN: Leopold de Maré.
OBOE: Alfred Barthel.
PIANOFORTE: Mrs. Fannie Bloomfield Zeisler; Eugéne d'Albert, Vladimir de Pachmann, Ignace J. Paderewski, Ernest Schelling.
VIOLA: Franz Esser.
VIOLIN: Ludwig Becker, Leopold Kramer, Fritz Kreisler, Charles Moerenhout, Emile Sauret.
VIOLONCELLO: Bruno Steindel.
VOCAL: Miss Muriel Foster, Mme. Louise Homer.

FIFTEENTH SEASON
(1905-1906)

Death of Arthur Orr, a sincere friend of the Orchestra—A gift of $15,000 from Daniel H. Burnham & Co. to The Orchestral Association, and one of $25,000 from Mrs. James M. Walker—Two friends of the Orchestra pass away, Marshall Field and President William R. Harper—Mr. Stock elected Conductor for three years—Extra concerts—First performance in Chicago of Elgar's "Apostles" by the Apollo Musical Club.

Arthur Orr, a member of our Board of Trustees and a strong friend of the Orchestra, died June 1, at Pasadena, California, where he had spent the winter in consequence of ill health. Mr. Orr came into the life of the Orchestra when the need for a new hall was first considered, and through his own generous contribution was a strong factor in the campaign for the Building Fund. The funeral services were held on Wednesday morning, June 7, from his late residence in Evanston, the brass choir of the Orchestra, under the direction of Frederick Stock, taking part.

The Trustees met on August 15, and arranged for a loan of $330,000 from Quincy A. Shaw of Boston, at four per cent per annum, to be secured on Orchestra Hall, land and building, to replace the loan carried at the bank.

A generous gift now came from the architects, Daniel H. Burnham & Company, a receipt in full of their fees of $15,000 for preparing plans, letting contracts and superintending the construction of Orchestra Hall and Building. This was in addition to the $10,000 given by Mr. Burnham personally.

All doubts the Trustees held regarding the success of the First Season in the new hall vanished with the close of the season ticket sale, the largest in the history of the Orchestra, and with the enthusiasm of the people at the first concerts, October 21 and 22.

I find this note on the Friday concert:

"Lovely day and a delightful program, so well played; house sold out; great enthusiasm over Stock, the man of the hour."

Suite No. 3, D Major, ... Bach
Symphony No. 5, C Minor, Opus 67, ... Beethoven
INTERMISSION
Tone Poem, "Don Juan," Opus 20, ... Strauss
Siegfried Idyl, ... Wagner
Symphonic Poem No. 3, "Les Préludes," . . . . . Liszt

FOURTH PROGRAM, NOVEMBER 10 AND 11
Soloist: David Bispham*

Songs:
"Hymnus," Opus 33, No. 3, . . . } . Richard Strauss
"Pilger's Morgenlied," Opus 33, No. 4, }
"Das Hexenlied" (Ballad for Recitation, with
   Orchestral Accompaniment), ... Schillings

At the concerts of December 1 and 2 an interesting work by one of our Chicago composers was heard: Grande Valse de Concert, by Duvivier.†

The Annual Meeting of the Association was held Wednesday afternoon, December 13, in Room 410 Orchestra Building, with an attendance of thirty-five Members in person or by proxy.

Trustees were elected for the ensuing year, Frederic A. Delano taking the place made vacant by the death of Arthur Orr.

Henry E. Voegeli was appointed Assistant Manager and Assistant Treasurer.

A gift of $25,000 from Mrs. Elia M. Walker‡ was accepted by the Association in accordance with the terms of a resolution adopted by the Executive Committee, December 8:

"That the President and Secretary are authorized to execute an agreement between The Orchestral Association and Mrs. Elia M.Walker, in which Mrs. Walker agrees to assign to the Association twenty-five thousand dollars ($25,000) of the claim allowed in her favor in the estate of Wirt D. Walker in the Probate Court of Cook County, together with interest to accrue on said sum from the first day of January, A. D. 1906, and in which agreement the Orchestral Association agrees to pay to Mrs. Elia M. Walker, or to her order, twelve hundred and fifty dollars ($1,250) in each year

---

*David Bispham died October 2, 1921, at his home in New York. A short time before his death he brought out an entertaining work on his artistic career, entitled "A Quaker Singer's Recollections." Mr. Bispham was born January 5, 1857, in Philadelphia.

†A. Devin Duvivier, a teacher of voice and theory in Chicago since 1892, was a picturesque figure in our musical life. In his youth he was a fellow-student at the Conservatoire in Paris with Saint-Saëns, Bizet and Massenet, and before coming to America had been (1887) a member of the Royal Academy of Music in London. His "Triumph of Bacchus" was played at the concerts of February 24 and 25, 1893, under his direction; at the concerts of March 2 and 3, 1900, he conducted the second and third movements from his "Dramatic Symphony." Mr. Duvivier died a few years later in Chicago.

‡Mrs. Walker died April 19, 1916.

Fifteenth Season—1905-1906

during her natural life, to date from the first day of January, A. D. 1906, to be payable to her in equal semi-annual installments."

The report of the Treasurer, Frederick J. Wessels, for the Fourteenth Season (1904-1905), ending June 30, 1905, showed:

Receipts		Expenses	
Chicago concerts	$ 98,789.75	Salaries of Conductor and Orchestra	$102,925.00
Out-of-town concerts	3,815.67	Business management and office expense	9,473.56
From Apollo Musical Club and other engagements	6,909.88	Auditorium rent, six weeks	4,800.00
Building rentals (net income, two months)	1,332.06	Soloists	6,250.00
Miscellaneous earnings	2,910.71	Advertising and other expenses	5,395.62
Deficit	15,086.11		
	$128,844.18		$128,844.18

BUILDING ACCOUNT

Receipts		Expenditures	
Subscriptions	$569,707.37	Cost of land	$450,000.00
Architects' fees (donated)	15,000.00	Cost of building	396,139.07
Interest on bank deposits	2,716.80	Cost of carrying charges	51,619.57
Dedicatory concert	3,851.00	Cost of organ on account	16,035.19
From loan at bank	330,000.00	Cost of electric fixtures and decorations	17,019.66
Balance needed to meet expenditures on land and building	23,911.90	Transferred to operating account	14,373.58
	$945,187.07		$945,187.07

The Executive Committee, in its report for the Fourteenth Season, stated:

"It is now happily evident that the Orchestra has passed, almost without a tremor, through the most dangerous crisis of its history. Had the death of Theodore Thomas occurred while it was a chronic though deserving mendicant, his Orchestra would by this time, in all probability, have become a beautiful but bitter memory. As it is, the hall for which he so long and ardently hoped, and whose value his ripe experience foretold, has proved to be the solid foundation of a great and permanent institution.

"Theodore Thomas' Musical Library has been presented to the Association by his wife and children, and is now being catalogued and placed in permanent order in these rooms. It contains the accumulation of his forty years of conductorship, and includes both scores and parts for an Orchestra of from 85 to 300 men, of literally every orchestral composition worthy of the name.

"It gives us sincere pleasure here to refer to a new and important extension of Musical Art in Chicago, made possible by the completion of our building, namely, the series of Chamber Concerts lately inaugurated, under the auspices of the Chicago Chamber Music Society, organized by Mrs. J. J. Glessner, Mrs. F. S. Johnson and Mrs. Theodore Thomas, and given in the foyer of the new hall. The first concert took place early in December, Messrs. Kramer, Becker, Esser, Steindel and Brueckner rendering the program, and it proved to be a complete success. The ladies of the Society have covered all expenses, including a moderate rent for the foyer, for a period of three years, by a season subscription and guarantee, and it now seems probable that this series of Chamber Concerts will become a permanent fixture for the future.

"Respectfully submitted for the Trustees,
BRYAN LATHROP.
DANIEL H. BURNHAM.
C. NORMAN FAY.
PHILO A. OTIS.
MAX BAIRD."

IN MEMORY OF THEODORE THOMAS
Born October 11, 1835
Died January 4, 1905

Twelfth Program: Friday afternoon, January 5, 1906
Saturday evening, January 6, 1906

Passacaglia and Fugue, C Minor, for Organ, . . Bach
   WILHELM MIDDELSCHULTE
Chorale, ... Abert
Symphony No. 3, "Eroica," E Flat, Opus 55, . Beethoven

INTERMISSION

"An Weber's Grabe," . . . . Wagner
Siegfried's Death Music, from "Die
   Götterdämmerung," . . . . Wagner
Tone Poem, "Death and Transfiguration,". . Strauss

Mme. Kirkby Lunn was the soloist at the concerts of January 12 and 13, Thirteenth Program":
Aria, "Divinités du Styx," from "Alceste," . . . . . Gluck
Sea Pictures, Opus 37, ... Elgar

Early in 1906 the Association lost by death two devoted friends: January 10, the Rev. William R.

Harper,* D.D., LL.D., President of the University of Chicago, and a member of the Board of Trustees of The Orchestral Association; January 16, at the Holland House in New York City, Marshall Field, a generous contributor to the Guarantee Fund of the Orchestra from its organization in 1891, and to the building of Orchestra Hall. A Memorial Service for Mr. Field was held in the Auditorium after the concert on Friday afternoon, January 19, conducted by the Rev. John Archibald Morison, D.D., minister of the First Presbyterian Church, and the Rev. William R. Notman, D.D., minister of the Fourth Presbyterian Church. The Orchestra, under the direction of Frederick Stock, played during the service:

Symphony No. 3, "Eroica," E Flat, Opus 55, . . *Beethoven*
(Two Movements)
"Death and Transfiguration," . . . . *Strauss*

The Trustees met on Friday, February 2, after the concert, and elected Chauncey Keep to fill the vacancy caused by the death of Dr. Harper. Mr. Stock was re-elected Conductor for a period of three years from July 1, 1906. Watson F. Blair and Charles H. Swift were elected Members of the Association to fill vacancies caused by the death of Arthur Orr and Dr. Harper. The Trustees passed this resolution:

"That the name of the hall to be placed on tickets, circulars, programs, advertisements, lettering on doors and windows, all forms of advertising and all printed matter shall be Orchestra Hall, and the name Theodore Thomas Orchestra Hall shall be used only in legal forms and documents."

A Memorial Concert for President William Rainey Harper was given by the Orchestra, under the direction of Frederick Stock, Tuesday evening, February 6, in Leon Mandel Assembly Hall, at the University of Chicago:

Chorale, ... *Bach—Abert*
Symphony No. 3 in E Flat, "Eroica," Opus 55, . . *Beethoven*
Marche Funèbre, ... *Chopin*

*William Rainey Harper was born July 26, 1856, in New Concord, Ohio; graduated (1870) from Muskingum College, near Zanesville, Ohio, going thence to Yale College, graduating in 1875; began his work July 1, 1891, as President of the University of Chicago; elected March 3, 1903, member of the Board of Trustees of The Orchestral Association. Dr. Harper once told me that his interest in orchestral music dated from early life, when he played second trombone in a theatre in Akron, Ohio: "I was undecided then whether to continue playing second trombone or go to Yale College and study theology."

Mme. Johanna Gadski was the soloist at the Twenty-fourth, and last, Program of the season, March 30 and 31:

Overture, "Oberon,"	Weber
Scene and Aria, "Ocean, Thou Mighty Monster" ("Oberon"), ...	Weber
Symphony No. 7, A Major, Opus 92, ...	Beethoven

INTERMISSION

Tone Poem, "Thus Spake Zarathustra,"	Strauss
Closing Scene from "Die Götterdämmerung," . . .	Wagner

Brünnhilde: MME. GADSKI

After the close of the regular season a series of extra concerts, with popular programs at popular prices, was given by the Orchestra, under Mr. Stock's direction, every Friday afternoon and Saturday evening through April. The concerts, covering a period of four weeks, were undertaken for the purpose of relieving the Conductor and Orchestra from the fatigue and discomforts of the "wearisome traveling."

Friday afternoon, April 6, Miss Zudie Harris (piano), soloist.

Saturday evening, April 7, Miss Lois Adler (piano), soloist.

Friday afternoon, April 13, Miss Marie Nichols (violin), soloist.

Saturday evening, April 14, Howard Wells (piano), soloist.

Friday afternoon, April 20, Mrs. Mabel Sharp Herdien (soprano) and Brahm Van der Burg (piano), soloists.

Saturday evening, April 21, the Musical Art Society (mixed voices), Clarence Dickinson, Conductor.

Friday afternoon, April 27, Mrs. Charlotte de Muth Williams (violin) and Glenn Hall (tenor), soloists.

Saturday evening, April 28, Wilhelm Middelschulte (organ), soloist.

The Apollo Musical Club closed its season Monday evening, April 23, with the performance, in the Auditorium, of Sir Edward Elgar's "Apostles," under the direction of Harrison M. Wild. Soloists: Mrs. Lillian French Read (soprano), Miss Janet Spencer (contralto), Glenn Hall (tenor), William W. Hinshaw (baritone), Marion Green (baritone) and Frank Croxton (bass);

Arthur Dunham (organist), and the Theodore Thomas Orchestra.

I heard the first performance of "The Apostles" under the direction of the composer, at the Birmingham Festival, October 14, 1903. The concert was given in the Town Hall, seating 1,700 people. Sir Edward had a choir of 350 and a band of 125, with Madame Albani, Miss Muriel Foster, John Coates, Kennerley Rumford, D. Ffrangcon Davis and Andrew Black, soloists. I find this note on the performance: "The work is on modern lines, but too mystic, *spirituelle* and dreamy for lasting results."

For the first time in the history of the May Festivals at Cincinnati the Theodore Thomas Orchestra did not take part in the Seventeenth Festival (1906). That honor was reserved for the Cincinnati Symphony Orchestra, whose Conductor, Frank Van der Stucken, became Musical Director of the Festivals on the death (1905) of Theodore Thomas.

FIFTEENTH SEASON
(1905-1906)

SOLOISTS

HARP: Enrico Tramonti.
ORGAN: Wilhelm Middelschulte.
PIANOFORTE: Miss Adele aus der Ohe; Rudolph Ganz, Waldemar Lütschg, Raoul Pugno, Alfred Reisenauer, Arthur Rubinstein.
READER: David Bispham.
VIOLIN: Ludwig Becker, Hugo Heermann, Leopold Kramer.
VIOLONCELLO: Robert Ambrosius, Bruno Steindel.
VOCAL: Mmes. Johanna Gadski, Louise Homer, Kirkby Lunn; David Bispham, Charles W. Clark, George Hamlin.

SIXTEENTH SEASON
(1906-1907)

Mr. Stock's early impressions of Theodore Thomas and the Orchestra —The out-of-town concerts under Mr. Wessels' management bring "peace and comfort" to the Conductor—A series of evening concerts at Mandel Hall and Ravinia Park—Four Thursday afternoon concerts in Orchestra Hall with noted soloists: Mme. Louise Homer, Saint-Saëns, Mmes. Schumann-Heink and Johanna Gadski—Mrs. Thomas Nelson Page establishes the Henry Field Memorial Fund—Sir Edward Elgar, Visiting Conductor—Festival Tour of the Orchestra.

During vacation days in 1906 Mr. Stock wrote his early impressions of Mr. Thomas and the Orchestra:

"I came to America in 1895, to join the Chicago Orchestra under Mr. Thomas. My recollections carry me back to the summer of the same year, 1895, when, on a pleasure trip to Europe, Mr. Thomas and his business representative, Mr. Henry Sachleben, happened to visit Cologne, where I was at that time one of the first violins in the Municipal Orchestra.

"I called on Mr. Thomas at his hotel and asked permission to play for him, which was granted. Thomas seemed pleased, and when I told him it was the ambition of my life to become a member of his Orchestra, he advised me to leave Europe and come to America, and that he would find a place for me in his Orchestra.

"I sailed for New York the end of September, 1895, arrived in Chicago the beginning of October, and again met Mr. Thomas at the first rehearsal of that season.

"I still have a very vivid impression of this, my first rehearsal under Thomas at the Auditorium Theatre, with the regular scenery set on the big stage for the concerts, as they used to be in those days. This was an interesting occasion. The magnificent Auditorium with its absolutely perfect acoustics, which made music 'sound' apparently without the least effort; the wonderful quality of tone produced by the finest Orchestra I had heard up to that time; Thomas' genial and forceful personality, the great skill of his leadership, shown in his attention to detail and in the ingenious manner with which he gained results and obtained desired artistic effects—all this was new and most interesting to me.

"I could notice from the beginning that as a leader Thomas had very distinctive qualities and characteristics, and that he was a man from whom I could learn a great deal. He was not only a great Conductor, a leader of musicians, but a born leader among men, a personality of great dynamic force, unlimited energy, and fine executive ability. He was far-seeing and sagacious, very human and idealistic, a man to whom it had been given to deliver a great message.   FREDERICK A. STOCK."

Sixteenth Season—1906-1907

The returns from the out-of-town concerts are ordinarily sufficient to meet salaries, traveling and local expenses; possibly a little more. In the early seasons, when we had a strong guarantee at home and the Trustees wished to exploit the Orchestra abroad, some chances were assumed in the out-of-town business. Many dates were made on the percentage plan of traveling theatrical companies, twenty per cent of the receipts to the local manager, and the balance to the "visiting attraction" (in the language of "stage folk"), a plan which does not always bring satisfaction to the "attraction." In recent years our Manager, Frederick J. Wessels, has worked up annual tours through the east and west, under contracts with ladies' clubs or responsible local committees, which have yielded profit; the only risks being railway accidents or delays, and the fatigue of travel for Conductor and men.

Mrs. Thomas, in her "Memoirs," says of Mr. Wessels:

"After this able assistant and good friend became the practical Business Manager of the Orchestra Mr. Thomas had such peace and comfort in his professional life as he had never known before, and even traveling engagements were robbed of much of their terror by the thought and care with which Mr. Wessels planned and carried out the details of the work."

Before the close of the Fifteenth Season the Trustees, in order to shorten the period of the out-of-town concerts, voted to lengthen the Chicago season from twenty-four to twenty-eight weeks, with a corresponding increase in prices: boxes from $500 to $600 and an addition of $1 to $5 on season tickets. The people were delighted with the prospect of four weeks more of the music they had learned to love, and responded with an advance sale of season tickets which reached the sum of $75,000 on September 15, the opening day of the sale, increasing to $79,000 before the concerts began; the increase due partly to the longer season and correspondingly higher prices for tickets.

Enthusiastic audiences assembled for the first concerts, October 12 and 13, to greet Mr. Stock and his men after vacation days:

Overture, "Euryanthe," . . . . *Weber*
Symphony No. 3, E Flat, "Eroica," Opus 55, . . *Beethoven*

INTERMISSION

Tone Poem, "Macbeth," . . . . *Strauss*
Vorspiel, "Die Meistersinger," . . . . *Wagner*

The Mandel Hall (University of Chicago) Concerts, inaugurated in the previous season under the direction of Mr. Stock, were continued during the season of 1906-1907:

October 23, November 20, with Mrs. Birdice Blye Richardson (piano), soloist.

December 18, January 22, 1907, with Miss Augusta Cottlow (piano), soloist.

March 5 and 26.

The Mandel Hall Concerts have been continued to the present date (1924) with liberal support by the people at the University and in the community.

A similar series of Tuesday Evening Concerts was started in the season of 1906-1907 at Ravinia Park Theatre: November 6, December 11, assisted by the Evanston Musical Society, Dean P. C. Lutkin, Conductor; January 11, 1907, January 29, March 12 and April 9.

The Ravinia Park Winter Concerts resulted in a loss, and were discontinued at the close of the season, owing to the distance of the theatre from the city and the lack of interest shown by the people in the vicinity of the Park.

From the opening of Orchestra Hall the demand for tickets at the Friday concerts had far exceeded the capacity of the hall. Early in October the Trustees announced four Thursday afternoon concerts with noted soloists, hoping that these extra concerts would meet the overflow from the Friday concerts and prove equally attractive.

The first concert of the series on Thursday afternoon, November 1, with Mme. Louise Homer, soloist, yielded only $453.

Camille Saint-Saëns was the soloist at the second concert, November 8, and at the regular concerts on Friday and Saturday of that week. He had been announced to play one of his organ works and conduct an orchestral number on Thursday and play his concerto for pianoforte in G minor, No. 2, on Friday and Saturday. Saint-Saëns arrived in Chicago Wednesday morning, far from well, and too ill to undertake all the works in which he was announced to appear. By the advice of his physician the organ selection was abandoned, and the orchestral works were conducted by Mr. Stock. Our

Sixteenth Season—1906-1907

distinguished visitor appeared, however, at each concert as a piano soloist, playing two numbers with Orchestra—his Fantasia "Africa," and Waltz Caprice, "Wedding Cake," on Thursday, and the concerto in G minor on Friday and Saturday. He received a tremendous ovation from Orchestra and audience when he appeared on the stage, an affectionate tribute from the American people to the illustrious Frenchman, for half a century one of the foremost artist-composers in Europe. The work of the veteran artist at the piano was of the highest order, playing with brilliancy, perfect ease and authority, showing that at seventy-two the age limit had no terrors for him,

The ticket sales ($1,650) did not represent half the house, and of this amount only $663 came to us. The attendance at the two "Extra Concerts" was so discouraging that the Trustees issued a statement to the public, November 10, regarding the remaining "Extra Concerts":

"These extra concerts are primarily intended for 'occasional' concert-goers, entertainment seekers rather than music lovers such as come week after week to the regular concerts. They are meant to provide for that overflow audience which occasionally (five or six times a year), added to the regular audience, used to tax the capacity of the Auditorium, and which is now shut out by the reduced capacity of the present hall. They are given in the afternoon rather than the evening because large numbers of applicants are turned away from the Friday matinées every week, while there are often vacant seats at the Saturday evening performances of the same program.

"They will be given only when especially eminent soloists engaged for concerts of the regular series can be engaged for an extra performance.

"Though popular in character, they will not be cheap in any sense of the word, the Theodore Thomas Orchestra knowing but one standard of performance—the best. The box office prices will be such as the cost of the soloists and the necessary advertising may dictate."

There were larger audiences at the remaining Thursday concerts, due rather to the attractive soloists than to any influence the letter of the Trustees had on the "occasional" concert-goers. Mme. Schumann-Heink delighted the people at the concert on Thursday, November 15, her numbers being the recitative and aria from Mozart's "La Clemenza di Tito," with clarinet obbligato by Joseph Schreurs, and two songs by Schubert, "The Young Nun" and "The Omnipotence." Mr. Stock's instrumentation of "The Omnipotence" was quite modern and picturesque, and especially effective in the use of the brasses. The box office receipts ($1,505) indicated more interest on the part of the general public.

Mme. Schumann-Heink appeared in the same selections at the regular Friday and Saturday concerts of the week, bringing out a large audience on Saturday evening.

The last of the Thursday concerts was given on November 29, Thanksgiving Day, with Mme. Johanna Gadski, soloist, who brought out the music lovers, with $2,043 in receipts. Mme. Gadski appeared in a program which included interesting numbers by the Orchestra in addition to her own:

Prelude, "The Deluge,". . . . . *Saint-Saëns*
    Violin Obbligato by Leopold Kramer
Scène Religieuse, from "Les Erinnyes," . . . . . *Massenet*
    Violoncello Obbligato by Bruno Steindel
Songs:
    "Gretchen at the Wheel," . . . . . . *Schubert*
    "Dreams," . . . . *Wagner*
Aria, "Dich theure Halle," from "Tannhäuser," . . *Wagner*

Mme. Gadski was the soloist at the regular Friday and Saturday concerts of the week of November 30 and December 1, Eighth Program, appearing in an aria from "Der Freischütz" (Weber) and "Isolde's Love-Death" (Wagner).

The Annual Meeting was held Tuesday afternoon, December 11, in the offices of the Association in Orchestra Building. Frederick J. Wessels presented his report as Treasurer for the Fifteenth Season (1905-1906), ending June 30, 1906:

Receipts		Expenses	
Chicago concerts	$ 93,498.75	Salaries of Conductor, Orchestra and expenses	$ 91,984.00
Extra four weeks (net)	4,069.00	Soloists	5,500.00
Mandel Hall, Apollo Club and other engagements	10,243.72	Business management	9,776.04
Hall rentals	21,638.42	Interest	11,568.27
Building rentals	24,098.15	Taxes	10,533.73
Program book, etc.	2,774.33	Advertising and musical instruments	3,498.96
Loss on season	917.82	Hall and building expenses	24,379.19
	$157,240.19		$157,240.19

The entire loss (including accounts charged off), $1,064.43, was paid by a generous subscription of $2,000 from one of our Members, O. W. Norton, leaving a balance of $936.57 in the hands of the Treasurer.

The Orchestra assisted the Apollo Musical Club in two performances of "The Messiah," Tuesday evening, December 25 (Christmas Day), and Wednesday evening, December 26, in the Auditorium, under the direction of Harrison M. Wild. Soloists: Mrs. Genevieve C. Wilson (soprano), Miss Christine Miller (contralto), John B. Miller (tenor) and William Harper (bass); Arthur Dunham (organist).

THIRTEENTH PROGRAM, JANUARY 4 AND 5
THEODORE THOMAS MEMORIAL
Soloist: Wilhelm Middelschulte

Overture to "Iphigénie en Aulide," . . . . . . *Gluck*
Organ Solo, Prelude and Fugue, E Minor, ... *Bach*
Andante con Variazioni, from the "Kreutzer" Sonata,
    Opus 47, ... *Beethoven*
        (Orchestration by Theodore Thomas)
"Träume" (A Study for "Tristan and Isolde"), . . . *Wagner*
        (Orchestration by Theodore Thomas)
Entrance of the Gods into Walhalla, from "Das Rheingold," *Wagner*

INTERMISSION

Tone Poem, "Ein Heldenleben," Opus 40, ... *Strauss*

FOURTEENTH PROGRAM, JANUARY 11 AND 12
Soloist: Moriz Rosenthal

Concerto for Pianoforte No. 1, B Minor, Opus 11, . . *Chopin*

"Eighteenth Program, February 8 and 9 (Wagner): Alois Burgstaller gave a vigorous interpretation of Lohengrin's 'Narrative' and Siegmund's 'Love Song' (Walküre); house sold out on Saturday night."

"Nineteenth Program, February 15 and 16: Horace Britt (violoncello), soloist; Saint-Saëns' concerto in A minor, Opus 33. Mr. Britt is a native of Antwerp; studied in Paris, and as a member of the Lamoureux Orchestra played Saint-Saëns' work under the direction of the composer."

Mr. Britt became a member of the Orchestra just before the opening of Orchestra Hall; his playing of Saint-Saëns' work was the feature of the concert this week. He left Chicago at the close of the season to become a member of the Philadelphia Symphony Orchestra.

The attendance at the "Extra Concerts" in November was not encouraging. The Trustees accordingly announced another concert, hoping for better results:

"February 21, Thursday afternoon: Mrs. Fannie Bloomfield Zeisler, soloist, playing Moszkowski's concerto for pianoforte in E major. The concerto was repeated at the Friday and Saturday concerts of the week."

"Twenty-fourth Program, March 22 and 23: Ossip Gabrilowitsch, soloist; Tschaikowsky's concerto for pianoforte in B flat minor, No. 1. The greatest performance of the work ever heard at these concerts. Mr. Gabrilowitsch played like a Cossack, showing his Slavic temperament, doing unexpected things, but always achieving artistic results.

"After the intermission came the Mahler Symphony No. 5, in C sharp minor, called by some writers the 'Giant Symphony'; a local critic called it the 'Ugly Symphony,' and expressed the hope that it might never be heard again at these concerts. Mr. Stock and the Orchestra (increased to one hundred men, including eight horns and an unusual assortment of percussion instruments) gave the work a brilliant interpretation."

During the week of March 22 The Orchestral Association received a generous gift of $50,000 from Mrs. Thomas Nelson Page*, widow of Henry Field, now the wife of Thomas Nelson Page, the novelist, and sister of Bryan Lathrop, for the foundation of the "Henry Field Memorial Fund." Mrs. Page had been a sincere and generous friend of the Association for many years, having paid $13,000 to the support of the Orchestra as a subscriber to the Guarantee Fund and contributed $18,000 to the building of Orchestra Hall.

The Trustees met on Friday, March 22, and adopted this resolution:

"In gratefully accepting the splendid endowment of $50,000 given by Mrs. Thomas Nelson Page of Washington, formerly Mrs. Henry Field of Chicago, to The Orchestral Association, and by her dedicated to its uses in the promotion of musical art, as 'The Henry Field Memorial Fund,' the Trustees desire the honor of placing on record their sense of the great fitness of such a memorial to so genuine and spontaneous a lover of good art as Henry Field ever was.

---

*Mrs. Thomas Nelson Page died June 6, 1921, at Southboro, Massachusetts.

FLORENCE LATHROP PAGE

"Also, with the keenest satisfaction and encouragement they note Mrs. Page's affectionate loyalty to her old home and the Theodore Thomas Orchestra, of which she has been a continuous supporter ever since it came to Chicago, though herself for long years resident of another city. They feel that under the circumstances this great gift, the first of its kind which they are able to announce, will have double value as a suggestion and stimulus to the generosity of other friends of this great institution; and they tender to Mrs. Page, on behalf of the Association and of all lovers of good art, their sincerest respect and most cordial thanks."

The Twenty-sixth Program (compositions by living writers), April 5 and 6, brought us the presence of Sir Edward Elgar, the greatest living British composer. The selections in the second part of the program were played under his direction:

Overture, "In the South" (Alassio), Opus 50, . . . ⎫
Variations, Opus 36, ... ⎬ *Elgar*
Military March, "Pomp and Circumstance," Opus 39, No. 1, ... ⎭

Sir Edward Elgar indicated to the members of the Orchestra, at the close of the rehearsal on Thursday morning, his thorough appreciation of their work:

"Gentlemen:

"I have never been in Japan or South Africa. Maybe they have better orchestras there, but in Europe they have none better than the Theodore Thomas Orchestra. I have never heard my works played so well."

TWENTY-EIGHTH, AND LAST, PROGRAM, APRIL 19 AND 20

Soloist: Hugo Heermann

Overture, "Im Frühling," Opus 36, ... *Goldmark*
"Elégie" and "Walzer," from Serenade, Opus 48, . *Tschaikowsky*
   String Orchestra
Concerto for Violin, D Minor, Opus 8, ... *Strauss*

INTERMISSION

March, "Marocaine," . . . . *Berlioz*
"Scène Religieuse," from Suite, "Les Erinnyes,"
   Opus 10, ... *Massenet*
   Violoncello Obbligato by Bruno Steindel
Spring Song, ... *Mendelssohn*
Valse de Concert No. 1, Opus 47, ... *Glazounow*
Overture to "Tannhäuser," . . . . *Wagner*

It has not been the purpose of this work to note all the concerts given by the Orchestra in each season; time and space would not permit, nor would my readers be interested in so many details; but I must now make an exception, and speak of the "Festival Tour" arranged by our Manager, Frederick J. Wessels, at the close of the season. This tour, coming after the Chicago season, had no support from the Trustees, and was entirely the venture of Mr. Wessels. Fortunately the concerts met the approval of the people and were well attended. Mr. Wessels was accompanied by sixty members of the Orchestra, Frederick Stock, Conductor, and a quartet of soloists—Mrs. Corinne Rider-Kelsey, Miss Janet Spencer, Edward Johnson and Herbert Witherspoon. A few details of the tour may be noted:

"May 16, 17 and 18 at Mount Vernon, Iowa, with the Cornell College Oratorio Society, George L. Pierce, Director. Thursday afternoon, May 16, piano recital by Rudolph Ganz. Friday evening, May 17, Grieg's 'Olaf Trygvason.' Saturday evening, May 18, Brahms' 'Requiem,' Wilhelm Middelschulte, organist.

"May 20 and 21 at Mitchell, South Dakota, with the Dakota Wesleyan Choir, E. W. Hobson, Conductor. Monday evening, May 20, and Tuesday afternoon, May 21, for soloists and Orchestra. Tuesday evening, May 21, Handel's 'Messiah.'

"May 22 and 23, second May Festival at Lincoln, Nebraska. Wednesday evening, May 22, Bruch's 'Fair Ellen' and miscellaneous program for soloists and Orchestra. Thursday evening, May 23, S. Coleridge-Taylor's 'Hiawatha's Wedding Feast' and miscellaneous program for soloists and Orchestra.

"May 24 and 25, with the State Normal School at Cedar Falls, Iowa. Friday evening, May 24, for soloists and Orchestra. Saturday afternoon, May 25, Howard Wells (piano) and Bruno Steindel ('cello), soloists with Orchestra. Saturday evening, May 25, Handel's 'Messiah,' C. A. Fullerton, Conductor."

The "Festival Tour" was then continued in Indiana, which brought me down from Chicago to Indianapolis, Monday, May 27, to hear the remaining concerts. The concert on Monday evening for soloists and Orchestra was held in the hall of the High School, a commodious room seating 1,500 people, and filled on this occasion. We stopped at the Claypool House, and after the concert Mr. Stock, soloists, Mr. and Mrs. Wessels, Mr. and Mrs. Voegeli and guests were entertained at supper by Mrs. Kelsey and Miss Spencer. One might call it "a family

MESSRS. WESSELS, STOCK AND OTIS
Taken on "Festival Tour"

Sixteenth Season—1906-1907

party," all the members having traveled and worked together so long and pleasantly with the Orchestra.

The next morning, Tuesday, we were up betimes for an early breakfast, and at eight o'clock Conductor Stock, Orchestra, soloists and other members of "the family party" boarded the train for Richmond, a ride of two hours, to assist in the May Festival in that city. In the afternoon there was a rehearsal in the Coliseum, to which the children of the public schools in Indianapolis were admitted, and it was a real pleasure to watch the little folks and note their enjoyment of the music. The important work at the concert in the evening was "The Swan and Skylark," by Arthur Goring Thomas, in which the Richmond chorus did credit to itself and its Director, Will Earhart. The rest of the program belonged to Mr. Stock, soloists and Orchestra.

With the afternoon concert on Wednesday, May 29, at which Louis Elbel played Rubinstein's concerto in D minor for pianoforte, and the performance of the Brahms "Requiem" in the evening under the direction of Mr. Earhart, the "Festival Tour" of 1907 came to an end, and the members of "the happy family" returned to their homes.

In September (1907) I was at the Chatham in Paris, and there I met Lawrence Maxwell, Jr., President of the Cincinnati Festival Association. On hearing that I was to return home on the "Kaiserin Augusta Victoria," leaving Cherbourg September 20, Mr. Maxwell said, "I have a letter I wish you would give to Mr. Van der Stucken, who will be on the ship leaving Hamburg." I made a few notes of the trip to New York:

"September 21, Saturday: At sea; on board are Van der Stucken, Conductor of the Cincinnati Orchestra; Leopold Kramer, Alfred Quensel and Curt Baumbach, of our Orchestra, and George E. Adams, Trustee, with his family."

"September 23, Monday: Long talks every day with Kramer and Van der Stucken (to whom I handed Mr. Maxwell's letter) about the last Festival and Cincinnati Orchestra, which may be disbanded after next season; in that event Van der Stucken said he would go to Europe to live. He will conduct the next Festival (1908). Van der Stucken is a poet as well as a composer; he translated the texts of Grieg's songs for New York publishers, and wrote the words of the cantata 'The Shepherd's Vision,' which Horatio Parker set to music."

SIXTEENTH SEASON
(1906-1907)
SOLOISTS

HARP: Enrico Tramonti.
ORGAN: Wilhelm Middelschulte.
PIANOFORTE: Mme. Olga Samaroff, Mrs. Fannie Bloomfield Zeisler; Ossip Gabrilowitsch, Rudolph Ganz, Joseph Lhevinne, Otto Neitzel, Moriz Rosenthal, Camille Saint-Saëns.
VIOLIN: Miss Maud Powell; Ludwig Becker, Hugo Heermann, Leopold Kramer, Francis Macmillen, Alexandre Petschnikoff.
VIOLONCELLO: Horace Britt, Bruno Steindel.
VISITING CONDUCTOR: Sir Edward Elgar.
VOCAL: Mmes. Johanna Gadski, Ernestine Schumann-Heink, Louise Homer; Alois Burgstaller, Herbert Witherspoon.

SEVENTEENTH SEASON
(1907-1908)

The alluring "Spell" of the Friday concerts—Pantomime and pageant for the beginnings of a Pension and Invalid Fund—A gift of $5,000 from Mrs. Marshall Field to The Orchestral Association— The Orchestra visits Toronto for the Annual Concerts of the Mendelssohn Choir—Frank Van der Stucken, Visiting Conductor at the Twenty-fourth Concerts—The Orchestra, with Frederick Stock as Associate Conductor, takes part in the Eighteenth Cincinnati Festival.

All hopes the Trustees had entertained of creating a Thursday afternoon *clientèle* vanished when an account was taken of the receipts from the "Extra Concerts." The "Friday Spell" had too strong a hold on the people to permit of any other afternoon series becoming a rival. It was only with the aid of noted soloists, though their fees absorbed a large part of the receipts, that the "Extra Concerts" were possible. The returns from the first "Extra" barely paid expenses. Music lovers were not interested in Saint-Saëns, the great French composer, nor did they care for Sir Edward Elgar, Visiting Conductor, when he appeared during the previous season.

One of the problems of the Manager's office is the soloist, and the drawing power of the artist. The people know what they want and will have what they want, be it Grand Opera or Thomas Concerts. They will not be treated like "dumb driven cattle," nor have they the slightest intention of becoming "heroes" in "the fight" for the musical uplift of the community. It was the lifelong desire of Theodore Thomas—and he lived to see it fulfilled—to make the program and the Orchestra the attraction of his concerts, without a soloist, whom he often regarded as an interruption.

No further attempt was made with "Extra Concerts" until the Twenty-third Season (1913-1914), when the "Popular Concerts" were resumed, with the co-operation of the City Club and the Civic Music Association.

The season ticket sale of $83,000 indicated an increasing interest on the part of the people in the work of the Orchestra, as was clearly shown by the large audiences at the first concerts, October 11 and 12, in a program which would have had little attraction for concert-goers ten years before:

Suite No. 3, in D Major, ...	Bach
Symphony No. 2, D Major, Opus 36, ...	Beethoven

INTERMISSION

Symphonic Poem (No. 6), "Mazeppa,"	Liszt
"Träume,"	Wagner
(Orchestration by Theodore Thomas)	
Polonaise, Opus 53, ...	Chopin
(Orchestration by Theodore Thomas)	

An annual concert for the benefit of the Presbyterian Hospital had been given in previous seasons, in which the Orchestra appeared, though, for lack of space, no mention of the concerts has been made in these records. The sixth concert for the benefit of the Hospital was given Monday evening, November 4, in Orchestra Hall. On this occasion the Musical Art Society (mixed voices), organized by Clarence Dickinson, made its initial appearance under Mr. Dickinson's direction, assisted by Mme. Olive Fremstad and the Theodore Thomas Orchestra. The Society showed excellent training in its singing of three *a cappella* numbers—"Gloria Patri" (Palestrina), "Alla Trinità" (traditional), "Herr, wie lange" (Georg Schumann)—and the "Chorus of Angels" from "Faust" (Liszt) with Orchestra. Mme. Fremstad contributed three songs by Richard Strauss, and "Isolde's Love-Death" (Wagner). The Orchestra, under Mr. Stock, played the "Academic Festival" overture (Brahms) and the "Scènes de Ballet" (Glazounow).

NINTH PROGRAM, DECEMBER 6 AND 7
SOLOIST: MME. TERESA CARREÑO
Concerto for Pianoforte No. 2, D Minor, Opus 23,   MacDowell

The Annual Meeting was held Tuesday afternoon, December 10, in Room 850 Orchestra Building, for the election of Trustees and officers. The report of the Treasurer for the Sixteenth Season (1906-1907), ending June 30, 1907, was read:

Seventeenth Season—1907-1908

Receipts		Expenses	
Chicago concerts	$109,369.00	Business management	$ 10,892.10
Mandel Hall, Apollo Club, out-of-town, etc.	10,770.25	Advertising	3,975.33
Hall and building rentals	55,361.35	Salaries of Conductor and Orchestra	99,330.39
Interest on Henry Field Fund	1,250.00	Soloists	10,150.00
Other receipts	3,034.79	Taxes	10,258.11
		Interest	14,450.00
		Building, hall and other expenses	28,159.97
		Profit on season	2,569.49
	$179,785.39		$179,785.39

After deducting some accounts and adding profit on former season, this balance was increased to $2,920.06.

TENTH PROGRAM, DECEMBER 13 AND 14
BEETHOVEN ANNIVERSARY
Soloist: Mrs. Corinne Rider-Kelsey

Beethoven Overture,	*Lassen*
Scene and Aria, "Ah! Perfido," Opus 46,	*Beethoven*
Overture, "Leonore," No. 3,	*Beethoven*
INTERMISSION	
Symphony No. 3, "Eroica," E Flat, Opus 55,	*Beethoven*

The Eleventh Program, December 20 and 21, included three attractive numbers:

Pastorale, "Christmas Oratorio,"	*Bach*
Concertstück for Harp and Orchestra, Opus 122,	*Wilm*
Enrico Tramonti	
"Four Character Pieces," Opus 48,	*Arthur Foote*

The *Chicago Tribune* said of Mr. Tramonti:

"If there be anything in the theory of re-incarnation, then surely Enrico Tramonti was in the days agone one of the master bards at some royal court. When he plays the harp we can easily believe the tales we read of the influence exerted by the bards of olden times, who took captive the hearts and spirits of men and maids who heard."

The "Four Character Pieces" are from the pen of one of America's foremost writers, Arthur Foote, who has been heard before at these concerts, but not often in such dainty work as appeared on this program. "They are all short," said Mr. Foote, "and are rather impressions or sketches than compositions written with any development, and were suggested by verses from the 'Rubaiyat' of Omar Khayyam." The setting of the second verse is the strongest:

"They say the lion and the lizard keep
The courts where Jamshyd gloried and drank deep."

Here the composer lets the "lion" loose with the fullest orchestra, including cymbals and tambourines.

The "Christmas Performance" of Handel's "Messiah" was given on Wednesday evening, December 25, in Orchestra Hall, and repeated Friday evening, December 27, under the direction of Harrison M. Wild. Soloists: Miss Sibyl Sammis (soprano), Miss Christine Miller (contralto), Reed Miller (tenor) and Arthur Middleton (bass); Arthur Dunham (organist), and the Theodore Thomas Orchestra.

THIRTEENTH PROGRAM, JANUARY 3 AND 4
THEODORE THOMAS MEMORIAL

Tragic Overture, Opus 81, ... *Brahms*
Sonata in F Minor, ... *Bach*
(Orchestration by Theodore Thomas)
Symphony No. 8, in B Minor (Unfinished), ... *Schubert*

INTERMISSION

Variations, Opus 26, ... *Elgar*
Tone Poem, "Death and Transfiguration," Opus 24, . *Strauss*

The beginnings of our Pension Fund date from the Seventeenth Season, when two concerts for the benefit of the Fund were given by the Orchestra, under the direction of Mr. Stock, on Monday and Tuesday evenings, January 6 and 7, in Orchestra Hall, illustrated by pantomime and dance, arranged by Joseph Lindon Smith, assisted by a group of society young men and women. The details of the concerts were in charge of an Executive Committee: Mrs. Bryan Lathrop, Chairman; Mrs. Russell Tyson, Vice-Chairman; Mrs. John J. Glessner, Treasurer; Mrs. George S. Isham, Secretary; Mrs. Watson F. Blair, Mrs. John M. Clark, Mrs. Frank S. Johnson, Mrs. Cyrus Bentley and Mrs. Theodore Thomas; the important numbers of the program being:

"Anitra's Dance," . . . . *Grieg*
(From the "Peer Gynt" Suite)
"The Close of Day" . . . . *Bizet*
(Incidental Music from the Suite "L'Arlésienne")
"Scène Religieuse," . . . . *Massenet*
(From the Suite "Les Erinnyes")
'CELLO OBBLIGATO BY BRUNO STEINDEL

(This represents the ceremony of decking the tomb of Agamemnon with flowers and garlands and pouring libations upon it, in accordance with the ancient classic rite.)

Seventeenth Season—1907-1908

"Jack Frost in the Garden in Midsummer."
(Incidental music composed especially for this occasion by
Edward Burlingame Hill.)
March, "Pomp and Circumstance," . . . . *Elgar*
(Introducing a grand pageant of all the characters.)

The program book for the concerts of January 17 and 18, Fifteenth Program, announced a gift from Mrs. Marshall Field:

"The Trustees have the great pleasure of announcing a gift of $5,000 to The Orchestral Association from Mrs. Marshall Field. This generous sum, which comes without solicitation and without conditions, the Trustees propose to set aside, invested in good securities, as the nucleus of a Sinking Fund for the retirement of the mortgage debt of $330,000 which rests upon the hall, and matures in August, 1910. By that time they hope many other generous friends will have joined Mrs. Field in contributing to the Fund, so that the debt may then be paid or materially reduced."

For the concerts of January 31 and February 1, Seventeenth Program, Mr. Stock had prepared a program of French classics, but in memory of Edward Alexander MacDowell, whose death occurred January 23, the composer's symphonic poem, "Lancelot and Elaine," was substituted for Chausson's symphonic poem, "Viviane." The soloist, Alfred Barthel, who has been with the Orchestra since the Thirteenth Season (1903-1904), chose for his number the concerto for oboe by a French woman, the Vicomtesse de Grandval. The concerto reveals all the possibilities of the oboe, and was played by Mr. Barthel with great skill and feeling, to the delight of the audience, who honored him with many recalls.

The program book of the concerts of February 7 and 8, Eighteenth Program, contained this notice of the passing of an old member of the Orchestra:

"The regular attendants at these concerts, who have missed the familiar presence of William Loewe at the kettledrum, will regret to learn of his death, which occurred a few days ago in New York City. He was a soldier in the Civil War, and, after being mustered out, in 1865, engaged with Mr. Thomas and remained until last season, when sickness compelled him to retire after a faithful, continuous service of thirty-four years."

Early in the autumn of the current season the Orchestra accepted an engagement with the Mendelssohn Choir of Toronto to play at its annual concerts in February, 1908. It was my good fortune to accompany the Orchestra and hear, for the first time, this famous Choir and meet its Conductor, Dr. A. S. Vogt. The entire Theodore

Thomas Orchestra, with Conductor Stock, Manager Wessels and a few Chicago friends, left on Sunday, February 9, at 5:30 P. M., by special train, and arrived in Toronto Monday, February 10, at 11:30 A. M. The first concert of the series was given that evening in Massey Hall, the important numbers being:

A Dramatic Cantata, "Olaf Trygvason," . . . . *Grieg*
    Soloists: Miss Janet Spencer and Gwilym Miles
Motet, "Hodie Christus Natus Est" (*a Cappella*), . *Palestrina*
Song, "Hey Nonino" (Eight Parts), ... *Brockway*
Symphonic Poem, "Les Préludes," . . . . . . *Liszt*
    Theodore Thomas Orchestra

    The work of the Choir was of the highest order, and a delightful surprise to the Chicago visitors, who had never heard before such perfection in choral singing. After the concert we were entertained at supper by Dr. and Mrs. Vogt at their home, and there learned some of the Conductor's methods with his singers, which are quite unlike those employed in other societies.

    The Choir was then in its Eleventh Season, and had among its officiary Lord Strathcona and Mount Royal, Patron, and Sir Edmund Walker, Honorary President. The rule with many societies—that once a member always a member—does not prevail with the Mendelssohn Choir in Toronto. At the end of each season all members, men and women, must resign, and before being admitted to membership in the next season must pass an examination before Dr. Vogt as to vocal ability. By this stern method no "dead wood" can accumulate in the Choir. In the autumn he assembles his singers in groups, on different days, reviewing them carefully as Samuel reviewed "the sons of Jesse." He will "line up" a section of tenors or sopranos, making them sing a passage or phrase, singly and collectively, and any voice that is harsh or strident and does not blend is at once discarded. In this manner Dr. Vogt tries out everyone who applies for membership in his Choir. These drastic rules might not be acceptable in the States, but they have made the Mendelssohn Choir the best singing society on this side of the Atlantic.

    We must bear in mind that Toronto is a musical and religious community, a city of church goers and church singers. The people love to sing. Toronto, with a popu-

Seventeenth Season—1907-1908

lation of 300,000, supported (1908) the Mendelssohn Choir and seven other singing societies.

At the concert on Tuesday evening, February 11, the Choir was heard in César Franck's sacred ode, "The One Hundred and Fiftieth Psalm," with some more *a cappella* numbers, notably Cui's ballad, "Spring's Delight," in eight parts. The Orchestra, under Mr. Stock, contributed, to close, the tone poem, "Death and Transfiguration" (Strauss). Later the two Conductors and guests were entertained at a banquet by the members of the Clef Club, an occasion of good fellowship, with interesting addresses from prominent guests.

The program of the last concert, on Wednesday evening, February 12, included the Brahms "Requiem" (Miss Marie Stoddard and Gwilym Miles, soloists) and a group of choruses *a cappella*, under the direction of Dr. Vogt:

"My Love Dwells in a Northern Land" (Eight Parts), . . *Elgar*
"Night Witchery" (Men's Voices), ... *Van Storch*
"Jubilate" (Soprano Solo and Women's Voices), . . *Scholz*
Ballad, "The Hero's Rest" (Baritone Solo and Mixed
    Voices), ... *Cornelius*

The concert closed with the Vorspiel from "Die Meistersinger," by Wagner, with the Theodore Thomas Orchestra, Mr. Stock, Conductor.

We left Toronto by special train at midnight for the return home, arriving in Chicago in the afternoon of the following day, carrying delightful remembrances of Toronto, the people and the concerts, and with plans already in hand for bringing the Choir to Chicago the following season.

"The Children's Crusade," one of the important works of recent years, by Gabriel Pierné, a French composer, was given in Orchestra Hall by the Apollo Musical Club, under the direction of Harrison M. Wild, Monday evening, February 17, and Tuesday evening, February 18. Soloists: Frank Ormsby (tenor) and Gustav Holmquist (bass); Arthur Dunham (organist); the Theodore Thomas Orchestra.

Herbert Witherspoon, the soloist for the Twenty-first Program, February 28 and 29, gave us two songs by Beethoven, "In Questa Tomba Oscura" and "Mit Mädeln sich vertragen," a "Madrigale" by Floridia, and the Air du Tambour-Major from "Le Cid" (Ambroise Thomas).

TWENTY-THIRD PROGRAM, MARCH 13 AND 14
"Three Episodes," Opus 38, ... *Adolf Weidig*

The words were suggested to Mr. Weidig by Clärchen's song from Goethe's "Egmont." The work, written in 1906, published in 1910, besides performances in Chicago, Minneapolis and Detroit, has been played by the symphony orchestras in Berlin, Hamburg, Frankfort and Wiesbaden.

For the Twenty-fourth Program, March 20 and 21, Leopold de Maré, first horn of the Orchestra, was the soloist; Frank Van der Stucken, Visiting Conductor. Mr. de Maré played the concerto for waldhorn, by Richard Strauss, which we had heard at the concerts of January 29 and 30, 1892 (First Season), when Herman Dutschke was our first horn. The concerto, written when Strauss was a young man, for his father, a horn player of note at Munich, and abounding in pitfalls for the unwary, had no terrors for Mr. de Maré, who interpreted the intricate passages of Strauss' work with perfect ease and with a lovely quality of tone.

Frank Van der Stucken, who succeeded Theodore Thomas as Conductor of the Cincinnati Festivals, led the Orchestra in the first performance (at these concerts) of his symphonic prologue, "William Ratcliff," written in 1879 and brought out in 1883 at Weimar.

While the Friday concert, April 3, Twenty-sixth Program, was in progress, Joseph Beckel, a faithful member of the Orchestra from its organization (1891) and principal of the double-basses from the Fifth Season, passed away. Owing to the absence of the Orchestra from the city, the funeral was delayed until Wednesday afternoon, April 8, when the services were held in the chapel of Graceland Cemetery, attended by Frederick Stock (Conductor), Frederick J. Wessels (Manager), members of the Executive Committee and Orchestra. Two chorales were played by the brass choir during the services.

Mr. Paderewski was the soloist at the concerts of April 10 and 11, Twenty-seventh Program (Beethoven), playing the "Emperor" concerto as Paderewski alone can play it. The *Inter-Ocean* said of the Polish artist:

Seventeenth Season—1907-1908

"Where can one find words to convey to the hearer the subtle atmosphere of poetry and beauty with which he surrounds every phrase? How can the cold, hard lines of type be made to reflect the color that glowed and faded and glowed again in each passage?"

The Seventeenth Season closed with the Twenty-eighth Program (Wagner "Request"), April 17 and 18, consisting of selections for the Orchestra from "Die Meistersinger," "Tristan and Isolde," "Parsifal" and other operas, closing with "The Kaisermarsch."

The Orchestra resumed its old place at the Eighteenth Cincinnati Festival, May 5, 6, 7, 8 and 9, under Frank Van der Stucken, Musical Director, and Frederick Stock, Associate Conductor, assisted by a strong array of soloists: Mme. Johanna Gadski, Mrs. Corinne Rider-Kelsey, Mrs. Edith Chapman Goold and Mrs. Antoinette Werner-West (sopranos); Mme. Ernestine Schumann-Heink, Miss Janet Spencer and Mrs. Taylor-Jones (contraltos); Daniel Beddoe and Edward Johnson (tenors); Dalton Baker, Tom Daniel, Herbert Witherspoon and Hans Seitz (basses).

I have pleasant remembrances of this Festival:

"May 5, Tuesday: Left Chicago at 9:00 A. M., Cincinnati at 6:00 P. M.; to the Hotel Sinton, then to the Queen City Club; dinner with Mr. and Mrs. Witherspoon, Mr. and Mrs. Wessels, Edward Johnson and Stock; afterward to the first concert—Haydn's 'Seasons'—conducted by Van der Stucken. I had never heard this genial oratorio before—somewhat long; too distended for modern ears; delightful solo work by Mme. Gadski, Beddoe and Baker.

"May 6, Wednesday: Rehearsal of the 'Passion Music' in P. M. at Music Hall. Van der Stucken is exacting in his demands on the Orchestra—sometimes severe; but he is a Conductor who knows. A great performance of the work at night for solos, chorus and Orchestra. Mr. Van der Stucken used a small choir at back of stage for the 'Chorales.' To my mind this is a mistake—the 'Chorales' should be given by soloists, chorus, Orchestra and organ.

"May 7, Thursday: Norman Fay arrived at the Sinton this morning—joined us at breakfast. Wessels explained how our Orchestra did not get the engagement for the last Festival (1906). The supporters of the Cincinnati Orchestra are interested in the May Festivals, and insisted that the Cincinnati Orchestra should be used. Wessels made the stipulation that in accepting the engagement for the Thomas Orchestra at this (1908) Festival, Mr. Stock should be Associate Conductor—'and it was so.' Concert in afternoon by Mme. Gadski and Orchestra. Mr. Stock, Conductor, received an ovation after the performance of Strauss' 'Death and Transfiguration.'

"May 8, Friday: In the evening 'The Children's Crusade' (Pierné); 700 children take part. Their lovely singing will be long remembered. The concert this evening a triumph for Mr. Van der Stucken; would like to hear 'Olaf Trygvason' (Grieg) tomorrow, but am leaving at 11:30 this evening for home."

SEVENTEENTH SEASON
(1907-1908)
SOLOISTS

HARP: Enrico Tramonti.
HORN: Leopold de Maré.
OBOE: Alfred Barthel.
ORGAN: Wilhelm Middelschulte.
PIANOFORTE: Miss Katharine Goodson, Mmes. Teresa Carreño, Olga Samaroff, Mrs. Fannie Bloomfield Zeisler; Richard Buhlig, Josef Hofmann, Ignace J. Paderewski.
VIOLIN: Miss Maud Powell; Ludwig Becker, Leopold Kramer, Fritz Kreisler.
VIOLONCELLO: Miss May Mukle; Bruno Steindel.
VOCAL: Mme. Johanna Gadski, Mrs. Corinne Rider-Kelsey; Emilio de Gogorza, Lawrence Rea, Herbert Witherspoon.
VISITING CONDUCTOR: Frank Van der Stucken.

EIGHTEENTH SEASON
(1908-1909)

Death of Ezra Butler McCagg, an early Trustee and friend of the Orchestra—Felix Borowski succeeds Hubbard William Harris as editor of the program book—Some thoughts on program making—The Orchestra makes a second visit to Toronto for the concerts of the Mendelssohn Choir—The Choir visits Chicago —The Willow Grove Park engagement.

A sincere friend of the Orchestra, Ezra Butler Mc-Cagg, passed away on August 2.

He had an active part in its organization, and was a member of its Board of Trustees for the first three seasons (1891-1894). He was interested in other ways in the city's welfare—as an incorporator (1857) of the Chicago Historical Society; member of the Academy of Sciences, and one of the founders (1874) of the Chicago Bar Association. Few men have done more for this city in their day and generation than Mr. McCagg. Veterans of the Civil War will recall the Northwestern Sanitary Commission and the Fair held in Chicago (1865) and the work done by its President, Mr. McCagg. The *Chicago Tribune* said of Mr. McCagg:

> "He was one of those enthusiastic workers for the public good, to whom the men of this day owe so much, but of whose names they are often unmindful. Mr. McCagg was a member of the Lincoln Park Board, and prominent among the men to whom the Park owes its existence—the best memorial any man could have."

Mr. Stock and his men were in the best of form for the first concerts, October 16 and 17, and were greeted by an enthusiastic audience. The "Friday Spell" is too strong to cause many changes among the regular attendants at the afternoon concerts; all were present and in their accustomed places, eager to hear the glorious music.

The people noted the new iron canopy (most welcome in stormy weather) at the Michigan Avenue entrance, and the newly decorated hall, in warm, soft colors, from designs by D. H. Burnham & Co. The Executive Committee was pleased with the season ticket sale, $85,417, which exceeded that of the previous year by $2,000, showing sold-out houses for the Friday afternoon concerts, but with the usual empty seats on Saturday nights.

The program was attractive:

Overture, "Rienzi," . . . . Wagner
Symphony No. 8, F Major, Opus 93, ... Beethoven

INTERMISSION

Symphonic Variations, Opus 78, ... Dvořák
Symphonic Poem No. 2, "Tasso, Lamento e Trionfo," . . Liszt

Hubbard William Harris,* editor of the program book, retired during the summer and was succeeded by Felix Borowski, well known in the musical life of Chicago as composer, critic and President of the Chicago Musical College. It was a happy and unusual coincidence that Mr. Stock and Mr. Borowski, who had studied (1887-1893) with the same masters at the Conservatory of Music in Cologne, should meet in Chicago and work together in the Theodore Thomas Orchestra.

Mr. Borowski's analysis of the "Rienzi" overture contained much that was new and fascinating regarding the early struggles of Wagner for recognition and existence. The editor inserted a note from a work by Edmund Van Hagen, "Contributions to an Insight into the Being of Wagnerian Art," in which the author declares the trumpet call with which the overture opens, to be Wagner's "summons to freedom," and that "the trumpeter who sounds the A should know this," a statement suggesting "moonlight musings" or the growlings of some dyspeptic Carlyle.

A tendency exists among modern critics, largely for advertising purposes and program-making, to give new thoughts on the themes used by the old composers and their methods in composition, which are not always sustained by testimony. Reliable witnesses were present who heard Handel say of "The Hallelujah Chorus" after the first performance of "The Messiah": "I did think I did see all heaven before me and the great God Himself." Reams of descriptive matter for the edification of the audience at the intermission have been written regarding

---

*Hubbard William Harris, an able teacher of musical theory and a member of the faculty of the Cosmopolitan School of Music, died September 25, 1915, in Chicago.

the works of Russian composers, which would amuse Tschaikowsky, Rimsky-Korsakow and their followers, were they to come back to earth. One must draw the line somewhere, so I would draw the line at the "fate knockings" or "landlord knockings for rent," as some writers have called the first notes in the opening measure of Beethoven's fifth symphony.

Some thirty years ago there was a supper at the Calumet Club after one of the "Summer Garden Concerts," Mr. Thomas being present, when a discussion was started about the fifth symphony. Mr. Thomas was asked his opinion of the first phrase in the symphony. I shall always remember his answer: "Beethoven had to work for his living, and worked hard and fast. He often used the first phrases which came to his mind, if they suited his purpose. He understood his art and developed themes with little thought of any future poetic or romantic meaning. It was the modern writer, not Beethoven, who discovered 'fate knocking' in the first measure of the fifth symphony."

"November 30, Monday evening, Orchestra Hall: Miss Isadora Duncan danced to the music of Gluck's 'Iphigénie en Aulide,' accompanied by the Orchestra, under Mr. Stock's direction."

In this "Revival of the Greek art of 2,000 years ago," Miss Duncan was assisted by seventy Chicago *débutantes*, for the benefit of the Children's Memorial Hospital and the Pension Fund of the Orchestra; the performance was repeated Tuesday afternoon, December 8.

There was a large representation of society people present on both occasions, who were delighted with the music, scenery and the dancing of Miss Duncan. The substantial sum of $5,507.32 was realized from the two performances for the Pension Fund.

EIGHTH PROGRAM, DECEMBER 4 AND 5
Soloist: Albert Spalding
Concerto for Violin, No. 3, B Minor, ... Saint-Saëns

The Annual Meeting was held Tuesday afternoon, December 8, in Room 850 Orchestra Building, to elect Trustees and officers and hear the report of the Treasurer for the Seventeenth Season (1907-1908), ending June 30, 1908:

RECEIPTS		EXPENSES	
Chicago concerts	$108,078.00	Business management	$ 12,224.05
Miscellaneous concerts (net)	17,097.88	Advertising	3,595.05
Program book	1,957.54	Salaries of Conductor, Orchestra and expenses	103,925.09
Interest	513.49	Soloists	7,950.00
Interest Henry Field Fund	2,500.00	Music and instruments	2,129.85
Hall and building rentals and miscellaneous sources	66,747.63	Building and hall expenses, decorating, heating, insurance, ushers, etc.	29,765.72
		Interest on loans	14,450.00
		Taxes	7,269.79
			$181,309.55
		Profit on season	15,584.99
	$196,894.54		$196,894.54

At the adjourned Annual Meeting of the Association Friday afternoon, December 18, the resignation of F. F. Peabody as a Member of the Association, on account of absence from the city, was accepted, and David B. Jones was elected to fill the vacancy.

THIRTEENTH PROGRAM, JANUARY 8 AND 9
THEODORE THOMAS MEMORIAL
SOLOIST: WILHELM MIDDELSCHULTE

Prelude, Chorale and Fugue, ... *Bach—Abert*
Symphony No. 1, C Minor, Opus 68, ... *Brahms*

INTERMISSION

Prelude and Double Fugue, on a Theme by Brückner, for Organ, Four Trumpets and Four Trombones, *Friedrich Klose*
(First Time in America)
Tone Poem, "Death and Transfiguration," Opus 24, *Strauss*

Klose's work, constructed on modern lines, though somewhat academic in form, called for an unusual combination of instruments, and received a brilliant interpretation by Mr. Stock and his men. The lion's share fell to Mr. Middelschulte, who played with great breadth and repose, showing his thorough knowledge of organ technique.

Walter Unger* was the soloist in the concerts of January 22 and 23, Fifteenth Program, playing the

---
*Walter Unger was a member of the Orchestra from the First Season (1891), and, after twenty-nine years of faithful service, retired (1919) on a pension.

concerto No. 1 in D minor, Opus 32, by Jules de Swert, a composer of note and a virtuoso (violoncello) of high order in his day (1843-1891). Mr. Unger was very happy in his choice of de Swert's concerto, and pleased the audience with his delightful interpretation of the work.

The doctrine of reciprocity should be beneficial to countries so closely related as Canada and the United States. It proved so at this time (1908-1909) in our musical relations with Toronto. Soon after the Orchestra returned home from its first visit to Toronto (February, 1908) an invitation came from Dr. Vogt and the officers of the Mendelssohn Choir to visit Toronto the next season. The Trustees of The Orchestral Association, in accepting this cordial invitation, coupled with the acceptance the hope that Dr. Vogt would visit Chicago that winter with his Choir, and show American musicians his methods in chorus work. The details were soon perfected whereby the Orchestra should visit Toronto in February (1909) for the annual concerts of the Mendelssohn Choir, commemorating the centennial of Mendelssohn's birth (February 3, 1809), and that the Choir should visit Chicago in March, as guests of the Theodore Thomas Orchestra. This plan provided for concerts in Toronto on Monday, Tuesday and Wednesday evenings (February 8, 9 and 10); but the advance ticket sale in Toronto had been so large that the Secretary of the Choir telegraphed Manager Wessels, asking the Orchestra to stay another day, Thursday, the 11th, in Toronto.

The Trustees willingly gave the Orchestra another day in Toronto, and that there should be plenty of time for the return to Chicago, changed the Friday concert of the week to Saturday afternoon.

We left Chicago—Conductor Stock, the Secretary, Manager Wessels and Orchestra—Sunday, February 7, at 5:30 P. M., arriving in Toronto Monday morning, in time for the rehearsal in Massey Hall.

Dr. Vogt had prepared programs of a miscellaneous character for the concerts, employing Choir and Orchestra, interspersed with *a cappella* numbers, to show his singers in the various forms of ancient and modern music. The important numbers at each concert may be noted:

Monday evening, February 8:

Motet, "Judge Me, O God,"	Mendelssohn
Ballad, "Hey Nonino,"	Brockway
Choral Ballad, "The Challenge of Thor,"	Elgar

CHOIR AND ORCHESTRA

Tuesday evening, February 9:

"Cherubim Song,"	Tschaikowsky
Symphony No. 5, Opus 64,	Tschaikowsky

THEODORE THOMAS ORCHESTRA

Song, "Ave Maris Stella,"	Grieg
Motet, "Cum Sanctu Spirito,"	Bach

CHOIR, ORGAN AND ORCHESTRA

The only extended work given in the series was Elgar's "Caractacus" on Wednesday evening (the 10th) with Mrs. Corinne Rider-Kelsey, George Hamlin, Claude Cunningham and Frederick Martin as soloists.

The concert on Thursday night (the 11th) was a repetition of that on Tuesday, with the addition of two numbers for the Choir—"How Blest are They" (Tschaikowsky) and "How Sweet the Moonlight Sleeps" (Fanning).

Our visit to Toronto concluded with a banquet after the concert Thursday evening, at the King Edward Hotel, given by Sir Edmund Walker, Honorary President of the Mendelssohn Choir, to the two Conductors, Dr. Vogt and Mr. Stock, the Chicago visitors, officers of the Choir, and the Governor General of Canada and staff. It was a feast of fellowship and good cheer, lasting until an early hour Friday morning, when the Chicago men were hurriedly called away to take the "special" for the return home, pleased with the thought that the Toronto singers would soon visit Chicago.

The Choir left Toronto Tuesday evening, March 2, by two special Pullman trains, arriving in Chicago Wednesday morning, March 3. Concerts were given on Wednesday and Thursday evenings and Friday afternoon, March 3, 4 and 5.

The Mendelssohn Choir in that year consisted of sixty-five sopranos, fifty-one altos, fifty-two tenors and sixty basses, total of 228 voices. Its creation, development and success have been largely due to the genius of its Conductor, Dr. A. S. Vogt, who organized the Choir in 1894, and conducted its first concert in January, 1895. In 1900 it was reorganized on its present basis,

Eighteenth Season—1908-1909

and has since been engaged in carrying out the high artistic ideals of its Conductor.

It being necessary for the Choir to leave Chicago for Toronto immediately after the Friday concert, to enable the business men of the organization to have a full day at home on Saturday, our regular concert scheduled for Saturday evening, March 6, was changed to Wednesday evening, March 3.

These were busy days for the Secretary, as his journal will indicate:

"March 3, Wednesday, 6:30 A. M.: With Wessels and Voegeli to the Polk Street Station to meet Dr. Vogt and the Choir and escort them to the Auditorium, where we had secured two floors with the large dining room for their special use. . . . 10:00 A. M. short rehearsal in the hall—luncheon at 1:00 P. M. by the Trustees to Dr. Vogt and officers of the Choir in Mr. Burnham's office in the Railway Exchange; then to a reception for the members, at 4 o'clock at the home of Mr. and Mrs. John J. Glessner. . . . Concert at 8:15 P. M. by Choir and Orchestra in Orchestra Hall; we have never heard before such perfection in choral singing, such admirable balancing of voices, marvelous volume and beauty of tone. The principal numbers for the Choir were:

'Crucifixus' (a Cappella), ...	Lotti
'By Babylon's Wave,'	Gounod
'Ave Maris Stella,'	Grieg

"Thursday, March 4: Ladies of the Choir spent the morning at the Stock Yards, on invitation of Charles H. Swift, of our Trustees. . . . Luncheon at 1:00 P. M. at the Chicago Club to Dr. Vogt, Sir Edmund Walker, Honorary President, and other officers of the Choir and Trustees of the Orchestra. . . . Reception at 4 o'clock for the Choir in the rooms of the Cliff Dwellers. . . . At 8:15 concert in Orchestra Hall by Choir and Orchestra, in which we again heard delightful work by the Toronto singers; a few of their numbers may be noted:

'The Cherubim Song,'	Tschaikowsky
Ballad, 'A Love Symphony,'	Pitt
'How Blest Are They,'	Tschaikowsky

"After the concert, reception for the Choir by the members of the Apollo Musical Club in the foyer of Orchestra Hall.

"Friday, March 5, 2:15 P. M.: Last appearance of the Choir; a great audience—many people turned away; program of Wednesday concert repeated; Choir at its best in the 'Crucifixus' (Lotti). . . . After the concert Wessels and I had a busy time in getting Dr. Vogt and his singers to the train for their return home."

A few friends of the Orchestra made it possible to bring the Mendelssohn Choir to Chicago, by guaranteeing the expenses:

ADAMS, GEORGE E.
ADAMS, JOSEPH.
BAIRD, FRANK T.
BAIRD, MAX.
BARNHART, A. M.
BARTLETT, A. C.
BECKER, A. G.
BENTLEY, MRS. CYRUS.
BIRCH, MRS. HUGH T.
BLACKSTONE, MRS. T. B.
BLAINE, MRS. EMMONS.
BORLAND, MRS. JOHN JAY.
BURLEY, CLARENCE A.
BURNHAM, D. H.
BUTLER, E. B.
BROWN, WM. L.
CARR, CLYDE M.
CRANE, MRS. RICHARD T.
DELANO, F. A.
DICK, A. B.
ELLIOTT, FRANCKE C.
FARR, A. G.
FULLER, WM. A.
GLESSNER, JOHN J.
HAMILL, CHARLES H.
HAMILL, ERNEST A.
HAMLIN, GEORGE.
HATELY, WALTER C.
HEALY, PAUL J.
HUTCHINSON, CHARLES L.
INSULL, SAMUEL.
ISHAM, DR. GEO. S.
JONES, DAVID B.
KEEP, CHAUNCEY.
LATHROP, BRYAN.
LAWSON, VICTOR F.
LINDGREN, J. R.
LORD, J. B.
MCCORMICK, HAROLD F.
NORTON, O. W.
OTIS, PHILO A.
RIPLEY, E. P.
ROLOSON, R. W.
RYERSON, MARTIN A.
SMITH, BYRON L.
SPOOR, JOHN A.
SPRAGUE, ALBERT A.
SWEENEY, JOHN M.
SWIFT, CHARLES H.
WALKER, WM. B.
WOOLLEY, CLARENCE M.
WRENN, JOHN H.

The Executive Committee at its next meeting (April 2) adopted resolutions incidental to the appearance of the Mendelssohn Choir, which are worthy of record:

"That the Secretary of this Association shall at once perform the pleasant duty of expressing to the Director and members of the Mendelssohn Choir of Toronto our deep sense of their courtesy in undertaking to visit our distant city for our pleasure; together with our assurance of, and congratulations upon, the complete success of their mission, in public estimation and our own.

"That the Trustees of The Orchestral Association have the honor and pleasure of expressing to Mr. and Mrs. J. J. Glessner their appreciation of, and thanks for, their courtesy to the guests of the Association, the Mendelssohn Choir of Toronto, during their recent visit to Chicago.

"That the Trustees desire to put on record their gratification with the thorough and satisfactory way in which F. J. Wessels handled so complex a task as that of bringing the Mendelssohn Choir of Toronto to Chicago, and sending them home again in unalloyed happiness and comfort."

Mr. Paderewski appeared as composer and soloist at the concerts of March 12 and 13, Twenty-second Program, when his symphony in B minor had its first hearing in Chicago, a work written as a patriotic tribute to his native country, inspired by the fortieth anniversary of the Polish Revolution (1863-1864). After the intermission Mr. Paderewski played Saint-Saëns' concerto No. 4 in C minor, giving the work a magnificent performance.

The Apollo Musical Club gave Bach's Mass in B minor at its concert on Monday afternoon and evening, April 5, in Orchestra Hall, under the direction of Harrison M. Wild—one performance only, in two parts, with a recess. Soloists: Mrs. Edith Chapman Goold (soprano), Miss Christine Miller (contralto), George Hamlin (tenor) and Herbert Witherspoon (bass); Arthur Dunham (organist), and the entire Theodore Thomas Orchestra.

Mrs. Fannie Bloomfield Zeisler was the soloist at the concerts of April 16 and 17, Twenty-seventh Program, her eleventh engagement with the Orchestra, playing Liszt's concerto No. 1 in E flat.

The Eighteenth Season closed with the concerts of April 23 and 24, Twenty-eighth, and last, Program:

Overture to "Euryanthe," . . . . *Weber*
Symphony No. 6, "Pathetic," B Minor, Opus 74, . *Tschaikowsky*
INTERMISSION
Tone Poem, "Don Juan," Opus 20, ... *Strauss*
Siegfried Idyl, ... *Wagner*
"Festival March and Hymn to Liberty," . . . . . . *Kaun*

One of the important engagements for the Orchestra, two weeks in the summer of every year (1908-1915), has been at Willow Grove Park, an attractive suburb of Philadelphia, owned and controlled by the Philadelphia Traction Company, with whom the engagement with the Orchestra was made. On my way east that summer (1909) I stopped at Philadelphia and had a short season of artist life (July 2, 3, 4 and 5) at the Park, with Mr. Stock and the men of the Orchestra:

"July 2, Friday: Philadelphia at 12:15 P. M.; train for Willow Grove at 2:30; dinner 6:30 P. M. at the Casino, by officers of the Transit Company, to Stock, Wessels and out-of-town guests; 7:45, concert by the Orchestra in the Pavilion; last number on the program, Tschaikowsky's 'Capriccio Italien,' delightfully played.

"July 3, Saturday: At the Mineral Spring House, an ancient hostelry, famous in colonial days as a road house, where the stages stopped *en route* to New York. The park is laid out with lakes, walks and flower beds, moving pictures, miniature Venice with gondolas, and other attractions to amuse the Philadelphia people.

"July 4, Sunday: Concerts daily in the Pavilion; afternoons 2:30 to 3:30 and 4:30 to 5:30; evenings 7:45 to 8:30 and 9:30 to

10:30. There are seats for 3,500 in the Pavilion; 10,000 more can be seated around the Pavilion on the outside—and all hear! Programs prepared by Mr. Stock from the *répertoire* of the Orchestra, and require no rehearsing; solos by members of the Orchestra. The program for the first part of the afternoon concerts today included:

March, 'Marocaine,'	*Berlioz*
Overture, 'Fra Diavolo,'	*Auber*
'Cowkeeper's Tune,' } 'Country Dance,'	*Grieg*
'Valse Caprice,'	*Keller*
'Trot de Cavalerie,'	*Rubinstein*

"Dinner 6:30 at the Casino by W. R. Lester, Musical Editor of the *Philadelphia North American*, to Stock, Wessels, Park Officials and out-of-town guests.

"July 5, Monday: The 'Glorious Fourth' was celebrated today; crowds of people (fully 50,000) came out from Philadelphia to spend the day; 10,000 attended the afternoon concerts. Supper at the Casino after the second part of the evening concerts, with Stock, Wessels, Lester and other newspaper men."

The Orchestra returned to Chicago from Willow Grove for a two weeks' engagement at Ravinia Park, commencing July 12, with programs admirably prepared by Mr. Stock for the wishes of a summer audience. On Tuesday evening he introduced the "Pastoral" symphony of Beethoven to Ben Greet's presentation on the green of Shakespeare's "As You Like It." The Ben Greet players again appeared on Friday evening, July 16, in "King René's Daughter" and "Creatures of Impulse," accompanied by the Orchestra with music adapted by Mr. Stock.

EIGHTEENTH SEASON
(1908-1909)

SOLOISTS

HARP: Enrico Tramonti.
ORGAN: Wilhelm Middelschulte.
PIANOFORTE: Misses Katharine Goodson, Adele Verne, Mrs. Fannie Bloomfield Zeisler; Ernesto Consolo, Ignace J. Paderewski, Emil Sauer, Ernest Schelling.
VIOLIN: Ludwig Becker, Mischa Elman, Leopold Kramer, Alexander Petschnikoff, Albert Spalding.
VIOLONCELLO: Bruno Steindel, Walter Unger.
VOCAL: Mmes. Johanna Gadski, Marie Rappold.
CHORAL: Mendelssohn Choir of Toronto, Ont.

FREDERICK STOCK

NINETEENTH SEASON
(1909-1910)

Frederick Stock the logical successor of Theodore Thomas—Rachmaninow soloist in the Eighth Program—A Russian lady explains "La Mélancolie du Nord"—George W. Chadwick, Visiting Conductor—Third visit of the Orchestra to Toronto—Dinner to friends of the Orchestra in foyer of the hall to discuss the debt—Some thoughts on the contracts with members of the Orchestra —The Nineteenth Cincinnati Festival—President Taft unveils bronze statue of Theodore Thomas—The Willow Grove engagement—Ravinia Park.

In the five years which had now passed since Mr. Stock left his seat as a viola player for the Conductor's stand, he had won the unanimous support of the press and public and the entire confidence of the Trustees by his rare abilities as musician and Conductor. He had furthermore shown great tact in meeting the problems constantly arising in the work of the Orchestra, thus showing that he was in every way qualified to succeed Theodore Thomas.

The season ticket sale opened early in September with a return of $88,328 when the concerts began, an increase of $2,500 over the previous year. The house for the Friday concerts was entirely sold, "over-subscribed," with a long waiting list; but there were empty seats on Saturday nights.

The first concerts, October 15 and 16, brought large audiences to hear the delightful music, showing that Mr. Stock and the Orchestra are of the things in Chicago which make life worth living:

Overture to "Der Freischütz," . . . . *Weber*
Symphony No. 5, E Minor, "From the New World,"
 Opus 95, ... *Dvořák*

INTERMISSION

Symphonic Poem No. 4, "Orpheus," . . . . *Liszt*
Italian Serenade, ... *Wolf*
Rondo, "Till Eulenspiegel's Merry Pranks," Opus 28, . *Strauss*

Arthur Dunham was the soloist at the concerts of November 12 and 13, Fifth Program, playing his "Symphonic Fantasia" for organ and Orchestra. The work, which is in one movement, along modern lines, and constructed on a theme of César Franck's, received a vigorous interpretation at the hands of the composer.

During the last week in November Mr. Kramer,* our concertmeister, an artist of high attainments, tendered his resignation to the Executive Committee, and was succeeded by Ludwig Becker, the second concertmeister.

EIGHTH PROGRAM, DECEMBER 3 AND 4
SOLOIST: SERGEI RACHMANINOW

Symphonic Poem, "Die Toteninsel," . . . . Rachmaninow
(Conducted by the Composer)
(First Time in Chicago)
Concerto for Pianoforte, No. 2, C Minor, Opus 18, . Rachmaninow

Rachmaninow was inspired to the composition of "The Isle of Death" by the painting of the same name by Arnold Boecklin, which he saw in the summer of 1909 in Paris. The music is passionless, uncanny, even gruesome, and in a sombre mood, as are many of the Russian works; but it was magnificently played by the Orchestra.

One summer, in the White Mountains, I met a Russian lady with whom I had many talks about Tschaikowsky, Glazounow, Rimsky-Korsakow and other Russian writers. I asked, "Why is the Russian music so sad?" She replied:

"*C'est la mélancolie du nord!* Life in Russia is very trying through four months in the year. It is so bitter cold, even in Petrograd and Moscow; but in the rural community, where my home is situated, the cold is almost unendurable. Distances are so great, we cannot in the winter months visit the cities. Consider also the condition of the Russian people, who have lived for

---

*Leopold Kramer, a native of Bohemia, studied at the Conservatory in Prague, from which Kubelik and Kocian also graduated; later filled engagements in Berlin, Petrograd, Amsterdam and Cologne, coming from the latter city to accept the position of concertmeister with the Chicago Orchestra at the first concerts of the Seventh Season, October 22 and 23, 1897. He showed his virtuosity by the performance of the concerto in D minor (Sibelius) at the concerts of March 19 and 20, 1909 (Eighteenth Season). The concerto is more than difficult; it is ungrateful; and for some players would be impossible. But Mr. Kramer played it with ease and thorough artistic feeling. After leaving the Chicago Orchestra he was concertmeister in the Orchestra of the Chicago Opera Company until 1914, when he returned to Europe as concertmeister in the Orchestra of the Hamburg Municipal Opera. He was (1922) concertmeister in the Orchestra of the Metropolitan Grand Opera Company of New York, but later (1923) returned to Hamburg.

Nineteenth Season—1909-1910

centuries under the heel of the Romanoffs! If we dare to murmur or complain there is the prospect of a trip to Siberia. Do you wonder that our poets are sad, and that their songs are in minor moods?"

After listening to Rachmaninow's "Isle of Death" and his concerto in C minor I could now understand *"La mélancolie du nord."*

In the summer of 1919 Mme. Niessen Stone, of the Metropolitan Opera Company, was at our hotel, "The Balsams," at Dixville Notch, in the White Mountains. She told me of life in Russia, her home when a child, and that the words, *"La mélancolie du nord,"* are true—too true:

"This evening I am to sing some Russian songs at the concert in the hall, one by Gretschaninow, 'My Native Land,' words by Tolstoi. Come and hear it; note the last line, three words only, 'Wind, Steppes, Clouds.' That describes the vast solitudes and their loneliness. That is Russia! 'My native land.' "

The report of the Treasurer for the Eighteenth Season (1908-1909), ending June 30, 1909, was read at the Annual Meeting Tuesday afternoon, December 14:

RECEIPTS		EXPENSES	
Chicago concerts	$111,409.25	Business management	$ 14,036.13
Miscellaneous and outside concerts (net)	13,174.39	Salaries of Conductor and Orchestra	104,085.00
Program book, etc.	3,036.86	Soloists	9,054.00
Hall rentals	44,211.50	Advertising and concert expenses	5,401.85
Building rentals	25,490.30	Hall and building expenses, decorating, etc.	42,385.69
		Interest on loans	14,450.00
		Taxes	7,617.48
		Net profit	292.15
	$197,322.30		$197,322.30

To the profit of $292.15 must be added that of last season, $14,755.05, and after deducting accounts charged off, $713.45, we had $14,333.75 as the total profits at the close of the Eighteenth Season.

Vaclav Jiskra, principal of the double-bass section in the Orchestra, was the soloist at the "Popular" concerts of December 24 and 25. The double-bass had never been heard before in solo work at these concerts; but Mr. Jiskra is an artist who understands and can exploit the possibilities of the instrument, playing with grace and ease and producing a tone as beautiful as that of the 'cello.

Mr. Jiskra's numbers were a "Souvenir" by Franz Khodl, a famous player of other days in Vienna, and the "Tarantelle" by Giovanni Bottesini, the most noted performer on the double-bass in the history of the art.

Three symphonies have appeared in the last twelve months which are above the ordinary, the conventional: that by Sir Edward Elgar; Paderewski's No. 1, and the new work by Mr. Stock, in C minor, played at the concerts of December 31 and January 1, 1910, Twelfth Program. "There is always," said Felix Borowski in the program notes on Mr. Stock's symphony, "some poetic or dramatic significance in a large proportion of the music of the present day." Some writers "prefer to keep the purport of their work to themselves"; others would proclaim their thoughts from the housetops, unmindful of the saying of Talleyrand, that "the purpose of language," and of music, perhaps, "is to conceal thought." Let us now hear from Mr. Stock as to his interpretation of the symphony:

"Speaking of the present symphony, it should be said that the work is also meant to describe what so often has been described in works of the same character and form, human life, its sorrows as well as joys, the struggle of mortal man against fate, the spiritual trials to which he is subjected, his despair at the apparent futility of worldly existence, mingled with everlasting hope that victory will be his in the end. The first movement represents various phases of this struggle; as it surges to and fro, it depicts man's mind in a state of utter restlessness and determined resistance, a state of mind which does not recognize hope of lasting relief or comfort.

"The second part—*Scherzo*—speaks of life's joys in a more or less humorous fashion, while the third—*Andante*—depicts reminiscences of life's happiest moments. The fourth—*Finale*—explains itself when it is made known that it bears the motto which has become the 'motive of life' of the German nation: *Vorwärts* (Forward), *Aufwärts!* (Upward), which motto is, of course, to be taken in its broadest, most ideal and universal sense."

After the intermission Rubinstein's concerto No. 4 in D minor was brilliantly played by the American pianist, Mme. Olga Samaroff.

Nineteenth Season—1909-1910

THIRTEENTH PROGRAM, JANUARY 7 AND 8
THEODORE THOMAS MEMORIAL

Overture, "Coriolanus," Opus 62,	*Beethoven*
Symphony No. 3, "Eroica," E Flat, Opus 55,	*Beethoven*

INTERMISSION

Variations on a Theme by Haydn, Opus 56-A,	*Brahms*
"Träume,"	*Wagner*
(Orchestration by Theodore Thomas)	
Prelude to "Die Meistersinger,"	*Wagner*

"January 20; Thursday A. M.: To Orchestra Hall to meet George W. Chadwick, Visiting Conductor this week. After rehearsal of his 'Symphonic Sketches,' to the Chicago Club for luncheon, where we were joined by Messrs. Lathrop, Glessner, Wessels, Stock and Wallace Goodrich, one of the Conductors of the Metropolitan Opera Company, at the Auditorium. The talk through the luncheon was about Mr. Thomas, the Orchestra and the great work he had done for music in America.

"Fifteenth Program, January 21 and 22: Chadwick conducted his 'Symphonic Sketches.' He has been with us in other seasons, and is always welcome, having something new to say on each visit. The 'Sketches' consist of four numbers—'Jubilee,' 'Noël,' 'Hobgoblin,' 'A Vagrom Ballad'; the second number, 'Noël,' a little Christmas song, to my mind the most enjoyable."

It was necessary now that the Trustees should provide for the payment of the $330,000 secured by a mortgage on Orchestra Building for the completion (1905) of Orchestra Hall. A dinner was given by Mr. Lathrop at his residence, Thursday evening, January 27, to discuss ways and means to raise this money, there being present twenty-two friends of the Orchestra, including Trustees and Members of the Association. Among the guests were George E. Adams, Joseph Adams, A. G. Becker, William L. Brown, D. H. Burnham, C. Norman Fay, John J. Glessner, David B. Jones, Chauncey Keep and Philo A. Otis. It was decided that a vigorous campaign should be started among the friends of the Orchestra, everyone present to consider himself a committee of one for the work, and to secure as much of the indebtedness as possible. Mr. Lathrop suggested a dinner in the foyer of the hall to the Trustees and Members at an early date after the return of the Orchestra from Toronto.

"January 30, Sunday: Left Chicago at 4:00 P. M. with Stock, Wessels and Orchestra for Toronto, our third visit for the annual concerts of the Mendelssohn Choir—Mr. and Mrs. John J. Glessner, Mrs. Stock and Mrs. Wessels on train.

"January 31, Monday. Arrived in Toronto at 8:30 A. M. King Edward Hotel; rehearsal at 2:15 P. M., soloists, Choir and Orchestra, in Massey Hall, Dr. Vogt conducting. First concert in evening—miscellaneous selections by Choir and Orchestra, including two numbers for Choir *a cappella:* Legend, 'Christ when a Child' (Tschaikowsky), chorus, 'On Himalay,' (Bantock). After intermission Brahms' 'Requiem'; Mrs. Corinne Rider-Kelsey and Claude Cunningham, soloists.

"February 1, Tuesday: What a concert we heard last night! The same finish, attack and blending of voices! At 12:30 P. M. to the National Club, luncheon by officers of Choir to Mr. Stock, Mr. Wessels and out-of-town guests. President Parks, on behalf of the Choir, presented Mr. Wessels with a silver cigar box, in appreciation of his efforts in bringing the Orchestra to Toronto.

"Concert in evening by Choir and Orchestra; two numbers by the Choir again showed its perfection in *a cappella* work: 'Ave Maris Stella' (Grieg), 'Cherubim Song' (Tschaikowsky).

"February 2, Wednesday, 12:30 P. M.: Luncheon at the residence of Mrs. J. W. Flavelle, a patroness of the Choir, for Mr. and Mrs. Stock, Choir and Chicago guests.

"Concert in evening—'The Children's Crusade' (Pierné); soloists: Mrs. Corinne Rider-Kelsey, Mrs. Mabel Sharp Herdien, George Hamlin and Marion Green; Dr. Vogt, Conductor.

"After the concert, supper at the residence of Dr. and Mrs. Vogt for Mr. and Mrs. Stock, soloists and out-of-town guests.

"February 3, Thursday, 2:00 P. M.: Matinée—soloists and Orchestra. Busoni played the concerto for pianoforte No. 1, E flat (Liszt). Mr. Stock conducted his new symphony in C minor—brilliant performance.

"In the evening, repetition of 'Children's Crusade'; an immense audience—great enthusiasm; at 11:00 P. M., supper at Clef Club by officers of Choir for Mr. Stock, soloists and guests.

"February 4, Friday: Left Toronto at 12:30 A. M.; special train for Orchestra and Chicago people, in a furious snowstorm; cleared away when we arrived at Sarnia to cross the river. Long talk with Mr. Stock about taking the Orchestra to Boston next season."

In consequence of the Toronto trip the regular Friday afternoon concert, February 4, was given Saturday afternoon, February 5.

The combination of the Mendelssohn Choir and the Thomas Orchestra proved so effective that other cities were eager to hear them. The Choir and Orchestra, with Dr. Vogt and Mr. Stock as Conductors, appeared together in Buffalo, in Convention Hall, on Monday evening, February 14, the program consisting of works for Choir and Orchestra and several numbers *a cappella* for the Choir, concluding with Parts II and VI of the Brahms "Requiem"; Claude Cunningham (baritone) soloist.

Nineteenth Season—1909-1910

Choir and Orchestra appeared in Cleveland, at Gray's Armory, in two concerts: Tuesday evening, February 15, the Choir sang several *a cappella* numbers—"Crucifixus" (Lotti), "On Himalay" (Bantock)—and the legend, "Christ when a Child" (Tschaikowsky). Wednesday evening, February 16, the important numbers were a portion of Brahms' "Requiem" and Chadwick's ballad, "Young Lochinvar," with Herbert Witherspoon (bass), soloist.

Mr. Stock and his men were back in Chicago early Thursday morning to prepare for the concerts of February 18 and 19, Nineteenth Program, Bruno Steindel, soloist, playing the Goltermann concerto for violoncello in B minor, Opus 51.

Twentieth Program, February 25 and 26, called "aquatic" by the critics:

Overture, "Fingal's Cave," Opus 26,	*Mendelssohn*
Two Movements from "Das Meer,"	*Nicodé*
"La Mer,"	*Debussy*

INTERMISSION

Concerto for Pianoforte in C Sharp Minor, Opus 28, Hans Richard	*Schytte*
Overture, "Le Carnaval Romain," Opus 9,	*Berlioz*

Mr. Richard, a Swiss pianist, living then in Cincinnati, gave a brilliant interpretation of the concerto by the Danish composer. The work has no real claim to originality and force, further than that it affords the player opportunities for a display of technique.

Twenty-second Program, March 11 and 12. Heinrich Gebhard came from Boston and delighted the audience by his performance of the "Pagan Poem" by Charles Marie Loeffler, a former member of the Boston Symphony Orchestra. The poem, based on some verses in Virgil's "Eclogues" and constructed along modern lines with a fund of originality, calls for a large orchestra, pianoforte, with obbligato parts for English horn, and three trumpets; the work received a poetic reading at the hands of Mr. Gebhard.

A dinner was given Monday evening, March 14, by the Trustees to the friends of the Orchestra, in the foyer of the hall, to provide funds to meet the $330,000 indebtedness now due on Orchestra Building. There were present:

GEORGE E. ADAMS.	CHARLES H. HAMILL.
JOSEPH ADAMS.	DR. GEORGE S. ISHAM.
MAX BAIRD.	DR. F. S. JOHNSON.
A. M. BARNHART.	VICTOR F. LAWSON.
A. G. BECKER.	BLEWETT LEE.
HENRY S. BOUTELL.	PHILO A. OTIS.
WILLIAM L. BROWN.	RALPH POOLE.
W. J. BRYSON.	HAROLD SMITH.
DANIEL H. BURNHAM.	HENRY E. VOEGELI.
F. A. DELANO.	WILLIAM B. WALKER.
JOHN V. FARWELL, JR.	FREDERICK J. WESSELS.
C. NORMAN FAY.	WALTER H. WILSON.
I. L. GATZERT.	B. L. WINCHELL.
JOHN J. GLESSNER.	C. M. WOOLLEY.

Prior to the dinner the entire Orchestra, under the direction of Mr. Stock, played several numbers on the stage in the hall, and then Trustees and guests adjourned to the foyer for dinner, sitting around the tables with Steindel, Schreurs, Krauss, Zettelmann, Tramonti and other men of the Orchestra whose names are like household words, and discussed the needs of the great cause, in which all were working. At the close of the dinner Daniel H. Burnham, Vice-President, in the absence of Bryan Lathrop, President of the Board of Trustees, spoke of the work of the Orchestra and its influence on the moral and educational life of Chicago. He announced that $85,000 had been secured that evening, making, with the $15,000 previously subscribed, a total of $100,000. "I am hopeful," continued Mr. Burnham, "that the fund will reach $200,000 before the end of the week."

The evening closed with a vaudeville by the members of the Orchestra:

> "ONE PERFORMANCE ONLY—THE WORLD FAMOUS STOCK COMPANY OF OVERTRAINED MUSICIANS —UNDER THE DIRECTION OF TWO CONDUCTORS, SEVERAL ENGINEERS, ALSO SOME FIREMEN."

One does not often hear on the stage anything brighter or more amusing in acting and make-up, than the selections then given:

I. Signor Maximo Spaghetti and His Royal Italian Band of Fifty Pieces.
II. Double-bass Solo—Mme. Violet Jiskra.
III. The Hungry Bunch.
IV. The Celebrated Vienna Ladies' Orchestra of Fifteen Pieces.

Nineteenth Season—1909-1910   217

V. The Four Jolly Monks and Mme. Isabel Dontcome; Première Ball of the Royal Opera, Kokomo.

TWENTY-THIRD PROGRAM, MARCH 18 AND 19
Soloist: Mme. Teresa Carreño*

Concerto for Pianoforte, No. 1, B Flat Minor,
Opus 23, ...   *Tschaikowsky*

The remaining concerts of the Nineteenth Season may be briefly noted:

"Twenty-fifth Program, April 1 and 2: 'Popular' concerts: Alfred Quensel played Winkler's concerto for flute (orchestration by Alfred Quensel), and Hans Letz the Andante from Viotti's concerto for violin in A minor, and the Rondo from Vieuxtemps' concerto in E major."

"Twenty-sixth Program, April 8 and 9: Enrico Tramonti, soloist, played Zabel's concerto in C minor, in which the artist showed by his mastery of the instrument, that he is still the Paganini among harp players. Repetition of Mr. Stock's symphony No. 1 in C minor created great enthusiasm."

"Twenty-seventh Program, April 15 and 16, with the assistance of the Apollo Musical Club, Harrison M. Wild, Conductor, and soloists: Mabel Sharp Herdien (soprano), Rose Lutiger Gannon (contralto), John B. Miller (tenor), William Beard (bass), Dr. Wm. Carver Williams (bass); Arthur Dunham, organist."

Overture, "In Springtime," Opus 36, ...   *Goldmark*
"Cherubim Song," . . . .   *Tschaikowsky*
"Ave Maria," Opus 45, ...   *Franz*
Motet, "I Wrestle and Pray," . . . .   *Bach*
Three Choruses from "Ruth," Opus 50, ...   *Schumann*

INTERMISSION

Symphony No. 9, D Minor, Opus 125, ...   *Beethoven*

TWENTY-EIGHTH, AND LAST, PROGRAM, APRIL 22 AND 23

Overture to "The Flying Dutchman," . . . . .   *Wagner*
Symphony No. 3, F Major, Opus 90, ...   *Brahms*

INTERMISSION

Rondo, "Till Eulenspiegel's Merry Pranks," Opus 28, .   *Strauss*
"Invitation to the Dance," . . . .   *Weber—Weingartner*
Overture, "1812," Opus 49, ...   *Tschaikowsky*

Mr. Stock received an ovation after the performance of Tschaikowsky's "1812" overture.

The program book noted the death of three members of the Orchestra:

---
*Mme. Teresa Carreño died June 12, 1917, in New York City.

> **IN MEMORIAM**
>
> E. Kruschwitz
> August 29, 1908
>
> L. Mayer
> December 1, 1909
>
> C. Moerenhout
> March 20, 1910

The out-of-town concerts by the Orchestra had now become of such importance in the work of the Association that a brief record may be here noted of the principal cities visited by Mr. Stock and his men.

A few words about the contracts with the members of the Orchestra and provision for playing the out-of-town engagements may be also in order at this time:

Every member of the Orchestra agrees in his contract with the Trustees to play twenty-eight weeks in Chicago, two concerts per week (Friday afternoon and Saturday evening), making fifty-six concerts, and an equal number of other concerts in or out of Chicago during the period and for the salary named in the contract, making 112 concerts in all, besides the regular rehearsals. This enables the Manager to provide the Orchestra for the Apollo and Mendelssohn Clubs and other local organizations, and to accept engagements in St. Louis, Milwaukee, Detroit, Cleveland and points as far east as Toronto, provided such concerts do not interfere with the Friday and Saturday concerts at home; and with no additional salaries to the men further than paying their hotel bills and transportation.

The concerts after the close of the Chicago season have been undertaken by our Manager, Mr. Wessels, as his own venture, and often at a loss, but with the commendable thought of earning additional salaries for the men. In this way the Orchestra has played during the spring and summer months in Birmingham, Atlanta, Memphis, Louisville, St. Louis, St. Paul and other cities in the south and west.

For the Festivals at Cincinnati, Ann Arbor, Oberlin, and other cities and the North Shore Festival at Evanston,

Nineteenth Season—1909-1910

the Musicians' Union has fixed a separate scale of pay for the men, so that individual contracts must be made.

One of the best stopping places along the "Highway" is Cleveland, where Mr. Wessels has made yearly visits since 1901 in a series of symphony concerts, admirably managed by Mrs. Adella Prentiss Hughes, of that city. During the Nineteenth Season the Orchestra appeared there November 17, 1909, with Mrs. Tilly Koenen (contralto), soloist; February 16, 1910, with the Mendelssohn Choir, heretofore noted, and March 30 with Enrico Tramonti (harp), soloist.

The Nineteenth Cincinnati Festival was held May 3, 4, 5, 6 and 7 under the direction of Frank Van der Stucken, with Frederick Stock, Associate Conductor, and the Theodore Thomas Orchestra:

SOLOISTS

SOPRANOS: Mme. Emmy Destinn, of the Royal Opera, Berlin; Mrs. Corinne Rider-Kelsey, Mme. Mariska Aldrich, Mrs. Edith Chapman Goold, Mrs. Antoinette Werner West.

CONTRALTOS: Mme. Louise Homer, Mme. Ernestine Schumann-Heink, Miss Janet Spencer.

TENORS: Daniel Beddoe, N. Hougnard Nielsen, H. Evan Williams.

BASSES: Herbert Witherspoon, Claude Cunningham.

The important works given were Handel's "Judas Maccabæus," Beethoven's "Missa Solennis," Pierné's "Children's Crusade" and Berlioz's "Trojans in Carthage." I went to the first concert, Tuesday evening, May 3, to witness the unveiling of the bronze statue of Theodore Thomas, which stands in the foyer of Music Hall, and to hear the address of President Taft on the life and work of our leader. The statue was the gift of the people of Cincinnati, in amounts large and small, headed by a subscription of $5,000 from Howard A. Hinkle. Mr. Van der Stucken made a happy choice in selecting "Judas Maccabæus" as the musical setting for the dedication, a work written by Handel (1747) "to express the irresistible enthusiasm of a people for a victorious hero."

When the choral number ending Part I of the oratorio had been sung—

> "Hear us, O Lord; on Thee we call,
> Resolved on conquest or a glorious fall,"

President Taft was ushered to the platform with a great fanfare of trumpets. The President said in his eulogy of Theodore Thomas:

> "It is fitting that this concert of the May Festival be dedicated to this great man. It is not for me, however, with no knowledge of music, to comment on his high and fine art, but even if one is not a musician we cannot afford to have any but the highest regard for this man, who made an ideal of his art and lived up to it."

The draperies were then removed from the statue, and on leaving the hall at the conclusion of the concert we were permitted to view this fitting tribute of the people of Cincinnati to the founder of the May Festivals.

On my way east for the summer I had the pleasure of another visit at Willow Grove with the men of the Orchestra, who were filling their Third Season (June 17-July 9) in that attractive resort. I arrived at the Grove in the afternoon of July 5, in time to hear Part II of the concert and afterward go with Mr. Stock and Mr. Wessels to the Huntington Valley Club House, where we had rooms as guests of the officers of the Philadelphia Traction Company. After dinner on the porch of the Club House, affording a glorious view of the valley, we returned to the Grove for the evening concert.

The Willow Grove engagement afforded a pleasant outing for the men. Mr. Stock had prepared programs of a popular character from the repertoire of the Orchestra, which required but few rehearsals; the afternoons and evenings were given over to work, but the mornings belonged to the men for recreation and the delightful out-of-door life at the Grove.

Hans Letz, second concertmeister, was the soloist on Wednesday evening, July 7, in Saint-Saëns' prelude to "The Deluge," and Bruno Steindel (violoncello) on Friday evening, July 8, in "The Andante" (Goltermann) and "Serenade" (Glazounow).

The season at the Grove closed on Saturday evening, July 9, the final number on the program being Tschaikowsky's overture "1812." The next day Mr. Stock and the men returned to Chicago for two weeks of concerts at Ravinia Park.

NINETEENTH SEASON
(1909-1910)

SOLOISTS

DOUBLE-BASS: V. Jiskra.
FLUTE: Alfred Quensel.
HARP: Enrico Tramonti.
ORGAN: Wilhelm Middelschulte, Arthur Dunham.
PIANOFORTE: Mmes. Teresa Carreño, Olga Samaroff; Ferruccio Busoni, Anton Foerster, Heinrich Gebhard, Sergei Rachmaninow, Hans Richard.
VIOLIN: Miss Maud Powell; Hans Letz, Alexander Sebald.
VIOLONCELLO: Carl Brueckner, Bruno Steindel.
VOCAL: Mmes. Johanna Gadski, Ernestine Schumann-Heink, Mrs. Corinne Rider-Kelsey.
VISITING CONDUCTORS: George W. Chadwick, Sergei Rachmaninow.
CHORAL: The Apollo Musical Club of Chicago.

TWENTIETH SEASON
(1910-1911)

The Orchestral Association now an Endowed Institution—The friends of the Orchestra again respond with subscriptions to meet the debt on Orchestra Building—Clyde M. Carr elected a Member of The Orchestral Association—The St. Paul Symphony Orchestra assists the Apollo Musical Club—The Theodore Thomas Orchestra again visits Toronto for the Annual Concerts of the Mendelssohn Choir—Willow Grove engagement.

After six years of concerts in the new hall, the people of Chicago began to appreciate the value of this permanent home for the Orchestra. The period of embarrassing deficits and subscription papers had now passed. No longer would The Orchestral Association appear before the public as a perpetual mendicant; it had risen to the dignity of an endowed institution. With the completion of the Orchestra Building the Trustees were at once in receipt of rentals from hall, offices and stores, which, added to the earnings of the Orchestra, after paying salaries, concert expenses, cost of administration, taxes and interest, would assure a surplus for further needs.

The time had now come when another effort must be put forth by the friends of the Orchestra to meet the loan of $330,000, incurred for finishing the hall, and maturing in 1910. For this purpose a dinner was given to the Trustees and Members Monday evening, March 14, 1910, when subscriptions for upwards of $100,000 were secured. This amount was increased during the summer months to $130,000 by additional subscriptions and the surplus earnings of the Association. Once more did the men and women of Chicago nobly and unselfishly respond to the call of the Trustees, as they have never failed to do when the Trustees were in need. The balance of $200,000 on the debt was carried by the bank of the Association until the time came for placing a new loan on the property.

The Orchestral Association had now completed nineteen years of work in giving the best of music to the Chicago public—a work which was assuming the character of a well established business, in routine, detail and system. Season succeeded season, with few changes. The character of the programs prepared by Mr. Stock, the soloists and the work of the Orchestra continued to be of the highest order. The Executive Committee met every Friday, after the concert, for the transaction of the routine business, the Trustees meeting when matters of importance were to be considered. Thanks to the increasing rentals of hall and building, there were no immediate financial burdens for the Trustees to carry, although money would be needed ultimately to pay the remainder of the debt on the building, keep up and improve the hall.

The season ticket sale opened in September, showing a total of $86,229 when the concerts began, a decrease of $2,200 as compared with the sale of the previous season, owing to the Grand Opera and other attractions.

FIRST CONCERTS, OCTOBER 14 AND 15

Festival March, ... *Stock*
(First Performance)
Symphony No. 4, F Minor, Opus 36, ... *Tschaikowsky*
INTERMISSION
Overture, "Leonore," No. 3, ... *Beethoven*
Prelude to "Die Meistersinger von Nürnberg," . . . *Wagner*

It was an ideal day for the opening concert, with the regular Friday audience in attendance filling every seat. Mr. Stock's "March" was an attractive feature of the program, "composed in commemoration of the opening of the Twentieth Season of the Theodore Thomas Orchestra, and dedicated to the Officers and Members of The Orchestral Association."

The new concertmaster, Hans Letz,* appeared at the First Concerts, succeding Ludwig Becker, resigned.

The program book contained this tribute to an old member of the Orchestra:

> IN MEMORIAM
> REINHARD GLASS
>
> Died October 1, 1910
> A faithful member of
> THE THEODORE THOMAS ORCHESTRA
> for nineteen years

---

*Hans Letz, born March 1887, in Ittenheim, Alsace, came to America in 1908. On leaving Chicago he joined the Kneisel String Quartet, and on its disbandment, organized the Letz Quartet, of which he is still the first violinist. Mr. Letz now resides in New York City, and in addition to his work with the quartet, is head of the Violin Department of the New York College of Music.

A newspaper man said, "I could hardly recognize my old friends, 'The Star Spangled Banner,' 'Dixie' and 'Old Folks at Home' amid such gorgeous instrumental surroundings."

The Third Program, October 28 and 29, was arranged by Mr. Stock to commemorate the one hundredth anniversary of the birth of Schumann. The anniversary having occurred June 8, 1910, six weeks after the Nineteenth Season had closed, it became necessary to hold over the commemoration performance of Schumann's works until the beginning of the next season. The program included Schumann's overture, "The Bride of Messina" and the symphony No. 1 in B flat major. After the intermission Jaroslav Kocian played Lalo's Spanish symphony for violin with orchestra, the concert closing with "The Carnival in Paris" (Svendsen)

At the concerts of November 11 and 12, Fifth Program, Henry Hadley's symphony No. 3 in B minor was given under the direction of the composer.

Francis Macmillen was the soloist at the concerts of November 18 and 19, Sixth Program,* playing the concerto for violin in A minor, Opus 28, by Goldmark.

The Seventh Program ("Popular"); November 25 and 26, included:

Hungarian Rhapsody No. 2, ...	*Liszt*
"Peer Gynt" Suite, No. 1, Opus 46, ...	*Grieg*
Symphonic Waltz, Opus 8, ...	*Stock*

Mr. Stock's waltz was produced at the concerts of November 1 and 2, 1907, Fourth Program of the Seventeenth Season. On the occasion of this interpretation, Mr. Stock, being requested for a statement concerning the significance of his composition, provided the following:

"As to the waltz itself, we don't think that it should stand in need of either comparison or analysis, although it is meant to be symphonic—or at least pretends to be so. It is written in the key of D major and in 3-4 time, just like the 'Beautiful Blue Danube' by Johann Strauss, but the themes are treated in more elaborate fashion. We trust fully what is good in it will make itself felt in true waltz-like fashion—let's say spontaneously—and that its pretentious title will fully protect it against undue or unbecoming popularity."

---

*This concert was given as an "extra" Thursday afternoon (24th), Thanksgiving Day.

Twentieth Season—1910-1911

The Annual Meeting was held Tuesday afternoon, December 13, in the offices of the Association in Orchestra Building.

The Treasurer's report for the Nineteenth Season (1909-1910), ending June 30, 1910, was then read:

Receipts		Expenses	
Chicago concerts	$111,057.25	Salaries of Conductor and Orchestra, and expenses	$108,460.50
Outside concerts (net)	17,115.33	Business management and advertising	17,480.35
Program book, etc.	2,815.68	Soloists	8,150.00
Hall rentals	51,892.50	Music and instruments	1,633.80
Building rentals	27,105.50	Interest	14,450.00
		Taxes	7,701.90
		Hall and building expenses, heating, etc.	40,317.58
		Net profit on the season	11,792.13
	$209,986.26		$209,986.26

The resignation of Chauncey B. Borland as a Member of the Association was accepted, and Clyde M. Carr was elected to fill the vacancy.

TENTH PROGRAM, DECEMBER 16 AND 17
BEETHOVEN ANNIVERSARY
Soloist: Ernest Hutcheson

Overture, "Fidelio," ⎫
Concerto for Pianoforte No. 3, C Minor, ⎭ . . . *Beethoven*

INTERMISSION

Symphony No. 7, A Major, Opus 92, ... *Beethoven*

Alfred Quensel (flute) and Enrico Tramonti (harp) were the soloists in the Eleventh Program ("Popular"), December 23 and 24, in the concerto for flute and harp by Mozart.

In consequence of out-of-town engagements the Orchestra was unable to take part in the performance of "The Messiah," by the Apollo Musical Club, Friday evening, December 23, in Orchestra Hall; the St. Paul Symphony Orchestra taking its place. The visiting Orchestra was welcome, and under the direction of

Harrison M. Wild furnished a spirited accompaniment for the oratorio. Soloists: Mrs. Mabel Sharp Herdien (soprano), Mrs. Marie White Longman (contralto), H. Evan Williams (tenor), Albert Borroff (bass); Arthur Dunham (organist).

TWELFTH PROGRAM, DECEMBER 30 AND 31
SOLOIST: ALEXANDER ZUKOVSKY*

Concerto for Violin in D Major, ... *Tschaikowsky*

THIRTEENTH PROGRAM, JANUARY 6 AND 7
THEODORE THOMAS MEMORIAL
SOLOIST: WILHELM MIDDELSCHULTE

Tragic Overture, Opus 81, ... *Brahms*
Sinfonia Sacra, for Organ and Orchestra, Opus 81, . . . *Widor*

INTERMISSION

Symphony No. 3, "Eroica," E Flat, No. 55, . . . *Beethoven*

SIXTEENTH PROGRAM, JANUARY 27 AND 28
SOLOIST: XAVER SCHARWENKA

Concerto for Pianoforte No. 4, F Minor, Opus 82, . *Scharwenka*

SEVENTEENTH PROGRAM, FEBRUARY 3 AND 4

The program included attractive numbers by Mme. Schumann-Heink:

Aria, "Hellstrahlender Tag," Opus 41, ... *Bruch*
    (From "Odysseus")
"O Ma Lyre Immortelle," . . . . *Gounod*
    (From "Sappho")
"My Heart at Thy Dear Voice," . . . . . *Saint-Saëns*
    (From "Samson et Dalila")

"February 5, Sunday P. M.: To the Polk Street Station to see the Orchestra start for Toronto to assist the Mendelssohn Choir in their Annual Concerts; regret so much I could not go."

When the Orchestra returned home I received the programs, with enthusiastic reports of the singing of the Choir:

"February 6, Monday evening; Massey Hall; miscellaneous program for Choir and Orchestra; Dr. A. S. Vogt and Frederick Stock, Conductors.

"February 7, Tuesday evening: 'The Manzoni Requiem' (Verdi); Miss Florence Hinkle, Miss Janet Spencer, George Hamlin and Herbert Witherspoon, soloists; Dr. A. S. Vogt, Conductor.

*Alexander Zukovsky was born July 1, 1882, at Kieff. At the age of five he began the study of the violin, and when ten years old toured Russia as a *Wunderkind*. He entered the Moscow Imperial Conservatory, studying the violin with Hyrmali and *ensemble* with Wassily Ilyitch Safonnov. In 1898 Mr. Zukovsky was engaged by Safonnov as first concertmeister of the Moscow Imperial Orchestra, holding this position while in the Conservatory. During this period Mr. Zukovsky played under Rimsky-Korsakow, Tschaikowsky, Arthur Nikisch, Richard Strauss and other Conductors. In 1906-1907 he made his *début* in Prague and Dresden, playing with the Orchestras in those cities.

Mr. Zukovsky became a member of the Theodore Thomas Orchestra at the beginning of the Twentieth Season (1910-1911).

Twentieth Season—1910-1911

"February 8, Wednesday afternoon: Matinée by the Theodore Thomas Orchestra, Bruno Steindel (violoncello), soloist; Frederick Stock, Conductor.

"February 8, Wednesday evening, and February 9, Thursday evening: 'The Children's Crusade' by Pierné, with Mrs. Edith Chapman-Goold, Mrs. Mabel Sharp Herdien, George Hamlin and Herbert Witherspoon, soloists; Dr. A. S. Vogt, Conductor; A. L. E. Davies, Associate Conductor."

After the return of the Orchestra to Chicago the regular concerts were resumed. A few may be noted:

TWENTY-SECOND PROGRAM, MARCH 10 AND 11
SOLOIST: HENIOT LEVY
Concerto for Pianoforte, No. 2, F Minor, Opus 21, . . *Chopin*

At the Twenty-fourth Program, March 24 and 25, four of the principal players in the Orchestra were soloists —Barthel, Schreurs, Kruse and de Maré, giving the Concertante Quartet (for oboe, clarinet, bassoon and horn, with orchestra), by Mozart.

TWENTY-SIXTH PROGRAM, APRIL 7 AND 8
SOLOIST: MRS. FANNIE BLOOMFIELD ZEISLER
Concerto for Pianoforte in C Minor, ... *Mozart*

Twenty-eighth, and Last, Program, April 21 and 22: The principal numbers were:

Symphony No. 4, B Flat, Opus 60, ... *Beethoven*
"The Wand of Youth," No. 2, Opus 13, ... *Elgar*
"Festival March," . . . . *Stock*

TWENTIETH SEASON
(1910-1911)
SOLOISTS

BASSOON: Paul Kruse.
CLARINET: Joseph Schreurs.
FLUTE: Alfred Quensel.
HARP: Enrico Tramonti.
HORN: Leopold de Maré.
OBOE: Alfred Barthel.
ORGAN: Wilhelm Middelschulte.
PIANOFORTE: Mme. Yolando Mérö, Mrs. Fannie Bloomfield Zeisler; Adolphe Borchard, Ferruccio Busoni, Ernest Hutcheson, Heniot Levy, Xaver Scharwenka.
VIOLIN: Mischa Elman, Jaroslav Kocian, Hugo Kortschak, Hans Letz, Francis Macmillen, Alexander Zukovsky.
VIOLONCELLO: Paulo Gruppe, Boris Hambourg, Bruno Steindel.
VOCAL: Miss Perceval Allen, Mme. Ernestine Schumann-Heink.
VISITING CONDUCTOR: Henry Hadley.

The Orchestra, with Mr. Stock, visited Willow Grove at the close of the season for a three weeks' engagement, commencing June 12. These annual trips to the Grove were welcome experiences in the life of the Orchestra, affording change and recreation for Conductor and men. A pleasant surprise awaited me on my arrival Thursday (the 29th) at the Phoenix Hotel, where Mr. Stock and many of the men were staying, to note my name among the composers on the program of the concert the previous afternoon:

Overture, "The Barber of Seville," . . . . *Rossini*
Suite, "Peer Gynt," No. 2, ... *Grieg*
   a. "Arabian Dance."
   b. "Solveig's Song."
"Benedictus," . . . . *Otis*
Two Dances from "The Bavarian Highlands," . . . . *Elgar*

The "Benedictus," written for violin, 'cello, harp, organ and double-bass, was first used (1910) in a service in our church (First Presbyterian). Mr. Stock was so much interested in the work that he scored it for full Orchestra. The "Benedictus" was repeated Friday evening (the 30th) and under my direction, at Mr. Stock's request:

Overture, "Academic Festival," . . . . *Brahms*
"Benedictus," . . . . *Otis*
Suite, "Nutcracker," . . . . *Tschaikowsky*
   I. "Ouverture Miniature."
   II. "Danses Caractéristiques."
   III. "Valse des Fleurs."
Irish Rhapsody, ... *Herbert*

TWENTY-FIRST SEASON
(1911-1912)

"The Chamber Music Society"—Eastern tour of the Orchestra—People in Philadelphia and Boston not interested—New York kindly disposed towards the "Windy City" players—The return home and loss on the tour—Clyde M. Carr elected a member of the Board of Trustees—Bryan Lathrop gives a testimonial dinner to the members of the Orchestra—The Orchestra visits Toronto for the Mendelssohn Choir Concerts—Orchestra and Choir make an eastern tour—Death of Daniel Hudson Burnham—Willow Grove engagement.

The season came and went quietly and calmly, without disturbing influences, with no serious financial issues to meet, though the returns from the season ticket sale were disappointing—$84,271—some $2,000 less than the previous season, owing to the "spell" of the Friday afternoon concerts and lack of interest in the concerts on Saturday evenings.

Mr. Stock prepared an attractive program for the first concerts, October 13 and 14:

Overture to "Der Freischütz,"	Weber
Symphony No. 5, C Minor, Opus 67,	Beethoven

INTERMISSION

Suite, "Die Königskinder,"	Humperdinck
Legend for Orchestra, "Zorahayda," Opus 11,	Svendsen
Overture to "Tannhäuser,"	Wagner

The one hundredth anniversary of the birth (1811) of Franz Liszt was observed by Mr. Stock in the concerts of October 27 and 28, Third Program, with Rudolph Ganz, soloist:

Huldigungsmarsch,	Wagner
Concerto for Pianoforte, No. 1, E Flat,	Liszt

INTERMISSION

"A Faust Symphony," in Three Character Pictures (after Goethe),	Liszt

FAUST.
MARGARET (GRETCHEN).
MEPHISTOPHELES.

(With the assistance of John B. Miller and the Chicago Mendelssohn Club, Harrison M. Wild, Musical Director.)

Bruno Steindel was the soloist at the concerts of November 10 and 11, Fifth Program, playing the concerto for violoncello in A minor, Opus 33 (Saint-Saëns).

The program books since the opening of the season contained announcements by the Executive Committee of the Chicago Chamber Music Society (Mrs. Theodore Thomas, Mrs. John J. Glessner and Mrs. Frank S. Johnson) that ten concerts would be given during the season by the Chicago String Quartet, the Chicago Wood-Wind Choir, the Kneisel and the Flonzaley Quartets.

I was unable to attend the first concert by the Chicago String Quartet, November 24, but have a pleasant remembrance of the second concert of the series given by the Wood-Wind Choir: Alfred Quensel (flute), Alfred Barthel (oboe), Joseph Schreurs (clarinet), Leopold de Maré (horn), Paul Kruse (bassoon) and Miss Eleanor Scheib (piano), Saturday morning, December 9, in the foyer of Orchestra Hall, with an attractive program:

Quintet in E Flat, ... *Mozart*
Quintet, Opus 55, ... *Rubinstein*

A disturbing feature on Friday afternoons is the impatience of some people to leave before the close of the concert. A "Friday subscriber" expressed her views on the subject in the program book of December 1 and 2:

"AS THE PROGRAM ENDS

"To me the Thomas Orchestra programs are great, satisfying, inspiring. And the playing is simply wonderful. I want to go every Friday, and I want to hear all of the program—the beginning and the end. Apparently others have not that desire, for they come late, thereby missing the first number, and they leave at any time during the progress of the last number. The tardy ones, however, are not permitted to disturb the punctual ones, because they are not seated until after the close of the number. I wish some such rule could be enforced to save marring the close of the program. Those who do not care to listen to the last number could leave before it begins. At present someone is going out all through it, possibly to get wraps from the checkroom before the rush, and others are busy from the start of it, poising hats, borrowing hatpins, arranging mufflers and veils, struggling into coats, so as to be entirely ready to rush away before the Conductor's baton has fairly paused. If one is interested in listening to this part of the program—and it is just as good to me as the middle—it is decidedly distracting to have such restlessness all around you."

The doctrine of reciprocity in the musical relations between Toronto and Chicago took on a new form after the visit of the Mendelssohn Choir to Chicago during the Eighteenth Season, in the suggestion that Toronto and Chicago should make a tour of the eastern cities during the winter of 1911-1912. The suggestion was at once adopted by our Executive Committee and the officers of the Mendelssohn Choir, and the arrangements for the tour were placed in the hands of Manager Wessels, of the Orchestra. In preparing the programs for the tour a serious question arose: how to give Choir and Orchestra proper representation without making the concerts too long. Dr. Vogt wished to produce large choral works, for which, as an accompaniment, an orchestra of seventy-five men would suffice. Mr. Stock had important modern works in mind, which would require an orchestra of ninety men. Our committee therefore decided to send the Orchestra on a preliminary tour early in the winter.

Thirteen years had now passed since the Orchestra visited New York and Boston (1898) with Mr. Thomas, and it seemed now that the Orchestra should again go east—this time with the new Conductor, Frederick Stock.

The entire Orchestra, with Conductor Stock, Manager Wessels, Assistant Manager Voegeli and the Secretary, left Chicago Sunday noon, December 10, by special train over the Pennsylvania Road, arriving at Philadelphia Monday morning (the 11th). The concert took place in the evening at the Academy of Music with a program Mr. Stock had prepared for the three cities, Philadelphia, Boston and New York; Albert Spalding, soloist. The few people who came manifested little interest in the Orchestra which bore the name of the great leader, who had filled the hall to overflowing in other days. Does not Rip Van Winkle ask the question, "Are we so soon forgot, when we are gone?"

PROGRAM

Overture, "Coriolanus," Opus 62, ... *Beethoven*
Symphonic Poem, "Don Juan," Opus 20, ... *Strauss*
Concerto for Violin, B Minor, Opus 61, ... *Elgar*
(First Performance in America)

INTERMISSION

Symphony No. 2, D Major, Opus 73, ... *Brahms*

The *Philadelphia Record* of December 12 was in an appreciative mood:

"With so many good orchestras in our country it would be difficult to venture any adequate comparison of their respective merits, but there need be no hesitancy in declaring that for an absolute perfection of *ensemble* the Thomas Orchestra is unapproachable."

Leaving Philadelphia at midnight, we were in Boston at 2:00 P. M. Tuesday (the 12th), several hours late, owing to delays on the road. Concert at Symphony Hall in the evening; a better house than in Philadelphia, and somewhat more responsive.

The *Boston Press* was guarded in its opinion:

"Orchestras that come to this town from other cities may not win large audiences, but they do gain audiences of *connoisseurs*. Mr. Mahler and the Philharmonic Orchestra of New York once played here to a very small but a very distinguished and appreciative company. The audience for Mr. Stock and the Thomas Orchestra of Chicago in Symphony Hall last evening was happily larger, equally expert and discriminating and still more appreciative of the Conductor and the band. Such genuine, rattling and spontaneous applause has not been heard in Symphony Hall, even for the cherished 'soloists' of the symphony concerts, for many a day."

Mr. and Mrs. Bryan Lathrop came from Chicago especially to hear the concert and inspire Conductor and men by their presence. We left Boston at midnight, arriving in New York Wednesday (the 13th) at 7:30 A. M. Concert at 2:15 in Carnegie Hall; a good house.

The *New York Times* of December 14 felt kindly toward the players from "The Windy City":

"The Chicago Orchestra has not reached a point of high development. It is not yet the finest Orchestra in the country, but the 'Windy City by the Lake' has reason to be proud of it and of its firm establishment, and ought to find in its ministrations artistic delight of a high order."

After the concert, dinner with Mr. Lathrop at the New Astor for Mr. Stock; other guests, Fay, Wessels, Voegeli, Consolo (pianist) and wife, and the Secretary; thence to Brooklyn for the concert. Owing to delay in getting the music and instruments to the Academy of Music, Mr. Stock did not go on the stand until 8:30; a meagre attendance on the part of Brooklyn music lovers.

PROGRAM

SOLOIST: ALBERT SPALDING

Overture to "Der Freischütz," . . . . *Weber*
Symphony No. 5, C Minor, Opus 67, ... *Beethoven*

INTERMISSION

Concerto for Violin, No. 3, B Minor, Opus 61, . . *Saint-Saëns*
Andante Soave ("Gretchen"), from "A Faust Symphony," . *Liszt*
Finale from "Das Rheingold," . . . . *Wagner*

Later in the evening Mr. Stock, Mr. Spalding, members of the Orchestra and guests were delightfully entertained at supper by R. E. Johnston, Eastern Manager for the tour, at the Hofbrau Haus; an informal occasion of good fellowship and good cheer, which lasted until we were called to the train for the return home.

Our report of the tour to the Executive Committee showed artistic work worthy of the honored name the Orchestra bears; but the financial returns made "a melancholy exhibit":

Receipts: Philadelphia, $520; Boston, $711; New York, $1,846; Brooklyn, $635; total, $3,702; loss on tour, $5,000.

THIRTEENTH PROGRAM, JANUARY 5 AND 6
THEODORE THOMAS MEMORIAL

Overture to "Iphigénie en Aulide," . . . . . . *Gluck*
Symphony No. 3, "Eroica," E Flat, Opus 55, . . *Beethoven*

INTERMISSION

Selections from Music to "Rosamunde," Opus 26, . . *Schubert*
Träume. A Study to "Tristan and Isolde," . . . . *Wagner*
(Orchestration by Theodore Thomas)
Prelude to "Die Meistersinger von Nürnberg," . . . *Wagner*

The Annual Meeting of the Association, adjourned from December 12, 1911, was held January 9, 1912, at 4:00 P. M. in the offices of the Association in Orchestra Building; President Lathrop in the chair. The Treasurer's report for the Twentieth Season (1910-1911) ending June 30, 1911, was then read:

RECEIPTS		EXPENSES	
Chicago concerts	$108,657.25	Salaries of Conductor and Orchestra	$112,457.00
Other concerts (net)	14,690.48	Concert expenses	12,100.34
Program book	1,666.54	Business management	16,156.65
Interest (bank account)	467.58	Interest on mortgage	11,541.66
Hall and building (net)	22,134.22		
Deficit	4,639.58		
	$152,255.65		$152,255.65

The accumulated interest from the Field Memorial Fund amounted to $9,465 on June 30, 1911.

The action of the Executive Committee* in applying for a loan of $200,000 at four per cent on ten years' time to repay the loan now being carried by the Association's bank, was approved.

The resignation of Stanley McCormick as a Member of the Association was accepted, and Benjamin Carpenter was elected to fill the vacancy. Clyde M. Carr was elected a Trustee to fill the vacancy caused by the resignation of Frank O. Lowden.

In the informal discussion of the affairs of the Orchestra at the close of the meeting the suggestion was made that our friends be asked to make provision in their wills for the payment of the $200,000 indebtedness. In line with this thought Mr. Lathrop prepared an article for the program book of the concerts of January 19 and 20:

"THE BEST MUSIC FOR THE BEST PEOPLE
"No institution in the city contributes more to the pleasure of the intelligent and to the elevation of the masses than does the Theodore Thomas Orchestra.

"Public spirited citizens have in the past contributed hundreds of thousands of dollars by way of subsidies to enable the Orchestra to do its work. Within the last six years nearly nine thousand persons have contributed approximately $750,000 to provide ground and a building for it, on which property there is still a debt of $200,000.

"It needs to have this debt paid and an endowment to enable it to do its work better, and more of it. If sufficiently endowed to afford it, it would give a series of absolutely free concerts, in addition to the regular series.

"Bequests may be made to The Orchestral Association."

SIXTEENTH PROGRAM, JANUARY 26 AND 27
SOLOIST: HANS LETZ
Fantasie for Violin, Opus 46, ... *Bruch*

A testimonial dinner was given Friday evening, February 2, at the Bismarck, by Bryan Lathrop, President of The Orchestral Association, to the members of the Orchestra and Frederick Stock, Conductor. It was an occasion of frolic and fun, after the manner of the festivities the men have prepared in other years, when we

"Turn night time into day time
With the sunlight of good cheer."

---

*The Executive Committee at a subsequent meeting authorized the President and Secretary to execute the necessary papers for a loan of $200,000, secured on Orchestra Building and land, to be dated February 1, 1912, due ten years after date, at the rate of four per cent per annum, payable semi-annually.

Twenty-first Season—1911-1912

A few numbers of the program may be noted:

SIGNOR SPAGHETTI AND HIS ROYAL ITALIAN BAND
"Alt Wien."
    Violin, ... A. Van der Voort
    Viola Alto, ... O. Roehrborn
    Accordion (Chromatique), ... W. Speckin
    Bassalaute, ... K. Stiegelmayer
Wien bleibt Wien, ... J. Schrammel
The President's Waltz, ... Karl Stiegelmayer
            Dedicated to President Bryan Lathrop

Gemeinsamer Gesang.
Spatzen Kongress.
    First Violin, ... H. Letz
    Second Violin, ... H. Kortschak
    Viola, ... F. Esser
    Violoncello, ... B. Steindel
Iberia, ... Claude
    Disarranged and Decomposed from the Original Texture for a Modern Orchestra, with Profound Explanations by Willy Speckin.
    Owing to the Lamentable Absence of Ludwig Wuellner, the Decomposer will Substitute:
    No. I.   In the Streets and by the Wayside.
    No. II. The Odors of the Night.
    No. III. The Morning of a Fête Day.

    The Orchestra is composed of:

Violin, Siren, ... Otto Roehrborn
Violin, Bassoon, ... Hjalmar Rabe
Bass, Police Whistle, ... Robert Maedler
Flute, Piccolo, ... Alfred Quensel
Oboe, Guitar, ... Karl Stiegelmayer
Essclarinet, ... Karl Meyer
French Horn, Dog-bark, ... Leopold de Maré
French Horn, ... Wm. Frank
Trombone, Auto Horn, ... G. Stange
Harp, Violin, ... W. Singer
Wooden Ladles, Pot Lids, Cow Bells, Wooden
    Shoes, Trolley Car Bells, Trowels, Auto-
    smell, Cat-calls, Triangle, ... Joseph Zettelmann
Snare Drum, Tambourin, Castanets, . . . Max Wintrich
Bass Drum, Cymbals, Beer Barrel, Broken Beer
    and Wine Bottles, ... Frank Wagner

The Annual Concerts of the Mendelssohn Choir again called the Orchestra and Mr. Stock to Toronto:

    "February 5, Monday evening, Massey Hall: Miscellaneous program for Choir and Orchestra; Dr. A. S. Vogt and Frederick Stock, Conductors.

    "February 6, Tuesday evening: 'The New Life' (Wolf-Ferrari) and 'Te Deum' (Berlioz). Soloists: Miss Florence Hinkle (soprano), George Hamlin (tenor), Clarence Whitehill (bass); Dr. A. S. Vogt, Conductor.

"February 7, Wednesday evening: 'The Manzoni Requiem' (Verdi). Soloists: Miss Florence Hinkle (soprano), Miss Christine Miller (mezzo-soprano), George Hamlin (tenor), Clarence Whitehill (bass); Dr. A. S. Vogt, Conductor.

"February 8, Thursday evening: Miscellaneous program for Choir and Orchestra. Soloists: Miss Florence Hinkle (soprano), Miss Christine Miller (mezzo-soprano); Dr. A. S. Vogt and Frederick Stock, Conductors."

The Orchestra returned to Chicago for the concerts of February 9 and 10, Eighteenth Program, though the Friday concert did not start until 3:00 P. M., owing to railway delays.

NINETEENTH PROGRAM, FEBRUARY 16 AND 17
SOLOIST: MME. JOHANNA GADSKI

Aria, "Wie nahte mir der Schlummer," from "Der Freischütz," . . . . *Weber*
"Tristan and Isolde," . . . . *Wagner*
    ACT I. PRELUDE, "WIE LACHEND SIE MIR LIEDER SINGEN."
    ACT III. ISOLDE'S LOVE-DEATH.

Detailed plans for the tour of eastern cities by Choir and Orchestra had been made by Mr. Wessels while in Toronto on the recent trip. The entire Theodore Thomas Orchestra, with Conductor Stock, Manager Wessels, Assistant Manager Voegeli and the Secretary, left Chicago Sunday afternoon, February 25, by special train over the Michigan Central Road, joining Dr. Vogt and the Choir at the Hotel Statler in Buffalo. The first concert was given Monday evening, February 26, in Convention Hall, in the outskirts of Buffalo, and at some distance from the residential section; conditions, however, which did not keep the people from coming in crowds to the concert. The program included:

Sacred Motets:
    (a) "Crucifixus," . . . . *Lotti*
    (b) "Psalm CXXXVII," . . . . *Gounod*
        THE MENDELSSOHN CHOIR
Hymne et Prière from the "Te Deum," . . . . . *Berlioz*
    THE MENDELSSOHN CHOIR AND THEODORE THOMAS ORCHESTRA
Soprano Solo and Chorus from the "Manzoni Requiem,"
    "Libera Me," . . . . *Verdi*
    MISS FLORENCE HINKLE, THE MENDELSSOHN CHOIR AND THEODORE
        THOMAS ORCHESTRA
Symphonic Waltz, ... *Frederick Stock*

Our first contact with the cold, critical east was in every way successful, the audience being charmed with

Twenty-first Season—1911-1912

the work of Choir and Orchestra; especially the singing by the Choir, which showed the same sonorous body of tone, precision of attack and enunciation we had learned to appreciate in other concerts with the Toronto Choir.

The next morning (the 27th) we arrived in New York by special train, taking up our quarters at the Woodward Hotel, within a few blocks of Carnegie Hall.

In the afternoon at four o'clock Choir and Orchestra, with Conductors Vogt and Stock, were delightfully entertained at a reception at the New Astor Hotel, by the Mendelssohn Club of New York (Clarence Dickinson, Musical Director).

In the evening, concert at Carnegie Hall, using the program given at Buffalo, with a few changes; Miss Florence Hinkle, soloist, Dr. A. S. Vogt and Frederick Stock, Conductors.

The critics were kindly disposed toward the work of Choir and Orchestra, H. E. Krehbiel of the *New York Tribune*, on the 28th, Thursday, especially so:

"The great Choir under its able Conductor, Dr. A. S. Vogt, performed all and more than was expected of it. In volume, richness and resonance of tone, in precision and unanimity of attack, in delicacy of shading, in powers of *crescendo* and *diminuendo*, it was deserving of the highest praise. Especially beautifully sung, too, was Antonio Lotti's "Crucifixus.""

The *New York Herald* was enthusiastic in its review of the concert:

"Across the border came the Mendelssohn Choir of Toronto, yesterday, two special Pullman trains loaded with them and their enthusiastic friends, and gave the first of two concerts last night in Carnegie Hall, assisted by the Theodore Thomas Orchestra of Chicago. And musical New York sat up, listened and cheered.

"And how they sang! Five years ago they first visited this music-ridden city and surprised their hearers. Recollections of that visit still cling in the memory, but their singing last night passed all former records. For *finesse*, surety of attack, intonation and all those other technical things the Choir is beyond the reach of jaunty criticism. They sang like one perfect quartet magnified a hundred fold.

"The Theodore Thomas Orchestra, conducted by Mr. Stock, also earned laurels."

Thursday evening, Choir and Orchestra joined in the performance of Verdi's "Manzoni Requiem," assisted by Miss Florence Hinkle (soprano), Miss Christine Miller (mezzo-soprano), George Hamlin,* (tenor) and Clarence Whitehill (bass); Dr. A. S. Vogt, Conductor.

At the conclusion of the concert Choir and Orchestra left for Boston, arriving in that city at 8:30 Friday morning. The concert in the evening drew an audience which filled Symphony Hall; the program was the same as that used in Buffalo and at the first New York concert. We were honored by the presence at the concert of Sir Edmund Walker, Honorary President of the Choir, with Lady Walker. Many Boston musicians and critics were present, all of them enthusiastic over the work of the great Choir.

H. T. Parker said in the *Boston Evening Transcript:*

"In our musical generation Boston has heard no such choral singing as that of the Mendelssohn Choir in Symphony Hall last evening, and applauded no choral Conductor of such ability as its leader, Dr. Vogt. For two hours and a half it held an audience that filled every corner of the great room, interested, intent, receptive and rewarding. Its program traversed almost the whole range of choral music, from a motet of Lotti for the early Italian vocal contrapuntists to light pieces by the contemporary Brockway and Von Storch. It touched the classic, ancient and modern, of choral music in the 'Sanctus' of Bach's Mass in B minor; in the 'Judex Crederis' of Berlioz's 'Te Deum'; in the 'Libera Me' of Verdi's Requiem. It entered opera with the exclamation of Sachs from the final scene in Wagner's 'Die Meistersinger.' It skirted folk-song, and it dramatized the grave harmonies of Gounod in his setting of the 'Psalm of the Waters of Babylon.' The chorus sang some of these pieces without accompaniment, and when accompaniment was necessary, sixty-odd members of the Thomas Orchestra of Chicago played it.

"No choir, no choral Conductor, has so mastered these secrets or gone so far in high and various attainment in them as Dr. Vogt and these Torontoans."

After the concert that night Choir and Orchestra started for their respective homes, laden with honors

---

*George Hamlin, one of the first of American tenors, was the son of John H. Hamlin, well known in other days as the owner of the Grand Opera House in Chicago, then situated on Clark Street. After his graduation from Phillips Academy at Andover, Massachusetts, young Hamlin went abroad to study, and on his return made Chicago his home. Here he became widely known through his choir, concert and oratorio work. He was the first artist in America to introduce the songs of Richard Strauss. He made his *début* in opera with Mary Garden in the first production (1912) in Chicago of Victor Herbert's opera, "Natoma," by the Chicago Grand Opera Company. George Hamlin was born September 20, 1869, in Elgin, Illinois, and died January 10, 1923, in New York City, where he had made his home in recent years.

Twenty-first Season—1911-1912

and bearing, best of all, the good wishes and thorough appreciation of new friends formed in the east.

In consequence of the eastern engagement of the Orchestra, the concert for Friday, March 1, was postponed to Saturday, March 2, at 2:15 P. M.

Dr. Vogt,* some years later, wrote me of his remembrances of the tour:

"TORONTO, October 24, 1919.

"I was very much pleased to receive your note, more particularly since it refers to that most delightful joint tour of your Orchestra and our Choir to New York, Boston and Buffalo in 1912.

"I feel that in this trip there was attained the highest standard of *ensemble* work, as between chorus and Orchestra, in the history of the Mendelssohn Choir. The superb support rendered the Choir by the Orchestra reflected not only the splendid technique of the Orchestra, but in a convincing manner revealed the wholehearted interest and enthusiasm of Mr. Stock, who left no stone unturned to provide, in the accompaniments to the work of the Choir, the same high ideals for which the Orchestra has become famous in its own special sphere as a symphonic body."

TWENTY-FOURTH PROGRAM, MARCH 22 AND 23
SOLOIST: HUGO KORTSCHAK

Concerto for Violin No. 4 in D major, ... *Mozart*

Twenty-eighth, and last, Program, April 19 and 20, with the assistance of the Apollo Musical Club, Harrison M. Wild, Conductor. Soloists: Miss Florence Hinkle (soprano), Mme. Nevada Van der Veer (alto), Reed Miller (tenor), Frederick Weld (baritone); Arthur Dunham (organist).

Kaisermarsch, ... *Wagner*
Vorspiel to "Parsifal," . . . . *Wagner*
Selections from "Caractacus," . . . . *Elgar*
    I. DUET—SOPRANO AND TENOR.
    II. LAMENT—CARACTACUS AND CHORUS.
    III. THE SEVERN—DRUIDESSES AND A BARD.
    IV. THE PROCESSION—CHORUS.
    V. EPILOGUE—CHORUS.
(Conducted by Mr. Wild)

INTERMISSION

Symphony No. 9, D Minor, Opus 125, ... *Beethoven*

The Theodore Thomas Orchestra went to Cincinnati for the Twentieth Festival, May 7, 8, 9, 10 and 11;

---

*In 1917 Dr. Vogt gave up his work with the Mendelssohn Choir to accept the Directorship of the Toronto Conservatory of Music.

Frank Van der Stucken, Musical Director, Frederick Stock, Associate Conductor.

SOLOISTS

SOPRANOS: Mme. Johanna Gadski, Mrs. Corinne Rider-Kelsey, Mrs. A. Werner West.
CONTRALTOS: Mme. Schumann-Heink, Miss Christine Miller.
TENORS: Riccardo Martin, Alessandro Bonci.
BASSES: Clarence Whitehill, Herbert Witherspoon, Tom Daniels, Douglas Powell.
ORGANIST: A. Stadermann.
CHORUS CONDUCTOR: Alfred Hartzell.

I am glad now that I could be there for a few of the concerts, as it proved to be the last Festival in which our Orchestra took part. I could not leave home in time to hear "Elijah" on Tuesday evening (the 7th), but heard César Franck's "Beatitudes" on Wednesday evening (the 8th), with delightful work by chorus and Orchestra, Mr. Van der Stucken conducting.

"Thursday, May 9: Long conference at the Hotel Sinton with Stock, Wessels and Ulrich about affairs of our Orchestra. How can we compete with New York, Philadelphia and Cincinnati in salaries? If we are forced to take our Orchestra out of the union on account of their demands we shall require a larger income. How can we do it?

"Matinée at 2:15; great audience. Soloist, Mme. Schumann-Heink. In Liszt's symphony to Dante's 'Divina Commedia' 500 children from Cincinnati public schools sang the choral part without their notes—beautiful! Stock conducted entire program.

Overture, 'Hänsel and Gretel,' . . . . . *Humperdinck*
'Träume,' . . . . *Wagner*

"Mr. Van der Stucken may not conduct the next Festival; some friction between the supporters of the Orchestra and supporters of the Cincinnati Orchestra; a new Conductor, Ernest Kunwald, coming for the Orchestra; he may conduct the Festival.

"There being no concert Thursday evening, left for home."

The Festival closed with some important works:

FOURTH CONCERT, FRIDAY EVENING, MAY 10

"The New Life" (For Solos, Chorus and Orchestra), . *Wolf-Ferrari*
"Pax Triumphans," . . . . *Van der Stucken*
ORCHESTRA.

The Fifth Concert, Saturday matinée, May 11, presented an entire Wagner program, conducted by Mr. Stock.

DANIEL HUDSON BURNHAM

Twenty-first Season—1911-1912

SIXTH CONCERT, SATURDAY EVENING, MAY 11

"Requiem," . . . . *Berlioz*
    SOLOIST: ALESSANDRO BONCI (TENOR).
    CHORUS AND AUGMENTED ORCHESTRA.
    CONDUCTOR: FRANK VAN DER STUCKEN.

The death, June 1, in Heidelberg, Germany, of Daniel Hudson Burnham, "Genius in architecture; known wherever art is known," brought sorrow to the people of Chicago and the friends of the Orchestra. The *Chicago Tribune* said of his life and work:

"Mr. Burnham was not merely a builder. He will be remembered, indeed, as a dreamer—a practical dreamer of noble dreams. He will be remembered as a leading maker of the epoch-making Columbian Exposition (1893) and as the father of the city plan of Chicago, and the most effective and aggressive leader in the inspiring movement for the beautification of cities."

The name of Daniel Hudson Burnham will be long remembered and associated with that of Bryan Lathrop as the creators and builders of Orchestra Hall. Resolutions were adopted by the Trustees June 6, on the death of Mr. Burnham:

"The Trustees of The Orchestral Association, in appreciation of their loss in the death of Daniel Hudson Burnham, desire to make this minute in the records of the Association.

"Mr. Burnham's name and fame need no mention here. The high order of his public service to his city, his state and his country have received their appropriate recognition and comment. The notable work of the firm of architects which bore his name and worked under his leadershop and inspiration, was fully recognized. His services as Director of Works and Construction of the World's Columbian Exposition; his services to the City of Chicago in preparing a plan for the future growth and development of the city; his services to the nation as a planner of great works, as evidenced by his work in Washington, San Francisco, at Manila and elsewhere, have all received generous and well deserved praise.

"The Trustees of The Orchestral Association, in full recognition of Mr. Burnham's many services in this direction, and because there is no occasion to repeat what has been so well said by others, wish to record here Mr. Burnham's services to this Association.

"Early in its history he became a Guarantor, and in January, 1895, was elected a Trustee. In December, 1899, he was elected Vice-President and member of the Executive Committee, and held these offices at the time of his death.

"It is, perhaps, natural enough that a man of Mr. Burnham's tastes and temperament should have been interested in music, and, therefore, in The Orchestral Association. The remarkable part is that, devoted as he was to another field of art, and absorbed as he was in many great undertakings, he should have been willing to give so generously of his time, his energy and his means; for the records show that in the bad times of 1895 and 1896, Mr. Burnham, with other Trustees of the Association, struggled manfully and successfully to put it on a sound and permanent footing; and when it came to building our Orchestra Hall, gladly contributed the services of his firm to the preparation of plans and superintendence of construction.

"His value as a Trustee having been fully appreciated by those associated with him, this minute is here and now unanimously adopted in grateful recognition of his valuable help and inspiration."

Now came the Willow Grove engagement, those happy days of "rest and gladness" for Conductor and men, which I shared with them during the first week in July. I arrived at Philadelphia in the morning of the 2nd, going out to the Grove early in the afternoon. At the "Mineral Spring House" I found our Conductor and Manager Wessels with some of the men, and started with them for the afternoon concert. At the Pavilion I again experienced a pleasant surprise in finding my name among the composers on the program. The "Pastorale" played that afternoon was another work written for violin, 'cello, harp and organ, for a service in our church (First Presbyterian) and it interested Mr. Stock so much that he scored it for orchestra. The "Pastorale" was repeated at the afternoon concert on Friday (the 5th) and, at Mr. Stock's request, under my direction.

My real purpose in stopping at the Grove was to confer with the Conductor and Manager about Orchestra matters—how to meet the competition created by salary lists in other cities—and to discuss the question of a second concertmeister who could act as Assistant Conductor for the coming season. Mr. Stock had such a man in mind, now in Berlin, who wished to come to Chicago, and would be a great accession to the Orchestra; but no action was taken towards bringing him from Berlin, in consequence of the rule of the Musicians' Union which requires a residence of six months in the United States before an alien musician can become eligible to membership in the union.

From Willow Grove Mr. Stock and the men returned to Chicago for three weeks of concerts at Ravinia Park.

TWENTY-FIRST SEASON
(1911-1912)
SOLOISTS
HARP: Enrico Tramonti.
ORGAN: Wilhelm Middelschulte.
PIANOFORTE: Misses Priscilla Carver, Hazel Everingham, Edna Gunnar Peterson, Mrs. Fannie Bloomfield Zeisler; Wilhelm Bachaus, Harold Bauer, Arthur Friedheim, Rudolph Ganz, Arthur Shattuck.
VIOLIN: Miss Kathleen Parlow; Hugo Kortschak, Hans Letz, Albert Spalding, Efrem Zimbalist.
VIOLONCELLO: Bruno Steindel.
VOCAL: Misses Elena Gerhardt, Florence Hinkle, Mmes. Johanna Gadski, Nevada Van der Veer; Reed Miller, Frederick Weld, Clarence Whitehill.
VISITING CONDUCTORS: Peter C. Lutkin, Frank Van der Stucken, Harrison M. Wild.
CHORAL: The A Cappella Choir of the Northwestern University, Apollo Musical Club of Chicago, chorus of eighty ladies from the Chicago North Shore Festival.

TWENTY-SECOND SEASON
(1912-1913)

The Attorney General of the United States gives an opinion regarding the Musicians' Union—The Eighth Season of the Chicago Chamber Music Society—Trustees vote to change the name of the Orchestra, and make an announcement to the public—Willow Grove engagement.

The National Federation of Musicians, having its principal office in New York City, with branch offices or "locals" in all the important cities throughout the United States, aims to keep on its rolls the best orchestral players, who can become members only after a severe examination as to their musical attainments; and to demand for its members salaries which shall be uniform. Certain benefits in case of illness or disability belong to a membership in the Federation.

The Alien Contract Labor Bill, enacted some years ago by Congress, aims to prevent the importation into the United States of carpenters, masons, machinists and other men to be employed in skilled labor, but never was intended to include violinists or other players of orchestral instruments. The Federation, however, has always contended that the bill covered all ordinary band or orchestral players, but made this provision, that if the Conductor of any Orchestra wishes to bring a player from Berlin to the United States, the player may come, but must remain six months in this country without employment in theatres or concerts where union men are employed. He may appear at concerts as a soloist, or he may teach. At the end of the six months, and on payment of $100, he is admitted to the Federation. He may then apply for a "transfer card"—if living in New York—to the Chicago "local," which may or may not accept the candidate, according to the length of the waiting list.

At the close of vacation days (1912) passed in the hills of New Hampshire I went down to Bretton Woods, and at the Mount Washington Hotel met the Hon. George Wickersham, Attorney General of the United States:

"September 1, Sunday P. M.: Long interview with Mr. Wickersham; told him of our wish to bring a second concertmeister

Twenty-second Season—1912-1913

(as Assistant Conductor) from Berlin, and of the attitude of the Federation. He replied: 'The Musicians' Union has no love of art. Legally their position is strong. It is a private organization, like all social clubs, and can make its own by-laws and rules regarding admission of members. Go back to Chicago; get your strong supporters together and secure a fund to take your Orchestra out of the union, as Mr. Higginson has done in Boston. As conditions are now the President and Congress cannot help you."

Later in the month, while *en route* for home, I stopped a few days in New York City to meet Joseph N. Weber, President of the Federation:

"September 28, Saturday: Spent the afternoon with Mr. Weber in the office of the National Federation, to ask his consent that we might bring a violinist from Berlin to Chicago. At first Mr. Weber demurred. 'You do not need to go abroad for players; plenty of violinists in Chicago walking the streets, with nothing to do; quite good enough for the Thomas Orchestra any time.' I replied that 'Mr. Stock has prepared programs which will require players of a high order. The works announced for this season could not be given with the men you mention.' Finally Mr. Weber withdrew his objections, saying he would write Mr. Stock accordingly."

By this time all the members of the Orchestra for the new season having been secured, the Executive Committee took no further action towards securing foreign players.

The season ticket sale yielded $82,600, nearly $2,000 less than that of the previous season, showing the reluctance of the public to attend the Saturday night concerts.

The Twenty-second Season opened October 18 and 19:

Suite No. 3, D Major, ... *Bach*
Symphony No. 4, B Flat, Opus 60, ... *Beethoven*
INTERMISSION
Suite, "Les Erinnyes," . . . . *Massenet*
VIOLONCELLO OBBLIGATO BY BRUNO STEINDEL
Prelude to "Lohengrin," . . . . *Wagner*
Finale from "Das Rheingold," . . . . . . *Wagner*

A new concertmeister (Hans Letz having resigned) appeared at these concerts, Harry Weisbach,* a young artist of ability, who gave every promise of being a great acquisition to the Orchestra, a promise he fully redeemed in the nine years he was with us.

---

*Mr. Weisbach was born April 28, 1886, in Odessa, Russia, and emigrated to America in 1890; studied in New York with Conductor Volpe, and became concertmeister at fourteen years of age. Eugène Ysaye, while on a tour (1905) in America, heard Mr. Weisbach, and was so much interested in his work that the young violinist had a summer's tuition (1906) at Ysaye's country home. Later Mr. Weisbach went to the Berlin Hochschule and became a pupil of Carl Halir for two years, graduating with highest honors, and appearing as soloist in concerts with the Berlin Philharmonic. He retired from the Chicago Symphony Orchestra at the close (1921) of the Thirtieth Season, and is now engaged in concert work.

The program book of these concerts contained the announcement of the Eighth Season of the Chicago Chamber Music Society; seven concerts, to be given in the foyer of Orchestra Hall, on Thursday afternoons at three o'clock, in charge of the Executive Committee of the Society:

MRS. N. H. BLATCHFORD.
MRS. CLYDE M. CARR.
MRS. ALBERT M. DAY.
MRS. F. A. DELANO.
MRS. A. B. DICK.
MRS. HENRY L. FRANK.
MRS. JOHN J. GLESSNER.
MRS. FRANK S. JOHNSON.
MRS. HARRY P. JUDSON.
MRS. JOHN R. LINDGREN.
MRS. WILLIAM R. LINN.
MRS. RUDOLPH MATZ.
MRS. PHILO A. OTIS.
MRS. RUSSELL TYSON.
MRS. CLARA WOODYATT.

December 5, The Chicago String Quartet.
December 19, The Chicago String Quartet.
January 20, 1913, The Flonzaley Quartet.
February 20, The Chicago String Quartet.
March 6, The Chicago Wood-Wind Choir.
March 20, The Chicago String Quartet.
April 3, The Kneisel Quartet.

"December 5, Thursday, 3:00 P. M.: First concert in the foyer of Orchestra Hall by the Chicago String Quartet, Harry Weisbach (first violin), Otto Roehrborn (second violin), Franz Esser (viola) and Bruno Steindel (violoncello)":

Quartet in C Major, ... *Haydn*
Quartet in B Flat Major, ... *Brahms*

The Annual Meeting was held Tuesday, December 10, at 4:00 P. M., in the offices of the Association, there being present in person or by proxy thirty-seven of the thirty-nine Members; President Lathrop in the chair.

The Treasurer, in his report for the Twenty-first Season (1911-1912) ending June 30, 1912, showed:

RECEIPTS		EXPENSES	
Chicago concerts	$107,491.00	Business management	$ 16,667.87
Outside concerts (net)	10,658.41	Advertising	2,975.93
Program book	2,153.01	Salaries of Conductor, Orchestra and expenses	116,488.35
Interest	394.03	Soloists	7,200.00
Hall and building rentals	70,339.38	Music	1,697.55
		Interest on loan	10,626.22
		Building and hall expenses, heating, insurance, ushers, etc.	30,912.77
		Taxes	8,663.49
Deficit	7,442.64	Repairs	3,246.29
	$198,478.47		$198,478.47

Twenty-second Season—1912-1913

The accumulated interest from the Field Memorial Fund (part of which has been used for disabled musicians) at the close of the current season amounted to $11,215.

Seymour Morris was elected a Member and Trustee of the Association, to fill the vacancy caused by the death of Daniel H. Burnham.

Bruno Steindel was the soloist at the concerts of December 27 and 28, Eleventh Program, in the variations for violoncello and orchestra, Opus 23, by Boellmann.

At the conclusion of the number, brilliantly interpreted by the artist, he was presented with a laurel wreath by a member of the Executive Committee, in honor of his twenty-two years of faithful work with the Orchestra.

TWELFTH PROGRAM, JANUARY 3 AND 4
THEODORE THOMAS MEMORIAL

Overture, "Coriolanus," Opus 62, ...	*Beethoven*
Symphony No. 8, F Major, Opus 93, ...	*Beethoven*

INTERMISSION

Symphony No. 3, "Eroica," E Flat, Opus 55, . .	*Beethoven*

THIRTEENTH PROGRAM, JANUARY 10 AND 11
AMERICAN COMPOSERS
Soloist: Efrem Zimbalist

Overture, "In Bohemia," Opus 28, ...	*Hadley*
(First Performance in Chicago)	
Romance for Orchestra, "Festival of Pan," Opus 9, . .	*Converse*
Concerto for Violin, E Major, ...	*Powell*
(First Performance in Chicago)	

INTERMISSION

Theme and Variations for Orchestra, Opus 19, . . .	*Oldberg*
(First Performance)	
Suite, A Minor, Opus 42, ...	*MacDowell*

I find this note in my journal:

"January 17, Friday evening: Dinner at the home of Mr. and Mrs. John J. Glessner to Mr. Stock, officers of the Association and members of the Orchestra. The Vienna Ladies' Orchestra, fifteen members of our Orchestra who have appeared on other occasions, entertained host, hostess and guests with lovely music."

At the Fifteenth Program, January 24 and 25, Mischa Elman, soloist for the week, being detained at Madison, Wisconsin, by illness, Leon Sametini, of the Chicago Musical College, appeared in his place, playing Brahms' concerto for violin, in D major.

There was some delightful work by the Chicago Woodwind Choir in the concert on Thursday afternoon, March 6: Messrs. Alfred Quensel (flute), Alfred Barthel (oboe), Joseph Schreurs (clarinet), Paul Kruse (bassoon) and Leopold de Maré (horn), assisted by Rudolph Reuter (piano):

"Caprice sur des Airs Danois et Russes," . . . . *Saint-Saëns*
    Piano, Flute, Oboe and Clarinet.
"Pastorale, Mal du Pays and Eclogue," . . . . *Liszt—Lassen*
    Flute, Oboe, Clarinet, Bassoon and Horn.
Quintette, ... *Spohr*
    Piano, Flute, Clarinet, Bassoon and Horn.

SIXTEENTH PROGRAM, JANUARY 31 AND FEBRUARY 1

SOLOIST: MISS JULIA CULP

Aria, "Il Lamento d'Arianne," . . . . . . *Monteverde*
Symphony No. 3, in F Major, Opus 90, ... *Brahms*

INTERMISSION

Ellen's Songs Nos. 1, 2 and 3, from Sir Walter Scott's
  "Lady of the Lake," . . . . *Schubert*
    a. "SOLDIER, REST! THY WARFARE O'ER."
    b. "HUNTSMAN, REST! THY CHASE IS DONE."
    c. "AVE MARIA."

Miss Julia Culp was in early life a violinist, and as a prodigy her playing attracted much attention in Holland. At the age of fourteen her mother discovered that she had a remarkable voice, and it was then that she was taken to sing before the Queen Mother of Holland, who provided for her vocal education. Miss Culp studied two years at the Amsterdam Conservatory, and afterward went to Berlin for a finishing course with Etelka Gerster.

This was her first appearance as soloist amid these surroundings.

NAME OF THE ORCHESTRA CHANGED
to
THE CHICAGO SYMPHONY ORCHESTRA
Founded by Theodore Thomas

During the winter of 1912-1913 President Lathrop interviewed or wrote to every member of the Board of Trustees, suggesting important reasons for changing the name "The Theodore Thomas Orchestra" to "The Chicago Symphony Orchestra." Mr. Lathrop had always

Twenty-second Season—1912-1913

held to the belief that an institution depending largely on the public for its support suffers in bearing the name of its founder or benefactor, however honored or distinguished that name may be. The large givers in the community are not always ready to respond to appeals by the institution for funds, believing that such appeals concern the friends and relatives of the founder.

Mr. Lathrop favored the name "The Chicago Symphony Orchestra" for a further reason: that if we did not secure the name some other musical organization surely would.

Eleven of the fifteen Trustees having responded to Mr. Lathrop's letter with their approval of his recommendation, the Executive Committee at its meeting on Friday, February 21, 1913, adopted this resolution:

"WHEREAS, A vote of the Trustees has been taken by letter on the question of adopting as the official name of our Orchestra, 'The Chicago Symphony Orchestra, Founded by Theodore Thomas,' and eleven of the fifteen Trustees have expressed themselves in favor of the adoption of the foregoing name, and no vote has yet been received against it,

"*Resolved*, That hereafter the official name of the Orchestra shall be,
  'THE CHICAGO SYMPHONY ORCHESTRA
   'Founded by Theodore Thomas.'"

The program book of the concerts of February 28 and March 1, twentieth week, appeared with the new name of the Orchestra:

THE CHICAGO SYMPHONY ORCHESTRA
Founded by Theodore Thomas
FREDERICK STOCK, CONDUCTOR

"ANNOUNCEMENT

"The Trustees of The Orchestral Association announce a change in the name of the Theodore Thomas Orchestra to 'The Chicago Symphony Orchestra, Founded by Theodore Thomas.'

"The main object in the change of the name is to forestall and prevent the adoption by any other musical organization of the name 'Chicago Symphony Orchestra,' as this would involve endless embarrassment and complication, and possibly serious financial loss to The Orchestral Association.

"By incorporating in the name the words, 'Founded by Theodore Thomas,' the Trustees believe that they will indissolubly connect the name of our first great Conductor with that of the Orchestra, and indicate to the world what the present name fails to do, that he was the founder of our Orchestra, and it will commemorate the great work which he did in America for the cause of good music. The new name will also associate the Orchestra with the city and people of Chicago, and insure for it their continued aid and support."

The Trustees sent, March 6, the following statement to the press:

"There is no diminution of the respect and esteem which the Trustees had for Mr. Thomas in his life, or of their wish to honor his memory. When the name was changed to 'The Theodore Thomas Orchestra' it was in courtesy to the family, and without any consideration whatever. The Board that was competent to make that change is competent to make this change now, and the Trustees feel that in it they are honoring Mr. Thomas' memory, while at the same time doing what they conceive to be for the best interests of the institution and for the credit of the city where it was built up and has its home, and from the citizens of which it derives its support.

"The Thomas Musical Library was tendered to The Orchestral Association by the Thomas family on January 10, 1905, without any reference or conditions as to the name of the Orchestra, which on that date was known as 'The Chicago Orchestra.' On January 28, 1905, the name was changed to 'The Chicago Orchestra, Founded by Theodore Thomas,' and it was not until April 11, 1905, that the title 'Theodore Thomas Orchestra' was adopted without any reference whatever to the gift of the library. Subsequently, at Mrs. Thomas' request, the more valuable scores, consisting of manuscripts, rare editions, etc., were transferred to the Newberry Library."

The term "Symphony Orchestra" is largely an Americanism. The important Orchestras in Europe are not so designated, and they are the London Philharmonic, the Lamoureux, Pasdeloup and Colonne of Paris, the Gewandhaus of Leipzig and the Philharmonics of Berlin and Vienna. Not one of these organizations ever leaves the home city for an extended tour. The work of the London Philharmonic is confined to the metropolis, though occasional concerts are given in other large English cities. All England, with Wales added, is not so large as the State of Illinois. If the London Orchestra had to cover a circuit of 2,000 miles with a concert tour, as the Theodore Thomas Orchestra was obliged to do every season to earn salaries, and local conditions along the "Highway" called for a change in the name, the Philharmonic would be forced to make the change, as we were.

Theodore Thomas was "a tower of strength" in his day, but it is sad to apply to him the question asked by Rip Van Winkle: "Are we so soon forgot when we are gone?" It is, alas! too true. The name of Theodore Thomas was almost unknown in some places where the

Twenty-second Season—1912-1913

Orchestra has played. The "melancholy" financial exhibit of the eastern tour (1912) of the Theodore Thomas Orchestra has already been noted. Where were the friends of thirty years ago, who crowded the Philadelphia Academy of Music and the Brooklyn Academy of Music whenever Mr. Thomas conducted? Dead and gone, many of them. The concert-goers of today, not being interested, stayed at home. During Mr. Thomas' life our Manager, Mr. Wessels, occasionally used in the out-of-town business the phrase "Theodore Thomas and his matchless Orchestra," to which Mr. Thomas more than once objected, saying: "This is a Chicago institution; my name must die."

In suggesting the change in the name of the Orchestra Mr. Lathrop unconsciously followed the thought expressed by Mr. Thomas: "The Orchestra is a Chicago institution." The name of a city is greater than that of a citizen. An institution bearing the name of a city has a larger vision, a broader field of influence, and will interest more people in its work than the institution named for the citizen.

There was great reluctance, mingled with sad thoughts on the part of the Trustees, to see the time-honored name "The Theodore Thomas Orchestra," a household word in our midst, disappear from the programs. Mr. Lathrop was right: "The condition and future of the Orchestra" called for this sacrifice, and the judgment of the people now sustains the Trustees in their action.

Several conclusions grew out of the "Announcement" by the Trustees which sustained them in their decision to change the name of the Orchestra:

"(1) The new name 'The Chicago Symphony Orchestra' is practically the original name taken (1891) by the Trustees and Mr. Thomas, with the word 'Symphony' added, and with a further clause which sets forth the important fact that Theodore Thomas was the founder;

"(2) Whereas the former name, 'The Theodore Thomas Orchestra,' might not suggest to the people along the 'Highway,' where the out-of-town concerts are important factors in our business, that Theodore Thomas was the founder, or that he had ever had anything to do with the Orchestra; any more than the name of the Toronto Choir would necessarily mean that 'Mendelssohn' was its founder or that he had ever been its Conductor;

"(3) In the judgment of the Trustees, The Orchestral Association and no other organization should control the name, 'The

Chicago Symphony Orchestra.' In fact, the name had already been preëmpted by a Chicago manager, who courteously surrendered it when our position was explained to him;

"(4) The real strength of our case, however, was based on the request of the strong supporters, 'citizens of no mean city,' without whose money there would never have been an Orchestra in Chicago. These men gave freely and generously, asking in return neither public mention nor recognition; only this, that Chicago should have some credit for the existence of the Orchestra, and that the name of the city should now be linked with that of its great founder—Theodore Thomas."

A meeting of the Trustees was held Monday afternoon, March 17, to act on the resignation of Charles Norman Fay, Second Vice-President, Trustee and Member of The Orchestral Association. Present at the meeting: Messrs. George E. Adams, Baird, Carr, Glessner, Hamill, Keep and Otis. The Secretary read Mr. Fay's letter of March 10, and, on motion of Mr. Adams, seconded by Mr. Baird, the resignation was accepted, and the Secretary was authorized to advise Mr. Fay of the acceptance of the resignation, with the sincere regrets of the Trustees and with their thorough appreciation of his work in the creation and maintenance of the Orchestra.

Some attractive concerts now followed, which may be briefly noted:

"Madame Schumann-Heink was the soloist in the Twenty-third Program, March 21 and 22, in an aria and recitative from 'La Clemenza di Tito' (Mozart), with clarinet obbligato by Joseph Schreurs, followed by the scene and aria 'Gerechter Gott' from 'Rienzi' (Wagner); the concert closed with the Good Friday Spell, Transformation Scene and Glorification from 'Parsifal' (Wagner)."

Eugène Ysaye, the soloist for the Twenty-fourth Program, March 28 and 29, was caught in the floods in Ohio and Indiana, but, by traveling fifty miles in a carriage, managed to get the first train which had left Indianapolis in several days, and after a seventeen-hour trip arrived in Chicago, Friday (the 28th) at 12:30 P. M., in time for a brief rehearsal before the concert. His principal number was a concerto for violin by the Italian composer, Viotti (1753-1824), in which the work of the Belgian artist was of the highest order. After intermission he played the "Scotch Fantasia" (Bruch).

"April 3, Thursday evening: Concert for the benefit of the flood sufferers in Ohio and Indiana, by Mr. Stock and the Orchestra, all donating their services, and the Trustees the use of the hall. The principal numbers: Overture, 'Euryanthe' (Weber), 'The

Twenty-second Season—1912-1913

New World' Symphony (Dvořák), 'The Wand of Youth' (Elgar), and Mr. Stock's arrangement of the Minuet (Beethoven). Mr. Tramonti (harp), soloist, contributed the 'Tristesse' (Lebano). The entire gross receipts, $1,167, were given to the committee in charge of the relief work."

"April 7, Monday evening: Berlioz's 'Faust' by the Apollo Musical Club in the Auditorium, under the direction of Harrison M. Wild. Soloists: Mabel Sharp Herdien (soprano), George Harris, Jr. (tenor), Leon Raine and Herbert Miller (baritones); Arthur Dunham (organist), and the Chicago Symphony Orchestra."

TWENTY-SIXTH PROGRAM, APRIL 11 AND 12
Soloist: Wilhelm Middelschulte

Elegy, Chorale and Fugue, ... *Otterström*
    (First Performance)
Passacaglia for Organ and Orchestra, D Minor, . *Middelschulte*

TWENTY-EIGHTH, AND LAST, PROGRAM, APRIL 25 AND 26
WAGNER ANNIVERSARY

Overture to "The Flying Dutchman."
"Tristan and Isolde":
    Act I. Prelude.
    Act II. Introduction, Love Scene and Brangaene's Warning. Dreams
    —a Study to "Tristan and Isolde."
        (Orchestration by Theodore Thomas)
    Act III. Introduction, Tristan's Vision, Arrival of the Ships, Isolde's Love Death.

INTERMISSION

Overture to "Rienzi."
Siegfried Idyl.
Ride of the Valkyries, from "Die Walküre."
Overture to "Tannhäuser."

TWENTY-SECOND SEASON
(1912-1913)
SOLOISTS

Harp: Enrico Tramonti.
Organ: Wilhelm Middelschulte.
Pianoforte: Misses Tina Lerner, Germaine Schnitzer, Mme. Yolanda Mérö; Gottfried Galston, Leopold Godowsky, Ernest Schelling, Silvio Scionti.
Violin: Miss Maud Powell; Leon Sametini, Harry Weisbach, Eugène Ysaye (twice), Efrem Zimbalist.
Violoncello: Bruno Steindel.
Vocal: Mmes. Alma Gluck, Ernestine Schumann-Heink, Miss Julia Culp; Clarence Whitehill.

---

*Thorwald Otterström, composer of the "Elegy, Chorale and Fugue," born July 17, 1868, in Copenhagen, received his first instruction in piano playing and musical theory in that city, and later studied the piano with Mme. Sofie Menter, in Petrograd. Mr. Otterström has been a resident of Chicago since 1892.

TWENTY-THIRD SEASON
(1913-1914)

The Chicago Chamber Music Society announces a series of seven concerts—Meeting of the National Institute of Arts and Letters in Chicago—The Trustees make an "Appeal to the Friends of the Orchestra" for funds to pay the debt on Orchestra Hall—President Lathrop sends a telegram to Major Higginson in Boston—Popular Concerts started—The Orchestra visits Toronto for the Annual Concerts of the Mendelssohn Choir.

The returns from the season ticket sale showed a total of $85,234, an increase of $3,500 over the previous season, which indicated that the public was at last appreciating the worth of the Saturday night concerts. Mr. Stock and the Orchestra were enthusiastically received at the first concerts of the Twenty-third Season, October 17 and 18, notably Hugo Kortschak, who resumed his place as second concertmeister:

Academic Festival Overture, Opus 80, ... *Brahms*
Symphony No. 7, A Major, Opus 92, ... *Beethoven*
INTERMISSION
Rondo, "Till Eulenspiegel's Merry Pranks," Opus 28, . *Strauss*
Petite Suite, ... *Debussy*
(Orchestrated by Henri Büsser)
Symphonic Poem, No. 3, "Les Préludes," . . . . . *Liszt*

The program book announced seven concerts under the auspices of the Chicago Chamber Music Society in Orchestra Hall foyer, in charge of the Executive Committee, on Thursday afternoons at 3:00 o'clock:

EXECUTIVE COMMITTEE

MRS. N. H. BLATCHFORD.	MRS. H. P. JUDSON.
MRS. CLYDE M. CARR.	MRS. JOHN R. LINDGREN.
MRS. ALBERT M. DAY.	MRS. WILLIAM R. LINN.
MRS. F. A. DELANO.	MRS. RUDOLPH MATZ.
MRS. A. B. DICK.	MRS. PHILO A. OTIS.
MRS. HENRY L. FRANK.	MRS. RUSSELL TYSON.
MRS. JOHN J. GLESSNER.	MRS. CLARA WOODYATT.
MRS. FRANK S. JOHNSON.	

December 4, Chicago String Quartet.
December 18, Chicago String Quartet.
January 15, 1914, Chicago Wood-Wind Choir.
January 29, Kneisel Quartet.
February 19, Flonzaley Quartet.
March 19, Chicago String Quartet.
April 2, Chicago String Quartet.

Twenty-third Season—1913-1914

The National Institute of Arts and Letters, composed of representative musicians and scholars, assembled at the Art Institute for its convention during the week of November 10. In honor of this meeting Mr. Stock prepared a program of American music for the concerts of November 14 and 15, and invited the composers to conduct their works. Victor Herbert and Horatio W. Parker were unable to be present, but we had the pleasure of seeing George W. Chadwick, Edgar Stillman Kelley and Arthur Foote on the Conductor's stand. After the rehearsal on Thursday morning (the 13th) a luncheon was given at the Chicago Club for Mr. Foote and Mr. Kelley, at which were present Bryan Lathrop, John J. Glessner, Charles L. Hutchinson, H. H. Walker, Seymour Morris, Martin A. Ryerson, Philo A. Otis, Frederick J. Wessels, Henry E. Voegeli and Frederick Stock.

American composers and the possibilities of American music were thoroughly discussed.

The concerts of November 14 and 15, Fifth Program, Miss Edith Thompson, soloist, indicated what American composers can do:

Prelude to Act III, "Natoma,"	*Herbert*
A Northern Ballad, Opus 46,	*Parker*
*Dramatic Overture, "Melpomene,"	*Chadwick*
Concerto for Pianoforte No. 2, D Minor, Opus 23,	*MacDowell*

INTERMISSION

*The Defeat of Macbeth,"	*Kelley*
*Four Character Pieces, Opus 48,	*Foote*
Festival March and Hymn to Liberty,	*Stock*

The first concert of the Chamber Music Society was given Thursday afternoon, December 4, in the foyer of Orchestra Hall; program by the Chicago String Quartet: Harry Weisbach (first violin), Hugo Kortschak (second violin), Franz Esser (viola) and Bruno Steindel (violoncello), assisted by Luigi Galli (piano):

Quartet in A Major,	*Beethoven*
Piano Quartet in A Major,	*Brahms*

The Annual Meeting was held Tuesday afternoon, December 9, in the offices of the Association in Orchestra Building. The Treasurer presented his report for the Twenty-second Season, ending June 30, 1913:

---

*Conducted by the composer.

Receipts		Expenses	
Chicago concerts	$109,652.50	Business management	$ 17,223.09
Outside concerts (net)	14,497.98	Advertising	3,580.19
Program book	1,173.20	Salaries of Conductor and Orchestra	118,424.00
Interest at bank	712.26	Orchestra expenses	1,025.97
Hall and building rentals	35,055.06	Soloists	9,800.00
		Music and instruments	1,650.92
		Interest on loans	9,254.00
			$160,958.17
		Gain	132.83
	$161,091.00		$161,091.00

President Lathrop, in reviewing the finances of the last season, said of Orchestra Hall:

"The financial statements of the past two years admonish us that the present debt of $200,000 and the annual interest charge of $8,000 are a menace to the very existence of the Orchestra. We must undertake at no distant day to raise money to discharge this debt.

"Year before last showed a deficit of $7,400. We met this by using the surplus income which had been accumulated by careful management, but we have now no such fund in reserve. Last year's statement shows receipts and expenditures of over $161,000 and a margin of only $133.

"I am convinced that our great Orchestra in its twenty-three years of service has won a lasting place in the affections and pride of Chicago. It will not die, but neglect of sane precautions may some day cause it to languish and weaken. What is there to do? First, we can keep the public informed about the condition of the Orchestra, the work of education which it is doing in the field of the fine arts, and its future needs in order to carry on this work successfully and to adhere to the present high standard.

"Secondly, we can let the public know something of our aspirations. I hope that the future has great things in store for us. I believe in them, though I may not live to see them realized. We aspire to found a great Conservatory of Music, equal to any in Europe, and to make Chicago one of the musical centers of the world. This had always been the ambition and the dream of our beloved leader, Theodore Thomas. He maintained that such a Conservatory would greatly strengthen the Orchestra, since the professorships would bring to it the best musicians of Europe, and we could train men here for every instrument that we use, while the orchestral concerts would attract students of music from far and near. Together the Orchestra and the Conservatory would be a constant source of joy and pride to all the people.

"The dreams of Chicago usually come true in time. To use Du Maurier's phrase, let us set it to 'dreaming true.'

Twenty-third Season—1913-1914

"Thirdly, to all those men and women who value art, who value education, who value the welfare and the good name of Chicago, let us suggest that The Orchestral Association is worthy of a place among the most worthy to be remembered by bequests in their wills."

George F. Porter was elected a Member of the Association. The Members then proceeded to the election of Trustees:*

After adjournment of the Annual Meeting the Trustees met and elected officers for the ensuing year:

Bryan Lathrop, President; Clyde M. Carr, First Vice-President; Charles H. Hamill, Second Vice-President; Philo A. Otis, Secretary; and Frederick J. Wessels, Treasurer. Mr. Wessels was appointed Business Manager and Henry E. Voegeli Assistant Treasurer and Assistant Business Manager. Executive Committee: Clyde M. Carr, Charles H. Hamill, Philo A. Otis, Joseph Adams and Bryan Lathrop, with Mr. Lathrop, Chairman.

Following Mr. Lathrop's suggestion, an appeal to "The Friends of the Orchestra" appeared in the program book of December 26 and 27:

"The Association has a mortgage debt of $200,000 and an annual interest charge of over $9,000.

"The cost of giving the concerts has risen from $128,884 in 1905 to $161,606 in 1913.

"Last season's operations showed an excess of receipts from all sources over expenses of only $132.83.

"A trifling diminution in hall or office rents would turn this to a deficiency. Present conditions hold the threat of decreased revenues with no promise of lessened expense.

"After the payment of the debt the surest guaranty of permanence to the Orchestra would be a substantial Pension Fund, to which the players could look for protection in age or sickness. In the absence of a Pension Fund and the presence of a mortgage debt there is real danger.

"Believers in good music will bear these facts in mind, and give and urge their friends to give by will and otherwise to preserve the Orchestra.

"THE TRUSTEES."

---

*The Trustees met an hour before the Annual Meeting, and passed an amendment to the by-laws providing for the election of Trustees in three classes of five each, for one, two and three years:

ONE YEAR	TWO YEARS	THREE YEARS
CLYDE M. CARR.	MAX BAIRD.	GEORGE E. ADAMS.
FREDERIC A. DELANO.	WILLIAM L. BROWN.	JOSEPH ADAMS.
CHAUNCEY KEEP.	CHARLES H. HAMILL.	JOHN J. GLESSNER.
SEYMOUR MORRIS.	HAROLD F. MCCORMICK.	BRYAN LATHROP.
CHARLES H. SWIFT.	CLARENCE M. WOOLLEY.	PHILO A. OTIS.

258 *The Chicago Symphony Orchestra*

TWELFTH PROGRAM, JANUARY 2 AND 3
THEODORE THOMAS MEMORIAL
BEETHOVEN PROGRAM
SOLOISTS: RUDOLPH REUTER.
HARRY WEISBACH.
BRUNO STEINDEL.

Overture to "Egmont," Opus 84.
Concerto for Piano, Violin and Violoncello, C Major, Opus 56.

INTERMISSION

Symphony No. 3, "Eroica," E flat, Opus 55.

The Trustees voted on January 9 that three Popular Concerts should be given in February, March and April; but with some fears that the people might not respond, and that the "Pops" might interfere with the attendance at the regular concerts, if continued another season. The three concerts were given, however, on Thursday evenings, February 26, March 26 and April 23, with the co-operation of the City Club and Civic Music Association, who disposed of the tickets (fifteen to fifty cents each) in communities in the city where the different nationalities live. The people came to the concerts in crowds, filling the hall each evening to the last row, so eager were they to hear the attractive music Mr. Stock had prepared.

Charles H. Hamill, Second Vice-President, addressed the audience at the intermission of the first concert, on the purpose for which The Orchestral Association had battled for twenty-three years, to give to the people of Chicago the best of music. "You are hearing this evening," continued Mr. Hamill, "one of the great Orchestras of the world at prices of admission which hardly meet one-third of the cost."

The programs covered a wide range of attractive music—the "Larghetto" from the second symphony (Beethoven), Mendelssohn's "Midsummer Night's Dream" music, the "Nutcracker Suite" (Tschaikowsky), the "Meditation" from "Thaïs" (Massenet), with violin obbligato by Mr. Weisbach, "Scène Religieuse" from "Les Erinnyes" (Massenet), with violoncello obbligato by Mr. Steindel, a few Strauss waltzes, the overtures to "Mignon" (Thomas) and "Tannhäuser" (Wagner), etc.

Among the important novelties by American composers which have appeared on our programs in recent years was the symphony in D major by Eric DeLamarter,

Twenty-third Season—1913-1914 259

Conductor of the Musical Art Society, heard at the concerts of January 23 and 24, Fifteenth Program, and one of the best of the new symphonies, irrespective of the composer's nationality. The *Tribune* writer said of Mr. DeLamarter's work:

"Art is measured by the canons of art, before which all men are equal. The fact that Mr. DeLamarter was born February 18, 1880, in Lansing, Michigan, should not be a disadvantage. Mr. Stock and the Orchestra performed wonders with the new work."

Eugène Ysaye was the soloist at the concerts of January 30 and 31, Sixteenth Program, playing the concerto in G minor, for violin, organ and string orchestra, by Vivaldi.

After the intermission Mr. Ysaye played the concerto for violin, No. 3, in B minor, Opus 61, by Saint-Saëns.

Mr. Stock, Manager Wessels, the Secretary and the Orchestra spent the first week of February in Toronto for the Annual Concerts of the Mendelssohn Choir. It was a season of rest and change, good-fellowship with artists and officers of the Choir, and of delightful music. We left Chicago by special train Sunday afternoon, February 1, arriving in Toronto on Monday morning in time for a short rehearsal with soloists and Choir in Massey Hall. The concerts, under the direction of Dr. A. S. Vogt and Frederick Stock, were of the same high order as in previous seasons, with enthusiastic audiences in attendance. The important works given were selections from Verdi's "Requiem," on Monday evening, February 2; Elgar's Cantata, "The Music Makers," with S. Coleridge-Taylor's cantata, "A Tale of Old Japan," on Tuesday evening, February 4; a program by the Chicago Symphony Orchestra, with Harold Bauer, soloist, playing the Schumann concerto in A minor, on Thursday afternoon, February 5; a miscellaneous program for Choir and Orchestra, including two numbers from Verdi's "Requiem" for the last concert in the evening. Soloists: Miss Florence Hinkle (soprano), Miss Mildred Potter (contralto), Reed Miller* (tenor) and Horatio Connell (bass). The attractive features of the concerts, however, were the *a cappella* numbers by the Choir—"The Cherubim Song" (Tschaikowsky),

---

*Reed Miller was the solo tenor in St. Thomas Episcopal Church, New York City. He died December 29, 1923. In 1909 he married Nevada Van der Veer, who survives him.

"On Himalay" (Granville Bantock), Slumber Song, "Sleep, Little Baby, Sleep" (Colin Taylor), and the double chorus, "How Sweet the Moonlight Sleeps" (Eaton Fanning). The singing of these numbers by the Choir was the perfection of choral art.

In parting from our Toronto friends that evening after the concert, for our return home, we little thought that war was coming, and that years might pass before we again heard the Choir.*

"The Music Makers" (Elgar), (a work we had heard in Toronto, but which was new in the west), and the "Stabat Mater" (Dvořák) were given by the Apollo Musical Club Monday evening, February 23, in Orchestra Hall, under Mr. Wild's direction, with the assistance of the Chicago Symphony Orchestra and soloists: Miss Leonora A. Allen (soprano), Miss Mildred Potter (contralto), George Harris, Jr. (tenor) and Gustaf Holmquist† (bass); Edgar A. Nelson (organist).

The resignation of Max Baird‡ as a Member of the Association and Trustee was accepted with sincere regret at a meeting of the Trustees, Friday, March 6; Charles L. Hutchinson was chosen to fill the vacancy.

Mr. Baird came into the life of the Orchestra in 1903, and will long be remembered for his earnest work as Secretary of the Auxiliary Committee, of which Harry Gordon Selfridge was Chairman, representing the professional, religious, social and commercial interests of Chicago, in the campaign for funds to build Orchestra Hall. Mr. Baird was elected (1904) a member of the Board of Trustees.

Mr. Stock's overture, "Life's Spring Tide," had its first hearing at the concerts of March 27 and 28—

---

*Sir Edmund Walker, Honorary President of the Mendelssohn Choir, died March 27, 1924, in Toronto.

†Gustaf Holmquist, well known in choir and concert work in our city, died May 12, 1923. He was born February 14, 1872, in Sweden, and came to America at the age of thirteen. For many years he was an instructor at the Chicago Musical College and the Bush Temple of Music. In later years he was a member of the quartet in the Sunday Evening Club in Orchestra Hall, and of the choir of the First Congregational Church in Evanston.

‡Mr. Baird retired in 1913 from the practice of law, in consequence of ill health, and in January, 1914, with Mrs. Baird, went abroad, taking up his residence on the island of Sark, Channel Islands, England, where they still (1924) reside. During the World War Mr. Baird entered the American Red Cross service in Paris and was assigned to the Bureau of French Canteens, which, six months later, was consolidated with the Bureau of American Canteens, and he was then reassigned to the latter branch of the work, serving between the two for the better part of two years.

Twenty-fourth Program. The work, written at Munich during the summer of 1913 (finished September 12), having for its theme the buoyancy and exuberance of youth, received a brilliant interpretation by the men of the Orchestra.

TWENTY-FIFTH PROGRAM, APRIL 3 AND 4
Soloist: Heinrich Gebhard

Symphony on "A French Mountain Song," . . . . *d'Indy*
(For Pianoforte and Orchestra)
Variations Symphoniques, Opus 25, ... *Franck*
(For Pianoforte and Orchestra)

Glenn Dillard Gunn said in the *Tribune* of d'Indy's symphony:

"It is an artistic work dedicated to beauty, and altogether void of display. Mr. Gebhard is an ideal exponent of this aristocratic music."

Madame Clara Butt, the English contralto, was heard at the concerts of April 10 and 11, Twenty-sixth Program, and gave the audience a delightful interpretation of Elgar's "Sea Pictures."

TWENTY-SEVENTH PROGRAM, APRIL 17 AND 18
Soloist: Ignace J. Paderewski

Concerto for Pianoforte in A Minor, Opus 17, . . *Paderewski*

"Twenty-eighth, and last, Program, April 24 and 25: With the assistance of the Apollo Musical Club, under the direction of Mr. Stock. Soloists: Miss Lucille Stevenson (soprano), Mrs. Rose Lutiger Gannon (contralto), John B. Miller (tenor) and Albert Borroff (bass). The program included the ninth symphony (Beethoven) and selections from the third act of 'The Meistersingers' (Wagner)."

The second American Concert by the Chicago Symphony Orchestra, Glenn Dillard Gunn conducting, was given in Orchestra Hall Monday evening, April 27, 1914, with the assistance of Miss Lucille Stevenson (soprano) and Miss Prudence Neff (piano), soloists:

Overture, "To Spring," . . . . *Dunham*
(First Performance)
Aria, "O Bona Patria," from "Hora Novissima," . . *Parker*
Three Oriental Sketches, ... *Paulsen*
(First Performance in Chicago)
"Gitanjali" (Six Songs for Soprano and Orchestra), . *Carpenter*
INTERMISSION
Concerto for Pianoforte and Orchestra, ... *Borowski*
(First Performance)
"A Chippewa Vision," Romance for String Orchestra, . *Busch*
(First Performance in Chicago)
"A Village Festival," from "Indian Suite," . . . *MacDowell*

TWENTY-THIRD SEASON
(1913-1914)
SOLOISTS

HARP: Enrico Tramonti.
ORGAN: Wilhelm Middelschulte.
PIANOFORTE: Miss Edith Thompson, Mrs. Fannie Bloomfield Zeisler; Harold Bauer, Heinrich Gebhard, Leopold Godowsky, Ignace J. Paderewski, Rudolph Reuter.
VIOLIN: Carl Flesch, Hugo Kortschak, Fritz Kreisler, Albin Steindel, Harry Weisbach (twice) Eugène Ysaye.
VIOLONCELLO: Miss Beatrice Harrison; Jean Gerardy, Bruno Steindel (twice).
VOCAL: Miss Lucille Stevenson, Mmes. Clara Butt, Rose Lutiger Gannon; Albert Borroff, John B. Miller.
VISITING CONDUCTORS: George W. Chadwick, Arthur Foote, Edgar Stillman Kelley.
CHORAL: The Apollo Musical Club of Chicago.

TWENTY-FOURTH SEASON
(1914-1915)

The Executive Committee adopts a rule that ladies must remove hats; this calls forth angry protests, but the rule holds—Death of Albert Arnold Sprague, a devoted friend of the Orchestra—His daughter, Elizabeth Sprague Coolidge, makes a generous gift to The Orchestral Association to found the Pension and Invalid Fund—Mr. Lathrop announces another gift to the Fund—Six Popular Concerts.

The prospectus issued in the early summer announcing the season ticket sale and first concerts had no sooner gone to the subscribers than another announcement appeared, terrifying all mankind and threatening the existence of civilization—the Kaiser's declaration of war and his invasion of Belgium. War conditions weighed heavily on many activities in art and commerce, but the friends of the Orchestra responded promptly, with the result that the season ticket sale, $86,249.25, somewhat exceeded that of the previous season.

The first Friday concert brought the customary audience, filling every seat, eager to hear the delightful music, and seemed like the reunion of old friends who meet to discuss the happenings of the summer. It was not "war talk" which absorbed the thoughts of the audience that lovely October afternoon, but a peaceful subject, far from "war's alarms"—hats! The Executive Committee, on March 6, in response to many complaints from patrons of the concerts, passed a resolution, to take effect with the beginning of the Twenty-fourth Season, requiring ladies to remove their hats and keep them off during the entire performance at the Friday and Saturday concerts. That there might be no misunderstanding of the rule, this clause was printed on each ticket:

"The purchaser of this ticket accepts the same, subject to the rules of the house, including the removal of hats."

Indignant letters appeared in the papers and came to the Manager's office from angry ladies who declared they could not and would not remove their hats—all pointing to a possible hostile demonstration at the Friday concert.

Nothing happened, however; the good sense of the women prevailed, as they realized the justice of the rule. One angry ticket holder raised a noisy objection, but was silenced in short order by an usher, while the rest of the audience quietly settled back to enjoy one of Mr. Stock's choicest programs. Then, for the first time in its history, the Orchestra played to bared feminine heads:

FIRST CONCERTS, OCTOBER 16 AND 17

Overture to "Euryanthe,"	*Weber*
Symphony No. 5, C Minor, Opus 67, ...	*Beethoven*

INTERMISSION

Symphonic Poem, "Don Juan," Opus 20, ...	*Strauss*
Voices of the Forest, from "Siegfried,"	*Wagner*
Finale from "Die Götterdämmerung,"	*Wagner*

The program book of the concerts of October 23 and 24, Second Program, contained this announcement:

JOHANN RUINEN
(First Violin)

Died June 12, 1914.
A member of the Orchestra for four years.

FREDERICK OTTE
(Tuba)

Died October 8, 1914.
A member of the Orchestra for nineteen years.

FOURTH PROGRAM, NOVEMBER 6 AND 7
SOLOIST: JOSEF HOFMANN

Concerto for Pianoforte in A Minor, Opus 58, . . *Schumann*

The Annual Meeting was held Tuesday afternoon, December 8, in the offices of the Association, there being present in person or by proxy thirty-five Members; President Lathrop in the chair; Frederick J. Wessels, clerk. Julius Rosenwald was elected a Member of the Association.

Twenty-fourth Season—1914-1915

Five Trustees were elected for a period of three years: Clyde M. Carr, Frederic A. Delano, Chauncey Keep, Seymour Morris and Charles H. Swift.

The Treasurer's report for the Twenty-third Season (1913-1914), ending June 30, 1914, showed:

RECEIPTS		EXPENSES	
Chicago concerts...	$111,600.25	Business management and advertising..........	$ 20,543.64
Outside concerts (net)..........	19,108.77	Salaries of Conductor and Orchestra.	126,074.50
Three popular concerts (net)......	3,320.80	Soloists...........	9,975.00
Interest..........	780.11	Music and orchestral instruments.....	2,282.73
Program book (net).	849.65		
Total Orchestra earnings........	$135,659.56		$158,875.87
Hall and building rentals..........	80,582.50	Building expenses, heating, insurance, etc.............	34,798.29
		Taxes.............	9,159.53
		Interest on loans...	9,254.00
		Improvements.....	2,651.97
		Total............	$214,739.68
		Profit on season....	1,502.42
	$216,242.08		$216,242.08

President Lathrop then reviewed the work of the Twenty-third Season:

"The auditor's report for the year ending June 30, 1914,
    shows a profit of............................$1,502.42
Deducting claims not good........................ 728.50

The actual profit was............................$ 773.92

"During the last fiscal year we received from Orchestra Hall the large rental of $49,285 gross, and from Orchestra Building the largest gross rental since it was built, $31,297.50, and yet we barely escaped a deficit. With expense aggregating $214,740, the net income of about $774 is a very narrow margin, especially in view of the fact that we have no working capital.

"The Trustees should recognize the menace of a deficit in the near future, since it is practically impossible to reduce our expenses materially. The hall rents are less now by about $1,500 per month than they were last year.

"It is exceedingly fortunate that the management was able to make a lease of the hall last summer for a moving picture show which yielded about $12,000. This may save us this year from a large deficit, which otherwise would have been unavoidable."

TENTH PROGRAM, DECEMBER 18 AND 19

Symphonic Suite, ... *Weidig*
(First Performance)

Adolf Weidig, the composer of the suite and a former member of the Orchestra, is now the Associate Director of the American Conservatory of Music in this city. The second movement, "Romance," is a dainty piece of work, full of beauty and imagery, with a solo for violin, which Mr. Weisbach played to the delight of the audience.

After the concert an informal reception for Mr. and Mrs. Stock was held in the foyer, in honor of Mr. Stock's tenth year as Conductor of the Orchestra. A silver punch bowl, the gift to Mr. Stock by a committee of ladies, was on exhibition.

TWELFTH PROGRAM, JANUARY 1 AND 2
THEODORE THOMAS MEMORIAL
SOLOIST: HAROLD BAUER

Overture, "Coriolanus," Opus 62, . . . ⎫
Symphony No. 3, "Eroica," E Flat, Opus 55, ⎭ . . *Beethoven*

INTERMISSION

Concerto for Pianoforte No. 4, G Major, Opus 58, . *Beethoven*

In the death of Albert Arnold Sprague, January 10, 1915, The Orchestral Association lost an old and valued friend. He was born May 19, 1835, at Randolph, Vermont, was graduated (1859) from Yale College, and two years later came to Chicago to seek a home and a fortune. His opportunity soon came. In 1862, with Ezra J. Warner as a partner, he embarked his small capital in a wholesale grocery business at No. 14 State Street. His brother, Otho S. A. Sprague, coming (1864) from the east to join the young merchants, the firm reorganized under the name of Sprague, Warner & Company. Their business prospered as the years rolled along, keeping pace with the growth of a city which has been the marvel of the world, and today few firms are of greater importance in the "Metropolis of the West" than that founded by Albert A. Sprague, Ezra J. Warner and Otho S. A. Sprague.

Albert A. Sprague found time in the midst of a busy life to interest himself in the institutions which have made Chicago a better place to live in—the Chicago Relief and Aid Society, Orphan Asylum, the Presbyterian Hospital, the Art Institute and the Chicago

ALBERT ARNOLD SPRAGUE

Symphony Orchestra. From the organization of the Orchestra (1891) he had its welfare constantly at heart, as a subscriber to the original three-year Guaranty Fund, a Governing Member of The Orchestral Association, and as a generous contributor to the building of Orchestra Hall.

In memory of Albert A. Sprague the Orchestra played at the concerts of January 22 and 23, Fifteenth Program, the andante from the suite in F major (Bach).

By the terms of Mr. Sprague's will a fund of $200,000 was left to his daughter, Mrs. Elizabeth Sprague Coolidge, to be distributed as she might designate. Charles H. Hamill, Second Vice-President of the Association, announced from the stage of Orchestra Hall at the concert on Saturday evening, January 30, that Mrs. Coolidge had given $100,000, one-half of the fund, to The Orchestral Association, for a Pension and Invalid Fund, thereby gladdening the hearts of all friends of the Orchestra.

Mr. Lathrop prepared a statement for the program book of February 5 and 6:

"Mrs. Coolidge's gift of 'The Albert Arnold Sprague Memorial Fund' of $100,000 for a Pension and Invalid Fund for the Chicago Symphony Orchestra is a magnificent contribution to the cause of good music and of higher education. It is a fitting memorial to her father, Albert Arnold Sprague, who was one of the most public-spirited citizens and one of the most generally beloved men of Chicago, and who had always been deeply interested in our Orchestra, and had contributed very generously to its support.

"I have long felt that the most imperative need of the Orchestra was a large Pension Fund, in order to attract and keep artists of the first rank, and to maintain for the Orchestra the highest possible standard; and we ought not to be satisfied with anything lower.

"In view of the probable return, at some time, of a low rate of interest, the Pension and Invalid Fund should not be less than $300,000.

"There is still a debt of $200,000 on Orchestra Hall, and the interest on this is a constant hindrance to the improvement of the Orchestra, and a menace to its high standard."

"February 5, Friday P. M.: Meeting of Executive Committee. Present, Messrs. Lathrop, Hamill, Joseph Adams and Otis. Mr. Lathrop announced his own gift of $25,000 to the Pension and Invalid Fund. The good work is spreading! Let us hope more gifts will follow."

A luncheon was given at the Chicago Club by Mr. Lathrop to the Trustees, Thursday, February 18, there being present Messrs. Joseph Adams, Glessner, Hamill, Keep, Morris, Otis; Conductor Stock, Manager Wessels and Assistant Manager Voegeli by invitation. The generous gifts to the Pension and Invalid Fund by Mrs. Coolidge and Mr. Lathrop were formally accepted and resolution adopted:

"That, in accepting the gift of Mrs. Coolidge and undertaking to employ it to the purpose and ends designated by said donor, The Orchestral Association does now record its hearty gratitude for the generous gift so made, and of its sincere appreciation of the high purpose of Elizabeth Sprague Coolidge in devoting her gift to the noble end of a Pension Fund, and so constituting the most fitting memorial to him who was for so many years a most devoted friend of the Orchestra, Albert Arnold Sprague.

"That, in accepting the gift of Mr. Lathrop and agreeing to comply with the same, for the purposes so designated, The Orchestral Association does here record its most hearty gratitude to Bryan Lathrop for his splendid gift, which is but another, though un-needed, evidence of his devoted and self-forgetting interest in the welfare of the Association."

The program book of February 26 and 27 (Twentieth Program) announced another gift to the Pension and Invalid Fund:

"I have the pleasure of announcing a gift of $5,000 to The Orchestral Association. It comes, quite unsolicited, from a very dear friend, who does not live in Chicago. He writes to me simply: 'I wish to give $5,000 to your favorite institution, The Chicago Symphony Orchestra. Apply it as you like, without naming the donor. I am glad to feel that in making this gift I am helping a most worthy educational institution.'
"BRYAN LATHROP,
"*President, The Orchestral Association.*"

At the Twenty-third Program, March 19 and 20, after the intermission the Orchestra gave the first performance of John Alden Carpenter's Suite, "Adventures in a Perambulator."

The composer of this suite was a pupil of Bernard Ziehn in Chicago, and later of Sir Edward Elgar. He was taught the piano by Miss Amy Fay and W. C. E. Seeboeck. After graduation (1897) from Harvard College, where he studied with Prof. John K. Paine, Mr. Carpenter entered his father's office in Chicago (George B. Carpenter & Company, dealers in vessel supplies); since 1909 he has been Vice-President of the firm.

Karleton Hackett said in the *Evening Post:*

"There was wit, humor and tenderness, and through it all the feeling that Mr. Carpenter had something to say, something that he had actually felt and wished to express. The suite has distinction, and we are all proud that it came out of Chicago."

"March 30; Tuesday evening: Concert in Orchestra Hall by the Orchestra, Mr. Stock conducting, for the benefit of the Pension and Invalid Fund. Soloist: Mme. Julia Claussen. The program (Wagner) included the overture to 'The Flying Dutchman,' prelude to 'Lohengrin,' scenes from 'Tristan and Isolde' and 'Die Götterdämmerung'; $3,600 added to the Fund."

TWENTY-SIXTH PROGRAM, APRIL 9 AND 10
Soloist: Fritz Kreisler
Concerto for Violin, D Major, Opus 61, ... *Beethoven*

Pablo Casals, the Spanish 'cellist, soloist at the concerts of January 8 and 9, 1915, Thirteenth Program, made such a sensation that he came for a return appearance in the Twenty-seventh Program, April 16 and 17:
Concerto in A Minor, Opus 129, ... *Schumann*
"Kol Nidrei," for Violoncello and Orchestra, . . . *Bruch*

The theme of the latter work is a ritual melody, recited in the synagogues on the Day of Atonement, at the beginning of the evening service; it was played with great effect by Mr. Casals.

TWENTY-EIGHTH, AND LAST, PROGRAM, APRIL 23 AND 24
Overture, "In Spring Time," Opus 36, ... *Goldmark*
Symphony No. 6, "Pathetic," B Minor, Opus 74, . *Tschaikowsky*
INTERMISSION
Overture, "Leonore," Opus 72, No. 3, ... *Beethoven*
"Die Walküre": The Ride of the Valkyries,. . . . *Wagner*
"Die Götterdämmerung": Siegfried's Death Music, . *Wagner*
"Tannhäuser": Overture, ... *Wagner*

THE POPULAR CONCERTS

The "Pops" of the previous season, undertaken with the co-operation of the City Club and Civic Music Association, proved so successful that the Trustees announced six concerts, on Thursday evenings of the current season: November 5, December 3, January 7, 1915, January 28, February 11, March 4, and a seventh concert (extra), April 8.

The programs of the Popular Series contained music the people wanted to hear, and the people came in throngs, filling Orchestra Hall to its capacity at every concert. The enthusiasm of the audience reacted on Conductor and men, inspiring and cheering them in their work. The programs were at first (1913) light and pleasing in character—"Ave Maria" (Bach—Gounod),

"Berceuse" (Godard), "Scène Religieuse" (Massenet), Strauss waltzes, etc.—but educational and progressive.

An unusual feature of the concerts was the rush of the people at intermission to the box office to secure seats for the next concert—a provision by the management for the working people who had no spare hours during the day.

The concerts of the Chamber Music Society were again attractive features of the season, given Thursday afternoons in the foyer of the hall, December 17, January 21, 1915, February 18, March 18 and April 1.

Two of the series may be noted: That of the Chicago Wood-Wind Choir, on February 18; Alfred Quensel (flute), Alfred Barthel (oboe), Paul Kruse (bassoon) and Leopold de Maré (French horn); assisting artists, Franz Esser (viola) and Henry Purmort Eames (piano):

Quintet, Opus 81, ... *Onslow*
Two Rhapsodies, ... *Loeffler*
    I. "L'ETANG" (THE POOL).
    II. "LA CORNEMUSE" (THE BAGPIPE).
        (For Viola, Oboe and Piano).
Sextet, ... *Van Cromphout*

The last concert of the series was given by the Chicago String Quartet, April 1: Harry Weisbach (first violin), Otto Roehrborn (second violin), Franz Esser (viola) and Bruno Steindel (violoncello):

Quartet in C Major, ... *Haydn*
Quartet No. 1, in F Major, ... *Beethoven*

The Civic Music Association, founded (1913-1914) for "the development of musical talent throughout the community," held its First Spring Festival Sunday, May 23, 1915, at 3:00 P. M., in the Harrison Technical High School. The program consisted of choral selections by local groups, organized by the Association, with the assistance of the American Symphony Orchestra, Glenn Dillard Gunn, Conductor.

For the past ten years the Chicago Symphony Orchestra, Frederick Stock, Conductor, with the co-operation of the Civic Music Association, has also done great work for the educational uplift of the community, through the Popular and Children's Series of Concerts, and the organization of the Civic Orchestra of Chicago, the purpose of which is to train players for Symphony Orchestras.

TWENTY-FOURTH SEASON
(1914-1915)
SOLOISTS

HARP: Enrico Tramonti.
OBOE: Alfred Barthel.
PIANOFORTE: Miss Tina Lerner, Mme. Olga Samaroff; Harold Bauer, Ferruccio Busoni, Rudolph Ganz, Josef Hofmann, Arthur Shattuck.
VIOLIN: Frank Gittelson, Hugo Kortschak, Fritz Kreisler, Albert Spalding, Harry Weisbach, Alexander Zukovsky.
VIOLONCELLO: Pablo Casals (twice), Bruno Steindel, Emmeran Stoeber.
VOCAL: Mmes. Julia Claussen, Alma Gluck, Louise Homer.

TWENTY-FIFTH SEASON
(1915-1916)

Mr. Lathrop makes an appeal for the Pension Fund—The annual Toronto engagement of the Orchestra cancelled by war conditions— The "Silver Jubilee" of the Orchestra—Fifteen members decorated for twenty-five years of faithful service—George W. Chadwick, Visiting Conductor—Death of Theodore F. McNicol, librarian of the Orchestra for twenty-five years—Elizabeth Sprague Coolidge gives another $100,000 to the Pension and Invalid Fund—The Popular Concerts—Death of Bryan Lathrop, President of The Orchestral Association—His life and work— He bequeaths $700,000 to The Orchestral Association to found a School of Music.

Mr. Lathrop concluded his "Appreciation" (February 5 and 6) of the generous gifts of Mrs. Coolidge and other friends of the Orchestra, with an earnest appeal for further contributions to enlarge the Pension Fund and pay the debt on Orchestra Hall:

"I hope that these gifts to the Orchestra will encourage others to make liberal contributions to its funds, and I am confident that in time Chicago will provide the $400,000 required to complete the Pension Fund and remove the debt.

"The people of Chicago love the Orchestra and are proud of it, but I doubt whether they appreciate its full significance.

"In our city there are two institutions of a public nature, and only two, which represent the artistic side of life—the Art Institute and the Chicago Symphony Orchestra. Chicago may well be proud of both of them, but it has reason to be especially proud of the Orchestra, because it has no superior.

"Chicago, more than most cities, needs these two artistic institutions to lift the mind above the dead level of materialism, and to bring into our lives inspiration, beauty, poetry and joy.

"Without the Art Institute and the Symphony Orchestra life would not be worth living in Chicago, even for those who care little themselves for artistic things.

"Who would choose as a home for his wife and his children a city which openly confessed to having no sympathy for the higher things of life?

"This is the full significance of our Orchestra. It is a symbol of the highest aspirations of our people and a means to promote them."

The funds held by The Orchestral Association at the close of the Twenty-fourth Season were:

ELIZABETH SPRAGUE COOLIDGE

Twenty-fifth Season—1915-1916

Gift from the estate of Charles A. Chapin	$ 5,000.00
Pension and Invalid Fund created by the efforts of The Orchestral Association	22,000.00
The Albert Arnold Sprague Memorial Fund	100,000.00
Available for Pension and Invalid Fund	$127,000.00
The Henry Field Memorial Fund, given by Mrs. Thomas Nelson Page, in securities of a present value of	62,500.00
Gift from Bryan Lathrop	25,000.00
Gift from a friend	5,000.00
	$219,000.00

The opportunities for the Orchestra to earn money were, in 1915, considerably diminished through the suspension of much of the out-of-town business, as a result of the European war. The engagement of the Orchestra for the Annual Concerts of the Mendelssohn Choir in Toronto (February, 1915) was canceled in November, 1914, and the concerts suspended for reasons assigned by the officers of the Choir:

"The women of the Choir were too busy making bandages; men preparing to go to war; many Canadian boys dead on the battlefields, so that the people of Toronto were in no mood for entertainments of any kind."

The advance ticket sale for the Twenty-fifth Season of Chicago concerts opened favorably in June, and in spite of war conditions reached the sum of $85,480.50 by the opening of the first concerts, October 15 and 16. In honor of the Twenty-fifth Season, the "Silver Jubilee of the Orchestra," the audience was requested to rise and sing the National Hymn, which concluded Weber's overture. In further recognition of our "Jubilee," fifteen members of the Orchestra came on the stage decorated with white ribbons, indicating that they took part in the first concerts, October 16 and 17, 1891:

Alexander Krauss, First Violin.
Richard Seidel, First Violin.
Lothar Nurnberger, First Violin.
Herman Braun, First Violin.
George Meyer, Viola.
Frank Mittelstaedt, Viola.
Bruno Steindel, Violoncello.
Walter Unger, Violoncello.
Joseph Schreurs, First Clarinet.
Carl Meyer, Second Clarinet.
Leopold de Maré, First Horn.
Albert Ulrich, First Trumpet and Orchestra Manager.
Joseph Zettelmann, Timpani.
Edward Wagner, Percussions.
Theodore F. McNicol, Librarian.

PROGRAM

Overture, "Jubilee," . . . . Weber
Symphony No. 7, A Major, Opus 92, ... Beethoven

INTERMISSION

Festival Prologue, ... Stock
(Written for the Twenty-fifth Anniversary of the Chicago Symphony Orchestra)
(First Performance)

Siegfried Idyl, ... Wagner
Prelude to "Die Meistersinger von Nürnberg," . . Wagner

THIRD PROGRAM, OCTOBER 29 AND 30

SOLOISTS: HARRY WEISBACH
ALEXANDER ZUKOVSKY

Overture to "Fidelio," . . . . Beethoven

Nocturne . . *Mendelssohn*

IN MEMORY OF
PROF. J. HENRY KAPPES

Born September 19, 1824
Died October 25, 1915

Concerto for Two Violins, D Minor, ... Bach

The program book of the concerts of December 10 and 11, Ninth Program, announced another gift to our Pension Fund:

"The Trustees of The Orchestral Association have pleasure in announcing the gift of $1,500 from a good friend of the Orchestra; the only condition attaching to the gift is that the name of the donor shall not be revealed."

Thirty-three Members were present in person or by proxy at the Annual Meeting, Tuesday afternoon, December 14, in the offices of the Association; President Lathrop in the chair.

The Treasurer's report for the Twenty-fourth Season (1914-1915), ending June 30, 1915, showed:

Twenty-fifth Season—1915-1916

RECEIPTS		EXPENSES	
Chicago concerts	$113,565.25	Business management	$ 17,650.19
Outside concerts (net)	16,293.55	Advertising	2,908.62
Seven Popular concerts (net)	6,184.04	Salaries of Conductor and Orchestra	123,985.00
Interest	851.51	Concert expenses	533.24
Program book (net)	1,510.93	Music	599.82
Hall rentals	56,418.60	Soloists	9,950.00
Building rentals	31,001.00	Building and hall expenses and improvements	37,699.35
		Heating, insurance, ushers, water, etc.	25,466.92
			$218,793.14
		Excess of receipts over expenses	7,031.74
	$225,824.88		$225,824.88

Albert A. Sprague II was elected a Member of the Association to fill the vacancy caused by the death of his uncle, Albert A. Sprague.

The Apollo Club, augmented to 1,000 voices, gave two performances of "The Messiah" in Medinah Temple, Thursday evening, December 23, and Monday evening, December 27, under the direction of Harrison M. Wild. Soloists: Miss Marie Stoddard (soprano), Miss Christine Miller (contralto), John Campbell (tenor) and Willard Flint (bass); Edgar A. Nelson (organist), and the Chicago Symphony Orchestra.

THIRTEENTH PROGRAM, JANUARY 7 AND 8
THEODORE THOMAS MEMORIAL

SOLOISTS: ALFRED BARTHEL (Oboe)
JOSEPH SCHREURS (Clarinet)
PAUL KRUSE (Bassoon)
LEOPOLD DE MARÉ* (Horn)

---

*Leopold de Maré, among the foremost of living players on the French horn, was born February 13, 1862, in Rotterdam, Holland. He began the study of music with his father, who was a member of the Rotterdam Orchestra, later taking up the violin with Herman Scillag and the French horn with Edward Preuss. In 1877, at the age of fifteen, Mr. de Maré became a member of the Rotterdam Orchestra, as a violinist for two years, afterward as first horn, a position he held for seven years. He then removed to Berlin, taking the position of first horn in the Berlin Philharmonic, playing under Joachim, Von Bulow and other Conductors. Leopold de Maré has been a member of the Orchestra since the First Season (1891); retired (1921) on a pension.

Concerto No. 3, G Major, ... Bach
(For String Orchestra)
VIOLIN OBBLIGATO BY HARRY WEISBACH
Concertante Quartet, ... Mozart
(For Oboe, Clarinet, Bassoon and Horn)
INTERMISSION
Symphony No. 3, "Eroica," E Flat, Opus 55, . . Beethoven

George W. Chadwick, Visiting Conductor, was tendered a luncheon at the Chicago Club, Thursday, January 20, there being present Bryan Lathrop, Frederick Stock, Clyde M. Carr, Charles H. Hamill, John J. Glessner, Joseph Adams, Philo A. Otis, Henry H. Walker, Frederick J. Wessels and Henry E. Voegeli. Greetings were extended by Mr. Lathrop and Mr. Stock to Mr. Chadwick, one of the foremost American composers, with the hope that when he had new works to produce he would again come west and let his many friends in Chicago hear them.

Ossip Gabrilowitsch was the soloist at the concerts of January 14 and 15, Fourteenth Program:

Concerto for Pianoforte, D Minor (Köchel 466), . . Mozart
Concertstücke for Pianoforte and Orchestra, Opus 79, . Weber

FIFTEENTH PROGRAM, JANUARY 21 AND 22
GEORGE W. CHADWICK, VISITING CONDUCTOR.
SOLOIST: WALTER FERNER

Ballade, "Tam O' Shanter," for Orchestra, . . . Chadwick
(Conducted by the Composer)
(First Performance in Chicago)
Concerto No. 2 for Violoncello, Opus 38, ... de Swert

February 3, Thursday evening: Concert by the Orchestra and Mr. Stock, for the benefit of the Pension and Invalid Fund, yielding $2,182. The program included:

Two Movements from a String Quartet, *Elizabeth Sprague Coolidge*
  a. ADAGIO LAMENTOSO.
  b. SCHERZO.
(In Memory of Albert Arnold Sprague)
Symphony No. 6, B Minor, "Pathétique," . . Tschaikowsky
Prelude to "Lohengrin," . . . . Wagner

The concert was followed by a reception for Mrs. Coolidge in the foyer of the hall.

SEVENTEENTH PROGRAM, FEBRUARY 4 AND 5
SOLOIST: MRS. H. H. A. BEACH.

Concerto for Pianoforte, C Sharp Minor, ... Beach

"February 12, Saturday P. M.: With Stock and Wessels to the funeral of Otto Wolf, for twenty-one years a double-bass player in the Orchestra. The services were conducted by a minister of the Lutheran Church, the brass choir of the Orchestra playing a Bach chorale."

The program book of the concerts for the week contained this tribute to Mr. Wolf:

IN MEMORIAM
OTTO WOLF

Died February 9, 1916
A member of the Orchestra
since 1895

At the concerts of March 10 and 11, Twenty-second Program, soloist, Percy Grainger, the program included the Grieg concerto for pianoforte in A minor and two numbers by Chicago composers:

Symphonic Prelude, ... *Cole*
Concertino for Pianoforte and Orchestra, ... *Carpenter*

Rossetter Gleason Cole, the composer of the Symphonic Prelude, born February 5, 1866, at Clyde, Michigan, was graduated in 1888 from the University of Michigan. His musical education was acquired largely in Berlin. Mr. Cole spent two years as Director of the School of Music in Ripon College, seven years in Grinnell College, and two years at the University of Wisconsin. In recent years he has resided in Chicago as composer, teacher of composition and theory, and musical writer. The Symphonic Prelude, composed in 1913, had its first performance at the Concert of American Music in Orchestra Hall, by the Chicago Symphony Orchestra, March 11, 1915, Glenn Dillard Gunn conducting.

Mr. Carpenter says of his work, composed in 1915:

"The Concertino is in effect a light-hearted conversation between piano and orchestra, as between two friends who have traveled different paths and become a little garrulous over their separate experiences. The conversation is mostly of rhythms—American, Oriental and otherwise."

TWENTY-THIRD PROGRAM, MARCH 17 AND 18
SOLOISTS: MISS MAUD POWELL* (VIOLIN).
WILHELM MIDDELSCHULTE (ORGAN).

Symphony No. 3, E Minor, Opus 96, ... *Kaun*
(First Performance in Chicago)
Concerto for Violin, A Major (Köchel 219), ... *Mozart*

INTERMISSION

Allegro de Concert, for Organ and Orchestra, . . . *Borowski*
Introduction and Rondo Capriccioso for Violin, Opus 28, ... *Saint-Saëns*
"Midsummer Wake," Swedish Rhapsody, ... *Alfvén*

The Allegro de Concert, composed in 1915, was brought out at a concert in Medinah Temple October 18, 1915, under the direction of the composer, with the assistance of Dr. J. Lewis Browne (organist) and members of the Chicago Symphony Orchestra.

The program book of the concerts of March 17 and 18, Twenty-third Program, contained a tribute to the memory of another old member of the Orchestra:

THEODORE F. MCNICOL

Died March 15, 1916
Aged Fifty-nine Years

Librarian of the Orchestra for twenty-five years; with Theodore Thomas eight years before location in Chicago—a continuous, faithful service of thirty-three years.

George P. Upton wrote of McNicol's invaluable service at the time he was preparing the biography of Mr. Thomas:

"Of course that necessitated many interviews with Mr. Thomas, either at his house or mine, and often when neither of us could fix a needed date or run down a needed fact, Thomas would say, 'Ask Mac; he will know'—and 'Mac' always knew."

"March 18, Saturday, 9 A. M.: With Mr. and Mrs. F. J. Wessels, George F. Wessels and Stock to the funeral of McNicol at the Queen of Angels' Church, North Western Avenue; High

---

*Maud Powell, the foremost of women violinists, was born August 22, 1868, at Peru, Illinois; died January 8, 1920, at Uniontown, Pennsylvania, while on a concert tour.

NANCY SPRAGUE

Mass; many members of the Orchestra came. The officiating priest spoke in high terms of 'Mac's' devotion to his church."

TWENTY-FOURTH PROGRAM, MARCH 24 AND 25
Soloist: Ernest Schelling

Symphony No. 2, C Minor, Opus 34, ... *Oldberg*
(First Performance in Chicago)

Impressions (From an Artist's Life) in the Form of Variations on an Original Theme for Pianoforte and Orchestra, ... *Schelling*
(First Performance in Chicago)

The symphony, sketched in the mountains of Colorado in the summer of 1911, and completed the following year, won the first prize offered by the National Federation of Music Clubs in 1915, and was first performed in Los Angeles, California, in June, 1915, under the direction of Mr. Oldberg.

THE ALBERT AND NANCY SPRAGUE MEMORIAL FUND

The following announcement was made by Charles H. Hamill, Second Vice-President of The Orchestral Association, at the concert Saturday evening, April 15, 1916:

"Fifteen months ago the Trustees of The Orchestral Association were privileged to announce to a concert audience that the memory of Albert Arnold Sprague, a devoted friend of the Orchestra, was to be perpetuated by a fund of $100,000 bearing his name, given by his daughter, Elizabeth Sprague Coolidge. The income of this was to be used as pensions for retired members of the Orchestra. Inspired doubtless by this noble example, other friends of the Orchestra have since given $37,500 more, available for pensions.

On the twenty-eighth day of March of this year, the death of Nancy A. Sprague, for over fifty years the beloved companion of Albert A. Sprague, and herself one of the best friends of the cause of good music, again brought sorrow to their daughter, and again she has found the great soul's comfort in grief. Today there has been received from her a telegram advising that she has signed a deed of gift by which the Fund now known as the 'Albert Arnold Sprague Memorial Fund,' is hereafter to be known as the 'Albert and Nancy Sprague Memorial Fund,' and is increased by her from $100,000 to $200,000. The purposes to which this gift of mag-

---

*Arne Oldberg, the composer of the symphony, born July 12, 1874, at Youngstown, Ohio, acquired his early musical training in Chicago from August Hyllested (piano); later studying composition and orchestration with Adolf Koelling, Frederick Grant Gleason and Wilhelm Middelschulte. In 1893 Mr. Oldberg went to Vienna, studying two years with Leschetizky; later with Rheinberger in Munich. Since 1899 Mr. Oldberg has been connected with the Department of Music in the Northwestern University in Evanston.

nificent generosity is to be devoted are the same as those for which the original amount was intended—pensions for our players.

"In the words used by Mrs. Coolidge when she first announced her intention of thus joining the two names so dear to her—and, may I add, so dear to us—the Trustees are assured that you, the patrons of these concerts, and you, the members of the Orchestra, will rejoice with them in making the name of Sprague a symbol of devotion to Chicago and to beauty."

TWENTY-SIXTH PROGRAM, APRIL 7 AND 8

Selections from "Fairyland," Opus 77, Prelude, Intermezzo and Ballad, ... *Parker

TWENTY-EIGHTH, AND LAST, PROGRAM, APRIL 21 AND 22

Suite No. 3, D Major, ... Bach
Symphony No. 4, E Minor, Opus 98, ... Brahms

INTERMISSION

"Death and Transfiguration," Opus 24, ... Strauss
Symphonic Poem No. 3, "Les Préludes," . . . . . . Liszt

THE POPULAR CONCERTS

Ten concerts in the "Popular" Series were given in the Twenty-fifth Season in Orchestra Hall with the co-operation of the City Club and Civic Music Association, on Thursday evenings, October 21, November 4 and 25, December 9 and 30, January 13 and 27, 1916, February 10 and 24, and March 9.

Two of the programs may be noted, which indicate that the tastes of the people, under Mr. Stock's leadership, are improving:

OCTOBER 21, FIRST CONCERT

Hungarian Rhapsody No. 12, ... Liszt
    FLUTE OBBLIGATO BY MR. QUENSEL
"The Wand of Youth," . . . . Elgar
a. May Blossoms, ... Hubay—Stock
b. To a Water Lily, ... MacDowell—Stock

---

*Horatio W. Parker, one of the first among American composers, was born September 15, 1863, at Auburndale, Massachusetts. Parker acquired his first lessons in music from his mother, a versatile and accomplished woman, and made such progress that at the age of sixteen he was organist and director of music of St. Paul's Church at Dedham, Massachusetts. After a course of study in Boston with Stephen Emery and in composition with George W. Chadwick, Parker went to Munich and became a pupil of Rheinberger. After his return to America Parker held various positions in Boston and New York, and in 1894 was appointed Professor of Music at Yale University, a post he held until his death. Parker won his greatest fame with his choral work, "Hora Novissima," which was produced May 3, 1893, in the Church of the Holy Trinity, New York. Horatio W. Parker died December 18, 1919.

Dr. Parker's "Fairyland" won the prize of $10,000 offered by the citizens of Los Angeles for the best opera written by an American. "Fairyland" was produced for the first time July 1, 1915, at the Temple Auditorium, Los Angeles.

BRYAN LATHROP

MARCH 9, 1916, TENTH, AND LAST, CONCERT

Overture, "The Magic Flute," . . . . Mozart
Symphony No. 6, "Pastoral," F Major, Opus 68, . Beethoven
Souvenir, ... Van der Stucken
Ball Scene, ... Helmesberger
          PLAYED BY ALL THE VIOLINS

BRYAN LATHROP

Mr. Lathrop was taken ill in February (1916), and was removed to the Presbyterian Hospital for an operation. In a few weeks he rallied sufficiently to return to his home, 120 Bellevue Place, but the disease was serious, and the end came suddenly on Saturday morning, May 13. When the sad news came to the office of the Orchestra, we realized that Chicago had lost a great benefactor, and the Orchestra one of its best friends. Who would now take up the work and "carry on" with the unselfish enthusiasm and generosity of our beloved President?

The funeral services were held Monday afternoon, May 15, conducted by the Rev. Frederick G. Budlong, at the Chapel in Graceland Cemetery, an institution founded by Mr. Lathrop, of which he was President for half a century. Active pallbearers: Cyrus H. McCormick, J. A. Holabird, Walter M. Ellis, Charles H. Hamill, John P. Wilson, Jr., Arthur Hall, Russell Tyson and J. S. Schleyelmilch. Honorary pallbearers: Thomas Jones, Jesse L. Moss, E. L. Ryerson, H. H. Kohlsaat, J. Dorr Bradley, R. Hall McCormick, John S. Runnells, John A. Spoor, Charles L. Hutchinson, Martin A. Ryerson, O. C. Simonds, Frederick Stock, Frank Cramer, Slason Thompson, Horace H. Martin, John P. Wilson, Watson F. Blair, William Holabird, Martin Roche and Philo A. Otis.

Bryan Lathrop was born August 6, 1844, in Alexandria, Va., the son of Jedidiah H. and Mariana Bryan Lathrop. He acquired his education in the Dinwiddie School, in Virginia; later went abroad for study under private tutors in Germany and France. He came to Chicago in 1865, entering the office of his uncle, Thomas B. Bryan, who was a strong factor in other days in the development of Chicago. Bryan Hall, on Clark Street north of Washington, dedicated in September, 1860, was named for him—a hall associated with early concerts by

Adelina Patti, Clara Louise Kellogg, Louis Moreau, Gottschalk and the Chicago Musical Union, conducted by Hans Balatka. In the office of Thomas B. Bryan Mr. Lathrop began his work as one of the most conservative and successful real estate investors in Chicago.

He was truly one of those rare men who had higher ideals than business and the accumulation of money. In the progress of a long business career he acquired a fortune, but only that it might be used for the betterment of the social and civic conditions of our city. The Chicago Relief and Aid Society, Newberry Library, Art Institute and Lincoln Park Board are institutions to which he gave much time and thought.

His name appears for the first time in the records of the Association as a subscriber in the Fourth Season (1894-1895) to "The Fund for the Support of the Orchestra." One day in March, 1894, while I was in Mr. Fay's office to discuss some matters of the Orchestra, Mr. Fay handed me a letter from Mr. Lathrop enclosing his check for $250 "Towards the support of the great cause to which you are giving so much time and thought." The check came entirely unsolicited, and was, therefore, the more welcome. This was the beginning of twenty-two years of work, in which he gave willingly and cheerfully of his time and money, towards the maintenance of our Orchestra.

Bryan Lathrop was elected, January 19, 1895, Trustee and Vice-President of the Association, and on the resignation of George E. Adams, December 19, 1899, was elected President.

By the terms of his will the munificent bequest of $700,000 was made to The Orchestral Association to found in Chicago a School of Music after the order of the Conservatoire in Paris:

"It is, in my opinion, very desirable that an institution should be founded in Chicago in connection with the Orchestra, maintained by The Orchestral Association, in which an education can be obtained in the higher branches of music and musical composition not inferior to that found in the cities of Europe."

Mr. Lathrop expressly provided that the School shall not bear his name, believing that the name of the founder attached to an institution often prevents other people from making gifts and bequests.

The bequest does not become operative during the lifetime of Mrs. Lathrop. The will further provides that the Trustees have the right—

"if they shall deem it necessary and expedient, to apply not to exceed $10,000 in one year, out of the income, to the supply and maintenance of the Orchestra."

The Trustees may also use $50,000 of the principal or accumulated income toward the Pension Fund, if they wish.

An editorial published on the day Mr. Lathrop was laid away contained these words:

"It is an unusual man, as Americans go nowadays, whose life is to be estimated first of all in terms of æsthetic service. Yet it is in such terms that all Chicago will estimate the career of the gentle, cultured, yet strong spirited and keen minded man who is buried today."

TWENTY-FIFTH SEASON
(1915-1916)
SOLOISTS

BASSOON: Paul Kruse.
CLARINET: Joseph Schreurs.
FLUTE: Alfred Quensel.
HARP: Enrico Tramonti.
HORN: Leopold de Maré.
OBOE: Alfred Barthel.
ORGAN: Wilhelm Middelschulte.
PIANOFORTE: Mrs. H. H. A. Beach, Mrs. Fannie Bloomfield Zeisler; Harold Bauer, Ossip Gabrilowitsch, Percy Grainger, Ernest Hutcheson, Rudolph Reuter, Ernest Schelling.
VIOLIN: Miss Maud Powell; Mischa Elman, Samuel Gardner, Harry Weisbach, Alexander Zukovsky.
VIOLONCELLO: Pablo Casals, Walter Ferner, Bruno Steindel.
VOCAL: Misses Sophie Braslau, Marcella Craft, Mmes. Julia Claussen, Olive Fremstad.
VISITING CONDUCTOR: George W. Chadwick.

TWENTY-SIXTH SEASON
(1916-1917)

The Trustees adopt a resolution on the death of Bryan Lathrop—Clyde M. Carr elected successor to Bryan Lathrop as President of The Orchestral Association—The Seventh Program a memorial to Mr. Lathrop—The "Rules and By-laws of the Pension Fund" are adopted—The Twenty-sixth Season closed with the Chicago Musical Festival and first performance in Chicago of Mahler's Symphony of "One Thousand"—Ten Popular Concerts.

The Trustees were called together Monday afternoon, May 29, to take action on the death of our President, and to elect his successor. There were present Joseph Adams, William L. Brown, Clyde M. Carr, Charles H. Hamill, Chauncey Keep, Seymour Morris, Philo A. Otis and Charles H. Swift.

A resolution prepared by Mr. Hamill was then read and adopted:

"Bryan Lathrop is dead. For more than sixteen years he served as President of this Association, and from its foundation he was a warm sympathizer with its aims and a generous contributor to its purse. The Trustees who have been privileged through many years of happy service to work with him, now record their appreciation of his self-forgetful devotion to the cause of orchestral music, of his prodigal gifts of time, intelligently directed energy and money, and of his lovable and tactful character, which made co-operation with him in every endeavor a pleasure and inspiration to his associates. He was open to conviction but firm in decision; gracious in attention but unyielding in principle. Unrelenting in industry, he was also charming in companionship. His initiative, enthusiasm, work and generosity made possible the success of the campaign for popular subscriptions to build our hall, a monument to his courageous struggle and wise foresight. Under his skillful guidance the Association, true to the ideals of its founders, and despising commercialism, has persisted in the endeavor to produce the best in music, and, growing in artistic stature, has yet not failed to gain in financial strength. Indeed, the organization was still in its infancy, promising but frail, when he took charge, and by his wise care he leaves it strong and self-reliant in robust maturity.

"Giving the best of himself during his lifetime, that this organization might fulfill its mission, he has by his will shown his affectionate concern for its future. With splendid generosity he has made certain the growth of the Association and the extension of its work into wider fields of artistic endeavor. Future generations of music lovers will rise up to call blessed the name a modest man refused to attach to his gift.

"As Bryan Lathrop's enterprise and effectiveness are recorded in Orchestra Hall, as his artistic aspirations are expressed by the Orchestra, here on the minutes of the Association be written the record of our admiration of the man, our esteem for and thankfulness to the Association-officer, our love for the friend, and our grief (which cannot be said) for his loss. And that she, who through long years has been his closest comrade, may be comforted by the thought that she grieves not alone, let there be transmitted to her a copy of this record."

The Trustees then proceeded to fill the vacancy caused by the death of Mr. Lathrop: Clyde M. Carr to succeed Mr. Lathrop as President; Charles H. Hamill to succeed Mr. Carr as First Vice-President; Joseph Adams to succeed Mr. Hamill as Second Vice-President; John J. Glessner to fill the vacancy on the Executive Committee; Clyde M. Carr, Chairman.

The Pension and Invalid Fund having now been established through the generosity of Elizabeth Sprague Coolidge, Bryan Lathrop and other friends, the Executive Committee decided at its meeting, September 16, to make further provision for the welfare of the members of the Orchestra by placing—

"Group insurance on the active members of the Orchestra and as many others of the employes of the Association as to bring the total number insured up to approximately 100.

"The insurance to be for One Thousand Dollars ($1,000) each, the premium to be paid out of the income of the Invalid Fund or the Henry Field Memorial Fund, as may be hereafter determined.

"The whole amount of the insurance to be paid to the estate or family of the decedent."

The by-laws of the Pension Fund provide for old age pension, the amount of pension depending on years of service, with provision in event of death for widow and minor children. The members of the Orchestra are not assessed for pensions or life insurance.

The ticket sale for the Twenty-sixth Season aggregated $87,260 at the date of the opening concerts, a larger sum than we had expected, in view of war conditions.

Karleton Hackett said in the *Evening Post* of the first concerts, October 13 and 14:

"Friday afternoon was quite on its good behavior, everybody glad to see everybody else, and giving a full measure of its kindliness to Mr. Stock and the artists of the Orchestra.

"As the players came to their seats they were greeted as old friends; and why should they not be? Mr. Stock naturally came in for a special demonstration, and all through the afternoon the people manifested their good will in an emphatic manner."

Overture to "Euryanthe," . . . . *Weber*
Symphony No. 2, D Major, Opus 36, ... *Beethoven*

INTERMISSION

A Romantic Suite, Opus 125, ... *Reger*
"The Swan of Tuonela," Opus 22, ... *Sibelius*
Valse Triste, Opus 44, ... *Sibelius*
Symphonic Poem, "Finlandia," Opus 26, No. 7, . . . *Sibelius*

SIXTH PROGRAM, NOVEMBER 17 AND 18
SOLOIST: EFREM ZIMBALIST

Concerto for Violin, D Minor, ... *Stock*
(First Performance in Chicago)

The concerto was finished in 1915 and heard for the first time June 3 of that year at the Litchfield County Choral Festival, held in the Music Shed in the grounds of Carl Stoeckel, Norfolk, Connecticut. The composer conducted, and the solo was played by Efrem Zimbalist.

The concerts of November 24 and 25, Seventh Program, were prepared by Mr. Stock as an affectionate tribute from the Association and the Orchestra to the memory of Bryan Lathrop, a man whose whole life was given over to doing good for others. Monuments in stone and tablets in brass are an inadequate return for the work such men accomplish!

BRYAN LATHROP MEMORIAL

Prelude, Choral and Fugue, ... *Bach—Abert*
Dance of the Happy Spirits, from "Orfeo ed Euridice," . *Gluck*
FLUTE OBBLIGATO BY ALFRED QUENSEL

Symphony No. 3, "Eroica," E Flat Major, Opus 55, . *Beethoven*
  a. ALLEGRO CON BRIO.
  b. MARCIA FUNEBRE.

INTERMISSION

Entrance of the Gods into Walhalla, from "Das Rheingold," *Wagner*
Prelude to "Lohengrin," . . . . *Wagner*
Träume, a Study to "Tristan and Isolde," . . . *Wagner*
(Orchestration by Theodore Thomas)
Tone Poem, "Death and Transfiguration," . . . . *Strauss*

The Annual Meeting called for Tuesday afternoon, December 12, was adjourned to Tuesday, December 19, at 12:45 P. M., at the Chicago Club; luncheon with President Carr. There were present at the luncheon, besides the host:

Twenty-sixth Season—1916-1917

EDWARD E. AYER.
ABRAHAM G. BECKER.
WILLIAM L. BROWN.
WILLIAM J. BRYSON.
CLARENCE A. BURLEY.
WATSON F. BLAIR.
EDWARD B. BUTLER.
BENJAMIN CARPENTER.
JOHN J. GLESSNER.
CHARLES H. HAMILL.
CHARLES L. HUTCHINSON.
DR. GEORGE S. ISHAM.
SEYMOUR MORRIS.
PHILO A. OTIS.
ALBERT A. SPRAGUE.
CHARLES H. SWIFT.

Seventeen Members were represented by proxy, making a total of thirty-four present in person or by proxy out of a total of thirty-eight Members.

There were also present at the luncheon by invitation Frederick Stock, Conductor; Frederick J. Wessels, Manager, and Henry E. Voegeli, Assistant Manager, of the Orchestra.

Frederick J. Wessels presented the Treasurer's report for the Twenty-fifth Season (1915-1916), ending June 30, 1916:

RECEIPTS		EXPENSES	
Chicago concerts	$108,916.75	Business management	$ 21,066.43
Outside concerts (net)	20,159.10	Advertising	2,116.55
Popular concerts	7,440.45	Salaries of Conductor and Orchestra	130,242.00
Interest at bank	588.76	Orchestra expenses	758.41
Program book (net)	1,677.83	Soloists	9,100.00
Hall rentals	58,022.57	Music and instruments	1,129.36
Building	30,258.50	Building expenses	10,199.93
		Heating	2,859.48
		Insurance	2,377.60
		Hall expenses	18,432.19
		Ushers	6,732.28
		Water	521.29
		Taxes (1915)	3,740.00
		Interest on mortgage	9,003.43
		Hall improvements	6,638.44
		Gain on season	2,146.57
	$227,063.96		$227,063.96

President Carr, after an eloquent tribute to the memory of our deceased President, urged the Members to provide for the debt on Orchestra Building in order that the Association might be relieved of the heavy interest charge:

"I fear that many Members of the Association have considered the Orchestra financially independent, and have failed to appreciate the increased expenses, which have been increased in line only with all salaries, general expenses, etc., in our industrial and civic life.

"We must bear in mind that the Orchestra is one of Chicago's greatest assets, one of the greatest orchestras of the world, and as Members of our Association, we cannot allow the reputation of the Orchestra to suffer in any particular.

"These references to the record of the past year may seem to be discouraging, but fortunately other things have brightened the picture—

"Mr. Lathrop's most generous gift provided for the ultimate founding of a School of Music in Chicago, by creating a trust fund approximating 80 per cent of his estate. This fund will amount to about $700,000, but will not be available during Mrs. Lathrop's lifetime. From this fund the Trustees of the Association, if they deem it necessary and expedient, may apply not exceeding $10,000 in any one year, out of the income, to support and maintain the Chicago Symphony Orchestra.

"During the past year the Association has been able to make provision for a Pension Fund, which will be operative shortly after the first of the year. Mrs. Elizabeth Sprague Coolidge added $100,000 to her gift of the year before, making a fund of $200,000, as a memorial to Albert and Nancy Sprague.

"This splendid foundation enables us to announce a total Pension Fund of $268,623, made up of the

Sprague Fund	$200,000.00
Mr. Lathrop	25,000.00
Mrs. M. A. Meyer	1,000.00
Benefit Orchestra Concert accumulation	27,260.00
Interest	13,195.00
Profits	2,168.00
	$268,623.00"

Mr. Stock then addressed the Members on the work of the past year, dwelling on the importance of the Popular Concerts, with the suggestion that the number should be increased for the Twenty-seventh Season. He outlined the plans for the performance of Mahler's eighth symphony at the Festival to be given in April, 1917, at the Auditorium, with soloists, augmented Orchestra and chorus: all of which was approved by the Members.

Robert J. Thorne and Cyrus McCormick were elected Members of the Association.

"December 29, Friday: Meeting of the Executive Committee after concert; arranged extension of the $200,000 mortgage on Orchestra Building and land, now held by the Provident Life and Trust Co. of Philadelphia, for a period of five years from February 1, 1917—4¼ per cent per annum."

Twenty-sixth Season—1916-1917

"December 29, Friday evening: Handel's 'Messiah' by the Apollo Musical Club in the Auditorium under the direction of Harrison M. Wild. Soloists: Anita Rio (soprano), Christine Miller (contralto), Theodore Karle (tenor) and Wilfred Glenn (bass). The oratorio was repeated Sunday evening, December 31, with the same soloists, excepting Carl Cochems (bass) in place of Wilfred Glenn; Arthur Dunham (organist), and the Chicago Symphony Orchestra."

THIRTEENTH PROGRAM, JANUARY 5 AND 6
THEODORE THOMAS MEMORIAL

Overture to "Don Giovanni," . . . . *Mozart*
Symphony No. 7, E Major, ... *Bruckner*

INTERMISSION

March, E Flat, Opus 40, No. 1, ... *Schubert*
(Orchestration by Theodore Thomas)
Andante con Variazioni, from the "Kreutzer" Sonata,
Opus 47, ... *Beethoven*
(Orchestration by Theodore Thomas)
Polonaise, A Flat Major, Opus 53, ... *Chopin*
(Orchestration by Theodore Thomas)

A special meeting of the Trustees was held at 4:00 o'clock Friday afternoon, February 9, there being present Charles H. Hamill, John J. Glessner, Charles L. Hutchinson, Seymour Morris and Philo A. Otis; Frederick Stock, Conductor, Frederick J. Wessels, Manager, and Henry E. Voegeli, Assistant Manager, by invitation.

At this meeting Ferdinand Starke was retired on a pension.

"The Rules and By-laws of the Pension Fund," which had been under consideration by the Trustees for some months past, were read and adopted.

Vice-President Hamill then read a letter from Mrs. Lathrop, which, on motion, was ordered spread on the records:

"216 BEACON STREET, BOSTON, February 5, 1917.
"DEAR MR. HAMILL:

"In Mr. Carr's absence I am going to ask you to convey to the Trustees of The Orchestral Association my grateful thanks for the beautiful memorial to my beloved husband which they have been kind enough to send me.

"I appreciate it deeply, and it will always be one of my most valued treasures. To feel that my husband's character and his unselfish aims and work were understood and valued in the community where he had lived so long, is now the dearest thing on earth to me.

"With heartfelt thanks and my earnest wish for the future prosperity and success of The Orchestral Association, believe me,

"Sincerely and gratefully yours,
"(Signed) HELEN LATHROP."

290 *The Chicago Symphony Orchestra*

TWENTIETH PROGRAM, FEBRUARY 23 AND 24
SOLOIST: WALTER FERNER*
Concerto for Violoncello No. 2, Opus 104, ... *Dvořák*

The Program Book of the concerts of March 9 and 10, Twenty-second Program, announced the death of a faithful member of the Orchestra:

> IN MEMORIAM
>
> WALFRIED SINGER
>
> Died March 3, 1917
> A member of the Orchestra
> since 1893

The Executive Committee met after the concert, Friday, March 16, and granted pensions to Mrs. Helen Wolf, widow of Otto Wolf, and Mrs. McNicol, widow of Theodore F. McNicol, librarian of the Orchestra for twenty-five years.

TWENTY-FOURTH PROGRAM, MARCH 23 AND 24
SOLOISTS: HAROLD BAUER
OSSIP GABRILOWITSCH

Overture to "The Secret of Susanne," . . . *Wolf-Ferrari*
Symphony No. 4, B Flat, Opus 60, ... *Beethoven*
Concerto for Two Pianofortes, E Flat (Köchel 365), . *Mozart*

INTERMISSION

Symphonic Poem, "Don Juan," Opus 20, ... *Strauss*
Variations on a Theme by Beethoven for Two Pianofortes, Opus 35, ... *Saint-Saëns*

March 23, Friday: At the close of the concert the Executive Committee met and voted a pension to Mrs. Vera R. Singer, widow of Walfried Singer.

---

*Walter Ferner was born February 14, 1880, in Baltimore, Maryland. His first teacher was Bruno Steindel, with whom he studied several years, and then, at the age of sixteen, he went to Leipzig, where he won a free scholarship in the Conservatory. From Leipzig he went to Wiesbaden as first 'cellist in the Orchestra of that city, remaining there four years, then to Berlin as a member of the Berlin Philharmonic Orchestra. Mr. Ferner returned to America and joined the Chicago Symphony Orchestra at the beginning of the Twenty-fifth Season, sitting at the same stand with his first teacher, Bruno Steindel. He left Chicago at the close of the Twenty-eighth Season, and is now (1924) first 'cellist of the San Francisco Orchestra.

"April 3, Thursday P. M.: meeting of the Trustees; in consequence of increased salaries for members of the Orchestra, a new scale of prices for season tickets was adopted:

> Main Floor: All $35 tickets increased to $45.
> Main Floor: All $23 tickets increased to $30.
> Balcony: All $23 tickets increased to $30.
> Balcony: All $18 tickets increased to $21.
> Balcony: All $12 tickets increased to $14.
> Boxes increased to $350 and $400, according to location."

TWENTY-SEVENTH PROGRAM, APRIL 13 AND 14
Soloist: Mme. Louise Homer

a. Aria, "Ombra Mai Fu," from "Serse," . . . . *Handel*
b. Aria, "Che Faro Senza Euridice," from "Orfeo ed Euridice," . . . . *Gluck*
Symphony No. 7, A Major, Opus 92, ... *Beethoven*

INTERMISSION

Aria, "O Don Fatale," from "Don Carlos," . . . . . *Verdi*
Aria, "Il Est Doux, Il Est Bon," from "Hérodiade," . *Massenet*

TWENTY-EIGHTH, AND LAST, PROGRAM, APRIL 20 AND 21

Overture, "Leonore," Opus 72, No. 3, ... *Beethoven*
Symphony No. 2, D Major, Opus 73, ... *Brahms*

INTERMISSION

Rondo, "Till Eulenspiegel's Merry Pranks," . . . . *Strauss*
Siegfried Idyl, ... *Wagner*
Prelude to "Die Meistersinger von Nürnberg," . . . *Wagner*

THE CHICAGO MUSIC FESTIVAL

The Chicago Music Festival, announced for the last week in April, was undertaken by Mr. Stock and The Orchestral Association for the first performance in Chicago of Gustav Mahler's eighth symphony, "The Symphony of One Thousand" (meaning that 1,000 performers—Orchestra, chorus and soloists—are needed for its performance).

The work of preparing the chorus for the Festival began early in the winter, under the general direction of Mr. Stock, though the weekly rehearsals were in charge of the Conductors of the assisting societies. A mass rehearsal was held Monday evening, April 23, in the Auditorium, under Mr. Stock's direction, for all the performers in "The Symphony of One Thousand" and other choral works given at the Festival. The Festival Chorus (850) included:

APOLLO MUSICAL CLUB
CHICAGO MENDELSSOHN CLUB } Harrison M. Wild, Conductor.
PHILHARMONIC SOCIETY, O. Gordon Erickson, Conductor.
SWEDISH CHORAL CLUB, Edgar A. Nelson, Conductor.
AMERICAN CHORAL SOCIETY
BELL TELEPHONE MALE CHORUS } Daniel Protheroe, Conductor.
CHICAGO SINGVEREIN, William Boeppler, Conductor.
TWO HUNDRED BOYS FROM THE OAK PARK AND RIVER FOREST GRADE AND HIGH SCHOOLS, O. Gordon Erickson, Conductor; Clara Thomas, Assistant.

Eight soloists were required for the Mahler symphony:

MISS MABEL GARRISON (soprano), *Una Pœnitentium.*
MISS ADELAIDE FISCHER (soprano), *Mater Gloriosa.*
MISS INEZ BARBOUR (soprano), *Magna Peccatrix.*
MISS MARGARET KEYES (contralto), *Mulier Samaritana.*
MISS SUSANNA DERCUM (contralto), *Maria Ægyptiaca.*
LAMBERT MURPHY (tenor), *Doctor Marianus.*
REINALD WERRENRATH (baritone), *Pater Ecstaticus.*
CLARENCE WHITEHILL (bass), *Pater Profundis.*

From the extended analytical notes by Felix Borowski in the Festival Program Book we may gather interesting data regarding the symphony and Mahler's methods in work. The eighth symphony, begun in 1906, was finished in 1909 and brought out September 12, in Munich, but not until many rehearsals had been held. "Time after time the score was modified after experiments in symphonic color had been made." Visitors from all parts of the world came to the Munich performance, Frederick Stock among the number.

The first performance of the eighth symphony in America was given by the Philadelphia Orchestra, under the direction of Leopold Stokowski, March 2, 1916, in the Academy of Music, Philadelphia.

Mahler's symphony is divided into two large divisions. The first is a setting of the ancient hymn "Veni, Creator Spiritus," and the second the closing scene of the second part of Goethe's "Faust." "The hymn 'Veni, Creator Spiritus' is used," says Mr. Borowski,

"as a song of yearning, to fill the universe with love—an invocation of the creative spirit. Faust's course to heaven is the answer to and the fulfillment of the opening invocation."

Four of Mahler's symphonies contain vocal parts, the texts of which are concerned with "metaphorical ideas." His reasons for using the second part of "Faust" in the eighth symphony are set forth in a letter written (1909) to his wife:

"Everything [he said] is but the image of something whose realization can be only the insufficient expression of that which is here required. Transitory things perhaps may be described, but what we feel and surmise and never reach—that is, what never can be realized, but is durable and imperishable behind all appearance—is indescribable, and that which draws us forward with mystical power—that which every creature, perhaps even stones, feels implicitly to be the center of its being (what Goethe calls here—once more in imagery—the 'eternal womanly')—that is, the element of repose, the goal, in opposition to the eternal longing, striving, forward-straining toward this goal—that is the eternal manly characteristic. You are quite right to designate it as the might of love."

Does any mortal know what all this means? Can any mortal explain the connection between the glorious hymn "Veni, Creator Spiritus," inspired of God for the use of the Fathers of the Church, and Goethe's godless poem? The connection is probably one of Mahler's "metaphorical ideas."

As for the music, that is another matter. The eighth symphony represents the highest form of the new order of music, requiring "a larger apparatus" (to use Mr. Borowski's words) for orchestra, chorus and soloists than that found in any work of modern times, excepting Berlioz's "Te Deum." After the rehearsal on Monday (the 23rd) Mr. Stock said to me, "Note the first eight bars in the symphony and the changes of rhythm, 4-4, 2-4, 3-4; only a genius can do this. Mahler's instrumentation is not as interesting as that of Wagner. He stays too long in the valleys, picking dainty flowers; does not dwell long enough on the mountain tops."

Gustav Mahler was born July 7, 1860, at Kalischt, Bohemia; died May 18, 1911, at Vienna.

The Mahler symphony was given on Tuesday, Thursday and Saturday evenings, April 24, 26 and 28, in the Auditorium, under the direction of Frederick Stock.

The concert on Wednesday evening, April 25, for Orchestra and soloists, included:

Overture, "Coriolanus," . . . . *Beethoven*
Symphony No. 6, "Pathetic," B Minor, Opus 74, . *Tschaikowsky*
Aria, "Ernani Involami," from "Ernani,". . . . . . *Verdi*
        Miss Frieda Hempel
Festival March and Hymn to Liberty, ... *Stock*

Orchestra, chorus and soloists appeared in a Wagner program on Friday evening, April 27, consisting of selections from "Tannhäuser," "Die Walküre," "Die Götterdämmerung," "Tristan and Isolde" and "Die Meistersinger." Soloists: Mme. Margaret Matzenauer, Lambert Murphy and Clarence Whitehill.

The Festival was an important event in the musical life of Chicago and a well earned triumph for the Conductor, Frederick Stock, who received an ovation from the audience at the close of the Saturday night concert.

The financial returns from the Festival made "a melancholy exhibit." Our music lovers were not interested in the Mahler symphony, the greatest choral work ever heard in Chicago. The American people were thinking of other matters. President Wilson read, on April 2, his message to Congress, recommending a declaration of war on Germany. Four days later Congress declared war, and at once the whole country was aflame with patriotism and war enthusiasm. The men and women were busy getting their boys ready for the Expeditionary Force to France, and were in no mood for the Festival and Mahler's eighth symphony.

THE POPULAR CONCERTS

The series consisted of ten concerts, with the cooperation of the City Club and Civic Music Association, under the direction of Frederick Stock in Orchestra Hall on Thursday evenings, October 26, November 9 and 30, December 28, January 11, 1917, February 1 and 22, March 8 and 29 and April 19. Soloists: Harry Weisbach, Alexander Zukovsky, Bruno Steindel, Alfred Quensel, Leopold de Maré and Enrico Tramonti. The Orchestra played music the people wanted to hear:

Symphonic poem, "The Moldau" (Smetana); suite, "The Wand of Youth" (Elgar); symphony No. 1 in B flat major, Opus 38 (Schumann); suite, "Nutcracker" (Tschaikowsky); serenade for flute and horn (Titl); overture to "Fingal's Cave" (Mendelssohn), and overture to "Oberon" (Weber).

The program of the Tenth Concert (April 19) contained works of a more advanced order, indicating that "the plain people" are now appreciating the best in music. The concerts were given to "sold-out houses" with net returns of $8,480.32 to the Association.

Twenty-sixth Season—1916-1917

The Executive Committee met Monday afternoon, April 30, and granted pensions to Ferdinand Volk and Louis Novak.

June 1, Friday afternoon, the Executive Committee met to discuss pensions again, and retired two old members of the Orchestra on pensions—Joseph Nicolini and William Zeller, trombone players.

TWENTY-SIXTH SEASON
(1916-1917)
SOLOISTS

PIANOFORTE: Mrs. Fannie Bloomfield Zeisler, Mme. Olga Samaroff; Harold Bauer, Ossip Gabrilowitsch, Rudolph Ganz, Percy Grainger, Josef Hofmann, Alexander Raab, Ernest Schelling.

VIOLIN: Eddy Brown, Mischa Elman, Albert Spalding, Theodore Spiering, Harry Weisbach (twice), Efrem Zimbalist, Alexander Zukovsky.

VIOLONCELLO: Walter Ferner, Bruno Steindel.

VOCAL: Mmes. Marcella Craft, Alma Gluck, Louise Homer; Clarence Whitehill.

TWENTY-SEVENTH SEASON
(1917-1918)

Death of George Everett Adams—The Second Program in memory of Mr. Adams—The Executive Committee adopts a memorial—President Carr answers the newspaper attacks on the loyalty of Frederick Stock and members of the Orchestra—Annual Festival of the Civic Music Association—Vice-President Hamill addresses the audience regarding the loyalty of the members of the Orchestra—Ten Popular Concerts.

The Twenty-seventh Season was about to open when the sad news came of the death of George Everett Adams, in whose passing the Orchestra lost a sincere friend and one of its generous supporters.

My friendship with Mr. Adams dates from the year 1894, when both of us came into the life of the Orchestra. He was elected Trustee and President in February of that year; my election as Trustee came in the following June. It was a trying period in the history of the Orchestra, owing to the indifference and lack of interest on the part of the general public. The Third Season (1893-1894) had just closed with a large deficit, and the indications for the future were not encouraging. The Trustees held many serious meetings during Mr. Adams' presidency (1894-1899) to discuss finances and secure guarantors. Though there were difficult financial situations to meet, Mr. Adams never had any misgivings as to the future of the Orchestra. He was a generous contributor to the "Fund," by which the Orchestra was maintained after the expiration of the first three years' guaranty, and was one of the ten men to secure the Michigan Avenue property, and made a large contribution to the construction of Orchestra Hall.

George Everett Adams was born June 18, 1840, in Keene, New Hampshire; died October 5, 1917, at Peterborough, New Hampshire.

The World War was still raging in Europe, creating an unrest throughout the United States which was not conducive to the success of Mahler Festivals and symphonic concerts. The established orchestras in some

GEORGE EVERETT ADAMS

Twenty-seventh Season—1917-1918

cities could be maintained only by levying assessments on the guarantors. In the face of these serious conditions the prospectus for the Twenty-seventh Season brought renewals from our subscribers aggregating $103,152 prior to the opening of the season.

FIRST PROGRAM, OCTOBER 12 AND 13
The Star Spangled Banner

Overture to "Rienzi,"	*Wagner*
Symphony No. 6, "Pastoral," in F Major, Opus 68,	*Beethoven*

INTERMISSION

Ballade, "Tam O'Shanter,"	*Chadwick*
a. Prelude, "The Afternoon of a Faun,"	*Debussy*
b. A Dance Rhapsody,	*Delius*
Rhapsody, "Italia," Opus 11,	*Casella*

At the close of the intermission Vice-President Charles H. Hamill addressed the audience on a patriotic subject, "Liberty Bonds."

Horace K. Tenney spoke on the same subject at the concert on Saturday evening.

The Second Program, October 19 and 20, included:

Symphony No. 1, ... *John Alden Carpenter*

Arioso from the St. Matthew Passion Music, . . . *Bach*

(Orchestration by Frederick Stock)

IN MEMORY OF

GEORGE E. ADAMS

Died October 5, 1917

Trustee (1894-1917) and President (1894-1899) of The Orchestral Association

---

Mr. Carpenter began the symphony July 31, 1916, and finished the work March 6, 1917. It was given for the first time under the direction of Frederick Stock at the Litchfield County Choral Union Festival, held in the Music Shed in the grounds of Carl Stoeckel's residence at Norfolk, Connecticut, June 5, 1917.

The score bears the motto: "Sermons in Stones," This occurs in Act II, Scene 1, of Shakespeare's "As You Like It."

A meeting of the Executive Committee was held Friday, October 19, at 4 P. M., there being present Messrs. Carr, Hamill, Adams and Otis; Frederick J. Wessels, Business Manager, Henry E. Voegeli, Assistant Manager, and Frederick Stock, Conductor, by invitation. The following memorial, offered by Mr. Hamill, was adopted and ordered spread upon the minutes of the meeting:

"George E. Adams is no more of this earth.

"It is rare that a community is blessed in the possession of a citizen of such high attainments in so many fields of endeavor. He was not only a lawyer of learning and a legislator of sagacity, he was, too, a patient and intelligent student of history, and an appreciative reader of good literature. Both his willingness to serve and the respect in which he was held are indicated by his activities. Besides sitting one term in the State Senate and four in the United States Congress, he was at different times an overseer of Harvard College, President of both the Union League and Commercial Clubs and Trustee of the Newberry Library and the Field Columbian Museum.

"He was one of the Trustees of this Association from 1894 until his death, and served as its President from 1894 to 1899. As a man of broad cultivation and public spirit he was prompt to recognize the cultural value to the community of a great Symphony Orchestra. Accordingly he gave generously of his means, his time and his wisdom to further the purposes of this Association. Warm in his sympathies, courteous in his manner, eloquent in his appeals, wise in his judgments, his efforts to better our city were fruitful of results, and the accomplishments of this Association are due in no small measure to his labors, which were prompted always by unselfish zeal for the public good.

"It is with the highest appreciation of his worth as a citizen, his character as a man, his charm as a friend and his devotion to the Association that we, his fellow-Trustees, record upon the minutes of this meeting our profound grief at his loss."

After the intermission at the concerts of November 2 and 3, Fourth Program, the Rev. Howard Agnew Johnston, D.D., addressed the audience on an essential in those war times, "Food Saving."

FIFTH PROGRAM, NOVEMBER 9 AND 10
SOLOIST: HAROLD HENRY
The Star Spangled Banner
Overture to a Fantastic Comedy, "The Faun," . . *DeLamarter*
Concerto for Pianoforte No. 2, D Major, Opus 23, . *MacDowell*

Twenty-seventh Season—1917-1918

Harry Weisbach was the soloist at the concerts of December 7 and 8, Ninth Program, playing Mendelssohn's concerto for violin in E major, Opus 64. The program included the first performance in Chicago of Goldmark's tone poem, "Samson."

The Annual Meeting of The Orchestral Association was adjourned from Tuesday afternoon, December 11, to Thursday, December 20, at the Chicago Club, the Members assembling at 1 P. M. for luncheon as guests of President Carr. There were present in person or by proxy thirty-four out of a total of thirty-nine Members.

The Treasurer presented his report for the Twenty-sixth Season (1916-1917), ending June 30, 1917:

RECEIPTS		EXPENSES	
Chicago concerts	$112,821.75	Business management	$ 21,760.32
Outside concerts (net)	19,211.00	Advertising	2,792.39
Popular concerts (net)	8,480.23	Salaries of Conductor and Orchestra	127,678.00
Interest at bank	676.14	Orchestra expenses	866.45
Program book	1,728.75	Soloists	11,000.00
Miscellaneous	54.50	Music and instruments	840.45
Hall rentals	57,441.17	Building expenses	1,144.53
Building rentals	23,757.50	Heating	2,926.62
		Insurance	1,300.18
		Hall expenses	14,936.21
		Ushers	5,173.45
		Water	621.16
		Taxes (1916)	9,711.29
		Interest on mortgage	10,000.00
		Hall improvements	6,117.07
		Gain on season	7,005.92
	$234,171.04		$234,171.04

From the gross gain of $7,005.92 on the season must be deducted the loss on the Mahler Festival, leaving $2,804.24 as the net gain for the season.

President Carr said of the Festival and the Mahler symphony:

"It was the climax of Chicago's musical season—for that matter, the climax of its musical life. To Conductor Stock belongs the credit of having brought about a magnificent performance of a gigantic work."

In answer to newspaper attacks on the loyalty of Conductor Stock and members of the Orchestra, the President said:

"There have been rumors circulated reflecting on the Americanism of the Chicago Symphony Orchestra, and it may interest you to know that out of approximately one hundred members there are only two who have not taken out their final papers. These two have their first papers."

The President then referred to the Pension Fund as being well established, and said:

"We have securities in this Fund amounting to $375,170.05, which put it on a permanent basis.

"During the past year we have taken out group insurance for 100 members of the Orchestra and employes, which will provide insurance of $1,000 on each member of the Orchestra and employe."

Horace S. Oakley was elected a Member of the Association, and Trustee to fill the vacancy caused by the death of George E. Adams.

THIRTEENTH PROGRAM, JANUARY 4 AND 5
THEODORE THOMAS MEMORIAL
The Star Spangled Banner

Suite No. 3, D Major, ... *Bach*
Symphony No. 3, "Eroica," E Flat, Opus 55, . . *Beethoven*

INTERMISSION

Bacchanale from "Tannhäuser," . . . . *Wagner*
Dreams, a Study to "Tristan and Isolde," . . . *Wagner*
(Orchestration by Theodore Thomas)
Prelude to "Die Meistersinger," . . . . *Wagner*

The Orchestra and Mr. Stock assisted the Civic Music Association in its Annual Festival on Wednesday evening, January 9, in Orchestra Hall, in a program consisting of folk-songs of the Allied Nations by the Children's Chorus of the Association, under the direction of Herbert E. Hyde; songs by 250 "Jackies" from the United States Training School at the Great Lakes Station, led by Herbert Gould; and children's songs by Tom Dobson.

FIFTEENTH PROGRAM, JANUARY 18 AND 19
Soloist: Efrem Zimbalist
The Star Spangled Banner

Symphonic Prelude, ... *Cole*
Symphony No. 3, B Minor, Opus 42, "Ilia Mourometz," . *Glière*

INTERMISSION

Concerto for Violin No. 3, G Minor, Opus 99, ... *Hubay*

HORACE S. OAKLEY

Twenty-seventh Season—1917-1918

The symphony by Glière was one of a number of Russian works, scores and parts, brought by Cyrus Hall McCormick on his recent return from Europe, and presented by him to the Orchestra. The Executive Committee met after the Friday concert and passed a resolution thanking Mr. McCormick for his "thoughtfulness in bringing this music, which will be of great value to the Association and its work."

SIXTEENTH PROGRAM, JANUARY 25 AND 26
Soloist: John McCormack

America

Recitative, "Deeper and Deeper Still,"
Aria, "Waft her, Angels, through the Skies," from "Jephtha," . . . . } *Handel*
Recitative, "Jehovah! Hear, O Hear Me," . . . *Beethoven*
Aria, "O My Heart is Sore within Me," from "Christ on the Mount of Olives," . . . . *Beethoven*

The program included "Peintures," by Borowski (first performance).

NINETEENTH PROGRAM, FEBRUARY 15 AND 16
Soloist: Willem Willeke

The Star Spangled Banner

"A Set of Four," . . . . **Sowerby*
(First Performance)
Concerto for Violoncello, C Major, Opus 20, ... *d'Albert*

Mr. Sowerby says of the last movement, "Lively, on the jump. It consists of all sorts of bits of what one often hears termed 'ordinary' character, thrown together in a ring, in which each one tries to out-do the others."

TWENTY-THIRD PROGRAM, MARCH 15 AND 16
Soloist: Ossip Gabrilowitsch

The Star Spangled Banner

Symphony No. 4, "Italian," A Major, Opus 90, . . *Mendelssohn*
Overture to a Romantic Comedy, ... *Stock*
(First Performance)
Concerto for Pianoforte No. 2, B Flat, Opus 38, . . *Brahms*

---

*Leo Sowerby, born May 1, 1895, at Grand Rapids, Michigan, came to Chicago at the age of fourteen to continue his studies with Calvin Lampert (piano) and Arthur Olaf Anderson (composition). In 1918 Mr. Sowerby was a member (clarinet) of the band of the 302d Field Artillery at Camp Grant, going abroad (1919) with the regiment as bandmaster.

On his return from France he entered the American Conservatory of Music in Chicago, as teacher of musical theory. In 1921 Mr. Sowerby went abroad as the first member of the new Music Department of the American Academy in Rome.

Mr. Stock began the overture in August, 1917, during the vacation which he spent at Lake George, New York, and finished it in Chicago, January 27, 1918. He says of the work:

"The characteristic quotation which serves as the text in the final fugue of Verdi's greatest work—his lyric comedy 'Falstaff'—is intended to be the leading motive:

" 'Jesting is man's vocation;
Wise is he who is jolly.' "

Mischa Elman was the soloist at the concerts of March 22 and 23, Twenty-fourth Program, playing the concerto for violin, in D major, Opus 61, by Beethoven.

TWENTY-SIXTH PROGRAM, APRIL 5 AND 6
SOLOIST: MISS ETHEL LEGINSKA
America
Fable of the Hapless Folk-Tune, ... *DeLamarter*
Concerto for Pianoforte No. 4, D Minor, Opus 70, . *Rubinstein*

After the intermission Charles H. Hamill, First Vice-President of The Orchestral Association, addressed the audience regarding the loyalty of the members of the Orchestra. In reply to the newspaper charges that some of the men were out-and-out "Pro-German" in their war views, Mr. Hamill declared that the entire Orchestra was faithful to America, from the Conductor to the drummer. In support of this statement he read a resolution adopted at a recent meeting of the members of the Orchestra:

"WHEREAS, The loyalty of the members of the Orchestra has been questioned,

"*Resolved*, That our attitude is one of unswerving loyalty to the Government of the United States in the great cause for which it has taken up arms against the rulers of the German people;

"*Resolved*, That we are in full accord with the measures taken by our Government to bring the war to a speedy and successful conclusion; that we have abiding faith in our country's Government and unfailing pride in our country's glory and the inspiring history of its flag;

"*Resolved*, That we pledge our moral and material support to the Government in its conduct of the war."

"April 11, Thursday evening, Orchestra Hall: Apollo Club concert under the direction of Harrison M. Wild: 'The Manzoni Requiem' (Verdi) and the Epilogue from 'Caractacus' (Elgar). Soloists: Adelaide Fischer (soprano), Emma Roberts (contralto), Theodore Karle (tenor), and Henri Scott (bass); Edgar A. Nelson (organist), the Chicago Symphony Orchestra."

I attended the first performance (1874) of the "Requiem" in Paris, under the direction of the composer, and made this note:

"June 9, Tuesday, 2 P. M.: To the Opéra Comique to hear 'The Manzoni Requiem' (Verdi), which was brought out May 22 at St. Mark's in Milan. Soloists today, Mmes. Soltz (soprano), Waldman (contralto), Messieurs Capponi (tenor) and Maim (bass); chorus of forty, including eighteen boys on the stage at the right of Verdi, and orchestra of eighty on his left. The 'Requiem' is operatic in style, rather than religious, reminding me of 'Aïda.' The duet in octave for the soprano and alto soloists was received by the audience with tremendous applause; the composer called out again and again."*

TWENTY-SEVENTH PROGRAM, APRIL 12 AND 13
SOLOIST: JASCHA HEIFETZ
The Star Spangled Banner

Suite, "American Negro,"	Otterström
Concerto for Violin, D Major, Opus 77,	Brahms

Mr. Otterström says of the suite, written in March, 1916:

"I have used seven negro songs, six of which have been drawn from 'Slave Songs of the United States.' In using the title 'Suite,' I had in mind the scope of the orchestral suites by Bach—an extensive first movement, followed by six short ones."

TWENTY-EIGHTH, AND LAST, PROGRAM, APRIL 19 AND 20
America

Fanfare Inaugurale,	Gilson
Symphony No. 5, E Minor, Opus 64,	Tschaikowsky

INTERMISSION

Symphonic Poem, No. 2, "Le Chasseur Maudit,"	Franck
Suite No. 2, "Indian," Opus 48,	MacDowell
Festival March,	Stock

The Star Spangled Banner

THE POPULAR CONCERTS

Ten concerts, with the co-operation of the City Club and the Civic Music Association, were given in Orchestra Hall, under the direction of Frederick Stock, on Thursday evenings, October 25, November 15, 29, December 27, January 19, 1918, January 31, February 21, March 14, 28 and April 18. Soloists: Harry Weisbach, Bruno Steindel, Franz Esser, Francesco Napolilli and Alexander Zukovsky.

---

*"Impressions of Europe" (1873-1874), by Philo A. Otis (1922).

The "Carnival of Venice" (Gungl), played at the tenth concert, April 18, was first heard at the Madison Square Garden Concerts in New York City, under the direction of Theodore Thomas, forty-five years ago, and was a favorite selection everywhere with the Thomas Orchestra of those days. The net returns to the Association from the Popular Concerts of the season were $7,911.93.

TWENTY-SEVENTH SEASON
(1917-1918)
SOLOISTS

HARP: Enrico Tramonti.
OBOE: Alfred Barthel.
ORGAN: Wilhelm Middelschulte.
PIANOFORTE: Misses Lillian Ammalee, Marie Kryl, Ethel Leginska, Mme. Yolanda Mérö; Ossip Gabrilowitsch, Harold Henry, Josef Hofmann, Mischa Levitzki, Arthur Shattuck.
VIOLIN: Eddy Brown, Mischa Elman, Jascha Heifetz (twice), Jacques Thibaud, Harry Weisbach, Efrem Zimbalist.
VIOLONCELLO: Willem Willeke.
VOCAL: Miss Mabel Garrison, Mmes. Julia Claussen, Povla Frijsch; John McCormack.
VISITING CONDUCTORS: Ernest Bloch, Henry Hadley, Adolf Weidig.

TWENTY-EIGHTH SEASON
(1918-1919)

Frederick Stock tenders his resignation until the question of his loyalty has been determined—Resignation of Bruno Steindel—Eric DeLamarter appointed Assistant Conductor—Conducts First Program—Letter from President Carr to Frederick Stock—Annual Festival of the Civic Music Association—A gift of $1,000 from Mrs. Jessie Spalding Walker to the Pension Fund—Visiting Conductors—Mr. Stock returns and conducts Nineteenth Program—A gala occasion—Death of George Putnam Upton.

Soon after the opening of the season the World War ended by the signing of terms between the allies and Germany, Monday, November 11, a day to be famous in the annals of history, and known as "Armistice Day." When the United States of America entered the war, the authorities at Washington started a rigid inquiry as to all native-born Germans residing in this country, regarding their loyalty, and requiring all such persons to show their naturalization papers. Frederick Stock, Conductor of the Chicago Symphony Orchestra, took out his first papers on his arrival (1895) in America, but in consequence of his absorbing duties in connection with the Orchestra, neglected to apply for his second papers until 1916, when he found his first papers had lapsed and it was necessary to take out new ones. Before the time for issuance of his final papers arrived, the United States had entered the war against Germany. Mr. Stock decided, therefore, in order to relieve the Trustees from possible embarrassment, to tender his resignation:

"MERRILL, NEW YORK, August 17, 1918.

"THE TRUSTEES OF THE ORCHESTRAL ASSOCIATION:

"*Gentlemen*—To you, with whom I have worked these many years in sympathy and mutual confidence, it is unnecessary that I should protest my devotion to this country, which I originally sought not only as a place in which to make a living, but as a home, in whose air of freedom, buoyancy and generosity my spirit could breathe and my art develop and flower.

"To some of you it is known that as a youth, while still living in Germany, the land of my birth, I disapproved of the autocracy of its government and combated the growing spirit of militarism. In the quarter of a century I have lived in Chicago my dearest hopes have been fulfilled.

"I have come to love the United States as my native land, to cherish her institutions, to identify myself with her cause and to regard myself as one of her dutiful and grateful sons. My devotion to and love for this country I count among the finest assets of my inner self.

"From the beginning of this awful war, and long before this country became a belligerent, I felt and said freely that Germany was in the wrong and should be defeated, and no one who knows me has ever questioned the sincerity of my then views, which, since April 6, 1917, have become with me, as with all Americans, the most profound convictions of my soul.

"I do not hesitate to classify myself as American, because all who know me are aware that at heart, in thought and in spirit, as well as in action and in deed, I am American, just as willing as any patriot to give my last drop of blood and my last penny for the land of my adoption and of my affections.

"While all this has been known to you, it unhappily is true that because my primary interest has been artistic and not political, I omitted the step which would have given legal effect to what was a spiritual accomplishment, and did not take out my second papers and become before the law an American citizen; and so now when most of all I wish to feel myself a part of this great republic in its struggle to make the world free from the menace of recurring wars, I find myself technically—almost, I would say, ironically—styled 'alien enemy.' For this, I know, I have no one to blame but myself, and it is I who must atone.

"However deeply I may feel my heart throb with love of this country, however ardently I may long to serve her, however sure may be your confidence in me—and it has been too often expressed to admit of question—it remains true that many of the music-loving public to whom our Orchestra must appeal are unable or unwilling to know the sentiments of my heart, or to distinguish between those who are alien enemies from conviction and choice and one whose greatest grief it is to be so classed.

"There has never been a moment when I have consciously put my own interest or ambitions above the welfare of the Orchestra to whose service I have given twenty-three years of my life, and now, after careful self-searching, I have come to the painful conclusion that the best interests of that Orchestra and of your Association demand that I withdraw from my position as Conductor until the day comes, for which I earnestly hope, when papers of full citizenship can be issued to me and make me before the law, as I am in spirit, an American citizen.

"I firmly believe that my withdrawal will afford a solution of the problems now confronting you, and will tend to relieve a delicate and vexing situation. I have, therefore, respectfully to request that you will relieve me of the duties of Conductor until that happier day shall dawn.

"Let me say in conclusion that it is impossible for me to express adequately my gratitude for the support and encouragement given me through all these years by the Trustees and Members of our Association and the music-loving public in general, and to express

the hope that the same consideration will be bestowed upon my successor. Respectfully,
"Frederick A. Stock."

Before Mr. Stock's letter of resignation had reached Chicago the Trustees were called together by President Carr, on Monday, August 19, to take action on an inquiry started by the Department of Justice concerning the loyalty of certain members of the Orchestra; there being present Clyde M. Carr, Charles H. Hamill, Charles L. Hutchinson, Seymour Morris and Horace S. Oakley; Frederick J. Wessels, Manager of the Orchestra, present by invitation.

I received a telegram August 15 at Dixville Notch, New Hampshire, from President Carr, asking for the use of my name as Trustee of The Orchestral Association "in a statement to the press expressing our determination to have no disloyal members in the Orchestra, also our absolute confidence in Mr. Stock." I replied expressing my unqualified approval of Mr. Carr's statement to the press.

Before taking up the business for which the meeting was called, the resignations of Frederic A. Delano and Clarence M. Woolley, as Trustees, were accepted; and Clarence A. Burley and Edward B. Butler were elected to fill the vacancies. On being notified by telephone of their election, Messrs. Burley and Butler came to the meeting. President Carr then advised the Trustees that certain members of the Orchestra had been summoned before the United States District Attorney for examination as to their loyalty. The Trustees, to show their faith in the loyalty of the men of the Orchestra, adopted the following preamble and resolution:

"*Be It Resolved*, That the Trustees of The Orchestral Association do co-operate in every way in their power to assist the Department of Justice or any governmental agency in securing all possible information which may secure a just and certain determination as to the loyalty of any member of the Orchestra under investigation, to the end that those members of the Orchestra, if any, who are disloyal or who have been guilty of acts or expressions of disloyalty may be dealt with according to law, and that the Orchestra may be purged of disloyal members; and to the end further that there may be put, once for all, an end to idle and malicious gossip concerning those members of the Orchestra whose loyalty to the country shall be found to be beyond reproach; and

"*Resolved Further*, That a committee of four be appointed from the Trustees to carry out the purpose of these resolutions, to co-operate with all appropriate governmental agencies in their efforts to discover and deal appropriately with disloyalty, and to advise the press and public of the steps taken and results achieved, so far as such advice shall not be inconsistent with the public interest as determined by the district attorney.

"TRUSTEES OF THE ORCHESTRAL ASSOCIATION:

JOSEPH ADAMS.	CHARLES L. HUTCHINSON.
WILLIAM L. BROWN.	CHAUNCEY KEEP.
CLARENCE A. BURLEY.	HAROLD F. MCCORMICK.
EDWARD B. BUTLER.	SEYMOUR MORRIS.
CLYDE M. CARR.	HORACE S. OAKLEY.
JOHN J. GLESSNER.	PHILO A. OTIS.
CHARLES H. HAMILL.	MAJOR A. A. SPRAGUE.
CHARLES H. SWIFT."	

A committee was then appointed, consisting of President Carr, Charles H. Hamill, Charles L. Hutchinson and Horace S. Oakley, to co-operate with the Department of Justice in determining the loyalty of the members of the Orchestra.

The *Chicago Tribune* of Wednesday, August 22, said of this action by the Trustees:

"The position taken by the Trustees of The Orchestral Association in the resolutions published today is exactly correct. The character of the Trustees is a guarantee that no disloyalist will be allowed to remain in the Orchestra after his disloyalty is disclosed or discovered. But the same character guarantees that faithful and loyal members of the Orchestra will not be expelled because of mere gossip or innuendo."

One of the most important meetings in the history of The Orchestral Association was held on Tuesday afternoon, October 1, when the Trustees met to consider Mr. Stock's letter, there being present Clyde M. Carr, Edward B. Butler, Clarence A. Burley, Charles H. Hamill, Charles L. Hutchinson, Seymour Morris, Horace S. Oakley and Philo A. Otis. The Trustees thoroughly appreciated Mr. Stock's request to be relieved of his duties as Conductor until the question of his citizenship had been determined, and therefore granted, though reluctantly, his request.

A letter was also read from Bruno Steindel,* principal 'cellist of the Orchestra, tendering his resignation, which

---

*Bruno Steindel was born in Zwickau, Saxony, where his father was Director of Music. He began the study of the violin at an early age, and as he progressed in his studies manifested a strong inclination for the 'cello, to which instrument he devoted his entire attention. He was for several years the first 'cellist of the Berlin Philharmonic Orchestra, playing under Brahms, Tschaikowsky, Dvořák, Grieg and Joachim. Mr. Steindel has been a member of The Chicago Symphony Orchestra from its organization (1891), and made his first appearance as a soloist in the Seventh Program, January 22 and 23, 1892. He was placed on the pension roll in 1919.

Twenty-eighth Season—1918-1919

was accepted with regret, Mr. Steindel having been with the Orchestra twenty-seven years, since its organization in 1891. President Carr stated that the Orchestra should now have a permanent Assistant Conductor, and that he had engaged Eric DeLamarter for the position. This action was approved by the Trustees, as was also Mr. Carr's reply to Mr. Stock's letter:

REPLY OF THE ORCHESTRAL ASSOCIATION

"CHICAGO, October 1, 1918.

"MY DEAR MR. STOCK:

"Your letter of August 17, 1918, long under consideration, was acted upon by the Trustees of The Orchestral Association today, and I was directed to say to you that in complying with your suggestion and relieving you from the duties of Conductor until your legal status as an American citizen can be established, the Trustees appreciate the noble motives which have prompted you to this course, and yield to your suggestion, not because they have now, or ever have had, any doubt of your loyalty to the country of our birth and your adoption, and of the equal affections of us all, but only because, as you so generously point out, a portion of the public who cannot know you as intimately as we have been privileged to know you, may be misled as to your sentiments by an appellation which, intended only for the enemies of our country, can nevertheless technically be affixed to you.

"To those who do not know you, the expressions of your letter and other declarations by you since the outbreak of war might not be convincing, but the faith of us who do know you, though it requires no support beyond our knowledge of you, is nevertheless confirmed by many facts, among which may be noted:

"Within four days of your arrival in this country, twenty-three years ago, you declared your intention of becoming a citizen, not, as has been intimated, to qualify you for admission to a musicians' union, for there was then no such requirement, but because, as we have reason to know, that declaration comported with your convictions and desires.

"In 1914, notwithstanding the tradition of twenty years and the fact that the directions on nearly all musical scores are in German, you, on your own initiative, changed the language of rehearsals from German to English, and since then have given all spoken directions in English.

"You, first among the Conductors of leading Orchestras, gave all-American programs, and on one of them included your own admirable composition, 'Festival March,' concluding with a beautiful orchestration of our national anthem, thus publishing to all the world that you regarded yourself as an American composer.

"Your several addresses on the subject of the war to the men of the Orchestra, as reported to us, have all manifested a fine sense of the obligations owed to this country by residents of foreign birth, and have left on the minds of your hearers no doubt as to your feelings.

"In permitting you to part for a time from us we wish to assure you of our regard for you as a man, our confidence in you as an American and our admiration and respect for you as a musical artist.

"In the quarter of a century of your association with our Orchestra, as player and Conductor, you have shown yourself always to be actuated by the highest musical ideals, and have brought to the performance of your duties the finest artistic skill and musical learning.

"No one who has followed your development as a Conductor or has known the artistic life of the body of musicians under your direction can, if he be at all sensible of the relation between integrity of character and nobility of musical expression, question your sincerity.

"We who have witnessed your untiring devotion to the cause of good music and the welfare of our Orchestra gratefully acknowledge that your present offer is but another evidence of that devotion and of the fine unselfishness which has governed you in all your relations to our Association.

"It is with the greatest reluctance, and only because we desire to relieve you from embarrassment which might result to you from the fact that the passions of our people are rightly inflamed against the government, from allegiance to which you have never been fully and technically released, that we accede to your proposal.

"Permit us to assure you that our grief in this separation finds its greatest comfort in the belief that it is but temporary, and that the omission of the past may be soon repaired. Then it will be our joy to welcome to our Conductor's stand Citizen Stock.
"Sincerely yours,
"CLYDE M. CARR, *President.*

"THE TRUSTEES OF THE ORCHESTRAL ASSOCIATION:

JOSEPH ADAMS.	CHAUNCEY KEEP.
WILLIAM L. BROWN.	HAROLD F. MCCORMICK.
CLARENCE A. BURLEY.	SEYMOUR MORRIS.
EDWARD B. BUTLER.	HORACE S. OAKLEY.
JOHN J. GLESSNER.	PHILO A. OTIS.
CHARLES H. HAMILL.	MAJOR A. A. SPRAGUE.
CHARLES L. HUTCHINSON.	CHARLES H. SWIFT."

The announcements through the press that Mr. Stock would not conduct for the present had a depressing effect on the interest of the public in the concerts. The season ticket sale at the date of the opening concerts was $91,767, showing a loss of $10,000 as compared with $101,620, the sale of the previous season.

ERIC DeLAMARTER

Eric DeLamarter,* organist and composer, whose works had been heard at the concerts in other seasons, made his first appearance as Assistant Conductor at the

FIRST CONCERTS, OCTOBER 11 AND 12

The Star Spangled Banner

Overture to "Benvenuto Cellini," Opus 23,	Berlioz
Symphony in D Minor,	Franck

INTERMISSION

Overture, Fantasia, "Romeo and Juliet,"	Tschaikowsky
Symphonic Poem, "The Sirens," Opus 33,	Glière
Irish Rhapsody,	Herbert

I made this note on the Friday concert:

"To the Conductor's room to meet Mr. DeLamarter and congratulate him. Tall and graceful, he made a great impression as he came to the stand. Mr. DeLamarter had the Orchestra and audience with him from the very start. What an opportunity for this young Conductor, who proved to be a man of genuine force, fulfilling all our expectations!"

The concerts of October 18 and 19, 25 and 26 were deferred, owing to the epidemic of influenza then prevalent in Chicago. Orchestra Hall and other places of amusement were closed by order of the Board of Health. People were advised to stay at home, or to wear "masks" if they went out. The epidemic soon abated, and the concerts were resumed November 1 and 2.

The Annual Festival for the benefit of the Civic Music Association was given Tuesday evening, November 5, in Orchestra Hall, in which Claudia Muzio (soprano), of the Metropolitan Opera Company, the Children's Chorus (800 voices) of the Association, led by Herbert E. Hyde, and the Chicago Symphony Orchestra, Eric DeLamarter, conducting, took part.

---

*Eric DeLamarter was born February 18, 1880, at Lansing, Michigan, and came to Chicago in 1899 to enter on his life work. He acquired his musical education from Wilhelm Middelschulte (organ) and Mary Wood Chase (piano). After a season in Paris, where he continued his organ studies with Charles Marie Widor, he returned to Chicago and resumed his studies, being largely aided by the counsels of Adolf Weidig and Adolf Brune in musical theory, and in orchestral writing by the criticisms of Frederick Stock. Mr. DeLamarter was musical critic (1908-1909) for the *Record-Herald*. In 1910 he substituted for W. L. Hubbard on the *Chicago Tribune*, and in 1911 was critic for the *Inter-Ocean*. Since 1914 he has been organist and choirmaster of the Fourth Presbyterian Church.

A letter from Mrs. Jessie Spalding Walker, enclosing a Liberty Bond of $1,000 for the Pension and Invalid Fund, was read at the Executive Committee meeting, Wednesday afternoon, November 27. This generous gift came from Mrs. Walker as a memorial to her husband, Henry Harrison Walker.

During Mr. Stock's absence the Executive Committee arranged for the appearance of Visiting Conductors:

SIXTH PROGRAM, NOVEMBER 29 AND 30
Visiting Conductor: Nikolai Sokoloff
Soloist: Raoul Vidas

Concerto Russe for Violin and Orchestra, Opus 29, . . . Lalo
Symphony No. 1, E Minor, Opus 39, ... Sibelius

SEVENTH PROGRAM, DECEMBER 6 AND 7
Visiting Conductor and Soloist: Serge Prokofieff

Concerto for Pianoforte, D Flat Major, Opus 10, } . Prokofieff
Scythian Suite, "Ala and Lalli," Opus 20, . . }
(Conducted by the Composer)
(First Performance in Chicago)

I was at the hall Thursday morning when Mr. Prokofieff, with coat off, was rehearsing the "Scythian" suite. The din and noise created by the "Dance of the Pagan Monsters" (second movement) suggested the music at the Temple in Jerusalem when the Queen of Sheba came to visit King Solomon. After the rehearsal Mr. Prokofieff told me of his trip to America, through Japan, across the Pacific to San Francisco, where he was "held up" two weeks in a detention camp.

At the Friday concert he played his concerto like a Slav, and with perfect ease and astonishing memory. He is only twenty-seven; has high thoughts and great intellectuality. His music is "hyper-modern." Will this be "the music of the future"?

The Annual Meeting of The Orchestral Association was held Tuesday afternoon, December 10, in the offices of the Association, there being present in person or by proxy thirty-six of the forty Members of the Association; President Carr in the chair; Frederick J. Wessels, Clerk.

The report of the Treasurer for the Twenty-seventh Season (1917-1918), ending June 30, 1918, was then read:

Twenty-eighth Season—1918-1919

RECEIPTS		EXPENSES	
Chicago concerts	$131,808.05	Business management	$ 21,632.26
Outside concerts (net)	17,870.11	Advertising	2,927.14
Popular concerts (net)	7,911.93	Salaries of Conductor and Orchestra	142,359.00
Interest at bank	935.68	Orchestra and concert expenses	1,207.14
Program book (net)	707.51	Soloists	12,300.00
Hall rentals	52,427.53	Music and instruments	620.00
Building rentals	32,938.50	Building expenses	10,830.26
		Heating	3,399.96
		Insurance	2,628.19
		Hall expenses	13,259.66
		Ushers	4,565.00
		Water	587.88
		Taxes	14,494.70
		Interest	8,500.00
Loss on season	1,549.68	Improvements	6,836.90
	$246,148.99		$246,148.99

The President then reviewed the work of the Twenty-seventh Season:

"Mr. Stock's absence from the Conductor's stand is a very great temporary loss to the Orchestra, but there are many compensating features. During this season Mr. Stock will be able to visit all of the cities of the country maintaining leading Orchestras. He has already been in Boston, New York and Philadelphia observing the work of the Orchestras in those cities, and gaining an insight into many interesting phases of the musical life in the east. He plans to hear the best Orchestras in the central west before the season ends. He has generously offered his services in assisting Mr. DeLamarter both at rehearsals and in coaching. The Trustees will call to mind that Mr. DeLamarter at the beginning of the season was appointed Assistant Conductor and organist. For some years past we have needed the services of an Assistant Conductor, and this season will offer Mr. DeLamarter an exceptional opportunity to be trained for his duties in the future.

"The Trustees are pleased to advise the Members that Mr. Stock is busily engaged on plans for increasing the field of usefulness of the Orchestra by giving concerts in a larger number of centers in Chicago, and in stimulating the interest in groups of music lovers in all sections of the city in the Chicago Symphony Orchestra, to the end that the hearers of the symphony concerts may be increased from possibly ten or fifteen thousand of our citizens per year to at least one hundred thousand.

"The Executive Committee is confident that these lists of Mr. Stock's activities are very great compensation for his temporary loss, and are convinced that without this season at his disposal, and without an assistant, he would have been altogether unable to devote his time to such necessary activities. It may be of interest to the Members that Mr. Stock, previous to this season, had never missed a concert or rehearsal in his twenty-three years of service to the institution."

The election of Trustees followed: William L. Brown, Charles H. Hamill, Charles L. Hutchinson, Harold F. McCormick and Edward B. Butler for the term of three years; Clarence A. Burley for the term of two years, to fill the vacancy caused by the resignation of Frederic A. Delano.

The Trustees assembled after the Annual Meeting, John J. Glessner in the chair, Frederick J. Wessels, Clerk, and elected Clyde M. Carr, President; Charles H. Hamill, First Vice-President; Joseph Adams, Second Vice-President; Philo A. Otis, Secretary; Frederick J. Wessels, Treasurer.

Section 4, Article III of the by-laws was amended to read as follows:

"The Board of Trustees at their Annual Meeting shall select out of their own number an Executive Committee, composed of seven persons, one of whom shall be the President, and shall, at the same time, select a member of the Committee as Chairman thereof."

Section 6, Article IV of the by-laws was also amended:

"The Executive Committee shall, subject only to the direction of the Board of Trustees, have full control of all the affairs of every kind of the Association, and exercise each and all of the powers, rights and duties of the whole Board of Trustees. Three members present shall constitute a quorum for the transaction of business."

In accordance therewith, Charles H. Hamill, Joseph Adams, Philo A. Otis, John J. Glessner, Charles L. Hutchinson and Horace S. Oakley were elected members of the Executive Committee. Clyde M. Carr, *ex officio* member of the Committee, was elected Chairman.

Frederick J. Wessels was appointed Business Manager, Henry E. Voegeli, Assistant Business Manager and Assistant Treasurer.

TENTH PROGRAM, DECEMBER 27 AND 28
SOLOIST: RUDOLPH GANZ

Concerto for Pianoforte No. 1, E Flat, ... *Liszt*
INTERMISSION
Concerto for Pianoforte No. 2, A Major, ... *Liszt*

After the Friday concert the members of the Orchestra, with their wives and children, and members of the Executive Committee, gathered in the foyer of the hall for the annual Christmas festivities. Joseph Polak (violoncello) in gorgeous attire acted as Santa Claus, and distributed presents from the tree. Then followed supper, prepared by the women, a genuine feast of good things; afterwards dancing, in which young and old took part.

ELEVENTH PROGRAM, JANUARY 3 AND 4
THEODORE THOMAS MEMORIAL
COMPOSER-CONDUCTOR: GEORGE W. CHADWICK
The Star Spangled Banner

Suite No. 4, D Major,	Bach
Symphony No. 3, F Major,	Chadwick

INTERMISSION

Symphony No. 5, C Minor, Opus 67,	Beethoven

TWELFTH PROGRAM, JANUARY 10 AND 11
VISITING CONDUCTOR: OSSIP GABRILOWITSCH
SOLOIST: MME. HELEN STANLEY

Symphony No. 1, C Minor, Opus 68,	Brahms
Recitative and Aria from "L'Enfant Prodigue,"	Debussy
Aria, "Pallas Athéné," Opus 98,	Saint-Saëns

FOURTEENTH PROGRAM, JANUARY 24 AND 25
ADOLPH WEIDIG CONDUCTING, IN CONSEQUENCE OF THE ILLNESS OF MR. DELAMARTER
SOLOIST: JOSEPH BONNET

Concerto for Organ No. 10, D Minor,	Handel
Symphony No. 3, F Major, Opus 76,	Dvořák
ORGAN SOLOS:	
Chorale-Prelude, "Out of Deep Need,".	Bach
(Six Parts, Double Pedal and Trombones)	
"Ariel" (after a Reading of Shakespeare),	Bonnet
Rhapsodie Catalane,	Bonnet
(With Pedal Cadenza)	

FIFTEENTH PROGRAM, JANUARY 31 AND FEBRUARY 1
VISITING CONDUCTOR: FRANZ KNEISEL
SOLOIST: JACQUES THIBAUD

Symphony No. 7, A Major, Opus 92,	Beethoven
Concerto for Violin No. 6, E Flat Major,	Mozart

SIXTEENTH PROGRAM, FEBRUARY 7 AND 8
AMERICAN COMPOSERS
Composer-Conductor: David Stanley Smith
Soloist: Miss Frances Nash

Overture, "The Taming of the Shrew," Opus 49, . . . *Avery*
Symphony No. 2, D Major, Opus 42, ... *Smith*
      Violoncello Solo by Theodore Du Moulin
      (First Performance in Chicago)

INTERMISSION

Concerto for Pianoforte, No. 2, D Minor, Opus 23, . *MacDowell*
March, "Louisiana,". . . . . *Van der Stucken*

"February 10, Monday evening: To Orchestra Hall to hear the Apollo Club in two important works, 'The Veil' (Cowen) and the 'Forty-seventh Psalm' (Schmidt). Mr. Wild conducted. Soloists: Cora Libberton (soprano), Frances Ingram (contralto), Warren Proctor (tenor) and Louis Kreidler (baritone), assisted by Julia Blish (contralto); Edgar A. Nelson (organist), and the Chicago Symphony Orchestra.

An important work at the concerts of February 14 and 15, Seventeenth Program, was the suite from the ballet-pantomime "Boudour," by Borowski (first performance), conducted by the composer.

EIGHTEENTH PROGRAM, FEBRUARY 21 AND 22
Guest-Conductor: Victor Herbert*
Soloist: Ossip Gabrilowitsch

Concerto for Pianoforte No. 1, B Flat Minor, Opus 23, *Tschaikowsky*
Suite, "Woodland Fancies," . . . . *Herbert*

The war now being over and peace declared, there seemed to be no valid reason why Mr. Stock could not return to the Conductor's stand.

A meeting of the Trustees was held on Friday, February 14, after the concert, there being present Joseph Adams, Clarence A. Burley, John J. Glessner, Chauncey Keep, Seymour Morris, Philo A. Otis and Charles H. Swift.

Manager Wessels reported to the Trustees that—

"Mr. Stock had complied with all the requirements of the law, having filed his application for second papers February 7, the first day under the law when he was permitted to do so. Ninety days

---

*Victor Herbert, one of the most successful among American composers of light opera, died May 26, 1924, in New York. He was born (1859) in Dublin, the grandson on his mother's side of Samuel Lover, the novelist. For some years after he came to America he was principal 'cellist in the Theodore Thomas Orchestra, and was often heard in solo work at the "Summer Garden Concerts" in Chicago. Among his works may be noted "Natoma," "Madeline," "The Wizard of the Nile" and "Babes in Toyland."

Twenty-eighth Season—1918-1919

from that date Mr. Stock will become a citizen, there being nothing in his long residence in the United States against his record."

The Trustees voted to refer the whole subject to the Executive Committee, with power to act.

The Executive Committee met on Wednesday afternoon, February 19, in the offices of the Association, there being present Joseph Adams, John J. Glessner and Philo A Otis; Frederick Stock, Conductor, and Frederick J. Wessels, Manager, by invitation.

The committee passed a unanimous resolution that Mr. Stock should resume his position as Conductor the following week.

It was a gala occasion when Mr. Stock appeared on the stage at the concert of Friday, February 28. Cheers came from the galleries; the men in the Orchestra gave him a prolonged "fanfare," while the vast audience rose to utter its gladness in shouts of applause and waving of handkerchiefs to our Conductor, who had come back to his own. When all was quiet, Mr. Stock, in a happy speech, thanked the people for the cordial support given to the Orchestra and the Association during this trying period. He gave special thanks to Mr. DeLamarter for the loyal manner in which he had performed his difficult task, and to Adolf Weidig for his aid in an emergency.

The concert closed with Mr. Stock's "March and Hymn to Democracy," "his confession of faith," in the words of the *Evening Post*, which had on this occasion its first hearing.

TWENTY-SECOND PROGRAM, MARCH 21 AND 22
Soloist: John McCormack

Air, "O Mort," . . . . } *Rameau*
Ariette, "Accourez Riante Jeunesse," from "Les Fêtes d'Hébé," . . . . }
Suite from "The Betrothal," . . . . *DeLamarter*
(First Performance in Chicago)
(Conducted by the Composer)

Maeterlinck's "The Betrothal," sequel to "The Blue Bird," was produced at the Schubert Theater, New York, on November 19, 1919, with an elaborate set of pictures by Herbert Paus, and incidental music by Eric DeLamarter; Theodore Spiering conducting.

TWENTY-THIRD PROGRAM

Monday afternoon, March 24, and Tuesday evening, March 25, postponed from October 18 and 19, on account of the epidemic of influenza.

GUEST CONDUCTOR: GIORGIO POLACCO

Symphony No. 3, "Eroica," E Flat, Opus 55, . . *Beethoven*

INTERMISSION

"La Mer," . . . . *Debussy*
Notturno, ... *Martucci*
Prelude and Isolde's Love-Death from "Tristan and Isolde," . . . . *Wagner*

TWENTY-FIFTH PROGRAM, APRIL 4 AND 5

SOLOIST: THEODORE DU MOULIN

Concert Overture, Opus 65, ... *Weidig*
(First Performance in Chicago)
(Conducted by the Composer)

Concerto for Violoncello, A Minor, Opus 33, . . . *Saint-Saëns*

The concert overture by Adolf Weidig, written in the summer of 1918, was brought out at a concert of the Minneapolis Symphony Orchestra, Minneapolis, February 23, 1919. Readers of the program book were afforded some information by Mr. Weidig regarding the evolution of a musical idea from its inception to the performance of the finished work:

"My overture was sketched in about three days, but the working out of its manifold details occupied the better part of six months. The score was then ready for the copyist—in this case my father.* It took him over two weeks, working seven to eight hours daily, to make a copy of the score, which comprises over seventy pages. The copying of the parts then began—about 400 pages in all. From the time of the inception of the work to the day on which it was ready for rehearsal, about four months intervened."

April 18, Friday: the Executive Committee held a meeting after the concert, and voted pensions to Walter Unger, Curt Baumbach and Frank A. Mittelstaedt.

TWENTY-EIGHTH, AND LAST, PROGRAM, APRIL 25 AND 26

The Star Spangled Banner

Overture, "Leonore," Opus 72, No. 3, ... *Beethoven*
Symphony No. 6, "Pathetic," B Minor, Opus 74, . *Tschaikowsky*

INTERMISSION

Tableau Musical, "Le Printemps," Opus 34, . . . *Glazounow*
A Dance Rhapsody, ... *Delius*
March and Hymn to Democracy, ... *Stock*

---

*Ferdinand Weidig, born (1841) in Saxony, was an excellent musician, and for thirty-eight years a member of the Hamburg Opera Orchestra. He was noted for his wonderful penmanship, specimens of his writing having been periodically exhibited in the Congressional Library at Washington, District of Columbia. Ferdinand Weidig came (1902) to Chicago to make his home with his son Adolf. Here his death occurred March 16, 1921.

GEORGE PUTNAM UPTON

Twenty-eighth Season—1918-1919

At a meeting of the Executive Committee, April 28, a new scale of prices of tickets for the coming season was adopted, in order to meet the increased salaries for members of the Orchestra:

$45 increased to $50.
$30 increased to $35.
$20 increased to $25.
$14 increased to $15.

All gallery tickets to be increased from twenty-five to fifty cents.

"May 20; Tuesday: The *Tribune* this morning contained the announcement of the death of a beloved friend of the Orchestra, George P. Upton, who passed away last night (the 19th) in his eighty-fifth year."

George Putnam Upton, one of the foremost of American critics and journalists, was born October 25, 1834, in Boston, and after his graduation from Brown University, in 1855, came to Chicago, and in 1856 became city editor of the *Chicago Evening Journal*. My friendship with him dates from 1868, after he had entered on his life work as music critic and editorial writer for the *Chicago Tribune*. I came to know him best in the Apollo Musical Club, when he was our first President (1872), and later as a staunch friend of Theodore Thomas in the early years of the Orchestra. Mr. Upton was the only Chicago critic who stood by the Conductor in the trying period of the World's Fair (1893).

Mr. Upton was the author of numerous works; a few of his "Standard" series may be noted: "Operas" (1886); "Oratorios" (1887); "Cantatas" (1888), and "Symphonies" (1889); "Theodore Thomas. A Musical Autobiography" (1905); "Musical Memoirs" (1908). The last services were held in the chapel of Oakwoods Cemetery, Thursday afternoon, May 22, conducted by the Rev. Frank W. Gunsaulus, D.D.

Mr. Upton closed his autobiography of Theodore Thomas with these words:

"His work was a public benefaction. His life is a noble example. His memory will be cherished by his contemporaries."

May we not use the same words in speaking of the life and work of George Putnam Upton?

THE POPULAR CONCERTS

The series consisted of nine concerts, with the cooperation of the City Club and the Civic Music Association, in Orchestra Hall on Thursday evenings, November 14, 28, December 26, January 16, 30, 1919, February 20, March 13, 27 and April 17.

The first four concerts were under the direction of the Assistant Conductor, Eric DeLamarter; the fifth on January 30, 1919, under the direction of Franz Kneisel, Guest Conductor for the week. Mr. DeLamarter directed the sixth, and then Mr. Stock resumed his old position March 13, conducting the remaining concerts of the series. Soloists: Harry Weisbach, Theodore Du Moulin, Franz Esser and Francesco Napolilli.

Louis Victor Saar conducted his suite "Roccoco" at the first concert, which had been heard at the third concerts of the regular series, November 8 and 9.

Borowski's "Allegro de Concert," with Herbert E. Hyde at the organ, was heard at the third concert, December 26.

June 2, Monday afternoon: Meeting of the Executive Committee. Carl Hillman was retired on a pension.

TWENTY-EIGHTH SEASON
(1918-1919)
SOLOISTS

ORGAN: Joseph Bonnet.
PIANOFORTE: Misses Frances Nash, Guiomar Novaes, Mrs. Vera Kaplan Aronson; Harold Bauer, Ossip Gabrilowitsch, Rudolph Ganz, Josef Hofmann, Mischa Levitzki, Serge Prokofieff.
VIOLIN: Miss Thelma Given; Leon Sametini, Toscha Seidel, Jacques Thibaud, Raoul Vidas, Harry Weisbach, Efrem Zimbalist.
VIOLONCELLO: Theodore Du Moulin.
VOCAL: Misses Sophie Braslau, May Peterson, Mmes. Hulda Lashanska, Helen Stanley; John McCormack, Reinald Werrenrath.
GUEST CONDUCTORS: Felix Borowski, George W. Chadwick, Rossetter G. Cole, Eric DeLamarter, Ossip Gabrilowitsch, Victor Herbert, Franz Kneisel, Giorgio Polacco, Serge Prokofieff, Louis Victor Saar, David Stanley Smith, Nikolai Sokoloff, Adolf Weidig.

TWENTY-NINTH SEASON
(1919-1920)

Mr. Stock now an American citizen—"The Children's Concerts" inaugurated—Organization of the "Civic Music Student Orchestra"—Bequest of $3,000 to The Orchestral Association from Cathrina Seipp—Death of Edward P. Ripley—Ten Popular Concerts—The Children's Concerts—The Student Orchestra First Concert.

The loss of $14,812.77 on the Twenty-eighth Season, due largely to the lack of interest on the part of the public in the concerts during Mr. Stock's absence, was met by the Trustees from the accumulated interest of the Field Memorial Fund.

Many of our regular patrons did not care at all for the concerts (especially on Saturday evenings) while Mr. Stock was away. The musical public did not fully realize that Frederick Stock voluntarily resigned all professional work until his status as an American citizen had been established, thus showing loyalty to his adopted country. With a little patriotism on the part of the public, the hall could have been filled at every concert, whoever conducted, thus supporting the Trustees and showing some courtesy to the distinguished musicians who came to our help as Visiting Conductors.

The season ticket sale for the current season aggregated $115,849 at the opening concerts, larger than that of the previous season, now that Mr. Stock was returning to the Orchestra as an American citizen. He appeared on May 22 before Judge Merritt W. Pinckney, of the Circuit Court, received his second papers and took the oath of allegiance to the Government of the United States.

FIRST CONCERTS, OCTOBER 17 AND 18

Symphony No. 3, "Eroica," Opus 55, ... Beethoven
Variations, Opus 36, ... Elgar
Symphonic Poem, "Finlandia," Opus 26, No. 7, . . . Sibelius

There was a great audience at the Friday concert, the men being greeted with applause as they appeared on the stage. Mr. Stock was received with cheers and waving of handkerchiefs when he came to the Conductor's stand.

The Executive Committee, April 4, 1919, adopted a suggestion of Mr. Stock, introducing a new feature in the educational work of the Association, which has since proved an attractive feature in the activities of the Orchestra, "The Children's Concerts." The program book of the first concerts contained this announcement:

"The present season will witness the launching of a series of Children's Concerts, with programs of about an hour's duration, and as the name given the concerts implies, especially constructed for the instruction and enjoyment of children. These concerts will be given at intervals during the season, on Thursday afternoons at four o'clock. The first is scheduled for Thursday, November 20. The prices will be the same as prevail for the Popular Concerts: Main floor, 25 cents, 35 cents, 50 cents; balcony, 25 cents, 50 cents; gallery, 15 cents; box seats, $1."

October 31, Friday: The Executive Committee met after the concert, and retired Bruno Kuehn (principal of the second violins) on a pension.

"November 3, Monday evening: 'Elijah' (Mendelssohn) in Orchestra Hall, under the direction of Harrison M. Wild. Soloists: Lois H. Johnston (soprano), Anna S. Imig (contralto), Robert Quait (tenor) and Theodore Harrison (baritone), Elwood Gaskell (boy soprano); Edgar A. Nelson (organist), and the Chicago Symphony Orchestra.

FOURTH PROGRAM, NOVEMBER 7 AND 8
SOLOIST: JOSEPH MALKIN*

Fantaisie, D Major, ... *Ropartz*
(First Performance in Chicago)
Concerto for Violoncello, D Minor, ... *Lalo*

SEVENTH PROGRAM, NOVEMBER 28 AND 29
SOLOIST: CARLOS SALZÉDO

Symphony No. 4, E Flat, Opus 48, ... *Glazounow*
Introduction and Allegro for Harp with String Orchestra,
Flute and Clarinet, ... *Ravel*
(First Performance in Chicago)
Symphonic Poem, "Enchanted Isles," for Harp and
Orchestra, Opus 35, ... *Salzédo*
(First Performance in Chicago)

Another important action in the promotion of "Music as a vital element in the civic growth of the community" was taken by the Executive Committee on December 4, in connection with the Civic Music Association, in the organization of the Civic Music Student Orchestra. The resolution adopted provided that:

―――
*Joseph Malkin, the new principal of the violoncellos, was born at Odessa, Russia, and received his first lessons from Ladislas Alois. On the advice of Anton Rubinstein Mr. Malkin went to Paris, entering the Conservatoire in 1895, receiving the first prize in 1898; then followed concert tours through France and Germany until 1902, when he was appointed first 'cellist of the Philharmonic Orchestra in Berlin, Arthur Nikisch, Conductor. He came to America in 1908, making his first appearance in December, 1909, with the New York Symphony Orchestra, Walter Damrosch, Conductor. In 1914 Mr. Malkin was engaged as first 'cellist in the Boston Symphony Orchestra, continuing until 1919, when he was engaged for the Chicago Symphony Orchestra, continuing until the close of the Thirty-first Season (1921).

"1. The Director of the Orchestra shall be Frederick Stock, and in his absence Eric DeLamarter, and in the absence of both, such person as Mr. Stock might appoint.

"2. The number of students to be admitted to the Orchestra shall be approximately fifty-four; though the number may be increased in the discretion of the Director.

"3. In the discretion of the Director, women may be admitted to the Orchestra.

"4. Permission is given for the use of scores and orchestral parts from the library of The Orchestral Association.

"5. The Music Association shall assume all expenses, costs and charges incurred in the work of the Student Orchestra."

A letter under date of November 21 to Herbert E. Hyde, Superintendent of the Music Association, from Joseph F. Winckler, President of the Musicians' Union, was then read, showing that the directors of the union were in hearty accord with the proposition to found the Student Orchestra, provided:

"The Orchestra as a collective body, or the members thereof individually, do not come in competition with the members of this organization upon professional engagements."

On motion, it was decided to convene the Annual Meeting on December 9, and then adjourn to December 16, at 2:00 P. M., also to notify the Board of Trustees that at its Annual Meeting on the same date the following amendments to the by-laws would be acted upon:

"*Resolved*, That Section 3 of Article III of the by-laws be amended so as to read as follows:

" 'SECTION 3—The Annual Meeting of the Trustees shall be held within one week after the Annual Meeting of the Association, and may be adjourned by a majority vote of the Trustees present at such meeting, without giving notice of such adjournment, to any date within one month thereafter. The Trustees shall elect a President, Vice-President, Second Vice-President, Third Vice-President, Secretary and Treasurer. The President, Vice-President, Second Vice-President, Third Vice-President and Secretary shall be elected from the Trustees. The Treasurer need not be a Trustee or a Member of the Association.'

"*Resolved*, That Section 4 of Article III be amended so as to read as follows:

" 'SECTION 4—The Board of Trustees at their Annual Meeting shall select, out of their own number, an Executive Committee, composed of eight persons, one of whom shall be the President, and shall at the same time select a member of the committee as Chairman thereof.'

"*Resolved*, That a section, to be known as Section 3-A, be added to Article IV, to follow immediately after Section 3 of said Article IV, as follows:

" 'SECTION 3-A—The Third Vice-President shall exercise all the powers and perform all the duties of the President, in case of the absence or inability to act of the President, Vice-President and Second Vice-President.'

"*Resolved*, That Section 5 of Article IV be amended to read as follows:

" 'SECTION 5—The Treasurer shall receive and keep the funds of the Association, and shall disburse the same only under the direction of the Trustees or of the Executive Committee by checks countersigned by the Secretary, or in the absence or inability of the Secretary to act, by the President or one of the Vice-Presidents. His books shall be open at all times to the inspection of the Trustees. He shall make a full financial report at the Annual Meeting of the Association, and shall make such other reports from time to time to the Association or the Board of Trustees or the Executive Committee, as from time to time may be required by any one of them. He shall give a bond in such amount and with such sureties as shall be approved by the Executive Committee, for the faithful performance of the duties of his office.' "

The Annual Meeting was held Tuesday, December 9, at 4:00 P. M. in the offices of the Association, there being present in person or by proxy twenty-five of the thirty-nine Members; Charles H. Swift in the chair, Frederick J. Wessels, Clerk.

The meeting then adjourned to Tuesday, December 16, at 2:00 P. M., there then being present in person or by proxy thirty-four of the thirty-nine Members; Vice-President Charles H. Hamill in the chair, Frederick J. Wessels, Clerk.

The Treasurer's report for the Twenty-eighth Season (1918-1919), ending June 30, 1919, showed:

RECEIPTS		EXPENSES	
Chicago concerts	$129,577.85	Business management	$ 23,150.12
Outside concerts (net)	3,939.08	Advertising	2,688.51
Popular concerts (net)	6,766.70	Salaries of Conductor and Orchestra	143,891.00
Interest	860.38	Orchestra and concert expenses	1,358.29
Program book	.00	Program	679.37
		Soloists	15,550.00
		Music	323.28
	$141,144.01		$187,640.57
Hall rentals	61,060.81	Building expenses	11,636.45
Building rentals	33,846.30	Heating and water	4,333.35
		Insurance and taxes	9,030.88
	$236,051.32	Hall expenses and ushers	21,173.90
		Interest	8,500.00
Loss	12,747.02	Improvements	6,483.19
	$248,798.34		$248,798.34

Twenty-ninth Season—1919-1920

William O. Goodman was elected a Member to fill the vacancy caused by the death of William B. Walker.* The Members then proceeded to the election of five Trustees for the period of three years: Joseph Adams, John J. Glessner, Horace S. Oakley, Philo A. Otis and Albert A. Sprague.

On adjournment the Trustees assembled; present, Messrs. Adams, Glessner, Hamill, Hutchinson, Keep, Morris, Oakley, Otis and Swift. The amendments to the by-laws, suggested by the Executive Committee at its meeting December 4, were then adopted: Section 3, Article III; Section 4, Article III; Section 3-A and Section 5, Article IV.

Horace S. Oakley was elected Third Vice-President, and Charles L. Hutchinson a member of the Executive Committee, in accordance with the revised by-laws.

ELEVENTH PROGRAM, DECEMBER 26 AND 27
SOLOIST: PERCY GRAINGER

Concerto for Pianoforte No. 2, G Minor, ... *Saint-Saëns*

INTERMISSION

"The Warriors" (Music to an Imaginary Ballet), . *Grainger*
(First Performance in Chicago)
(The Composer at the Piano)

TWELFTH PROGRAM, JANUARY 2 AND 3
THEODORE THOMAS MEMORIAL
SOLOISTS: HARRY WEISBACH
JOSEPH MALKIN

Symphony No. 7, A Major, Opus 92, ... *Beethoven*
Symphonic Poem, "The Angel of Death," . . . *Chadwick*
(First Performance in Chicago)

INTERMISSION

Concerto for Violin and Violoncello, A Minor, Opus 102, . *Brahms*
Siegfried's Death Music and Finale, from "The Twilight of the Gods," . . . . *Wagner*

THIRTEENTH PROGRAM, JANUARY 9 AND 10
SOLOIST: MRS. THEODORA STURKOW-RYDER

Symphony No. 3, A Minor (Scotch), Opus 56, . . *Mendelssohn*
Concerto for Pianoforte, F Minor, Opus 2, ... *Arensky*

A meeting of the Executive Committee was held on Saturday morning, January 24; present, Messrs. Carr, Glessner, Hamill, Oakley, Otis and Swift. President Carr read a letter, dated November 20, from William Sherman Hay, informing The Orchestral Association that

---
*William B. Walker died July 2, 1919, at Manchester, Massachusetts.

by the terms of the will of Cathrina Seipp, widow of Conrad Seipp, a bequest of $3,000 had been left to the Association for the benefit of the Pension and Invalid Fund. This generous bequest was greatly appreciated by the Executive Committee, and the Secretary was instructed to convey the thanks of the Association to Mr. Hay.

The Orchestra lost a friend in the death, February 4, at Santa Barbara, California, of Edward P. Ripley, President of the Santa Fe Railroad System. Mr. Ripley was elected a Member of The Orchestral Association at the time (1905) of its reorganization.

TWENTIETH PROGRAM, FEBRUARY 27 AND 28
SOLOIST: MISS KATHARINE GOODSON
Symphony No. 2, D Minor, Opus 70, ... *Dvořák*
Concerto for Pianoforte No. 2, Opus 38 (in One Movement), ... *Liapounow*
(First Performance in Chicago)

TWENTY-FIRST PROGRAM, MARCH 5 AND 6
SOLOIST: LEO SOWERBY
Symphony No. 2, D Major, Opus 36, ... *Beethoven*
Concerto for Pianoforte, F Major, ... *Sowerby*

TWENTY-FIFTH PROGRAM, APRIL 2 AND 3
SOLOIST: ERIC DELAMARTER
Symphony No. 2, D Major, ... *Sibelius*
Concerto for Organ, E Major, ... *DeLamarter*
(First Performance)

TWENTY-EIGHTH, AND LAST, PROGRAM, APRIL 23 AND 24
Overture to "Egmont," Opus 84, ... *Beethoven*
Symphony No. 2, E Minor, Opus 27, ... *Rachmaninow*

INTERMISSION
Bacchanale from "Tannhäuser," . . . . *Wagner*
Ride of the Valkyries, from "The Valkyries," . . . *Wagner*
March and Hymn to Democracy, ... *Stock*

THE POPULAR CONCERTS

Ten concerts were given under the direction of Frederick Stock in Orchestra Hall, on Thursday evenings, October 23, November 13, 27, December 18, January 8, 29, 1920, February 19, March 11, 25 and April 15. Soloists: Franz Esser, Joseph Malkin, Francesco Napolilli, Harry Weisbach and Alexander Zukovsky.

THE CHILDREN'S CONCERTS

The series consisted of six concerts, under the direction of Frederick Stock, in Orchestra Hall on Thursday afternoons at 4 o'clock, November 20 and December 11, January 15, 1920, February 12, March 18 and April 22. Soloists: Alfred Quensel, Joseph Malkin, Miss Anita Malkin and Harry Weisbach.

The programs, with analytical notes by Anne Faulkner Oberndorfer, were prepared by Mr. Stock with due regard to the tastes of the little folks, and, with the Conductor's explanations, filled an hour of delight for old and young.

The program of the fourth concert, February 12, Miss Anita Malkin, soloist, will show the character of the music Mr. Stock selected to please and educate the children:

March, "Rakoczy,"	Berlioz
Allegro Molto from Symphony in G Minor,	Mozart
Concerto for Violin, E Minor (First Movement),	Rode
Military Polonaise,	Chopin

(Orchestration by Theodore Thomas)

THE CIVIC MUSIC STUDENT ORCHESTRA

Before the close of the year 1920, plans were completed by The Orchestral Association and Civic Music Association for the organization of the Civic Music Student Orchestra, with Frederick Stock, Musical Director; Eric DeLamarter and George Dasch, Assistant Directors. When the announcement was made to the public, 500 young men and women applied at once for membership in the new Orchestra, from whom, after examination as to their musical qualifications, eighty-six players were accepted.

The first rehearsal was held on January 27, 1920, in Orchestra Hall, Mr. Stock conducting, and with such excellent results that the first concert by the Student Orchestra was given Monday evening, March 29, in Orchestra Hall:

March, Triumphant Entry of the Boyards,	Halvorsen
Adagio Pathétique, Opus 128, No. 3,	Godard
Symphony No. 5, E Minor, Opus 64,	Tschaikowsky

INTERMISSION

Suite "Peer Gynt," No. 1, Opus 46,	Grieg
Two Pieces for String Orchestra, Opus 15,	Keller
Military March, "Pomp and Circumstance,"	Elgar

Herbert E. Hyde, Superintendent of the Civic Music Association, said in his Seventh Annual Report (1919-1920):

"Never in this city has a concert created so much enthusiasm and excitement. At its conclusion the audience stood and cheered, and elaborate reviews appeared in the press. It is a safe statement to make that every person in the audience realized that this concert marked the beginning of music in this country 'by Americans and for Americans,' for every member of the Orchestra has received his training in this country and was awaiting only such an opportunity to acquire the necessary routine in symphonic *ensemble* to place himself on a competitive basis with foreign trained players. There is a wealth of capable, finely equipped players in this city alone who are denied membership in our Orchestras just because of their lack of familiarity with orchestral repertoire and discipline, and one of the objects of the Civic Music Student Orchestra is to give them the opportunity of acquiring it. The vision, interest and enthusiasm of Mr. Stock are beyond all praise, for without his whole-hearted co-operation the idea would have been impossible of accomplishment."

TWENTY-NINTH SEASON
(1919-1920)
SOLOISTS

HARP: Carlos Salzédo, Enrico Tramonti.
ORGAN: Eric DeLamarter.
PIANOFORTE: Miss Katherine Goodson, Mrs. Fannie Bloomfield Zeisler, Mrs. Theodora Sturkow-Ryder; Alfred Cortot, Percy Grainger, Josef Lhevinne, Benno Moiseiwitsch, Leo Ornstein, Sergei Rachmaninow, Leo Sowerby.
VIOLIN: Miss Ruth Ray; Mischa Elman, Jascha Heifetz, Albert Spalding, Harry Weisbach.
VIOLONCELLO: Joseph Malkin (twice).
VOCAL: Misses Mabel Garrison, Maggie Teyte, Mrs. Merle Alcock; Edward Johnson.

THIRTIETH SEASON
(1920-1921)

The men who worked for "The Condition and Future of the Orchestra"—Death of Oliver W. Norton—Eleven members of the Orchestra (1891-1921) honored at the first Friday concert—Gift of $3,000 from Edward G. Uihlein—Eastern trip of the Orchestra, with comments of the press—Banquet by the men of the Orchestra in honor of Mrs. Elizabeth Sprague Coolidge—The Children's Concerts—The Popular Concerts—The Student Orchestra.

The *Chicago Tribune* said of the opening of the season:

"The great value of the Orchestra to the city is not confined to the concerts, high and educational as the standard of their music is. The Orchestral Association is active. It is never contented with success."

The *Tribune* called particular attention to the Children's Concerts and the Student Orchestra as being "the most important steps forward in the development of American orchestral music that Chicago has ever taken." "Chicago is a real center of musical education now," due to the intelligent development of many people working with "unselfish spirit to this end." "The Orchestra has crystallized this devotion, and to the men who have made the Orchestra what it is today there are thousands and thousands who are truly grateful."

The hearts of the founders (some, alas! have passed from our midst) would surely have rejoiced had they been permitted to be with us at the first concerts of this season, to witness the fruits of their labors. They were inspired with rare devotion in their work for "The Condition and Future of the Orchestra," and their work abides.

The season ticket sale, at the date of the first concerts, showed a total of $126,958.06—the largest in the history of the Orchestra, and an increase of $10,000 over the sale of the previous season.

A sincere friend and generous supporter of the Orchestra, Oliver W. Norton, passed away October 1. From 1894 until the completion (1904) of Orchestra Hall, Mr. Norton had contributed annually to the "Fund for the Support of the Orchestra." He never failed at any time to respond to a call of the Trustees, and, with a subscription of $10,000, was one of the first to answer "The Appeal" for funds to build Orchestra Hall. His son, R. H. Norton, in a letter of December 21, says:

"My mother wishes me to thank you and the Association for the expression of sympathy contained in your letter.

"As you may know, my father has been blind for a great many years. One of the few sources of pleasure available to him was music. He was always genuinely interested in the work and development of the Orchestra, and enjoyed keenly its concerts for many years."

Mr. Stock prepared an attractive program for the first concerts, commencing with the appearance, amid a tumult of applause, of eleven of the ninety-five members of the Orchestra, decorated with white ribbons, indicating that they had been with the Orchestra since the First Season (1891):

JOSEPH SCHREURS.	ALBERT ULRICH.
CARL MEYER.	GEORGE F. MEYER.
LEOPOLD DE MARÉ.	LOTHAR NURNBERGER.
ALEXANDER KRAUSS.	HERMAN BRAUN.
RICHARD SEIDEL.	JOSEPH FITZEK.

JOSEPH ZETTELMANN.

"The intelligent devotion and unselfish spirit" of these faithful men (some of them have not missed a concert in all these years) have made the Chicago Symphony Orchestra what it is today.

FIRST PROGRAM, OCTOBER 15 AND 16

Overture, "Husitzká," Opus 67, ... *Dvořák*
Symphony No. 5, C Minor, Opus 67, ... *Beethoven*

INTERMISSION

Suite, "Impressions d'Italie," . . . . *Charpentier*
Prelude, "L'Après-midi d'un Faune," . . . . . *Debussy*
Overture, "Le Carnaval Romain," Opus 9, ... *Berlioz*

Joseph Malkin was the soloist in the concerts of November 5 and 6, Fourth Program:

Symphony No. 8, F Major, Opus 93, ... *Beethoven*
Concerto for Violoncello, D Major, Opus 101, . . . *Haydn*
Symphonic Poem, "Finlandia," Opus 26, No. 7, . . *Sibelius*

SIXTH PROGRAM, NOVEMBER 19 AND 20
SOLOIST: BENNO MOISEIWITSCH

Concerto for Pianoforte, A Minor, Opus 54, . . *Schumann*
Fantastic Suite for Piano and Orchestra, . . . *Schelling*

Thirtieth Season—1920-1921

The Annual Meeting of The Orchestral Association was held in Orchestra Hall, Tuesday, December 14, at 4 P. M., there being present in person or by proxy thirty-four of the thirty-eight Members; Vice-President Hamill in the chair, Frederick J. Wessels, Clerk. Edward L. Ryerson and Frank Cramer were elected Members to fill the vacancies caused by the death of Edward P. Ripley and Oliver W. Norton.

Frederick J. Wessels presented the Treasurer's report for the Twenty-ninth Season (1919-1920), ending June 30, 1920:

RECEIPTS		EXPENSES	
Chicago concerts	$156,796.50	Business management	$ 30,051.42
Outside concerts (net)	16,453.96	Advertising	3,805.21
Popular concerts (net)	8,463.55	Salaries of Conductor and Orchestra	161,295.00
Children's concerts (net)	4,815.48	Orchestra expenses	1,186.01
Interest	1,407.26	Program	543.69
		Soloists	13,850.00
	$187,936.75	Music	1,189.03
			$211,920.36
Hall rentals	$ 78,477.87	Building expenses	14,039.01
Building rentals	34,301.00	Heating	3,495.42
		Insurance	2,008.87
	$112,778.87	Hall expenses	18,869.90
		Ushers	6,459.50
Old accounts paid	$ 252.57	Water	770.68
		Taxes	9,614.84
		Interest	8,500.00
		Improvements	2,374.75
		Total	$278,053.33
		Profit	22,914.86
	$300,968.19		$300,968.19

Orchestra expenses (as above)	$211,920.36
Add hall rent	18,000.00
Add office rent	1,500.00
	$231,420.36
Deduct share of business management, account of hall	12,000.00
Orchestra expenses	$219,420.36
Orchestra earnings	187,936.75
Loss on operation of Orchestra	$ 31,483.61

ELEVENTH PROGRAM, DECEMBER 23 AND 24
Soloist and Guest Conductor: Cyril Scott

Concerto for Pianoforte, ...	Scott
(First Performance in Chicago)	
Two Passacaglias, ...	Scott
(First Performance in Chicago)	

A gift of $3,000 from Edward G. Uihlein to The Orchestral Association was announced at a meeting of the Executive Committee Wednesday afternoon, December 29. It was voted that this money should be added to the Endowment Fund, and that the Secretary be authorized to acknowledge receipt of the same with the sincere thanks of the Association to Mr. Uihlein for his generosity.

THIRTEENTH PROGRAM, JANUARY 7 AND 8, 1921
THEODORE THOMAS MEMORIAL
Soloist: Enrico Tramonti

Symphony No. 3, "Eroica," Opus 55, ...	Beethoven
Chorale and Variations for Harp and Orchestra, . . .	Widor

INTERMISSION

Symphonic Poem, "The Garden of Fand,"	Bax
Tone Poem, "Death and Transfiguration,"	Strauss

EASTERN TOUR
(1921)

The entire Orchestra, with Frederick Stock, Conductor; Eric DeLamarter, Assistant Conductor; Frederick J. Wessels, Business Manager, and Henry E. Voegeli, Assistant Manager, left Chicago at 8:25 A. M. Sunday, January 23, by the Michigan Central Railroad, arriving in Boston at 10:25 A. M. Monday, January 24. Concert in the evening in Symphony Hall:

Overture, "The Magic Flute,"	Mozart
Symphony No. 2, ...	Rachmaninow

INTERMISSION

Symphonic Poem, "The Garden of Fand,"	Bax
Prelude and Love-Death, from "Tristan and Isolde," .	Wagner

Tuesday evening, January 25, in New York. Concert in Carnegie Hall:

Symphony No. 3, ...	Brahms
Fantasia, "Francesca da Rimini," . . .	Tschaikowsky
Symphonic Poem, "The Garden of Fand,"	Bax
Tone Poem, "Death and Transfiguration,"	Strauss

Thirtieth Season—1920-1921

The people of New York had plenty of good music to occupy their attention at this time. Three Orchestras of the first order gave concerts on the same day, January 25: the National Symphony (Willem Megelberg, Conductor), the Orchestra of the Teatro de la Scala, Milan (Arturo Toscanini, Conductor), and the Chicago Symphony (Frederick Stock, Conductor). This was not all: the Chicago Opera Company, Mary Garden leading the cast, was playing at the Manhattan Opera House. Henry E. Krehbiel, in the *Tribune*, had kind things to say of our Conductor and his men: "The Chicago Orchestra, under Leadership of Mr. Stock, Wins Enthusiastic Admiration in Superb Program!"

In Philadelphia the Orchestra was assisted by Mme. Olga Samaroff on Wednesday evening, January 26, in the Academy of Music:

Overture, "The Magic Flute,". . . . . *Mozart*
Symphony, E Minor, Opus 27, ... *Rachmaninow*
Concerto for Piano and Orchestra, Opus 54, . . . *Schumann*
Symphonic Poem, "Finlandia," . . . . *Sibelius*

The concert in Washington was given at the National Theatre, Thursday, January 27, at 4:30 P. M., with the assistance of Vasa Prihoda, soloist:

Overture, "Carneval," . . . . *Dvořák*
Symphony No. 4, ... *Tschaikowsky*
Concerto for Violin in D Minor, ... *Mendelssohn*
Tone Poem, "Finlandia," . . . . *Sibelius*

Mr. Stock and the men of the Orchestra were entertained at a delightful lunch by Mrs. Marshall Field at her residence, No. 2600 Sixteenth Street. Each member of the Orchestra at the concert wore a pink carnation as a souvenir of her hospitality.

After the return of the Orchestra to Chicago a detailed account of the trip, with comments by the eastern press, was prepared by Manager Wessels, entitled "As Others See Us," and mailed to our season ticket subscribers.

All of the eastern critics spoke in the highest terms of the work of Conductor Stock and the men of the Orchestra.

Alfred Cortot was the soloist at the concerts of February 4 and 5, Seventeenth Program, playing the Concerto for Pianoforte, No. 3, D Minor, Opus 30, by Rachmaninow.

TWENTY-SECOND PROGRAM, MARCH 11 AND 12
Soloist: Harry Weisbach

Concerto for Violin, D Minor, ... Stock

The concerto was heard for the first time at these concerts November 17 and 18, 1916, Twenty-sixth Season.

TWENTY-FOURTH PROGRAM, MARCH 25 AND 26
THE FLONZALEY QUARTET:

Adolfo Betti (First Violin)   Alfred Pochon (Second Violin)
Louis Bailly (Viola)   Iwan d'Archambeau (Violoncello)

Concerto for String Quartet and Orchestra, ... Moór
(First Performance in Chicago)[1]

At a meeting of the Executive Committee held Tuesday afternoon, March 29, there being present Messrs. Hamill, Adams, Glessner, Hutchinson and Otis, the following letter was read:

"March 29, 1921.

"To the Orchestral Association:
"*Gentlemen*—I herewith hand you:
Securities.................................$24,950.00
Check.. 50.00
                                             ──────────
                                             $25,000.00

"the income from which is to be applied to any use deemed best by your Association.

"Yours truly,
"Henry L. Frank."

On motion this generous gift from Mr. Frank was accepted, and the Secretary was instructed to convey to Mr. Frank the sincere thanks and thorough appreciation of the Committee and the Orchestral Association.

At the concerts of April 8 and 9, Twenty-sixth Program, the soloists were Guy Maier and Lee Pattison, who appeared in works for two pianofortes: concerto in E flat major by Mozart, and the scherzo by Saint-Saëns.

Ruth Miller (*Chicago Tribune*) said of the soloists:

"Messrs. Maier and Pattison came to us with eulogistic press notices from the far east. But these notices do not give an adequate verbal portrait of the charm and deft *finesse*, the exquisite style of their playing."

Another interesting number was the symphonic poem, "Attis," by A. A. Stanley, professor of music at the University of Michigan, Ann Arbor.

Thirtieth Season—1920-1921

Friday evening, April 15, the members of the Orchestra gave a banquet in the foyer of the hall in honor of Mrs. Elizabeth Sprague Coolidge and "the artists of thirty years' service with the Chicago Symphony Orchestra," from the First Season (1891):

JOSEPH SCHREURS.	ALBERT ULRICH.
CARL MEYER.	GEORGE F. MEYER.
LEOPOLD DE MARÉ.	LOTHAR NURNBERGER.
ALEXANDER KRAUSS.	HERMAN BRAUN.
RICHARD SEIDEL.	JOSEPH FITZEK.
JOSEPH ZETTELMANN.	

After the banquet came "A Veritable Riot and Wave of Crime," entitled "The Seemphunny Foolies of 1921," consisting of a series of "skits" and "stunts" by the men, introducing clever bits of comedy, burlesque and even tragedy. It was an evening of genuine fun and frolic, ending with a dance and supper, in which the women and children took part. Among the guests were Mr. and Mrs. Frederick Stock, Mr. and Mrs. Charles H. Hamill, Mr. and Mrs. Philo A. Otis, Mr. and Mrs. William O. Goodman, Mr. and Mrs. Charles L. Hutchinson, Mr. and Mrs. Joseph Adams, Mr. and Mrs. Frederick J. Wessels and Mr. and Mrs. Henry E. Voegeli.

The Apollo Musical Club closed its Forty-ninth Season with the first performance in Chicago of Edgar Stillman Kelley's "Pilgrim's Progress," under the direction of Harrison M. Wild, in Orchestra Hall, Monday evening, April 18. Soloists: Mae Graves Atkins, Ethel Benedict, Theodore Harrison, Walter Boydston, Arthur Kraft, Eugene Dressler and Herbert Gould. The Club was assisted by the Chicago Woman's Chorus and the Chicago Symphony Orchestra; Edgar A. Nelson (organist).

"April 20, Wednesday evening: In Orchestra Hall; Annual Festival of the Civic Music Association. There was good singing by the Children's Chorus (1,000 voices), led by Herbert E. Hyde, and the Florence Nightingale Chorus (125 student nurses), led by John W. Norton. The Civic Orchestra (student) contributed effective numbers under the direction of Frederick Stock, Conductor, Eric DeLamarter and George Dasch, Assistant Conductors.

"The hall was filled with Chicago music lovers, who now appreciate what these young men and women are doing in community work for our city."

TWENTY-EIGHTH, AND LAST, PROGRAM, APRIL 22 AND 23

Overture, "Coriolanus," . . . . Beethoven
Symphony No. 4, E Minor, Opus 98, ... Brahms

INTERMISSION

"The Planets," Opus 32, ... Holst
    MARS, THE BRINGER OF WAR.
    VENUS, THE BRINGER OF PEACE.
    JUPITER, THE BRINGER OF JOLLITY.

"Ride of the Valkyries," from "The Valkyries," . . ⎫
Siegfried's Death Music, from "The Twilight of the ⎬ Wagner
    Gods," . . . . ⎪
Finale, ... ⎭

THE CHILDREN'S CONCERTS

The programs prepared by Mr. Stock for the little folks in the previous season were so attractive that the patrons of the regular Friday and Saturday concerts were eager to attend "The Children's Concerts," regardless of the rule that "adults will be admitted only when accompanied by children."

For the Thirtieth Season two series were therefore arranged: "Series A" consisting of seven concerts in Orchestra Hall on Thursday afternoons at four o'clock—October 28, November 18, December 16, January 20, 1921, February 17, March 17 and April 21; "Series B" included six concerts on Thursday afternoons—November 4, December 2, January 6, 1921, February 3, March 3 and April 7. Soloists: Alfred Quensel, Harry Weisbach, Joseph Malkin, Franz Esser and Francesco Napolilli. Miss Anita Malkin, eight years of age, daughter of Joseph Malkin, was the soloist at the fourth concert ("Series A"), January 20, 1921:

Suite, "The Wand of Youth," . . . . Elgar
Introduction and Rondo Capriccioso for Violin and
    Orchestra, ... Saint-Saëns
Tarantelle from "The Costume Ball," . . . . Rubinstein

Regular concert-goers who were admitted to "The Children's Concerts" could not but be impressed with the educational methods adopted by Mr. Stock in teaching the children. He would ask the Orchestra to play a few bars of some selection heard at a previous concert, and then, turning to the little folks, would ask them to name the title. At once they would respond, "The Spring Song" (Mendelssohn). Thus they learned to recognize "The Serenade" (Moszkowski), "The Humoresque" (Dvořák), and "The Moment Musical" (Schubert). The spirit and promptness with which the children sang Carpenter's "Home Road" at the fourth concert ("Series B") must have rejoiced the heart of the composer, if he were present.

The program notes by Eric DeLamarter and Anne Faulkner Oberndorfer were interesting and instructive.

THE POPULAR CONCERTS

The series as announced included eleven concerts under the direction of Frederick Stock in Orchestra Hall on Thursday evenings during the season: October 21, November 11, 25, December 9, 30, January 13, 1921, February 10, 24, March 10, 24, and April 14.

So great was the demand for tickets at the "sub-agencies" in the various communities in our city, that two extra concerts were given: December 20, Monday evening, March 30, 1921, Wednesday evening, making thirteen concerts in all.

Miss Josephine Rosensweet was the soloist at the concert of December 30, playing Saint-Saëns' concerto for pianoforte No. 4, C minor.

Bach's suite No. 2, B minor, was the feature of the concert on February 24. Soloists: Flute obbligatos, Alfred Quensel; solo string quartet, Messrs. Weisbach, Roehrborn, Esser and Malkin; double-bass obbligato, Vaclav Jiskra.

Soloists at other concerts in the series: Alfred Quensel, Joseph Schreurs, Harry Weisbach, Francesco Napolilli, Leopold de Maré and Alexander Zukovsky.

Program notes by Anne Faulkner Oberndorfer.

THE STUDENT ORCHESTRA

The Civic Music Association of Chicago, co-operating with The Orchestral Association, gave three concerts during the season, designed for the students of orchestral *ensemble*. Frederick Stock, Musical Director; Eric DeLamarter and George Dasch, Assistant Conductors. The first concert was given in Orchestra Hall, Monday evening, December 6:

Polonaise from "Eugene Onegin," . . . . *Tschaikowsky*
Symphony No. 6, E Minor, ... *Dvořák*

INTERMISSION

Overture, "Fingal's Cave," . . . . . *Mendelssohn*
Prelude to "The Deluge," . . . . *Saint-Saëns*
    Violin Obbligato by Mr. John Weicher
Berceuse, ... *Järnefelt*
Minuetto, ... *Balzoni*
Waltz, "Wine, Woman and Song," . . . . . *Strauss*

SECOND CONCERT, WEDNESDAY EVENING,
JANUARY 12

March from "Boabdil," . . . . *Moszkowski*
Andante con Moto, }Symphony, E Flat, ... *Mozart*
Minuetto, . . . }
Symphonic Poem, "Waves of Spring," . . . . *Scharwenka*
Waltz, "Roses from the South," . . . . . . *Strauss*

THIRD CONCERT, MONDAY EVENING,
FEBRUARY 28

March of the Boyards, ... *Halvorsen*
Suite, "Sigurd Jorsalfar," . . . . *Grieg*
Symphonic Poem, No. 3, Opus 40, "Danse Macabre," *Saint-Saëns*
"Under the Linden Tree," from Scènes Alsaciennes, . *Massenet*
    Violoncello and Clarinet Obbligatos by Alvin Jacobson and
    D. de Capio

THIRTIETH SEASON
(1920-1921)

SOLOISTS

Flonzaley Quartet: Adolfo Betti, Alfred Pochon, Louis Bailly, Iwan d'Archambeau.
Harp: Enrico Tramonti.
Pianoforte: Benno Moiseiwitsch, Harold Bauer, Arthur Shattuck, Alfred Cortot, John Powell, Guy Maier, Lee Pattison; Miss Carol Robinson, Mrs. Fannie Bloomfield Zeisler.
Violin: Efrem Zimbalist, Albert Spalding, Harry Weisbach, Sasha Culbertson.
Violoncello: Joseph Malkin.
Vocal: Mmes. Hulda Lashanska, Louise Homer, Margaret Matzenauer; Edward Johnson, Lambert Murphy.
Guest Conductor: Cyril Scott.

THIRTY-FIRST SEASON
(1921-1922)

Death of Seymour Morris—Death of Joseph Schreurs, an old member of the Orchestra—A new concertmeister, Jacques Gordon—Vincent d'Indy, Visiting Conductor—Six members of the Orchestra retired on pensions—Death of Adolphus Clay Bartlett—He Bequeaths $10,000 to The Orchestral Association—Fiftieth Anniversary of the Apollo Musical Club—Death of Hermann Paepcke—He bequeaths $10,000 to The Orchestral Association—Popular Concerts—Children's Concerts—Civic Orchestra.

The season ticket sale aggregated $127,715 by the first week of concerts, fully $1,000 in excess of the sale of the previous season—a pleasant surprise to the Executive Committee, in view of the deficit of $8,798 on that season. I find a note on the first concert:

"October 14, Friday P. M.: A great house; everybody there and ready for the delightful music prepared by Mr. Stock."

Overture, "Leonore," Opus 72, No. 3, ... *Beethoven*
Symphony No. 5, E Minor, Opus 64, ... *Tschaikowsky*
INTERMISSION
Suite for Orchestra, Opus 19, ... *Dohnányi*
"Dance of Nymphs and Satyrs," from "Amor and Psyche," Opus 3, ... *Georg Schumann*
Overture to "Tannhäuser," . . . . *Wagner*

Before the season opened The Orchestral Association met with a great loss in the death, on September 27, of Seymour Morris, a sincere friend of the Orchestra. Mr. Morris was elected a Member of the Association, and Trustee, December 10, 1912, to fill the vacancy caused by the death of Daniel Hudson Burnham.

In other ways Mr. Morris was interested in the welfare of the community: As a founder (1894) of the Illinois Society of Colonial Wars, Secretary of the Chicago Historical Society, and Treasurer of the Chicago Orphan Asylum.

The Executive Committee of The Orchestral Association on October 17 adopted the following preamble and resolution:

"WHEREAS, Death has removed from our midst Seymour Morris, our long-time associate on the Board of Trustees of The Orchestral Association.

"*Resolved*, That we record our appreciation of his valuable services to the Association and his worth as a member of the community;

"*Resolved*, That we convey to his stricken family our sympathy in their bereavement."

SECOND PROGRAM, OCTOBER 21 AND 22

Concerto for Violin, Opus 82, ... *Glazounow*

Jacques Gordon, our new concertmaster, succeeding Harry Weisbach (resigned), made his first appearance at these concerts.

The program book contained a worthy tribute to the memory of one long associated with the Orchestra, and an artist of high rank†:

JOSEPH SCHREURS

Died July 15, 1921

An honored member of the Orchestra, and its principal clarinet for the entire thirty years of its existence.

Josef Lhevinne, the soloist at the concerts of November 11 and 12, Fifth Program, delighted the audience with his interpretation of Rubinstein's concerto for pianoforte No. 5 in E flat. The real interest of the Friday concert, however, was created by Frederick Stock, who reminded the audience that this was the Third Anni-

---

*Jacques Gordon, came to America from Russia, where his musical studies had been pursued under Franz Stupka, now Conductor of the Prague Philharmonic Orchestra. In this country Mr. Gordon continued his studies at the Institute of Musical Art in New York, under Franz Kneisel. For three seasons Mr. Gordon was a member of the Berkshire String Quartette, and also appeared in chamber concerts with Harold Bauer and Benno Moiseiwitsch.

†Joseph Schreurs, born April 20, 1863, in Brussels, acquired his early musical training at home from his father, a clarinet player, and at the age of six entered the Conservatory of Brussels, receiving the first prize, when ten years old, from King Leopold of Belgium. In a few years, after making a concert tour of Europe as a *Wunderkind* with his teacher, young Schreurs turned his thoughts towards America. When eighteen years old he arrived in New York, and secured an engagement at once with Grau's Opera Company for a tour in Mexico. In that country the company met with financial reverses, and Mr. Schreurs, to earn money for his return to New York, played the clarinet or piano in Mexican cafés. On arriving in New York he was engaged by Anton Seidl for his orchestral concerts. Some of the members of the Theodore Thomas Orchestra attended the first concert, and after hearing Mr. Schreurs recommended him to Mr. Thomas, who engaged him at once. From that time (1883) Mr. Schreurs was a member of the Thomas Orchestra and, later, the Chicago Symphony Orchestra, and was one of the eleven men who appeared at the first concerts of the Thirtieth Season (1920) wearing white ribbons, indicating they had been members of the Orchestra since its organization in 1891.

Thirty-first Season—1921-1922

versary of Armistice Day (November 11, 1918), and then asked that they rise and join with the Orchestra in singing our National Anthem.

The Annual Meeting was held Tuesday, December 13, at 4 P. M. in the offices of the Association. There were present in person Clyde M. Carr, John J. Glessner, Horace S. Oakley, Philo A. Otis, Albert A. Sprague and Charles H. Swift, making a total of thirty-two present in person or by proxy out of a membership of thirty-nine.

Frederick J. Wessels presented the Treasurer's report for the Thirtieth Season (1920-1921), ending June 30, 1921:

RECEIPTS		EXPENSES	
Chicago concerts	$165,502.50	Business management	$ 30,676.66
Outside concerts (net)	13,834.82	Advertising	3,904.13
Popular concerts (net)	10,904.60	Salaries of Conductor and Orchestra	189,410.00
Children's concerts (net)	8,962.38	Orchestra and concert expense	1,274.17
Interest	2,734.88	Program	3,374.71
	$201,939.18	Soloists and music	15,459.47
Hall rentals	94,411.65	Building expenses, heating, insurance	24,353.59
Building rentals	38,761.00	Hall expenses, ushers	32,926.43
Program book	00.00	Water, taxes, interest	20,557.32
		Improvements and repairs	8,911.61
		Eastern trip	12,682.01
		Accounts charged off	380.00
			$343,910.10
		Loss on season	8,798.27
	$335,111.83		$335,111.83

President Carr, in his annual report, said of the finances of the Thirtieth Season:

"An analysis of the general fund as compared with the previous season shows an increase in receipts of $34,200, accounted for as follows:

Orchestra earnings	$ 14,000.00
Hall rentals	16,000.00
Building rentals	4,200.00
	$ 34,200.00

"The expenses increased nearly $66,000, the principal items being:

Orchestra salaries	$ 28,000.00
Music	1,000.00
Program book	3,000.00
Building, miscellaneous expenses	1,500.00
Heating	3,300.00
Hall, miscellaneous expenses	3,800.00
Ushers	4,000.00
Taxes	1,700.00
Improvements and repairs	6,600.00
Eastern trip	12,600.00
	$ 65,500.00

"The net loss on the season was $8,798.16. This was paid out of a surplus carried forward from the previous season, and there still remained a credit in the profit and loss account of $9,653.46.

"For comparison, let us assume that by a journal entry the Orchestra was charged a flat rental of $300 for each of the fifty-six symphony, thirteen popular and thirteen children's concerts which it gave last season (total eighty-two), and a division of the cost of business management was made between Orchestra and hall expenses. The total expenses for the Orchestra would then have been $253,699, while its earnings were $201,939, or a loss of $51,760.

"Looking into the future, we face increased expenses and probable deficits. The negotiations with the Musicians' Union last spring resulted in a compromise, which added some $10,000 to the payroll. One or two needed musicians have been engaged, also a new concertmaster, and with an addition to the Conductor's salary the Orchestra will cost $18,000 more than last season.

"The hall rentals, owing to poor business last summer, show a decrease for July, August and September of $11,500, while October and November have added a further decrease of $4,000. An estimate of $15,000 of new rentals to be booked for the period ending June 30, 1922, will show a total decrease of $24,000 from this source.

"The estimate for Orchestra earnings shows an increase of $4,800, building rentals increase $3,900, total $8,700; hall rentals a decrease of $24,000, leaving a net decrease in receipts of $15,300.

"The increases in expenses are: Business management $3,000, orchestra salaries $18,000, soloists $1,700, insurance $500, taxes $4,000, interest on loan $2,250, new organ console $3,500, changes in the offices of the Association $4,000, a total of $36,950. This will be reduced by decreases in cost of programs, ushers, miscellaneous expenses and last year's eastern trip, to a net of about $25,000, which added to the $15,300 decrease in revenue will give us a deficit on the Thirty-first Season of $40,300.

The Members then proceeded to elect Daniel H. Burnham a Governing Member.

William O. Goodman was elected to fill the vacancy on the Board of Trustees caused by the death of Seymour Morris.

TENTH PROGRAM, DECEMBER 16 AND 17
Soloist and Guest Conductor: Serge Prokofieff

Concerto for Pianoforte, No. 3, C Major, . . . *Prokofieff*
Classical Symphony, D Major, Opus 25, ... *Prokofieff*

Mr. Prokofieff left Russia in 1918, and was the soloist with our Orchestra in the concerts of December 6 and 7, Seventh Program, thrilling the audience with his artistic work.

In this, his second appearance in Chicago, the young Russian was even more successful, showing great art and intellectuality as pianist and Conductor. I had the pleasure of meeting Mr. Prokofieff* at the intermission on Friday in the Conductor's room, and heard further details of his experiences in leaving Russia and the terrible condition of life in that country.

Mr. Prokofieff said further that this second visit to Chicago had a two-fold interest for him—in conducting for the Chicago Opera Company his opera, "The Love of Three Oranges," and in again playing with our Orchestra.

The concerts of December 23 and 24, Eleventh Program, "Holiday Concerts," contained attractive numbers:

Symphony No. 1, "The Rustic Wedding," Opus 26, . *Goldmark*

Prelude to "The Deluge," Opus 45, . *Saint-Saëns*

Charles Camille Saint-Saëns

Born October 9, 1835; died December 16, 1921.

"Krazy Kat," a Jazz Pantomime, ... *Carpenter*
(First Performance)

TWELFTH PROGRAM, DECEMBER 30 AND 31
Guest Conductor: Vincent d'Indy

Prelude to Act I, "Fervaal," . . . . *d'Indy*
"La Queste de Dieu," from "La Légende de Saint-Christophe," Opus 67, ... *d'Indy*
Variations Symphoniques, "Istar," Opus 42, ... *d'Indy*

INTERMISSION

Symphony No. 2, B Flat, Opus 57, ... *d'Indy*

---

*See page 312, where mention is made of Mr. Prokofieff's first appearance in Chicago.

I had the pleasure of entertaining Mr. d'Indy at luncheon on Saturday (the 31st) at the Chicago Club, the other guests being Clyde M. Carr, Clarence A. Burley, John J. Glessner, William O. Goodman, Charles H. Hamill, Charles H. Swift, A. Barthelémy (French Consul), Frederick Stock, Eric DeLamarter, Frederick J. Wessels and Henry E. Voegeli. At the conclusion of the luncheon some happy remarks were made by Mr. Barthelémy and Mr. Stock in welcoming to our city the distinguished French artist, to which Mr. d'Indy replied by assuring us of the great pleasure he had enjoyed in meeting Mr. Stock and hearing his works interpreted by the Chicago Symphony Orchestra.

THIRTEENTH PROGRAM, JANUARY 6 AND 7
THEODORE THOMAS MEMORIAL

Overture, "Coriolanus," Opus 62, ... *Beethoven*
Symphony No. 3, "Eroica," Opus 55, ... *Beethoven*
INTERMISSION
Tone Poem, "Ein Heldenleben," . . . . *Strauss*

In consequence of the serious illness of her husband, Mme. Yolanda Mérö was unable to appear at the concerts of January 13 and 14, Fourteenth Program. Mme. Elly Ney was engaged in her place:

Four Ancient Dances, ... *Respighi*
Symphony No. 4 in E Minor, Opus 36, . . . *Tschaikowsky*
INTERMISSION
Concerto for Pianoforte, No. 2, B Flat, ... *Brahms*

Mme. Ney gave a delightful interpretation of Brahms' work, and interested the audience through her distinguished ancestry, she being the daughter of an ancient Alsatian family, and a direct descendant of Napoleon's famous marshal, Michel Ney (1769-1815).

EIGHTEENTH PROGRAM, FEBRUARY 10 AND 11
SOLOIST: MLLE. CLAIRE DUX

Aria, "Ruhe sanft," from "Zaide," . . . . . . *Mozart*
Aria, "L'Amerò, Sarò Costante, "from "Il Re Pastore," . *Mozart*
INTERMISSION
Four Songs with Orchestra:
   "Liebesfeier," . . . . *Weingartner*
   "Wiegenlied," . . . . *Humperdinck*
   "Morgen," . . . . *Strauss*
   "Ständchen," . . . . *Strauss*

Thirty-first Season—1921-1922

In the Twentieth Program, February 24 and 25, Great Britain and America were happily represented at these concerts by works of two of their modern composers:

"On the Cliffs of Cornwall," . . . . *Smyth*
Concerto No. 2, A Major, for Organ, with Orchestra, . *DeLamarter*

Felix Borowski, in his program notes, gave a sketch of the life and work of Ethel Mary Smyth. She was the daughter of the late General J. H. Smyth of the Royal Artillery; went to Leipzig at the age of nineteen, and entered (1877) the Conservatory. Later, after spending some years in Italy, she returned (1884) to Leipzig, where a string quartet of her composition was brought out at a Gewandhaus Concert. Tschaikowsky came to Leipzig in 1888, and at a dinner with the Brodskys, met Miss Smyth, of whom he wrote in his diary:

'There was another lady at this party, about whom I should like to say a few words. In a few moments a tall Englishwoman, not handsome, but having what people call an 'intelligent' or 'expressive' face, walked into the room, and I was at once introduced as a fellow-composer. Miss Smyth is one of the comparatively few woman composers who may seriously be welcomed among the workers in this sphere of music."

"On the Cliffs of Cornwall" is the prelude to Act II of her opera, "The Wreckers," brought out (1896) at Leipzig and produced March 1, 1910, at the Covent Garden Theatre in London under the direction of Sir Thomas Beecham.

Eric DeLamarter, the composer of the organ concerto, has been since 1917 organist and Assistant Conductor of our Orchestra. The concerto, written in 1921, had at these concerts its first public hearing. Without going into a technical, scientific analysis of his work, I can truly say it contains interesting themes, melodious in character, which are so well employed that the listener hears not only good music, but something better than our modern music, and it is music he will want to hear again.

Mr. Stock and his men gave Mr. DeLamarter a vigorous, sympathetic support in his performance of the concerto.

The Executive Committee, at its meeting March 23, placed six members of the Orchestra on the pension list, in accordance with the by-laws: Herman Braun, Leopold de Maré, Joseph Fitzek, Otto Hesselbach, Carl Meyer and George F. Meyer. It has been only by the earnest work of these and other faithful men, through their years of service, that the Orchestra has reached its present high standard in art.

TWENTY-FIFTH PROGRAM, MARCH 31 AND APRIL 1
Soloist: Rudolph Reuter

The interest in this program centered about the works of two Chicago composers:

Concertino for Pianoforte and Orchestra, ... *Carpenter*
Rhapsody No. 2, Opus 39, ... *Oldberg*

The concertino by John Alden Carpenter, written in 1915, had its first performance at the concerts of March 10 and 11, 1916, with Percy Grainger as the interpreter of the solo part.

The city of Chicago may well be proud of John Alden Carpenter, recognized at home and abroad as one of the first of modern composers, on whom the French Government in 1922 bestowed the Order of the Legion of Honor.

Arne Oldberg, the composer of the rhapsody, is Professor of Composition and Director of the Piano Department in the School of Music in the Northwestern University at Evanston. The rhapsody had its first performance under the direction of the composer at the fifth concert, June 5, 1919, of the Chicago North Shore Festival at Evanston.

At the concerts of April 7 and 8, Twenty-sixth Program, an important work by another Chicago composer was heard for the first time at these concerts: symphony No. 1, by Leo Sowerby.

The symphony was written (1921-1922) at Palisades Park, Michigan. Mr. Sowerby is as characteristic in the analytical notes he prepares as in the music itself. He speaks of the three movements in this manner:

"Fast, with restless energy."
"With quiet languor."
"With triumphal sweep. Fairly fast."

Henry Eichheim appeared as Guest Conductor at the concerts of April 14 and 15, Twenty-seventh Program, giving his "Oriental Impressions" (first performance in Chicago).

Mr. Eichheim spent several years in Japan and other eastern countries, making a careful study of Oriental music. This work was written at the request of Mrs.

Frederick S. Coolidge, and brought out under the direction of the composer October 1, 1921, at the Music Festival at Pittsfield, Massachusetts.

There were old-time concert-goers in our audience who were interested to see Mr. Eichheim on the Conductor's stand. Their memories went back to early days in Chicago when his father, Meinhard Eichheim, was our first 'cellist, and was often heard in concerts and musicales. Meinhard Eichheim, with Robert Goldbeck (piano) and William Lewis (violin), played the Beethoven trio, Opus 19, at the first concert in the Second Season of the Apollo Musical Club, September 30, 1873, in Kingsbury Hall. Meinhard Eichheim was one of twenty-four Chicago musicians selected by Mr. Thomas for the First Season (1890-1891) of the Chicago Orchestra.

TWENTY-EIGHTH, AND LAST, PROGRAM, APRIL 21 AND 22

Overture, "Le Carnaval Romain," Opus 9, ... *Berlioz*
Symphony No. 4, E Minor, Opus 98, ... *Brahms*

INTERMISSION

Scherzo, "L'Apprenti Sorcier," . . . . *Dukas*
Prelude and Isolde's Love-Death, from "Tristan and Isolde," . . . . *Wagner*
Overture, "1812," Opus 49, ... *Tschaikowsky*

Adolphus Clay Bartlett, member of the firm of Hibbard, Spencer, Bartlett & Co., died May 30 in Pasadena, California. He was greatly interested in the work of the Orchestra, as a subscriber to the Guaranty Fund and a member of the Board of Trustees in the first three seasons (1891-1894). His will contained a generous bequest of $10,000 to The Orchestral Association.

The Apollo Musical Club celebrated this season its Fiftieth Anniversary (1871-1921), an important event in the Club's history and in the musical life of our city. Its whole season was devoted to the celebration of the Anniversary in the preparation for and performance of a series of concerts in Orchestra Hall under the direction of Harrison M. Wild, with the assistance of the Chicago Symphony Orchestra. The last concerts of the "Anniversary" series may be noted:

May 1, 1922, Monday evening: Mass in B minor, by Bach. Soloists: Else Harthan Arendt (soprano), Mary Welch (contralto), Arthur Boardman (tenor), Walter Allen Stults (bass); Edgar A. Nelson (organist).

May 2, Tuesday evening: "Rock of Liberty" by Rossetter G. Cole. Soloists: Gladys Swarthout (soprano), Mina Hager (contralto), James Hamilton (tenor), René S. Lund (baritone), Blake Wilson (bass); Edgar A. Nelson (piano).

The concert closed with a reproduction of the first concert, or "Reception," as it was called, "fifty years ago," when the Club was a männerchor, stirring the hearts of the few men in the audience that evening who took part in that "Reception" given under the direction of Adolph W. Dohn in Standard Hall, at the southwest corner of Michigan Avenue and Thirteenth Street. I was a second tenor, and remember well the enthusiasm aroused when we sang "The Loyal Song" (Kücken) and Schroeter's "Champagne Song." The program included some attractive solo numbers:

"He, of All, the Best, the Noblest," . . . . . . Schumann
"Greeting," . . . . Taubert
           Miss Jessica Haskell*
"The Meeting at the Sea," . . . . Loewe
           Fritz Foltz†
Piano Solos: "La Serenata," and "Rhapsody," . . . Liszt
           Robert Golbeck‡
"The Erl King," . . . . Schubert
           Miss Haskell
"Salute a Bergamo," . . . . Siebert
           Frank A. Bowen§

By the terms of the will of Hermann Paepcke, one of our successful business men, who died July 22, a generous bequest of $10,000 was left to The Orchestral Association. Mr. Paepcke was a patron of music, the drama and literature, and for many years a subscriber and regular attendant at the concerts of the Chicago Symphony Orchestra.

---

*Miss Jessica Haskell is now Mrs. Edward Fuller, and resides in Madison, Wisconsin.

†Fritz Foltz, a well known choir and concert singer, an early member of the Apollo Musical Club, and member of the firm of Treat & Foltz, architects, died in Chicago February 1, 1916.

‡Robert Golbeck came to Chicago in 1864 and established a Conservatory of Music. In 1873 he moved to St. Louis and was associated with the Beethoven Conservatory of that city. He remained in St. Louis until 1874, and then returned to New York; later he was in London (1899-1903) and then returned to St. Louis, where his death occurred May 16, 1908.

§Frank A. Bowen is now living in London, England.

Thirty-first Season—1921-1922

THE POPULAR CONCERTS

The Children's Concerts and the "Pops" now constitute a distinctive feature in each season of the Orchestra. It is impossible to estimate the good thus accomplished for the moral and educational uplift of the young men and women of the community. No work of similar importance has ever before been attempted in our city. Each concert in the Children's and Popular series represents a cost to the Association of $2,000, and as the receipts do not exceed $1,000 at each performance, the practical man of business may well ask, "How can this be done?" Simply through the generosity of the noble men and women of Chicago who have given us an endowment represented by Orchestra Hall, and other funds. These good friends have never yet failed to respond to any call when the Trustees are in need.

The "Pops," starting in the Twenty-third Season (1914) with three concerts, have so steadily grown in interest that the Trustees announced fifteen concerts for the Thirty-first Season, under the direction of Frederick Stock, in Orchestra Hall on Thursday evenings, October 20, 27, November 10, 24, December 8, 29, January 2, 1922, 12, 26, February 9, 23, March 9, 23, 30 and April 13. Soloists: Jacques Gordon, Joseph Malkin, Miss Anita Malkin, Miss Sarah Suttle (piano), Alexander Zukovsky, Franz Esser and Francisco Napolilli. Program notes by Eric DeLamarter.

THE CHILDREN'S CONCERTS

Two series of six concerts each were given under the direction of Frederick Stock in Orchestra Hall on Thursday afternoons at 4 o'clock: "Series A": November 3, December 1, January 5, 1922, February 2, March 2 and April 6; "Series B": November 17, December 15, January 19, 1922, February 16, March 16 and April 20. Soloist, Joseph Malkin.

It was a charming sight, those bright young faces all turned towards the Conductor, eager to catch every word, as he showed on the screen portraits of Berlioz, Tschaikowsky and other composers, and told of their lives and work. The little folks are just as eager to sing, and, with the "grown-ups," joined heartily with the

Orchestra in Carpenter's "Home Road" and "The Battle Hymn of the Républic."

The program notes by Mr. DeLamarter added interest to the concerts.

THE CIVIC ORCHESTRA

Six concerts were given, with the co-operation of the Civic Music Association and The Orchestral Association, in Orchestra Hall, with Frederick Stock, Musical Director, Eric DeLamarter and George Dasch, Assistant Conductors, on Sundays, October 23, November 27, January 22, 1922, February 19, March 19 and April 30, at 3:30 P.M.

Four programs may be noted:

JANUARY 22
SOLOIST: MISS DOROTHY BELL

Chorale and Variations for Harp and Orchestra, . . . *Widor*

FEBRUARY 19
SOLOIST: MRS. ZOE KENDALL AMES

Aria, "Hérodiade," . . . . *Massenet*
Four Songs:
   "The Star," . . . . *Rogers*
   "Pale Moon," . . . . *Logan*
   "Cradle Song," . . . . *MacFadyen*
   "The Nightingale," . . . . *Stephens*

(Miss Beulah Taylor Porter, Accompanist for Mrs. Ames.)

MARCH 19
SOLOIST: ERIC DELAMARTER

Concerto for Organ, No. 1, E Major, ... *DeLamarter*

APRIL 30
SOLOIST: MISS FLORENCE TRUMBULL

Concerto for Pianoforte, A Minor, Opus 16, ... *Grieg*

The Annual Festival of the Civic Music Association was held in Orchestra Hall Wednesday, April 19, 1922, at 8:15 P. M. The combined children's choruses of the Association (1,000 voices) were led by Herbert E. Hyde, assisted by the Civic Orchestra, with Frederick Stock, Musical Director, Eric DeLamarter and George Dasch, Assistant Conductors. Community singing was led by Frederick W. Carberry.

THE CIVIC ORCHESTRA OF CHICAGO
1921—SEASON—1922

FIRST VIOLINS
Rink, Carl, *Principal.*
Smith, Miss C. W.
Levitt, W.
Marshall, Miss J.
Hrych, C.
Early, Miss G.
Swanson, E.
McCann, Miss C.
Hyna, H.
Hunt, Mrs. A.
Caldwell, R. H.
Dvorak, Miss H.
Elkins, Miss E.
Callow, Mrs. G. G.
Clarke, Mrs. R. S.
Silberhorn, Miss D.
Fisher, M.

SECOND VIOLINS
Willihnganz, W., *Principal.*
Paltz, H.
Mayerson, B.
Beilfus, H. A.
Bernstein, S.
Dirks, Miss E.
Polleyea, S.
Turek, Miss D.
Woolett, Miss M.
Lamont, H. J.
Olivadoti, J.
Friedman, Miss E.
Waskevicz, Miss M.
Polacek, Miss S.
Peterson, H.
Fischer, Miss Helen

VIOLAS
Kribben, Miss B., *Principal.*
Ferry, Miss M.
Stirn, E.

VIOLAS—Continued
Lenhard, J.
Huslik, C.
Wessling, J.
Cheeseman, W.

VIOLONCELLOS
Jacobsen, A., *Principal.*
Gross, Miss G.
Novy, J.
Davis, Miss M.
Slack, Miss A.
Ewert, E.
Esser, W.
Hughes, Miss M.
Beidel, R.
Zimberoff, N.
Kirsch, Miss G.

STRING BASSES
Clifford, J. B., *Principal.*
Andel, J.
Hrudka, G.
Fleischmann, W.
Stanko, L.
Ludvik, O.
Berhold, B.
Beilfus, A.

CLARINETS
DeCaprio, D.
Sheerer, Miss J.

FLUTES
Dell' Aquila, R. L.
Rizzo, F.

OBOES
Mueller, F.
Baldwin, T. B.

ENGLISH HORN
Baldwin, T. B.

BASSOONS
Fox, H.
Hedges, A.
Kessler, C.

CONTRA-BASSOON
Hartman, L. C.

FRENCH HORNS
Babbe, C. H.
Bruno, G. A.
Grant, E.
Jackson, C.

TRUMPETS
Kase, V.
Swerdlow, L.
Sweringen, C.
Florent, V.

TROMBONES
Lomonte, L.
Gish, A.
Bozek, A.
Anderson, O.

TUBA
Stanko, L.

HARPS
Bell, Miss D.

TIMPANI AND PERCUSSIONS
Robertson, G.
Minnema, J.

LIBRARIAN
Handke, P.

THIRTY-FIRST SEASON
(1921-1922)
SOLOISTS

ORGAN: Eric DeLamarter.
PIANOFORTE: Mmes. Yolanda Mérö, Elly Ney; William Bachaus, Josef Hofmann, Josef Lhevinne, Guy Maier, Lee Pattison, Serge Prokofieff, Rudolph Reuter, Ernest Schelling.
VIOLIN: Miss Erika Morini; Jacques Gordon, Jascha Heifetz, Paul Kochanski, Hans Muenzer, Alexander Zukovsky.
VIOLONCELLO: Joseph Malkin.
VOCAL: Misses Sophie Braslau, Claire Dux, Maria Ivogun.
VISITING CONDUCTORS: Henry Eichheim, Vincent d'Indy, Serge Prokofieff.

THIRTY-SECOND SEASON
(1922-1923)

A gift of $5,000 from Mr. and Mrs. Ernest A. Hamill to the Endowment Fund—Trustees vote to change date of Annual Meeting from December to May—Charles H. Swift gives $12,000 to the Endowment Fund—The Civic Orchestra—Popular Concerts—Children's Concerts—The Musicians' Union demands increase in salaries—The Executive Committee makes a settlement with the union—Death of Milward Adams.

There was a substantial increase in the season ticket sale, aggregating $144,545, by the first week of concerts, a gain of $17,000 over the previous season, due largely to an increase in the prices of tickets for main floor and balcony, adopted by the Executive Committee at its meeting on April 6.

"To the Friday concert early, to meet the men of the Orchestra; some new faces: Hoss (first horn) and Wallenstein* (first 'cello). The usual Friday audience; house sold out. The Orchestra played as it always plays, with delicacy and authority. Mr. Stock had some delightful numbers on the program:

FIRST PROGRAM, OCTOBER 13 AND 14

Symphony No. 6, "Pathetic," B Minor, Opus 74, . *Tschaikowsky*
"Iberia," Images pour Orchestre No. 2, ... *Debussy*
Four Movements from Suite, "Ruses d'Amour,"
    Opus 61, ... *Glazounow*
    INTRODUCTION.
    VALSE.
    "GRAND PAS DES FIANCÉS."
        MESSRS. GORDON AND WALLENSTEIN
    FINALE, "LA FRICASSÉE."

Mr. Wallenstein made his first appearance as soloist in the concerts of October 27 and 28, Third Program, playing Saint-Saëns' concerto for violoncello in A minor, Opus 33, and delighted the audience with his artistic interpretation of the work.

The program book contained a tribute to an old member of the Orchestra:

---

*Alfred Wallenstein, the new first 'cellist of the Orchestra, was born in Chicago, but spent his youth in California, beginning the study of the 'cello when eight years old. His studies in America were followed by a long period under Professor Klengel in Leipzig. Then came orchestral experience under Nikisch, one season with Bodamzky and concert tours through Central Europe and North and South America.

Thirty-second Season—1922-1923

> **IN MEMORIAM**
> DAVID ROSENSWEET
>
> 1886—1923
>
> A member of the first violin section of the Chicago Symphony Orchestra for eight years.

President Carr brought a letter from Ernest A. Hamill to the meeting of the Executive Committee, Tuesday afternoon, October 31, enclosing a check for $5,000 from Mrs. Hamill and himself as a memorial to their daughter, Eleanor Corwith Clow. This gift was gratefully accepted, and the Secretary was requested to convey to Mr. and Mrs. Hamill the thorough appreciation of the committee for their thoughtful generosity.

At the concerts of November 24 and 25, Seventh Program, Mr. Stock presented a number of works illustrating scenes from Shakespeare's plays. Among them may be noted:

Overture to "The Merry Wives of Windsor,"	*Nicolai*
Overture to "A Midsummer Night's Dream," Opus 21,	*Mendelssohn*
Tone Poem, "Macbeth," Opus 23,	*Strauss*
Overture, "King Lear," Opus 4,	*Berlioz*
Overture-Fantasia, "Romeo and Juliet,"	*Tschaikowsky*

EIGHTH PROGRAM, DECEMBER 1 AND 2
Soloist: Arthur Rubinstein

Concerto No. 1, B Flat Minor, Opus 23, . . . *Tschaikowsky*

The Annual Meeting was held Tuesday afternoon, December 12, in the offices of the Association, there being present in person: Joseph Adams, Clarence A. Burley, John J. Glessner, Charles H. Hamill, Charles L. Hutchinson, Chauncey Keep, Philo A. Otis, Horace S. Oakley and Charles H. Swift. Twenty-seven Members were represented by proxy, making a total of thirty-six present out of a membership of thirty-nine.

Charles H. Hamill was elected Chairman and Frederick J. Wessels, Clerk.

The report of the Treasurer for the Thirty-first Season (1921-1922), ending June 30, 1922, was then read:

Expenses

Business management		$ 34,345.30
Advertising		4,101.04
Orchestra and Conductors		206,765.00
Orchestra and concert expenses		1,273.73
Soloists		13,800.00
Music and instruments		1,298.76
Building expenses—general	$ 4,687.26	
Building, light and power	608.76	
Building employes	10,705.11	
Building management	1,750.14	
		17,751.27
Heating		6,448.64
Insurance		3,237.58
Hall expenses—general	$ 1,539.62	
Hall, light and power	4,971.98	
Hall, employes	14,288.20	
Hall, organ and licenses	625.00	
		21,424.80
Ushers		9,138.90
Water		458.04
Taxes		14,831.08
Interest on loan		8,590.00
Improvements and repairs		10,863.08
Accounts charged off		485.00
		$354,812.22

Receipts

Symphony series		$164,706.50
Extra concerts (net)	$ 1,464.10	
Milwaukee concerts (net)	8,614.91	
Mandel Hall concerts (net)	5,278.21	
Aurora concerts (net)	3,239.18	
		18,596.40
Popular concerts (net)		12,695.37
Children's concerts (net)		9,769.75
Interest		2,064.93
Program		101.39
Old accounts		505.15
Subscriptions		1,065.00
Hall rentals	$ 74,775.00	
Building rentals	43,847.71	
		118,622.71
Receipts		$328,127.20
Expenses		354,812.22
Deficit*		$ 26,685.02

*Paid from accumulated interest of the Henry Field Memorial.

Thirty-second Season—1922-1923

Comments of the Treasurer

"At the last Annual Meeting, in December, 1921, it was estimated that the current season would close with a deficit of $40,000. At that time the outlook was discouraging; therefore the estimates were conservative. Afterwards conditions grew brighter; hall and building rentals increased $5,600, and other sources of income $2,700, giving us $8,300 more receipts, while expenditures were $5,500 less, leaving a loss of $26,685.02.

"This was paid out of the accumulated interest of the Henry Field Memorial, and there remained in this fund $14,693. In addition there was an accumulated interest of $7,096 on General Endowment, making a total of $21,789, which is available for deficits. The annual interest from endowment now amounts to $5,000 a year. These accounts are carried as trust funds, and the income is to be used only in case of necessity. We had one gift, in October, of $5,000 from Mr. and Mrs. Ernest A. Hamill as a memorial to their daughter, and two bequests of $10,000 each by wills of A. C. Bartlett and Herman Paepcke. Payment of these bequests can be expected in due course. . . .

"One thing I wish to impress on the members at this Annual Meeting: If we are to maintain our standing in the musical world as the *first* Orchestra we shall have great need for further endowment.

"The net returns from the hall and building this season should be about $60,000. This is on the supposition that the Orchestra pays rent for all its concerts and offices. In addition we have $5,000 from endowments, or a total of $65,000, and that is all. . . .

"The standard of the Orchestra must be maintained and, if possible, improved. We have some excellent players, whose salaries must be increased if we are to keep them, and as vacancies occur in the principal positions we shall have to pay much more for competent men than we are paying now."

The five Trustees whose terms of office expired this season were re-elected for three years: Joseph Adams, John J. Glessner, Horace S. Oakley, Philo A. Otis and Albert A. Sprague.

The Annual Meeting of the Trustees was held on adjournment of the meeting of the Members. Officers were elected for the ensuing year: Clyde M. Carr, President; Charles H. Hamill, Vice-President; Joseph Adams, Second Vice-President; Horace S. Oakley, Third Vice-President; Philo A. Otis, Secretary; Frederick J. Wessels, Treasurer and Business Manager; Henry E. Voegeli, Assistant Treasurer and Assistant Business Manager.

356 *The Chicago Symphony Orchestra*

EXECUTIVE COMMITTEE

Joseph Adams.
Clyde M. Carr.
John J. Glessner.
Charles H. Hamill.

Charles L. Hutchinson.
Horace S. Oakley.
Philo A. Otis.
Charles H. Swift.

Charles H. Hamill, *Chairman.*

The Trustees voted to change the date of the Annual Meeting to the last Tuesday in May of each year.

TENTH PROGRAM, DECEMBER 15 AND 16
FRENCH COMPOSERS
Soloist: Alfred Cortot

Feuillets de Voyage, Opus 26, ... *Schmidt*
Concerto for Pianoforte No. 5, F Major, Opus 103, . *Saint-Saëns*

INTERMISSION

César Franck

Born December 10, 1822, at Liège

Died November 8, 1890, at Paris

Symphony, D Minor, ... *Franck*
Variations Symphoniques (for Pianoforte and Orchestra), . *Franck*

The Orchestra assisted the Apollo Musical Club in the Christmas performance of "The Messiah," under the direction of Harrison M. Wild, in Orchestra Hall, Sunday afternoon, December 24. Soloists: Muriel Kyle (soprano), Eva Horadesky (contralto), Robert Quait (tenor), John Barclay (baritone); Edgar A. Nelson (organist).

THIRTEENTH PROGRAM, JANUARY 5 AND 6
THEODORE THOMAS MEMORIAL

Symphony No. 3, "Eroica," . . . . . . *Beethoven*

INTERMISSION

Tone Poem, "Ein Heldenleben," . . . . . . *Strauss*
Finale from "Das Rheingold," . . . . . . *Wagner*

At the adjourned Annual Meeting on Tuesday afternoon, January 9, Arthur B. Hall was elected a Member of the Association, to fill the vacancy caused by the death of A. C. Bartlett.

Thirty-second Season—1922-1923

Soon after the Annual Meeting an unexpected and generous gift came from Charles H. Swift, of our Executive Committee:

"January 15, 1923.

"THE ORCHESTRAL ASSOCIATION:
>   Attention, Mr. Wessels, Manager.

"*Gentlemen*—In accordance with my letter of January 3rd to Mr. Charles H. Hamill, Chairman Executive Committee, I enclose herewith my check for $6,000 in payment of the first two quarters of my pledge of $12,000 during the calendar year 1923—this gift to go to the general Endowment Fund of The Orchestral Association, with the privilege of transfer at any time to the Pension and Invalid Fund, or being applied to the payment of the $200,000 debt, on favorable vote of the Executive Committee.

"Yours very truly,
"CHARLES H. SWIFT."

Mr. Swift sent, on July 15, his check of $6,000 for the remaining two quarters of his generous pledge for the Endowment Fund.

At the next meeting of the committee this gift from Mr. Swift was gratefully received, and the Secretary was instructed to convey to him the thorough appreciation and thanks of the committee.

Mr. Stock prepared a "Literary Program" for the concerts of March 2 and 3, Twelfth Program, illustrating poems of Byron and Goethe:

Overture to "Manfred,".	*Schumann*
Symphony after Byron's "Manfred," B Minor, Opus 58, ...	*Tschaikowsky*

INTERMISSION

Scherzo, "L'Apprenti Sorcier,"	*Dukas*
Andante ("Marguerite"), from "A Faust Symphony," . .	*Liszt*
Rakoczy March, from "The Damnation of Faust," .	*Berlioz*

TWENTY-FOURTH PROGRAM, MARCH 23 AND 24
SOLOIST AND GUEST CONDUCTOR: ALFREDO CASELLA

Spanish Rhapsody for Pianoforte and Orchestra, Opus 70, ... (First Performance in Chicago)	*Albeniz—Casella*
Pupazzetti, "Five Pieces for Marionettes,"	*Casella*
Rhapsody, "Italia,"	*Casella*

TWENTY-SIXTH PROGRAM, APRIL 6 AND 7
Soloist: Albert Spalding

"Horace Victorieux," . . . . *Honegger*
Concerto for Violin, D Minor, Opus 27, . . . *Dohnányi*

TWENTY-EIGHTH, AND LAST, PROGRAM, APRIL 20 AND 21

Marche Joyeuse, ... *Chabrier*
Symphony No. 2, D Major, Opus 73, ... *Brahms*

INTERMISSION

"The Waltz," Choreographic Poem, ... *Ravel*
Dance of the Seven Veils, from "Salome," . . . *Strauss*
Prelude and Isolde's Love-Death, from "Tristan and Isolde," . . . . *Wagner*
Finale, from "Die Götterdämmerung," . . . . . *Wagner*

THE CIVIC ORCHESTRA
FOR THE DEVELOPMENT OF SYMPHONY PLAYERS

The season consisted of six concerts under the direction of Frederick Stock, with Eric DeLamarter and George Dasch, Assistant Conductors, in Orchestra Hall, Sundays, October 29, November 26, December 31, January 28, 1923, February 25 and March 25, at 3:30 P. M. Soloists: Miss Mildred Brown, Mrs. Louise Harrison Slade, Paul Snyder, Joseph Novy, Hilda Edwards.

THE POPULAR CONCERTS

The "Series" consisted of fifteen concerts in Orchestra Hall under the direction of Frederick Stock, with Eric DeLamarter, Assistant Conductor, on Thursday evenings, October 19, 26, November 9, 23, 30, December 14, 28, January 1, 1923, 11, 25, February 8, 22, March 8, 22 and April 12. Soloists: Miss Mildred Brown, Miss Margaret Farr, Jacques Gordon, Alfred Quensel, Enrico Tramonti, George G. Smith, Miss Nesta Smith, Alfred Wallenstein and Alexander Zukovsky.

Instructive and entertaining program notes were contributed by Eric DeLamarter.

THE CHILDREN'S CONCERTS

Twelve concerts were given in Orchestra Hall, under the direction of Frederick Stock, on Thursday afternoons at 4 o'clock. "Series A," November 2, December 7, January 4, 1923, February 1, March 1 and April 5; "Series B," November 16, December 21, January 18, 1923, February 15, March 15 and April 19.

Thirty-second Season—1922-1923

There were no soloists. The children were the attraction, and their singing of national airs, Balfe's "Song of Victory" and "The Sturdy Blacksmith" (Mozart) delighted fathers and mothers, "sisters and brothers, cousins and aunts," who filled the hall at every concert. Mr. Stock's talks on the lives of the composers, with analyses of their works, were not only interesting but instructive to the "grown-ups" as well as "the little folks," and of a like character were the program notes contributed by Eric DeLamarter.

The closing weeks of the season were largely concerned in a serious discussion between the Executive Committee of the Orchestra and the Musicians' Union, regarding increased salaries for the season of 1923-1924. In reply to the statement by the committee that the increase might mean the dissolution of the Orchestra, their answer indicated how serious the situation was, and that it was fraught with grave danger to the musical life of the city.

The announcement, April 21, to the season ticket subscribers, of the opening of the Thirty-third Season, showed clearly why the Executive Committee could not meet the demands of the union:

"March 19, the Musicians' Union sent word to the office of the Orchestra that a delegation from the Federation desired a conference. Accordingly, on the afternoon of Wednesday, March 21, a delegation of eight, headed by President Petrillo, presented and discussed a demand that the minimum salary paid by the Orchestra be increased twenty-five per cent (from $60 to $75 per week). It was conceded that this increase would require a horizontal increase of the like amount throughout the Orchestra. After a very full explanation of the situation the delegation was informed that it was impossible to meet the demand in whole or in part. The delegation withdrew, and on the following Saturday (March 24) served notice that none of the musicians of the Orchestra should enter into any contracts for the season 1923-1924 until the matter of the scale had been adjusted. The concessions finally offered by the union were coupled with conditions that made it impossible to consider them."

The Executive Committee could not adopt the suggestion of the union that we go among the friends of the Orchestra and raise the $40,000 needed annually to meet increased salaries for the men. Nor did the committee approve of any further increase in prices of tickets for the Subscription, Children's and Popular Concerts. The announcement to the season ticket subscribers concluded with these prophetic words:

"As the matter now stands three courses are open: to discontinue the concerts for the next season and to disband the Orchestra; to meet the demands of the union and reduce the Orchestra to sixty-five players; to renew the contracts upon the scale of 1922-1923."

There were many conferences between the Executive Committee and the directors of the union during the weeks that followed, resulting in the union reducing the minimum to $67.50 per week. This we could not consider. Final action was not taken until the Annual Meeting in May.

The Annual Meeting, in accordance with the revised by-law adopted at the meeting on December 12, 1922, was held Tuesday afternoon, May 29, in the offices of the Association, there being present in person, Clarence A. Burley, William O. Goodman, Arthur B. Hall, Chauncey Keep, Harold F. McCormick, Horace S. Oakley, Philo A. Otis, A. A. Sprague and Charles H. Swift, and twenty Members by proxy, making twenty-nine present out of a total of thirty-nine Members.

Horace S. Oakley was elected Chairman and Frederick J. Wessels, Clerk.

The first matter for consideration was the report of the Treasurer for the Thirty-second Season, ending April 30:

RECEIPTS

Chicago concerts		$180,763.00
Extra concerts (net)	$ 1,579.10	
Outside concerts (net)	271.00	
Milwaukee concerts (net)	10,309.85	
Mandel Hall concerts (net)	6,114.48	
Aurora concerts (net)	3,255.50	
		21,529.93
Popular concerts		13,307.82
Children's concerts		10,809.70
Interest		2,095.89
Subscriptions		1,000.00
Hall rentals	$68,375.00	
Building rentals	41,510.00	
		109,885.00
		$339,391.34

Thirty-second Season—1922-1923

Expenses

Business management		$ 28,815.48
Advertising		3,382.73
Orchestra and Conductor		208,705.00
Orchestra and concert expenses		817.32
Soloists		13,150.00
Music and instruments		1,999.93
Building, expenses, general	$ 4,475.10	
Building, light and power	594.50	
Building, employes	8,984.39	
Building, management	1,660.40	
		15,714.39
Heating		7,833.63
Insurance		1,421.46
Hall, expense, general	$ 1,143.80	
Hall, light and power	3,583.40	
Hall, employes	11,561.30	
Hall, organ and license	743.57	
		17,032.25
Ushers		6,940.55
Water		420.52
Taxes		15,101.39
Interest on loan		12,000.00
Improvements and repairs		8,142.46
Accounts charged off		275.00
Total expenses		$341,752.11
Total receipts		339,391.34
Loss		$ 2,360.77
Subscription		1,000.00
Actual loss		$ 3,360.77

Treasurer's Comments

"The statement presented covers a period of ten months, the fiscal year closing April 30, but the result is approximately the same as if we had run two months longer and closed the books June 30.

"The advance in season tickets brought an addition of $17,000 at the beginning of the season, the number of tickets sold being about thirty less than the year before. This advance was maintained until well along in the season, when poor business, caused probably by the epidemic of influenza, possibly in a measure by the radio craze, caused a falling off in single ticket sales of about $3,000 from the amount we were justified in anticipating.

"Returns from outside concerts were very satisfactory, running $3,500 over the former season. A portion of this was due to a reduced railway rate between Chicago and Milwaukee.

"The Popular Concert receipts are $600 more, the Children's Concerts $1,000 more.

"Hall business is good, the returns for ten months being $68,375 against $64,500 for the same ten months last season. A rental contract for the entire summer has been made, subject to a three weeks' cancellation clause, but in any case the summer returns will be better than last year, and should be sufficient to take care of regular overhead expenses for the period and leave a profit.

"The loss on operation after using the receipts from hall and building is $3,360, against a loss last season of $27,750, a gain of $24,390.

"We have not, therefore, had to draw on our Trust Funds. There is a balance in the General Account of $10,607, and the accumulated interest in the Field Memorial and General Endowment amounts to $28,530. This will be increased $7,500 during the coming year, which will give us a total available reserve for deficits next season of $46,637.

"The Trust Funds outside of real estate have increased in ten months $33,500.

"I desire to make mention of a plan, which was outlined at the last Annual Meeting, for a further endowment. Since then we have received $6,000 from Charles H. Swift and $10,000 from the estate of A. C. Bartlett. The $10,000 from the estate of Hermann Paepcke is still in the Probate Court, and a gift of $10,000 from Mrs. Pauline Dohn Rudolph is on the way.

"Without the last two we have a principal fund of $125,000."

The five Trustees whose terms of office expired in 1923 were re-elected for a period of three years: Clarence A. Burley, Clyde M. Carr, William O. Goodman, Chauncey Keep and Charles H. Swift.

At the Trustees' meeting which followed, the present officers and members of the Executive Committee were re-elected.

The action of Third Vice-President Oakley and Secretary Otis in signing the papers in regard to a gift of $10,000 from the estate of Franklin Rudolph was approved.

The Secretary was authorized to send a vote of thanks to Ernest Schelling for his gift of $200 to the Pension Fund of the Orchestra.

The next business in order was the consideration of the demand by the Chicago Federation of Musicians for an increase in the salaries of members of the Orchestra for next season.

Third Vice-President Oakley presented five plans, as follows:

"1. Discontinue the Orchestra concerts.

"2. Accept union demands of $67.50 minimum salary per week at yearly cost of about $18,000.

"3. Make contracts for a season of forty-two weeks at present minimum of $60. This would add $140,000 a season. From the extra fourteen weeks it is estimated we could secure a net return of about $9,000, thus facing a loss of $5,000.

"4. Contract for seventy-three men at a minimum of $75, which would cost same as ninety-one men at former minimum.

"5. Contract for a regular Orchestra of seventy-eight men at a minimum of $75, securing the right to play an average of four and a half concerts weekly in place of four. This organization would cost $9,500 more than our former payroll. These men would play all the concerts—Symphony, Popular, Children's, Milwaukee, Aurora, Mandel Hall and as many more as we could consistently contract for, up to a total of 126.

"To the seventy-eight men we should add twelve who would play only the Friday and Saturday symphony series. This can probably be done at a cost of $16,800, making a total of $26,300, which should be materially reduced by receipts from the additional concerts."

These plans were considered in turn by the Trustees, and after due consideration the following resolution was unanimously adopted:

"That the Executive Committee be authorized and empowered to compose the differences between the Association and the Chicago Federation of Musicians, Local No. 10, in substantial accordance with plan No. 5, which the Board prefers, and that upon settlement with the Federation of such a plan, to proceed with the making of contracts with the men on that basis for the ensuing year."

On motion, it was ordered "that the Association acknowledges with grateful appreciation the generous donation of $10,000 from the Franklin Rudolph estate, and that the Secretary be directed to spread a memorandum thereof upon the records of the Board of Trustees, and to convey to Mrs. Rudolph the thanks and acknowledgment of the Orchestral Association."

In accordance with the action of the Trustees at the Annual Meeting, an agreement substantially as follows was entered into with the Chicago Federation of Musicians, Local No. 10, under date of May 31, 1923, for the seasons of 1923-1924 and 1924-1925:

"In place of the minimum of $67.50, demanded by the Federation, the Association has decided to advance the minimum to $75 per week. In return for this advance in salary the men are to play a total of 126 concerts, an average of four and a half per week, in place of 112, an average of four per week, as in former years.

"Four rehearsals per week are allowed, but in place of being limited to nine hours per week they are changed to thirty-six hours in every four weeks. With this method eight hours can be used one week and ten hours the next, at the discretion of the Conductor. Heretofore the hours have not been cumulative, each week being separate in itself.

"The season is to be for twenty-nine weeks, with a vacation of one week, in which there will be no performances and for which the members of the Orchestra will receive no salaries. This will permit the Association to declare a vacation the week before Christmas, if it seems advisable.

"Under the new arrangement the Orchestra will be divided into two classes—seventy-eight men who will play all the concerts, and twelve in addition, making a total of ninety who will play the symphony concerts."

My journal records a sad note in the closing days of the Thirty-second Season:

"June 21, Thursday, 2:30 P. M.: Funeral services of an old friend, Milward Adams, in the parlors of the Auditorium Hotel, conducted by the Rev. Josiah Sibley, D.D., minister of the Second Presbyterian Church, assisted by the choir of the church."

Milward Adams, long associated with Theodore Thomas and his Orchestra, first Manager of the Auditorium Theatre and first Manager of the Chicago Orchestra (1890-1894), died Wednesday, June 18, 1923, at the Auditorium Hotel. He was born January 6, 1857, in Lexington, Kentucky; came to Chicago in 1870 and began work as an errand boy for Wilson Brothers, clothiers. He soon found a more congenial situation in the office of Carpenter & Sheldon, of the Star Lecture Course. Mr. Adams was long associated with George B. Carpenter in the management of the Summer Garden Concerts, and after the death (1881) of Mr. Carpenter, assisted Mrs. Carpenter in managing the concerts. Later the concerts were managed by Mr. Adams himself. In 1887 Mr. Adams became Manager of Central Music Hall, where he remained until the Auditorium Theatre was opened in 1889.

The *Evening Post* said of Milward Adams: "His life was given to the promotion of sane amusements. He believed that instruction and amusement should go hand in hand, and under his direction they did so go."

MILWARD ADAMS

THIRTY-SECOND SEASON
(1922-1923)
SOLOISTS

PIANOFORTE: Miss Josephine Rosensweet; Wilhelm Bachaus, Alfredo Casella, Alfred Cortot, Josef Hofmann, Mischa Levitzki, Arthur Rubinstein, Ernest Schelling, Artur Schnabel.

VIOLIN: Miss Erika Morini, Miss Erna Rubinstein; Jacques Gordon, Miron Poliakin, Toscha Seidel, Albert Spalding.

VIOLONCELLO: Alfred Wallenstein.

VOCAL: Miss Claire Dux, Mme. Maria Ivogun; Paul Bender.

VISITING CONDUCTOR: Alfredo Casella.

THIRTY-THIRD SEASON
(1923-1924)

Death of President Clyde Mitchell Carr—Trustees adopt an appreciation of his life and work—A bequest of $1,000,000 in his will to the Chicago Symphony Orchestra—First Program a tribute to his memory—The Executive Committee decides to name Mr. Carr's bequest "The Clyde M. and Lillian Carr Fund"—Mr. Stock visits Philadelphia as Guest Conductor of its Orchestra—A gift of $5,000 each from Mrs. Edward Kemp and her daughter, Miss Frances Kemp, to the Endowment Fund—Dedication of the Theodore Thomas Memorial—Mandel Hall Concerts—Milwaukee Concerts—Popular Concerts—Children's Concerts—Civic Orchestra Concerts—Aurora Symphony Concerts—Ann Arbor Festivals—North Shore Festivals—Postlude—Appendix.

We come now to a sad page in this history, which records the illness and death of a beloved friend of the Orchestra, who was devoted heart and soul to its welfare,

CLYDE MITCHELL CARR

Though in failing health for nearly two years, he presided at the Annual Meeting December 13, 1921, and presented a thorough analysis of the finances of the Association, but was too ill to attend the meeting December 12, 1922, and that of May 29, 1923. The end soon came, his "Death and Transfiguration," Tuesday, June 5, 1923. The last services were held from his home, 1130 Lake Shore Drive, Thursday, June 7, conducted by the Rev. James G. K. McClure, D.D., who had known Mr. Carr in his student days at Lake Forest University. Dr. McClure, in his address, dwelt especially on Mr. Carr's forceful character—always an optimist, "Looking forward! Facing the front! It was this element in his life that led to success in the world of commerce."

Clyde Mitchell Carr was born July 7, 1869 (of Virginia parentage) in Will County, Illinois, the son of Richard Baxter Carr and Margaret Mitchell Carr. He prepared for college at Lake Forest University, and after a two years' course at the Northwestern University at Evanston, entered Princeton in the class of 1889, but did not graduate, owing to his father's death.

CLYDE MITCHELL CARR

Thirty-third Season—1923-1924

On leaving Princeton he came to Chicago, and later became associated with the firm of Joseph T. Ryerson & Son, continuing with them many years, and at the time of his resignation in January, 1923, he was President of the firm.

Mr. Carr was not only an earnest friend of the Orchestra, but in other ways was interested in the city's welfare; as a Trustee of the Art Institute and of the Chicago Plan Commission.

In 1894 Mr. Carr married Lillian Van Alstyne of Evanston, who survives him.

By the terms of his will one-half of the residuary estate is bequeathed to The Orchestral Association, the income to be used by the Trustees in their discretion. This magnificent bequest of approximately $1,000,000 does not become available during the life of Mrs. Carr.

A meeting of the Trustees was held Friday afternoon, October 5, to fill the vacancy caused by the death of President Carr. Present, Messrs. Hamill, Adams, Burley, Hutchinson, Oakley, Otis and Swift; Manager Wessels by invitation. Charles H. Hamill was elected President and Horace S. Oakley Vice-President; the election of a Third Vice-President (in place of Horace S. Oakley) was deferred.

The following appreciation of the life and work of Mr. Carr was adopted, and a copy directed to be published in the first program book (October 12 and 13) of the season:

"Once again death has taken the President of this Association. On June 5, 1923, after a long illness, Clyde M. Carr died. He joined the Association in 1910, became a Trustee in 1912, and was made Vice-President the same year. In this position his services were such that when in 1916 the presidency became vacant by the lamented death of Bryan Lathrop, Mr. Carr was unanimously chosen his successor. As President, Mr. Carr was devoted to the welfare of the Association and the promotion of all its aims. He never failed to keep in mind its problems, or to give to them the same earnest and intelligent deliberation which had made him successful in his own affairs. Considerate of the opinion of others and modest in the expression of his own, he yet invariably showed such maturity of judgment that it was rare his conclusions failed to commend themselves to his colleagues. He was gentle in his manners, devoted to the highest ideals of art, and generous in his gifts of time, effort and money to the advancement of musical culture. By his will he has given eloquent expression to his sympathy, devotion and generosity by providing that in time one-half of his ample fortune—the fruit of his industry and foresight—shall come to the treasury of this Association, to be forever applied to its uses and purposes.

"To us, his fellow-Trustees, association with him has been an inspiration, and his death is a bereavement which impels us to record on the minutes of our meeting this inadequate appreciation of him who was our friend.

"From the country has been taken one of its best citizens, The Orchestral Association has been deprived of a leader who cannot be replaced, and to the cause of good music his benefaction, munificent though it be, is but slight recompense for his loss."

At this meeting pensions were granted to Alexander Krauss, Wilfred Woollett, Rudolph Fitzek, Carl Sauter, and the widow of Paul Kruse.

Frederick J. Wessels, Treasurer, reported the payment, on August 1, of the $10,000 bequest from the estate of Hermann Paepcke. The Trustees expressed their thorough appreciation of this generous gift from Mr. Paepcke's estate, which was added to the funds of the Association.

I find in my journal this note on the First Concert of the season, on Friday, October 12:

"Came early to greet old friends. Some new faces in the Orchestra. Alexander Krauss (first violin), after thirty-two years of faithful service, retires on a pension."

The program included:

Symphony No. 5, C Minor, Opus 67, ...	*Beethoven*
Elegy, ...	*Stock*
(Dedicated to the Memory of Clyde M. Carr)	
(First Performance)	
Prelude, "The Afternoon of a Faun,"	*Debussy*

The interest of the concert centered largely in Mr. Stock's "Elegy," written as a tribute to the memory of one of his dearest friends, Clyde M. Carr, President of The Orchestral Association. The "Elegy" depicts in tone the fine qualities of character that distinguished Mr. Carr.

The program book announced the passing of an old member of the Orchestra:

PAUL KRUSE

Died July 3, 1923

A member of the Orchestra (bassoon section) for twenty-four years.

Thirty-third Season—1923-1924

FIFTH PROGRAM, NOVEMBER 9 AND 10
Soloist: Enrico Tramonti

Introduction and Allegro for Harp, with String Orchestra, Flute and Clarinet,	Ravel
Harp Solo, "Féerie," Prelude and Dance,	Tournier

SEVENTH PROGRAM, NOVEMBER 23 AND 24
Soloist: Moriz Rosenthal

Concerto for Pianoforte No. 1, E Minor, Opus 11, . . *Chopin*

After the Friday concert the Executive Committee met. Present, Messrs. Hamill, Otis and Swift. The following resolution was adopted:

"Because it is known to the Board that the interest in music of our late President was stimulated and sustained by his wife, Lillian Carr,

"*Resolved*, That when his bequest shall become available to the Association it shall be designated and known as 'The Clyde M. and Lillian Carr Fund.'"

Mr. Stock selected three soloists for the early concerts of the season from the artists of the Orchestra, whose work is of a high order and is always enjoyed by the people: Enrico Tramonti on November 9 and 10; Alfred Wallenstein, November 30 and December 1, Eighth Program:

"Schelomo," Hebrew Rhapsody for Violoncello and Orchestra,	Bloch
Symphonic Variations for Violoncello and Orchestra, Opus 25,	Boellmann

and Jacques Gordon, Tenth Program, December 14 and 15:

Concerto for Violin, A Minor, with String Orchestra and Organ Accompaniment,	Vivaldi—Nachez
Fantasie for Violin and Orchestra, Opus 46,	Bruch

In the meantime another important soloist appeared at the concerts, who must be mentioned: Benno Moiseiwitsch in the Ninth Program, December 7 and 8, playing the Tschaikowsky concerto No. 1, B flat minor, Opus 23.

The Orchestra assisted the Apollo Musical Club in two Christmas performances of "The Messiah," under the direction of Harrison M. Wild, Sunday evening, December 23, when the soloists were: Edith Bideau Normelli (soprano), Betty Baxter (contralto), Arthur Kraft (tenor), Edgar Fowlston (bass); and Monday evening, December 24, when the soloists were: Muriel Magerl Kyle (soprano), Kathryn Meisle (contralto), Arthur Boardman (tenor), and Edgar Fowlston (bass).

TWELFTH PROGRAM, JANUARY 4 AND 5
THEODORE THOMAS MEMORIAL

Overture, "Coriolanus," Opus 62, ...	*Beethoven*
Symphony No. 3, "Eroica," Opus 55, ...	*Beethoven*

INTERMISSION

Das Rheingold, ... *Wagner*
    RAINBOW SCENE.
    RHINE DAUGHTERS' LAMENT.
    ENTRANCE OF THE GODS INTO VALHALLA.

Siegfried, ... *Wagner*
    ASCENT OF BRÜNNHILDE'S ROCK.
    FINALE.

Die Meistersinger von Nürnberg, ... *Wagner*
    INTRODUCTION TO ACT III.
    PROCESSION OF THE GUILDS.
    FINALE.

Mr. Stock was the Guest Conductor for the concerts that week of the Philadelphia Orchestra, in the absence of its Conductor, Leopold Stokowski. Eric DeLamarter, our Assistant Conductor, in the absence of Mr. Stock led the Orchestra in the concerts of January 18 and 19, Fourteenth Program:

SOLOIST: CECILIA HANSEN
Concerto for Violin, No. 3, B Minor, Opus 61, . . *Saint-Saëns*

At the concerts of January 25 and 26, Fifteenth Program, the important numbers were:

Symphony in D Minor, ...	*Franck*
"Tema con Variazioni,"	*Panizza*

    (First Performance in America)
    (Conducted by the Composer)

Mr. Stock's return to the Conductor's stand from his visit to Philadelphia was the event of the Friday concert. In response to the enthusiasm with which he was greeted by the Orchestra, Mr. Stock spoke of the brilliant work of the Philadelphia Orchestra, but he preferred our own Orchestra—"The playing of our men is more musicianly, more artistic."

After the concert there was a meeting of the Executive Committee; present, Messrs. Hamill, Adams, Glessner, Oakley, Otis and Swift; Messrs. Wessels, Voegeli and Stock by invitation. On motion the Secretary was instructed to write to Mrs. Edward Kemp and her daughter, Miss Frances D. Kemp, conveying the thanks of The Orchestral Association for their generous gifts of $5,000 each to the Endowment Fund of the Association.

EIGHTEENTH PROGRAM, FEBRUARY 15 AND 16
Soloists: Guy Maier.
Lee Pattison.
Arthur Shattuck.

Concerto for Two Pianofortes and String Orchestra,
  E Flat Major, ... *C. P. E. Bach*
       (First Performance in America)
Ballad for Two Pianofortes and Orchestra, ... *Sowerby*
       (First Performance in Chicago)
Symphonic Poem, "The Fountains of Rome," . . . *Respighi*
Concerto for Three Pianofortes and String Orchestra,
  C Major, ... *Bach*
       (First Performance in Chicago)

TWENTIETH PROGRAM, FEBRUARY 29 AND MARCH 1
Soloist: Claire Dux

Concert Aria, "Bei diesen schönen Augen," . . . . *Mozart*
       Double-bass Obbligato by Vaclav Jiskra
       (First Performance in Chicago)
Symphony No. 4, G Major, ... *Mahler*
       Soprano Solo by Miss Dux
Aria, "Me voila seule," from "Les Pêcheurs de Perles,". . *Bizet*

TWENTY-SECOND PROGRAM, MARCH 14 AND 15
Soloist: Wanda Landowska

Concerto for Harpsichord, B Flat Major, ... *Handel*
   Andante—Allegro.
   Larghetto.
              (Cadenza Improvised by Wanda Landowska)
   Allegro moderato.
Harpsichord Solos:
   The Harmonious Blacksmith, ... *Handel*
   Gavotte, from English Suite No. 3, ... *Bach*
   Sonata, A Major, ... *Scarlatti*

TWENTY-THIRD PROGRAM, MARCH 21 AND 22

"A Pilgrim Vision," . . . . *Carpenter*
       "This composition was written for the Mayflower Celebration held in Philadelphia in 1920 to mark the tercentenary of the landing of the Pilgrims, and it was performed for the first time at concerts of the Philadelphia Orchestra. Leopold Stokowski was the Conductor."
Symphony, E Minor (Two Movements), ... *Brune*

TWENTY-SIXTH PROGRAM, APRIL 11 AND 12
Soloist: Fannie Bloomfield Zeisler

Symphonic Poem, "The Dying Swan," . . . . . *Perinello*
       (First Performance in America)
Concerto for Pianoforte, E Major, Opus 59, . . . *Moszkowski*

THE THEODORE THOMAS MEMORIAL

A noble and worthy tribute was made to the memory of our leader in the dedication, Monday afternoon, April 14, of the Theodore Thomas Memorial. The monument, representing the "Spirit of Music," stands in Grant Park, Michigan Avenue, south of the Art Institute, and was erected from the income of the B. F. Ferguson Monument Fund: Albin Polasek, sculptor; Howard Shaw, architect.

PROGRAM IN ORCHESTRA HALL
EDWARD J. KELLY, Chairman

Chorale and Fugue, ... *Bach—Abert*
    THE CHICAGO SYMPHONY ORCHESTRA,
    Frederick Stock, Conductor

Address: "Life and Work of Theodore Thomas."
    CHARLES H. HAMILL,
    President of The Orchestral Association

First Movement, Allegro con Brio from Symphony No. 3, "Eroica," Opus 55, ... *Beethoven*
    THE CHICAGO SYMPHONY ORCHESTRA

Presentation of the Memorial.
    CHARLES L. HUTCHINSON,
    President of the B. F. Ferguson Monument Fund

Acceptance of the Memorial.
    EDWARD J. KELLY,
    President of the South Park Commissioners

Prelude to "The Mastersingers of Nuremberg," . . . *Wagner*
    THE CHICAGO SYMPHONY ORCHESTRA

President Hamill in his address said of Theodore Thomas:

"He believed in his art; to him it was the great thing of life, and from his earliest day he nurtured it and developed it. The time never came when he felt he had nothing more to learn or could live upon his past accomplishments. The time never came when he felt he could conduct a concert without the most painstaking preparation, even of numbers which he had played countless times before. And his industry was fortified by sublime courage and faith."

At the conclusion of the program the audience gathered around the monument and witnessed the unveiling by Mrs. Minna Thomas Sturgis, daughter of Theodore Thomas.

THE THEODORE THOMAS MEMORIAL

Thirty-third Season—1923-1924

TWENTY-EIGHTH, AND LAST, PROGRAM, APRIL 25 AND 26

Overture, "Leonore," Opus 72, No. 3, ... *Beethoven*
Symphony No. 4, E Minor, Opus 98, ... *Brahms*

INTERMISSION

Iberia, Images pour Orchestre No. 2, ... *Debussy*
 "In the Streets and by the Wayside."
 "The Odors of the Night."
 "The Morning of the Fête Day."
Ride of the Valkyries, from "Die Walküre," . . . . *Wagner*
Overture to "Tannhäuser," . . . . *Wagner*

The Annual Festival of the Civic Music Association was held in Orchestra Hall Sunday, April 27, at 3 P. M. The attractive numbers on the program were the songs for the Children's Chorus, led by Herbert E. Hyde. A few may be noted:

"Rain Song," . . . . . . } . . . *Reinecke*
"When the Little Children Sleep," }
Jolly Jinks Songs, ... *Edith Lobdell Reid*
 "A Candle, a Candle."
 "A Penny Down a Crack."
 "Off to Yakima."
 "Our Old Horse."

The Civic Orchestra, Frederick Stock, Musical Director, and Eric DeLamarter, Assistant Conductor, contributed:

Overture to "The Secret of Susanne," . . . . *Wolf-Ferrari*
"March," . . . }
"The Lake," . . } . . . . . *Elizabeth Sprague Coolidge*
"Somersaults," . }

Community singing led by Frederick W. Carberry.

THE CIVIC ORCHESTRA OF CHICAGO
1924—SIXTH SEASON—1925

FIRST VIOLINS
Hyna, H., *Principal.*
Marshall, Miss J.
Hrych, C. V.
Sutton, G. A.
Swanson, E. T.
Clarke, Mrs. R. S.
Senescu, B.
Cherry, Mrs. J. H.
Fuchs, M.
Sindelar, C.
Lyngby, C. N.
Gross, H.
Smith, W.
Filerman, J.
Larsen, W. L.
Willianganz, W.
Pollyea, S.
Bruck, Ed., Jr.

SECOND VIOLINS
Emanuel, L., *Principal.*
Polacek, Miss S.
Quiriconi, A.
Waskevicz, Miss M.
Katznelson, J.
Bernstein, H.
Norton, J.
Kailin, L.
Roehrborn, W.
Tempkins, A.
Silvestri, C.
Mack, W.
Stolzberg, Miss F.
Brandt, H.
Zimberoff, B.

VIOLAS
Bernstein, S., *Principal.*
Roth, A.
Lehnhard, J. L.
Sher, H.
Baehrend, H. W., Jr.
Braverman, L.
Filerman, P.

VIOLONCELLOS
Mundry, P. H., *Principal.*
Davis, Miss M.
Beidel, R.
Whitney, Miss G.
Coleman, T. G.
Snyder, Miss M.
Feigen, Miss S.
Swanson, Miss R.
Matuska, J.
Kosloff, N.

BASSES
Fleischman, W., *Principal.*
Andel, J. S.
Hyde, P. M.
Stanko, L.
Gangursky, N.

FLUTES
Noack, H. C.
Snauffer, J. E.
Linhart, F.

OBOES
Salathiel, D.
Montgomery, J. M.

OBOE AND ENGLISH HORN
Baldwin, T. B.

CLARINETS
Sheerer, Miss J.
Halac, A. J.

BASSOONS
Kessler, C. S.
Johnson, H.
Jordan, S.

FRENCH HORNS
Babbe, C. H.
Bruno, G. A.
Griswold.
Williams, R.

TRUMPETS
Goldman, B.
Brabrook, A. N.
Kutson, R. C.
Branch, W.

TROMBONES
Lomonte, L.
Bozek, A.
Anderson, O. W.

TUBA
Stanko, L.

HARPS
Van Bramer, Miss F.
Murphy, Miss L.

TIMPANI AND PERCUSSIONS
Metzenger, E. M.
Glenicke, T. J.
Mann, H. R.

LIBRARIAN
Handke, P.

Thirty-third Season—1923-1924

The Annual Meeting of The Orchestral Association was held Tuesday afternoon, May 27, 1924, at 4:00, in the offices of the Association.

There were present in person Messrs. Joseph Adams, Clarence A. Burley, Charles H. Hamill, Chauncey Keep, Harold F. McCormick, Philo A. Otis and Charles H. Swift, and by proxy twenty-one, making a total of twenty-eight out of the present membership of thirty-eight. Mr. Hamill was elected Chairman of the meeting, and Mr. Otis, Clerk.

The report of the Treasurer, Frederick J. Wessels, for the Thirty-third Season, ending April 30, 1924, was then read:

Receipts

		Thirty-third Season (1923-1924)	Thirty-second Season 1922-1923)
Symphony series		$ 181,357.00	$181,763.00
Extra hall concerts (net)	$ 6,503.90		
Miscellaneous outside concerts (net)	2,105.96		
Milwaukee concerts (net)	11,987.26		
Mandel Hall concerts (net)	5,136.53		
Aurora concerts (net)	5,129.26		
		30,862.91	21,529.93
Popular concerts (net)		14,292.35	13,307.82
Children's concerts (net)		10,055.45	10,809.70
Interest		2,297.20	2,095.89
		$238,864.91	$229,506.34
Hall rentals	$ 97,232.00		
Building rentals (ten months)	50,851.00		
		$148,083.00	109,885.00
Total		$386,947.91	$329,391.34

Expenses

	Thirty-third Season (1923-1924)	Thirty-second Season (1922-1923)
Business management	$ 34,814.89	$ 28,815.48
Advertising	3,246.87	3,382.73
Orchestra and Conductors	237,510.00	208,705.00
Miscellaneous concert expenses	1,435.06	817.32
Soloists	10,350.00	13,150.00
Music and instruments	1,313.28	1,999.93
	$288,670.10	$256,870.46
Building expenses (ten months)	18,012.14	15,664.39
Heating	5,773.17	7,833.63
Insurance	3,802.69	1,421.46
Hall expenses	25,774.95	17,082.25
Ushers (ten months)	10,416.52	6,940.55
Taxes, special......$ 3,054.65		
Taxes, general........ 9,492.00		
	12,546.65	15,101.39
Water (ten months)	563.05	420.52
Interest	12,000.00	12,000.00
Improvements and repairs	4,086.39	8,142.46
Total	$381,615.66	$341,477.11
Profit (charged off)	5,332.25	275.00
		$341,752.11
Loss		2,360.77
	$386,947.91	$339,391.34

Treasurer's Comments

"It is not possible to make exact comparisons with the Thirty-second Season. The changing of the fiscal year from June 30 to April made the Thirty-second Season consist of but ten months.

"The Orchestra earnings are fully covered in both seasons, and show an increase of $9,348, due to additional concerts and increases in rates for outside concerts.

"The only increase in Orchestra expenses was $28,800 for salaries. Some items show a decrease, notably the soloist account —$2,800 less.

"We were fortunate in making a contract for moving pictures which kept the hall running the entire summer, and the hall rentals were $97,232, about $3,000 more than the largest previous year.

"The building rentals increased $1,000, and the general result shows a profit of $5,300.

"The hall is now rented for five summers at a rate of $2,000 per week for eighteen weeks each year.

"The Trust Funds show the following increases:

Thirty-third Season—1923-1924

Henry Field Memorial:
Accumulated interest..........................$ 4,386.76

Pension Fund:
Hermann Paepcke bequest.........$ 10,000.00
Ernest Schelling, gift..............   200.00
Accumulations...................   8,701.39
                                              ————————
                                                         18,901.39
Endowment Fund:
Subscriptions:
Charles H. Swift................$ 6,000.00
Mrs. Franklin Rudolph.......... 10,000.00
Mrs. E. M. Kemp..............   5,000.00
Miss Frances D. Kemp..........   5,000.00
Interest accumulations..........   4,114.09
                                              ————————
                                                         30,114.09
Page Memorial:
Accumulated interest............................   2,245.67

There is available for deficits:
General account................................ 15,939.92
Field Memorial interest.......................... 22,857.63
General endowment............................. 13,502.41
                                                         ————————
                                                         $52,299.96"

Augustus C. Peabody and Frank G. Logan were elected Members of the Association.

Benjamin Carpenter's resignation as a Member was read and, on motion of Mr. Adams, seconded by Mr. Otis, it was unanimously voted that the resignation be not accepted.

William L. Brown, Edward B. Butler, Charles H. Hamill, Charles L. Hutchinson and Harold F. McCormick were elected Trustees for three years, to succeed themselves.

Augustus S. Peabody was elected Trustee for two years, to fill the vacancy caused by the death of Clyde M. Carr.

THE MANDEL HALL CONCERTS

For nearly twenty years the Chicago Symphony Orchestra has contributed greatly to the social and musical life of the University of Chicago. The Leon Mandel Assembly Hall was dedicated with a concert directed by Theodore Thomas, December 22, 1903. Theodore Thomas also conducted the first concerts of the following season, November 2 and December 5, 1904.

On the death of Mr. Thomas the remaining concerts of the season were given under the direction of Frederick Stock, and under his direction the work has been carried on for nineteen years (1905 to 1924) without interruption.

In the early years the concerts were given at the University in the evening. In order to strengthen the support of the series a new organization was formed in 1909, the University Orchestral Association, and one of the first things arranged was an afternoon hour for the concerts—4:15—an hour which permitted students and professors to come to Mandel Hall directly from classroom, library and laboratory. The change of hour has been a vital element in the increased success of the University series.

During the year 1922, 496 students purchased seats for the season. All of the 1,100 seats were sold before the first concert, in spite of the increase in prices. The series has been sold out for three years.

The first meeting of the University Orchestral Association was called to order May 10, 1909, by Dr. A. K. Parker. Among those who were present at that meeting were Mrs. Harry Pratt Judson, James R. Angell, William G. Hale, James H. Breasted, George H. Mead, James A. Field, Walter A. Payne and David A. Robertson. The constitution was adopted May 24, and the following officers were elected: President, George H. Mead; Vice-President, Mrs. Sherwood J. Larned; Secretary-Treasurer, Walter A. Payne; Directors, Mrs. Harry Pratt Judson, Wallace Heckman, Mrs. Francis W. Parker, James H. Breasted.

The officers for 1922-1923 were: President, James A. Field; Vice-President, Mrs. Harry Pratt Judson; Secretary-Treasurer, David A. Robertson; Assistant Secretary-Treasurer, Miss V. Virginia Cates; Directors, Mrs. Henry Gordon Gale, Mrs. Frederic Woodward, Mrs. Ferdinand Schevill, and Edgar J. Goodspeed.

Eight regular concerts were given by the Orchestra in the season 1922-1923 in Mandel Hall, October 24, November 21, December 5, January 16 and 30, 1923, February 13, March 13 and April 10. The program of the first concert, Tuesday evening, October 24, 1922, may be noted:

Thirty-third Season—1923-1924

"March of Homage," . . . . *Wagner*
Symphony No. 1, C Minor, ... *Brahms*
Symphonic Poem, "The Spinning Wheel of Omphale," *Saint-Saëns*
Spanish Rhapsody, ... *Chabrier*

In addition there were two concerts for young people, at which were presented programs like those offered at the Children's Concerts in Orchestra Hall.

Before each concert the Director of the University Choir, Robert W. Stevens, gives a lecture recital on the program. Program notes are also published by the college paper, the *Daily Maroon*, which also gives a large amount of space to a review of each concert, thus showing a creditable appreciation of the program and of the Orchestra.

The officers for 1923-1924 are: President, Gerald B. Smith; Vice-President, Mrs. Harry P. Judson; Secretary-Treasurer, Mrs. Ernest Freund; Assistant Secretary-Treasurer, Miss V. Virginia Cates; Directors: Thomas H. G. Gale, Mrs. Marcus Hirsahl, Paul MacClintock and Robert W. Stevens.

Eight concerts were given by the Orchestra in the season 1923-1924 in Mandel Hall, under the direction of Frederick Stock, on Tuesday evenings, October 23, November 6 and December 4, January 15, 1924, February 12, 26, March 11 and April 8.

THE MILWAUKEE CONCERTS

Ever since its organization in 1891 the Chicago Symphony Orchestra has played several concerts a year at the Pabst Theatre in Milwaukee.

In 1913 and 1914 the Orchestra went for a series of three concerts each year, under the auspices of the Milwaukee Musical Society. In 1915, for the first time, an organized effort was made to establish these concerts on a permanent basis, so as to assure the city a minimum of ten subscription concerts a year. As was inevitable, difficulties arose during the years of the war, and for a time the plan did not seem feasible. However, in 1919 the Milwaukee Orchestral Association was reorganized, with the following officers and directors:

CLARENCE R. FALK, *President.*   DAVID A. EDGAR, *Vice-President.*
CLEMENT C. SMITH, *Treasurer.*   MARGARET RICE, *Secretary.*

DIRECTORS

CLARENCE R. FALK.   WILLIAM C. WHITE.
DAVID A. EDGAR.   CLEMENT C. SMITH.
CLAIRE JACOBS.   MARGARET RICE.
           WILLIAM C. QUARLES.

The financial success was assured by 160 guarantors, who pledged themselves to support the undertaking for five years. So great has been the interest in the concerts that capacity houses are the rule for every performance, and the series has been made entirely self-supporting. Since the reorganization in 1919 the concerts have been under the management of Miss Margaret Rice, who is also Secretary of the Association. Ten performances are given on alternate Monday evenings; over ninety per cent of the capacity of the theatre is sold by subscription.

In addition to the evening concerts several matinée concerts are given each year for children.

The success of the symphony series in Milwaukee is the more remarkable when it is explained that while soloists are occasionally engaged, no soloists are featured in the advance work. Thus it can truthfully be claimed that in Milwaukee the Orchestra and not the soloist is the attraction. All the concerts for both evening and matinée performances are given under the direction of Frederick Stock.

PROGRAM OF THE LAST CONCERT, SEASON OF 1922-1923,
MONDAY EVENING, APRIL 2, 1923

Symphony, B Major, ... *Schumann*
Variations on an Original Theme, Opus 7, ... *Stock*

INTERMISSION

Magic Fire Scene, from "Die Walküre," . . . . . *Wagner*
Selections from "Siegfried," . . . . *Wagner*
   SIEGFRIED IN THE FOREST (ACT II).
   SIEGFRIED ASCENDING BRÜNNHILDE'S ROCK.
   BRÜNNHILDE'S AWAKENING—FINALE (ACT III).

Prelude and Isolde's Love-Death, from "Tristan and
   Isolde," . . . . *Wagner*

Ten concerts were given in the season of 1923-1924 in Pabst Theatre, by the Chicago Symphony Orchestra under the direction of Frederick Stock, on Monday evenings, November 5, 26 and December 10, January 7,

21, 1924, February 4, 18, March 3, 17 and 31. Soloists: Gilbert Ross (violin), Alfred Wallenstein ('cellist).

Two children's matinées were given during the season, by the Chicago Orchestra—one in Shorewood School on January 7, and one at the Pabst Theatre, March 31. Mr. Stock directed at both, giving brief talks before each number.

THE POPULAR CONCERTS

The Eleventh Season of the "Popular Series" consisted of sixteen concerts in Orchestra Hall under the direction of Frederick Stock, with Eric DeLamarter, Assistant Conductor, on Thursday evenings at 8:15, October 18, 25, November 8, 22, 29, December 27, Monday evening December 31, January 10, 24, 1924 (Eric DeLamarter conducting), 31, February 14, 28, March 13, 27, April 10 and 24.

Soloists: Alfred Wallenstein, Jacques Gordon, Alexander Zukovsky and Lillian Magnuson.

The appearance of the soloists, who were prize winners in the competition held annually by the American Society of Musicians added interest to the concerts: Hilda Hinrichs (violoncello), February 14, 1924, Harvey Noack (flute) and J. Henry Welton (tenor), February 28, and Olga Eitner (violin), March 13.

Program notes by Eric DeLamarter.

THE CHILDREN'S CONCERTS

The Fifth Season consisted of thirteen concerts in Orchestra Hall, under the direction of Frederick Stock, with Eric DeLamarter, Assistant Conductor: "Series A," Thursday afternoons at 4 o'clock, November 1, 1923, December 6, January 3, 1924, February 7, March 6 and April 3. Extra Concert, Wednesday afternoon, December 3, at 3:45 o'clock. "Series B," Thursday afternoons at 4 o'clock, November 15, December 13, January 17, 1924 (Mr. DeLamarter conducting), February 21, March 20, and April 17.

Again have the Children's Concerts proved to be an attractive feature of our Thirty-third Season. All were given to enthusiastic audiences, including 1,000 children, filling Orchestra Hall at every performance. Mr. Stock has talked to the little folks so often of the instruments in the orchestra that they can now discriminate between the French horn and bassoon, the clarinet and oboe.

Program notes by Eric DeLamarter.

THE CIVIC ORCHESTRA
(For the Development of Symphony Players)

The Fifth Season consisted of five concerts in Orchestra Hall, under the direction of Frederick Stock, with Eric DeLamarter, Assistant Conductor, on Sunday afternoons at 3:30 o'clock, November 25, December 30, January 27, 1924, February 24 and March 30.

Soloists: Helen Freund (coloratura), Bernice Violle-McChesney (piano), Mary Welch (contralto), Mabel Lyons (piano) and Goldie Gross (violoncello).

THE AURORA SYMPHONY CONCERTS

The beginnings and development of the Aurora Concerts are all set forth in a letter (April 22, 1923) from the Manager, Mrs. Theodore Worcester:

"The Chicago Symphony Orchestra, Frederick Stock, Conductor, has just closed its Eleventh Season in Aurora, and we trust there will be many more. We have never had any committees or association, though there is now some thought of forming an organization to place the concerts on a permanent basis. The concerts have been entirely under my management, and it has at times been a struggle to keep them going.

"There was only one concert in the First Season, October 29, 1912, in the Grand Opera House, Aurora:

PROGRAM
SOLOIST: MRS. THEODORE WORCESTER

Overture, "Oberon," . . . . *Weber*
Symphony No. 8, B Minor, Unfinished, ... *Schubert*
Concerto for Pianoforte No. 1, B Flat Minor,
    Opus 23, ... *Tschaikowsky*

INTERMISSION

Suite, "The Wand of Youth," No. 2, ... *Elgar*
"Dance of the Angels," from "The New Life," . . *Wolf-Ferrari*
"Under the Linden Trees," . . . . *Massenet*
    VIOLONCELLO AND CLARINET OBBLIGATOS BY BRUNO STEINDEL AND JOSEPH SCHREURS
"Ride of the Valkyries," from "Die Walküre," . . . *Wagner*

"We continued thereafter with only one concert a year until the new building, 'Sylvandell,' was completed, with a much larger seating capacity. We were given the privilege of opening this new auditorium with a symphony concert May 3, 1915, assisted by the entire Chicago Symphony Orchestra, Frederick Stock, Conductor, and the Apollo Musical Club, Harrison M. Wild, Conductor; soloists: Lambert Murphy and Clarence Whitehill.

"We then began a series of three symphony concerts each season, which have continued until the present time.

"The 'Sylvandell' building was rebuilt in 1919, and is now the 'Theatre Rialto,' where our concerts are given.

"In later years we have added two 'Children's Concerts' for each season. In this work we have the support of the entire community throughout the Fox River Valley, who are calling for more concerts, especially for the children. Among our soloists in past seasons may be noted Mmes. Margaret Matzenauer, Alma Gluck, Hulda Lashanska and Miss Maud Powell (violin).

"At the last concert of the Eleventh Season, Monday evening, April 16, 1923, we had the Chicago Symphony Orchestra as usual, Frederick Stock, Conductor; soloist, Jacques Gordon; the important numbers being:

Symphony, D Major, ... *Mozart*
Concerto for Violin, E Minor, Opus 64, ... *Mendelssohn*
"Ride of the Valkyries," } from "Die Walküre," . . *Wagner*
"Magic Fire Scene," . . }
March, "Pomp and Circumstance," . . . . . . *Elgar*

In a letter of May 9, 1923, Mrs. Worcester announced the organization of

THE AURORA SYMPHONY ASSOCIATION

Mrs. James H. Bliss (Chairman), Albert M. Snook (Vice-Chairman), Frank G. Plain (Treasurer), Mrs. Theodore Worcester (Secretary and Manager).

Three concerts were given by the Orchestra in the Twelfth Season (1923-1924), under the direction of Frederick Stock, on Monday evenings, October 22, 1923, January 24 and April 14, 1924; and two School Concerts on Monday afternoons at two o'clock and four o'clock, January 14 and April 14, 1924.

This Association went out of existence at the close of the Twelfth Season with quite a deficit. Mrs. Theodore Worcester at once started on the Thirteenth Season with no organization to assist, but firmly convinced that the Fox River Valley community would support the concerts.

THE ANN ARBOR FESTIVALS

Among notable musical events in the Middle West must now be counted the Annual Festivals of the University of Michigan, founded by an enthusiastic worker in the musical life of the University—Albert A. Stanley.

The First Festival was held May 18 and 19, 1894, with the assistance of the Boston Festival Orchestra, Emil Mollenhauer and Albert A. Stanley, Conductors. From 1905 to 1921 Frederick Stock has been associated with Mr. Stanley in the direction of the Festivals. Mr. Stanley then withdrew, and was succeeded by Earl V. Moore, who, with Mr. Stock, conducted the Twenty-ninth (1922), Thirtieth (1923) and Thirty-first (1924) Festivals. Since 1913 the Festivals have been held in the Hill Auditorium; prior to that date they were given in the University Hall.

THE TWENTY-FIRST FESTIVAL
May 13, 14, 15, 15, 1914

May 13, Wednesday evening: Miscellaneous program. Mme. Alma Gluck (soloist) and Orchestra.

May 14, Thursday evening: "The Messiah" (Handel). Soloists: Miss Inez Barbour (soprano), Miss Margaret Keyes (contralto), Lambert Murphy (tenor) and Henri G. Scott (bass); Albert A. Stanley, Conductor; the Chicago Symphony Orchestra.

May 15, Friday afternoon: Riccardo Martin (tenor), soloist; special Children's Chorus and Orchestra.

May 15, Friday evening: Miscellaneous program. Pasquale Amato (baritone), soloist, and Orchestra.

May 16, Saturday evening: "Caractacus" (Elgar). Soloists: Miss Florence Hinkle (soprano), Lambert Murphy (tenor), Reinald Werrenrath (baritone), and Henri G. Scott (bass); the University Choral Union and Orchestra.

THE THIRTY-FIRST FESTIVAL
May 21, 22, 23 and 24, 1924

May 21, Wednesday evening: Miscellaneous program. Miss Emmy Krueger, soloist, and Orchestra. An important number was the concerto No. 2 for organ and Orchestra (DeLamarter), played by Palmer Christian, the composer conducting.

Thursday evening, May 22: Choral concert, "Sea Drift" (Delius), and B Minor Mass (Bach). Soloists: Claire Dux (soprano), Royal Dadmun (baritone) and Sylvia Lent (violinist); the University Choral Union and Orchestra.

Friday afternoon, May 23: Children's concert. Alberto Salvi (harp), soloist.

Friday evening, May 23: Miscellaneous concert. Soloists: Sophie Braslau (contralto), Tito Schipa (tenor), and Orchestra.

Saturday afternoon, May 24: Symphony concert. Harold Bauer, soloist, and Orchestra.

Saturday evening, May 24: Choral concert; "La Primavera" (Respighi). Soloists: Dusolina Gianinni (soprano), Vicente Ballester (baritone), Forest Lamont (tenor) and Cesare Baromeo (bass); the University Choral Union and Orchestra, Frederick Stock, Conductor.

THE CHICAGO NORTH SHORE FESTIVAL ASSOCIATION

The North Shore Festivals were organized (1908-1909) by that energetic worker in the musical life of Evanston, Dean Peter Christian Lutkin of the Northwestern University, and have been held in the spacious gymnasium of the University. One of our critics said recently, "A great festival under the wing of a university must do something for the more serious side of the art." Dean Lutkin, with his co-workers of the North Shore Association, has indeed done "something" in showing the young men and women of the University "the serious side" of musical art.

A few of the Festivals may be noted:

First Festival: June 3, 4 and 5, 1909, in which Dean Lutkin had the assistance of Mme. Ernestine Schumann-Heink, David Bispham and other soloists, his choral forces, and the entire Theodore Thomas Orchestra. Frederick Stock, Orchestral Conductor.

Second Festival: June 1, 2 and 4, 1910:

Soloists: Mrs. Jane Osborn Hannah (soprano), Mme. Ernestine Schumann-Heink and Mrs. Rose Lutiger Gannon (contraltos), H. Evan Williams and David Duggan (tenors), David Bispham, Marion Green, Allen Hinckley and Albert Borroff (basses); Festival Chorus of 600 and Children's Chorus of 1,200; the entire Theodore Thomas Orchestra. Frederick Stock, Orchestral Conductor.

The important works given were "Samson and Delilah" (Saint-Saëns) and the "Manzoni Requiem" (Verdi). The real interest of the festival centered in the Children's Chorus. The singing of these fresh young voices selected from the schools in Evanston, and carefully trained by Dean Lutkin, brought fathers, mothers and relations to every Children's Concert.

Fifth Festival, May 26, 27, 29 and 31, 1913:

Soloists: Eugène Ysaye (violinist), Miss Helen Stanley, Miss Florence Hinkle, Mrs. Edith Chapman Gould, Mrs. Mabel Sharp Herdien and Miss Mary Ann Kaufman (sopranos), Mme. Ernestine Schumann-Heink and Miss Christine Miller (contraltos), Reed Miller and Paul Althouse (tenors), Clarence Whitehill and Herbert Miller (baritones), Henri Scott and Gustaf Holmquist (basses); the Festival Chorus of 600 singers—for "Messiah" performance, 1,000 singers—Young Ladies' Chorus of 500 voices; Children's Chorus of 1,500 voices; the entire Chicago Symphony Orchestra. Frederick Stock, Orchestral Conductor.

First Concert, Monday evening, May 26—"The Messiah" (Handel).

Second Concert, Tuesday evening, May 27—"Artist's Night," for soloists and Orchestra.

Third Concert, Thursday evening, May 29—"The Children's Crusade" (Pierné).

Fourth Concert, Saturday afternoon, May 31—"Young People's Matinée."

Fifth Concert, Saturday evening, May 31—"Wagner Anniversary Concert."

Sixteenth Festival, May 26, 27, 28, 29, 30 and 31, 1924:

PETER CHRISTIAN LUTKIN, Musical Director.
FREDERICK STOCK, Orchestral Conductor.
OSBOURNE MCCONATHY, Associate Conductor.
ERNEST SCHELLING and DEEMS TAYLOR, Guest Conductors.

Thirty-third Season—1923-1924

SOLOISTS

MERLE ALCOCK (Metropolitan Opera),	*Contralto*
PAUL ALTHOUSE (Metropolitan Opera),	*Tenor*
MARY ANN BROWN,	*Soprano*
RICHARD CROOKS,	*Tenor*
FLORENCE EASTON (Metropolitan Opera),	*Soprano*
MARY FABIAN (Chicago Civic Opera),	*Soprano*
LOUIS GRAVEURE,	*Baritone*
FRIEDA HEMPEL (Metropolitan Opera),	*Soprano*
KATHRYN MEISLE (Chicago Civic Opera),	*Contralto*
GLADYS SWARTHOUT (Chicago Civic Opera),	*Soprano*
ERNESTINE SCHUMANN-HEINK,	*Contralto*
ROLLIN PEASE,	*Baritone*
TITO SCHIPA (Chicago Civic Opera),	*Tenor*
HENRI SCOTT,	*Bass*
LOUISE HARRISON SLADE,	*Contralto*
MONICA GRAHAM STULTS,	*Soprano*
CLARENCE WHITEHILL (Metropolitan Opera),	*Baritone*

Festival Chorus of 600 Singers (Enlarged to 1,000 Singers for the "Elijah" Performance)
Children's Chorus of 1,500 Voices
A Cappella Choir
Chicago Symphony Orchestra
Organist, MARY PORTER PRATT

First Concert, Monday evening, May 26: "Elijah" (Mendelssohn). Soloists, Festival Chorus and Orchestra; Peter C. Lutkin, Conductor.

Second Concert, Tuesday evening, May 27: "Jenny Lind Concert" (in costume). Frieda Hempel, soloist, and Orchestra.

Third Concert, Wednesday evening, May 28: First Artists' Night. Tito Schipa, soloist, and Orchestra.

Orchestral Composition Contest, Thursday evening, May 29: Chicago Symphony Orchestra, Frederick Stock, Conductor. The program consisted of five works selected by the judges from the eighty-three submitted by competitors for the prize of $1,000 offered by the Chicago North Shore Festival Association. Judges, Deems Taylor, Ernest Schelling and Adolf Weidig. The prize was won by Charles M. Loeffler.

Young People's Concert, Friday afternoon, May 30: Miscellaneous program for Orchestra. Frederick Stock, Conductor.

Fourth Concert, Second Artists' Night, Friday evening, May 30: Miscellaneous program. Ernestine Schumann-Heink, soloist, and Orchestra. The winning composition in the $1,000 prize competition was played at this concert.

Fifth Concert, Young People's Matinée, Saturday, May 31: Children's Chorus and Orchestra.

Sixth Concert, Wagner Night, Saturday evening, May 31: Miscellaneous program for soloists, Festival Chorus, *a Cappella* Choir and Orchestra.

THIRTY-THIRD SEASON
(1923-1924)

SOLOISTS

HARP: Enrico Tramonti.
PIANOFORTE: Mmes. Fannie Bloomfield Zeisler, Wanda Landowska; Claudio Arrau, Ernst von Dohnányi, Carl Friedberg, Guy Maier, Benno Moiseiwitsch, Lee Pattison, Moriz Rosenthal, Arthur Shattuck (twice).
VIOLA: Lionel Tertis.
VIOLIN: Miss Cecilia Hansen (twice); Carl Flesch, Jacques Gordon (twice).
VIOLONCELLO: Felix Salmond, Alfred Wallenstein (twice).
VOCAL: Misses Sophie Braslau, Claire Dux.
VISITING CONDUCTORS: Carl Busch, Ettore Panizza.

POSTLUDE

After many years passed in research work I can appreciate the words of Edward Eggleston in the preface to "The Beginners of a Nation" (1914):

> "As year after year was consumed in toilsome preparation, the magnitude of the task became apparent, and I began to feel the fear so felicitously expressed by Sir Walter Raleigh, 'That the darkness of age and death would cover over both it and me before the performance.' "

The story of the Chicago Symphony Orchestra for the thirty-three seasons ending June 30, 1924, has now been told. "The performance" is over; but before the curtain descends, the author would beg the customary indulgence of the audience for many of the shortcomings in his efforts to relate the progress of music in Chicago and the events which led up to the establishment of our Orchestra, its "Organization, Growth and Development."

Philo Adams Otis.

APPENDIX

Officers, Trustees and
Members of

The Orchestral Association

and

Members of the Orchestra

for the

Thirty-three Seasons
(1891-1924)

Pension Roll, 1924

THE ORCHESTRAL ASSOCIATION

Trustees and Officers, until the Thirty-second Season, were elected at the Annual Meeting on the second Wednesday in December of each year. At the Annual Meeting on December 12, 1922, the date was changed to the last Tuesday of May in each year.

FIRST, SECOND AND THIRD SEASONS
(1891-1894)

OFFICERS

NATHANIEL K. FAIRBANK, *President.*
C. NORMAN FAY, *Vice-President.*
P. A. MCEWAN, *Secretary and Treasurer.**
MILWARD ADAMS, *Manager.*

TRUSTEES

ADOLPHUS C. BARTLETT.   CHARLES D. HAMILL.
NATHANIEL K. FAIRBANK.   EZRA B. MCCAGG.
C. NORMAN FAY.

FOURTH SEASON
(1894-1895)

The Association adopted a by-law at the adjourned Annual Meeting, January 19, 1895, increasing the number of Trustees from five to nine and creating an Executive Committee, consisting of three members of the Board of Trustees, "clothed with such powers as the Board may from time to time confer."

OFFICERS

GEORGE E. ADAMS, *President.*
BRYAN LATHROP, *Vice-President.*
GEORGE H. WILSON, *Secretary and Manager.*
PHILO A. OTIS, *Treasurer.*
MISS ANNA MILLAR, *Manager of the Season Ticket Sale.*

EXECUTIVE COMMITTEE

CHARLES D. HAMILL.   PHILO A. OTIS.
C. NORMAN FAY.

TRUSTEES

GEORGE E. ADAMS.   CHARLES D. HAMILL.
ALLISON V. ARMOUR.   BRYAN LATHROP.
DANIEL H. BURNHAM.   PHILO A. OTIS.
C. NORMAN FAY.   HENRY B. STONE.†
WILLIAM A. FULLER.

---

*Resigned 1893; succeeded by Charles E. Anderson.

†Henry B. Stone to fill the vacancy caused by the resignation of Charles H. Wacker, who declined to serve.

FIFTH SEASON
(1895-1896)

OFFICERS

GEORGE E. ADAMS, *President.*
BRYAN LATHROP, *Vice-President.*
PHILO A. OTIS, *Secretary.*
P. A. MCEWAN, *Treasurer.*
MISS ANNA MILLAR, *Manager.*

EXECUTIVE COMMITTEE

CHARLES D. HAMILL.
C. NORMAN FAY.
PHILO A. OTIS.

PRESIDENT ADAMS,
Member ex-officio.

TRUSTEES

GEORGE E. ADAMS.
ALLISON V. ARMOUR.
DANIEL H. BURNHAM.
CHARLES R. CORWITH.
C. NORMAN FAY.

CHARLES D. HAMILL.
BRYAN LATHROP.
PHILO A. OTIS.
HENRY B. STONE.

SIXTH SEASON
(1896-1897)

OFFICERS

GEORGE E. ADAMS, *President.*
BRYAN LATHROP, *Vice-President.*
PHILO A. OTIS, *Secretary.*
FREDERICK J. WESSELS, *Treasurer.*
MISS ANNA MILLAR, *Manager.*

EXECUTIVE COMMITTEE

CHARLES D. HAMILL.
C. NORMAN FAY.
PHILO A. OTIS.

PRESIDENT ADAMS,
Member ex-officio.

TRUSTEES

GEORGE E. ADAMS.
ALLISON V. ARMOUR.
DANIEL H. BURNHAM.
CHARLES R. CORWITH.
C. NORMAN FAY.

CHARLES D. HAMILL.
BRYAN LATHROP.
PHILO A. OTIS.
HENRY B. STONE.

394 *The Chicago Symphony Orchestra*

SEVENTH SEASON
(1897-1898)

OFFICERS

GEORGE E. ADAMS, *President*.
  BRYAN LATHROP, *Vice-President*.
    PHILO A. OTIS, *Secretary*.
      FREDERICK J. WESSELS, *Treasurer*.
        MISS ANNA MILLAR, *Manager*.

EXECUTIVE COMMITTEE

CHARLES D. HAMILL.	PRESIDENT ADAMS,
C. NORMAN FAY.	*Member ex-officio*.
PHILO A. OTIS.	

TRUSTEES

GEORGE E. ADAMS.	CHARLES D. HAMILL.
ALLISON V. ARMOUR.	BRYAN LATHROP.
DANIEL H. BURNHAM.	PHILO A. OTIS.
CHARLES R. CORWITH.	WILLIAM B. WALKER.*
C. NORMAN FAY.	

EIGHTH SEASON
(1898-1899)

The by-laws were amended at the Annual Meeting, December 14, 1898, increasing the number of Trustees from nine to fifteen.

OFFICERS

GEORGE E. ADAMS, *President*.
  BRYAN LATHROP, *Vice-President*.
    PHILO A. OTIS, *Secretary*.
      FREDERICK J. WESSELS, *Treasurer*.
        MISS ANNA MILLAR, *Manager*.

EXECUTIVE COMMITTEE

CHARLES D. HAMILL.	PRESIDENT ADAMS,
C. NORMAN FAY.	*Member ex-officio*.
PHILO A. OTIS.	

TRUSTEES

GEORGE E. ADAMS.	CHARLES D. HAMILL.
JOSEPH ADAMS.	THEODORE A. KOCHS.
DANIEL H. BURNHAM.	BRYAN LATHROP.
WILLIAM L. BROWN.	FRANK O. LOWDEN.‡
WILLIAM T. CARRINGTON.	ARTHUR ORR.
CHARLES R. CORWITH.†	PHILO A. OTIS.
C. NORMAN FAY.	WILLIAM B. WALKER.
JOHN J. GLESSNER.	

---

*William B. Walker to fill the vacancy caused by the death of Henry B. Stone, July 5, 1897.
†Resigned December 13, 1899; died December 8, 1915.
‡Frank O. Lowden to fill the vacancy caused by the resignation of Allison V. Armour, November 9, 1894.

Appendix

NINTH SEASON
(1899-1900)
OFFICERS

BRYAN LATHROP, *President.*
 DANIEL H. BURNHAM, *Vice-President.*
  PHILO A. OTIS, *Secretary.*
   FREDERICK J. WESSELS, *Treasurer and Manager.*

EXECUTIVE COMMITTEE

CHARLES D. HAMILL.	PRESIDENT LATHROP,
C. NORMAN FAY.	*Member ex-officio.*
PHILO A. OTIS.	

TRUSTEES

GEORGE E. ADAMS.	THEODORE A. KOCHS.*
JOSEPH ADAMS.	BRYAN LATHROP.
DANIEL H. BURNHAM.	FRANK O. LOWDEN.
WILLIAM L. BROWN.	ARTHUR ORR.
WILLIAM T. CARRINGTON.	PHILO A. OTIS.
C. NORMAN FAY.	WILLIAM B. WALKER.
JOHN J. GLESSNER.	(One vacancy).
CHARLES D. HAMILL.	

TENTH SEASON
(1900-1901)
OFFICERS

BRYAN LATHROP, *President.*
 DANIEL H. BURNHAM, *Vice-President.*
  PHILO A. OTIS, *Secretary.*
   FREDERICK J. WESSELS, *Treasurer and Manager.*

EXECUTIVE COMMITTEE

CHARLES D. HAMILL.	PRESIDENT LATHROP,
C. NORMAN FAY.	*Member ex-officio.*
PHILO A. OTIS.	

TRUSTEES

GEORGE E. ADAMS.	CHARLES D. HAMILL.
JOSEPH ADAMS.	BRYAN LATHROP.
WILLIAM L. BROWN.	FRANK O. LOWDEN.
DANIEL H. BURNHAM.	ARTHUR ORR.
WILLIAM T. CARRINGTON.	PHILO A. OTIS.
CHARLES R. CRANE.†	WILLIAM B. WALKER.
C. NORMAN FAY.	(One vacancy).
JOHN J. GLESSNER.	

---

*Theodore A. Kochs died March 13, 1924.
 †Charles R. Crane was elected December 19, 1900, to fill the vacancy caused by the resignation of Charles R. Corwith.

ELEVENTH SEASON
(1901-1902)

OFFICERS

BRYAN LATHROP, *President*.
　DANIEL H. BURNHAM, *Vice-President*.
　　PHILO A. OTIS, *Secretary*.
　　　FREDERICK J. WESSELS, *Treasurer and Manager*.

EXECUTIVE COMMITTEE

MAX BAIRD.
DANIEL H. BURNHAM.
C. NORMAN FAY.
PHILO A. OTIS.

CHARLES D. HAMILL.
PRESIDENT LATHROP,
　Member ex-officio.

TRUSTEES

GEORGE E. ADAMS.
JOSEPH ADAMS.
WILLIAM L. BROWN.
DANIEL H. BURNHAM.
WILLIAM T. CARRINGTON.
C. NORMAN FAY.
JOHN J. GLESSNER.
CHARLES H. HAMILL.

BRYAN LATHROP.
FRANK O. LOWDEN.
HAROLD F. MCCORMICK.*
ARTHUR ORR.
PHILO A. OTIS.
WILLIAM B. WALKER.
(One vacancy).

TWELFTH SEASON
(1902-1903)

OFFICERS

BRYAN LATHROP, *President*.
　DANIEL H. BURNHAM, *Vice-President*.
　　PHILO A. OTIS, *Secretary*.
　　　FREDERICK J. WESSELS, *Treasurer and Manager*.

EXECUTIVE COMMITTEE

DANIEL H. BURNHAM.
C. NORMAN FAY.
PHILO A. OTIS.

CHARLES D. HAMILL.
PRESIDENT LATHROP,
　Member ex-officio.

TRUSTEES

GEORGE E. ADAMS.
JOSEPH ADAMS.
WILLIAM L. BROWN.
DANIEL H. BURNHAM.
C. NORMAN FAY.
JOHN J. GLESSNER.
CHARLES H. HAMILL.

BRYAN LATHROP.
FRANK O. LOWDEN.
HAROLD F. MCCORMICK.
ARTHUR ORR.
PHILO A. OTIS.
WILLIAM B. WALKER.
(Two vacancies).

*Harold F. McCormick to fill the vacancy caused by the resignation of Charles R. Crane December 11, 1901.

Appendix 397

THIRTEENTH SEASON
(1903-1904)
OFFICERS

BRYAN LATHROP, *President.*
   DANIEL H. BURNHAM, *Vice-President.*
      PHILO A. OTIS, *Secretary.*
         FREDERICK J. WESSELS, *Treasurer and Manager.*

EXECUTIVE COMMITTEE

DANIEL H. BURNHAM.	CHARLES D. HAMILL.
C. NORMAN FAY.	PRESIDENT LATHROP,
PHILO A. OTIS.	*Member ex-officio.*

TRUSTEES

GEORGE E. ADAMS.	BRYAN LATHROP.
JOSEPH ADAMS.	FRANK O. LOWDEN.
WILLIAM L. BROWN.	HAROLD F. MCCORMICK.
DANIEL H. BURNHAM.	ARTHUR ORR.
C. NORMAN FAY.	PHILO A. OTIS.
JOHN J. GLESSNER.	WILLIAM B. WALKER.
CHARLES D. HAMILL.	(One vacancy).
WILLIAM R. HARPER.	

FOURTEENTH SEASON
(1904-1905)
OFFICERS

BRYAN LATHROP, *President.*
   DANIEL H. BURNHAM, *Vice-President.*
      PHILO A. OTIS, *Secretary.*
         FREDERICK J. WESSELS, *Treasurer and Manager.*

EXECUTIVE COMMITTEE

MAX BAIRD.	CHARLES D. HAMILL.
DANIEL H. BURNHAM.	PRESIDENT LATHROP,
C. NORMAN FAY.	*Member ex-officio.*
PHILO A. OTIS.	

TRUSTEES

GEORGE E. ADAMS.	WILLIAM R. HARPER.
JOSEPH ADAMS.	BRYAN LATHROP.
MAX BAIRD.*	FRANK O. LOWDEN.
WILLIAM L. BROWN.	HAROLD F. MCCORMICK.
DANIEL H. BURNHAM.	ARTHUR ORR.
C. NORMAN FAY.	PHILO A. OTIS.
JOHN J. GLESSNER.	CLARENCE M. WOOLLEY.
CHARLES H. HAMILL.†	

*Max Baird to fill the vacancy caused by the resignation of William B. Walker, December 14, 1904.

†Charles H. Hamill was elected at theadjourne d Annual Meeting, January 28, 1905, to fill the vacancy caused by the death of his father, Charles D. Hamill, January 11, 1905.

FIFTEENTH SEASON
(1905-1906)

"At the adjourned Annual Meeting, January 31, 1905, the Association adopted a 'Plan for the Reorganization of The Orchestral Association,' which provided that the Association shall hereafter consist of forty persons whose names here follow, who will be known as Members. The Members shall elect from out of their number each year at the Annual Meeting a Board of not exceeding fifteen Trustees."

MEMBERS

GEORGE E. ADAMS.
JOSEPH ADAMS.
EDWARD E. AYER.
MAX BAIRD.
ADOLPHUS C. BARTLETT.
ABRAHAM G. BECKER.
CHAUNCEY B. BORLAND.
WILLIAM L. BROWN.
WILLIAM J. BRYSON.
CLARENCE A. BURLEY.
DANIEL H. BURNHAM.
EDWARD B. BUTLER.
FREDERIC A. DELANO.
C. NORMAN FAY.
JOHN J. GLESSNER.
CHARLES H. HAMILL.
WILLIAM R. HARPER.
ARTHUR HEURTLEY.
CHARLES L. HUTCHINSON.
GEORGE S. ISHAM.
CHAUNCEY KEEP.
BRYAN LATHROP.
VICTOR F. LAWSON.
JOHN R. LINDGREN.
FRANK O. LOWDEN.
HORACE H. MARTIN.
CYRUS H. McCORMICK.
HAROLD F. McCORMICK.
STANLEY McCORMICK.
OLIVER W. NORTON.
ARTHUR ORR.
PHILO A. OTIS.
FREDERICK F. PEABODY.
HENRY H. PORTER, JR.
EDWARD P. RIPLEY.
MARTIN A. RYERSON.
JOHN A. SPOOR.
ALBERT A. SPRAGUE.
WILLIAM B. WALKER.
CLARENCE M. WOOLLEY.

OFFICERS

BRYAN LATHROP, *President.*
DANIEL H. BURNHAM, *First Vice-President.*
C. NORMAN FAY, *Second Vice-President.*
PHILO A. OTIS, *Secretary.*
FREDERICK J. WESSELS, *Treasurer and Business Manager.*
HENRY E. VOEGELI, *Assistant Treasurer and Assistant Business Manager.*

EXECUTIVE COMMITTEE

BRYAN LATHROP, *Chairman.*
MAX BAIRD.
DANIEL H. BURNHAM.
C. NORMAN FAY.
PHILO A. OTIS.

Appendix

TRUSTEES

GEORGE E. ADAMS.
JOSEPH ADAMS.
MAX BAIRD.
WILLIAM L. BROWN.
DANIEL H. BURNHAM.
FREDERIC A. DELANO.*
C. NORMAN FAY.
JOHN J. GLESSNER.

CHARLES H. HAMILL.
WILLIAM R. HARPER.
BRYAN LATHROP.
FRANK O. LOWDEN.
HAROLD F. MCCORMICK.
PHILO A. OTIS.
CLARENCE M. WOOLLEY.

SIXTEENTH SEASON
(1906-1907)

OFFICERS

BRYAN LATHROP, *President.*
DANIEL H. BURNHAM, *First Vice-President.*
C. NORMAN FAY, *Second Vice-President.*
PHILO A. OTIS, *Secretary.*
FREDERICK J. WESSELS, *Treasurer and Business Manager.*
HENRY E. VOEGELI, *Assistant Treasurer and Assistant Business Manager.*

EXECUTIVE COMMITTEE

BRYAN LATHROP, *Chairman.*

MAX BAIRD.
DANIEL H. BURNHAM.

C. NORMAN FAY.
PHILO A. OTIS.

TRUSTEES

GEORGE E. ADAMS.
JOSEPH ADAMS.
MAX BAIRD.
WILLIAM L. BROWN.
DANIEL H. BURNHAM.
FREDERIC A. DELANO.
C. NORMAN FAY.
JOHN J. GLESSNER.

CHARLES H. HAMILL.
CHAUNCEY KEEP.†
BRYAN LATHROP.
FRANK O. LOWDEN.
HAROLD F. MCCORMICK.
PHILO A. OTIS.
CLARENCE M. WOOLLEY.

MEMBERS

WATSON F. BLAIR and CHARLES H. SWIFT to fill the vacancies caused by the death of ARTHUR ORR and of DR. HARPER.

---

*Frederic A. Delano to fill the vacancy caused by the death of Arthur Orr, June 1, 1905.

†Chauncey Keep to fill the vacancy caused by the death of William R. Harper, January 10, 1906.

SEVENTEENTH, EIGHTEENTH, NINETEENTH AND TWENTIETH SEASONS
(1907-1911)

OFFICERS

BRYAN LATHROP, *President.*
DANIEL H. BURNHAM, *First Vice-President.*
C. NORMAN FAY, *Second Vice-President.*
PHILO A. OTIS, *Secretary.*
FREDERICK J. WESSELS, *Treasurer and Business Manager.*
HENRY E. VOEGELI, *Assistant Treasurer and Assistant Business Manager.*

EXECUTIVE COMMITTEE
BRYAN LATHROP, *Chairman.*

MAX BAIRD.	C. NORMAN FAY.
DANIEL H. BURNHAM.	PHILO A. OTIS.

TRUSTEES

GEORGE E. ADAMS.	CHARLES H. HAMILL.
JOSEPH ADAMS.	CHAUNCEY KEEP.
MAX BAIRD.	BRYAN LATHROP.
WILLIAM L. BROWN.	FRANK O. LOWDEN.
DANIEL H. BURNHAM.	HAROLD F. MCCORMICK.
FREDERIC A. DELANO.	PHILO A. OTIS.
C. NORMAN FAY.	CLARENCE M. WOOLLEY.
JOHN J. GLESSNER.	

MEMBERS

GEORGE E. ADAMS.	DAVID B. JONES.†
JOSEPH ADAMS.	CHAUNCEY KEEP.
EDWARD E. AYER.	BRYAN LATHROP.
MAX BAIRD.	VICTOR F. LAWSON.
ADOLPHUS C. BARTLETT.	JOHN R. LINDGREN.
ABRAHAM G. BECKER.	FRANK O. LOWDEN.
WATSON F. BLAIR.	HORACE H. MARTIN.
WILLIAM L. BROWN.	CYRUS H. MCCORMICK.
WILLIAM J. BRYSON.	HAROLD F. MCCORMICK.
CLARENCE A. BURLEY.	STANLEY MCCORMICK.
DANIEL H. BURNHAM.	OLIVER W. NORTON.
EDWARD B. BUTLER.	PHILO A. OTIS.
CLYDE M. CARR.*	HENRY H. PORTER, JR.
FREDERIC A. DELANO.	EDWARD P. RIPLEY.
C. NORMAN FAY.	MARTIN A. RYERSON.
JOHN J. GLESSNER.	JOHN A. SPOOR.
CHARLES H. HAMILL.	ALBERT A. SPRAGUE.
ARTHUR HEURTLEY.	CHARLES H. SWIFT.
CHARLES L. HUTCHINSON.	WILLIAM B. WALKER.
GEORGE S. ISHAM.	CLARENCE M. WOOLLEY.

*Clyde M. Carr elected Member December 13, 1910, to fill the **vacancy** caused by the resignation of Chauncey B. Borland.
†David B. Jones to fill the vacancy caused by the resignation of Frederick F. Peabody, December 18, 1908.

TWENTY-FIRST SEASON
(1911-1912)
OFFICERS

BRYAN LATHROP, *President.*
DANIEL H. BURNHAM, *First Vice-President.*
C. NORMAN FAY, *Second Vice-President.*
PHILO A. OTIS, *Secretary.*
FREDERICK J. WESSELS, *Treasurer and Business Manager.*
HENRY E. VOEGELI, *Assistant Treasurer and Assistant Business Manager.*

EXECUTIVE COMMITTEE
BRYAN LATHROP, *Chairman.*

DANIEL H. BURNHAM. C. NORMAN FAY.
CLYDE M. CARR. PHILO A. OTIS.

TRUSTEES

GEORGE E. ADAMS. JOHN J. GLESSNER.
JOSEPH ADAMS. CHARLES H. HAMILL.
MAX BAIRD. CHAUNCEY KEEP.
WILLIAM L. BROWN. BRYAN LATHROP.
DANIEL H. BURNHAM. HAROLD F. MCCORMICK.
CLYDE M. CARR.* PHILO A. OTIS.
FREDERIC A. DELANO. CLARENCE M. WOOLLEY.
C. NORMAN FAY.

MEMBERS

BENJAMIN CARPENTER to fill the vacancy caused by the resignation of STANLEY MCCORMICK, January 9, 1912.

*Clyde M. Carr to fill the vacancy caused by the resignation of Frank O. Lowden, January 9, 1912.

TWENTY-SECOND SEASON
(1912-1913)
OFFICERS

BRYAN LATHROP, *President.*
CLYDE M. CARR, *First Vice-President.*
C. NORMAN FAY, *Second Vice-President.*
PHILO A. OTIS, *Secretary.*
FREDERICK J. WESSELS, *Treasurer and Business Manager.*
HENRY E. VOEGELI, *Assistant Treasurer and Assistant Business Manager.*

EXECUTIVE COMMITTEE
BRYAN LATHROP, *Chairman.*

JOSEPH ADAMS.	C. NORMAN FAY.
CLYDE M. CARR.	PHILO A. OTIS.

TRUSTEES

GEORGE E. ADAMS.	CHARLES H. HAMILL.
JOSEPH ADAMS.	CHAUNCEY KEEP.
MAX BAIRD.	BRYAN LATHROP.
WILLIAM L. BROWN.	HAROLD F. McCORMICK.
CLYDE M. CARR.	SEYMOUR MORRIS.*
FREDERIC A. DELANO.	PHILO A. OTIS.
C. NORMAN FAY.	CLARENCE M. WOOLLEY.
JOHN J. GLESSNER.	

*Seymour Morris to fill the vacancy as a Member of the Association and of the Board of Trustees caused by the death of Daniel H. Burnham, June 1, 1912.

Appendix

TWENTY-THIRD SEASON
(1913-1914)

At a meeting of the Trustees, Tuesday afternoon, December 9, 1913, prior to the Annual Meeting, an amendment to the by-laws was adopted, providing for the election of Trustees in three classes of five each, for one, two and three years.

OFFICERS

BRYAN LATHROP, *President.*
　CLYDE M. CARR, *First Vice-President.*
　　CHARLES H. HAMILL, *Second Vice-President.*
　　　PHILO A. OTIS, *Secretary.*
　　　　FREDERICK J. WESSELS, *Treasurer and Business Manager.*
　　　　　HENRY E. VOEGELI, *Assistant Treasurer and Assistant Business Manager.*

EXECUTIVE COMMITTEE
BRYAN LATHROP, *Chairman.*

JOSEPH ADAMS.　　　　　CHARLES H. HAMILL.
CLYDE M. CARR.　　　　　PHILO A. OTIS.

TRUSTEES

ONE YEAR	TWO YEARS
CLYDE M. CARR.	MAX BAIRD.
FREDERIC A. DELANO.	WILLIAM L. BROWN.
CHAUNCEY KEEP.	CHARLES H. HAMILL.
SEYMOUR MORRIS.	HAROLD F. MCCORMICK.
CHARLES H. SWIFT.*	CLARENCE M. WOOLLEY.

THREE YEARS
GEORGE E. ADAMS.
JOSEPH ADAMS.
JOHN J. GLESSNER.
BRYAN LATHROP.
PHILO A. OTIS.

MEMBERS

GEORGE F. PORTER to fill the vacancy caused by the resignation of C. NORMAN FAY.

---

*Charles H. Swift to fill the vacancy caused by the resignation of C. Norman Fay, March 19, 1913.

TWENTY-FOURTH SEASON
(1914-1915)
OFFICERS

BRYAN LATHROP, *President.*
CLYDE M. CARR, *First Vice-President.*
CHARLES H. HAMILL, *Second Vice-President.*
PHILO A. OTIS, *Secretary.*
FREDERICK J. WESSELS, *Treasurer and Business Manager.*
HENRY E. VOEGELI, *Assistant Treasurer and Assistant Business Manager.*

EXECUTIVE COMMITTEE
BRYAN LATHROP, *Chairman.*

JOSEPH ADAMS. CHARLES H. HAMILL.
CLYDE M. CARR. PHILO A. OTIS.

TRUSTEES

ONE YEAR	TWO YEARS
WILLIAM L. BROWN.	GEORGE E. ADAMS.
CHARLES H. HAMILL.	JOSEPH ADAMS.
CHARLES L. HUTCHINSON.*	JOHN J. GLESSNER.
HAROLD F. McCORMICK.	BRYAN LATHROP.
CLARENCE M. WOOLLEY.	PHILO A. OTIS.

THREE YEARS
CLYDE M. CARR.
FREDERIC A. DELANO.
CHAUNCEY KEEP.
SEYMOUR MORRIS.
CHARLES H. SWIFT.

MEMBERS

JULIUS ROSENWALD to fill the vacancy caused by the resignation of MAX BAIRD.

---

*Charles L. Hutchinson to fill the vacancy caused by the resignation of Max Baird, March 6, 1914.

TWENTY-FIFTH SEASON
(1915-1916)
OFFICERS

BRYAN LATHROP, *President.*
CLYDE M. CARR, *First Vice-President.*
CHARLES H. HAMILL, *Second Vice-President.*
PHILO A. OTIS, *Secretary.*
FREDERICK J. WESSELS, *Treasurer and Business Manager.*
HENRY E. VOEGELI, *Assistant Treasurer and Assistant Business Manager.*

EXECUTIVE COMMITTEE
BRYAN LATHROP, *Chairman.*

JOSEPH ADAMS.
CLYDE M. CARR.
CHARLES H. HAMILL.
PHILO A. OTIS.

TRUSTEES

ONE YEAR
GEORGE E. ADAMS.
JOSEPH ADAMS.
JOHN J. GLESSNER.
BRYAN LATHROP.
PHILO A. OTIS.

TWO YEARS
CLYDE M. CARR.
FREDERIC A. DELANO.
CHAUNCEY KEEP.
SEYMOUR MORRIS.
CHARLES H. SWIFT.

THREE YEARS
WILLIAM L. BROWN.
CHARLES H. HAMILL.
CHARLES L. HUTCHINSON.
HAROLD F. MCCORMICK.
CLARENCE M. WOOLLEY.

MEMBERS

ALBERT A. SPRAGUE II to fill the vacancy caused by the death of ALBERT A. SPRAGUE, January 10, 1915.

TWENTY-SIXTH SEASON
(1916-1917)

OFFICERS

CLYDE M. CARR, *President.*
CHARLES H. HAMILL, *First Vice-President.*
JOSEPH ADAMS, *Second Vice-President.*
PHILO A. OTIS, *Secretary.*
FREDERICK J. WESSELS, *Treasurer and Business Manager.*
HENRY E. VOEGELI, *Assistant Treasurer and Assistant Business Manager.*

EXECUTIVE COMMITTEE

CLYDE M. CARR, *Chairman.*

JOSEPH ADAMS. CHARLES H. HAMILL.
JOHN J. GLESSNER. PHILO A. OTIS.

TRUSTEES

ONE YEAR
CLYDE M. CARR.
FREDERIC A. DELANO.
CHAUNCEY KEEP.
SEYMOUR MORRIS.
CHARLES H. SWIFT.

TWO YEARS
WILLIAM L. BROWN.
CHARLES H. HAMILL.
CHARLES L. HUTCHINSON.
HAROLD F. MCCORMICK.
CLARENCE M. WOOLLEY.

THREE YEARS
GEORGE E. ADAMS.
JOSEPH ADAMS.
JOHN J. GLESSNER.
PHILO A. OTIS.
ALBERT A. SPRAGUE II.*

MEMBERS

ROBERT J. THORNE and CYRUS MCCORMICK to fill the vacancies caused by the death of JOHN R. LINDGREN, April 29, 1915, and of BRYAN LATHROP, May 13, 1916.

---

*Albert A. Sprague II to fill the vacancy caused by the death of Bryan Lathrop.

TWENTY-SEVENTH SEASON
(1917-1918)

OFFICERS

CLYDE M. CARR, *President.*
CHARLES H. HAMILL, *First Vice-President.*
JOSEPH ADAMS, *Second Vice-President.*
PHILO A. OTIS, *Secretary.*
FREDERICK J. WESSELS, *Treasurer and Business Manager.*
HENRY E. VOEGELI, *Assistant Treasurer and Assistant Business Manager.*

EXECUTIVE COMMITTEE
CLYDE M. CARR, *Chairman.*

JOSEPH ADAMS.   CHARLES H. HAMILL.
JOHN J. GLESSNER.   PHILO A. OTIS.

TRUSTEES

ONE YEAR	TWO YEARS
WILLIAM L. BROWN.	JOSEPH ADAMS.
CHARLES H. HAMILL.	JOHN J. GLESSNER.
CHARLES L. HUTCHINSON.	HORACE S. OAKLEY.*
HAROLD F. MCCORMICK.	PHILO A. OTIS.
CLARENCE M. WOOLLEY.	ALBERT A. SPRAGUE.

THREE YEARS
CLYDE M. CARR.
FREDERIC A. DELANO.
CHAUNCEY KEEP.
SEYMOUR MORRIS.
CHARLES H. SWIFT.

---

*Horace S. Oakley elected December 20, 1917, for the term of two years to fill the vacancy caused by the death of George E. Adams, October 5, 1917.

TWENTY-EIGHTH SEASON
(1918-1919)

The Trustees at the Annual Meeting December 10, 1918, adopted an amendment to the by-laws increasing the membership of the Executive Committee to seven.

OFFICERS

CLYDE M. CARR, *President.*
CHARLES H. HAMILL, *First Vice-President.*
JOSEPH ADAMS, *Second Vice-President.*
PHILO A. OTIS, *Secretary.*
FREDERICK J. WESSELS, *Treasurer and Business Manager.*
HENRY E. VOEGELI, *Assistant Treasurer and Assistant Business Manager.*

EXECUTIVE COMMITTEE
CLYDE M. CARR, *Chairman.*

JOSEPH ADAMS.   CHARLES L. HUTCHINSON.
JOHN J. GLESSNER.   HORACE S. OAKLEY.
CHARLES H. HAMILL.   PHILO A. OTIS.

TRUSTEES

ONE YEAR	TWO YEARS
JOSEPH ADAMS.	CLYDE M. CARR.
JOHN J. GLESSNER.	CLARENCE A. BURLEY.*
HORACE S. OAKLEY.	CHAUNCEY KEEP.
PHILO A. OTIS.	SEYMOUR MORRIS.
ALBERT A. SPRAGUE.	CHARLES H. SWIFT.

THREE YEARS
WILLIAM L. BROWN.
EDWARD B. BUTLER.*
CHARLES H. HAMILL.
CHARLES L. HUTCHINSON.
HAROLD F. MCCORMICK.

*The resignations of Frederic A. Delano and Clarence M. Woolley were received August 19, 1918. Clarence A. Burley and Edward B. Butler were elected at the Annual Meeting December 10, 1918, to fill these vacancies.

TWENTY-NINTH SEASON
(1919-1920)

At the adjourned Annual Meeting, December 16, 1919, amendments to the by-laws were adopted increasing the membership of the Executive Committee to eight and creating the office of Third Vice-President.

OFFICERS

CLYDE M. CARR, *President.*
 CHARLES H. HAMILL, *First Vice-President.*
  JOSEPH ADAMS, *Second Vice-President.*
   HORACE S. OAKLEY, *Third Vice-President.*
    PHILO A. OTIS, *Secretary.*
     FREDERICK J. WESSELS, *Treasurer and Business Manager.*
      HENRY E. VOEGELI, *Assistant Treasurer and Assistant Business Manager.*

EXECUTIVE COMMITTEE
CLYDE M. CARR, *Chairman.*

JOSEPH ADAMS.	HORACE S. OAKLEY.
JOHN J. GLESSNER.	PHILO A. OTIS.
CHARLES H. HAMILL.	CHARLES H. SWIFT.
CHARLES L. HUTCHINSON.	

TRUSTEES

ONE YEAR	TWO YEARS
CLARENCE A. BURLEY.	WILLIAM L. BROWN.
CLYDE M. CARR.	EDWARD B. BUTLER.
CHAUNCEY KEEP.	CHARLES H. HAMILL.
SEYMOUR MORRIS.	CHARLES L. HUTCHINSON.
CHARLES H. SWIFT.	HAROLD F. MCCORMICK.

THREE YEARS
JOSEPH ADAMS.
JOHN J. GLESSNER.
HORACE S. OAKLEY.
PHILO A. OTIS.
ALBERT A. SPRAGUE.

MEMBERS

WILLIAM OWEN GOODMAN to fill the vacancy caused by the death of WILLIAM B. WALKER, July 2, 1919.

THIRTIETH SEASON
(1920-1921)

OFFICERS

CLYDE M. CARR, *President.*
CHARLES H. HAMILL, *First Vice-President.*
JOSEPH ADAMS, *Second Vice-President.*
HORACE S. OAKLEY, *Third Vice-President.*
PHILO A. OTIS, *Secretary.*
FREDERICK J. WESSELS, *Treasurer and Business Manager.*
HENRY E. VOEGELI, *Assistant Treasurer and Assistant Business Manager.*

EXECUTIVE COMMITTEE

CLYDE M. CARR, *Chairman.*

JOSEPH ADAMS.
JOHN J. GLESSNER.
CHARLES H. HAMILL.
CHARLES L. HUTCHINSON.
HORACE S. OAKLEY.
PHILO A. OTIS.
CHARLES H. SWIFT.

TRUSTEES

ONE YEAR
WILLIAM L. BROWN.
EDWARD B. BUTLER.
CHARLES H. HAMILL.
CHARLES L. HUTCHINSON.
HAROLD F. McCORMICK.

TWO YEARS
JOSEPH ADAMS.
JOHN J. GLESSNER.
HORACE S. OAKLEY.
PHILO A. OTIS.
ALBERT A. SPRAGUE.

THREE YEARS
CLARENCE A. BURLEY.
CLYDE M. CARR.
CHAUNCEY KEEP.
SEYMOUR MORRIS.
CHARLES H. SWIFT.

MEMBERS

FRANK CRAMER and EDWARD L. RYERSON were elected to fill vacancies caused by the death of EDWARD P. RIPLEY, February 4, 1920, and of OLIVER W. NORTON, October 1, 1920.

THIRTY-FIRST SEASON
(1921-1922)

OFFICERS

CLYDE M. CARR, *President.*
CHARLES H. HAMILL, *Vice-President.*
JOSEPH ADAMS, *Second Vice-President.*
HORACE S. OAKLEY, *Third Vice-President.*
PHILO A. OTIS, *Secretary.*
FREDERICK J. WESSELS, *Treasurer.*
HENRY E. VOEGELI, *Assistant Treasurer.*

EXECUTIVE COMMITTEE

CLYDE M. CARR, *Chairman.*

JOSEPH ADAMS.	HORACE S. OAKLEY.
JOHN J. GLESSNER.	PHILO A. OTIS.
CHARLES H. HAMILL.	CHARLES H. SWIFT.
CHARLES L. HUTCHINSON.	

TRUSTEES

ONE YEAR	TWO YEARS
JOSEPH ADAMS.	CLARENCE A. BURLEY.
JOHN J. GLESSNER.	CLYDE M. CARR.
HORACE S. OAKLEY.	WILLIAM OWEN GOODMAN.*
PHILO A. OTIS.	CHAUNCEY KEEP.
ALBERT A. SPRAGUE.	CHARLES H. SWIFT.

THREE YEARS

WILLIAM L. BROWN.
EDWARD B. BUTLER.
CHARLES H. HAMILL.
CHARLES L. HUTCHINSON.
HAROLD F. MCCORMICK.

---

*William Owen Goodman to fill the vacancy caused by the death of Seymour Morris, September 27, 1922.

THIRTY-SECOND SEASON
(1922-1923)

OFFICERS

CLYDE M. CARR, *President*.
CHARLES H. HAMILL, *Vice-President*.
JOSEPH ADAMS, *Second Vice-President*.
HORACE S. OAKLEY, *Third Vice-President*.
PHILO A. OTIS, *Secretary*.
FREDERICK J. WESSELS, *Treasurer and Business Manager*.
HENRY E. VOEGELI, *Assistant Treasurer and Assistant Business Manager*.

EXECUTIVE COMMITTEE

CHARLES H. HAMILL, *Chairman*.

JOSEPH ADAMS.
CLYDE M. CARR.
JOHN J. GLESSNER.
CHARLES L. HUTCHINSON.

HORACE S. OAKLEY.
PHILO A. OTIS.
CHARLES H. SWIFT.

TRUSTEES

ONE YEAR
CLARENCE A. BURLEY.
CLYDE M. CARR.
WILLIAM OWEN GOODMAN.
CHAUNCEY KEEP.
CHARLES H. SWIFT.

TWO YEARS
WILLIAM L. BROWN.
EDWARD B. BUTLER.
CHARLES H. HAMILL.
CHARLES L. HUTCHINSON.
HAROLD F. MCCORMICK.

THREE YEARS
JOSEPH ADAMS.
JOHN J. GLESSNER.
HORACE S. OAKLEY.
PHILO A. OTIS.
ALBERT A. SPRAGUE.

MEMBERS

Joseph Adams.
Edward E. Ayer.
Abraham G. Becker.
Watson F. Blair.
William L. Brown.
William J. Bryson.
Daniel H. Burnham.*
Clarence A. Burley.
Edward B. Butler.
Benjamin Carpenter.
Clyde M. Carr.
Frank Cramer.
Frederic A. Delano.
John J. Glessner.
William Owen Goodman.
Arthur B. Hall.†
Charles H. Hamill.
Arthur Heurtley.
Charles L. Hutchinson.
George S. Isham.
David B. Jones.‡
Chauncey Keep.
Victor F. Lawson.
Frank O. Lowden.
Horace H. Martin.
Cyrus H. McCormick.
Cyrus McCormick.
Harold F. McCormick.
Horace S. Oakley.
Philo A. Otis.
George F. Porter.
Henry H. Porter.
Julius Rosenwald.
Edward F. Ryerson.
Martin A. Ryerson.
John A. Spoor.
Albert A. Sprague.
Charles H. Swift.
Robert J. Thorne.
Clarence M. Woolley.

*Daniel H. Burnham, son of Daniel H. Burnham the architect and builder of Orchestra Hall, was elected December 13, 1921.

†Arthur B. Hall to fill the vacancy caused by the death of Adolphus C. Bartlett, May 20, 1922.

‡David B. Jones died August 22, 1923.

THIRTY-THIRD SEASON
(1923-1924)

OFFICERS

CHARLES H. HAMILL, *President.*
HORACE S. OAKLEY, *Vice-President.*
JOSEPH ADAMS, *Second Vice-President.*
PHILO A. OTIS, *Secretary.*
FREDERICK J. WESSELS, *Treasurer and Business Manager.*
HENRY E. VOEGELI, *Assistant Treasurer and Assistant Business Manager.*

EXECUTIVE COMMITTEE
CHARLES H. HAMILL, *Chairman.*

JOSEPH ADAMS.
JOHN J. GLESSNER.
CHARLES L. HUTCHINSON.
HORACE S. OAKLEY.
PHILO A. OTIS.
CHARLES H. SWIFT.

TRUSTEES

ONE YEAR
WILLIAM L. BROWN.
EDWARD B. BUTLER.
CHARLES H. HAMILL.
CHARLES L. HUTCHINSON.
HAROLD F. MCCORMICK.

TWO YEARS
JOSEPH ADAMS.
JOHN J. GLESSNER.
HORACE S. OAKLEY.
PHILO A. OTIS.
ALBERT A. SPRAGUE.

THREE YEARS
CLARENCE A. BURLEY.
WILLIAM OWEN GOODMAN.
CHAUNCEY KEEP.
CHARLES H. SWIFT.
One vacancy.

MEMBERS

JOSEPH ADAMS.
EDWARD E. AYER.
ABRAHAM G. BECKER.
WATSON F. BLAIR.
WILLIAM L. BROWN.
WILLIAM J. BRYSON.
DANIEL H. BURNHAM.
CLARENCE A. BURLEY.
EDWARD B. BUTLER.
BENJAMIN CARPENTER.
FRANK CRAMER.
FREDERIC A. DELANO.
JOHN J. GLESSNER.
WILLIAM OWEN GOODMAN.
ARTHUR B. HALL.
CHARLES H. HAMILL.
ARTHUR HEURTLEY.
CHARLES L. HUTCHINSON.
GEORGE S. ISHAM.
CHAUNCEY KEEP.
VICTOR F. LAWSON.
FRANK O. LOWDEN.
HORACE H. MARTIN.
CYRUS H. MCCORMICK.
CYRUS MCCORMICK.
HAROLD F. MCCORMICK.
HORACE S. OAKLEY.
PHILO A. OTIS.
GEORGE F. PORTER.
HENRY H. PORTER.
JULIUS ROSENWALD.
EDWARD F. RYERSON.
MARTIN A. RYERSON.
JOHN A. SPOOR.
ALBERT A. SPRAGUE.
CHARLES H. SWIFT.
ROBERT J. THORNE.
CLARENCE M. WOOLLEY.

THE CHICAGO ORCHESTRA
FIRST SEASON
(1891–1892)

First Violins
Bendix, M., *Principal.*
Schnitzler, J.
Knoll, E.
Krauss, A.
Hildebrandt, Ch.
Human, Th.
Czerny, J.
Braun, H.
Seidel, R.
Rissland, R.
Troll, C.
Marum, L.
Beresina, F.
Schmidt, O.
Mittelstaedt, F.
Nurnberger, H.

Second Violins
Poltmann, R., *Principal*
Zeiss, A.
Schmitz, P. R.
Starke, G.
Heiland, F.
Liefke, A.
Donati, R.
Ulrich, A.
Zettelmann, J.
Wagner, E.
Du Moulin, G.
Katsch, Th.
Busse, H.
Seifert, L.
Nurnberger, L.
Busse, L.

Violas
Wigger, A., *Principal.*
Laendner, J.
Meyer, G.
Riedelsberger, C.
Meigross, J.
Dietrich, W.

Violas—Cont.
Maurer, A.
Fitzek, G.
Hoffmann, C.
Krauss, Ph.

Violoncellos
Steindel, B., *Principal.*
Unger, W.
Corell, L.
Amato, L.
Schippe, E.
Sachleben, H.
Eichheim, M.
Hess, F.
Metzdorf, A.
Clussmann, E.

Basses
Wiegner, A., *Principal.*
Beckel, J.
Klemm, L.
Dreibrodt, F.
Helm, R.
Helleberg, A.
Glass, R.
Kramer, A.
Kretlow, J.

Harp
Schuecker, E.

Flutes
Andersen, V.
Valck, F.

Piccolo
Ballmann, M.

Oboes
Bour, F.
Friedrich, L.

English Horn
Schoenheinz, E.

Clarinets
Schreurs, J.
Quitson, A.

Bass Clarinet
Meyer, C.

Bassoons
Litke, H.
Friedrich, L.
Kirchner, A.

Contra-Bassoon
Friedrich, L.

Horns
Dutschke, H.
Schütz, A.
de Maré, L.
Walker, A.

Cornets
Rodenkirchen, Ch.
Dietz, F.
Ulrich, A.
Braun, W.

Tenor Trombones
Gebhardt, O.
Zeller, W.
Nicolini, J.

Bass Trombone
Helms, Ch.

Tuba
Helleberg, A.

Kettledrums
Loewe, W.

Bass Drum
Katsch, Th.

Small Drum
Zettelmann, J.

Cymbals
Wagner, E.

Librarians
McNicol, Theo.
Bairstow, W.

THE CHICAGO ORCHESTRA
SECOND SEASON
(1892–1893)

FIRST VIOLINS
Bendix, M., *Principal.*
Marquardt, J.
Boegner, E.
Knoll, E.
Schoeniger, L.
Krauss, A.
Esser, F.
Czerny, J.
Seidel, R.
Braun, H.
Spiering, Th.
Marum, L.
Schmidt, O.
Beresina, T.
Weidig, A.
Nurnberger, H.

SECOND VIOLINS
Poltmann, R., *Principal*
Zeiss, A.
Starke, G.
Schmitz, Ph.
Heiland, F.
Mittelstaedt, F.
Donati, R.
Ulrich, A.
Zettelmann, J.
Wagner, E.
Du Moulin, G.
Krauss, P.
Hausen, M.
Krauss, A.
Martin, T.
Lockert, J.

VIOLAS
Junker, A., *Principal.*
Laendner, J.
Meyer, G.
Riedelsberger, C.
Dietrich, W.
Katsch, F.
Volk, F.
Meyroos, J.
Fitzek, G.
Andauer, A.

VIOLONCELLOS
Steindel, B., *Principal.*
Unger, W.
Amato, L.
Grienauer, C.
Mingels, E.
Sachleben, H.
Hess, F.
Wagner, F.
Metzdorf, A.
Poltmann, C.

BASSES
Wiegner, A., *Principal.*
Beckel, J.
Klemm, L.
Dreibrodt, F.
Helm, R.
Helleberg, A.
Glass, R.
Kramer, A.
Mayer, L.

HARPS
Schuecker, E.
Winch, Mrs. Lawrence A.

FLUTES
Andersen, V.
Baumbach, C.
Wiesenbach, H.

PICCOLO
Ballmann, M.

OBOES
Bour, F.
Allner, F.
Bareither, J.

ENGLISH HORN
Schoenheinz, E.

CLARINETS
Schreurs, J.
Quitson, A.
Weisenbach, H.

BASS CLARINET
Meyer, G.

BASSOONS
Lipke, H.
Schon, J.
Leroux, W.

CONTRA-BASSOON
Friedrich, L.

HORNS
Dutschke, H.
Schütz, A.
de Maré, L.
Walker, A.
Müller, A.
Beyer, C.
Chapek, F.
Preller, F.

CORNETS
Rodenkirchen, Ch.
Dietz, F.

TRUMPETS
Ulrich, A.
Scherzberg, F.

BASS TRUMPET
Andauer, A.

TENOR TROMBONES
Gebhardt, O.
Zeller, W.
Nicolini, J.

BASS TROMBONE
Braun, H.

TUBA
Helleberg, A.

KETTLEDRUMS
Loewe, W.
Zettelmann, J.

BASS DRUM
Katsch, Th.

SMALL DRUM
Wagner, E.

CYMBALS
Donati, R.

LIBRARIANS
McNicol, Theo.
Hansen, J.

THE CHICAGO ORCHESTRA
THIRD SEASON
(1893–1894)

First Violins
Bendix, M., *Principal*.
Körner, C.
Boegner, E.
Knoll, E.
Schoeniger, L.
Krauss, A.
Spiering, Th.
Esser, F.
Seidel, R.
Braun, H.
Marum, L.
Weidig, A.
Schmidt, O.
Vilim, J.
Nurnberger, H.
Kruschwitz, E.

Second Violins
Hillman, C., *Principal*.
Zeiss, A.
Hladky, F.
Kühn, B.
Mittelstaedt, F.
Hilliges, R.
Roehrborn, O.
Ulrich, A.
Zettelmann, J.
Wagner, E.
Du Moulin, G.
Jenning, H.
Baumgärtner, J.
Meyer, R.
Fink, R.
Rischar, L.

Violas
Junker, A., *Principal*.
Laendner, J.
Meyer, G.
Wunderle, C.
Dietrich, W.
Katsch, Th.
Volk, F.
Goebert, A.
Maurer, A.
Andauer, A.

Violoncellos
Steindel, B., *Principal*.
Unger, W.
Amato, L.
Diestel, H.
Brückner, C.
Sachleben, H.
Hess, F.
Wagner, F.
Metzdorf, A.
Kalas, J.

Basses
Wiegner, A., *Principal*.
Beckel, J.
Klemm, L.
Dreibrodt, F.
Glass, R.
Helleberg, A.
Bruus, C.
Kramer, A.
Seydel, Th.

Harps
Schuecker, E.
Wunderle, Mrs. C.

Flutes
Andersen, V.
Baumbach, C.
Helms, O.

Piccolo
Ballman, M.

Oboes
Starke, F.
Bertram, C.
De Vaux, E.

English Horn
Hesselbach, O.

Clarinets
Schreurs, J.
Quitson, A.
Wiesenbach, W.

Bass Clarinet
Meyer, C.

Bassoons
Modess, O.
Schon, J.
Leroux, W.

Contra-bassoon
Friedrich, L.

Horns
Dutschke, H.
Lange, R.
de Maré, L.
Walker, A.

Tubas
Müller, A.
Beyer, C.
Forkert, R.
Fritsch, C.

Cornets
Rodenkirchen, Ch.
Dietz, F.

Trumpets
Ulrich, A.
Scherzberg, F.

Bass Trumpet
Andauer, A.

Tenor Trombones
Gebhardt, O.
Zeller, W.
Nicolini, J.

Bass Trombone
Braun, H.

Bass Tuba
Helleberg, A.

Kettledrums
Loewe, W.
Zettelmann, J.

Bass Drum
Katsch, Th.

Small Drum
Wagner, E.

Cymbals
Bunge, C.

Librarian
McNicol, Theo.

THE CHICAGO ORCHESTRA
FOURTH SEASON
(1894-1895)

First Violins
Bendix, M., *Principal.*
Boegner, E.
Spiering, Th.
Esser, F.
Knoll, E.
Schoeniger, L.
Krauss, A.
Marum, L.
Seidel, R.
Braun, H.
Schmidt, O.
Weidig, A.
Vilim, J.
Nurnberger, H.
Kruschwitz, E.
Chapek, J.

Second Violins
Kuehn, B., *Principal.*
Zeiss, A.
Hladky, F.
Hillmann, C.
Mittelstaedt, F.
Hillieges, R.
Roehrborn, O.
Ulrich, A.
Zettelmann, J.
Wagner, E.
DuMoulin, G.
Fink, A.
Baumgaertner, J.
Meyer, R.
Guttenberger, G.
Wenning, F.

Violas
Junker, A., *Principal.*
Laendner, J.
Meyer, G.
Wunderle, C.
Dietrich, W.
Katsch, Th.
Volk, F.
Goebert, A.
Maurer, A.
Andauer, A.

Violoncellos
Steindel, B., *Principal.*
Unger, W.
Amato, L.
Diestel, H.
Brueckner, C.
Sachleben, H.
Hess, F.
Wagner, F.
Metzdorf, A.
Schoersling, P.

Basses
Wiegner, A., *Principal.*
Beckel, J.
Klemm, L.
Dreibrodt, F.
Glass, R.
Helleberg, A.
Bruus, C.
Kramer, A.
Meyer, L.

Harps
Schuecker, E.
Wunderle, Mrs. C.

Flutes
Andersen, V.
Baumbach, C.
Helms, O.

Piccolo
Ballmann, M.

Oboes
Starke, F.
Bertram, C.
Bareither, J.

English Horn
Hesselbach, O.

Clarinets
Schreurs, J.
Quitson, A.
Wiesenbach, W.

Bass Clarinet
Meyer, C.

Bassoons
Modess, O.
Schon, J.
Fernschild, F.

Contra-Bassoon
Friedrich, L.

Horns
Dutschke, H.
Lange, R.
de Maré, L.
Walker, A.

Tubas
Mueller, A.
Beyer, C.
Forkert, R.
Fritsch, C.

Cornets
Rodenkirchen, Ch.
Dietz, F.

Trumpets
Ulrich, A.
Scherzberg, F.

Bass Trumpet
Andauer, A.

Tenor Trombones
Gebhardt, O.
Zeller, W.
Nicolini, J.

Bass Trombone
Braun, H.

Bass Tuba
Helleberg, A.

Kettledrums
Loewe, W.
Zettelmann, J.

Bass Drum
Katsch, Th.

Small Drum
Wagner, E.

Cymbals
Bunge, C.

Organist
Middelschulte, Wm.

Librarian
McNicol, Theo.

THE CHICAGO ORCHESTRA
FIFTH SEASON
(1895-1896)

FIRST VIOLINS
Bendix, M., *Principal.*
Boegner, E.
Spiering, Th.
Esser, F.
Knoll, E.
Schoeniger, L.
Krauss, A.
Schmidt, O.
Seidel, R.
Braun, H.
Weidig, A.
Nurnberger, H.
Kruschwitz, E.
Chapek, J.
Nurnberger, L.
Verdier, A.

SECOND VIOLINS
Kuehn, B., *Principal.*
Roehrborn, O.
Hladky, F.
Hillman, C.
Mittelstaedt, F.
Hilliges, R.
Rabe, H.
Ulrich, A.
Zettelmann, J.
Wagner, E.
Baumgaertner, J.
Diestel, W.
Guttenberger, G.
Meyer, R.
Woollett, W.
Bertram, A.

VIOLAS
Junker, A., *Principal.*
Stock, F.
Meyer, G.
Wunderle, C.
Voellmar, Ch.
Katsch, Th.
Volk, F.
Goebert, A.
Andauer, E.
Fitzek, J.

VIOLONCELLOS
Steindel, B., *Principal.*
Unger, W.
Diestel, H.
Amato, L.
Brueckner, C.
Sachleben, H.
Jennisen, P.
Metzdorf, A.
Schoessling, P.
Heinickel, A.

BASSES
Beckel, J., *Principal.*
Klemm, L.
Dreibrodt, F.
Parbs, H.
Glass, R.
Wolf, O.
Otte, F.
Kramer, A.
Bruus, C.

HARPS
Schuecker, E.
Wunderle, Mrs. C.

FLUTES
Buchheim, A.
Baumbach, C.
Wagner, E.

PICCOLO
Ballmann, M.

OBOES
Starke, F.
Bertram, A.
Bareither, J.

ENGLISH HORN
Hesselbach, O.

CLARINETS
Schreurs, J.
Meyer, H.
Quitson, A.

BASS CLARINET
Meyer, C.

BASSOONS
Lange, H.
Schon, J.
Fernschild, F.

CONTRA-BASSOON
Friedrich, L.

HORNS
Ketz, E.
Wieder, C.
de Maré, L.
Walker, A.

TUBAS
Mueller, C.
Meyer, C.
Forkert, R.
Fritsche, R.

CORNETS
Rodenkirchen, Ch.
Dietz, F.

TRUMPETS
Ulrich, A.
Scherzberg, F.

BASS TRUMPET
Andauer, E.

TENOR TROMBONES
Gebhardt, O.
Zeller, W.
Nicolini, J.

BASS TROMBONE
Braun, H.

BASS TUBA
Otte, F.

KETTLEDRUMS
Loewe, W.
Zettelmann, J.

SMALL DRUM
Wagner, E.

BASS DRUM
Katsch, Th.

CYMBALS
Wunderle, C.

ORGANIST
Middelschulte, W.

LIBRARIANS
McNicol, Theo.
Hansen, J.

THE CHICAGO ORCHESTRA
SIXTH SEASON
(1896-1897)

FIRST VIOLINS
Wendel, E., *Principal.*
Boegner, E.
Esser, F.
Krauss, A.
Knoll, E.
Schoeniger, L.
Seidel, R.
Schmidt, O.
Becker, L.
Braun, H.
Nurnberger, H.
Nurnberger, L.
Troll, C.
Chapek, J.
Woollett, W.
Novak, L.

SECOND VIOLINS
Kuehn, B., *Principal.*
Roehrborn, O.
Hladky, F.
Hillman, C.
Mittelstaedt, F.
Hilliges, R.
Rabe, H.
Ulrich, A.
Zettelmann, J.
Wagner, E.
Diestel, W.
Guttenberger, G.
Meyer, R.
Busse, H.
Schmidt, E.
Ohlheiser, J.

VIOLAS
Junker, A., *Principal.*
Stock, F.
Meyer, G.
Wunderle, C.
Voellmar, Ch.
Katsch, Th.
Volk, F.
Fitzek, J.
Andauer, E.
Fitzek, R.

VIOLONCELLOS
Steindel, B., *Principal.*
Unger, W.
Diestel, H.
Amato, L.
Brueckner, C.
Sachleben, H.
Schoessling, P.
Heinickel, A.
Clusmann, E.
Kalas, J.

BASSES
Beckel, J., *Principal.*
Klemm, L.
Dreibrodt, F.
Parbs, H.
Glass, R.
Wolf, O.
Otte, F.
Kramer, A.
Mayer, L.

HARPS
Schuecker, E.
Wunderle, Mrs. C.

FLUTES
Quensel, A.
Baumbach, C.
Wagner, E.

PICCOLO
Ballmann, M.

OBOES
Starke, F.
Allner, F.
Bareither, J.

ENGLISH HORN
Hesselbach, O.

CLARINETS
Schreurs, J.
Meyer, H.
Gross, J.

BASS CLARINET
Meyer, C.

BASSOONS
Lange, H.
Schon, J.
Rabe, H.

CONTRA-BASSOON
Friedrich, L.

HORNS
de Maré, L.
Wieder, C.
Walker, A.
de Maré, A.

TUBAS
Mueller, C.
Beyer, C.
Forkert, R.
Chapek, F.

CORNETS
Rodenkirchen, Ch.
Dietz, F.

TRUMPETS
Ulrich, A.
Scherzberg, F.

BASS TRUMPET
Andauer, E.

TENOR TROMBONES
Gebhardt, O.
Zeller, W.
Nicolini, J.

BASS TROMBONE
Braun, H.

BASS TUBA
Otte, F.

KETTLEDRUMS
Loewe, W.
Zettelmann, J.

SMALL DRUM
Wagner, E.

BASS DRUM
Katsch, Th.

CYMBALS
Wunderle, C.

ORGANIST
Middelschulte, W.

LIBRARIANS
McNicol, Theo.
Hansen, J.

Appendix

THE CHICAGO ORCHESTRA
SEVENTH SEASON
(1897-1898)

FIRST VIOLINS
Kramer, L., *Principal.*
Baré, E.
Esser, F.
Krauss, A.
Becker, L.
Schoeniger, L.
Seidel, R.
Schmidt, O.
Braun, H.
Chapek, J.
Kruschwitz, E.
Troll, C.
Woollett, W.
DuMoulin, G.
Novak, L.

SECOND VIOLINS
Kuehn, B., *Principal.*
Hladky, F.
Hillman, C.
Mittelstaedt, F.
Busse, A.
Rabe, H.
Ulrich, A.
Zettelmann, J.
Wagner, E.
Baumgartner, J.
Romanes, F.
Rychlik, C.
Fitzek, R.
Schmidt, E.
Ohlheiser, J.

VIOLAS
Keller, J., *Principal.*
Stock, F.
Meyer, G.
Wunderle, C.
Katsch, Th.
Volk, F.
Fitzek, J.
Andauer, E.
Voellmar, Ch.

VIOLONCELLOS
Steindel, B., *Principal.*
Unger, W.

VIOLONCELLOS—Cont.
Brueckner, C.
Amato, L.
Klammsteiner, C.
Sachleben, H.
Schoessling, P.
Heinickel, A.
Clusmann, E.
Kalas, J.

BASSES
Beckel, J., *Principal.*
Klemm, L.
Dreibrodt, F.
Parbs, H.
Glass, R.
Wolf, O.
Otte, F.
Kramer, A.
Mayer, L.

HARPS
Schuecker, E.
Wunderle, Mrs. C.

FLUTES
Quensel, A.
Baumbach, C.
Wagner, E.

PICCOLO
Ballmann, M.

OBOES
Starke, F.
Allner, F.
Bareither, J.

ENGLISH HORN
Hesselbach, O.

CLARINETS
Schreurs, J.
Busse, L.
Gross, J.

BASS CLARINET
Meyer, C.

BASSOONS
Bachmann, F.
Schon, J.
Rabe, H.

CONTRA-BASSOON
Friedrich, L.

HORNS
de Maré, L.
Wieder, C.
Pieper, C.
Walker, A.

TUBAS
Mueller, C.
Beyer, C.
Forkert, R.
Chapek, F.

CORNETS
Rodenkirchen, Ch.
Dietz, F.

TRUMPETS
Ulrich, A.
Scherzberg, F.

BASS TRUMPET
Andauer, E.

TENOR TROMBONES
Gebhardt, O.
Zeller, W.
Nicolini, J.

BASS TROMBONE
Braun, H.

BASS TUBA
Otte, F.

KETTLEDRUMS
Loewe, W.
Zettelmann, J.

SMALL DRUM
Wagner, E.

BASS DRUM
Katsch, Th.

CYMBALS
Wunderle, C.

ORGANIST
Middelschulte, W.

LIBRARIANS
McNicol, Theo.
Hansen, J.

Through changes in the *personnel* of the Orchestra the following men played for a portion of the season: L. Nurnberger, first violin, and M. Eichheim, 'cello.

THE CHICAGO ORCHESTRA
EIGHTH SEASON
(1898-1899)

FIRST VIOLINS
Kramer, L., *Principal*.
Baré, E.
Krauss, A.
Becker, L.
Seidel, R.
Schoeniger, L.
Braun, H.
Marx, L.
Nurnberger, H.
Nurnberger, L.
Chapek, J.
Kruschwitz, E.
Troll, C.
Dimond, H.
Silberstein, J.

SECOND VIOLINS
Kuehn, B., *Principal*.
Hladky, F.
Hillmann, C.
Mittelstaedt, F.
Busse, A.
Rabe, H.
Ulrich, A.
Zettelmann, J.
Wagner, E.
Dasch, G.
Woollett, W.
Baumgaertner, J.
Novak, L.
Recoschewitz, J.
Lamprecht, W.

VIOLAS
Esser, F., *Principal*.
Stock, F.
Meyer, G.
Wunderle, C.
Katsch, Theo.
Volk, F.
Fitzek, J.

VIOLAS—Cont.
Fitzek, R.
Andauer, E.
Strobach, C.

VIOLONCELLOS
Steindel, B., *Principal*.
Unger, W.
Brueckner, C.
Amato, L.
Corell, L.
Eicheim, M.
Heinickel, A.
Clusmann, E.
Kalas, J.
Ambrosius, R.

BASSES
Beckel, J., *Principal*.
Klemm, L.
Dreibrodt, F.
Parbs, H.
Glass, R.
Wolf, O.
Kramer, A.
Mayer, L.

HARP
Schuecker, E.

FLUTES
Quensel, A.
Baumbach, C.

PICCOLO
Ballmann, M.

OBOES
Starke, F.
Allner, F.

ENGLISH HORN
Hesselbach, O.

CLARINETS
Schreurs, J.
Busse, A.

BASS CLARINET
Meyer, C.

BASSOONS
Bachmann, M.
Schon, J.

CONTRA-BASSOON
Friedrich, L.

HORNS
de Maré, L.
Wieder, C.
Pieper, C.
Albrecht, C.

TRUMPETS
Rodenkirchen, Ch.
Dietz, F.
Ulrich, A.

BASS TRUMPET
Andauer, E.

TROMBONES
Gebhardt, O.
Zeller, W.
Nicolini, J.

BASS TUBA
Otte, F.

TIMPANI
Loewe, W.

SIDE DRUM, TRIANGLE, TAMBOURINE, ETC.
Zettelmann, J.
Wagner, E.

BASS DRUM
Katsch, Theo.

ORGANIST
Middelschulte, W.

LIBRARIANS
McNicol, Theo.
Hansen, J.

THE CHICAGO ORCHESTRA
NINTH SEASON
(1899-1900)

FIRST VIOLINS
  Kramer, L., *Principal.*
  Baré, E.
  Krauss, A.
  Becker, L.
  Seidel, R.
  Kuiper, Jr.
  Schoeniger, L.
  Braun, H.
  Marx, L.
  Malcherek, K.
  Nurnberger, H.
  Nurnberger, L.
  Chapek, J.
  Kruschwitz, E.
  Troll, C.
  Schulze, W.

SECOND VIOLINS
  Kuehn, B., *Principal.*
  Hladky, F.
  Hillmann, C.
  Dasch, G.
  Busse, A.
  Rabe, H.
  Ulrich, A.
  Nickell, M.
  Wagner, E.
  Silberstein, J.
  Woollett, W.
  Du Moulin, G.
  Novak, L.
  Baumgaertner, J.
  Recoschewitz, J.
  Lampert, C.

VIOLAS
  Esser, F., *Principal.*
  Stock, F.
  Meyer, G.
  Wunderle, C.
  Mittelstaedt, F.
  Volk, F.
  Fitzek, J.
  Fitzek, R.
  Andauer, E.
  Strobach, C.

VIOLONCELLOS
  Steindel, B., *Principal.*
  Unger, W.
  Brueckner, C.
  Amato, L.
  Corell, L.
  Borch, G.
  Heinickel, A.
  Clusmann, E.
  Kalas, J.
  Ambrosius, R.

BASSES
  Beckel, J., *Principal.*
  Klemm, L.
  Dreibrodt, F.
  Parbs, H.
  Glass, R.
  Wolf, O.
  Kramer, A.
  Mayer, L.

HARPS
  Suppantschitsch, R.
  Singer, W.

ORGANIST
  Middelschulte, W.

FLUTES
  Quensel, A.
  Baumbach, C.

PICCOLO
  Ballmann, M.

OBOES
  Starke, F.
  Allner, F.

ENGLISH HORN
  Hesselbach, O.

CLARINETS
  Schreurs, J.
  Busse, A.

BASS CLARINET
  Meyer, C.

BASSOONS
  Kruse, P.
  Schon, J.

CONTRA-BASSOON
  Friedrich, L.

HORNS
  de Maré, L.
  Wieder, C.
  Pieper, C.
  Albrecht, C.

TRUMPETS
  Rodenkirchen, Ch.
  Dietz, F.
  Ulrich, A.

BASS TRUMPET
  Andauer, E.

TROMBONES
  Gebhardt, O.
  Zeller, W.
  Nicolini, J.

BASS TUBA
  Otte, F.

TIMPANI
  Zettelmann, J.

SIDE DRUM, TRIANGLE, ETC.
  Nickell, M.
  Wagner, E.

BASS DRUM
  Mittelstaedt, F.

LIBRARIANS
  McNicol, Theo.
  Hansen, J.

THE CHICAGO ORCHESTRA
TENTH SEASON
(1900-1901)

FIRST VIOLINS
  Kramer, L., *Principal.*
  Baré, E.
  Krauss, A.
  Becker, L.
  Seidel, R.
  Kuiper, J.
  Schoeniger, L.
  Braun, H.
  Marx, L.
  Malcherek, K.
  Nurnberger, H.
  Nurnberger, L.
  Chapek, J.
  Kruschwitz, E.
  Troll, C.
  Schulze, W.

SECOND VIOLINS
  Kuehn, B., *Principal.*
  Hladky, F.
  Hillmann, C.
  Dasch, G.
  Busse, A.
  Rabe, H.
  Ulrich, A.
  Singer, W.
  Silberstein, J.
  Woollett, W.
  DuMoulin, G.
  Novak, L.
  Baumgaertner, J.
  Recoschewitz, J.
  Lampert, C.
  Itte, F.

VIOLAS
  Esser, F., *Principal.*
  Stock, F.
  Meyer, G.
  Wunderle, C.
  Mittelstaedt, F.

VIOLAS—Cont.
  Volk, F.
  Fitzek, J.
  Fitzek, R.
  Andauer, E.
  Strobach, C.

VIOLONCELLOS
  Steindel, B., *Principal.*
  Unger, W.
  Brueckner, C.
  Amato, L.
  Corell, L.
  Heinickel, A.
  Clusmann, E.
  Kalas, J.
  Ambrosius, R.
  Felber, H.

BASSES
  Beckel, J., *Principal.*
  Klemm, L.
  Dreibrodt, F.
  Parbs, H.
  Glass, R.
  Wolf, O.
  Kramer, A.
  Mayer, L.

HARPS
  Wunderle, Mrs. C.
  Singer, W.

ORGANIST
  Middelschulte, W.

FLUTES
  Quensel, A.
  Baumbach, C.

PICCOLO
  Ballmann, M.

OBOES
  Starke, F.
  Allner, F.

ENGLISH HORN
  Hesselbach, O.

CLARINETS
  Schreurs, J.
  Busse, A.

BASS CLARINET
  Meyer, C.

BASSOONS
  Kruse, P.
  Schon, J.

CONTRA-BASSOON
  Friedrich, L.

HORNS
  de Maré, L.
  Wieder, C.
  Pieper, C.
  Albrecht, C.

TRUMPETS
  Rodenkirchen, Ch.
  Dietz, F.
  Ulrich, A.
  Felber, H.

TROMBONES
  Gebhardt, O.
  Zeller, W.
  Nicolini, J.

BASS TUBA
  Otte, F.

TIMPANI
  Zettelmann, J.

SIDE DRUM, TRIANGLE,
    TAMBOURINE, ETC.
  Wintrich, M.
  Wagner, E.

BASS DRUM
  Mittelstaedt, F.

LIBRARIANS
  McNicol, Theo.
  Hansen, J.

THE CHICAGO ORCHESTRA
ELEVENTH SEASON
(1901-1902)

FIRST VIOLINS
Kramer, L., *Principal.*
Baré, E.
Krauss, A.
Becker, L.
Seidel, R.
Marx, L.
Schoeniger, L.
Braun, H.
Kuiper, J.
Malcherek, K.
Nurnberger, L.
Chapek, J.
Kruschwitz, E.
Fischer, G.
Schulze, W.
Rhys, S.

SECOND VIOLINS
Kuehn, B., *Principal.*
Hladky, F.
Hillmann, C.
Dasch, G.
Busse, A.
Rabe, H.
Ulrich, A.
Singer, W.
Silberstein, J.
Woollett, W.
DuMoulin, G.
Novak, L.
Baumgaertner, J.
Itte, F.
Bichl, J.

VIOLAS
Esser, F., *Principal.*
Stock, F.
Meyer, G.
Wunderle, C.
Mittelstaedt, F.
Volk, F.
Fitzek, J.

VIOLAS—Cont.
Fitzek, R.
Andauer, E.
Strobach, C.

VIOLONCELLOS
Steindel, B., *Principal.*
Unger, W.
Brueckner, C.
Ambrosius, R.
Corell, L.
Herner, J.
Heinickel, A.
Clusmann, E.
Kalas, J.
Felber, H.

BASSES
Beckel, J., *Principal.*
Klemm, L.
Dreibrodt, F.
Parbs, H.
Glass, R.
Wolf, O.
Otte, F.
Kramer, A.
Mayer, L.

HARPS
Wunderle, Mrs. C.
Singer, W.

ORGANIST
Middelschulte, W.

FLUTES
Quensel, A.
Baumbach, C.

PICCOLO
Ballmann, M.

OBOES
Starke, F.
Allner, F.

ENGLISH HORN
Hesselbach, O.

CLARINETS
Schreurs, J.
Busse, A.

BASS CLARINET
Meyer, C.

BASSOONS
Kruse, P.
Schon, J.

CONTRA-BASSOON
Friedrich, L.

HORNS
de Maré, L.
Wieder, C.
Frank, W.
Albrecht, C.

TRUMPETS
Rodenkirchen, Ch.
Dietz, F.
Ulrich, A.
Felber, H.

TROMBONES
Gebhardt, O.
Zeller, W.
Nicolini, J.

BASS TUBA
Otte, F.

TIMPANI
Zettelmann, J.

SIDE DRUM, TRIANGLE,
TAMBOURINE, ETC.
Wintrich, M.
Wagner, E.

BASS DRUM
Mittelstaedt, F.

LIBRARIANS
McNicol, Theo.
Hansen, J.

THE CHICAGO ORCHESTRA
TWELFTH SEASON
(1902-1903)

First Violins
Kramer, L., *Principal.*
Franke, C.
Krauss, A.
Becker, L.
Seidel, R.
Marx, L.
Schoeniger, L.
Braun, H.
Moerenhout, C.
Nurnberger, L.
Chapek, J.
Rhys, S.
Schulze, W.
Bass, G.
Kruschwitz, E.

Second Violins
Kuehn, B., *Principal.*
Hladky, F.
Hillmann, C.
Dasch, G.
Busse, A.
Rabe, H.
Ulrich, A.
Silberstein, J.
Woollett, W.
Novak, L.
Lampert, C.
Bichl, J.
Itte, F.
Singer, W.

Violas
Esser, F., *Principal.*
Stock, F.
Meyer, G.
Wunderle, C.
Volk, F.
Mittelstaedt, F.
Fitzek, J.
Fitzek, R.
Andauer, E.
Strobach, C.

Violoncellos
Steindel, B., *Principal.*
Unger, W.
Brueckner, C.
Ambrosius, R.
Corell, L.
Herner, J.
Heinickel, A.
Clusmann, E.
Kalas, J.
Felber, H.

Basses
Beckel, J., *Principal.*
Klemm, L.
Dreibrodt, F.
Parbs, H.
Glass, R.
Wolf, O.
Kramer, A.
Mayer, L.
Otte, F.

Harps
Tramonti, E.
Wunderle, Mrs. C.
Singer, W.

Organist
Middelschulte, W.

Flutes
Quensel, A.
Baumbach, C.

Piccolo
Ballmann, M.

Oboes
Starke, F.
Allner, F.

English Horn
Hesselbach, O.

Clarinets
Schreurs, J.
Busse, A.

Bass Clarinet
Meyer, C.

Bassoon
Kruse, P.
Rabe, H.

Contra-Bassoon
Friedrich, L.

Horns
de Maré, L.
Wieder, C.
Frank, W.
Albrecht, C.

Trumpets
Steffens, P.
Llewellyn, J.
Ulrich, A.
Felber, H.

Trombones
Gebhardt, O.
Zeller, W.
Nicolini, J.

Bass Tuba
Otte, F.

Timpani
Zettelmann, J.

Side Drum, Triangle, Tambourine, etc.
Wintrich, M.
Wagner, E.

Bass Drum
Mittelstaedt, F.

Librarians
McNicol, Theo.
Hansen, J.

THE CHICAGO ORCHESTRA
THIRTEENTH SEASON
(1903-1904)

FIRST VIOLINS
Kramer, L., *Principal.*
Meyer, P.
Krauss, A.
Becker, L.
Seidel, R.
Marx, L.
Moerenhout, C.
Braun, H.
Tak, E.
Nurnberger, L.
Chapek, J.
Combel, A.
Kruschwitz, E.
Bass, G.
Rhys, S.

SECOND VIOLINS
Kuehn, B., *Principal.*
Hladky, F.
Hillmann, C.
Dasch, G.
Silberstein, J.
Woollett, W.
Novak, L.
Lampert, C.
Bichl, J.
Itte, F.
Fitzek, R.
Singer, W.
Busse, A.
Ulrich, A.

VIOLAS
Esser, F., *Principal.*
Stock, F.
Meyer, G.
Wunderle, C.
Volk, F.
Hesselbach, O.
Fitzek, J.
Andauer, E.
Mittelstaedt, F.
Strobach, C.

VIOLONCELLOS
Steindel, B., *Principal.*
Unger, W.
Brueckner, C.
Ambrosius, R.
Corell, L.
Heinickel, A.
Klammsteiner, C.
Clusmann, E.
Kalas, J.
Felber, H.

BASSES
Beckel, J., *Principal.*
Klemm, L.
Parbs, H.
Glass, R.
Wolf, O.
Kramer, A.
Mayer, L.
Krausse, J.
Otte, F.

HARPS
Tramonti, E.
Singer, W.

ORGANIST
Middelschulte, W.

FLUTES
Quensel, A.
Baumbach, C.

PICCOLO
Ballmann, M.

OBOES
Barthel, A.
Bour, F.

ENGLISH HORNS
Starke, F.
Hesselbach, O.

CLARINETS
Schreurs, J.
Gross, J.

BASS CLARINET
Meyer, C.

BASSOON
Kruse, P.
Rabe, H.

CONTRA-BASSOON
Friedrich, L.

HORNS
de Maré, L.
Wieder, C.
Frank, W.
Albrecht, C.

TRUMPETS
Handke, P.
Llewellyn, J.

CORNETS
Ulrich, A.
Felber, H.

TROMBONES
Gebhardt, O.
Zeller, W.
Nicolini, J.

BASS TUBA
Otte, F.

TIMPANI
Zettelmann, J.

PERCUSSIONS
Wintrich, M.
Wagner, E.
Mittelstaedt, F.

LIBRARIANS
McNicol, Theo.
Whitcomb, W.

THE THEODORE THOMAS ORCHESTRA
FOURTEENTH SEASON
(1904-1905)

FIRST VIOLINS
  Kramer, L., *Principal.*
  Becker, L.
  Krauss, A.
  Seidel, R.
  Marx, L.
  Moerenhout, C.
  Braun, H.
  Tak, E.
  Nurnberger, L.
  Chapek, J.
  Rhys, S.
  Combel, A.
  Bass, G.
  Roehrborn, O.
  Kruschwitz, E.

SECOND VIOLINS
  Kuehn, B., *Principal.*
  Hladky, F.
  Hillmann, C.
  Dasch, G.
  Silberstein, J.
  Woollett, W.
  Novak, L.
  Lampert, C.
  Bichl, J.
  Itte, F.
  Fitzek, R.
  Busse, A.
  Singer, W.
  Ulrich, A.
  Rabe, H.

VIOLAS
  Esser, F., *Principal.*
  *Stock, F.
  Meyer, G.
  Haferburg, C.
  Volk, F.
  Hesselbach, O.
  Fitzek, J.
  Andauer, E.

VIOLAS—Cont.
  Mittelstaedt, F.
  Strobach, C.

VIOLONCELLOS
  Steindel, B., *Principal.*
  Unger, W.
  Brueckner, C.
  Ambrosius, R.
  Corell, L.
  Stelle, F.
  Klammsteiner, C.
  Clusmann, E.
  Kalas, J.
  Felber, H.

BASSES
  Beckel, J., *Principal.*
  Klemm, L.
  Parbs, H.
  Glass, R.
  Wolf, O.
  Kramer, A.
  Mayer, L.
  Krausse, J.
  Otte, F.

HARPS
  Tramonti, E.
  Singer, W.

ORGANIST
  Middelschulte, W.

FLUTES
  Quensel, A.
  Baumbach, C.

PICCOLO
  Ballmann, M.

OBOES
  Barthel, A.
  Bour, F.

ENGLISH HORNS
  Starke, F.
  Hesselbach, O.

CLARINETS
  Schreurs, J.
  Gross, J.

BASS CLARINET
  Meyer, C.

BASSOONS
  Kruse, P.
  Rabe, H.

CONTRA-BASSOON
  Friedrich, L.

HORNS
  de Maré, L.
  Crass, M.
  Frank, W.
  Albrecht, C.

TRUMPETS
  Handke, P.
  Llewellyn, J.

CORNETS
  Ulrich, A.
  Felber, H.

TROMBONES
  Stange, G.
  Zeller, W.
  Nicolini, J.

BASS TUBA
  Otte, F.

TIMPANI
  Zettelmann, J.

PERCUSSIONS
  Wintrich, M.
  Wagner, E.
  Mittelstaedt, F.

LIBRARIANS
  McNicol, Theo.
  Whitcomb, W.

*Frederick Stock was elected Conductor April 11, 1905.

THE THEODORE THOMAS ORCHESTRA
FIFTEENTH SEASON
(1905-1906)

FIRST VIOLINS
  Kramer, L., *Principal.*
  Becker, L.
  Krauss, A.
  Seidel, R.
  Marx, L.
  Roehrborn, O.
  Moerenhout, C.
  Nurnberger, H.
  Braun, H.
  Nurnberger, L.
  Chapek, J.
  Rhys, S.
  Bass, G.
  Itte, F.
  Silberstein, J.
  Kruschwitz, E.

SECOND VIOLINS
  Kuehn, B., *Principal.*
  Hladky, F.
  Hillmann, C.
  Dasch, G.
  Woollett, W.
  Novak, L.
  Bichl, J.
  Lampert, C.
  Konrad, W.
  Fitzek, R.
  Busse, A.
  Singer, W.
  Rabe, H.
  Ulrich, A.

VIOLAS
  Esser, F., *Principal.*
  Meyer, G.
  Haferburg, C.
  Volk, F.
  Diestel, W.
  Fitzek, J.
  Hesselbach, O.

VIOLAS—Cont.
  Andauer, E.
  Mittelstaedt, F.
  Strobach, C.

VIOLONCELLOS
  Steindel, B., *Principal.*
  Unger, W.
  Brueckner, C.
  Ambrosius, R.
  Corell, L.
  Britt, H.
  Klammsteiner, C.
  Clusmann, E.
  Kalas, J.
  Felber, H.

BASSES
  Beckel, J., *Principal.*
  Klemm, L.
  Parbs, H.
  Glass, R.
  Wolf, O.
  Kramer, A.
  Mayer, L.
  Otte, F.

HARPS
  Tramonti, E.
  Singer, W.

ORGANIST
  Middelschulte, W.

FLUTES
  Quensel, A.
  Baumbach, C.

PICCOLO
  Ballmann, M.

OBOES
  Barthel, A.
  Bour, F.

ENGLISH HORNS
  Starke, F.
  Hesselbach, O.

CLARINETS
  Schreurs, J.
  Gross, J.

BASS CLARINET
  Meyer, C.

BASSOONS
  Kruse, P.
  Rabe, H.

CONTRA-BASSOON
  Friedrich, L.

HORNS
  de Maré, L.
  Cras, R.
  Frank, W.
  Albrecht, C.

TRUMPETS
  Handke, P.
  Llewellyn, J.

CORNETS
  Ulrich, A.
  Felber, H.

TROMBONES
  Stange, G.
  Zeller, W.
  Nicolini, J.

BASS TUBA
  Otte, F.

TIMPANI
  Zettelmann, J.

PERCUSSIONS
  Wintrich, M.
  Wagner, E.
  Mittelstaedt, F.

LIBRARIANS
  McNicol, Theo.
  Whitcomb, W.

THE THEODORE THOMAS ORCHESTRA
SIXTEENTH SEASON
(1906-1907)

First Violins
Kramer, L., *Principal.*
Becker, L.
Krauss, A.
Seidel, R.
Marx, L.
Schulz, M.
Braun, H.
Nurnberger, L.
Moerenhout, C.
Chapek, J.
Roehrborn, O.
Nurnberger, H.
Bass, G.
Itte, F.
Silberstein, J.
Kruschwitz, E.

Second Violins
Kuehn, B., *Principal.*
Hladky, F.
Hillmann, C.
Woollett, W.
Novak, L.
Barker, O.
Bichl, J.
Meinken, C.
Recoschewitz, J.
Lampert, C.
Konrad, W.
Fitzek, R.
Busse, A.
Singer, W.
Rabe, H.
Ulrich, A.

Violas
Esser, F., *Principal.*
Meyer, G.
Dasch, G.
Schroeter, R.
Haferburg, C.
Volk, F.
Fitzek, J.
Diestel, W.
Hesselbach, O.

Violas—Cont.
Andauer, E.
Mittelstaedt, F.
Strobach, C.

Violoncellos
Steindel, B., *Principal.*
Unger, W.
Brueckner, C.
Ambrosius, R.
Corell, L.
Britt, H.
Klammsteiner, C.
Clusmann, E.
Kalas, J.
Felber, H.

Basses
Beckel, J., *Principal.*
Klemm, L.
Parbs, H.
Glass, R.
Wolf, O.
Hase, A.
Kramer, A.
Mayer, L.
Otte, F.

Harps
Tramonti, E.
Singer, W.

Organist
Middelschulte, W.

Flutes
Quensel, A.
Baumbach, C.

Piccolos
Ballmann, M.
Schroeter, R.

Oboes
Barthel, A.
Bour, F.

English Horns
Starke, F.
Hesselbach, O.

Clarinets
Schreurs, J.
Gross, J.
Busse, A.

Bass Clarinet
Meyer, C.

Bassoons
Kruse, P.
Rabe, H.
Kruschwitz, E.

Contra-Bassoon
Friedrich, L.

Horns
de Maré, L.
Cras, R.
Frank, W.
Albrecht, C.

Trumpets
Handke, P.
Llewellyn, J.

Cornets
Ulrich, A.
Felber, H.

Bass Trumpet
Andauer, E.

Trombones
Stange, G.
Zeller, W.
Nicolini, J.

Bass Tuba
Otte, F.

Timpani
Zettelmann, J.

Percussions
Wintrich, M.
Wagner, E.
Mittelstaedt, F.
Strobach, C.

Librarian
McNicol, Theo.

THE THEODORE THOMAS ORCHESTRA
SEVENTEENTH SEASON
(1907-1908)

FIRST VIOLINS
Kramer, L., *Principal.*
Becker, L.
Krauss, A.
Seidel, R.
Marx, L.
Kortschak, H.
Braun, H.
Nurnberger, L.
Moerenhout, C.
Chapek, J.
Schulz, M.
Wunderle, C.
Nurnberger, H.
Bass, G.
Itte, F.
Silberstein, J.

SECOND VIOLINS
Hillmann, C., *Principal.*
Hladky, F.
Woollett, W.
Kruschwitz, E.
Novak, L.
Mangold, R.
Busse, A.
Ulrich, A.
Singer, W.
Rabe, H.
Bichl, J.
Lampert, C.
Meinken, C.
Recoschewitz, J.
Fitzek, R.
Konrad, W.

VIOLAS
Esser, F., *Principal.*
Roehrborn, O.
Meyer, G.
Dasch, G.
Schroeter, R.
Hesselbach, O.
Mittelstaedt, F.
Strobach, C.
Volk, F.

VIOLAS—Cont.
Fitzek, J.
Diestel, W.
Andauer, E.

VIOLONCELLOS
Steindel, B., *Principal.*
Unger, W.
Brueckner, C.
Ambrosius, R.
Corell, L.
Felber, H.
Klammsteiner, C.
Clusman, E.
Kalas, J.
Heinickel, A.

BASSES
Beckel, J., *Principal.*
Klemm, L.
Parbs, H.
Glass, R.
Wolf, O.
Hase, A.
Maedler, R.
Mayer, L.
Otte, F.

HARPS
Tramonti, E.
Singer, W.

ORGANIST
Middelschulte, W.

FLUTES
Quensel, A.
Baumbach, C.

PICCOLOS
Ballmann, M.
Schroeter, R.

OBOES
Barthel, A.
Allner, F.

ENGLISH HORNS
Starke, F.
Hesselbach, O.

CLARINETS
Schreurs, J.
Gross, J.
Busse, A.

BASS CLARINET
Meyer, C.

BASSOONS
Kruse, P.
Rabe, H.
Kruschwitz, E.

CONTRA-BASSOON
Friedrich, L.

HORNS
de Maré, L.
Pottag, M.
Frank, W.
Albrecht, C.

TRUMPETS
Schubert, O.
Handke, P.

CORNETS
Ulrich, A.
Felber, H.

BASS TRUMPET
Andauer, E.

TROMBONES
Stange, G.
Zeller, W.
Nicolini, J.

BASS TUBA
Otte, F.

TIMPANI
Zettelmann, J.

PERCUSSIONS
Wintrich, M.
Wagner, E.
Mittelstaedt, F.
Strobach, C.

LIBRARIAN
McNicol, Theo.

THE THEODORE THOMAS ORCHESTRA
TWENTIETH SEASON
(1910-1911)

First Violins
Letz, H., *Principal.*
Kortschak, H.
Zukovsky, A.
Krauss, A.
Seidel, R.
Ruinen, J.
Marx, L.
Culp, S.
Van der Voort, A.
Nurnberger, L.
Roehrborn, O.
Itte, F.
Mangold, R.
Uterhart, C.
Rhys, S.
Braun, H.

Second Violins
Hillmann, C., *Principal.*
Silberstein, J.
Barker, O.
Woollett, W.
Novak, L.
Singer, W.
Busse, A.
Ulrich, A.
Woelfel, P.
Bichl, J.
Meinken, C.
Du Moulin, G.
Fitzek, R.
Fitzek, J.
Konrad, W.
Demuth, F.

Violas
Esser, F., *Principal.*
Dasch, G.
Meyer, G.
Nurnberger, H.
Schroeter, R.
Hesselbach, O.
Mittelstaedt, F.
Strobach, C.
Volk, F.
Andauer, E.

Violoncellos
Steindel, B., *Principal.*
Unger, W.
Brueckner, C.
Ambrosius, R.
Corell, L.
Felber, H.
Klammsteiner, C.
Clusmann, E.
Kalas, J.
Heinickel, A.

Basses
Jiskra, V., *Principal.*
Klemm, L.
Parbs, H.
Wolf, O.
Maedler, R.
Speckin, W.
Stelle, Fr.
Sauter, C.
Otte, F.

Harps
Tramonti, E.
Singer, W.

Organist
Middelschulte, W.

Flutes
Quensel, A.
Baumbach, C.

Piccolos
Furman, J.
Schroeter, R.

Oboes
Barthel, A.
Stiegelmayer, K.
Hesselbach, O.

English Horn
Starke, F.

Clarinets
Schreurs, J.
Hoffmeester, T.
Busse, A.
Parbs, H.

Bass Clarinet
Meyer, C.

Bassoons
Kruse, P.
Rabe, H.
Schon, J.

Contra-Bassoon
Friedrich, L.

Horns
de Maré, L.
Pottag, M.
Frank, W.
Albrecht, C.

Trumpets
Schubert, O.
Handke, P.

Cornets
Ulrich, A.
Felber, H.

Bass Trumpet
Andauer, E.

Trombones
Stange, G.
Zeller, W.
Nicolini, J.

Bass Tuba
Otte, F.

Timpani
Zettelmann, J.

Percussions
Wintrich, M.
Wagner, E.
Mittelstaedt, F.
Strobach, C.

Librarian
McNicol, Theo.

THE THEODORE THOMAS ORCHESTRA
TWENTY-FIRST SEASON
(1911-1912)

FIRST VIOLINS
Letz, H., *Principal.*
Kortschak, H.
Zukovsky, A.
Krauss, A.
Seidel, R.
Culp, S.
Ruinen, J.
Hillmann, C.
Van der Voort, A.
Korb, A.
Nurnberger, L.
Itte, F.
Mangold, R.
Rhys, S.
Bass, G.
Du Moulin, G.

SECOND VIOLINS
Roehrborn, O., *Principal.*
Silberstein, J.
Braun, H.
Woollett, W.
Barker, O.
Novak, L.
Singer, W.
Busse, A.
Rabe, H.
Ulrich, A.
Woelfel, P.
Bichl, J.
Fitzek, R.
Fitzek, J.
Konrad, W.

VIOLAS
Esser, F., *Principal.*
Dasch, G.
Meyer, G.
Nurnberger, H.
Schroeter, R.
Hesselbach, O.
Mittelstaedt, F.
Strobach, C.
Volk, F.
Andauer, E.

VIOLONCELLOS
Steindel, B., *Principal.*
Unger, W.
Brueckner, C.
Ambrosius, R.
Corell, L.
Felber, H.
Klammsteiner, C.
Heinickel, A.
Polak, J.

BASSES
Jiskra, V., *Principal.*
Parbs, H.
Wolf, O.
Maedler, R.
Speckin, W.
Gatterfeld, E.
Friedrich, O.
Sauter, C.
Otte, F.

HARPS
Tramonti, E.
Singer, W.

ORGANIST
Middelschulte, W.

FLUTES
Quensel, A.
Baumbach, C.

PICCOLOS
Furman, J.
Schroeter, R.

OBOES
Barthel, A.
Stiegelmayer, K.
Hesselbach, O.

ENGLISH HORN
Starke, F.

CLARINETS
Schreurs, J.
Busse, A.
Parbs, H.

BASS CLARINET
Meyer, C.

BASSOONS
Kruse, P.
Krieglstein, W.
Rabe, H.

CONTRA-BASSOON
Friedrich, O.

HORNS
de Maré, L.
Pottag, M.
Frank, W.
Albrecht, C.

TRUMPETS
Borodkin, J.
Handke, P.

CORNETS
Ulrich, A.
Felber, H.

TROMBONES
Stange, G.
Zeller, W.
Gunther, A.

BASS TUBA
Otte, F.

TIMPANI
Zettelmann, J.

PERCUSSIONS
Wintrich, M.
Wagner, E.
Mittelstaedt, F.
Strobach, C.

LIBRARIAN
McNicol, Theo.

THE CHICAGO SYMPHONY ORCHESTRA
TWENTY-FOURTH SEASON
(1914-1915)

FIRST VIOLINS
Weisbach, H., *Principal*
Zukovsky, A.
Krauss, A.
Seidel, R.
Itte, F.
Hillmann, C.
Bass, G.
Nurnberger, L.
Felber, H., Jr.
Bramhall, J.
Rhys, S.
Du Moulin, G.
Silberstein, J.
Rosensweet, D.
Hecker, C.

SECOND VIOLINS
Roehrborn, O., *Principal*.
Woelfel, P.
Barker, O.
Braun, H.
Novak, L.
Woollett, W.
Recoschewitz, J.
Bichl, J.
Konrad, W.
Rogers, H.
Schoeniger, L.
Hand, A.
Fitzek, R.
Singer, W.
Rabe, H.
Busse, A.

VIOLAS
Esser, F., *Principal*.
Dasch, G.
Meyer, G.
Strobach, C.
Volk, F.
Schroeter, R.
Andauer, E.
Elander, C.
Fitzek, J.
Hesselbach, O.
Mittelstaedt, F.

VIOLONCELLOS
Steindel, B., *Principal*.
Stoeber, E.
Unger, W.
Brueckner, C.
Ambrosius, R.
Du Moulin, T.
Felber, H., Sr.
Klammsteiner, C.
Polak, J.
Heinickel, A.

BASSES
Jiskra, V., *Principal*.
Parbs, H.
Wolf, O.
Maedler, R.
Speckin, W.
Houdek, J.
Sauter, C.
Wemheuer, O.
Gatterfeld, E.

HARPS
Tramonti, E.
Singer, W.

ORGANIST
Middelschulte, W.

FLUTES
Quensel, A.
Baumbach, C.

PICCOLOS
Furman, J.
Schroeter, R.

OBOES
Barthel, A.
Stiegelmayer, K.
Hesselbach, O.

ENGLISH HORN
Napolilli, F.

CLARINETS
Schreurs, J.
Gross, J.
Busse, A.

BASS CLARINET
Meyer, C.

BASSOONS
Kruse, P.
Weiss, A.
Rabe, H.

CONTRA-BASSOON
Krieglstein, W.

HORNS
de Maré, L.
Pottag, M.
Frank, W.
Albrecht, C.
Johnson, H.
Kryl, F.

TRUMPETS
Llewellyn, E.
Hartl, J.

CORNETS
Ulrich, A.
Felber, H., Sr.

BASS TRUMPET
Andauer, E.

TROMBONES
Stange, G.
Gunther, A.
Kuss, R.

BASS TUBA
Gatterfeld, E.

TIMPANI
Zettelmann, J.

PERCUSSIONS
Wintrich, M.
Wagner, E.
Mittelstaedt, F.

LIBRARIAN
McNicol, Theo.

THE CHICAGO SYMPHONY ORCHESTRA
TWENTY-FIFTH SEASON
(1915-1916)

FIRST VIOLINS
Weisbach, H., *Principal*
Zukovsky, A.
Gardner, S.
Krauss, A.
Seidel, R.
Itte, F.
Bass, G.
Hillmann, C.
Nurnberger, L.
Felber, H., Jr.
Bramhall, J.
Rhys, S.
Du Moulin, G.
Silberstein, J.
Rosensweet, D.
Hecker, C.

SECOND VIOLINS
Roehrborn, O., *Principal*.
Woelfel, P.
Barker, O.
Braun, H.
Novak, L.
Woollett, W.
Recoschewitz, J.
Hladky, F.
Bichl, J.
Konrad, W.
Hand, A.
Fitzek, R.
Christensen, T.
Singer, W.
Rabe, H.
Busse, A.

VIOLAS
Esser, F., *Principal*.
Dasch, G.
Meyer, G.
Strobach, C.
Volk, F.
Schroeter, R.
Andauer, E.
Elander, C.
Fitzek, J.
Hesselbach, O.
Mittelstaedt, F.

VIOLONCELLOS
Steindel, B., *Principal*.
Ferner, W.
Unger, W.
Brueckner, C.
Ambrosius, R.
Du Moulin, T.
Felber, H., Sr.
Klammsteiner, C.
Polak, J.
Heinickel, A.

BASSES
Jiskra, V., *Principal*.
Parbs, H.
*Wolf, O.
Maedler, R.
Speckin, W.
Houdek, J.
Braunsdorf, E.
Sauter, C.
Wemheuer, O.
Krieglstein, W.
Gatterfeld, E.

HARPS
Tramonti, E.
Singer, W.

ORGANIST
Middelschulte, W.

FLUTES
Quensel, A.
Baumbach, C.

PICCOLOS
Furman, J.
Schroeter, R.

OBOES
Barthel, A.
Stiegelmayer, K.
Hesselbach, O.

ENGLISH HORN
Napolilli, F.

CLARINETS
Schreurs, J.
Meyer, C.
Busse, A.
Parbs, H.

BASS CLARINET
Meyer, C.

BASSOONS
Kruse, P.
Weiss, A.
Guetter, W.
Rabe, H.

CONTRA-BASSOON
Krieglstein, W.

HORNS
de Maré, L.
Pottag, M.
Frank, W.
Albrecht, C.
Johnson, H.
Kryl, F.

TRUMPETS
Llewellyn, E.
Hebs, W.

CORNETS
Ulrich, A.
Felber, H., Sr.

BASS TRUMPET
Andauer, E.

TROMBONES
Stange, G.
Gunther, A.
Kuss, R.

BASS TUBA
Gatterfeld, E.

TIMPANI
Zettelmann, J.

PERCUSSIONS
Wintrich, M.
Wagner, E.
Mittelstaedt, F.

LIBRARIAN
†McNicol, Theo.

*Died February 9, 1916.
†Died March 15, 1916.

THE CHICAGO SYMPHONY ORCHESTRA
TWENTY-SIXTH SEASON
(1916-1917)

First Violins
Weisbach, H., *Principal.*
Zukovsky, A.
Krauss, A.
Seidel, R.
Itte, F.
Bass, G.
Nurnberger, L.
Bramhall, J.
Rhys, S.
Du Moulin, G.
Silberstein, J.
Rosensweet, D.
Hecker, C.
Harris, G.
Hand, A.
Ginsburg, R.

Second Violins
Roehrborn, O., *Principal.*
Woelfel, P.
Barker, O.
Braun, H.
Novak, L.
Woollett, W.
Recoschewitz, J.
Martinson, M.
Bichl, J.
Konrad, W.
Christensen, T.
Fitzek, R.
Fitzek, J.
*Singer, W.
Rabe, H.
Busse, A.
Ulrich, A.

Violas
Esser, F., *Principal.*
Dasch, G.
Hillmann, C.
Meyer, G.
Strobach, C.
Volk, F.
Elander, C.
Schroeter, R.
Andauer, E.
Hesselbach, O.
Mittelstaedt, F.

Violoncellos
Steindel, B., *Principal.*
Ferner, W.
Unger, W.
Brueckner, C.
Ambrosius, R.
Du Moulin, T.
Felber, H., Sr.
Klammsteiner, C.
Polak, J.
Heinickel, A.

Basses
Jiskra, V., *Principal.*
Parbs, O.
Maedler, R.
Speckin, W.
Houdek, J.
Braunsdorf, E.
Sauter, C.
Wemheuer, O.
Krieglstein, W.
Gatterfeld, E.

Harps
Tramonti, E.
*Singer, W.

Organist
Middelschulte, W.

Flutes
Quensel, A.
Baumbach, C.

Piccolos
Furman, J.
Schroeter, R.

Oboes
Barthel, A.
Stiegelmayer, K.
Hesselbach, O.

English Horn
Napolilli, F.

Clarinets
Schreurs, J.
Meyer, C.
Busse, A.
Parbs, H.

Bass Clarinet
Meyer, C.

Bassoons
Guetter, W.
Rabe, H.
Kruse, P.
Krieglstein, W.

Contra-bassoon
Kruse, P.

Horns
de Maré, L.
Pottag, M.
Frank, W.
Albrecht, C.
Johnson, H.
Kryl, F.

Trumpets
Llewellyn, E.
Hebs, W.

Cornets
Ulrich, A.
Felber, H.

Bass Trumpets
Andauer, E.

Trombones
Stange, G.
Gunther, A.
Kuss, R.

Bass Tuba
Gatterfeld, E.

Timpani
Zettelmann, J.

Percussions
Wintrich, M.
Ludwig, W.
Mittelstaedt, F.

Librarian
Handke, P.

---
*Died March 3, 1917.

THE CHICAGO SYMPHONY ORCHESTRA
TWENTY-SEVENTH SEASON
(1917-1918)

First Violins
Weisbach, H., *Principal*
Zukovsky, A.
Krauss, A.
Seidel, R.
Itte, F.
Bass, G.
Nurnberger, L.
Bramhall, J.
Rhys, S.
Du Moulin, G.
Silberstein, J.
Rosensweet, D.
Hecker, C.
Selinger, H.
Ginsburg, R.
Paley, B.

Second Violins
Roehrborn, O., *Principal*.
Woelfel, P.
Hand, A.
Braun, H.
Barker, O.
Woollett, W.
Schulte, K.
Recoschewitz, J.
Martinson, M.
Bichl, J.
Konrad, W.
Christensen, T.
Fitzek, R.
Fitzek, J.
Busse, A.
Ulrich, A.

Violas
Esser, F., *Principal*.
Dasch, G.
Hillmann, C.
Meyer, G.
Elander, C.
Fiala, R.
Strobach, C.
Schroeter, R.
Andauer, E.
Hesselbach, O.
Mittelstaedt, F.

Violoncellos
Steindel, B., *Principal*.
Ferner, W.
Unger, W.
Brueckner, C.
Ambrosius, R.
Du Moulin, T.
Felber, H., Sr.
Klammsteiner, C.
Polak, J.
Heinickel, A.

Basses
Jiskra, V., *Principal*.
Parbs, H.
Maedler, R.
Speckin, W.
Houdek, J.
Braunsdorf, E.
Sauter, C.
Wemheuer, O.
Krieglstein, W.
Gatterfeld, E.

Harps
Tramonti, E.
Jiskra, Mrs. M.

Organist
Middelschulte, W.

Flutes
Quensel, A.
Baumbach, C.

Piccolos
Furman, J.
Schroeter, R.

Oboes
Barthel, A.
Stiegelmayer, K.
Hesselbach, O.

English Horn
Napolilli, F.

Clarinets
Schreurs, J.
Meyer, C.
Busse, A.
Parbs, H.

Bass Clarinet
Meyer, C.

Bassoons
Guetter, W.
Rabe, H.
Kruse, P.
Krieglstein, W.

Contra-bassoon
Kruse, P.

Horns
de Maré, L.
Pottag, M.
Frank, W.
Albrecht, C.
Hoss, W.
Johnson, H.

Trumpets
Llewellyn, E.
Hebs, W.

Cornets
Ulrich, A.
Felber, H.

Bass Trumpets
Andauer, E.

Trombones
Stange, G.
Gunther, A.
Kuss, R.

Bass Tuba
Dietrichs, W.

Timpani
Zettelmann, J.

Percussions
Wintrich, M.
Ludwig, W.
Mittelstaedt, F.

Librarian
Handke, P.

THE CHICAGO SYMPHONY ORCHESTRA
TWENTY-EIGHTH SEASON
(1918-1919)

FIRST VIOLINS
Weisbach, H., *Principal*
Zukovsky, A.
Krauss, A.
Seidel, R.
Itte, F.
Bass, G.
Nurnberger, L.
Rhys, S.
Du Moulin, G.
Silberstein, J.
Rosensweet, D.
Hecker, C.
Selinger, H.
Ginsburg, R.
Shostac, H.
Linden, H.

SECOND VIOLINS
Roehrborn, O., *Principal*.
Woelfel, P.
Hand, A.
Braun, H.
Barker, O.
Woollett, W.
Recoschewitz, J.
Martinson, M.
Bichl, J.
Konrad, W.
Fitzek, R.
Wiley, E.
Kopp, E.
Leviton, S.
Busse, A.
Ulrich, A.

VIOLAS
Esser, F., *Principal*.
Dasch, G.
Hillmann, C.
Meyer, G.
Elander, C.
Fiala, R.
Strobach, C.
Schroeter, R.
Andauer, E.
Fitzek, J.
Mittelstaedt, F.

VIOLONCELLOS
Du Moulin, T., *Principal*.
Ferner, W.
Unger, W.
Brueckner, C.
Ambrosius, R.
Klammsteiner, C.
Polak, J.
Heinickel, A.
Felber, H., Sr.
Williams, D.

BASSES
Jiskra, V., *Principal*.
Parbs, H.
Maedler, R.
Speckin, W.
Houdek, J.
Zweifel, J.
Sauter, C.
Wemheuer, O.

HARPS
Tramonti, E.
Jiskra, Mrs. M.

ORGAN
DeLamarter, E.

FLUTES
Quensel, A.
Baumbach, C.

PICCOLOS
Furman, J.
Schroeter, R.

OBOES
Barthel, A.
Stiegelmayer, K.
Napolilli, F.

ENGLISH HORN
Napolilli, F.

CLARINETS
Schreurs, J.
Meyer, C.
Busse, A.
Parbs, H.

BASS CLARINET
Meyer, C.

BASSOONS
Rabe, H.
Kruse, P.
Janovsky, E.

CONTRA-BASSOON
Kruse, P.

HORNS
de Maré, L.
Frank, W.
Pottag, M.
Johnson, H.
Albrecht, C.

TRUMPETS
Llewellyn, E.
Hebs, W.

CORNETS
Ulrich, A.
Felber, H., Sr.

BASS TRUMPETS
Andauer, E.

TROMBONES
Stange, G.
Gunther, A.
Beilschmidt, W.

BASS TUBA
Dietrichs, W.

TIMPANI
Zettelmann, J.

PERCUSSIONS
Wintrich, M.
Ludwig, W.
Mittelstaedt, F.
Strobach, C.

LIBRARIAN
Handke, P.

Appendix

THE CHICAGO SYMPHONY ORCHESTRA
TWENTY-NINTH SEASON
(1919-1920)

FIRST VIOLINS
Weisbach, H., *Principal.*
Zukovsky, A.
Krauss, A.
Seidel, R.
Itte, F.
Bass, G.
Rosensweet, D.
Nurnberger, L.
Bramhall, J.
Rhys, S.
Selinger, H.
Du Moulin, G.
Silberstein, J.
Ginsburg, R.
Paley, B.
Hand, A.

SECOND VIOLINS
Roehrborn, O., *Principal.*
Woelfel, P.
Barker, O.
Braun, H.
Schulte, K.
Woollett, W.
Recoschewitz, J.
Martinson, M.
Bichl, J.
Leviton, S.
Konrad, W.
Ulrich, A., Jr.
Wiley, E.
Kopp, E.
Busse, A.
Ulrich, A., Sr.

VIOLAS
Esser, F., *Principal.*
Dasch, G.
Meyer, G.
Fiala, R.
Schein, S.
Schroeter, R.
Fitzek, J.
Fitzek, R.
Andauer, E.
Hesselbach, O.
Strobach, C.

VIOLONCELLOS
Malkin, J., *Principal.*
Du Moulin, T.
Brueckner, C.
Ambrosius, R.
Klammsteiner, C.
Polak, J.
Heinickel, A.
Singer, C.
Felber, H.
Hoffman, A.

BASSES
Jiskra, V., *Principal.*
Parbs, H.
Maedler, R.
Speckin, W.
Houdek, J.
Zweifel, J.
Sauter, C.
Wemheuer, W.
Krieglstein, W.
Dietrichs, W.

HARPS
Tramonti, E.
Jiskra, Mrs. M.

ORGAN
DeLamarter, E.

FLUTES
Quensel, A.
Knauss, R.

PICCOLOS
Furman, J.
Schroeter, R.

OBOES
Barthel, A.
Stiegelmayer, K.
Hesselbach, O.

ENGLISH HORN
Napolilli, F.

CLARINETS
Schreurs, J.
Meyer, C.
Busse, A.
Parbs, H.

BASS CLARINET
Meyer, C.

BASSOONS
Guetter, W.
Rabe, H.
Krieglstein, W.

CONTRA-BASSOON
Kruse, P.

HORNS
de Maré, L.
Johnson, H.
Pottag, M.
Frank, W.
Albrecht, C.

TRUMPETS
Llewellyn, E.
Hebs, W.

CORNETS
Ulrich, A.
Felber, H.

BASS TRUMPETS
Andauer, E.

TROMBONES
Stange, G.
Gunther, A.
Beilschmidt, W.

BASS TUBA
Dietrichs, W.

TIMPANI
Zettelmann, J.

PERCUSSIONS
Wintrich, M.
Veseley, B.
Strobach, C.
Kopp, E.

LIBRARIAN
Handke, P.

THE CHICAGO SYMPHONY ORCHESTRA
THIRTIETH SEASON
(1920-1921)

FIRST VIOLINS
  Weisbach, H., *Principal.*
  Zukovsky, A.
  Krauss, A.
  Seidel, R.
  Itte, F.
  Bass, G.
  Rosensweet, D.
  Nurnberger, L.
  Bramhall, J.
  Rhys, S.
  Selinger, H.
  Du Moulin, G.
  Silberstein, J.
  Ginsburg, R.
  Paley, B.
  Hand, A.

SECOND VIOLINS
  Roehrborn, O., *Principal.*
  Woelfel, P.
  Barker, O.
  Braun, H.
  Schulte, K.
  Woollett, W.
  Recoschewitz, J.
  Martinson, M.
  Bichl, J.
  Leviton, S.
  Konrad, W.
  Ulrich, A., Jr.
  Wiley, E.
  Kopp, E.
  Busse, A.
  Ulrich, A., Sr.

VIOLAS
  Esser, F., *Principal.*
  Dasch, G.
  Evans, C.
  Meyer, G.
  Schein, S.
  Schroeter, R.
  Fitzek, J.
  Fitzek, R.
  Andauer, E.
  Hesselbach, O.
  Strobach, C.

VIOLONCELLOS
  Malkin, J., *Principal.*
  Du Moulin, T.
  Brueckner, C.
  Ambrosius, R.
  Klammsteiner, C.
  Polak, J.
  Heinickel, A.
  Felber, H.
  Hoffman, A.
  Ratzer, T.

BASSES
  Jiskra, V., *Principal.*
  Parbs, H.
  Maedler, R.
  Speckin, W.
  Houdek, J.
  Zweifel, J.
  Sauter, C.
  Wemheuer, O.
  Krieglstein, W.

HARPS
  Tramonti, E.
  Jiskra, Mrs. M.

ORGAN
  DeLamarter, E.

FLUTES
  Quensel, A.
  Knauss, R.

PICCOLOS
  Furman, J.
  Schroeter, R.

OBOES
  Barthel, A.
  Ruckle, L.
  Hesselbach, O.

ENGLISH HORN
  Napolilli, F.

CLARINETS
  Schreurs, J.
  Meyer, C.
  Busse, A.
  Parbs, H.

BASS CLARINET
  Meyer, C.

BASSOONS
  Guetter, W.
  Rabe, H.
  Krieglstein, W.

CONTRA-BASSOON
  Kruse, P.

HORNS
  de Maré, L.
  Johnson, H.
  Pottag, M.
  Frank, W.
  Albrecht, C.

TRUMPETS
  Llewellyn, E.
  Hebs, W.

CORNETS
  Ulrich, A.
  Felber, H.

BASS TRUMPET
  Andauer, E.

TROMBONES
  Stange, G.
  Martin, C.
  Gunther, A.

BASS TUBA
  Hamburg, G.

TIMPANI
  Zettelmann, J.

PERCUSSIONS
  Wintrich, M.
  Veseley, B.
  Strobach, C.
  Kopp, E.

LIBRARIAN
  Handke, P.

THE CHICAGO SYMPHONY ORCHESTRA
THIRTY-FIRST SEASON
(1921-1922)

VIOLINS
  Gordon, J.,
    Concertmaster
  Zukovsky, A.,
    Principal.
  Krauss, A.
  Seidel, R.
  Itte, F.
  Rosensweet, D.
  Nurnberger, L.
  Bramhall, J.
  Rhys, S.
  Selinger, H.
  Du Moulin, G.
  Silberstein, J.
  Ginsburg, R.
  Paley, B.
  Hand, A.
  Hancock, W.

SECOND VIOLINS
  Roehrborn, O., *Principal.*
  Schulte, K.
  Braun, H.
  Martinson, M.
  Woollett, W.
  Recoschewitz, J.
  Bichl, J.
  Leviton, S.
  Konrad, W.
  Wiley, E.
  Ulrich, A., Jr.
  Perkins, H.
  Kopp, E.
  Ulrich, A., Sr.

VIOLAS
  Esser, F., *Principal.*
  Dasch, G.
  Evans, C.
  Meyer, G.
  Schein, S.
  Schroeter, R.
  Fitzek, J.
  Fitzek, R.
  Andauer, E.
  Hesselbach, O.
  Strobach, C.

VIOLONCELLOS
  Malkin, J., *Principal.*
  Du Moulin, T.
  Brueckner, C.
  Ambrosius, R.
  Klammsteiner, C.
  Polak, J.
  Heinickel, A.
  Felber, H.
  Ratzer, T.
  Brauer, W.

BASSES
  Jiskra, V., *Principal.*
  Houdek, J.
  Speckin, W.
  Zweifel, J.
  Sauter, C.
  Cerney, E.
  Wemheuer, O.
  Pytlowski, W.
  Krieglstein, W.

HARPS
  Tramonti, E.
  Jiskra, Mrs. M.

ORGAN
  DeLamarter, E.

FLUTES
  Quensel, A.
  Knauss, R.

PICCOLOS
  Furman, J.
  Schroeter, R.

OBOES
  Barthel, A.
  Ruckle, L.
  Hesselbach, O.

ENGLISH HORN
  Napolilli, F.

CLARINETS
  Meyer, C.
  Siniscalchi, J.
  Busse, A.
  Parbs, H.

BASS CLARINET
  Parbs, H.

BASSOONS
  Guetter, W.
  Rabe, H.
  Krieglstein, W.

CONTRA-BASSOON
  Kruse, P.

HORNS
  de Maré, L.
  Johnson, H.
  Pottag, M.
  Frank, W.
  Albrecht, C.

TRUMPETS
  Llewellyn, E.
  Masacek, E.

CORNETS
  Ulrich, A.
  Felber, H.

BASS TRUMPET
  Andauer, E.

TROMBONES
  Stange, G.
  Geffert, E.
  Gunther, A.

BASS TUBA
  Hamburg, G.

TIMPANI
  Zettelmann, J.

PERCUSSIONS
  Wintrich, M.
  Veseley, B.
  Strobach, C.
  Kopp, E.

LIBRARIAN
  Handke, P.

THE CHICAGO SYMPHONY ORCHESTRA
THIRTY-SECOND SEASON
(1922-1923)

FIRST VIOLINS
Gordon, J., *Concertmaster.*
Zukovsky, A., *Principal.*
Katz, T.
Selinger, H.
Krauss, A.
Itte, F.
Ginsburg, R.
Hancock, W.
Bramhall, J.
Koerner, C.
Rhys, S.
Du Moulin, G.
Silberstein, J.
Hand, A.
Martinson, M.
Fantozzi, W.

SECOND VIOLINS
Dasch, G., *Principal.*
Barker, O.
Nurnberger, I.
Woollett, W.
Recoschewitz, J.
Morello, C.
Konrad, W.
Rink, C.
Bichl, J.
Leviton, S.
Wiley, E.
Ulrich, A., Jr.
Charbulak, V.
Dolnick, S.
Busse, A.
Kopp, E.

VIOLAS
Esser, F., *Principal.*
Evans, C.
Roehrborn, O.
Seidel, R.
Schein, S.
Fiala, R.
Schroeter, R.
Perkins, H.
Fitzek, R.
Wessling, J.
Andauer, E.
Strobach, C.

VIOLONCELLOS
Wallenstein, A., *Principal.*
Du Moulin, T.
Brueckner, C.
Ambrosius, R.
Klammsteiner, C.
Polak, J.
Heinickel, A.
Felber, H.
Ratzer, T.
Brauer, W.

BASSES
Jiskra, V., *Principal.*
Houdek, J.
Speckin, W.
Zweifel, J.
Sauter, C.
Cerney, E.
Wemheuer, O.
Pytlowski, W.
Krieglstein, W.

HARPS
Tramonti, E.
Jiskra, Mrs. M.

ORGAN
DeLamarter, E.

FLUTES
Quensel, A.
Kitti, A.

PICCOLOS
Furman, J.
Schroeter, R.

OBOES
Barthel, A.
Ruckle, L.
Napolilli, F.

ENGLISH HORN
Napolilli, F.

CLARINETS
Siniscalchi, J.
De Caprio, A.
Busse, A.
Parbs, H.

BASS CLARINET
Parbs, H.

BASSOONS
Fox, H.
Rabe, H.
Kruse, P.
Krieglstein, W.

CONTRA-BASSOON
Kruse, P.

HORNS
Hoss, W.
Pottag, M.
Frank, W.
Albrecht, K.

TRUMPETS
Llewellyn, E.
Masacek, E.
Ulrich, A., Sr.

CORNETS
Ulrich, A., Sr.
Felber, H.

BASS TRUMPET
Andauer, E.

TROMBONES
Stange, G.
Geffert, E.
Gunther, A.

BASS TUBA
Hamburg, G.

TIMPANI
Zettelmann, J.

PERCUSSIONS
Wintrich, M.
Veseley, B.
Strobach, C.
Kopp, E.

LIBRARIAN
Handke, P.

THE CHICAGO SYMPHONY ORCHESTRA
THIRTY-THIRD SEASON
(1923-1924)

FIRST VIOLINS
Gordon, J., *Concertmaster.*
Zukovsky, A., *Principal.*
Hancock, W.
Selinger, H.
Itte, F.
Bass, G.
Charbulak, V.
Silberstein, J.
Rhys, S.
Koerner, C.
Weicher, J.
Bramhall, J.
Hand, A.
Du Moulin, G.
Martinson, M.
Fantozzi, W.

SECOND VIOLINS
Roehrborn, O., *Principal.*
Polesny, F.
Barker, O.
Nurnberger, I.
Recoschewitz, J.
Rink, C.
Morello, C.
Leviton, S.
Konrad, W.
Bichl, J.
Ulrich, A., Jr.
Wiley, E.
Dolnick, S.
Finerman, A.
Busse, A.
Kopp, E.

VIOLAS
Esser, F., *Principal.*
Evans, C.
Seidel, R.
Fiala, R.
Linke, C.
Schroeter, R.
Hesselbach, O.
Wessling, J.
Schein, S.
Perkins, H.
Andauer, E.
Strobach, C.

VIOLONCELLOS
Wallenstein, A., *Principal.*
Brueckner, C.
Lingeman, J.
Klammsteiner, C.
Polak, J.
Heinickel, A.
Felber, H.
Hendrickson, R.
Brauer, W.
Ratzer, T.

BASSES
Jiskra, V., *Principal.*
Houdek, J.
Parbs, H.
Speckin, W.
Zweifel, J.
Cerney, E.
Wemheuer, O.
Pytlowski, W.

HARPS
Tramonti, E.
Jiskra, Mrs. M.

ORGAN
DeLamarter, E.

FLUTES
Quensel, A.
Kitti, A.

PICCOLOS
Eck, E.
Schroeter, R.

OBOES
Barthel, A.
Ruckle, L.
Napolilli, F.
Hesselbach, O.

ENGLISH HORN
Napolilli, F.

CLARINETS
Lindemann, R.
Evenson, S.
Meyer, C.
Busse, A.

BASS CLARINET
Meyer, C.

BASSOONS
Fox, H.
Rabe, H.
Krieglstein, W.

CONTRA-BASSOON
Krieglstein, W.

HORNS
Frank W.
Pottag, M.
Johnson, H.
Albrecht, K.

TRUMPETS
Llewellyn, E.
Masacek, E.
Ulrich, A., Sr.

CORNETS
Ulrich, A., Sr.
Felber, H.

BASS TRUMPET
Andauer, E.

TROMBONES
Stange, G.
Geffert, E.
Gunther, A.

BASS TUBA
Hamburg, G.

TIMPANI
Zettelmann, J.

PERCUSSIONS
Wintrich, M.
Veseley, B.
Strobach, C.
Kopp, E.

LIBRARIAN
Handke, P.

THE PENSION ROLL

AT THE CLOSE OF THE

THIRTY-THIRD SEASON

(1923-1924)

	Pension Began	Years of Service
ERNEST FRANK WAGNER (continued to widow). .	1916	25
MRS. THEODORE F. MCNICOL (widow of member).	1916	25
(Continued to minor children until 1924)		
MRS. OTTO WOLF (widow of member). . . .	1916	20
FERDINAND VOLK	1917	26
LOUIS NOVAK	1917	20
WILLIAM ZELLER	1917	21
JOSEF NICOLINI (continued to widow) . . .	1917	20
FREDERICK STARKE	1917	20
LOUIS FRIEDRICH.	1917	20
MRS. WALFRIED SINGER (widow of member) . .	1917	17
MRS. FRITZ OTTE (widow of member) . . .	1917	19
W. G. A. UNGER	1919	28
FRANK A. MITTELSTAEDT	1919	28
CURT BAUMBACH (continued to widow) . . .	1919	27
CARL HILLMANN	1919	26
BRUNO KUEHN	1919	14
BRUNO STEINDEL	1919	27
MRS. JOSEPH SCHREURS (widow of member) . .	1921	30
HERMAN BRAUN	1922	31
GEORGE F. MEYER	1922	31
JOSEPH FITZEK	1922	31
LEOPOLD DE MARÉ	1922	31
ALEXANDER KRAUSS	1923	32
WILFRED WOOLLETT	1923	28
RUDOLPH FITZEK	1923	27
CARL SAUTER	1923	15
MRS. PAUL KRUSE (widow of member) . . .	1923	24

The following pensioners have passed away:
    ERNEST FRANK WAGNER.
    MRS. THEODORE F. MCNICOL.
    JOSEF NICOLINI.
    LOUIS FRIEDRICH.
    CURT BAUMBACH.
    BRUNO KUEHN.

INDEX

INDEX

Adams, George E.: Trustee and President, 55; at dinner to Mr. Thomas, 81; letter from F. W. Peck, 82; luncheon to Trustees, 109; resignation as President, 116; subscribes to the purchase of the Michigan Avenue lot, 135; address at dedication of hall, 152; resolutions on death of Mr. Thomas, 157-158; 187; death, 296; memorial concert, 297; memorial by Trustees, "A man of broad cultivation and public spirit," 298.

Adams, Joseph: at dinner to friends of the Orchestra 104; Trustee, 109; Second Vice-President, 285.

Adams, Milward: Manager of the Summer Garden Concerts, 15; Chicago Festival, 17; 23; Manager of the Orchestra, 27; resignation, 59; death and funeral services, 364.

Adler, Miss Lois: 176.

Ahner, Henry: early Conductor, 9; 10.

Alien Contract Labor Bill: 244.

Amato, Louis: 54; plays solo on a double-bass at "show"; death, 110.

Anderson, Charles E.: Secretary and Treasurer, 54; resignation, 61.

Ann Arbor Festivals: 383-385.

Anschutz, Carl: 11, 123, 160.

Apollo Musical Club:
Conductors: Adolph W. Dohn (1873-1875), William L. Tomlins (1875-1898), Harrison M. Wild 1898—), 8; organization; Schumann's "Paradise and the Peri," 14; Festival (1877); "Saint Paul" (Part First) (Mendelssohn); "Israel in Egypt" (Handel), 15; "Faust" (Berlioz), 16; 17; 33; 77; 78; 253; "Rose of Sharon" (Mackenzie); report of Music Committee (1885), 21; "Messiah," 32, 116, 122, 143-144, 183, 192, 225, 275, 289, 356, 369; "Wage Workers' Concerts," 32; Twentieth Anniversary (1892), 35-36; Columbian Exposition, 39; 44; Ninth Symphony (Beethoven), 41, 56, 81, 123, 146; "Elijah," 42-43, 46, 92, 100-101, 322; "Passion Music" (Bach), 46; "Samson et Dalila" (Saint-Saëns), 55; "Hora Novissima" (Parker), "Frithjof" (Bruch), 56; "Israel in Egypt" (Handel) selections; "Golden Legend" (Sullivan), 66; "Stabat Mater" (Dvořák); "Swan and Skylark" (Thomas), 89-90; "Creation" (Haydn), 110; "Requiem" (Stanford), 98; "Te Deum" (Berlioz); "Hiawatha's Wedding Feast" (Coleridge-Taylor), 124; "Dream of Gerontius" (Elgar), 139; Dedicatory Concert (Orchestra Hall), 152; "Apostles" (Elgar), 176; "The Children's Crusade"(Pierné), 195; "Bach Mass," 207; assists the Orchestra, 217; assists the Orchestra, selections from "Caractacus" (Elgar), 239; "The Music Makers" (Elgar); "Stabat Mater" (Dvořák), 260; assists the Orchestra, ninth symphony and Wagner selections, 261; assists in Music Festival, 292; "Manzoni Requiem" (Verdi); "Epilogue" from "Caractacus" (Elgar), 302; "The Veil" (Cowen); "Forty-seventh Psalm" (Schmidt), 316; "Pilgrim's Progress" (Kelley), 335; Fiftieth Anniversary, Mass in B Minor (Bach), 347; "Rock of Liberty" (Cole); reproduction of first concert (1873), 348.

Armour, Allison V.: Trustee, 55; 64; dinner by Trustees at Chicago Club; subscribes $5,000, 104; resignation, 105.

Aurora Symphony Concerts: 382-383.

Aus der Ohe, Miss Adèle: 68.

Auxiliary Committee: a strong factor in the campaign for building fund, 141.

Baernstein, Joseph S.: 100.

Baird, Max: Secretary of Auxiliary Committee, 141; Trustee, 151; Member, 166; resignation, 260.

Balatka, Hans: "The forerunner of Theodore Thomas," 10; death, 11.

Baré, Emil: concertmeister, 95.

Barthel, Alfred: 146; "played with great skill and feeling," 193; 227; 230; 248; 270; 275.

Bartlett, A. C.: Trustee, 27; resignation, 57; death; bequest of $10,000 to The Orchestral Association, 347.

Bauer, Harold: 131, 266, 290.

Baumbach, Curt: 187; retired on pension, 318.

Beach, Mrs. H. H. A.: 276.

Beard, William: 217.

Beckel, Joseph: death; funeral services, 196.

Becker, Ludwig: 164; concertmeister, 210; resignation, 223.

Bendix, Max: 29; 56; at Cincinnati Festival, 58; 65; 76; 81; resignation, 85.

Bispham, David: death, 172.
Blackstone, T. B.: 62; death; resolution by Trustees, "His constant and generous support," 118.
Blair, Watson F.: Member, 175.
Blauvelt, Mrs. Lillian: 61.
Boeppler, William: Chicago Music Festival, 292.
Bonnet, Joseph: 315.
Borland, Chauncey B.: Member, 166; resignation, 225.
Borroff, Albert: 146; 261.
Borowski, Felix: editor of program book; "New thoughts" on program making, 200-201; Mr. Stock's symphony, 212; Allegro de Concert, 278; suite from "Boudour," 316; 320; Miss Ethel Mary Smyth, 345.
Boston Symphony Orchestra: at Exposition, 46.
Braun, Herman: "Silver Jubilee," 273; "white ribbon," 330; retired on pension, 345.
Breitner, Ludwig: ill, 131.
Brentano, Mrs. Minna: 41.
Britt, Horace: 183.
Browne, Dr. J. Lewis: 278.
Brown, William L.: Trustee, 109; subscribes to the purchase of the Michigan Avenue lot, 135; Member, 166.
Brueckner, Carl: 145.
Buckley, Miss Helen: 95.
Bull, Ole: 11.
Burgstaller, Alois: "a vigorous interpretation," 183.
Burley, Clarence A.: Member, 166; Trustee, 307.
Burnham, Daniel H.: one of the "creators of the Exposition," 45; 62; Trustee, 64; 73; Committee on Finance, 101; Committee on Organization, 104; 105; subscribes to the purchase of the Michigan Avenue lot, 135; plans for new hall, 142; dinner in foyer of hall, 216; death; *Chicago Tribune;* resolution by Trustees, "In recognition of his valuable help and inspiration," 241-242.
Burnham, Daniel H. (son): Member, 342.
Burnham, Daniel H., & Co.: architects of Orchestra Hall, 145; a gift of $15,000, 171.
Busoni, Ferruccio: 145; 214.
Butler, Edward B.: Member, 166; Trustee, 307.
Butt, Mme. Clara: 261.

Cady, C. M.: 123.
Campanari, Giuseppe: 95.
Campanini, Cleofonte: death, 43.
Campanini, Italo: 17; 29; "sang as Orpheus sang," 34; death, 43.
Carberry, Frederick W.: 350; 373.

Carpenter, Benjamin: Member, 234.
Carpenter, George Benedict: Manager Summer Garden Concerts, 15; address on "Ideals"; builder of Central Music Hall; death, 16-17; 140.
Carpenter, Mrs. George B.: Manager, 15.
Carpenter, John Alden: suite, "Adventures in a Perambulator," 268; Concertino, 277, 346; symphony No. 1, 297; "Home Road," 337; "Legion of Honor," 346; "A Pilgrim Vision," 371.
Carr, Clyde M.: Member, 225; Trustee, 234; President, 285; luncheon to Members, 286; necessity of paying debt on hall, 287; praise of the Music Festival and Mr. Stock, 299; loyalty of members of the Orchestra, 300; letter to Mr. Stock, 309-310; reviews Treasurer's report, 313-314, 341; death; funeral services, 366; bequest of $1,000,000 to The Orchestral Association, 367; an appreciation by the Trustees, "devoted to the highest ideals of art," 367-368.
Carreño, Mme. Teresa: 88; 190; death, 217.
Carrington, William T.: Trustee, 109; subscribes to the purchase of the Michigan Avenue lot, 135; resignation, 136.
Casals, Pablo: 269.
Casella, Alfredo: soloist and Guest Conductor, 357.
Chadwick, George W.: Visiting Conductor, 213; 255; luncheon and guests, 276; composer-Conductor, 315.
Chase, Miss Mary Wood: 139.
Chicago Biennial Musical Festival Association: organization; First Festival; soloists, 17; loss, 18; Second Festival; soloists, 18; loss, 20.
Chicago Chamber Music Society: announcement; Executive Committee, 174; 230; Eighth Season, 246; 254; 255; 270.
Chicago Evening Post (Karleton Hackett): Carpenter's suite, 268; opening of Twenty-sixth Season, 285-286; Stock's "Confession of Faith," 317; tribute to Milward Adams, 364.
Chicago Herald: 51.
Chicago Music Festival: Choral societies, Conductors, soloists, programs, 290.
Chicago North Shore Festival Association: dates, programs and soloists, 385-388.
Chicago String Quartet: 230, 246, 254, 255, 270.
Chicago Symphony Orchestra, known prior to 1913 as The Chicago Orchestra (1891-1905) and The Theodore Thomas Orchestra (1905-1913):

Index

First Season (1891-1892): "Twentieth Anniversary Concerts" (Apollo Club), 35-36; public not interested in the Orchestra, 36; soloists for season, 37.

Second Season (1892-1893): opening of the Columbian Exposition; inaugural exercises, 40; two People's Concerts, 42; soloists for season, 44; Exposition, 46-47.

Third Season (1893-1894): soloists for season, 57.

Fourth Season (1894-1895): People's Institute Program, 65; out-of-town concerts, 67; tour of the Orchestra, 68; soloists for the season, 71.

Fifth Season (1895-1896): W. S. B. Mathews, editor of program book, 74; Popular Program, 75; program of music at the dedication of the "Silver Bowl"; "Till Eulenspiegel," 76; eastern tour; comments of the press, 78-79; ninth symphony; soloists for season, 81.

Sixth Season (1896-1897): chorus; Arthur Mees, Assistant Conductor, 82; First Program; patriotic ending, 86; Promenade Concert, with chorus, 90-92.

Seventh Season (1897-1898): ninth symphony, 96; eastern tour; soloists, 98; comments of press, 99; return home; loss on tour, 100; soloists for season, 102.

Eighth Season (1898-1899): banquet and "show" by men of the Orchestra, 110; out-of-town concerts; spring tour; Children's Concert, 111; soloists for season, 112.

Ninth Season (1899-1900): southern tour, 117-118; soloists for season, 119.

Tenth Season (1900-1901): "Beethoven Cycle," 121, 122, 123; western tour, 124; soloists for season, 125.

Eleventh Season (1901-1902): First "Historical" Concert; vaudeville for Mr. Thomas and Trustees, 128-130; Third and Fourth "Historical" Concerts, 130; Fifth "Historical" Concert; Sixth "Historical" Concert, 131; soloists for season, 133.

Twelfth Season (1902-1903): soloists for season, 140.

Thirteenth Season (1903-1904): Young People's Concerts, 146-147; soloists for season, 148.

Fourteenth Season (1904-1905): dedicatory (Orchestra Hall) concert, 152; Beethoven program, 153; Popular Program, 154; Trustees announce an annual Memorial Concert for Mr. Thomas, 156; memorial for Charles D. Hamill, 164; named changed to "The Theodore Thomas Orchestra,"168; two extra concerts; organ concerts, 169; soloists for season, 170.

Fifteenth Season (1905-1906): Thomas Memorial, 174; extra concerts, 176; soloists for season, 177.

Sixteenth Season (1906-1907): season lengthened to twenty-eight weeks, 179; Mandel Hall Concerts; Ravinia Park; four Thursday afternoon concerts, 180-181; Thomas Memorial Concert, 183; another extra concert, 184; soloists "Festival Tour," 186-187; soloists for season, 188.

Seventeenth Season (1907-1908): the "spell" of the Friday concerts; "Extra Concerts" did not interest the public; problems of the Manager, 189; concert for Presbyterian Hospital, 190; Beethoven Program, 191; Thomas Memorial, 192; two concerts for Pension Fund, 192-193; visit to Toronto, 193; concerts and soloists, 194-195; return home, 195; soloists for season, 198.

Eighteenth Season (1908-1909): the "Friday spell"; new decorations in Orchestra Hall, designed by D. H. Burnham & Company, 199-200; Thomas Memorial, 202; second visit to Toronto, 203; programs and soloists, 204; Choir comes to Chicago, 204-205; programs and soloists, 205; friends who guaranteed cost, 206; Willow Grove, 207-208; Ravinia Park; soloists for season, 208.

Nineteenth Season (1909-1910): Popular Concerts, 211-212; Thomas Memorial; third visit to Toronto, 213; programs and soloists, 214; Choir and Orchestra in Buffalo, 214; in Cleveland; programs and soloists; return home; "Aquatic" Program, 215; vaudeville by men of Orchestra, 216; contracts with members of the Orchestra, 218; Willow Grove, 220; soloists for season, 221.

Twentieth Season (1910-1911): Thomas Memorial, 226; Toronto visit; programs and soloists, 226-227; soloists for season, 227; Willow Grove, 228.

Twenty-first Season (1911-1912): Third Program (Liszt Anniversary), 229; letter from "a Friday subscriber," 230; eastern tour of Orchestra, 231; comments of press, 232; Thomas Memorial, 233; Mr. Lathrop gives testimonial dinner

454   *The Chicago Symphony Orchestra*

to Orchestra, 234-235; Toronto; programs and soloists, 235-236; eastern tour of Choir and Orchestra; programs and soloists; Buffalo and New York; comments of press; reception by Mendelssohn Club, New York, 236-237; Boston; press comments, 238; soloists for season, 243.

Twenty-second Season (1912-1913): Thomas Memorial, 247; name changed to "The Chicago Symphony Orchestra, Founded by Theodore Thomas," 248; Twenty-third Program; concert for benefit of flood sufferers, 252; soloists for season, 253.

Twenty-third Season (1913-1914): First and Fifth Programs, 254-255; Thomas Memorial; three Popular Concerts, 258; Fifteenth Program, symphony by Eric DeLamarter, 258-259; with Mendelssohn Choir, Toronto; programs and soloists, 259-260; Second American Concert, 261; soloists for the season, 262.

Twenty-fourth Season (1914 - 1915): Thomas Memorial, 266; Twenty-third Program (John Alden Carpenter), 268; concert for Pension Fund, 269; six Popular Concerts, 269-270; soloists for season, 271.

Twenty-fifth Season (1915-1916): Toronto engagement canceled by European war, 273; First Program ("Silver Jubilee"), 273-274; Thomas Memorial, 275; concert for Pension Fund, 276; ten Popular Concerts, 280-281; soloists for the season, 283.

Twenty-sixth Season (1916 - 1917): Bryan Lathrop Memorial, 286; Thomas Memorial, 289; Chicago Music Festival, programs and soloists, 291-294; Popular Concerts; soloists for the season, 295.

Twenty-seventh Season (1917-1918): every concert now opened with the playing of some patriotic number; Second Program in memory of George E. Adams, 297; Thomas Memorial; Civic Music Festival, 300; Popular Concerts, 303; soloists for season, 304.

Twenty-eighth Season (1918-1919): Civic Music Festival, 311; Christmas festivities; Thomas Memorial, 315; Popular Concerts; soloists for season, 320.

Twenty-ninth Season (1919-1920): Children's Concerts established, 322; Thomas Memorial, 325; Popular Concerts, 326; Children's Concerts, 327; soloists for season, 328.

Thirtieth Season (1920-1921): First Concerts; "eleven men decorated with white ribbons," 330; Thomas Memorial; eastern tour; Boston, New York, 332; Philadelphia, Washington, 333; banquet for Mrs. Elizabeth Sprague Coolidge and "artists of thirty years' service"; guests, 335; Children's Concerts, 336; Popular Concerts, 337; soloists for season, 338.

Thirty-first Season (1921-1922): Fifth Program; third anniversary of Armistice Day, 340-341; Thomas Memorial, 344; Popular Concerts; Children's Concerts, 349; soloists for season, 351.

Thirty-second Season (1922-1923): Seventh Program (Shakespeare), 353; Tenth Program (César Franck); Thomas Memorial, 356; Twelfth Program ("Literary"), 357; Popular Concerts, 358; Children's Concerts, 358-359; soloists for season, 365.

Thirty-third Season (1923-1924): First Concerts, tribute to President Carr, 368; Thomas Memorial, 370; dedication of Theodore Thomas Memorial, 372; Popular Concerts, 381; Children's Concerts, 381-382; soloists for season, 388.

Chicago Times: "Request Programs," 38.

Chicago Tribune: 7; first appearance of Theodore Thomas in Chicago, 11; Thomas Orchestra, 11; 12; "might be our leader," 22; 29; "Wage Workers' Concerts," 42; financial conditions in Chicago, 88; Enrico Tramonti, 191; Ezra B. McCagg, 199; Daniel H. Burnham, 241; d'Indy's symphony, 261; George P. Upton, 319; opening of Thirtieth Season, 329; an appreciation by Ruth Miller of Maier and Pattison, 334.

Chicago Woodwind Choir: 230; 246; 248; 254; 270.

Chorus of the Association: organization, 82-83; Mr. Thomas sends letter to Chicago singers, 84; first rehearsal; Chorus Committee, 85; first appearance of chorus, 88; public not interested in chorus, 90; Promenade Concert, 91; "Festival March" (Kaun), 94; "A Midsummer Night's Dream" (Mendelssohn), 95; ninth symphony, 96; best work the chorus had done, 98; selections from "Parsifal," 100; chorus disbanded, 103.

Cincinnati Festivals: Sixth, 19; Eleventh; soloists, 57-58; Sixteenth; program; soloists, 147-148; Seventeenth; Theodore Thomas Orchestra did not

Index

appear, 177; Eighteenth; soloists, 197; Nineteenth; soloists, 219; Twentieth; soloists, 239-241.
Civic Music Association Festivals: organization, 270; 300; 311; 335; 350; 373.
Civic (Student) Orchestra: organization, 322-323; first concert, 327; 335; three concerts, 337; 350; *personnel*, 351; six concerts, 358; *personnel*, Sixth Season (1924-1925), 374; 382.
Clark, Charles W.: 81; 100; 123; 128.
Clark, Rev. W. G.: People's Institute, 64.
Claussen, Mme. Julia: 269.
Cleveland, S. E.: 14.
Coffin, Warren C.: 14.
Cole, Rossetter G.: symphonic prelude, 277.
Coolidge, Mrs. Elizabeth Sprague: 8; gift of $100,000 to Pension Fund, 267; resolution by Trustees, 268; reception, 276; banquet by members of the Orchestra, 335.
Cortot, Alfred: 333; 356.
Corwith, Charles R.: Trustee, 77; resignation; death, 116.
Cottlow, Miss Augusta: 180.
Cramer, Frank: Member, 331.
Crane, Charles R.: Trustee, 116; resignation, 127.
Culp, Miss Julia: 248.
Cunningham, Claude: 204; 214.
Curtiss, Charles C.: first Secretary of the Apollo Musical Club, 14; plans for a new hall, 82.

Dasch, George: Assistant Director, Student Orchestra, 327; 335; 337; Annual Festival, Civic Music Association, 350; Civic Orchestra, 358.
Davies, A. L. E.: Associate Conductor, Mendelssohn Choir, 227.
Davies, Ben: "in glorious voice," 58; 118.
Davies, D. Ffrangcon: 88.
DeLamarter, Eric: symphony in D major, 258; Assistant Conductor, 309; first appearance as Conductor, "made a great impression," 311; suite from "The Betrothal," 317; concerto for organ, E major, 326; eastern tour, 332; Civic Music Festival, 335; program notes; Student Orchestra, 337; concerto No. 2, A major, for organ, 345; program notes, 349-350; Assistant Conductor, Civic Orchestra; Annual Festival Civic Music Association, 350; Civic Orchestra; Popular Concerts; program notes, 358-359; conducts in absence of Mr. Stock, 370; program notes, 381.

Delano, Frederic A.: Member, 166; Trustee, 172; resignation, 307.
de Maré, Leopold: 86; 146; "lovely quality of tone," 196; 227; 230; 248; 270; "Silver Jubilee," 273; 275; "white ribbon," 330; retired on pension, 345.
Dermitt, Edward H.: 90.
Desvignes, Miss Carlotta: 64.
Dickinson, Clarence: 176; 190; 237.
d'Indy, Vincent: Guest Conductor, 343; luncheon; guests, 344.
Dobson, Tom: leads children's songs, 300.
Dohn, Adolph W.: 9; 12; first Conductor of the Apollo Club, 14; editor of program book, 32; 56; resignation, 59; death; funeral services; life and work, 122-123; 348.
Dreier, Mrs. Christine N.: 96.
DuMoulin, Theodore: 318.
Duncan, Miss Isadora: 201.
Dunham, Arthur: 209; 217; 239.
Dunlap, George L.: 17.
Durno, Miss Jeannette: 103.
Dutschke, Herman: 196.
Duvivier, A. Devin: 172.
Dyhrenfurth, Julius: an early Conductor, 9.
Dux, Mlle. Claire: 344; 371.

Eames, Henry Purmort: 270.
Eames, Mme. Emma: 56.
Eddy, Clarence: 65; 87; 97.
Eichheim, Henry: 346-347.
Elgar, Sir Edward: first performance of "The Apostles" in Birmingham, 177; "no better Orchestra in Europe than the Theodore Thomas Orchestra," 185; 189.
Ellsworth, James W.: Chairman of the Committee on Music at the Exposition, 51.
Elman, Mischa: ill, 247; 302.
Elwell, John D.: letter, 22.
Erickson, O. Gordon: Chicago Music Festival, 292.
Esser, Franz: 164; 246; 255; 270.
Evanston Musical Society: 180.
Exposition Building: on the Lake Front, 15; 17; 18; 19; 134.

Fairbank, Nathaniel K.: 17; President, 27; resignation, 55; death, 139-140.
Fay, Charles Norman: wedding reception for Mr. and Mrs. Theodore Thomas, 24; story of organization of Orchestral Association (from *The Outlook*), 25-27; Vice-President' 27; letter, 28; dinner by Trustees, 104; "Appeal to Friends of Music," 137-138; "The Orchestra will be disbanded," 139; committee on reorganization, 152; Member, 166; conference with Mr. Stock, 168; 232; resignation, 252.

Fay, Miss Rose: wedding, 24.
Ferner, Walter: 276; 290.
Field, Henry: "Memorial Fund," 184.
Field, Marshall: death; memorial service, 175.
Field, Mrs. Marshall: gift of $5,000, 193; luncheon in Washington for Mr. Stock and Orchestra, 333.
Finck, Henry T.: *Evening Post*, New York, 80.
Fish, Miss Minnie: 41. (See Mrs. Minnie Fish Griffin.)
Fisk, Mrs. Katharine: 118.
Fitzek, Joseph: "white ribbon," 330; retired on pension, 345.
Fitzek, Rudolph: retired on pension, 368.
Flonzaley Quartet: 230; 246; 254; 334.
Foote, Arthur: "Four Character Pieces," 191; 255.
Formes, Carl: 11; 12; 123.
Foster, Miss Muriel: 147.
Fremstad, Mme. Olive: 190.
Frank, Henry L.: gift of $25,000, 334.
Fuller, Miss Loie: 80.
Fuller, William A.: Trustee, 64; resignation, 77.
Furbeck, Mrs. Sue Harrington: 123; 146.

Gabrilowitsch, Ossip: 136; 184; 276; 290; 301; Visiting Conductor, 315; soloist, 316.
Gadski, Mme. Johanna: 176; 182; 236.
Galli, Luigi: 255.
Gannon, Mrs. Rose Lutiger: 217; 261.
Ganz, Rudolph: 139; 229; 314.
Gebhard, Heinrich: 215; 261.
Gifford, Miss Electa: 76; 81; 130.
Glass, Reinhard: death, 223.
Gleason, Frederick Grant: 80; 98; "The Song of Life"; death, 121.
Glessner, John J.: 62; Trustee, 109; subscribes to the purchase of the Michigan Avenue lot, 135; Member, 166; on Executive Committee, 285.
Glessner, Mr. and Mrs. John J.: reception for Professor Parker, 136; reception for Toronto Choir, 205; dinner to Mr. Stock, officers and Orchestra, 247.
Glover, Lyman B.: on "Till Eulenspiegel," "a fantastical piece of musical horseplay," 76.
Goodman, William O.: Member, 325; Trustee, 342.
Goodson, Miss Katharine: 326.
Gordon, Jacques: concertmeister, 340; 352; 369.
Gould, Herbert: leads chorus of "Jackies," 300.
Grainger, Percy: 277; 325.
Greene, Plunkett: "delighted the audience," 55; 58.
Gregorowitsch, Charles: 127.

Griffin, Mrs. Minnie Fish: 56; 100; 122.
Guilmant, Alexandre: "the eminent French organist," 96; at Mr. Irwin's dinner, 96; death, 98.
Gunn, Glenn Dillard: 261; 270; 277.
Gunsaulus, Rev. Frank W., D.D.: tribute to Theodore Thomas, "Goodbye to a priest and prophet," 162.

Hall, Arthur B.: Member, 356.
Hall, Glenn: 176.
Hallé, Lady: 110; 113.
Hamill, Charles D.: one of the founders of the Mendelssohn Society, 9; 17; 19; 23; Trustee, 27; at Cincinnati Festival, 58; Chairman Executive Committee, 64; 73; at dinner to Mr. Thomas, 81; Chorus Committee, 85; Committee on Finance, 101; 126; Trustees meet to consider Building Fund, 144; serious illness, 151; "whose presence and counsel we needed so much," 157; death; funeral services, 162; memorial by Executive Committee, "the first lover and promoter of good music," 163; death notice in program book, 164.
Hamill, Charles H.: 163; Trustee, 167; Trustees give dinner to Friends of the Orchestra, 216; Second Vice-President and Executive Committee, 257; "You are hearing one of the great Orchestras of the world," 258; "Sprague Memorial Fund," 279-280; First Vice-President, 285; address on Liberty Bonds, 297; address on "Loyalty of the Orchestra," 302; Committee on "Loyalty of the Orchestra," 308; President, 367; address on the Theodore Thomas Memorial, 372.
Hamill, Mr. and Mrs. Ernest A.: gift of $5,000, 353.
Hamlin, George: 81; 88; 96; 101; "delightful work," 110; 123; 146; 204; 214; death, 238.
Hansen, Miss Cecilia: 370.
Harper, President William R.: Trustees did not favor affiliation of Orchestra with University of Chicago, 119; Trustee, 140; Member, 166; death, 174-175; Memorial Concert, 175.
Harrington, Miss N. Estelle: 90; 95.
Harrington, Miss Sue Aline: 88; 90; (See Mrs. Furbeck.)
Harris, Hubbard William: editor of program book, 104; resignation; death, 200.
Harris, Miss Zudie: 176.
Heerman, Hugo: 139; 185.
Heifetz, Jascha: 303.
Henry, Harold: 298.
Herbert, Victor: 23; 29; 255; Guest Conductor; death, 316.

Index

Herdien, Mrs. Mabel Sharpe: 176; 214; 217.
Hesselbach, Otto: retired on pension, 345.
Hill, Edward Burlingame: 193.
Hillman, Carl: retired on pension, 320.
Hinkle, Miss Florence: 239.
Hinkle, Howard A.: 219.
Hlavac, M.: Russian Conductor, at the Exposition, 47; 51.
Hofmann, Josef: engaged for eastern tour, 94; 99; "played with wonderful spirit and fire," 100; 264.
Holmes, George E.: 41; 43; death, 96.
Homer, Mme. Louise: 149; 180; 291.
Hopkins, Rev. John Henry: funeral of Theodore Thomas, 155.
Huberman, Bronislaw: 89.
Hughes, Mrs. Adella Prentiss: Manager of the Cleveland Concerts, 219.
Hutcheson, Ernest: 225.
Hutchinson, Charles L.: 62; Member, 166; Trustee, 260; Executive Committee, 325.
Hyde, Herbert E.: conducts Children's Chorus, 300, 311, 320, 335, 350, 373; Superintendent of Civic Music Association; report on Student Orchestra, "music by Americans and for Americans," 328.

Inter-Ocean, Chicago: of Paderewski's playing, 196-197.
Iroquois Theatre fire: 144.
Irwin, Charles D.: dinner to Alexandre Guilmant, 96-98.

Jackson, Miss Leonora: 117.
Jahn, Miss Marie: 29.
Januschowsky, Mme. Georgine von: 88.
Jiskra, Vaclav: 211-212.
Johnson, Edward: 186.
Johnson, Samuel: 10.
Johnston, Rev. Howard Agnew, D.D.: address on "Food Saving," 298.
Johnston, R. E.: Eastern Manager, 233.
Jones, David B.: Member, 202.
Joseffy, Rafael: 23; 32; 65.
Junker, August: resignation, 95.

Kappes, Prof. J. Henry: death, 274.
Kaselowska, Mme.: 12.
Keep, Chauncey: Member, 166; Trustee, 175.
Keller, J.: 95.
Kelley, Edgar S.: 255.
Kemp, Mrs. Edward: gift of $5,000, 370.
Kemp, Miss Frances D.: gift of $5,000, 370.
Kneisel, Franz: Visiting Conductor, 315; 320.

Kneisel String Quartet: 230; 246; 254.
Knorr, Charles A.: 41; 43; 56.
Kochs, Theodore A.: Trustee, 109; death, 395.
Kocian, Jaroslav: 224.
Koenen, Mrs. Tilly: 219.
Kohlsaat, H. H.: 62.
Kortschak, Hugo: 239; 254; 255.
Kramer, Leopold: concertmeister, 95; "the violin solo celestial," 123; 145; 149; 153; at sea, 187; resignation, 210.
Krauss, Alexander: "Silver Jubilee," 273; "white ribbon," 330; retired on pension, 368.
Kreisler, Fritz: 269.
Kruschwitz, E.: death, 218.
Kruse, Paul: 227; 230; 248; 270; 275; death, 368.
Kruse, Mrs. Paul: receives pension, 368.
Kuehn, Bruno: retired on pension, 322.

Landowska, Mme. Wanda: 371.
Lathrop, Bryan: "thoughtful generosity," 8; Trustee and Vice-President, 64; dinner to Mr. Thomas, 81; meets a financial situation "quietly and calmly"; Committee on Finance, 101; dinner by Trustees to Friends of the Orchestra; guests, 104; President, 116; "a tower of strength," 127; luncheon to President Harper, 132; with other Trustees buys the Michigan Avenue lot, 135; luncheon at the Chicago Club, 137; "Building Fund," 144; Committee on "Organization," 152; letter from Mrs. Thomas donating the Thomas library to "The Orchestral Association," 157; Committee on "Organization and By-Laws" makes a report, 164; "Henry Field Memorial Fund," 184; dinner to friends of the Orchestra; guests, 213; dinner in New York, 232; articles on "The Best Music"; testimonial dinner to Mr. Stock and Orchestra, 234-235; suggests change in name of the Orchestra, 248; "Condition and future of the Orchestra" demands change, 251; reviews finances of Twenty-second Season, 256-257; and Twenty-third Season, 265; appreciation of Mrs. Coolidge's gift, $100,000; his own gift of $25,000; luncheon to Trustees, 267; an earnest appeal to pay debt on hall, 272; illness and death; funeral services; pall bearers, 281; bequest of $700,000 to "The Orchestral Association," 282-283; resolution by the Trustees, "A gentle, cultured man," 284; Memorial Concert, 286.
Ledochowski, Count Napoleon: 98.

Leginska, Miss Ethel: 302.
Lester, W. R.: dinner at Willow Grove, 208.
Letz, Hans: 217; 220; concertmeister, 223; 234; resignation, 245.
Levy, Heniot: 227.
Lhevinne, Josef: 340.
Liebling, Emil: death, 34.
Lloyd, Edward: "a revelation to American audiences," 35-36; at the Exposition, 46.
Locke, Charles E.: 18.
Loewe, William: death, 193.
Logan, Frank G.: Member, 377.
Lowden, Frank O.: Trustee, 105; subscribes to purchase of Michigan Avenue lot, 135; address on need for endowment fund, 139; Member, 166; resignation as Trustee, 234.
Ludwig, William: 33; death, 122.
Lutkin, Dean P. C.: 180; 385; 386.

MacCarthy, Miss Maud: 139.
MacDowell, Edward A.: 55.
Macmillen, Francis: 224.
Maier, Guy: 334; 371.
Mahler, Gustav: Eighth Symphony, 291-294.
Malkin, Joseph: 322; 325; 330.
Malkin, Miss Anita: 327; 336.
Mandel Hall Concerts: 180; organization of the University Orchestral Association; officers, 377; concerts, 378-379.
Maretzek, Mme. Bertucca: 11.
Marteau, Henri: 98.
Martin, Frederick: 204.
Massenet, Jules: 50.
Materna, Mme. Amalie: 55.
Mathews, W. S. B.: editor of program book, 74; resignation; death, 86.
Maxwell, Lawrence, Jr.: 187.
Mayer, L.: death, 218.
McCagg, Ezra B.: Trustee, 27; resignation, 55; death, 199.
McConathy, Osbourne: 336.
McCormack, John: 301; 317.
McCormick, Cyrus: Member, 288.
McCormick, Cyrus H.: 62; Chairman of Committee on Organization, 63; sends letter to people of Chicago, 72; Member, 166; presents Russian works to Orchestra, 301.
McCormick, Harold F.: Trustee, 127; subscribes to the purchase of the Michigan Avenue lot, 135; Member, 166.
McCormick, Stanley: Member, 166; resignation, 234.
McEwan, P. A.: Secretary and Treasurer, 27; resignation, 54; Treasurer, 73; resignation, 83.
McNicol, Theodore F.: "Silver Jubilee," 273; death, 278.
McNicol, Mrs. Theodore F.: granted a pension, 290.

Mees, Arthur: Assistant Conductor, 82; assembles chorus, 84-85; editor of program book, 86; 88; 94; best work the chorus had done, 98; returns east; death, 103.
Mehlig, Miss Anna: 12; 163.
Mendelssohn Choir, Toronto: first visit of the Orchestra, 193-195; second visit, 203; Choir visits Chicago, 204-205; third visit, 213-214; Buffalo, 214; Cleveland, 215; fourth visit, 226-227; fifth visit, 235-236; tour with Orchestra; soloists; press comments, 236-239; last visit, 259-260.
Mendelssohn Club: 110; dedicatory concert, Orchestra Hall, 152; 229; Chicago Festival, 292.
Mendelssohn Society: 9.
Mérö, Mme. Yolanda: ill, 344.
Meyer, Carl: "Silver Jubilee," 273; "white ribbon," 330; retired on pension, 345.
Meyer, George F.: "Silver Jubilee," 272; "white ribbon," 330; retired on pension, 345-346.
Middelschulte, Wilhelm: 89; 98; 101; funeral of Mr. Thomas, 155; dedicates organ in hall, 169; 176; 183; 202; 226; 253; 278.
Miles, Gwilym: 194; 195.
Millar, Miss Anna: in charge of season ticket sale, 60; report on sales, 66; takes Orchestra on tour, 58; appointed Manager; arranges eastern trip, 74; good report on season sale, 75; prospectus Sixth Season, 84; effective management, 87; goes to San Francisco, 89; goes to Europe to secure soloists, 93; Josef Hofmann engaged, 94; eastern tour, 98; encouraging season sale, 104; resignation, 116; resolution by Trustees, 117.
Mittelstaedt, Frank A.: "Silver Jubilee," 273; retired on pension, 318.
Miller, John B.: 217; 229; 261.
Miller, Reed: 239; death, 259.
Milwaukee Concerts: Milwaukee Musical Society; Milwaukee Orchestral Association, 379-381.
Mockridge, Whitney: 117.
Moerenhout, C.: death, 218.
Moiseiwitsch, Benno: 330; 369.
Moore, Francis S.: 162.
Morison, Rev. John A., D.D.: 162; 175.
Morris, Seymour: Member and Trustee, 247; death, 339; resolution by Executive Committee, 339-340.
Mosenthal, Julius: 11.
Mottl, Felix: cables "No," 167; 168.
Musical Art Society: 176; 190; 259.
Musicians' Union: 30; demands increased salaries, 359-360.
Muzio, Mlle. Claudia: 311.

Nash, Miss Frances: 316.
National Federation of Musicians: 244; interview with President of Federation, 245.
National Institute of Arts and Letters: convention and luncheon; guests, 255.
Neff, Miss Prudence: 261.
Nelson, Edgar A.: Chicago Music Festival, 292.
New York Tribune: 237; H. E. Krehbiel says of Chicago Orchestra, 333.
Ney, Mme. Elly: of distinguished ancestry, 344.
Nichols, Miss Marie: 176.
Nicolini, Joseph: retired on pension, 295.
Nikisch, Arthur: 50.
Nordica, Mme. Lillian: 43.
Norton, Edward: 62.
Norton, John W.: conducts Florence Nightingale Chorus: 335.
Norton, Oliver W.: 62; Member, 166; pays loss on season, 183; death, 329-330.
Norton, R. H.: letter, "my father was always interested in the development of the Orchestra," 330.
Notman, Rev. William R., D.D.: 175.
Novak, Louis: retired on pension, 295.
Noyes, D. A.: Chorus Committee, 85.
Nurnberger, Lothar: "Silver Jubilee," 273; "white ribbon," 330.

Oakley, Horace S.: Member and Trustee, 300; Third Vice-President, 325; arranges settlement with Union, 362-364; Vice-President, 367.
Oberndorfer, Anne Faulkner: notes on programs, 327; 337.
Oldberg, Arne: 279; symphony No. 2, 346.
Olmstead, Frederick Law: one of "the creators of the Exposition," 45.
Ondricek, Franz: 76.
Oordt, Jan van: 87.
Orchestral Association, The: (For names of Officers, Trustees, Members of the Association, and *personnel* of the Orchestra, see pages 392-448.)
 Incorporation: first Board of Trustees; officers, 27; Guarantee Fund; contract with Theodore Thomas, 28; fifty-one Guarantors, 29.
 First Season (1891-1892): prospectus, 31; financial difficulties; report of Treasurer, 37.
 Second Season (1892-1893): criticisms of the press, 38; prospectus, "Associate Members" and "Option Tickets," 39; newspapers offer advice to the Trustees, 41; report of Treasurer, 43.
 Third Season (1893-1894): outlook not cheerful; criticisms by a Chicago paper, 53; resignation of P. A. McEwan, Treasurer; succeeded by Charles E. Anderson, 54; resignation of N. K. Fairbank, President; succeeded by George E. Adams; resignation of Ezra B. McCagg; succeeded by Allison V. Armour, 55; prospectus, 56; resignation of A. C. Bartlett; succeeded by Philo A. Otis, 57; report of Treasurer, 57.
 Fourth Season (1894-1895): resignation of Milward Adams (Manager); succeeded by George H. Wilson, 59; "Fund for the Support of the Orchestra"; Miss Anna Millar, Manager of season ticket sale; meeting of Trustees; prospectus, 60; meeting of Trustees, 61; meeting of subscribers to "Fund for Support of the Orchestra"; Committee, Cyrus H. McCormick, Chairman, to formulate plans; meeting of Trustees, 62; report of Mr. McCormick's Committee, 63; amendments to by-laws adopted; Executive Committee appointed; Trustees and Officers elected, 64; report on ticket sales, 66; report of Treasurer, 70.
 Fifth Season (1895-1896): letter to the people of Chicago by Mr. McCormick's committee, for Governing Members, 72; meeting of Trustees; season lengthened to twenty-two weeks; resignation of George H. Wilson as Secretary; Philo A. Otis succeeds; P. A. McEwan succeeds Philo A. Otis as Treasurer, 73; Miss Anna Millar, Manager; meeting of Trustees, 74; Annual Meeting, 77.
 Sixth Season (1896-1897): Charles C. Curtiss presents plans for a new hall, 82; Frederick J. Wessels, Treasurer, 83; offices of Association moved to Isabella Building; Annual Meeting; report of Treasurer, 87; large deficit, 88.
 Seventh Season (1897-1898): offices of Association back in Auditorium Tower, 93; death of George M. Pullman and Henry B. Stone; resolution of Trustees, 94; Annual Meeting; report of Treasurer, Sixth Season, 95; report of Treasurer, Seventh Season, 101.
 Eighth Season (1898-1899): dinner to Friends of the Orchestra, 104; guests, 104-105; financial statement for eight seasons, 106; list of generous friends who have supported the Orchestra, 106-108; Annual Meeting, 108; report of

Treasurer; election of fifteen Trustees, 109; dinner to Mr. Thomas; guests, 110-111.

Ninth Season (1899-1900): Annual Meeting, 115; report of Treasurer; election of Officers, 116; resolution on death of Timothy B. Blackstone, 118; proposition from Dr. Harper to found a School of Music, 119.

Tenth Season (1900-1901): three matters considered by Trustees, 120; Annual Meeting; report of Treasurer, 122; season lengthened to twenty-four weeks, 123; ticket sales, 124.

Eleventh Season (1901-1902): meetings of Executive Committee, 126; Annual Meeting; report of Treasurer, 127; Northwestern University proposes plan for new hall, 130; "Condition and Future of the Orchestra," 131; President Harper again proposes plan for "School of Music"; President Lathrop presents memorandum "for the School," 132; not approved by Trustees, 133.

Twelfth Season (1902-1903): Bryan Lathrop and seven other friends of the Orchestra buy land on Michigan Avenue, 135; Annual Meeting; report of Treasurer; beginnings of the new hall, 136; C. N. Fay writes "An Appeal to Chicago Friends of Music," 137-138; Trustees agree as to need of new hall, 140.

Thirteenth Season (1903-1904): money in response to the "Appeal"; Auxiliary Committee, 141; proved the salvation of the Orchestra, 142; Annual Meeting; report of Treasurer; D. H. Burnham hopeful for balance of hall fund, 143; meeting of Trustees; Building Fund, 144; purchase of Michigan Avenue lot formally consummated, 145; Trustees announce opening of new hall, 147.

Fourteenth Season (1904-1905): Friends of the Orchestra now in a hopeful frame of mind, 149; opening of hall deferred, 150; Annual Meeting; election of Trustees; report of Treasurer, 151; names of men and women paying loss on season; Committee on "Organization and By-Laws," 152; makes a report, 165; meeting of subscribers to Building Fund; organization, 165; forty Members, 166; election of Trustees, 167; approve action of Trustees; Pullman Company and Standard Office Company, 167-168.

Fifteenth Season (1905-1906): Annual Meeting; gift from Mrs. Elia M. Walker, 172; report of Treasurer, 173.

Sixteenth Season (1906-1907): Annual Meeting; report of Treasurer, 182; resolution by Trustees on gift from Mrs. Thomas Nelson Page, 184-185.

Seventeenth Season (1907-1908): Annual Meeting; report of Treasurer, 190-191.

Eighteenth Season (1908-1909): Annual Meeting; report of Treasurer, 201-202; resolution of Executive Committee on visit of Toronto Choir, 206.

Nineteenth Season (1909-1910): Annual Meeting; report of Treasurer, 211; dinner in foyer to friends of the Orchestra; guests, 215-216; $85,000 subscribed towards debt, 216.

Twentieth Season (1910-1911): the Orchestral Association no longer a perpetual mendicant; has now completed nineteen years of work, 222; Annual Meeting; report of Treasurer, 225.

Twenty-first Season (1911-1912): Annual Meeting; report of Treasurer, 233-234.

Twenty-second Season (1912-1913): Annual Meeting; report of Treasurer, 246-247; action of Trustees in changing name, 249; statement to press, 250; conclusions growing out of the announcement, 251; resignation of Charles Norman Fay, 252.

Twenty-third Season (1913-1914): Annual Meeting; report of Treasurer, 255-256; President Lathrop reviews report, 256-257; election of Trustees in classes of five each for one, two and three years; election of Officers; appeal to the "Friends of the Orchestra," 257.

Twenty-fourth Season (1914-1915): ladies requested to remove hats, 263-264; Annual Meeting, 264; election of Trustees; report of Treasurer; President Lathrop reviews Treasurer's report, 265.

Twenty-fifth Season (1915-1916): Annual Meeting; report of Treasurer, 274-275.

Twenty-sixth Season (1916-1917): Clyde M. Carr elected President to fill vacancy caused by the death of Bryan Lathrop, 285; Annual Meeting; luncheon by President Carr, 286; guests; report of Treasurer, 287; address by President Carr, 287-288; address by Mr. Stock, 288; special meeting; letter from Mrs. Lathrop, 289; prices of season tickets increased, 291.

Twenty-seventh Season (1917-1918): the World War still raging, 294; memorial by Executive Committee on death of George E. Adams, 298; Annual Meeting; luncheon by President Carr; report of Treasurer, 299.

Twenty-eighth Season (1918-1919): Trustees' action on loyalty of the Orchestra, 307-308; committee appointed, 308; Annual Meeting, 312; report of Treasurer, 313; President Carr reviews report, 313-314; election of Trustees; by-laws amended; Executive Committee of seven Trustees, 314; Committee votes that Mr. Stock should return to Conductor's stand, 317; increase in prices of tickets, 319.

Twenty-ninth Season (1919-1920): Annual Meeting; amendments to by-laws adopted, 323-324; report of Treasurer, 324.

Thirtieth Season (1920-1921): largest season ticket sale in the history of the Orchestra, 329; Annual Meeting; report of Treasurer, 331; gift of $3,000 for the Endowment Fund from Edward G. Uihlein, 332; gift of $25,000 from Henry L. Frank, 334.

Thirty-first Season (1921-1922): Annual Meeting; report of Treasurer, 341; President Carr reviews report, 341-342; six members of the Orchestra retired on pension, 345-346; bequest of $10,000 from estate of Adolphus C. Bartlett, 347.

Thirty-second Season (1922-1923): increase in season ticket sale, 352; gift of $5,000 from Mr. and Mrs. Ernest A. Hamill; Annual Meeting, 353; report of Treasurer, 354; comments of Treasurer; election of Trustees and Officers, 355; Executive Committee; Trustees change date of Annual Meeting, 356; Annual Meeting in accordance with the revised by-laws, 360; report of Treasurer, Thirty-second Season, 360-361; comments of Treasurer, 361-362; election of Trustees, Officers and Executive Committee, 362; an appreciation of bequest of $10,000 from estate of Franklin Rudolph adopted, 363; settlement with Musicians' Union effected, 363-364.

Thirty-third Season (1923-1924): death of President Carr, 366-367; meeting of Trustees to fill the vacancy, 367; Executive Committee decides to call President Carr's bequest "The Clyde M. and Lillian Carr Fund," 369; meeting of Executive Committee; gift of $5,000 from Mrs. Edward Kemp and $5,000 from Miss Frances D. Kemp for Endowment Fund, 370; Annual Meeting; report of Treasurer, 375-376; comments of Treasurer, 376-377.

Orr, Arthur: Trustee, 109; subscribes to the purchase of the Michigan Avenue lot, 135; Member, 166; death, 171.

Osborn, Miss Jenny: 146.

Otis, James: brings his family to Chicago, 9.

Otis, Philo Adams: member of Music Committee of the Apollo Musical Club, 14; Secretary of Chicago Musical Festival Association, 17; notes on second Festival, 19; letter from Mr. Thomas, 31; notes on Twentieth Anniversary Concerts (Apollo Club), 35-36; Inaugural Exercises (Exposition), 40; concerts at the Exposition, 46-47; ninth symphony, 56; Trustee, 57; meets Mr. Thomas at Cincinnati, 58; Treasurer, 61; meets Mr. Thomas at rehearsal, 62-63; Executive Committee, 64; People's Institute Concert, 64-65; resignation as Treasurer; Secretary, 73; Chorus Committee, 85; dinner by Trustees at Chicago Club, 104-105; Children's Concert, 111; meets Wessels at the opera; Mr. Thomas' resignation, 114-115; funeral of A. W. Dohn, 122; closing concerts of Twelfth Season, 139; campaign for new hall fund, 141; closing concerts of Thirteenth Season, 146-147; Sixteenth Cincinnati Festival, 147-148; "Committee on Reorganization," 152; "Festival Tour," 186; notes on trip from Cherbourg to New York, 187; with the Orchestra to Toronto, 193-195; Eighteenth Cincinnati Festival, 197-198; Toronto, 203-204; Choir visits Chicago, 204-205; Willow Grove, 207-208; dinner at Mr. Lathrop's home, 213; Toronto, 213-214; Choir and Orchestra in Buffalo and Cleveland, 214-215; Willow Grove, 228; eastern tour of Orchestra, 231-232; tour of Choir and Orchestra, 236-239; Twentieth Cincinnati Festival, 239-241; Willow Grove; conference with Stock and Wessels, 242; funeral of Theodore F. McNicol, 278; funeral of Bryan Lathrop, 281; telegram from President Carr, 307; funeral of Milward Adams, 364; note on First Concerts, Thirty-third Season, 368.

Otte, Frederick: death, 264.

Paderewski, Ignace J.: 32; 42; at the Exposition, 49; letter, 50; 78; presents loving cup to Theodore Thomas, 79; 168; "an atmosphere of poetry and beauty," 196-197; 206-207; 261.
Paepcke, Hermann: bequest of $10,000 to The Orchestral Association, 348.
Page, Mrs. Thomas Nelson; 101; gift of $50,000; death, 184.
Panizza, Ettore: Guest Conductor,370.
Parker, Horatio W.; 136; 255; death, 280.
Patti, Amalia: 11.
Pattison, Lee: 332; 334; 371.
Payne's Livery Stable: 134.
Peabody, Augustus C.: Member; Trustee, 377.
Peabody, F. F.: Member, 166; resignation, 202.
Peck, Ferdinand W.: letter to President Adams, "The Orchestral Association the salvation of the Auditorium," 82.
Pension and Invalid Fund: 8; its beginnings; Executive Committee in charge of concerts, 192; Miss Isadora Duncan dances, 201; gift of $100,000 from Mrs. Elizabeth Sprague Coolidge; gift of $25,000 from Mr. Lathrop, 267; gift of $5,000 from "a friend," 268; concert, 269; funds, 272-273; gift of $1,500, 274; concert, 276; group insurance, 285; rules and by-laws adopted, 289; "well established," 300; bequest of $3,000 from Cathrina Seipp, 325-326.
Pension Roll: 448.
Perring, Ernest: 11.
Philharmonic Society (Chicago): 9; 10.
Pinckney, Judge Merritt W.: "Stock an American citizen," 321.
Polacco, Giorgio: Guest Conductor, 318.
Polak, Joseph: as "Santa Claus," 315.
Polasek, Albin: 372.
Porter, George F.: Member, 257.
Powell, Miss Maud: 124; death, 278.
Pratt, Silas G.: founder of the Apollo Musical Club, 14.
Prihoda, Vasa: 333.
Proctor, George: 144.
Prokofieff, Serge: Visiting Conductor and soloist; "played like a Slav," 312; second visit, "great art and intellectuality," 343.
Protheroe, Daniel: Chicago Music Festival, 292.
Pugno, Raoul: "Artist of the highest order," 96; 136.
Pullman, George M.: "A lover of art and music"; death, 94.

Quensel, Alfred: 86; 146; 187; 217; 225; 230; 248; 270; 280; 286.

Rachmaninow, Sergei: 210.
Ravinia Park: 180; 208; 220; 242.
Reuter, Rudolph: 248; 258; 346.
Rice, Miss Margaret: Manager of the Milwaukee Concerts, 380.
Rich, Mrs. Ella Dahl: 130.
Richard, Hans: 215.
Richardson, Mrs. Birdice Blye: 180.
Richter, Hans: 50; 168.
Riddle, George: 130.
Rider-Kelsey, Mrs. Corinne M.: 186; 191; 204; 214.
Ripley, Edward P.: Member, 166; death, 326.
Roehrborn, Otto: 246; 270.
Root, John W.: one of the "Creators of the Exposition," 45.
Rosensweet, David: death, 353.
Rosenthal, Moriz: ill, 87; 105; 113; 183; 369.
Rosenwald, Julius: Member, 264.
Rubinstein, Arthur: 353.
Rudolph, Franklin: bequest of $10,000 to The Orchestral Association, 123.
Rudolph, Mrs. Pauline Dohn: 123.
Ruinen, Johann: death, 264.
Ryerson, Edward L.: Member, 331.

Saar, Louis Victor: conducts suite "Roccoco," 320.
Sachleben, Henry: death, 62.
Saint Paul Symphony Orchestra: (Apollo Club), 225.
Saint-Saëns, Camille: 50; received a tremendous ovation, 180-181; 189.
Salzédo, Carlos: 322.
Samaroff, Mme. Olga: 212; 333.
Sametini, Leon: 247.
Sauer, Emil: 113.
Sauret, Emile: 78.
Sauter, Carl: retired on pension, 368.
Scharwenka, Xaver: 226.
Scheib, Miss Eleanor: 230.
Schelling, Ernest: 168; 279; gift of $200 to Pension Fund, 362; 387.
Schoenfeld, Henry: 55.
Schreurs, Joseph: 146; 181; 227; 230; 248; "Silver Jubilee," 273; 275; "white ribbon," 330; death, 340.
Schuecker, Edmund: 65; 96; resignation, 117.
Schumann, Mme.: 11.
Schumann-Heink, Mme. Ernestine: 181; 182; 226; 252.
Scott, Cyril: soloist and Guest Conductor, 332.
Seeboeck, W. C. E.: 64; 268.
Seidel, Richard: "Silver Jubilee," 273; "white ribbon," 330.
Seipp, Cathrina: bequest of $3,000, 325-326.
Selfridge, Harry G.: 141; 260.
Shattuck, Arthur: 371.
Shaw, Howard: 372.
Shepherd, Dr. Robert D.: suggests a new hall, 130.

Index

Sherman, Miss Blanche: 146.
Sherwood, William H.: 42; death, 110.
Shortall, John G.: 10.
Singer, Mrs. Vera R.: granted a pension, 290.
Singer, Walfried: death, 290.
Smith, David Stanley: composer-Conductor, 316.
Smith, Joseph Linden: Pension Fund Concerts, 192.
Smith, Mrs. Proctor: 76.
Smyth, Miss Ethel Mary: "On the Cliffs of Cornwall," 345.
Sokoloff, Nikolai: Visiting Conductor, 312.
Sowerby, Leo: "A Set of Four," 301; concerto for pianoforte, F major, 326; symphony No. 1, 346.
Spahn, Louis: member of Chorus Committee, 85.
Spalding, Albert: 201; 231; 232; 233; 358.
Spencer, Miss Janet: 186; 194.
Spiering, Theodore: 317.
Sprague, Albert A.: 62; subscribes to the purchase of the Michigan Avenue lot, 135; Member, 166; death, 266; bequest of $100,000 to The Orchestral Association, 267.
Sprague, Albert A., II: Member, 275; Trustee, 325.
Sprague, Albert and Nancy, Memorial Fund: 279.
Sprague, William: 14; funeral of A. W. Dohn, 122.
Stanley, A. A.: symphonic poem, "Attis," 334.
Stanley, Mme. Helen: 315.
Starke, Ferdinand: retired on pension, 289.
Stein, Mrs. Gertrude May: 131.
Steindel, Bruno: 40; 61; 87; "played delightfully," 92; 96; 118; 136; 150; 192; 215; 226; 227; 230; 246; presented with a laurel wreath, 247; 255; 258; 270; "Silver Jubilee," 273; resignation, 308.
Stevenson, Miss Lucille: 261.
Stock, Frederick: 8; "sitting quietly among the viola players," 74-75; the "young viola player" conducts, 118; "Symphonic Variations," 146; funeral of Theodore Thomas, 155; temporary Conductor, 156; funeral of Charles D. Hamill, 162; "Symphonic Poem," Conductor, 168; early impressions of Mr. Thomas and Orchestra, 178; "Festival Tour," 186; concert in memory of Edward A. MacDowell, 193; Toronto, 194-195; Eighteenth Cincinnati Festival, 197; Toronto, 203-204; Mendelssohn Choir visits Chicago, 205; Willow Grove, 207-208; the logical successor of Theodore Thomas, 209; symphony in C minor, 212; Toronto, 213-214; Buffalo, 214; Cleveland, 215; received an ovation, 217; Nineteenth Cincinnati Festival, 219; Willow Grove, 220; "Festival March," 223; "Symphonic Waltz," 224; Toronto, 226; Willow Grove, 228; eastern tour of Orchestra, 231-233; Toronto, 235-236; eastern tour of Mendelssohn Choir and Orchestra, 236-239; Twentieth Cincinnati Festival, 239-241; National Federation of Musicians, 245; dinner at Mr. and Mrs. Glessner's, 247; benefit concert, flood sufferers, 252-253; Toronto, 259-260; overture, "Life's Spring Tide," 260; reception for Mr. and Mrs. Stock, 266; concerto for violin, 286; Chicago Music Festival, 291; "a triumph for the Conductor," 294; "Overture to a Romantic Comedy," 301-302; tenders resignation pending citizenship, 305-307; resignation accepted, 307; returns to Conductor's stand; a gala occasion; "March and Hymn to Democracy," 317; now an American citizen, 321; eastern tour, 332-333; "Armistice Day," 340-341; prepares Shakespeare Program, 353; Literary Program, 357; conducts Philadelphia Orchestra, 370; Children's Concerts; "the little folks can now discriminate between the French horn and the bassoon," 381-382.
Stoddard, Miss Marie: 195.
Stone, Miss Helen: 117.
Stone, Henry B.: 62; Trustee, 64; 74; death, "a strong character, a loyal associate," 94.
Stone, Rev. James S.: funeral of Theodore Thomas, 155.
Stone, Mme. Niessen: "La Mélancolie du Nord," 211.
Strakosch, Max: 11.
Strathcona, Lord: 194.
Strauss, Dr. Richard: Visiting Conductor; "Death and Transfiguration"; made a deep impression, 146.
Strauss, Mme. Pauline: 146.
Sturges, George: 17.
Sturgis, Mrs. Minna Thomas: unveils monument of Theodore Thomas, 372.
Sturkow-Ryder, Mrs. Theodora: 325.
Summer Garden Concerts: 15.
Suppantschitsch, R.: 117.
Swift, Charles H.: Member, 175; entertains Toronto Choir, 205; Trustee, 265; gift of $12,000, 357.
Swing, Rev. David: 16-17.

Taft, President William H.: unveils statue of Theodore Thomas, 219-220.
Taylor, Deems: 386.

Tenney, Horace K.: address on "Liberty Bonds," 297.
Thibaud, Jacques: 144; 315.
Thomas, Miss Clara: Chicago Music Festival, 290.
Thomas, Franz C.: death, 130.
Thomas, Mrs. Rose Fay: "Memoirs of Theodore Thomas," 8; marriage to Theodore Thomas, 24; reception by Apollo Musical Club, 31; at the Exposition, 49; 68; letter of Mr. Thomas, "This traveling must stop," 69; reception by Mr. and Mrs. Thomas, 75; Orchestra in New York, 79; patriotic ending of concert, 86; death of Theodore Thomas, 155-157; praise for Manager Wessels, 179.
Thomas, Theodore: 7; 8; first appearance in Chicago; as soloist; Thomas Orchestra, 11; 12; 13; 14; Summer Garden Concerts, 15; conducts "Faust" (Berlioz) for Apollo Club; Chicago Festivals, 17; 18; 19-20; conducts "Rose of Sharon" (Mackenzie) for Apollo Club, 21; "Testimonial Tour," 22-23; marriage of Miss Rose Fay and Theodore Thomas, 24; first meeting with C. Norman Fay, 26; "Farewell Concerts" in the east; "Six Popular Concerts" (Chicago), 29; "Summer Night Series" (New York); reception by Apollo Club, 31; conducts "Faust" for Apollo Club, 33; conducts the "Passion Music" at the Anniversary Concerts, Apollo Club, 35; 36; Director of Bureau of Music at Exposition, 39; conducts ninth symphony, "an inspiration," 41; at the Exposition; "a man of stern integrity," 44; concerts, 46; unjust charges by the *Chicago Herald*, 47; Director-General Davis demands resignation, 50; tenders resignation, 51; more bitter comments by Chicago papers; asked to return and resume the work of the Bureau; invitation declined, 52; invitation from Henry L. Higginson to conduct the Boston Symphony Orchestra; declined; letter from Charpentier, 54; declines offer from New York, 58; discusses programs and soloists, 63; "in a delightful mood," 65-66; an authority on out-of-town concerts, 67; serious thoughts of resigning; dinner by Trustees at Chicago Club, 69; presented with a silver punch bowl, the gift of thirty-six ladies in Chicago; guests, 70; views on French music; reception by Mr. and Mrs. Thomas, 75-76; talks to Apollo Club about Berlioz, 77; eastern tour; Paderewski presents silver loving cup; bitter press comments, 78-80; "must have regular rehearsals," 80; complimentary dinner; guests, 81; letter about chorus, 83-84; Promenade Concert, 90-92; dinner by C. D. Irwin, 96-98; dinner at Chicago Club; guests, 98; eastern tour; good friends among newspaper men, 99; "Parsifal," 100; banquet and "show" by men of the Orchestra; plays (violin) a jig; dinner at Chicago Club, guests, 110; on works of young composers, 113; letter of resignation, 114; action of Trustees, 115; dinner to Mr. Thomas; guests, 124; "does not need any committees," 126; six Historical Concerts; vaudeville by men of Orchestra, 128-129; "sad news," death of his son, Franz C. Thomas, 130; Sixteenth Cincinnati Festival, 147-148; Orchestra Hall the joint creation of Theodore Thomas and D. H. Burnham; sends telegram to Mr. Burnham, 150; dedicatory concert, 152; a proud moment; not in best of health, 153; last concerts conducted, 154; last illness and death; funeral services, 155; pallbearers; Memorial Concert, 156; life and work, 158-162; views on fifth symphony, 201; bronze statue at Cincinnati, 219-220; Theodore Thomas Memorial; dedication program, 372.
Thompson, Miss Edith: 255.
Thompson, Miss Fanchon H.: 56; 81.
Thorne, Robert J.: Member, 288.
Tinkham, Edward I.: 10.
Tomlins, William L.: Conductor of the Apollo Musical Club, 14; Festival (1877), 15; First Chicago Festival, 17; Second Festival, 18; "called out again and again," 20; Twentieth Anniversary Concerts, 35-36; Choral Director at Exposition, 45; 47; farewell concert, "Elijah" (Mendelssohn), 100; resignation, 101.
Tramonti, Enrico: 138; 191; "the Paganini among harp players," 217; 219; 225; 253; 332; 369.

Uihlein, Edward G.: gift of $3,000, 332.
Ullman, Manager: 11.
Ulrich, Albert: "Silver Jubilee," 273; "white ribbon," 330.
Unger, Walter: 138; 202; "Silver Jubilee," 273; retired on pension, 318.
Upton, George P.: critic and author, 9; first visit of Theodore Thomas to Chicago; critic ("Peregrine Pickle") for the *Chicago Tribune*, 11; "Now come the people to hear Theodore Thomas' Orchestra," 12; President of the Apollo Musical Club, 14; death of Theodore F. McNicol, 278; one of the foremost of American critics; death, 319.

Index

Van der Burg, Brahm: 176.
Van der Stucken, Frank: 177; "poet as well as composer," 187; Conductor of Cincinnati Festivals, 196; Eighteenth Festival, 197; "a triumph for Mr. Van der Stucken," 198; Nineteenth Festival, 219; Twentieth Festival, 239-241.
Van der Veer, Mme. Nevada: 239.
Vidas, Raoul: 312.
Voegeli, Henry E.: "began his work," 120; Assistant Manager and Assistant Treasurer, 172; visit of the Toronto Choir to Chicago, 205; eastern tour of Orchestra, 231; tour of Choir and Orchestra, 236; eastern tour of Orchestra, 332-333.
Vogt, Dr. A. S.: Conductor of the Toronto Choir, 193; his drastic rules, 194; visit of the Orchestra to Toronto, 203; Choir visits Chicago, 204-205; conducts "Children's Crusade" (Pierné), 214; "Manzoni Requiem" (Verdi), 226; "The New Life" (Wolf-Ferrari) and "Te Deum" (Berlioz), 235; letter, 239; Orchestra visits Toronto, 259-260.
Volk, Ferdinand: retired on pension, 295.
Von Dohnányi, Ernst: 121.

Wacker, Charles H.: Trustee; declines to serve, 64.
Wagner, Ernest Frank: retired on a pension; death, 156; "Silver Jubilee," 273.
Walker, Sir Edmund: 194; 204; 205; 238; death, 260.
Walker, Mrs. Elia M.: gift of $25,000; death, 172.
Walker, Mrs. Jessie Spalding: gift of $1,000 to Pension Fund, 312.
Walker, Lady: 238.
Walker, William B.: 105; Trustee, 109; resignation, 151; death, 325.
Wallenstein, Alfred: 352; 369.
Weber, Joseph N.: 245.
Weidig, Adolf: 117; 196; symphonic suite, 266; Visiting Conductor, 315; concert overture, 318.
Weidig, Ferdinand: death, 318.
Weingartner, Felix: 148; 165; 168.
Weisbach, Harry: concertmeister, 245; 246; 255; 258; 266; 270; 274; 276; 299; 325; 334; resignation, 340.
Weld, Frederick: 239.
Wells, Howard: 176.
Wendel, Ernest: concertmeister, 85; resigned, 95.
Werbke-Burchard, Mrs. Martha: 41.
Wessels, Frederick J.: Treasurer, 83; Chorus Committee, 85; 87; 95; 101; 109; meets Secretary Otis at opera, 114; Manager, 117; 122; 127; 136; 143; 151; 173; Mrs. Thomas says of Manager Wessels, 179; 182; Festival Tour, 186-187; 190; Toronto, 194; 203; Choir visits Chicago, 205; resolution of Executive Committee, 206; Willow Grove, 207-208; Toronto; receives a present, 214; out-of-town concerts, 218; 219; Willow Grove, 220; 225; Toronto, 226-227; eastern tour of Orchestra, 231; 233; tour of Choir and Orchestra, 236-239; 246; 255; 257; Toronto, 259; 265; 274-275; funeral of Theodore F. McNicol, 278; 287; 299; 314; reports to Trustees that "Mr. Stock has complied with all legal requirements," 316; 331; eastern tour of Orchestra, 332; pamphlet on tour, "As Others See Us," 333; 341; 354; "need for further endowment," 355; 360; comments on finance, 361-362; 375-377.
Wessels, George F.: funeral of Theodore F. McNicol, 278.
Wickersham, Hon. George, Attorney General of United States: regarding demands of the Musicians' Union; "the President and Congress cannot help you," 244-245.
Wild, Harrison M.: Conductor Apollo Musical Club, 101; 217; 229; 239; Chicago Music Festival, 292.
Willeke, Willem: 301.
Williams, Mrs. Charlotte DeMuth: 176.
Williams, Dr. William Carver: 217.
Willow Grove: 207-208; 220; 228; 242.
Wilson, Mrs. Genevieve C.: 96; 123.
Wilson, George H.: Secretary of Bureau of Music at the Exposition, 45; Secretary of Orchestral Association, 57; editor of program book, 60; 61; resignation; death, 73.
Winckler, Joseph F.: letter, 323.
Winkelmann, Hermann: 18; 20.
Witherspoon, Herbert: 186; 195; 215.
Wolf, Mrs. Helen: granted a pension, 290.
Wolf, Otto: death; funeral services, 277.
Wolfsohn, Henry: 148.
Woollett, Wilfred: retired on pension, 368.
Woolley, Clarence M.: Member, 166; Trustee, 167; resignation, 307.
Worcester, Mrs. Theodore: Aurora concerts, 382-383.
World's Columbian Exposition: 44; "Bureau of Music"; fourteen varieties of concerts; societies in United States and Canada invited to come as guests, 45; dissatisfaction among piano exhibitors; demand that Steinway piano shall not be used, 48; that Mr. Paderewski should not use Steinway piano; Bureau of Music placed in charge of a Music Committee; friends of Musical Director,

49; Mr. Paderewski did use the Steinway piano, 50; resignation of Musical Director, 51.
Ysaye, Eugène: 64; 95; 99; 252; 259.

Zeisler, Mrs. Fannie B.: 130; 143; 149; 184; 207; 227; 371.

Zeller, William: retired on pension, 295.
Zettelmann, Joseph: "Silver Jubilee," 273; "white ribbon," 330.
Ziegfeld, Dr. Florenz: 165.
Zimbalist, Efrem: 247; 286; 300.
Zukovsky, Alexander: 226; 274.